Pine to Prairie Cookbook Volume II

Telephone Pioneers of America
C.P. Wainman - Chapter #18

ACKNOWLEDGMENTS

I want to thank all of the telephone industry members and their families who contributed their recipes, so this volume II could be printed.

The response was overwhelming. We received more than 2,600 recipes, and need to limit the number to around 2,000. Those not used are in a permanent file at the chapter office to be kept for possible future use.

It is most gratifying to see the accomplishments of our pioneer chapter, in helping our own and others, with special items and projects, that could not have been undertaken without the proceeds of Volume I.

It is with a deep sense of gratitude, I acknowledge the pioneer partners of C.P. Wainman Chapter. Their willingness to accept the challenge of sorting, typing and checking for duplication of all the recipes submitted, along with their time and effort will not be forgotten.

Thanks are also due the administrator and officers of the chapter, councils and clubs of C.P. Wainman for their continued support of this project.

John G. Norton
President
C.P. Wainman Chapter
Telephone Pioneers of America

Published By
Cookbook Publishers, Inc.
P.O. Box 12918
Lenexa, Kansas 66212

B

OFFICERS

John G. Norton .... Chapter President
George W. Rehschuh .... Pioneer Administrator
Roy B. Bergstrom................ Chapter Life Member Rep.
Marie Entringer .... Chapter Life Member Rep.
Marion Iverson .... Bismarck Council President
Arvid W. Torgerson .... Detroit Lakes Council President
Bob Broas .... Duluth Council President
Cathy Rudolph .... Range Club President
R. J. (Dick) Wenberg .... Lake Agassiz Council President
Bob Lewis .... Minneapolis Council President
Bruce Hoeke .... Anoka Club President
Eleanor Erdahl .... Red River Valley Council President
Virginia Hermanson .... Rochester Council President
Ray Thompson .... St. Cloud Council President
Buddy Christenson .... Western Plains Club President
Ron Christy.................... St. Paul Council President
Vada Thompson .... Life Member Club President
Blanche L. Claxton .... Life Member Club President
Leo Speare.................... Life Member Club President
Blanche Masica .... Life Member Club President
E. J. Fox .... Life Member Club President
Bernard F. Marren............. Life Member Club President
Wm. H. Hayden .... Life Member Club President
Art Steinbeck .... Life Member Club President

c

COOKBOOK COMMITTEE

Ruth Rehschuh
Vivian Bergstrom
Jane Hallin
Laurie Johnston
Joan Lewis
Lovise Lorenz
Toni Larson
Eileen Thompson
Mary Boe
Marty Shaw
Dolores Klosterman
Roy Bergstrom
Art Larson

D

TABLE OF CONTENTS

APPETIZERS

PICKLES

RELISHES

RULES FOR USING HERBS

1 Use with a light hand - the aromatic oils are strong and objectional ⸱ᶜ too much is used.

2. Blend or heat with butter, margarine or oil to draw out and extend the flavor. Unsalted butter is best. When using herbs in French dressing, have the oil tepid.

3. Cut or chop leaves very fine. The more cut surface exposed, the more completely the aromatic oil is absorbed.

4 Dried herbs are two to four times as strong as fresh herbs, so that if you substitute dried for fresh herbs use 1/4 to 1/2 the amount. Experimentation is the best guide.

5. The flavoring of herbs is lost by extended cooking.

6. To taste the true flavor of an herb you have not used before, mix 1/2 tsp. crushed herb with 1 Tbsp. cream cheese or sweet butter, let stand 10 - 15 minutes. Taste on a cracker.

7. The beginner should err on the side of too little rather than too much. It is easy to overseason and one flavor should never be allowed to overpower another. A person should not be able to recognize the presence of an herb or what accounts for the delicious flavor. More of an herb can be added, but it cannot be taken out.

8. Herbs are used in addition to salt and pepper.

9. For **herb butters**, 1 Tbsp. of the minced fresh herb is mixed into 1/4 lb. softened butter or margarine. Let stand at room temperature for at least one hour preferably more. After flavor has been absorbed into butter, it should be chilled in refrigerator. This will keep for several days if covered tightly so it does not absorb odors from refrigerator.

APPLE DIP

1/2 c. sugar
1 tsp. dry mustard

1 tsp. salt
1/2 tsp. grated onion

Mix well. Add 2 tablespoons vinegar and 1 cup salad oil. Add slowly, beating constantly. Add 3 more tablespoons vinegar and 1 tablespoon celery seed; continue beating until thick. Makes 1 1/2 cups. Serve with sliced fresh apples.

Bev. Jensen, Willmar, Mn.

HOT MEXICAN BEAN DIP

1 (16 oz.) can refried beans
1 (8 oz.) jar Cheez Whiz
1 large tomato, diced

1 (4 oz.) can diced green
chiles
Salsa to taste
Corn chips to dip

Mix all but the chips together; microwave with full power about 5 minutes or until cheese is melted. Stir once while cooking. Dip corn chips.

Dee Olson, St. Paul, Mn.

CHEESE DIP

2 lb. Velveeta cheese
2 cans Hormel chili without
beans

1 can green chili peppers,
diced

Melt cheese in double boiler, then add chili and green peppers.
Note: This cheese dip can also be put over taco salad for extra added flavor.

Mary Andrew, St. Paul, Mn.

CHEESE DIP

1 (8 oz.) pkg. cream cheese
1 (5 oz.) jar Kraft Roka
  Blue cheese spread
1 (5 oz.) jar Kraft Old
  English cheese spread

1 (5 oz.) jar Kraft bacon
  cheese spread
2 drops onion juice
4 drops liquid smoke
2 tsp. cooking sherry
Season salt to taste

    Mix together. (Freezes well.)
             Jeanie Rose, Tracy, Mn.

HOT CHEESE DIP

6 slices bacon
1/2 c. milk
1 tsp. Worcestershire sauce
1/4 tsp. dry mustard

1/4 tsp. onion salt
3 drops hot pepper sauce
1 (8 oz.) pkg. cream cheese
2 c. (8 oz.) shredded
  Cheddar cheese

    Cut bacon into 1/4 inch pieces. In skillet, fry bacon until crisp; drain on absorbent toweling. Meanwhile in heavy saucepan, combine milk, Worcestershire sauce, mustard, onion salt and hot pepper sauce. Add cream and Cheddar cheeses. Heat over medium heat, stirring occasionally, until cheese melts and mixture is hot. Add bacon Yield: 2 cups.
    Note: Dip may be served in warmer and will hold well for several hours if stirred occasionally. If mixture becomes too thick, stir in additional milk.
             Mankato, Mn.

HOT CHEESE DIP

3 c. Cheddar cheese, grated
2 c. Hellmann's mayonnaise

1/2 c. grated onion
Dash of white pepper

    Mix together and bake in 8 inch pie plate at 350° F. for 45 minutes until brown.
             Ruth Rehschuh, Minneapolis, Mn.

E-Z PICANTE CHEESE DIP

1 can Frito-Lay picante dip   Velveeta cheese, as needed

Heat picante dip; add cheese, either cubed or sliced. Stir until smooth. Serve in fondue pot.

Debbie Burgum, Dickinson, N.D.

Similar recipe submitted by: Anne Aune, Minneapolis, Mn.

CHEEZY ALL-PURPOSE DIP

Melt 2 pounds Velveeta cheese. Saute:

1/2 small onion, diced   1 small green pepper, diced

1/2 c. butter

Combine with melted cheese and add:

1 small can mushrooms, drained   1 can tomatoes, cut in pieces

Serve hot with just about any chip or cracker.

Judy Burton, Duluth, Mn.

CHIP DIP

1 large pkg. Philadelphia cream cheese
1 can tuna
1/2 c. chili sauce
2 tsp. mayonnaise

Dash of Worcestershire sauce
1/4 tsp. salt
2 tsp. chopped onion
2 hard boiled eggs (can be omitted)

Mix and serve with chips.

Pearl Paulsrud, Montevideo, Mn.

CHILE CON QUESO DIP

1 (4 oz.) can diced green chiles
1 lb. Velveeta cheese, cubed

1 (1 lb.) can whole tomatoes, drained and diced
1 Tbsp. minced dried onion
Corn chips for dipping

Heat all but the chips in pan over low heat till cheese is melted. Serve with chips for dipping.

1507-82   Dee Olson, St. Paul, Mn.   5

CHILI CON QUESO

In the top of a double boiler, melt together 1/2 pound Velveeta cheese, cut up, and 1 pound grated sharp Cheddar cheese. Add 2 medium onions, well chopped, and 1 small can of tomatoes, well drained. When well blended, add 1 large can chopped green chili peppers, well drained, 1 tablespoon white wine and 1/2 cup milk. Serve with corn chips or French bread, broken in small pieces. It is best when it is frozen and then reheated. This is my adaptation of the hot cheese dips we've enjoyed in Latin America.

Annette Erspamer, Duluth, Mn.

CHILI DIP

1 pkg. cream cheese
Chili sauce
Onion salt
Garlic salt
Chopped onion

Whip cream cheese until smooth; add chili sauce until red in color. Sprinkle garlic and onion salts. Add 1 chopped onion. Serve with chips.

Renee Andreasen, Duluth, Mn.

CHILI DIP

1/2 small pkg. Kraft
   Velveeta cheese
1 can Hormel chili with beans

Pour chili into pan and mash beans. Cut cheese into cubes; add to the chili. Heat under low fire until cheese is melted. Serve warm.

Debbie Tuft, St. Paul, Mn.

BOBBY'S CRABMEAT DIP

1 c. crabmeat, sorted
1 (8 oz.) pkg. cream
   cheese, beaten
1/2 c. Miracle Whip
1/2 onion (small), grated
1 tsp. Worcestershire sauce
Dash of Tabasco sauce
Salt to taste

Mix and refrigerate.

Beverly Fox, Fargo, N.D.

STEVE'S HOT CRAB DIP

1 (8 oz.) pkg. Philadelphia cream cheese
3/4 lb. Velveeta cheese, cubed
1 (6 oz.) pkg. Wakefield shredded crabmeat
1/8 tsp. garlic powder
Few shakes of Worcestershire sauce
Few shakes of Maggi sauce
Few shakes of Tabasco sauce to taste

Melt cheeses together and add rest of the ingredients. If too thick, add a little cream or milk. Keep warm in a chafing dish. Serve with French onion crackers and Bacon Thins.

Alice Nelson, Minneapolis, Mn.

CUCUMBER DIP

2 (8 oz.) pkg. cream cheese
1 Tbsp. grated onion
1 small cuke, peeled
1 Tbsp. green pepper, chopped
1 chicken bouillon cube
1 Tbsp. chives

Put in blender and mix well. Good with all vegetables (raw).

M. Paul, Minneapolis, Mn.

DEVILED DIP

1 1/2 c. creamed cottage cheese
1 (2 1/4 oz.) can deviled ham
1 tsp. finely chopped parsley
1 Tbsp. finely chopped onion
Dash of freshly ground pepper

Combine all ingredients; mix until well blended, either by hand or electric mixer.

K., St. Cloud, Mn.

GOOD DILL DIP

1 c. sour cream
1 c. real mayonnaise
2 tsp. Beau Monde seasoning
2 tsp. dill weed
1 tsp. grated onion

Blend and refrigerate. Excellent for chips, vegetables or whatever. Chill 4 hours.

Key Barck, Rochester, Mn.

Similar recipes submitted by: Mrs. Norma Applen, Minneapolis, Mn., Mary Paul, Minneapolis, Mn.

DILLY DIP

1 c. salad dressing
1 c. sour cream
1 Tbsp. parsley flakes

1 Tbsp. minced onion flakes
1 tsp. dill weed
1 tsp. seasoning salt

Mix together and chill about 8 hours.

Grayce Funke, Minneapolis, Mn.

FRUIT DIP

1 (8 oz.) pkg. Philadelphia
  brand cream cheese

1 (7 oz.) jar Kraft
  marshmallow creme
Assorted fruit

Combine marshmallow creme and softened cream cheese; mix until well blended. Serve with fruit.

Adeline Jasken, St. Cloud, Mn.

FRUIT DIP

12 oz. sour cream
1/2 tsp. powdered sugar

1 small can orange juice
  (concentrated)

Mix sour cream, juice and sugar. Serve with pieces of apple, banana, muskmelon, honeydew, orange or any fruits.

Pam Stomberg, Fargo, N.D.

GARY'S DIP

8 oz. cream cheese
1/3 c. catsup

1/3 c. French dressing
Several slices of onion

Blend.

Helen Teeuwen, Minneapolis, Mn.

DEVILED HAM DUNK

1 (5 oz.) jar pimento
  cheese spread
1 (2 1/4 oz.) can deviled
  ham

1/2 c. mayonnaise
1 Tbsp. minced onion
A few drops of bottled hot
  pepper sauce

Combine ingredients and chill. Makes 1 1/3 cups.
Bette Thistle, Minneapolis, Mn.
Similar recipe submitted by: Anne Aune, Minneapolis, Mn.

HAMBURGER CHEESE DIP

Brown 1/2 pound of ground beef; drain. Add:

1 can cream of mushroom
  soup, undiluted
1 stick jalapeno cheese

1 stick garlic cheese
1/2 can chopped green
  chilies

Heat until all cheese is melted and everything is blended.
Esther Stevens, Council Bluffs, Ia.

HOT DIP

2 big cans tomatoes, cut
  up and drained
1/2 lb. Velveeta cheese,
  grated
1/2 lb. sharp Cheddar
  cheese, grated

1 (7 oz.) can Ortega green
  chilies, chopped
1/2 - 1 Tbsp. garlic powder
1/2 - 1 Tbsp. chili powder
Red pepper to taste (opt.)

Mix tomatoes and spices together in 2 quart casserole. Add other ingredients. Bake at 350°, uncovered. Serve with taco chips.
Geri Running, St. Paul, Mn.

HOT DIP

2 lb. Velveeta cheese,
  grated
4 Tbsp. butter

1 tsp. Worcestershire sauce
2 tomatoes (fresh), diced
Green pepper

Heat until melted.
1507-82

Anne Aune, Minneapolis, Mn. 9

QUICK HOT DIP

Brown 1 pound hamburger. Add:

1/2 (8 oz.) jar jalapeno pepper relish

1 small box Velveeta cheese

Cook till cheese melts. Serve with Dorito chips.

Marian Nelson, Dickinson, N.D.

DIP LEMON

1 pt. Hellmann's mayonnaise
1/2 bunch green onions
1/2 c. fresh parsley

1 clove of garlic
1/2 tsp. salt
2 Tbsp. lemon juice

Put ingredients in blender. Mix well and refrigerate.
Serve with chips or vegetables.

Maryann Skelton, Duluth, Mn.

LIEDERKRANZ DIP

1 (4 oz.) pkg. Liederkranz
  cheese
1/2 c. butter
1/2 tsp. salt
1/2 tsp. prepared mustard
1/4 tsp. pepper

1/2 tsp. paprika
1/4 tsp. Worcestershire sauce
3 Tbsp. green pepper,
  chopped
2 Tbsp. onion, chopped

Blend all together and serve with potato chips.

Vivian Bergstrom, Forest Lake, Mn.

MEXICAN CHILI DIP

1 c. chopped ripe olives
1/2 - 1 can chopped green
  chilies (mild)
4 medium tomatoes, diced

1/2 c. chopped onion
3 Tbsp. oil
1 Tbsp. vinegar
Garlic salt to taste

Mix all together. Serve with nacho cheese Doritos.
Can be made a day before serving.

Mary J. Sward, New Hope, Mn.

NACHO DIP

Brown 1 pound hamburger; drain grease. Add 1 package taco seasoning mix. Add 1 (10 ounce) can refried beans and 1 cup of water; cover and simmer for 30-40 minutes. Line 8 or 9 inch pie pan with mixture. Spread 1 small carton sour cream over. Pour 1/2 (8 ounce) bottle La Victoria taco sauce; top with 1 cup shredded cheese. Bake at 350° for 25 minutes. Excellent for chip dip.

Becky Carlson, Fargo, N.D.

SMOKED OYSTER DIP

1 (3 oz.) pkg. cream cheese
2 Tbsp. mayonnaise
2 Tbsp. milk
1 Tbsp. finely chopped onion
2 tsp. chopped pimento
1 (4 oz.) can smoked
   oysters, drained, chopped

Combine all ingredients and chill.

Sally Bartsch, Blaine, Mn.

PEASANT BREAD DIP

1 loaf unsliced round dark
  bread or peasant bread
3 containers onion dip
  (Bermuda)
3 small cans deviled ham
1 pkg. dried beef, chopped
  fine
1 tsp. dill weed

Mix together the night before. To serve, take out center of loaf of bread and break into pieces. Put dip in center of loaf of bread and spread the broken pieces around loaf.

Jeanne Regnier, Marshall, Mn.

HOT PECAN DIP

8 oz. softened Philadelphia
  cream cheese
2 Tbsp. evaporated milk
1 (2 1/2 oz.) jar dried beef,
  chopped
2 Tbsp. instant minced onion
2 Tbsp. chopped green
  pepper
1/2 c. sour cream

Mix the above and spread in ovenproof baking dish.

Garnish with 1/4 cup chopped pecans. Bake at 350° for 15 minutes. Serve with Triscuits.

Fernando Gomez, Minneapolis, Mn.
Similar recipes submitted by: Judy Burton, Duluth, Mn., Mildred Nelson, St. Paul, Mn.

SHRIMP DIP

1 stick sharp Cheddar
  cheese, grated
1 medium size onion, grated
1/2 tsp. garlic salt

2 cans cooked shrimp,
  mashed
Dash of Worcestershire sauce
1 qt. Miracle Whip

Mix all of the above together. Chill several hours. This makes a large batch. This is a yummy dip; good with all types of chips and crackers.

Bev Denyes, Grand Marais, Mn.

SHRIMP DIP

1 can small shrimp
1 (8 oz.) pkg. cream cheese
1/2 - 1 c. mayonnaise

1 tsp. Worcestershire sauce
Dash of chili powder
1 Tbsp. ketchup

Mix all ingredients well, except the shrimp. When well blended, then add the shrimp. Chill.

Dorothy Bowe, Duluth, Mn.

SHRIMP DIP

1 can cream of shrimp soup
1 (8 oz.) pkg. cream cheese
1 small can shrimp, drained

Dash of garlic powder
Dash of paprika

Beat together. Overbeating will cause thin dip.
Jeanie Rose, Tracy, Mn.

SHRIMP COCKTAIL DIP

1 container soft Philadelphia
  cream cheese
1 jar shrimp cocktail sauce

1 can tiny cocktail shrimp,
  drained and soaked in ice
  water

12

On a pizza pan or round serving tray, spread soft cream cheese; add cocktail sauce and spread it on top of the cheese. Sprinkle with the shrimp. To serve, let guests spread the dip on crackers.

Jeannie Regnier, Marshall, Mn.

CHEDDAR AND SHRIMP DIP

1/2 lb. Cheddar cheese, grated	1 small onion, chopped fine
5 oz. shrimp, cooked and chopped	1 c. Kraft mayonnaise
	1 tsp. Worcestershire sauce
	Dash of garlic salt

Mix well. Refrigerate 2 hours and serve.

Linda Landsman, Bloomington, Mn.

SPINACH DIP

2 pkg. frozen chopped spinach, thawed and drained	2 cans water chestnuts, chopped
2 c. mayonnaise	2 bunches of green onions, chopped
16 oz. sour cream	2 pkg. Knorr dry vegetable soup mix

Mix and chill. Hollow out a loaf of sourdough or whole wheat bread. Pour the dip in this hollowed out area. Use remaining dough to dip into this mixture. Also good with vegetables.

Carole Justin, St. Cloud, Mn.
Similar recipes submitted by: Maryann Skelton, Duluth, Mn., Pearl Mohn, Montevideo, Mn.

SPINACH DIP FOR VEGETABLES

2 jars baby spinach	3/4 tsp. salt
2 c. mayonnaise	1/2 tsp. pepper
1/2 c. chopped parsley	1/2 tsp. lemon juice
1/2 c. chopped green onions	Small clove of grated garlic

Mix together a day ahead.

Ginny Harwood, St. Cloud, Mn.

HOT SPINACH DIP

1 (10 oz.) pkg. frozen
   chopped spinach, thawed
   and well drained
1 (8 oz.) pkg. cream
   cheese, softened
1/2 c. milk

2 Tbsp. butter or margarine
2 tsp. chicken flavored
   instant bouillon
1/8 tsp. ground nutmeg
1 Tbsp. ReaLemon juice

In medium saucepan, combine cheese, milk, butter, bouillon and nutmeg; cook and stir over low heat until thickened and smooth. Stir in spinach; heat through. Remove from heat; stir in ReaLemon juice. Serve hot with crackers. Refrigerate leftovers.

Inez Hagen, Duluth, Mn.

SPINACH-VEGETABLE DIP

1 (10 oz.) pkg. chopped
   frozen spinach, thawed
   and well drained
1 pkg. Knorr vegetable soup
1 c. Miracle Whip

8 oz. cream cheese or sour
   cream
8 oz. water chestnuts,
   drained and chopped
4-6 strips bacon, fried and
   broken into bits
Round loaf of bread

Combine ingredients. Slice top off of loaf and tear out middle. Break into dipping pieces; fill loaf with dip. Serve with fresh vegetables (cauliflower, mushrooms, tomatoes, carrots, celery) and with the dipping pieces of bread from the center of the loaf.

R. Mielke, Chisholm, Mn.

TACO DIP

1 lb. Velveeta cheese
8 oz. taco sauce

1/2 lb. ground beef,
   browned and drained

Melt cheese in top of double boiler. Add cooked ground beef and taco sauce. Serve hot with Dorito chips for dipping.

Alice Nelson, Minneapolis, Mn.

TACO DIP

8 oz. cream cheese   1 pkg. taco mix
8 oz. sour cream

Mix together and put on bottom of 9x12 inch pan or Tupperware pan. Place over this: Lettuce, broken up and dried a bit with paper towels; tomatoes, cut in pieces; cheese, shredded; onions, cut small (about 1 tablespoon or what you like); 1 can ripe olives, chopped. Cover with a bottle of mild taco sauce; refrigerate. Serve with taco chips.

Mary Jane Schmitz, Wadena, Mn.
Similar recipe submitted by: Dorothy Bowe, Duluth, Mn.

TACO DIP

Mix together:
3 medium ripe avocados,   1/2 tsp. salt
  peeled and mashed   Pepper to taste
2 tsp. lemon juice

Set aside. Mix together and set aside:

1 c. sour cream   1 (1/4 - 1 1/8 oz.) pkg. taco
1/2 c. mayonnaise or salad   seasoning
  dressing

2 (10 1/2 oz.) cans plain or   2 c. pitted ripe olives,
  jalapeno bean dip   chopped
1 large bunch green onions   1 (8 oz.) pkg. Cheddar
  and tops, chopped   cheese, shredded
3 medium tomatoes, cored
  and halved

Layer bean dip first, then avocado mixture, then sour cream mixture. Sprinkle vegetables over layers; cover with cheese. Serve with tortilla chips. Makes a 13x9 inch pan. I use two 8x8 or 9x9 inch pans; it's easier to serve.

Lovise Lorenz
St. Paul Life Member Club

TACO DIP

Mix together:

1 ripe avocado, mashed
1 (8 oz.) ctn. sour cream
3 (8 oz.) pkg. cream cheese
1 pkg. taco seasoning mix

1 tsp. seasoned salt
Garlic, chopped fine
Onion, chopped fine
Salt to taste

Place in large dish with sides (such as a platter). Garnish top with:

Finely chopped lettuce
Tomatoes, cut fine

Sliced black olives
Shredded Cheddar cheese

Dip Tostidos.

Ginny Harwood, St. Cloud, Mn.

HOT TACO DIP

1 large can refried beans
1 medium can tomatoes and
   green chilies
3/4 c. "hot" taco sauce

1 lb. hamburger, sauteed
   with 1 onion, drained
2 c. Mozzarella cheese
1 can chopped ripe olives

In 9 inch glass pan, layer: 1. Refried beans; 2. Hamburger, mixed with tomatoes and chilies; spread over beans; 3. Spread on taco sauce; 4. Sprinkle on cheese; 5. Top with chopped ripe olives. Bake at 400° for 20 minutes. Serve with large regular flavored taco chips.

Maryann Skelton, Duluth, Mn.

TACO LAYERED HOT DISH DIP

Layer in the following order:

1 (16 oz.) can refried beans
1 small can diced chilies
2 avocados, mashed with a
   little lemon juice
1 c. sour cream and 1/2 pkg.
   taco seasoning, mixed
   together

1 c. sharp Cheddar cheese,
   shredded
1 c. Monterey Jack cheese,
   shredded
4-5 chopped green onions
1 (6 oz.) can black olives,
   diced
2 small tomatoes, diced

Use 10x10 inch dish. Bake at 350° for 1/2 hour or until bubbly.

Sue Hetland, Grand Forks, N.D.

TACO PLATE DIP

2 (8 oz.) pkg. Philadelphia cream cheese, room temperature

2 Tbsp. sour cream

Beat the above together. Add 1 jar El Paso taco sauce. Spread on large plate. Spread 2 cartons avocado dip on top. Layer with:

Chopped onion
Chopped lettuce
2 cans chopped green chilies

Chopped tomatoes
1 can black olives, chopped

Sprinkle 2 cups grated cheese. Serve with taco chips.
Sue Hetland, Grand Forks, N.D.

VEGETABLE DIP

1 qt. Hellmann's mayonnaise (do not substitute)
2 c. buttermilk
2 Tbsp. minced onion

1 Tbsp. parsley
4 tsp. Accent
1 tsp. garlic salt
Scant pepper

Mix well. Refrigerate overnight before using.
M.L. Roskoski, Virginia, Mn.

VEGETABLE DIP

1/2 c. mayonnaise, room temperature
1/4 c. sugar

2 Tbsp. prepared mustard (or more)
2 Tbsp. salad oil
1/2 tsp. garlic powder

Mix together.

Mrs. Robert L. Benson
Stillwater, Mn.

VEGETABLE DIP

1 (16 oz.) ctn. sour cream

1 (1.3 oz.) pkg. Italian Good Seasons dressing

Mix together. Refrigerate a few hours before using so flavor mixes through. Good with any raw vegetables.
1507-82   Betty Drier, Rochester, Mn.   17

YUMMY CHEESE DIP

1 lb. Velveeta cheese,
  melted in double boiler
3 hard boiled eggs, chopped
  fine
1 (4 oz.) jar pimento,
  chopped

1 - 1 1/2 Tbsp. onion,
  chopped fine
1/2 tsp. salt
Dash of red pepper (or more
  to taste)
2 Tbsp. vinegar
1 Tbsp. melted butter

In separate pan, cook until thick over low heat:

1/2 c. whipping cream
1 Tbsp. flour

1 Tbsp. sugar

Mix all ingredients together and cool. Serve on sesame crackers. Remove from refrigerator an hour or so before serving.

Barb Discher, Bismarck, N.D.

GARDEN PATCH VEGETABLE DUNK

Blend:
1 (8 oz.) pkg. cream cheese
1/3 c. mayonnaise
1 Tbsp. horseradish
1/2 tsp. garlic salt
1/3 c. shredded cucumber,
  drained

1/2 c. shredded carrots
1 (2 oz.) jar pimento,
  drained
2 Tbsp. shredded radish,
  drained
1 tsp. grated onion

Mix all ingredients; chill 1 hour. Dip fresh vegetables or crackers.

Jeanne Shaver, Minneapolis, Mn.

ALMOND PINE CONES

1 1/4 c. whole almonds
1 (8 oz.) pkg. cream cheese
1/2 c. mayonnaise
1 Tbsp. chopped onion

5 crisp bacon slices,
  crumbled
1/2 tsp. dill weed
1/8 tsp. pepper

Spread almonds in a single layer in shallow pan. Bake at 300° for 15 minutes; stir often. Combine softened cream cheese and mayonnaise; mix well. Add bacon, onion, dill and pepper; mix well. Cover; chill overnight. Form cheese mixture into pine cones. Begin at narrow end; press almonds at a straight angle into cheese, in rows. Continue overlapping rows until cheese is covered. Serve with crackers. Makes 1 1/2 cups.

Renee Andreasen, Duluth, Mn.

ARTICHOKE SPREAD

2 cans water packed
   artichokes, drained
2 c. mayonnaise

1 (8 oz.) can grated
   Parmesan cheese
1 tsp. garlic powder

Chop artichokes; add mayonnaise, cheese and garlic powder. Mix into 1 quart pan. Bake at 350° for 30 minutes. This goes well on Triscuits.

Katie Johnson, Duluth, Mn.

BAMBINOS

1 (6 oz.) can tomato paste
1 tsp. garlic powder
1 tsp. oregano

1 long stick pepperoni,
   sliced
Sharp Cheddar cheese,
   shredded

Mix the tomato paste and spices together in bowl. Spread it on top of Ritz crackers. Put cheese and slice of pepperoni on top. Bake in 375° oven till cheese melts, about 3 minutes. Serve hot.

Joan Norton, Hibbing, Mn.

CHIPPED BEEF SPREAD

8 oz. cream cheese

1/3 - 1/2 c. sour cream with
   onion and chives

Cream with mixer.

1 pkg. chipped beef
1/4 c. finely chopped onion

1/2 c. pimentos, chopped
1/2 c. olives, chopped

Mix. Serve with snack bread.

Char Reno, Duluth, Mn.

BRAUNSCHWEIGER ROLL

Mix equal amounts of Braunschweiger and cream cheese; add chopped onion. Serve with crackers. Can be made into a ball and rolled in chopped nuts.

Virginia Miller, Anoka, Mn.

QUAN'S POORMAN'S CAVIAR

1 can chopped black olives
1 1/2 inch anchovy paste
1/2 tsp. lemon juice

1 (8 oz.) pkg. Philadelphia cream cheese

Mix and serve as a spread on Club crackers.

Kris Riley, So. St. Paul, Mn.

CHEESE BALL

1 (8 oz.) pkg. Philadelphia cream cheese

1/4 lb. butter (must be butter)
1/4 tsp. garlic powder (must be powder)

Soften cream cheese and butter; add garlic powder and mix till well blended. Roll in 1 large ball or 2 small ones. Can also be rolled in chopped walnuts or chopped parsley or left plain.

Fran Toler, Minneapolis, Mn.

CHEESE BALL

2 (8 oz.) pkg. cream cheese, softened
2 c. (8 oz.) shredded sharp Cheddar cheese
1 Tbsp. chopped pimiento
1 Tbsp. finely chopped onion
2 tsp. Worcestershire sauce

1 tsp. lemon juice
1 Tbsp. chopped green pepper (opt.)
Dash of cayenne red pepper
Dash of salt
Finely chopped pecans or walnuts

Combine cream cheese and Cheddar cheese, mixing until well blended. Add remaining ingredients, except nuts; mix well. Chill. Shape into ball; roll in nuts. Serve with crackers. (See following note.)

Note: Cheese balls freeze well. Make 2 small balls, if desired, and freeze one for future use.

Kathy Michalski, Duluth, Mn.
Similar recipe by: Ann Aune, Minneapolis, Mn.

CHEESE BALL

1 (8 oz.) pkg. cream cheese
2 or 3 dashes of Tabasco
   sauce
2 or 3 dashes of
   Worcestershire sauce
2-3 pkg. dried beef
Parsley flakes

Cream the cheese; add sauces and mix. Chop the beef fine; add cream cheese mixture. Mix; form a ball and roll in parsley flakes.

Jeanne Regnier, Marshall, Mn.

BLUE CHEESE BALL

1 (4 oz.) pkg. Blue cheese
1 (8 oz.) pkg. cream cheese
1/4 c. black olives, chopped
1/4 c. onion, chopped
1 Tbsp. butter
1 tsp. garlic salt
Chopped walnuts or parsley

Soften cheeses and mix with olives, onion, butter and garlic salt. Roll in walnuts or parsley.

Jean Schultz, Duluth, Mn.

BUTTERY CHEESE BALL

2 jars Kraft Old English
   cheese
1/2 lb. butter

Let both come to room temperature; mix well with mixer. Refrigerate for 1 hour or until able to shape into a ball. Roll ball in crushed nuts; refrigerate overnight. Remove from refrigerator 4 hours before serving.

Jan Eschbach, Duluth, Mn.

CHICKEN CHEESE BALL

1 (8 oz.) pkg. cream
  cheese, softened
1/2 c. finely chopped
  canned chicken
1 Tbsp. chopped pimento

1 tsp. chicken flavored
  instant bouillon
1 c. French fried onions,
  crushed

In small bowl, combine all ingredients, except onions; mix well. Shape into a ball; roll in onions to coat. Chill. Garnish as desired. Serve with Melba rounds. Makes 1 cheese ball.

Inez Hagen, Duluth, Mn.

HOLIDAY CHEESE BALL

4 (3 oz.) pkg. cream cheese
6 oz. Bleu cheese
6 oz. Cheddar cheese spread
1 pkg. smoked cheese
  spread
1 tsp. Worcestershire sauce

2 tsp. grated onion or onion
  flakes
1/8 tsp. monosodium
  glutamate
1 c. finely ground pecans
1/2 c. finely chopped parsley
  or parsley flakes

In bowl, combine cheeses, onion, Worcestershire sauce and monosodium glutamate. Beat until well blended. Stir in 1/2 cup pecans and 1/4 cup parsley; shape into a ball. Wrap in damp towel and place in refrigerator overnight. About 1 hour before serving, roll in remaining pecans and parsley. Place on serving plate and surround with crackers.

Gemma Pierson, St. Cloud, Mn.

PORT WINE CHEESE BALL

8 oz. cream cheese
1 1/2 c. grated mild
  Cheddar cheese

1 (5 oz.) jar Port wine cheese
1/2 tsp. salt
1/2 tsp. mustard

Mix thoroughly. Before shaping into ball, may add chopped ripe olives, chopped green pepper. Roll ball in chopped parsley or chopped dried beef or nuts.

Mary J. Sward, New Hope, Mn.

CHEESE FOR CRACKERS

1 jar Old English cheese   3/4 cube butter, softened

Blend together and roll in crushed pecans (small bag). Roll to the size of your Hi-Ho crackers. Chill overnight and slice when ready to serve.

Gloria Smith, Jackson, Mn.

CHEESE BITES

2 pkg. Pillsbury baking   1 c. melted butter
   powder biscuits   1 c. grated Parmesan cheese

Cut biscuits into 2 pieces; dip in butter and grated cheese. Bake at 375° for 8 minutes. Very good with beer or wine.

Bev Denyes, Grand Marais, Mn.

PHILADELPHIA CREAM CHEESE AND DRIED BEEF LOG

2 large (8 oz.) pkg.   1/2 small onion, chopped
   cream cheese   fine
1 (2 1/2 oz.) glass jar dried   1/2 c. finely chopped pecans
   beef, chopped fine

Let cheese soften. Mix all ingredients together, except for pecans. Shape into 2 logs and roll in pecans. Chill thoroughly. Serve with small crackers.

Mrs. Norma Applen
Minneapolis, Mn.

CHEESE FONDUE

1 lb. any processed cheese   1 stick butter
   (you can use more than   1 pkg. frozen crabmeat
   one kind as long as
   they're pasteurized)

Can also use as a sauce for broccoli.

Anne Aune, Minneapolis, Mn.

CHEESE LOG

1 lb. Colby cheese,
   shredded or grated
1/4 c. mayonnaise
1/2 c. crushed saltine
   crackers
1 egg, hard boiled

3 Tbsp. green pepper
3 Tbsp. dill pickle
1/2 tsp. onion (or more to
   taste)
10 stuffed olives
1/2 tsp. salt

Shred cheese in blender until fine. Chop egg, green pepper, pickle, onion and olives as fine as possible. Mix into a log or ball. Serve with crackers.

Barb Discher, Bismarck, N.D.

PLANTATION CHEESE LOG

1 c. pecans (or walnuts)   2 cloves of garlic

Chop the above in a blender until fine. Combine:

1 (8 oz.) pkg. cream cheese,
   soft

1/8 tsp. Worcestershire sauce
1/8 tsp. soy sauce
4 drops Tabasco sauce

Add nuts and cloves to cheese mixture. Shape into roll about 1 1/2 inches in diameter. Sprinkle 1 1/2 teaspoons chili powder on sheet of wax paper; roll log to coat evenly. Wrap and chill for at least 4 hours.

Mary Jean Voss, Owatonna, Mn.

CHEESE ROLL

2 (8 oz.) pkg. Philadelphia
   cream cheese
4 oz. grated Blue cheese
4 oz. grated sharp Cheddar
   cheese

2 or 3 tsp. Worcestershire
   sauce
Garlic salt to taste
Ground nuts and parsley
   leaves to roll in

Mix together.

Martie Athey, Osage, Mn.

CHEESE SPREAD

Mix:

1 (8 oz.) pkg. Philadelphia
cream cheese
1 pkg. Good Seasons mild
Italian salad dressing mix

Enough Miracle Whip to make
a good spreading
consistency

Refrigerate overnight. Spread on Pepperidge Farm
rye bread and top with a slice of cucumber.

Mavis Ann Hjulberg
Minneapolis, Mn.

CHEESE SPREAD FOR 100

6 1/4 lb. diced American
cheese
1 Tbsp. salt

3 tall cans evaporated milk
4 Tbsp. dry mustard

Cook in double boiler till cheese melts; cool.

Marion Round, Faribault, Mn.

HELL FIRE CHEESE

1/2 lb. cream cheese
1 Tbsp. melted butter
1 Tbsp. Worcestershire
sauce
1/2 tsp. or more onion juice
1/2 tsp. salt

1/2 tsp. dry mustard
Chopped parsley
2 dashes of Tabasco sauce
6 chopped stuffed olives or
olive spread
1 Tbsp. catsup

Blend all together and serve with chips.

Vivian Bergstrom, Forest Lake, Mn.

CHEESE WAFERS

1/2 c. butter or margarine
2 c. shredded Cheddar
cheese
3/4 c. flour

1/4 tsp. salt
Dash of cayenne pepper
1 1/2 c. Rice Krispies

Cream butter and cheese until fluffy. Add remaining
ingredients. Form into balls and press down with a dampened fork. Bake at 350° for 10-12 minutes until brown.

Marilyn Radakovich, Duluth, Mn.

CHILIES CHEESE SQUARES

1 (4 oz.) can diced, peeled
    green chilies, drained
8 oz. Cheddar cheese,
    shredded
1 c. Bisquick

1 c. light cream
4 eggs
1/4 tsp. salt
1/4 c. sliced, stuffed olives

    Sprinkle chilies and cheese in the bottom of a lightly greased 9 inch pan. Combine the Bisquick, cream, eggs and salt. Beat until thoroughly blended. Pour over the chili cheese mixture. Bake in 375° oven for 30 minutes or until puffed and golden. Garnish with olives. Let stand 10 minutes. Cut into squares and serve.

                    Dee Olson, St. Paul, Mn.

HOT CHEESE PUFFS

    Beat 2 egg whites until stiff. Beat in 1/2 teaspoon baking powder, 1/4 teaspoon salt and 1/4 teaspoon paprika. Fold in 1/2 cup grated sharp American cheese. Heap on 1 1/2 inch rounds of prepared toast beds. Broil about 5 minutes until delicately browned.

                    K., St. Cloud, Mn.

TORTILLA CHEESE SNACKS

24 tortilla chips
1/4 lb. (4 oz.) cheese (your
    favorite), cut in 1/8 inch
    slices

1/4 lb. (4 oz.) hot Italian
    sausage, cooked, drained
    and crumbled

    Place chips in single layer on large ovenproof serving platter. Top each chip with sausage and cheese strip. Bake in preheated 400° oven for 3-5 minutes until cheese melts. Serves 6-8.

                    K. Ells, Duluth, Mn.

SESAME CHICKEN BITS

1/2 c. mayonnaise
1 tsp. dry mustard
1 tsp. instant onion flakes
1/4 c. sesame seeds

1/2 c. fine, dry bread
    crumbs
2 c. cubed, cooked chicken
    or turkey

Mix the first 3 ingredients; set aside. Mix crumbs and sesame seeds. Coat the chicken with the mayonnaise mixture, then with the crumb mixture. Place on a baking sheet; bake at 425° for 12 minutes. Serve hot. Serves 6.

Dee Olson, St. Paul, Mn.

CHICKEN SALAD FILLING

2 whole chickens (about
   3 lb. each)
1 qt. salad dressing
1 medium onion

1/2 bunch celery, chopped
   fine
3/4 pt. sweet pickle relish
Salt and pepper to taste

Grind chicken and onion, then add rest of ingredients. Fills about 100 cocktail buns, open faced.

Marion Round, Faribault, Mn.

CHICKEN WINGS

2 lb. chicken wings
1/3 c. soy sauce
2 Tbsp. salad oil
2 Tbsp. chili sauce
1 Tbsp. dry sherry

1/3 c. honey
2 tsp. salt
1/2 tsp. fresh grated ginger
2 cloves garlic, pressed
4 drops of Tabasco sauce

Cut wings at joints; remove tip of wing. Wash and pat dry on paper toweling. Combine remaining ingredients in 9x13 inch pan. Arrange wings single layer in marinade. Cover; refrigerate overnight. Bake, uncovered, in 375° oven till tender, 30-40 minutes.

Hai Shan Ellis, Minneapolis, Mn.

CHICKEN WINGS

Cut 40 wings in halves; discard tips. Mix:

1/2 c. soy sauce
1 1/2 c. pure maple syrup
1/2 tsp. dry mustard

1/2 tsp. (pinch) ginger
3 caps lemon juice
1 tsp. garlic

Mix and pour over wings in pan for 24 hours. Bake 2 1/2 hours at 350°. When it starts to thicken, put in crock pot and serve.

Mary Boyd, Minneapolis, Mn.

CHICKEN WINGS IN WINE SAUCE

Cut tips off 24 chicken wings; cut rest of wings in halves. Dip in milk and egg mixture, then dust with flour. Brown and place in large broiler pan. Mix:

1/2 c. sugar   1 (6 oz.) bottle soy sauce
1/2 c. white wine

Pour this mixture over wings. Bake 3 hours at 250°; turn every 1/2 hour.

Ellie Cox, Rochester, Mn.

APRICOT CHICKEN WINGS

1 pkg. onion soup mix   1 (10 or 12 oz.) jar apricot
1 bottle Russian dressing   preserves

Pour above ingredients over chicken wings. Bake at 350° until done (8 pounds chicken wings). Don't refrigerate. (You won't need to worry about it as there won't be any left.)

Vivian Knutson, Bismarck, N.D.

SWEET AND SOUR CHICKEN WINGS

1/3 c. honey   1 tsp. salt
1/3 c. mustard   Garlic powder
1 tsp. ginger   Sesame seed

Cut wings in halves. Lay in pan and pour half of above mixture over them. Bake 1/2 hour; turn and cover with rest of honey mixture. Bake 1 hour at 350°. Covers at least 2 dozen wings.

Anne Aune, Minneapolis, Mn.

SWEET AND SOUR CHICKEN WINGS

20-25 chicken wings,   1 tsp. ginger
  cut up   1/4 c. sweetened pineapple
1 c. water   juice
1 c. soy sauce   1 c. granulated sugar
1/4 c. salad oil   1 tsp. garlic powder

Mix ingredients; add wings. Let stand at least 5 hours (overnight). Drain off marinade and save. Place wings on foil lined cookie sheet. Bake at 350° for at least 1 hour; check at 45 minutes. May need turning; baste.

Evelyn Swing, Anoka, Mn.

TERIYAKI CHICKEN WINGS

2 c. soy sauce
1 c. sugar
2 tsp. Accent
1/2 c. oil

1 c. sherry
4 tsp. ginger, grated, or
1-2 tsp. canned
1 clove garlic, chopped

Marinate overnight. Bake 10 minutes at 450°, then turn and bake 10 minutes more. Reduce heat to 350° and bake 20 minutes longer.

Mary J. Sward, New Hope, Mn.

CLAM AND CHEESE CANAPES

2 (6 oz.) pkg. cream cheese
1 Tbsp. lemon juice
1 Tbsp. Worcestershire
  sauce

1 (10 oz.) can minced clams,
  drained
48 (3 x 1/2 inch) toast
  strips

Cream the cheese well with the lemon juice and Worcestershire sauce; mix in the drained clams. Spread on toast strips and garnish with paprika. Yield: 48 canapes.

Gladys Turk, Duluth, Mn.

CORNUCOPIAS

Roll salami slices into cornucopias; fasten with a pick. Fill with white cream cheese, seasoned with horseradish.

K., St. Cloud, Mn.

CRABMEAT HORS D'OEUVRES

1 c. crabmeat or 1 frozen
  pkg.
1/2 stick butter

1 1/2 c. grated Cheddar
  cheese
1/4 tsp. onion powder
1 loaf fresh sandwich bread

Melt butter and cheese in a double boiler on low heat; add onion powder and crabmeat. Cut crust off bread and roll out each slice a little with a rolling pin. Butter both sides of the bread; add cheese and crabmeat mixture and roll ends of slice of bread together. Put in pan, seam side up; sprinkle with sesame seeds. Bake in 400° oven until lightly browned, about 15 minutes. Cut slices into bite sized pieces and serve hot.

Jeanne Regnier, Marshall, Mn.

HOT CRABMEAT PUFFS

Whip 2 egg whites until stiff. Fold in 1 cup mayonnaise and 1 cup (7 ounce can) flaked crabmeat. Season and pile on toast beds. Sprinkle with paprika. Broil 3 minutes until puffy and lightly browned.

K., St. Cloud, Mn.

Similar recipe submitted by K. Ells, Duluth, Mn.

CRAB TOAST ROUNDS

6 English muffins, split and toasted
1 stick butter
1/2 tsp. garlic powder

1/2 tsp. onion powder
2 Tbsp. mayonnaise
4 oz. (1/2 c.) grated cheese
1 small can crabmeat

Blend the last 5 ingredients; spread on toasted English muffins. Place on cookie sheet 6 inches from heat and broil 5 minutes.

Ruth Rehschuh, Minneapolis, Mn.

QUICK CRACKERS AND SPREAD

Mix together and pour over 1 (8 ounce) package cream cheese:

1 can drained clams or shrimp

1/2 bottle Black & Crosswell shrimp cocktail sauce

Excellent spread on Triscuit crackers.

Lois Niemi, Duluth, Mn.

CURRIED APPETIZER BALLS

1/2 c. crushed herb
   seasoned stuffing mix
1/3 c. evaporated milk

1 1/2 tsp. curry powder
1/4 tsp. salt
1 lb. ground beef

Mix stuffing mix, milk, curry powder and salt. Add beef; mix well. Shape into about 40 small balls. Place in large shallow baking pan. Bake in 400° oven for 15 minutes.

Clifford H. Carlson, Saginaw, Mn.

DOG EARS

Spread dried beef with Philadelphia cream cheese (spread). Roll around a dill pickle; put in refrigerator. Cut in slices just before serving.

A.T. Isakson, Fargo, N.D.

Similar recipe submitted by: Jeanne Regnier, Marshall, Mn.

EGG ROLLS

1/3 c. water
2 c. cabbage, chopped fine
2/3 c. celery
1/2 c. onion
1/2 lb. ground beef or
   ground pork
2 1/2 c. bean sprouts
1 tsp. salt

2 tsp. peanut butter
1 1/2 tsp. MSG (or Accent)
1 Tbsp. sugar
2 2/3 soy sauce
2 pkg. egg roll wrappers
   (produce department of
   any grocery store has
   them)

Combine all ingredients in a large bowl. Put about 2 tablespoons filling (raw) into each egg roll wrapper. Fry seam side down in about 1 1/2 inches of oil on medium high heat. Turn till golden brown, about 5 minutes.

Marcia Theisen, Duluth, Mn.

STUFFED EGGS

12 hard cooked eggs
1 c. (8 oz. can) crabmeat,
   flaked
1 c. finely chopped celery

2 Tbsp. finely chopped
   green pepper
1 Tbsp. French salad
   dressing mix
1/3 c. sour cream

Slice eggs in halves lengthwise; remove yolks and mash. Combine yolks, crabmeat, celery, green pepper, salad dressing mix and sour cream, blending well. Stir until well mixed. Refill egg whites. Chill until serving time. Makes 24 stuffed eggs.

Gladys Turk, Duluth, Mn.

FISH HORS D'OEUVRES

Crush 40 saltine crackers. Beat 6 eggs with 2 tablespoons milk. Cut one 4-5 pound fish, filleted, into pieces 1 inch wide and 2 inches long. Salt and pepper both sides of fish strips. Dip into egg mixture, then into cracker crumbs. Dip back into egg mixture. Place strips into frying pan with Crisco. Turn until each side is golden brown. Cut into 1/2 inch pieces. Can be served hot or cold.

Dick Slotness, Duluth, Mn.

POLISH PICKLED FISH

A. Make a salt brine: 1 cup salt* to 2 cups water.
*Use Morton's Jewish "Kosher" salt (not iodized).
Fill pail with fish** (3/4 full). Soak for 48 hours in refrigerator; stir 3 times.
**Fish mush be frozen.
Note: Fish must be filleted (1 x 3 x 1/2 inch thick).

B. Drain off salt brine and soak for 24 hours in undiluted white vinegar in refrigerator. C. Drain off vinegar and make up pickling brine:

4 c. white vinegar   3 c. sugar

Bring to boil just so sugar dissolves. Remove from heat; let cool. Add 1 cup of Silver Satin wine (white). Add 1/2 cup of pickling spices (put in cloth) or sprinkle over fish. D. Put in plastic pail or glass jar: Layer of fish and a layer of raw onions, etc., etc. and put spices in center of pail or jar. Or, sprinkle between layers of fish (works best). E. Last, pour the brine over fish and onions; cover and let stand in refrigerator for 3 weeks. Stir occasionally. Keep cool at all times.

Dick Glodek, Minneapolis, Mn.

32

GREEN BALLS

Mix together:

1/2 c. grated Swiss cheese	1 egg yolk
1/2 c. minced, cooked ham	1/4 tsp. salt
1/2 tsp. prepared mustard	Dash of pepper

Form into balls; roll in minced chives or parsley.

K., St. Cloud, Mn.

CASHEW HAM SPREAD

1 c. ground, salted cashews	1/2 c. grated Cheddar
1 (4 1/2 oz.) can deviled	cheese (sharp)
ham	1 tsp. prepared mustard

Mix well and chill. (Sour cream or mayonnaise can be added.)

Linda Landsman, Bloomington, Mn.

SWEET AND SOUR HAM BALLS

1/2 c. dried bread crumbs	1 Tbsp. cornstarch
1 tsp. salt	1 1/2 c. brown sugar
1 Tbsp. parsley flakes	1 tsp. dry mustard
1 Tbsp. prepared mustard	1/2 c. vinegar
3/4 c. milk	1 1/4 c. water
1 lb. ham, ground	1/4 c. sherry (optional)
1 lb. pork, ground	

Put bread crumbs, salt, parsley, prepared mustard and milk in bowl. Mix well; add the ham and pork and mix well again. Form into 1 inch balls; place in a 9x13 inch pan. Bake at 350° for 1 hour. Pour off the fat and use the same pan for the next step. Combine cornstarch, brown sugar, dry mustard, vinegar, water and sherry in a saucepan. Boil till clear; stir occasionally. Pour over the balls and bake at 350° for 45 minutes. Serve hot. Can make ahead, freeze and reheat when needed.

Joan Norton, Hibbing, Mn.

HERRING

Take any fresh fish; cut in pieces to make 1 quart. Soak in brine strong enough to hold raw egg for 48 hours. Drain and rinse in cold water, then soak in vinegar 25 hours. Drain and rinse in cold water. In 1 quart jar, put 1 sliced onion, 3 tablespoons mixed spices, 5 heaping teaspoons sugar, 1/2 cup white wine and fish. Fill jar with vinegar and seal.

Mary Paul, Minneapolis, Mn.

LIVER PATE

1 (8 oz.) pkg. liver sausage
1 (8 oz.) pkg. Philadelphia
 cream cheese, softened
1 tsp. Worcestershire sauce
1 tsp. or Tbsp. onion,
 grated
Parsley
Salt and pepper

Mix sausage, cream cheese, salt and pepper together. Shape into ball and spread parsley on top. Refrigerate for a couple of hours before serving.

Maryann Skelton, Duluth, Mn.

LIVER PATE

1 lb. chicken livers
3/4 c. chicken bouillon
1/2 c. sauterne (wine gold)
1 sprig of parsley
1/4 tsp. ginger
1 Tbsp. soy sauce
1/2 c. soft butter
1 tsp. seasoned salt
1/2 tsp. dry mustard
1 Tbsp. brandy

Simmer chicken livers in a small saucepan with bouillon cube, wine, parsley, onion, ginger and sauce until tender. Cover and cool in the small amount of liquid that remains. (This keeps the chicken livers moist.) Drain and save liquid. Discard parsley. Put livers through a fine blade or food grinder or chop very fine. If you like a smooth paste, whirl livers in blender with just enough cooking liquid to blend them. Beat liver mixture with butter, salt, mustard and brandy until smooth. If necessary, add some of the cooking liquid to keep mixture soft. Cover and refrigerate overnight to mellow flavors. Makes about 1 1/2 cups.

Mary Ann Schwefel
Minneapolis, Mn.

FROSTED LIVERWURST PATE

1 lb. liverwurst
1 clove garlic, crushed
1/2 tsp. basil
1/4 c. minced onion

1 (8 oz.) pkg. cream cheese, softened
1 tsp. mayonnaise or salad dressing

Mash liverwurst with fork; thoroughly mix in garlic, basil and onion. Mound on serving platter and form into igloo shape. Cover and chill. Blend cream cheese and mayonnaise together well. Spread over liverwurst and chill at least 8 hours. Garnish with parsley and serve with your favorite crackers. Makes 12-16 servings.

Kathy Michalski, Duluth, Mn.

PROVINCIAL PATE

3/4 lb. bacon
3/4 lb. beef liver
1 can tomato soup
1 egg

3/4 tsp. bouquet garni (mixed herbs)
Pepper to taste
Melted butter

Put the bacon and the liver through the coarse blade of the meat grinder. Combine with all of the other ingredients, except the butter. Put the mixture in a baking dish; smooth the top and cover the dish. Cook 1 1/4 hours at 350°; remove the cover and cook 30 minutes more. Cool completely, then cover with a very thin layer of melted butter. Refrigerate. Serve as a "starter" (first course) with fingers of dry toast, or serve with assorted crackers as an hors d'oeuvre.

Eileen Thompson, Minneapolis, Mn.

LOBSTER BALLS

1 can lobster
1 (8 oz.) pkg. cream cheese
1 tsp. lemon juice

1/2 tsp. celery seed
Dash of pepper

Combine all ingredients; blend well and chill. Place a pretzel stick into each ball when ready to serve to be used as a handle.

Kim Kazmierczak, Duluth, Mn.

COCKTAIL MEAT BALLS

Meat Balls:

1 lb. ground beef	9 drops Tabasco sauce
2 eggs	Pinch of salt
1 c. cracker crumbs	1/4 tsp. garlic salt
2 Tbsp. instant minced onion	2 Tbsp. pepper flakes

Form into small meat balls. Place meat balls in shallow pan to brown in 325° oven for about 30 minutes.

Sauce:

3/4 c. catsup	1 1/2 Tbsp. instant minced
1/2 c. water	onion
1/4 c. vinegar	4 tsp. Worcestershire sauce
5 Tbsp. brown sugar	6 drops Tabasco sauce
1 tsp. mustard	1 1/2 tsp. salt

Simmer 1 hour with meat balls in sauce.
Mary Andrew, St. Paul, Mn.

COCKTAIL MEAT BALLS

1 lb. ground round	1 egg
Salt and pepper	1 c. chili sauce
Flour	1/2 c. grape jelly
1 Tbsp. cream	

Mix meat with seasonings, egg and cream. Add just enough flour to hold together. Make miniature balls and brown. Mix chili sauce and grape jelly in a saucepan; add meat balls. Cover and simmer 30 minutes. (Freezes well.)
Helen Lev Schmidt, Dent, Mn.

COCKTAIL MEAT BALLS

2 lb. ground beef	1 jar red currant jelly
3 eggs	1 bottle Heinz hot ketchup
1/2 c. dry bread crumbs	3 tsp. cornstarch
1/2 c. chopped onion	

Combine ground beef, eggs, bread crumbs, onion and salt; shape into small balls. Bake in cookie sheet at 350° for 20 minutes, 1 layer only. In a pan, bring to boil the last 3 ingredients. Pour over meat balls and bake at 200° for 2 hours.

36
Marilyn Radakovich, Duluth, Mn.

QUICK COCKTAIL MEAT BALLS

Mix 2 pounds lean ground beef with 1 package dry Lawry's spaghetti sauce mix. Form meat balls around large stuffed green olives. Bake at 350° on cookie sheet for about 20 minutes or until brown. Serve with toothpick in each one with a BBQ dipping sauce.

Ann Christensen, Litchfield, Mn.

SNACK MEAT BALLS

3 lb. hamburger
1/3 c. grated onion
1 1/2 c. bread crumbs
1 tsp. salt

1 1/2 tsp. Worcestershire
sauce
3 eggs
1 1/4 c. milk

Form into small meat balls. Bake 10 minutes in oven; cool.

Sauce:

1 (14 oz.) bottle hot catsup
1 (6 oz.) jar apple jelly

3 tsp. cornstarch

Bake meat balls in sauce for 2 hours in 200° oven or in crock pot on medium for 2 1/2 hours.

Karen Bergh, Duluth, Mn.

"MUNCIES"

1/2 c. margarine
1/2 c. grated Parmesan
cheese

4 c. Spoon Size Shredded
Wheat

In small saucepan, combine margarine and cheese. Heat over low heat until margarine is melted. Pour mixture over Shredded Wheat and toss until cereal is evenly coated. Place mixture in large shallow pan and bake at 300° for 20 minutes. Stir occasionally. Makes 4 cups.

Mary Paul, Minneapolis, Mn.

MUSHROOM HORS D'OEUVRE

1 small pkg. cream cheese
1 can mushrooms, drained
   and chopped

Salt and other seasonings
1 pkg. crescent rolls

Seal perforations in rolls, making 4 rectangles. Spread with mixture of mushrooms, cheese and seasonings. Roll up and cut into 1 inch pieces. Brush tops with egg yolk and poppy seed. Bake 10 minutes at 350°. Makes 2 cookie sheets full.

Anne Aune, Minneapolis, Mn.

BROILED CHEESE-STUFFED MUSHROOMS

24 large mushrooms
2 Tbsp. butter, plus
   butter for caps
3 Tbsp. scallions, chopped
   fine
3 Tbsp. shallots, chopped
   fine

3 Tbsp. basil, chopped fine
1 1/2 c. grated white
   Cheddar cheese
Salt and paprika
Freshly grated Parmesan
   cheese

Remove the stems from the mushrooms; wipe the caps with a damp cloth. Chop the stems very fine; simmer in the butter. Add the herbs, cheese and garlic. Season the mixture with the salt and paprika to taste and brush the caps with butter. Fill the caps with the mixture; sprinkle with Parmesan cheese. Place them in a preheated broiler, cap side up, on a well greased pan. Broil for about 5 minutes and serve hot.

K., St. Cloud, Mn.

STUFFED MUSHROOMS

1 (3 oz.) pkg. cream cheese
1 box whole, fresh
   mushrooms

1 onion, diced
Croutons

Chop mushroom stems and onion. Fry in saucepan with butter; sprinkle a little garlic salt over it. Mix mushroom stems, onion, cream cheese and a little chopped ham; stuff mushroom caps. Roll in crouton crumbs and set in foil pan. Sprinkle Mozzarella cheese and bacon pieces and close foil. Bake 20-25 minutes and serve.

Sue Kurtz, Minneapolis, Mn.

MUSHROOM TARTS

Mix:

2/3 c. butter   1/2 tsp. salt
2 1/2 c. flour

Add:

1/3 c. sour cream   1 egg, beaten

Cut with pastry blender and mix with hands. Put in cupcake tins. Bake at 400° for 12-15 minutes.

Filling: Saute -

1/2 lb. mushrooms   1/4 c. butter
2 Tbsp. minced onion

Stir in 1/4 cup flour and 1/2 teaspoon salt. Add 1 cup whipping cream (not whipped); cook until thick. Fill shells. Can be frozen and reheated at 400° for 10-12 minutes.

Renee Andreasen, Duluth, Mn.

FRESH STUFFED MUSHROOMS

Remove stems from 12 large caps. Wash mushrooms and stems; pat dry with towel. In a skillet, saute the following:

12 mushroom stems, chopped   2 Tbsp. chives
  fine   2 Tbsp. cooked bacon,
3 Tbsp. butter   crumbled
2 Tbsp. onion, chopped fine   2 Tbsp. crushed pecans
1 c. bread crumbs   1/2 c. sour cream

Stir until light and fluffy; fill mushroom caps. Place in skillet. Saute at 275° for 7 minutes.

Dorothy Bowe, Duluth, Mn.

NACHOS

Brown 1 pound hamburger; add 1/4 - 1/2 package taco seasoning. Add water as directed. Simmer while meat is simmering. Line cookie sheet with Tostitos. Grate Colby or Cheddar cheese and have hot sauce (examples: Lacampa or Mexican Village) on hand. On each shell, add a teaspoon

1507-82   39

of meat mixture, 1 teaspoon hot sauce and sprinkle with grated cheese. Place under hot broiler approximately 1 minute. Turn off broiler; close oven door and wait approximately 2 minutes. Serve.

Colleen Fahey, Grand Forks, N.D.

ONION EGG PIE

2 c. soda cracker crumbs
1/4 c. melted butter
2 large onions, sliced
1/4 c. butter

4 eggs
1 1/2 c. milk
1 1/2 tsp. salt
Grated cheese

Mix crumbs and melted butter; pat into 9x13 inch pan for thin crust. Saute onion slices and 1/4 cup butter until slightly browned. Place onions over crust. Beat eggs, milk and salt; pour over onions. Sprinkle with lots of cheese and bake at 350° for 35-40 minutes. Serve warm, cut into squares.

Jan Eschbach, Duluth, Mn.

OYSTER CRACKER APPETIZERS

1 (12 oz.) pkg. oyster crackers
1/2 c. warm vegetable oil
1/2 tsp. dill weed

1/2 tsp. garlic salt powder (opt.)
1 pkg. dry Hidden Valley salad dressing (Blue cheese is very good)

Mix and toss well.

Helen Lev Schmidt, Dent, Mn.

PEANUT BUTTER AND BACON APPETIZERS

Spread prepared toast bed with crunchy peanut butter. Sprinkle with crumbled crisp bacon. Trim with minced parsley.

K., St. Cloud, Mn.

FANCY PICKLE APPETIZERS

1 pkg. sliced smoked beef
1 jar large dill pickles

1 container soft Philadelphia
cream cheese

Take 1 slice of beef and spread the cream cheese on it; wrap it around a dill pickle. Do this to each pickle. To serve, cut the pickles crosswise in round, bite sized pieces.

Jeanne Regnier, Marshall, Mn.
Similar recipe submitted by A.T. Isakson.

MINIATURE PIGS IN BLANKETS

Wrap Vienna sausage halves in thinly rolled pastry or rich biscuit dough. Let ends show. Bake at 450° for 8 minutes. Serve hot.

K., St. Cloud, Mn.

PIZZA HORS D'OEUVRE

1 stick pepperoni, chopped
1/4 c. green pepper,
  chopped
1/4 c. chopped onion

1 Tbsp. mayonnaise
1 can chopped black olives
1 pkg. Swiss cheese,
  shredded

Cook in oven until bubbly. Serve hot on Triscuit crackers.

Kris Riley, So. St. Paul, Mn.

PORK SAUSAGE ROLLS

3 c. Bisquick
1 lb. pork sausage,
  browned

3/4 c. grated Cheddar
  cheese

Roll in balls the size of walnuts. Freeze until ready to use. Bake at 375° for 15 minutes.

Laverne M. Akerstrom
Duluth, Mn.

SALMON BALL

1 c. (7-8 oz.) drained,
  flaked salmon
8 oz. cream cheese
1 Tbsp. lemon juice

2 Tbsp. grated onion
1 tsp. horseradish
1/4 tsp. salt
1/4 tsp. liquid smoke

Combine and shape the above ingredients. Combine:

1/2 c. chopped pecans   3/4 Tbsp. chopped parsley

Roll salmon ball in above and chill. (Nuts will stick better if salmon ball is not too cold.)

Karen Moe, Duluth, Mn.

SALMON SPREAD

1 (16 oz.) can red salmon,
  drained, flaked
1 (8 oz.) pkg. cream
  cheese, softened
1/4 c. finely chopped green
  onions
2 tsp. lemon juice

1 Tbsp. horseradish
2 Tbsp. sweet pickle relish
1/4 tsp. salt
1/4 c. finely chopped parsley
1/2 c. chopped walnuts
Assorted appetizer crackers

In medium size bowl, blend salmon, cream cheese, onions, lemon juice, horseradish, pickle relish and salt. Wrap in wax paper and form into ball. Chill until firm, about 1 hour. Mix parsley and walnuts together; pat into salmon ball to garnish. Chill until ready to serve. Serve with crackers. Makes 1 large ball (about 2 cups).

Blánche B. Masica, Minneapolis, Mn.

SMOKED SALMON CANAPES

6 thin slices of white bread,
  fried on one side
2 Tbsp. butter

1/4 tsp. prepared mustard
6-10 thin slices of smoked
  salmon

Mix the butter and mustard; spread on the soft side of the bread. Cover the bread with smoked salmon; cut each slice into 3 strips. Sprinkle with a bit of lemon juice and pepper. (There should be enough salmon to cover the bread. Some salmon slices are small and must be pieced out to cover a piece of bread.) Yield: 18 canapes.

Gladys Turk, Duluth, Mn.

ITALIAN SAUSAGE SQUARES

1 lb. hamburger
1 lb. Italian sausage (hot)

1 lb. Velveeta cheese

Brown meat; skim fat. Add cheese till it melts. Spread on cocktail rye bread. Lay on cookie sheet and freeze. When ready to use, bake at 375° for 15 minutes.

Laverne M. Akerstrom, Duluth, Mn.

Similar recipe submitted by: Helen Teeuwen, Minneapolis, Mn.

SHRIMP CANAPES

2 Tbsp. butter
2 tsp. lemon juice

24 (1 1/2 - 2 inch) toast rounds
24 canned shrimp, cleaned

Cream the butter and lemon juice; spread on the toast rounds. Top each with a whole shrimp; garnish with parsley. Yield: 24 canapes.

Gladys Turk, Duluth, Mn.

SHRIMP MOLD

Heat together:
1 can tomato soup

1 env. Knox gelatine

Beat in 1 (8 ounce) package cream cheese. Add and mix:

2 (4 1/2 oz.) cans shrimp, cut fine
1 c. onion, cut very fine

1 c. celery, cut very fine
1 c. mayonnaise (not Miracle Whip)

Put in mold and refrigerate several hours. Great on Ritz crackers.

Lois Niemi, Duluth, Mn.

SHRIMP STUFFED CELERY

6 oz. Philadelphia cream
cheese
1 small can tiny shrimp
Celery

1 Tbsp. chives or onion
2 tsp. lemon juice
1/4 tsp. salt
2 dashes of Tabasco sauce
1/4 c. mayonnaise

Place all ingredients, except shrimp, into a blender; mix well. May also use a rotary beater. Fold in tiny shrimp. Using a knife, stuff the shrimp mixture into the celery and cut into 1 inch pieces. Serves 12.

Marlene U'Ren, Duluth, Mn.

SPINACH BALLS

2 pkg. frozen spinach
6 eggs, well beaten
2 c. Pepperidge Farm
stuffing

3/4 c. softened butter
1 c. Parmesan cheese
Salt and pepper

Combine all ingredients in bowl; shape into 1 inch balls. Quick-freeze balls on cookie sheet until firm. Place balls in plastic bags in quantities desired. When ready to use, place desired number in shallow baking dish or on cookie sheet. Bake 15 minutes at 375°.

Kim Kazmierczak, Duluth, Mn.

SPINACH BALLS
(You don't taste the spinach)

1 pkg. frozen chopped
spinach, thawed and
drained
1 medium onion, chopped
3 eggs, beaten

3/4 c. melted butter
3/4 c. Parmesan cheese
1/2 tsp. garlic salt
16 oz. Pepperidge Farm
herbed stuffing (crumbs,
not cubes)

Mix well; shape into balls (cocktail size on up). Refrigerate 1 hour. Bake at 350° for 20 minutes.

Optional: Add fried hamburger or sausage, chopped water chestnuts or chopped nuts.

Can be frozen and reheated. Size of ball can range from small cocktail size to the size of a tennis ball for side dishes to chicken and pork.

Linda Landsman, Bloomington, Mn.

44

GLORIA'S SPINACH BALLS

2 pkg. chopped frozen spinach, cooked and drained

2 c. Pepperidge Farm herbed stuffing

1 large onion, finely chopped

6 eggs, beaten lightly

1/2 c. melted butter

3/4 c. grated Parmesan cheese

1 1/2 tsp. garlic salt

1/4 tsp. nutmeg

1/2 tsp. dried, crushed thyme

1 tsp. black pepper

Mix all ingredients; form into balls about half dollar size. Place on well greased cookie sheet and freeze, then store in plastic bag. When ready to serve, bake in 350°-375° oven straight from freezer for about 20-25 minutes (until firm, but not hard).

Helen Teeuwen, Minneapolis, Mn.

BERT'S BREAD SPREAD

1 loaf round rye bread

1 pkg. chopped spinach, thawed, squeeze out moisture

Add:

1 c. sour cream

1 c. mayonnaise

1 can chopped water chestnuts

4 chopped green onions

1 pkg. dry country vegetable soup mix (Lipton)

Mix well. Cut hole in center of bread large enough for the spread. Break into bite size pieces and place around edge of loaf. Serves 10-15.

Roberta Martinson, Duluth, Mn.

SHRIMP HORS D'OEUVRE

1 small pkg. cream cheese

1 small can shrimp, mashed

1 pkg. crescent rolls

Seal roll perforations to make 4 rectangles; spread with mixture of softened cream cheese and shrimp. Cut into narrow strips and roll into pinwheels. Bake 10 minutes at 350°. Makes 2 cookie sheets full.

Anne Aune, Minneapolis, Mn.

SWEDISH NITEMARES

Grind together fine:

8 strips of raw bacon	1/2 lb. sharp Cheddar
1 large onion	cheese

Mix 8 tablespoons chili sauce into ground mixture. Store for 24 hours (can be frozen). Spread mixture on party snack rye bread and broil until mixture bubbles.

G.W. Seemans, Robbinsdale, Mn.

TOAST BEDS

Spread prepared toast beds with deviled ham, seasoned with horseradish, onion and mayonnaise. Or, smoked turkey or gooseliver paste, or smoked oysters with sliced cucumber and anchovy paste, minced clams and creamed cheese.

K., St. Cloud, Mn.

TRIPLE TREAT

Place on one pick a maraschino cherry, a pickled onion and a gherkin.

K., St. Cloud, Mn.

TURNOVERS

1 env. onion soup mix	1 lb. hamburger
1 c. shredded Cheddar	3 pkg. refrigerated crescent
cheese	rolls

Preheat oven to 375°. In fry pan, combine onion soup mix and hamburger; brown well. Blend in cheese. Separate crescent dough according to package directions, then cut in halves. Place spoonful of meat mixture in center of each triangle; fold over and seal edges. Place on ungreased cookie sheet. Bake 15 minutes or until golden brown. Makes 48 turnovers.

Ella Fennessy, Duluth, Mn.

BARBECUED WATER CHESTNUTS

1 (8 oz.) can water
  chestnuts, drained

Enough bacon slices, cut in
  halves, to wrap each
  chestnut

Use toothpick to hold in place while baking. Place on baking sheet with sides. Bake 1 hour at 325°; drain grease. Cover with 1/2 cup catsup and 1/3 cup brown sugar, mixed. Bake another 30-35 minutes at 325°. Serve while warm; leave toothpicks in for serving.

Mrs. Harry Osborn, Rochester, Mn.

WEDGIES

Spread 4 slices of large bologna or minced ham with softened cream cheese, seasoned with onion or chives and mustard. Place slices together (like a layered cake). Spread cheese over top and sides; decorate with sliced olives. Chill; cut in wedges.

K., St. Cloud, Mn.

COCKTAIL WIENERS ORIENTAL

1 (13 1/4 oz.) can pineapple
  chunks
1/2 c. brown sugar
1/2 tsp. salt
1 Tbsp. cornstarch
1/4 c. white vinegar
1/2 c. water

1/2 green pepper, cut in
  chunks
2 small bottles button
  mushrooms
2 pkg. (1 lb.) cocktail
  wieners

Drain pineapple, reserving 1/2 cup juice. Mix sugar, salt and cornstarch in pan. Stir in vinegar, 1/2 cup pineapple juice and water. Boil over medium heat for 5 minutes. Add pineapple chunks, green pepper, mushrooms and wieners; heat thoroughly. Spear with toothpicks.

Marilyn Radakovich, Duluth, Mn.

BARBECUE SAUCE FOR SMALL BARBECUE WIENERS

16 oz. barbecue sauce
  (original flavor)
10 oz. grape jelly

Dry onion
2 Tbsp. brown sugar

Simmer 10 minutes; add cocktail wieners and simmer 10 minutes longer.

1507-82   Gloria Smith, Jackson, Mn.   47

TO PRESERVE GREEN TOMATOES
(Ripen in House)

1 gal. water (cold)   1 tsp. Clorox bleach

Wash tomatoes in water and dry completely. This will keep them from rotting.

Mrs. Henry J. Vold, Wilton, Mn.
By: Bonnie Sovick, Marshall, Mn.

SWEET AND SOUR PICKLED CARROTS

18-20 carrots (about 2 lb.)   1 Tbsp. whole cloves
1 qt. vinegar   Mace
4 c. sugar   Whole allspice
1 stick cinnamon

Bring carrots to boil in a large kettle of water; simmer until the skins slip easily. Remove skins and slice carrots into thin strips. Combine vinegar and sugar in a large kettle. Add spices; bring to boil. Pour over drained carrots. Cover and refrigerate overnight. Drain liquid and heat for 5 minutes. Pour over carrots and refrigerate until cold. Makes 10 to 12 servings.

Mary Paul, Minneapolis, Mn.

APPLE CHUTNEY

16 apples (tart medium),   4 c. brown sugar
  chopped, cored, pared   1 qt. apple cider vinegar
1 c. chopped onion   2 "hot" red peppers
1 clove garlic, minced (put   3 Tbsp. mustard seed
  through press)   2 Tbsp. ground ginger
1 c. chopped sweet peppers   2 tsp. salt
  (optional)   2 Tbsp. ground allspice
2 lb. raisins

Combine ingredients; simmer until thick, about 1 1/4 to 1 1/2 hours. As mixture thickens, stir frequently to prevent sticking. Pour boiling hot into hot jars. Adjust caps; seal. Put jars into boiling water and boil for 10 minutes. Use after 6 to 8 weeks. Like a woman, it gets better with age.

Maryann Skelton, Duluth, Mn.

48

CINNAMON APPLE SLICES

3 lb. Jonathan apples   1/3 c. red cinnamon candies
2 c. white sugar   Few drops of red food
                                 coloring

Cut each apple in 8 pieces or core and cut in rings. Boil gently, uncovered, until tender. Remove from stove; cover until cool. Put in Tupperware container and store in refrigerator, covered. Keeps up to about 1 month.
Joan Norton, Hibbing, Mn.

BAKED CRANBERRIES

1 lb. cranberries   1/2 c. water
2 c. sugar

Set over low flame long enough to melt sugar. Bake 1 hour at 350°. Serve hot or cold with turkey or chicken.
Marie Capen, Duluth, Mn.

SWEET DILLS

Drain 1 quart of whole dill pickles (regular dills, not kosher type); cut in small chunks. Mix with 1 1/2 cups white sugar. Keep in Tupperware 24 hours at room temperature, then refrigerate. Keeps for weeks. The pickles will be crisp.
Mrs. Harry Osborn, Rochester, Mn.

FREEZER CUCUMBER PICKLES

3 qt. cucumbers   1 lb. onions
1 green pepper   1/4 c. salt
1 sweet red pepper   4 c. white vinegar
1 bunch of celery   6 c. sugar

Slice vegetables paper thin. Combine salt, sugar and vinegar; heat to dissolve and cool. Pour syrup over vegetables; weight down and let set overnight. In the morning, pack in freezer containers; cover with syrup. Keeps indefinitely.
Marion Round, Faribault, Mn.

FROZEN CUKES

3 qt. sliced cukes (don't peel)
2 large green peppers, cut in strips
2 lb. sliced onions

2 large red peppers, cut in strips, or 1 small jar pimentos
Several ribs of celery, cut in cubes

Mix together. In separate bowl, mix:

3 c. sugar
2 c. white vinegar

1/2 c. coarse salt

Pour over pickle mixture. Cover and set at least 3 hours or overnight. Put in plastic containers and fill with juice. Freeze; after defrosted, keep in refrigerator.
Mary Paul, Minneapolis, Mn.

RUSSIAN OR SWEET AND SOUR DILLS

Soak pickles in cold water overnight. Boil 5 minutes:

2 c. white vinegar
1 c. water

1 c. sugar
1/4 c. canning salt

Place 2 slices of onion, some garlic and dill in bottom of jars. Slice cukes lengthwise and pack in jars. Add some dill on top, then fill with brine and seal. Place in hot water up to necks; let cool overnight. Can be eaten in 12 hours. Carrots, green pepper, also hot peppers and celery can be added, too.
Mary Paul Minneapolis, Mn

BRANDIED PEACHES

1 (1 lb. 13 oz.) can peach halves
6 whole cloves

1 piece of stick cinnamon
2 Tbsp. brandy

Drain syrup from peaches into a small saucepan; add cinnamon stick and cloves. Heat to boiling; lower heat and simmer for 5 minutes. Stir in the brandy; pour over the peaches in a small bowl. Cover and chill at least overnight to blend the flavors.
Joan Norton, Hibbing, Mn.

BREAD AND BUTTER PICKLES

4 qt. sliced, unpared
  medium cucumbers
6 medium white onions,
  sliced (6 c.)
2 c. green peppers, sliced
  (1 2/3 c.)
3 cloves garlic

1/3 c. granulated pickling
  salt
5 c. sugar
3 c. cider vinegar
1 1/2 tsp. turmeric
1 1/2 tsp. celery seed
2 Tbsp. mustard seed

Combine cucumber, onion, green pepper and whole garlic cloves. Add salt; cover with cracked ice. Mix thoroughly. Let stand 3 hours; drain well. Remove garlic. Combine remaining ingredients; pour over cucumber mixture. Bring to boil. Fill hot jars to 1/2 inch from top; adjust lids. Process in boiling water bath for 5 minutes (start timing when water returns to boiling). Makes 8 pints.

Anne Aune, Minneapolis, Mn.

GOLDEN GLOW PICKLES

6 lb. ripe yellow or green
  cucumbers
6 large onions
3 sweet peppers
3 green peppers
1/4 c. salt

2 c. white sugar
2 c. brown sugar
2 c. brown vinegar
1 tsp. turmeric
1 tsp. celery seed
1 tsp. mustard seed

Peel cucumbers; cut and discard seeds and pulp. Peel onions and remove seeds from peppers. Cut cucumbers, onions and peppers; stir in salt. Let mixture stand overnight. Drain; rinse in cold water and drain again. Combine sugars, vinegar, turmeric, celery seeds and mustard seeds. Add to cucumber, onion and pepper mixture. Cook slowly until cucumbers are transparent, not mushy. Seal at once in jars, covering well with liquid.

Note: Cucumbers, onions and peppers can be chopped, sliced or just cut up, as desired.

Maryann Skelton, Duluth, Mn.

PERFECT DILL PICKLES

Boil for 15 minutes:
13 - 13 1/2 c. water   6 - 6 1/4 c. vinegar
1 c. salt

Pack cukes in jars with lots of dill or rounded teaspoon of dill seed. Add 1 tablespoon sugar per quart; do not boil sugar in brine. Pour boiling vinegar over cukes. Fill to top and seal tight. Set jars in boiling water to come over tops of jars. Let stand till cold.

Helen Martin, Fargo, N.D.

REFRIGERATOR PICKLES

2 c. sugar   1 Tbsp. salt
1 c. vinegar   1 tsp. celery seed

Boil together. In large jar, put 7 cups cucumbers, 1 cup onion. Pour boiled mixture over cucumbers; let stand 24 hours on counter.

Inez Wagner, Austin, Mn.

REFRIGERATOR PICKLES

3 c. vinegar   1/3 tsp. salt
3 c. sugar   1 tsp. celery seed
1/2 tsp. turmeric

Bring to boil. Slice cucumbers and put in container. Pour liquid over them. (Optional: Cut up onion and/or green pepper with it.) Leave in refrigerator for 2 weeks at least. You can save juice and use again also. (Double above recipe uses 5 quart pail and 6-7 large cukes.)

Anne Aune, Minneapolis, Mn.

TURMERIC PICKLES

1 doz. oversized ripe   1 tsp. whole allspice
   cucumbers   1 tsp. turmeric powder
1 pt. vinegar   1 tsp. ground mustard
3 heaping c. sugar   1/2 tsp. salt

Peel cukes; cut in fourths, lengthwise. Remove seeds.

Cut into desired size pieces. Put spices in cheesecloth bag. Heat sugar and vinegar until sugar is dissolved. I add a few drops of yellow food coloring to the syrup for a brighter yellow pickle. Add bag of spices to syrup; bring to a boil. Add cukes; cook, covered, only until they become clear in appearance. You'll need to turn them occasionally with a wooden spoon to attain even cooking. Don't overcook! Pack in hot jars and seal. Makes 7 pints.

Alicia Woodford, Montevideo, Mn.

ZUCCHINI PICKLES

1 qt. white vinegar	1 tsp. dry mustard
2 c. granulated sugar	5 lb. (5-6 inch long)
1/4 c. salt	zucchini, unpeeled, cut
2 tsp. celery seed	into 1/4 inch slices
2 tsp. ground turmeric	1 qt. thinly sliced onions
	(4-5 medium onions)

Combine first 6 ingredients; bring to boil. Pour over zucchini and onions; let stand 1 hour. Stir occasionally. Bring to boil and simmer 3 minutes; continue simmering while packing in clean, hot jars one at a time, making sure juice covers vegetables. Process 5 minutes in boiling water bath. Makes 6-7 pints.

Mary Paul, Minneapolis, Mn.

WATERMELON PICKLES

7 lb. rind, parboiled	1 pt. vinegar
3 1/2 lb. sugar (2 1/4 c.	1/2 tsp. cinnamon oil
equals 1 lb.)	1/2 tsp. clove oil

Pour syrup on rind; let stand overnight. Drain. Heat syrup; pour over rind again. Repeat for 3 days. Heat all together third day and seal hot. To prepare rind, cut off all outside green and inside red. Cut white meat into chunks and parboil in water until raw, white look is gone.

Mrs. Neva Kost, Fairmont, Mn.

BEET RELISH

1 (16 oz.) can whole beets, strained and chopped fine in blender
1 1/2 c. sugar

1 (5 oz.) jar creamy horseradish
1 tsp. chili sauce (opt., but nice if using the beet relish with seafood)

Combine the beets with horseradish, sugar and chili sauce; stir to dissolve sugar. Keep in covered container. Keeps well in refrigerator and is good with ham, pork, beef and cold cuts.

Fran Toler, Minneapolis, Mn.

CRANBERRY-ORANGE RELISH

1 lb. Ocean Spray fresh or frozen cranberries

1 small orange, quartered
1 1/2 c. sugar

Put fresh or frozen cranberries and orange sections through a food grinder. Add sugar; mix well and chill several hours before serving. This will keep for several weeks in refrigerator or it may be frozen for later use.

Clara O. Johnson, Chanhassen, Mn.

CRANBERRY ORANGE RELISH

1 (3 oz.) pkg. cherry jello

1 c. boiling water

Add:
1 (10 oz.) pkg. cranberry orange relish, partially thawed

1 (9 oz.) can crushed pineapple and juice
1 Tbsp. lemon juice

Chill till partially set. Fold in 1/2 cup chopped celery and 1/2 cup chopped walnuts. Place in mold.

Freida Paro, Crystal, Mn.

ZUCCHINI RELISH

10 c. zucchini, pared
2 c. onions, grated
2 green peppers

2 red peppers or 2 bottles pimento

Put all through food grinder; add 5 tablespoons salt. Let stand overnight. Combine:

3 c. vinegar	2 tsp. cornstarch
4 1/2 c. sugar	2 tsp. celery seed
1 tsp. cinnamon	1 tsp. mustard*
1 tsp. turmeric	

Cook till sugar is dissolved. Rinse zucchini under cold water till all is removed (salt). Add to sugar-vinegar mixture. Cook for 30 minutes. Seal while hot.

*Note: Instead of mustard called for, the mustard seed is required.

Esther Mungovan, Duluth, Mn.

ZUCCHINI RELISH

Grind:

10 c. zucchini	5 c. onions

Add 5 tablespoons salt; mix. Soak overnight. Drain; rinse in cold water and drain again. Add:

2 1/4 c. vinegar	1 Tbsp. cornstarch
5 c. sugar	2 Tbsp. celery seed
1 Tbsp. nutmeg	1/2 Tbsp. black pepper
1 Tbsp. mustard	1 red and 1 green pepper,
1 Tbsp. turmeric	chopped

Cook about 25 or 30 minutes on low heat. Stir; place in hot jars and seal. Makes about 2 3/4 quarts.

Marlys Swehla, Albert Lea, Mn.

SALADS
DRESSINGS
SAUCES

Approximate 100 Calorie Portions

Almonds (shelled) — 12 to 15 nuts
Angel cake — 1¾ inch cube
Apple — 1 large
Apple pie — 1/3 normal piece
Apricots — 5 large
Asparagus — 20 large stalks
Bacon — 4 or 5 small slices
Bananas — 1 medium
Beans — 1/3 cup canned baked
Beans — green string — 2½ cups
Beets — 1 1/3 cups sliced
Bread — all kinds — slice ½ inch thick
Butter — 1 tablespoon
Buttermilk — 1 1/8 cups
Cabbage — 4 to 5 cups shredded
Cake — 1¾ inch cube
Candy — 1 inch cube
Cantaloupe — 1 medium
Carrots — 1 2/3 cups
Cauliflower — 1 small head
Celery — 4 cups
Cereal — uncooked — ¾ cup
Cheese — 1 1/8 inch cube
Cottage cheese — 5 tablespoons
Cherries — sweet fresh — 20 cherries
Cookies — 1 to 3 inches in diameter
Corn — 1/3 cup
Crackers — 4 soda crackers
Crackers — graham — 2½ crackers
Cream — thick — 1 tablespoon
Cream — thin — 4 tablespoons
Cream sauce — 4 tablespoons
Dates — 3 to 4
Doughnuts — ½ doughnut
Eggs — 1 1/3 eggs
Fish — fat — size of 1 chop
Fish — lean — size of 2 chops
Flour — 4 tablespoons
Frankfurter — 1 small
French dressing — 1½ tablespoons
Grapefruit — ½ large
Grape juice — ½ cup
Grapes — 20 grapes
Gravy - 2 tablespoons
Ice cream — ½ cup
Lard — 1 tablespoon
Lemons — 3 large
Lettuce — 2 large heads

Macaroni — ¾ cup cooked
Malted milk — 3 tablespoons
Marmalade and jelly - 1 tablespoon
Marshmallows — 5 marshmallows
Mayonnaise - 1 tablespoon
Meat — cold sliced — 1/8 inch slice
Meat — fat — size ½ chop
Meat — lean — size 1 chop
Milk — 5/8 cup (regular)
Molasses — 1½ tablespoons
Onions — 3 to 4 Medium
Oranges — 1 large
Orange juice — 1 cup
Peaches — 3 medium fresh
Peanut butter — 1 tablespoon
Pears — 2 medium fresh
Peas — ¾ cup canned
Pecans — 12 meats
Pie — ¼ ordinary serving
Pineapple — 2 slices 1 inch thick
Plums — 3 to 4 large
Popcorn — 1½ cups
Potatoes — sweet — ½ medium
Potatoes — white — 1 medium
Potato salad — 1 cup
Prunes — dried 4 medium
Radishes — 3 dozen red button
Raisins — ¼ cup seeded or 2 table-
   spoons seeded
Rhubarb — stewed and sweetened
   — ½ cup
Rice — cooked ¾ cup
Rolls — 1 medium
Rutabagas — 1 2/3 cups
Sausage — 2 small
Sauerkraut — 2½ cups
Sherbet — 4 tablespoons
Spinach — 2½ cups
Squash — 1 cup
Strawberries — 1 1/3 cups
Sugar — brown — 3 tablespoons
Sugar — white — 2 tablespoons
Tomatoes — canned — 2 cups
Tomatoes — fresh— 2 to 3 medium
Turnips — 2 cups
Walnuts — 8 to 16 meats
Watermelon — ¾ slice 6 inches
   diameter

EASY ANTIPASTO SALAD
(All Ingredients Optional)

1/2 lb. asparagus, cut in chunks
1 head cauliflower
1 head broccoli
1 cucumber, cut in chunks, unpeeled
1 green pepper, cut in chunks
1 zucchini, cut in chunks
1 lb. mushrooms (fresh)
1 lb. cherry tomatoes

Couple large stalks of celery, cut in chunks
1/2 lb. cherry tomatoes, sliced in halves
1 pkg. sliced pepperoni, slices cut in halves
1 small jar green olives
1 can pitted black olives
2 pkg. Good Season's zesty salad dressing, mixed according to directions

Pour over vegetables; marinate 2 days.

Kris Riley, So. St. Paul, Mn.

APPLE-PINEAPPLE-CELERY SALAD

3 c. diced apples
2 c. diced celery
1 (No. 2) can crushed pineapple, drained (about 1 1/2 c. fruit, keep drained juice)

1/4 c. water
1/3 c. sugar
1 Tbsp. cornstarch
1/2 c. walnuts

Combine apples, celery and drained pineapple. Combine juice, water, sugar and cornstarch; cook until clear, stirring constantly. Cool dressing; pour over fruits. Stir well; add walnuts or garnish salad with them. Serve on lettuce leaves. Serves 8-10.

Joan Wichman, Duluth, Mn.

ZESTY ARTICHOKE SALAD

1 pkg. strawberry jello
2 c. tomato juice
1 can artichoke hearts, cut up
1/4 c. chopped onion

1/4 c. chopped celery
1/4 c. chopped green pepper
2 tsp. horseradish
2 tsp. lemon juice (optional)

1507-82

Heat 1 cup tomato juice to boiling point. Dissolve jello in juice; add cool juice. Blend all ingredients; mold. Chill several hours before serving.

Note: This recipe was given to me by Helen (Lev) Schmidt and is delicious. Also, I use V-8 juice for more flavor.

Phyllis Granum, Moorhead, Mn.

BANANA SALAD

1 c. sugar	3-4 Tbsp. butter
3 Tbsp. flour	1 Tbsp. lemon juice
2 eggs	Pinch of salt
3-4 Tbsp. milk	

Cook until thick; cool. Just before serving, add:

1 c. miniature marshmallows	3 bananas
Grapes, halved	Pineapple tidbits, drained

K., St. Cloud, Mn.

BEAN SALAD

1 can kidney beans	1 tsp. salt
1 can green beans	1/2 tsp. pepper
1 can yellow beans	3/4 c. sugar
1/2 c. chopped green pepper	1/2 c. salad oil
1/2 c. onion (rings)	1/2 c. vinegar

Combine spices, oil, sugar and vinegar. Pour over vegetables; let stand overnight.

Anne Aune, Minneapolis, Mn.

BEAN SPROUT SALAD

Drain:

2 c. bean sprouts	2 c. canned garbanzo beans
2 c. canned green beans	(optional)
2 c. canned yellow wax beans	2 c. canned kidney beans

Combine:

3/4 c. vinegar	3/4 c. sugar
1/2 c. oil	2 Tbsp. soy sauce

2 tsp. dry mustard   1 c. chopped onion
Salt and pepper to taste

Pour over beans and marinate 3-4 hours, covered, in refrigerator. Makes 10 one cup servings.

Margaret McKenney, Minneapolis, Mn.

BLUEBERRY SALAD

2 (3 oz.) boxes strawberry   2 c. hot water
    jello

Mix with jello and chill till syrupy. Fold in 2 cups sour cream with electric mixer on low. Add 1 cup blueberry pie filling. Chill until set, then serve. Walnuts may also be added.

Mary J. Sward, New Hope, Mn

BROCCOLI-BACON SALAD

1 bunch broccoli, in bite
    size pieces
1 bunch green onions,
    thinly sliced

1/2 lb. bacon, crisp,
    crumbled
1 1/2 c. Hidden Valley
    Ranch dressing
1/4 c. bacon grease, added
    to dressing

Toss broccoli, bacon and onion; chill well, overnight if possible. Add dressing just before serving.

Maryann Skelton, Duluth, Mn.

BROCCOLI AND CAULIFLOWER SALAD

1 head cauliflower, cut
    into small pieces
1 bunch broccoli, cut into
    small pieces
1 c. frozen peas, uncooked
1 grated carrot

2 c. Hellmann's mayonnaise
1 (8 oz.) ctn. sour cream
1 tsp. garlic juice (or garlic
    seasoning)
Salt and pepper to taste

Mix all together. (Make a day ahead, if possible.)

Ginny Harwood, St. Cloud, Mn.

CABBAGE SALAD

Shred 1/2 medium size head cabbage. Chill and pour over the cabbage this dressing:

1/2 c. cultured sour cream	1/8 tsp. pepper
2 Tbsp. lemon juice or vinegar	1/2 tsp. dry mustard
1/2 tsp. salt	2 Tbsp. sugar

Lorraine Rieger, Minneapolis, Mn.

CABBAGE AND KIDNEY BEAN SALAD

1 c. kidney beans, drained	1/3 c. minced onion
1 1/2 c. shredded cabbage	1 tsp. salt
1/2 c. diced celery	1/2 tsp. pepper
2 Tbsp. chopped parsley	5 strips bacon, crumbled

Combine all, except bacon. Mix 1/2 cup Hellmann's mayonnaise, 2 tablespoons vinegar and 1 or 2 tablespoons sugar. Pour over salad; toss lightly. Chill. Just before serving, add the crumbled bacon.

Ginny Harwood, St. Cloud, Mn.

MOM'S CABBAGE-PINEAPPLE SALAD

1 medium head of cabbage	1/2 c. mayonnaise or salad dressing
1 (16 oz.) can crushed pineapple, drained (reserve juice)	1/4 c. reserved pineapple juice
1 c. salad marshmallows	1/4 c. evaporated milk
Salt to taste	1 Tbsp. sugar

Slice cabbage on hand or electric slicer, but do not slice with knife; flavor is better when slicer is used. Add marshmallows and pineapple. Mix mayonnaise with juice, sugar and evaporated milk. Add to cabbage until well moistened. Store, covered, in refrigerator.

M.J. Nelson, Minneapolis, Mn.

SWEET SOUR CABBAGE

Cook 1 medium head cabbage, shredded, in salt water until almost done; drain. Add 1/2 cup white sugar, 1/3 cup vinegar, 2 tablespoons bacon drippings and 1 cup raisins. Simmer 1/2 hour.

Karleen Gerth, St. Paul, Mn.

CALICO SUPPER SALAD

1 (8 oz.) pkg. macaroni
  shells, cooked
1 can Spam, diced
1/2 c. chopped celery

1 green pepper
1/2 c. ripe olives, chopped
1 c. diced Cheddar cheese
Chopped onion

Mix the above together with mayonnaise till moist; sprinkle with Lawry's seasoning. This may be doubled.

Harriett Haggard, Anoka, Mn.

CARROT SALAD

1 c. sugar
1/2 c. oil
1 tsp. salt
1 tsp. pepper
1 tsp. dry mustard
3/4 c. vinegar

1 tsp. Worcestershire sauce
1 diced green pepper or
  onion
1 can tomato soup
5 c. sliced carrots, cooked
  and cooled

Mix together the day before using. Will keep a week or more.

Jo Nell Murack, Fargo, N.D.

CARROT TUNA SALAD

1 c. grated carrots
1 c. chopped celery
2 hard cooked eggs, chopped
2 cans tuna

1 c. salad dressing
1/4 tsp. grated onion
1 large can shoestring
  potatoes

Mix together all ingredients, except potatoes. Chill 1 hour. Just before serving, add potatoes.

Mary Paul, Minneapolis, Mn.

CAULIFLOWER SALAD

4 c. sliced, raw cauliflower
1 c. sliced, pitted black
  olives

2/3 c. sliced green pepper
1/2 c. sliced pimento
1/2 c. sliced onion

Dressing:

1/4 c. salad oil
3 Tbsp. lemon juice
4 Tbsp. white vinegar

4 Tbsp. sugar
1/2 tsp. pepper
2 tsp. salt

Mix dressing together and beat with rotary beater until well blended and frothy. Pour over salad. Cover and refrigerate at least 4 hours. Stir several times. Serves 8.

Alicia Woodford, Montevideo, Mn.

CAULIFLOWER-BROCCOLI SALAD

1 head cauliflower, cut in
  bite size pieces
3 green onions, chopped

1 bunch broccoli, cut in bite
  size pieces
1 c. frozen green peas

Dressing:

2 c. sour cream
1 tsp. garlic powder

1 tsp. garlic juice

With the onions, you can use more or less; this is up to you. I like to put dressing on an hour before serving. This keeps several days in refrigerator.

Harriett Haggard, Anoka, Mn.

CAULIFLOWER-RADISH MOLD

2 env. unflavored gelatin
1 c. cold water
1 env. instant vegetable
  broth
1/4 c. sugar
1/2 tsp. salt

1/4 c. lemon juice
1 1/2 c. ice water
1 c. thinly sliced cauliflower
Radishes
2 Tbsp. chopped green onion
Preferred salad dressing

Sprinkle gelatin over cold water in small saucepan. Cook and stir over low heat until gelatin dissolves, about 3 minutes. Remove from heat; stir in broth, sugar and salt until dissolved. Stir in ice water and lemon juice. Chill until thickened and very syrupy. Fold in cauliflower,

1/4 cup sliced radishes and green onion. Turn into 1 quart ring mold; chill until firm. Unmold on serving plate; fill center with whole radishes, if desired, and serve with salad dressing. Makes 4-6 servings. If you don't have cauliflower, cucumbers, green peppers, etc. are also very good.

Phyllis Granum, Moorhead, Mn.

CAULIFLOWER AND RADISH SALAD

1 medium head cauliflower, divided into flowerets, sliced paper thin

10 large radishes, sliced paper thin
5 scallions, chopped
1 small bunch watercress

Mix and chill at least 1/2 hour. Blend:

1/2 c. sour cream
2 Tbsp. Parmesan cheese

1/2 tsp. black pepper
1/4 c. mayonnaise

Pour over salad and toss.

Dee Olson, St. Paul, Mn.

COPPER PENNY CARROT SALAD

Slice and cook 2 pounds carrots just till tender. Drain and put on cold water till cold. Drain and add:

1 can tomato soup
1/2 c. sugar
1/4 c. vinegar
1/2 c. salad oil
Salt and pepper to taste

1 tsp. Worcestershire sauce
3 small onions, chopped
Green pepper (optional)
Celery (optional)

This keeps well.

Marlys Swehla, Albert Lea, Mn.

CHERRY SALAD

1 can Wilderness cherry pie filling
1 large can crushed pineapple, drained

1 can Eagle Brand milk
1 large bowl Cool Whip
1 (4 oz.) pkg. chopped pecans (more if desired)

Mix pie filling, pineapple and milk together. Add Cool Whip and pecans; mix well. Chill in refrigerator.

Marilyn Radakovich, Duluth, Mn.

Similar recipes submitted by: Lila Houser, Aitkin, Mn., Liz Tuft, St. Paul, Mn.

CHERRY   SALAD

1 (3 oz.) pkg. cherry jello   1 c. cold water
1 (3 oz.) pkg. lemon jello   1 can cherry pie filling
2 c. boiling water

Dissolve jello in boiling water; add cold water and pie filling. Stir until dissolved. Pour into mold and set.

Jeanie Rose, Tracy, Mn.

CHICKEN   SALAD

2 c. cooked, diced chicken   A little pimiento, for color
2 c. celery   1 can drained pineapple
1 c. peas   tidbits
2 eggs, hard boiled   Miracle Whip to moisten

Just before serving, add 1 can or package of chow mein noodles. Serve on crisp lettuce.

Anne Aune, Minneapolis, Mn.

CHINESE   CHICKEN   SALAD

2 c. chicken or turkey,   1 (8 1/2 oz.) can water
   cut up   chestnuts, drained, sliced
2 medium ribs of celery,   2 green onions, thinly sliced
   chopped (about 1 c.)   1 (10 oz.) can bamboo
     shoots, drained

Second Mixture:

3/4 c. mayonnaise   1 Tbsp. lemon juice
2 Tbsp. soy sauce

Chill both mixtures; combine just before serving. Serve on lettuce and pineapple slice. Serves 4-6.

Mrs. Carl Granrud
Montevideo, Mn.

CHINESE CHICKEN SALAD DRESSING FOR 2

1/2 c. salad oil
1 tsp. onion powder
1 tsp. garlic powder
1/4 - 1/2 tsp. black pepper

6 Tbsp. rice vinegar
2 tsp. salt
4 Tbsp. sugar

Mix the above to make dressing. Stir or shake before using.

To make salad, use salad greens and have bowls of tomatoes, fresh mushrooms, onion, green pepper, sliced radishes, bean sprouts, grated Cheddar cheese, roasted almonds and chicken. To make salad, have each person mix greens with any of the above toppings. Fry rice sticks in peanut oil; add to top off salad, then add dressing. Triple for 6 people.

Joan Wichman, Duluth, Mn.

DELUXE CHICKEN SALAD

1 c. chopped celery
1 c. shredded carrots
1 tsp. minced onion
1 c. Miracle Whip

1/2 c. sour cream
1 tsp. mustard
2 cans boned chicken
1 (8 oz.) can shoestring
potatoes

Mix everything together, except shoestring potatoes. Add them just before serving.

Esther Mungovan, Duluth, Mn

HOT CHICKEN SALAD

4 c. cooked, chopped
chicken
1 c. chopped almonds
2 cans cream of chicken soup
2 c. crushed potato chips
1/4 c. grated onion

2 c. thinly sliced celery
1 c. mayonnaise
1 c. grated Cheddar cheese
1 tsp. salt
2 Tbsp. lemon juice

Combine all ingredients, except cheese and crushed chips. Place in a 4 quart baking dish. Top with cheese and chips. Bake at 350° for 30 minutes. Serves 6.

D. Klosterman, Anoka, Mn.
Similar recipe submitted by: Eloise Hoff, Preston, Mn.

PARTY CHICKEN OR TURKEY SALAD

1 c. cubed chicken or
  turkey
1 Tbsp. minced onion
Salt to taste
1 c. green grapes, cut in
  halves
1 c. diced celery

1 c. mandarin oranges
1/2 c. slivered almonds
1 c. cooked macaroni rings
1 c. salad dressing (not
  mayonnaise)
1 c. heavy cream, whipped

Combine first 3 ingredients; refrigerate several hours
or overnight. Add grapes, celery, oranges, almonds,
macaroni rings and dressing; mix well. Refrigerate again.
Add whipped cream just before serving. Serves 12.

Mary Paul, Minneapolis, Mn.

TAJ MAHAL CHICKEN SALAD

1 c. rice (Minute or
  cooked, raw rice)
2 c. cooked chicken, diced
1/4 c. golden raisins
1/4 c. thinly sliced green
  onions and tops
1 tsp. salt

1 1/2 c. mayonnaise or salad
  dressing
2 Tbsp. lemon juice in
  dressing
1 1/2 tsp. curry powder (go
  easy)
1/4 tsp. pepper

Prepare chicken; add rice, raisins and onion. Mix
dressing, lemon juice, curry powder, salt and pepper. Stir
into rice mixture and chill 3 or 4 hours. Sprinkle over top
when ready to serve 1/2 cup toasted cocoanut or 1/2 cup
chopped, salted peanuts.

Helene Rice, Bradenton, Fl.

CINNAMON APPLE SALAD

1 large pkg. lemon jello
1/2 c. red hot cinnamon
  candies

1 1/2 c. boiling water
1 c. cold water
1 1/2 c. canned applesauce

Dissolve candy in boiling water. Add jello; dissolve.
Add the rest; let set.

Karleen Gerth, St. Paul, Mn.

CLUB SALAD

1 pkg. lemon jello
2 pkg. raspberry jello
1 large can crushed
   pineapple, drained
1/2 lb. small marshmallows

1 large pkg. Philadelphia
   cream cheese, mixed
   together with 3/4 c.
   Miracle Whip
1/2 pt. cream, whipped

Dissolve lemon jello in hot pineapple juice (only what juice is there, no water). Let cool, then beat; fold in whipped cream. Add pineapple and marshmallows, then add cream cheese mixture. Let this set preferably overnight. Make raspberry jello according to directions; cool. Pour over top of first mixture; let set.

Marie Capen, Duluth, Mn.

EASY COLE SLAW

1 large head of cabbage,
   shredded
2 carrots, shredded

1 tsp. celery seed
1-2 c. Miracle Whip
1/2 c. sugar

Mix well; refrigerate. May add more or less Miracle Whip to taste.

Julie Floth, Dent, Mn.

MAKE AHEAD CABBAGE SLAW

1 head cabbage, shredded
2 carrots, chopped fine
1 onion, chopped fine

1/2 green pepper, chopped
   fine
A little pimento

Mix and pour over vegetables:
2 c. sugar
1 1/2 c. white vinegar
1 Tbsp. salt

1 tsp. mustard seed
1 tsp. celery seed

Keep in refrigerator 24 hours or more. Will keep a week or more.

G.W. Seemans, Robbinsdale, Mn.

CARDINAL COLE SLAW

4 c. shredded cabbage   1/2 c. raisins
1 c. cubed, unpeeled apple   1/4 c. peanuts

Combine cabbage, apple, raisins and peanuts. Add enough salad dressing to moisten; toss lightly. Makes about 4 servings.

Bernice Fonos, Minneapolis, Mn.
Similar recipe submitted by: Coleen Landwehr, St. Cloud, Mn.

FROZEN CABBAGE COLE SLAW

1 head cabbage, grated   2 c. sugar
1 tsp. salt   1 c. white vinegar
1 large carrot, grated   1/4 c. water
1 large green pepper,   1 tsp. mustard seed
  finely chopped   1 tsp. celery seed

In a large bowl, add salt to grated cabbage; mix well. Let stand 1 hour. Squeeze out liquid; add grated carrot and green pepper. Make a syrup by combining sugar, vinegar, water and spices. Bring to boil; boil 1 minute. Cool until lukewarm. Pour over cabbage; mix well. Pack into containers and freeze. Leave room for expansion. Makes 4-5 pints.

Suzie Brainard, Minneapolis, Mn.

REFRIGERATOR COLE SLAW

2 qt. shredded cabbage   1 green pepper, chopped fine
                                2 Tbsp. salt

Soak in 4 cups water for 4 hours. Bring to a boil:

1 c. vinegar   2 c. sugar
1 c. water   2 Tbsp. mustard seeds

Cool the above; add to well drained cabbage. Also add 1 small can pimento, drained, 3 ribs celery, chopped fine, and 2 carrots, chopped fine. Put in covered container and refrigerate. Will keep up to 6 weeks.

Millie Monte, Chisholm, Mn.

COLORFUL SALAD

Chop or break into large chunks:

1 head cauliflower
1-2 c. celery
1 bunch of broccoli flowerets
1-2 c. carrots

1 pkg. cherry tomatoes or
    2 or 3 tomatoes, cut in
    wedges
Any other vegetables you
    wish

Add:

2 Tbsp. chopped, drained
    green olives

2 Tbsp. chopped black
    olives

Pour over this 1 (8 ounce) bottle Italian dressing (not the creamy). Refrigerate this mixture in a large covered bowl for 8 hours or overnight, stirring a few times while marinating. Salad will keep for 2 or 3 weeks in refrigerator. Will serve a large crowd.

D. Klosterman, Anoka, Mn.

COTTAGE CHEESE SALAD

Mix and chill:

8 oz. cottage cheese
1 small ctn. Cool Whip

1 (3 oz.) pkg. jello,
    sprinkled on dry
1 small can pineapple chunks

Virginia Miller, Anoka, Mn.

Similar recipe submitted by: Jackie Joenisch, Windom, Mn.

REGAL CRABMEAT SALAD

2 (6 1/2 oz.) cans crabmeat*
2 c. cool, cooked rice
1 (8 oz.) can green peas,
    drained
1 1/2 c. finely sliced celery

1/4 c. sliced pimientos
1 c. mayonnaise
1 1/2 Tbsp. lemon juice
1 tsp. salt
1/4 tsp. pepper

Combine crabmeat, rice, peas, celery and pimientos. Blend remaining ingredients; pour over crabmeat mixture. Toss lightly. Adjust seasonings, if necessary; chill. Serve in lettuce cups and garnish with tomato wedges, if desired. Makes 6 servings.

*Or, substitute 1 (12 ounce) package fresh or frozen cooked shrimp (about 2 cups).

Ann Christensen, Litchfield, Mn.

1507-82

CRANBERRY SALAD

1 pkg. cranberries
1 1/4 c. boiling water
1 1/4 c. sugar
1 (3 oz.) small pkg. cherry
  jello

1 c. broken pecans
1 c. diced pineapple, well
  drained (tidbits are fine)
1 c. grapes, cut up

Add sugar and cranberries to boiling water; stir well. When it begins to boil again, cook for 5 minutes. Remove from fire; stir in jello. When cranberry mixture begins to congeal, add pineapple tidbits, nuts and grapes. Let set until ready to use.

Mildred Sjostrom, St. Peter, Mn.
Similar recipe submitted by: Mary Vork, Duluth, Mn.

CRANBERRY SALAD

1 lb. cranberries, ground   1 c. sugar

Mix together; let stand 2 hours. Mix 1 can crushed pineapple, drained, with above and let stand 2 hours.

1 lb. miniature marshmallows   1/2 pt. cream, whipped

Mix with above and let stand 2 hours in refrigerator. Add 1/2 cup walnuts before serving.

Suzie Brainard, Minneapolis, Mn.
Similar recipe submitted by: Karleen Gerth, St. Paul, Mn.

CRANBERRY DELUXE SALAD

Grind 1 pound cranberries (fresh); add 1 cup sugar. Mix well; let stand 1/2 hour. Add:

1 lb. miniature marshmallows   2 c. cream, whipped

Mix well and pour into large salad bowl. Set in refrigerator overnight. Will keep several days. Delicious with turkey.

Maryann Skelton, Duluth, Mn.

MOLDED CRANBERRY SALAD

2 pkg. cherry jello
2 c. boiling water
1 can whole cranberry sauce

2 Tbsp. orange juice
1 can crushed pineapple (do
   not drain)
1/2 c. chopped walnuts

Dissolve jello in boiling water. Add cranberry sauce, orange juice, crushed pineapple and nuts; stir well. Pour into a large oiled jello mold. Refrigerate.

                     Gladys Turk, Duluth, Mn.

CRANBERRY AND APPLE SALAD

Grind together:
2 c. ground cranberries
  (raw)

1 medium apple

Cut small 16 marshmallows; mix with above and let stand overnight in refrigerator. Just before serving, add 1/2 cup whipped whipping cream. Arrange on lettuce leaf: Put a slice of pineapple, then cranberry mixture. Very good (delicious).

                     Mrs. Kermit A. Haugen
                     Clarkfield, Mn.

CRANBERRY-ORANGE-APPLE MOLD

2 c. boiling water
2 (3 oz.) pkg. fruit flavored
  gelatin (any red flavor)
1/8 tsp. salt
1 tsp. cinnamon
Dash of cloves

1 (16 oz.) can whole berry
  cranberry sauce
2 Tbsp. grated orange rind
1 c. chopped apple
1 c. diced orange sections
  (fresh)

Add boiling water to gelatin, salt and spices in bowl; stir until dissolved. Add cranberry sauce and rind. Chill until thickened. Fold in apple and orange sections. Pour into a 6 cup mold (or individual molds); chill until firm before unmolding. Makes 9-10 servings.

                     Edna V. Olson, Duluth, Mn.

CRANBERRY-RASPBERRY SALAD

1 (10 or 12 oz.) pkg. frozen   2 c. cold water, including
   red raspberries   raspberry juice
2 pkg. lemon jello   1 (1 lb.) can whole
2 c. hot water   cranberry sauce

    Thaw raspberries and reserve juice. Dissolve jello in hot water; add cold water and juice. Chill until it begins to thicken. Fold in cranberries and raspberries; refrigerate until firm.

                    Anne Aune, Minneapolis, Mn.

CRANBERRY RELISH AND SALAD

1 (1 lb.) pkg. cranberries   2 c. sugar
1 orange

    Grind fine; mix well with sugar and let stand.

1 pkg. lemon or orange   1 c. diced celery, extra fine
   gelatin (follow directions)   1/2 c. finely chopped
                      walnuts

    Mix well and cool overnight.

                  Marguerite Roth, Minneapolis, Mn.

TART CRANBERRY SALAD

1 pkg. apple jello   2 c. raw cranberries
1/3 c. sugar   1 c. diced celery
1 pt. warm water

    Dissolve jello and sugar in warm water; chill. Put cranberries through food chopper. When jello is slightly thickened, fold in cranberries and celery. Turn into mold; chill until firm. Unmold on crisp lettuce or romaine. Serve with mayonnaise. Serves 8. (Lemon jello may be used instead of apple jello, then use 1 cup diced red apples instead of celery.)

                  Harriett C. Kurek, Minneapolis, Mn.

FROSTED CRANBERRY SQUARES

1 (18 1/2 oz.) can crushed
   pineapple (1 2/3 c.)
2 (3 oz.) pkg. lemon jello
1 (7 oz.) bottle ginger ale
1 (1 lb.) can jellied
   cranberry sauce

1 (2 oz.) pkg. dessert
   topping mix (or Cool
   Whip)
1 (8 oz.) pkg. Philadelphia
   cream cheese, softened
1/2 c. chopped pecans

Drain pineapple; add water to juice to make 1 cup of liquid. Heat. Dissolve jello in hot liquid; cool. Gently stir in ginger ale; chill till partially set. Blend drained pineapple and cranberry sauce; fold into gelatin mixture. Turn into 9x9x2 inch pan; chill till set.

Topping: Add creamed cheese to topping, which has been prepared in the usual way; spread over gelatin. Toast pecans in 1 tablespoon butter in 350° oven for 10 minutes; watch carefully. Sprinkle over top and chill.

                    Esther Mungovan, Duluth, Mn.

CREAM CHEESE JELLO

Mix 1 small package lime jello with 1 small can crushed pineapple in small saucepan; boil until jello is dissolved. Add 3/4 cup cold water. Pour into bowl; chill until partially set. Into deep bowl, put 8 ounces softened cream cheese, 1/2 cup cold milk and 1 envelope Dream Whip. Beat together till smooth. Fold this into pineapple and jello mixture. Pour into 6 cup mold; chill 8 hours.

              Bernice Wicklund, Minneapolis, Mn.

Similar recipe submitted by: Ina Veal, Bismarck, N.D.

CUCUMBER SALAD

1 small pkg. lime jello
1 1/2 c. water
1 grated cucumber

1 Tbsp. horseradish
1 c. mayonnaise

Dissolve jello in water. Add mayonnaise; mix well with beater. Add rest of ingredients. Put in mold or square glass dish; chill. Good with meat.

              Norma Bergman, Two Harbors, Mn.

CUCUMBERS IN SOUR CREAM DILL SAUCE

4 cucumbers
1 c. boiling water
3/4 c. sour cream
2 Tbsp. cider vinegar

3 Tbsp. minced dill or 1 tsp. seed
1 1/2 tsp. salt
1/4 tsp. pepper
1 tsp. sugar

Peel cucumbers; slice very thin. Pour boiling water over them; drain immediately and cover with ice water. Drain again and dry. Mix together all the other ingredients and toss with cucumbers. Chill 30 minutes.

Betty M. Case, Hibbing, Mn.

CUCUMBERS AND RADISHES IN SOUR CREAM

1 cucumber, peeled and thinly sliced
1 pkg. radishes, sliced (2 c.)

1 medium onion, thinly sliced
8 oz. sour cream
2 Tbsp. vinegar
1 1/2 tsp. salt

Put vegetables in large bowl. Cover with ice water. Combine remaining ingredients; chill. To serve, drain vegetables; stir in sour cream. Stir until coated and serve.

Dee Olson, St. Paul, Mn.

MOLDED CUCUMBER AND COTTAGE CHEESE SALAD

1 pkg. lemon jello
3/4 c. boiling water
1 c. mayonnaise
1 medium cucumber, grated

1 small onion, grated
1/2 c. blanched almonds
2 tsp. lemon juice
1 c. dry cottage cheese

Dissolve jello in water. When it begins to set, stir in the mayonnaise and mix well. Add rest of ingredients and pour into mold; chill.

Jo Lynn Freitag, Minneapolis, Mn.
Similar recipe submitted by: K., St. Cloud, Mn.

DELLA ROBBIA SALAD

4 env. (4 Tbsp.) unflavored
gelatin
1 c. sugar
1/4 tsp. salt
1 1/2 c. water
1 (9 oz.) can (4 rings)
pineapple
Maraschino cherries
1 (11 oz.) can (1 1/3 c.)
mandarin orange sections,
drained
Green seedless grapes

2 (6 oz.) cans frozen pink
lemonade concentrate
2 tsp. aromatic bitters
(optional)
1 (28 oz.) bottle (3 1/2 c.)
lemon-lime carbonated
beverage, well chilled
1 fully ripe banana, halved
lengthwise and crosswise
1 (1 lb.) can (2 c.) pear
halves, drained
1 fully ripe banana, diced

Mix gelatin, sugar and salt; add water. Heat and stir until gelatin dissolves. Drain pineapple; reserve syrup. Add enough water to syrup to measure 1 1/2 cups; add to gelatin. Add lemonade concentrate and stir to melt. Add the bitters and slowly pour the carbonated beverage down side of bowl, to hold carbonation. Mix gently with up and down motion. Chill 4 cups of gelatin mixture until partially set; spoon a thin layer, about 1 cup, into an 11 cup mold. Arrange pineapple slices in bottom of mold; center each with a cherry. Ladle in about 2 cups more of chilled gelatin. Press in a fruit design 4 orange sections, the banana slices, 4 pear halves, 4 maraschino cherries and grapes. Layer in remaining partially set gelatin as you go along; chill until set. If fruit floats up, press down before gelatin becomes firm. Meanwhile, chill rest of gelatin until partially set. Dice rest of pears; fold into gelatin along with diced banana and oranges. Carefully pour over set gelatin in mold. Chill until firm, 6 hours or overnight. Unmold and offer some type of whipped cream, mayonnaise dressing or any one of your favorite fruit dressings.

Lorraine Follrath, Anoka, Mn.

DINNER SALAD

1 pkg. regular vanilla
pudding mix
1 pkg. lemon flavored gelatin
1 (9 oz.) ctn. Cool Whip

1 (11 oz.) can mandarin
oranges, drained, cut up
1 (15 oz.) can crushed
pineapple, drained

Mix pudding mix and gelatin with 2 cups boiling water. Refrigerate until partially set. Add fruit; fold in Cool Whip. Fill mold and chill until thick.

Clifford H. Carlson, Saginaw, Mn.

EASTER SALAD

2 pkg. lime jello, dissolved
   in 1 c. boiling water
1 cucumber
1 green pepper

2 large carrots
12 radishes, ground, drained
1/2 c. Spin Blend
1 c. cottage cheese

Combine all ingredients and chill until set. Add 1 cup whipped cream; pour into mold.

Ellie Cox, Rochester, Mn.

EGG SALAD FOR 100

Mix together:
1 qt. salad dressing
2 c. evaporated milk

2 1/2 Tbsp. salt
1/4 c. dry mustard

Add:
8 doz. chopped, hard
   cooked eggs
1 bunch chopped celery

1 - 1 1/2 lb. stuffed olives
   or sweet pickles or a
   mixture of both
A little sugar to taste

One-fourth cup scoop makes 100 sandwiches.

Marion Round, Faribault, Mn.

EVERLASTING SALAD

1 pkg. macaroni rings
1 (No. 2) can crushed
   pineapple, drained
   (save juice)
1/2 c. lemon juice
4 eggs, beaten

1/2 c. sugar
3 c. cut up apples
2 Tbsp. flour
1 pt. whipping cream
1 bottle cherries, drained,
   cut up small

Cook rings; drain and cool. Cook until thick the drained pineapple, juice, lemon juice, flour, sugar and beaten eggs. Add to cooled rings. Add fruit; let stand overnight. Add whipping cream before serving. (You may also add cut up seedless grapes, if you wish; adds more color, too.)

Edna V. Olson, Duluth, Mn.

FRESH GARDEN SALAD

1 head cauliflower, cut in little flowerets
1 bunch broccoli, cut in small pieces

1 box frozen peas, uncooked
6-8 green onions, sliced thin

Pour over the above:

1 c. sour cream
2 c. mayonnaise
1 Tbsp. sugar

1 tsp. salt
1 tsp. garlic salt

Mix all together and let stand overnight.
Phylliss Mac Johnson, Winona, Mn.

HAM AND EGG MAIN DISH SALAD

1 c. uncooked small pasta shells
2 c. diced, cooked ham
4 hard cooked eggs, sliced
10 cherry tomatoes, halved
1/2 c. chopped celery
1/4 c. sliced green onions
1/4 c. chopped dill pickle
3/4 c. dairy sour cream

1/4 c. chopped fresh parsley
1/4 c. grated Parmesan cheese
1 1/2 tsp. Worcestershire sauce
1/2 tsp. salt
1/8 tsp. pepper
Lettuce leaves

Cook pasta according to package directions; rinse and drain. Combine cooked pasta, ham, eggs, tomatoes, celery, onion and pickle in a large mixing bowl. Combine sour cream, parsley, cheese, Worcestershire sauce, salt and pepper in a small mixing bowl. Pour over ham mixture; mix well. Chill, covered, 3 to 4 hours to allow flavors to blend. Serve in lettuce lined, chilled salad bowl. Makes 6 to 8 servings.
Joan Norton, Hibbing, Mn.

JELLO SALAD

1 (12 oz.) ctn. small curd cottage cheese
1 (9 oz.) ctn. Cool Whip (frozen)

1 (13 oz.) can crushed pineapple, drained
1 (13 oz.) can mandarin oranges, drained

Combine well and add 1 (3 ounce) box of dry orange jello. Stir well. Will keep in refrigerator up to 10 days if fruit is well drained. For variety, change type of fruit and flavor of jello.

Suzie Brainard, Minneapolis, Mn.

15-LAYER JELLO MOLD

4 small pkg. jello (red, yellow, orange and green or purple)
1 1/4 c. sugar

1 pt. sweet cream
1 pt. sour cream
2 env. unflavored gelatin, softened in 1/2 c. cold water

Bring sugar and sweet cream to a boil; add unflavored gelatin. Cool; add sour cream. Dissolve red jello in a bowl with 1 1/2 cups boiling water. Repeat with other colors, putting each in a separate bowl. Using a 10-12 cup mold (mine is round and deep with a tube center), put a thin layer of red jello in the mold and put in refrigerator. When set (or almost), spoon a thin layer of cream mixture over it. Let set. Repeat, alternating colors, and allowing each layer to set, until all are used up.

Tips: If cream curdles, use it anyway; it'll taste and look OK. If it gets lumpy or too thick, soften it over a pan of hot water. I keep the bowl of cream and jello on the counter and the mold in the refrigerator because it sets faster. A real conversation piece--and yummy!

Elsie Nelson, St. Paul, Mn.

FIVE CUP ORANGE SALAD

Dissolve 2 (3 ounce) packages orange gelatin in 2 cups boiling water. Let the gelatin get a little syrupy, then add a pint of orange sherbet. Stir until it melts. Add 1 (11 ounce) can mandarin oranges; pour into a quart ring mold. When firm, turn it out on a plate. Fill the center with Five Cup Salad:

1 (No. 2) can pineapple tidbits, drained
1 (11 oz.) can mandarin oranges, drained
1 c. miniature marshmallows

1 c. Thompson seedless grapes, drained
1 (3 1/2 oz.) can coconut
2 c. sour cream
1/4 tsp. salt

Combine fruits, marshmallows and coconut. Stir in sour cream and salt; chill overnight.

Aster Paulsrud, Montevideo, Mn.
Similar recipe submitted by: Maxine Olsen, Duluth, Mn.

FLYING FARMER'S SALAD

2 Tbsp. salad oil
2 Tbsp. orange juice
1/2 tsp. salt
1 1/2 c. diced celery
5 c. cooked, chunked
   chicken
3 c. cooked rice

1 1/2 c. green seedless
   grapes
1 (13 1/2 oz.) can pineapple
   tidbits, drained
1 can mandarin oranges,
   drained
1 c. slivered almonds
1 1/2 c. mayonnaise

Mix all together. Let stand several hours or overnight. Serves 15.

Edna V. Olson, Duluth, Mn.

FROG EYE SALAD

1 c. sugar
3 egg yolks
1/2 tsp. salt
2 tsp. flour
Juice from drained fruit
1 large ctn. Cool Whip
1 (No. 303) can crushed
   pineapple, drained

1 (No. 303) can pineapple
   tidbits, drained
2 small cans mandarin
   oranges, drained
1 small pkg. miniature
   marshmallows
1 box acini-de-pepe macaroni
   (or any other kind of
   pasta)

Combine and cook until thick the sugar, flour, salt, juice and egg yolks. Melt marshmallows with cooked mixture. Cook macaroni; blanch and cool. Combine macaroni and cooked mixture; refrigerate overnight. Next day, add pineapple, oranges and Cool Whip. Any other kind of fruit may be added (bananas, grapes, etc.).

Lovise Lorenz, St. Paul, Mn.

FRUIT SALAD

12 oz. sour cream
1 pkg. instant coconut
  pudding
1 (20 oz.) can crushed
  pineapple and juice

4 tsp. sugar
1 (30 oz.) can fruit cocktail,
  drained
2 c. miniature marshmallows

Mix together the sour cream, pudding, pineapple and juice and sugar. Add drained fruit cocktail and marshmallows; can use colored ones for color. This is better if it stands for at least 24 hours. Serves 25.

Loretta VanEngelenhoven, Luverne, Mn.

Similar recipes submitted by: Esther Mungovan, Duluth, Mn., Gladys Turk, Duluth, Mn., Esther Lee, St. Paul, Mn.

FRUIT SALAD

1 pkg. lemon pie mix, fixed
  as directed
1 pkg. small circle macaroni,
  cooked and cooled

1 apple, diced
1 c. grapes
1 c. diced pineapple

Mix and let stand overnight. Add whipped cream before serving.

Marlys Swehla, Albert Lea, Mn.

FRUIT SALAD

1 small (8 oz.) can
  shredded pineapple
1/2 lb. miniature
  marshmallows

3 oz. Philadelphia cream
  cheese
1/2 pt. cream, whipped stiff
1 pkg. lime jello

Dissolve lime jello in 1 1/2 cups boiling water; add cheese and beat until mixed. Add pineapple and cool. Add whipped cream and marshmallows as jello congeals. Use 9x9 inch pan. Serves 9 or more. No dressing required. This salad is nice for dessert also. For Christmas, add 1 drop green coloring.

Linnea Anderson, Valley City, N.D.

FRUIT SALAD

Sauce:

1/2 c. sugar
Juice from 2 tall (No. 2)
   cans pineapple

1 egg, beaten a little
Dash of lemon juice
2 Tbsp. cornstarch

Cook to consistency of pudding. Cool to cold and mix with:

3 large sliced bananas
1 small can mandarin
   oranges
1 jar maraschino cherries

1/2 c. miniature
   marshmallows
2 (No. 2) cans chunk
   pineapple (use juice for
   sauce)

This salad keeps for several days in covered container. Serves 10.

Emogene Homan, Minneapolis, Mn.

FROZEN FRUIT SALAD

2 (10 oz.) pkg.
   strawberries (I use
   unsweetened - fresh
   berries are great)
6 sliced bananas

2 (20 oz.) cans crushed
   pineapple
1 (16 oz.) can mandarin
   oranges
1/3 c. lemon juice
2 (6 oz.) cans orange juice

Do not drain fruit. Put in plastic containers and freeze. Take out a half hour before serving.

Bev. Jensen, Willmar, Mn.

LEMON FRUIT SALAD

1 can Wilderness lemon
   pie filling
1/2 pt. cream, whipped
1 can fruit cocktail, drained

1 can pineapple tidbits,
   drained
1 can mandarin oranges,
   drained
1/2 pkg. miniature
   marshmallows

Fold pie filling into whipped cream. Add fruits and marshmallows.

Sue Hetland, Grand Forks, N.D.

MAE'S FRUIT SALAD

1 pkg. lemon chiffon
  pudding and pie mix,
  cooked according to
  directions, cooled, whipped
2 tall cans pineapple
  tidbits, drained

2 cans mandarin oranges,
  drained
1 jar maraschino cherries,
  drained
1 c. miniature marshmallows
1 c. seedless white grapes
1 c. cashew nuts

Fold all together with the lemon pie mix; chill. Just before serving, add 2 sliced bananas.

Dee Olson, St. Paul, Mn.

ONE-CUP FRUIT SALAD

Mix together:

1 c. mandarin oranges,
  drained
1 c. miniature marshmallows
1 c. Angel Flake coconut

1 c. chunk pineapple,
  drained
1 c. sour cream

Cover and chill for 8 hours before serving.

Ferne Plenke

OVERNIGHT FRUIT SALAD

2 eggs
1/4 c. sugar
1 Tbsp. lemon juice
2 Tbsp. butter or margarine
2 c. miniature marshmallows
2 c. pineapple chunks

2 c. white cherries (1 glass
  jar)
1 c. mandarin oranges
1/4 c. maraschino cherries
1 c. whipped cream or Cool
  Whip

Beat eggs; add sugar and lemon juice. Cook over low heat or in double boiler till thick. Stir in butter and cool. Add fruit, marshmallows and cream; let stand overnight.

Norma Bergman, Two Harbors, Mn.

7-UP FRUIT SALAD

2 pkg. lemon jello
2 c. boiling water
2 c. 7-Up

1 (No. 2) can crushed
  pineapple, drained
1 c. small marshmallows
2 large bananas

Dissolve jello in boiling water and add 7-Up. When partially set, add remaining ingredients. The 7-Up keeps bananas from turning dark and keeps well for several days in refrigerator.

Topping:

1/2 c. sugar
2 Tbsp. flour
1 c. pineapple juice
1 egg, beaten

2 Tbsp. butter
1 c. cream, whipped
1/4 c. shredded American
  cheese

Combine sugar and flour in saucepan; stir in pineapple juice and egg. Cook, stirring constantly. Add butter and cool. Fold in cream. Spread over jello and sprinkle with cheese. Use 9x12 inch pan.

Bessie Wilke, Detroit Lakes, Mn.

SUMMER FRUIT SALAD

Bring to a boil in small saucepan:
1 c. dry white wine
1/2 c. honey
1 Tbsp. cinnamon

Pour the heated mixture over the following fruit in a large bowl. Chill several hours.

1 large pkg. green
  seedless grapes
2 pt. strawberries, hulled
  and halved
2 large cans Dole pineapple
  chunks, in own juice,
  drained

1 large ripe cantaloupe,
  cubed
1 medium size ripe honeydew
  melon, cubed
3 large seedless oranges,
  sectioned, peeled, and
  removed of membrane

If desired, sprinkle fruit salad just before serving with any or all of the following:

1 large pkg. pecan halves,
  coarsely chopped

Baker's Angel Flake coconut
  (3/4 - 1 c.)
1 c. raisins

Brenda Aucutt, Minneapolis, Mn.

THREE FRUIT SALAD

2 (3 oz.) pkg. cream cheese, softened
1 c. mayonnaise or salad dressing
1/4 c. lemon juice
1/4 tsp. salt
1/4 c. sugar
2 c. canned pineapple tidbits, drained

2 c. diced mandarin orange sections
1 c. snipped maraschino cherries
1 c. canned, pitted Royal Anne cherries, quartered
1 c. pecans, chopped
2 c. heavy cream, whipped

In large bowl, blend the first 5 ingredients. Lightly mix the fruit, chopped pecans and whipped cream; pour into Bundt pan. Cover top tightly with freezer wrap and freeze. To thaw, unwrap mold; let stand in hot water 2-3 minutes. Unmold on serving plate. Thaw 1 hour in refrigerator. Garnish with fruit of season (melon balls, strawberries, etc.). Use sharp knife to cut into wedges to serve. Serves 16.

Thelma Olson, St. Cloud, Mn.

GERMAN SALAD

1 (No. 2 1/2) can or 1 qt. sauerkraut, drained
1 large onion, minced or chopped
1 green pepper, minced or chopped
2 c. celery, minced or chopped

1 c. shredded carrots (or 1 small jar pimento)
3/4 c. sugar
1/2 c. vinegar
1/2 c. salad oil
Celery seed
Salt to taste

Combine and chill 24 hours or more. Will keep for 2 weeks.

Thalia Fox, Willmar, Mn.

GRAPE-NUT SALAD

Beat 2 egg whites; add 2 tablespoons sugar. Beat well. Fold in:

1/3 c. maraschino cherries, finely chopped
1 Tbsp. juice

1/3 c. Grape-Nuts
1/4 c. slivered almonds

Whip 1 cup cream; add 1/4 cup powdered sugar and 1/2 teaspoon vanilla. Fold in egg white mixture; freeze. I like to freeze in foil cups and decorate with cut candied red and green cherries, especially at Christmas time.

Pearl Mohn, Montevideo, Mn.

GREEN BEAN SALAD

1/2 lb. fresh mushrooms,
  washed and sliced
1/2 small onion, chopped
1/4 c. butter
2 Tbsp. flour
1 1/2 c. milk
1/2 lb. diced sharp
  Cheddar cheese

1 tsp. soy sauce
1/2 tsp. salt
1/4 tsp. pepper
1 can water chestnuts,
  drained, sliced thin
2 pkg. French cut green
  beans
1/2 can French fried onions

Saute mushrooms and onion in butter; blend in flour. Add milk; cook and stir until thickened. Add cheese; stir until melted. Add vegetables, except French fried onions; these are put on top. Bake 1/2 hour at 350°. I used canned beans and instead of flour, milk and cheese, used diluted Cheddar cheese soup.

Thelma Olson, St. Cloud, Mn.

GREEN MIST SALAD

1/2 c. hot water
1 (3 oz.) pkg. lime jello
3 stalks celery, cut fine
6 oz. cottage cheese

1/2 c. half & half cream
1/2 c. mayonnaise
1 small can crushed
  pineapple, not drained

Pour hot water over jello; mix well. When cool, add cottage cheese, celery, cream, mayonnaise and pineapple (juice and all). Mix well; pour into pan or mold. Chill. Serves 8.

Marilyn Radakovich, Duluth, Mn.

GREEN PEA SALAD

2 stalks celery, sliced
4-6 green onions, with tops

1 can water chestnuts, sliced
1 pkg. frozen peas, thawed
  completely

Lay out vegetables in order given in a shallow pan.

Dressing:

1/2 c. Miracle Whip   2 Tbsp. vinegar
2 Tbsp. sugar

Pour dressing over top; sprinkle Parmesan cheese on top. Cover and refrigerate 24 hours.

Sally Bartsch, Blaine, Mn.

GRECIAN SALAD

1 head lettuce   1/4 c. onion, chopped
1 head cauliflower   1/4 c. sugar
1 lb. bacon, crisp and   1/2 c. Parmesan cheese
  crumbled   1 c. Hellmann's mayonnaise

Put in large bowl as listed; spread mayonnaise on top to seal. Cover with plastic wrap and refrigerate overnight. Mix and toss just before serving.

Maryann Skelton, Duluth, Mn.

JELLO SALAD

1 (28 oz.) ctn. small curd   1 (15 oz.) can crushed
  cottage cheese   pineapple, well drained
2 (3 oz.) pkg. lime jello   1/2 bag miniature
1 (8 oz.) ctn. Cool Whip   marshmallows

Combine all ingredients in large bowl; chill at least 4 hours or overnight. Serves about 20 people. Other flavors of jello can be substituted and other canned fruits, such as fruit cocktail, can be used.

Ella Fennessy, Duluth, Mn.

PARTY JELLO SALAD

1 (3 oz.) pkg. lime gelatin   1/4 c. chopped nuts
1 c. boiling water   1 (1 lb. 4 1/2 oz.) can
1/2 c. cottage cheese   crushed pineapple
1/4 c. maraschino cherries,   1 c. whipped Dream Whip
  chopped

Dissolve gelatin in boiling water; add 1/2 cup syrup

(saved from the pineapple). Chill to very thick. Fold in remaining ingredients; thoroughly chill before serving. A delicious salad and very colorful and festive.

"Addie" Mayer, St. Paul, Mn.

KRAUT SALAD

1 can kraut, drained	2/3 c. vinegar
1 can bean sprouts	2 c. sugar
2 c. chopped onions	2 tsp. celery salt
2 c. celery, chopped	1/2 tsp. salt
2 c. green peppers, chopped	1/2 tsp. pepper

Drain vegetables; add marinade. Let set 24 hours, then serve.

Grayce Funke, Minneapolis, Mn.

LEMON SALAD

Let partially set 1 package lemon jello, mixed with 1 cup hot water. Add:

1/2 pt. cream, whipped	Maraschino cherries
1 (3 oz.) pkg. cream cheese	1 c. crushed pineapple, drained

Sally Bartsch, Blaine, Mn.

TUTTI-FRUITI LEMON SALAD

1 (13 1/4 oz.) can pineapple tidbits or crushed	1/2 c. flaked coconut
1 (16 oz.) can mandarin orange sections, drained	2 c. miniature marshmallows
1 (17 oz.) can fruit cocktail	1 pkg. instant lemon pudding
	1 small container Cool Whip

In large bowl, combine the pineapple, fruit cocktail and the drained orange sections with the coconut and marshmallows (do not drain the pineapple or fruit cocktail). Sprinkle the pudding over ingredients; stir gently. Let stand 1 hour, then add Cool Whip. This recipe serves 12.

Adeline Jasken, St. Cloud, Mn.

WILTED LETTUCE OR SPINACH SALAD

Dice and brown 1 pound bacon (reserve 1/3 cup fat). Add 1/3 cup vinegar and 1/3 cup sugar to fat. Boil fat, vinegar and sugar until sugar is dissolved. Layer:

1 layer garden lettuce or spinach
Bacon bits

Hot vinegar, sugar, fat mixture
Drizzle on sweet cream

Repeat layers, ending with cream.
Ellen Kanthak, St. Cloud, Mn.

LIME SALAD

1 large pkg. cream cheese, softened
1 pt. whipping cream, whipped until stiff
1 large can crushed pineapple, juice drained

12 cherries, cut up
2/3 c. walnuts, chopped
Dash of salt
1 pkg. lime jello
Green food coloring, if desired

Bring pineapple juice to boil; add jello and dissolve. Mix pineapple, cream cheese, salt, cherries and walnuts; add jello mixture. Cool and fold in whipped cream; chill until firm.
Mary Jean Voss, Owatonna, Mn.

LIME JELLO MOLD

1 large pkg. lime jello
2 c. boiling water

1 can Wilderness lemon pie filling
1 c. cold water

Mix well; mold in large Tupperware mold.
Mary Paul, Minneapolis, Mn.

LIME JELLO SALAD

Melt 16 large marshmallows in 1 cup milk. Pour hot mixture over 1 small package lime jello; stir till dissolved. Stir in 2 (3 ounce) packages cream cheese, room temperature; stir till dissolved. Add No. 2 can undrained, crushed pineapple; let cool. Blend in 1 cup whipped cream. Pour into jello mold. Top with cherries.
88   Mary Vork, Duluth, Mn.

LIME JELLO SALAD

Dissolve 2 packages lime jello in 3 cups boiling water. Chill in bowl in refrigerator until starting to jell. Fold in:

1 grated carrot
1 small green pepper, cut
  fine

1 heaping Tbsp. grated
  onion
2 Tbsp. grated cucumber

Beat 1 cup whipping cream; fold into 1 cup Miracle Whip. Fold this into jello mixture. Pour into mold, which has been rinsed in cold water. Let set in refrigerator for several hours.

Esther Mungovan, Duluth, Mn.

LIME JELLO - PHILLY CREAM CHEESE SALAD

3 small pkg. lime jello,
  mixed as usual
1 c. diced celery

1 can crushed pineapple,
  drained
1 (8 oz.) pkg. Philadelphia
  cream cheese, cut in small
  pieces

Mix and refrigerate in 9x13 inch pan. Cut in squares; serve on lettuce.

Ruth Lee, Detroit Lakes, Mn.

LIME PARTY SALAD

Melt in top of double boiler 1/4 pound marshmallows (16 large) and 1 cup milk. Pour hot mixture over package of lime jello; stir until dissolved. Stir in until dissolved 2 (3 ounce) packages of cream cheese, room temperature, mashed. Add No. 2 can crushed pineapple, underained. Set until cooled. Blend in 1 cup whipped cream and refrigerate overnight.

Dode Desch, St. Paul, Mn.
Similar recipe submitted by: Karen Ireland, Montevideo, Mn.

LIME YOGURT SALAD

1 (8 1/2 oz.) can pear halves   2 c. boiling water
2 (3 oz.) pkg. lime flavored   1 container vanilla yogurt
  gelatin

Drain pears, reserving 1/2 cup syrup; slice pears. Dissolve gelatin in boiling water. Measure 1 cup of gelatin mixture and blend in yogurt. Pour into an 8 inch square pan. Chill until set, but not firm. Add measured syrup to remaining gelatin; chill until slightly thickened. Arrange pear slices on gelatin-yogurt layer and top with clear gelatin. Chill until firm, about 3 hours.

Adeline Hortsch, St. Cloud, Mn.

MANDARIN SALAD

1 pkg. orange jello   1 c. whipping cream
1 c. hot water   1 c. mandarin oranges
1/2 pt. orange sherbet   1 pkg. cream cheese

Dissolve jello in hot water; add juice of oranges. Add sherbet. Refrigerate till slightly thick. Beat cream cheese and whipping cream till smooth. Mix well; put in oiled mold. Drop oranges on top; refrigerate.

Marilyn Radakovich, Duluth, Mn.

MANDARIN ORANGE SALAD

1 qt. creamed cottage cheese   1 large (6 oz.) pkg. orange
2 c. refrigerated whipped   jello
  topping   2 (11 oz.) cans mandarin
                                 oranges, drained

Fold the whipped topping into the cottage cheese. Sprinkle the dry gelatin over the mixture and stir to combine. Stir in mandarin oranges. Refrigerate until firm.
Note: The salad may be garnished with maraschino cherries. Also 1 (1 pound) can drained fruit cocktail may be added.

Mary Paul, Minneapolis, Mn.

MOLDED SALAD

Bring 1 1/2 cups tomatoes and juice to boil. Add 1 large package lemon jello; heat until dissolved. Chill until thickened. Add:

1 tsp. lemon juice
1 cucumber, diced
1 c. celery, diced
1 c. pepper, diced

1/2 onion, diced
1/2 c. mayonnaise
1/2 c. sour cream

Pour into mold.

Vivian Bergstrom, Minneapolis, Mn.

QUICK MOLDED SALAD

1 pkg. lemon flavored
gelatin
1 c. boiling water

1 (10 oz.) pkg. frozen
raspberries
1 can mandarin oranges,
drained

Dissolve gelatin in boiling water; add raspberries. Break apart gently with fork to speed thawing. Add mandarin oranges and mix well. Pour into 1 quart mold. Salad is ready to serve in about 2 hours.

Margaret McKenney, Minneapolis, Mn.

FRESH MUSHROOM SALAD

1 lb. large mushrooms
6 Tbsp. lemon juice
1 Tbsp. snipped chives
1 Tbsp. chopped parsley
1 tsp. dried tarragon leaves
1/2 c. bottled Italian style
dressing

1/4 c. finely chopped
pimiento
1/2 tsp. salt
1/8 tsp. pepper
1 1/2 tsp. sugar
2 tsp. prepared mustard
1 small bunch watercress

1. Wash and dry mushrooms. 2. Thinly slice mushrooms into large bowl. Sprinkle with lemon juice, chives, parsley and tarragon; stir gently. Refrigerate, covered, 1 hour. 3. Meanwhile, in bowl, combine salad dressing, pimiento, salt, pepper, sugar and mustard; stir to mix well. Refrigerate, covered, about 1 hour. 4. To serve: Toss mushrooms with dressing. Arrange on bed of watercress on large platter. Makes 6 to 8 servings.

Lovise Lorenz, St. Paul, Mn.

MYSTERY SALAD

1 pkg. lemon jello (no
  water)
1 (No. 2) can crushed
  pineapple, drained
1 c. chopped celery
3/4 c. chopped nuts

2 small pkg. pimento
  Philadelphia cream cheese
  (or use regular and small
  jar of pimento)
1/2 pt. cream, whipped, or
  Rich's Whip

Add water to the pineapple juice to make 1 cup of liquid; heat and dissolve jello in it. Add cheese; cool. Fold in pineapple, celery, nuts and cream; pour into mold. Refrigerate.

Esther Mungovan, Duluth, Mn.

NEW SALAD

2 pkg. lemon jello
2 or 3 bananas
48 small marshmallows

1 can crushed pineapple,
  drained
1 can mandarin oranges,
  drained

Frost with custard: Use pineapple juice in a cup and add enough water to measure 1 cup.

1/2 c. sugar
1 egg, beaten
2 tsp. flour

2 tsp. butter
1 c. cream, whipped

Set jello as directed; let cool and slightly set. Add fruit and marshmallows. Put in bowl or mold. Cook the custard ingredients until spoon is coated; add whipped cream after custard is cooled. Spread on the jello. Serves 15.

Doris Lindgren, Duluth, Mn.

ORANGE SALAD

1 small pkg. orange jello
1 small pkg. lemon jello
2 c. hot water

1 c. pineapple juice
1 c. frozen orange juice
1 large can pineapple,
  drained

Dissolve jello in hot water; add reserved pineapple juice. Add pineapple to orange juice, then add to jello mixture; mold.

Anne Aune, Minneapolis, Mn.

FLUFFY ORANGE SALAD

1 (3 oz.) pkg. cream cheese
1 (5 oz.) jar Neufchatel
   cheese spread with
   pimento
1 (11 oz.) can mandarin
   oranges, drained

1 (16 oz.) can sliced peaches
1 (13 1/2 oz.) can pineapple
   tidbits or chunks, drained
1 c. miniature marshmallows
1 c. whipping cream,
   whipped

Beat the two kinds of cheese. Drain and cut up peaches; save 1/4 cup syrup. Beat syrup into cheese. Fold fruit and marshmallows into cheese mixture. Fold in whipped cream; chill. Serves 8.

Maryann Skelton, Duluth, Mn.

MOLDED ORANGE SALAD

1 c. water
1 orange, ground (rind
   and all)
1 small can crushed
   pineapple, drained

1/2 c. sugar
1 pkg. orange flavored
   gelatin
1 c. whipping cream,
   whipped

Mix together water, sugar, juice from the ground orange and juice from the drained pineapple; boil for 2 minutes. Remove from heat; add gelatin. Add fruit; mix well and cool until it thickens slightly. Fold in whipped cream; mold. Serves 6-8.

Aster Paulsrud, Montevideo, Mn.

ORANGE-COTTAGE CHEESE SALAD

Mix the following:
1 pt. cottage cheese
1 pkg. orange jello (dry)

1 can crushed pineapple,
   drained
1 can mandarin oranges

Fold in 1/2 of a pint size carton of Cool Whip.

Esther Mungovan, Duluth, Mn.

MANDARIN ORANGE AND COCONUT SALAD

Mix:

1/2 pt. sour cream	1/2 lb. miniature marshmallows

Let stand 3 hours or overnight. Add:

2 cans mandarin oranges, drained	1 (14 oz.) can pineapple tidbits or pineapple chunks, halved
1 c. Angel Flake coconut (more if desired)	

Mix together and let stand at least 1 hour before serving. Serve on lettuce; garnish with cherry on top. May be served with rolls, popovers or nut bread. Very good with ham.

Maryann Skelton, Duluth, Mn.

ORANGE TAPIOCA SALAD

2 pkg. vanilla tapioca pudding	2 c. juice from drained fruit
1 large can fruit cocktail, drained	2 (3 oz.) pkg. orange jello
	2 c. boiling water
1 can mandarin oranges, drained	1 c. whipping cream, whipped

Dissolve jello in boiling water. Cook tapioca pudding with juice as directed on box. Combine jello and tapioca; chill until congealed. Fold in fruit and whipped cream. Makes a large salad.

Jan Eschbach, Duluth, Mn.

ORANGE TOSSED SALAD

Candied Almonds: Use iron frying pan. Put in 2 to 4 tablespoons sugar, then 1/4 cup almonds. Stir constantly over low heat until sugar melts and almonds are brown and coated with sugar; cool on foil. A large quantity may be made at one time and stored in refrigerator.

Dressing:

1/2 tsp. salt	1/4 tsp. Tabasco sauce
2 Tbsp. sugar	2 Tbsp. cider vinegar
1/4 c. salad oil	

94

Put ingredients in a jar and shake well. To assemble salad: Place the following in a bowl -

1/2 head lettuce, shredded
1 c. celery, chopped
2 green onions and tops,
   shredded thinly

1 Tbsp. minced parsley
1 can mandarin oranges,
   drained
1/4 c. candied almonds

Pour dressing over salad and toss gently.
Lovise Lorenz, St. Paul, Mn.

OVERNIGHT SALAD

1 c. coconut
1 c. mandarin oranges,
   drained

1 c. crushed pineapple,
   drained
1 c. miniature marshmallows
1 pt. sour cream

Mix well and chill overnight.
Marilyn Radakovich, Duluth, Mn.

PARTY RAINBOW JELLO

Have 10 packages jello, two each of 5 assorted colors. Layer salad in 9x13 inch glass cake pan, oiled lightly with mayonnaise. Layer 1: Jello, 3/4 cup boiling water to dissolve jello and add 3/4 cup cold water. Let first layer set until firm. Layer 2: Jello, 3/4 cup boiling water to dissolve jello; add 3/4 cup cold sweetened condensed milk (keep in refrigerator before starting to make jello set faster). Let second layer set until firm. Repeat layers. When ready to serve, unmold; cut in squares on platter lined with lettuce and garnish with fresh fruit. Serves 24.
Ann Christensen, Litchfield, Mn.

PEA SALAD

2 cans peas (reserve juice
   if using macaroni)
3 hard boiled, chopped
   eggs
1/4 lb. cheese, cubed
1/2 onion, chopped

1 Tbsp. sugar
1 Tbsp. vinegar
1 c. salad dressing
1 c. chopped celery
Salt and pepper

Add to this mixture either cut up lettuce or 1 package cooked macaroni rings. If using macaroni rings, salad tends to get dry, so add pea juice and moisten to your liking.

Ellen Kanthak, St. Cloud, Mn.

PEACH SALAD

1 pkg. vanilla pudding (regular)

1 pkg. vanilla tapioca pudding
1 pkg. peach jello

Put puddings and jello in saucepan with 3 cups water. Boil for 1 minute; cool. Add 1 large container Cool Whip and 1 large can drained peach slices; refrigerate 1 hour.

Myrtle Bohline, Gamaliel, Ar.

MOLDED PEAR SALAD

1 pkg. lime flavored gelatin
1 (No. 2) can pears

2 small pkg. cream cheese
1/2 pt. whipping cream, whipped

Dissolve gelatin in 1 cup of warm pear juice. When slightly firm, add mashed pears and mashed cheese; fold in whipped cream. Place in a ring mold or custard cups and chill until firm. Makes 8 to 10 servings.

Aster Paulsrud, Montevideo, Mn.

PINEAPPLE-BANANA SALAD

2 (3 oz.) pkg. lemon jello
2 c. boiling water
2 c. miniature marshmallows
10 large ice cubes

1 (No. 2) can crushed, drained pineapple (reserve juice)
2 sliced bananas

Dissolve 2 packages lemon jello in 2 cups boiling water. Immediately, add 2 cups miniature marshmallows; stir until dissolved. Add 10 large ice cubes; stir for 2 minutes. Remove any cubes not dissolved; chill. When jello starts to set, approximately 15 minutes, add No. 2 can drained, crushed pineapple (reserve juice for topping). Add 2 sliced bananas. Pour into 8x12 or 9x13 inch pan. When completely set, cover with Custard Topping (follows).

Custard Topping:

1/2 c. sugar
2 beaten eggs
2 Tbsp. flour

1 c. pineapple juice (add water if necessary to make 1 c. liquid)

Cook above ingredients until thick; cool. Add 1/2 pint whipping cream, which has been whipped, or equal volume of Cool Whip or Dream Whip. Spread over set jello base. Sprinkle chopped nuts on top.

Karen Moe, Duluth, Mn.

MOLDED PINEAPPLE CHEESE SALAD

Boil together:
1 (No. 2) can crushed pineapple

1 c. sugar

Remove from heat. In 1/2 cup cold water, dissolve 2 packages Knox plain gelatine; add this to the pineapple mix. Cool well; add:

1 c. grated mild Cheddar cheese
1 c. chopped nuts
1 c. finely diced celery

3/4 c. mayonnaise or Miracle Whip
1 pkg. Dream Whip, prepared as directed on pkg.

Fold together; put into a 10x13 inch pan to refrigerate. Garnish with lettuce.

Liz Tuft, St. Paul, Mn.

PINEAPPLE MINT JELLY SALAD

Put 1 envelope gelatin in saucepan with 1/2 cup pineapple syrup from a 20 ounce can. Stir over heat till dissolved. Remove and add 1/3 cup apple mint jelly; stir until dissolved. Add pineapple and rest of syrup; mix together. Add 1 teaspoon powdered sugar to 1 cup whipping cream; beat until stiff. Fold into the first mixture and put in mold. Chill till firm.

Joan Norton, Hibbing, Mn.

PISTACHIO SALAD

1 small pkg. instant
   pistachio pudding
1 (9 oz.) ctn. Cool Whip

1 large can crushed
   pineapple, undrained
3 c. miniature marshmallows

Garnish with cherries and nuts, if desired.

Anne Aune, Minneapolis, Mn.
Similar recipe submitted by: Edna V. Olson, Duluth, Mn.

POTATO SALAD

4 good sized potatoes
3 eggs
1 large onion
1 dill pickle

1 Tbsp. pickle juice
2-3 Tbsp. mayonnaise
Salt and pepper to taste
Paprika

Boil the potatoes just until tender. Boil the eggs in another pan until solid. Dice the potatoes into a large bowl. Cut up the eggs, onion and pickles in average sized pieces; mix with potatoes. Add the juice, mayonnaise, salt and pepper; mix again lightly until all blends in well. Sprinkle paprika generously over all. Add tomato wedges on top, if preferred.

Colleen Landwehr, St. Cloud, Mn.

COLD GERMAN POTATO SALAD

Boil 12 potatoes. Mix:

1/4 c. Mazola oil
1/4 c. white vinegar

2 Tbsp. sugar
2 Tbsp. water

Let set until you peel and dice potatoes to dissolve sugar. Add 3/4 cup celery, diced, 1/4 cup onion and 1/2 teaspoon salt. Sprinkle with pepper.

Sue Helland, Grand Forks, N.D.

SOUR CREAM POTATO SALAD

2 c. cubed, cooked
  potatoes
2 hard cooked eggs,
  chopped
1/2 c. chopped green
  pepper
1/2 c. chopped celery
2 Tbsp. green onion slices

1/2 c. chopped, peeled
  cucumber
1/4 c. pickle relish
2 Tbsp. chopped pimiento
1/2 c. dairy sour cream
1 tsp. prepared mustard
3/4 tsp. salt
Dash of pepper

Combine potatoes, eggs, vegetables, pickle relish and pimiento. Add combined sour cream, mustard and seasonings; mix lightly. Chill. Makes 6 servings.

Mankato, Mn.

PRETZEL SALAD

Bottom: Mix together -

2 2/3 c. crushed pretzels
3 Tbsp. sugar

1 1/2 sticks margarine

Use as crust in 9x13 inch pan. Bake at 350° for 10 minutes; cool.

Middle: Mix -

1 (8 oz.) pkg. cream cheese
1 c. sugar

1 (8 oz.) container Cool
Whip

Spread over crust.

Top: Mix -

1 (6 oz.) pkg. strawberry
  jello

3 c. boiling water

Add 1 (10 ounce) package frozen strawberries when jello is slightly thickened. Pour over middle layer. Serve when set.

Bonnie Sorby, Moorhead, Mn.

PRUNE SALAD

24 unsweetened, cooked
   prunes, cut up
Rind of 1 orange, grated
Juice of 1 orange

1 pkg. lemon jello
1 c. hot water
3/4 c. prune juice (in bottle)
Walnuts

Melt jello in hot water; add prune and orange juices. Add rest of mixture. Makes 8 small molds.

Topping: Whip 1/4 cup cream. Mash 1/2 banana and cut 1/4 cup celery fine. Mix together; put on top of salad.

Aster Paulsrud, Montevideo, Mn.

PURPLE LADY SALAD

1 (6 oz.) pkg. raspberry
   jello
1 c. boiling water
1 (1 lb.) can blueberries

1 small can crushed pineapple
1 c. chopped pecans
1/4 pt. whipping cream

Dissolve jello in water; stir in blueberries (with syrup) and pineapple. Refrigerate until partially set. Fold in nuts and whipped cream. Refrigerate. Serves 8.

Elynor Pederson, Minneapolis, Mn.

MY FAVORITE RASPBERRY SALAD

1 (3 oz.) pkg. raspberry
   flavored gelatin
1 c. boiling water
1 (10 oz.) pkg. frozen
   raspberries and juice

1/2 - 1 c. cottage cheese
   (small curd)
1/4 - 1/2 c. chopped walnuts
   or pecans

First, partly thaw the frozen raspberries by submerging the package in warm water for about 20 minutes. Stir water into gelatin until gelatin is dissolved. Add raspberries and juice, stirring gently until raspberries are completely thawed. Add cottage cheese and nuts, mixing them in. Pour into a mold; chill until set. Unmold onto large plate, or cut into individual servings. Serve with a sweet, creamy salad dressing. Serves 6.

Bernice Fonos, Minneapolis, Mn.

RASPBERRY DELIGHT SALAD

1 pkg. raspberry jello
1 c. hot water
1 c. vanilla ice cream

3 Tbsp. orange juice
1 (9 oz.) can crushed
  pineapple, drained
1/2 c. chopped pecans

Dissolve jello in hot water. Mix in ice cream and orange juice; chill. When slightly set, add fruit and nuts.

Ruth Lee, Detroit Lakes, Mn.

RIBBON SALAD

Step 1:

1 (3 oz.) pkg. blackberry
  jello

3/4 c. hot water
3/4 c. cold water

Pour into 9x13 inch pan; chill until set.

Step 2:

1 (3 oz.) pkg. cherry jello
1/2 c. hot water

1/2 c. cold water
1/2 c. evaporated milk

Pour over first layer.

Step 3: Mix 1 (3 ounce) package lime jello the same as step 1.

Step 4: Mix 1 (3 ounce) package lemon jello the same as step 2.

Step 5: Mix 1 (3 ounce) package orange jello the same as step 1.

Step 6: Mix 1 (3 ounce) package orange-pineapple jello the same as step 2.

Step 7: Mix 1 (3 ounce) package strawberry jello the same as step 1.

As each layer is setting, mix next flavor of jello. Let it set so it is not hot when poured over the next layer of set jello.

Beverly Carlin, Austin, Mn.

TOMATO RIBBON SALAD

1/2 c. cold water
6 c. tomato juice
3 (1/4 oz.) env. unflavored
  gelatin

1 lemon, sliced
1/2 c. sugar
1/2 tsp. salt
6 whole cloves

1507-82

2 sticks cinnamon

1 (1 lb.) container cream style cottage cheese

In a small bowl, combine cold water and 1/2 cup of the tomato juice; sprinkle gelatin over liquids to soften. In a large saucepan, combine remaining tomato juice, lemon, sugar, salt and spices; stir well. Bring to a boil; reduce heat and simmer 10 minutes. Strain. Add gelatin mixture; stir to dissolve. Pour half of the mixture into a lightly oiled 8 inch square pan; chill until firm. Keep remaining mixture at room temperature. Spread chilled mold with cottage cheese to within 1/4 inch of edges. Carefully pour remaining gelatin mixture over mold; chill until set. At serving time, dip mold in warm water 10 seconds. To unmold, invert onto a serving platter. Slice into bars. Makes 8-10 servings.

Bernita Engel, Minneapolis, Mn.

DONNA'S RING SALAD

1 (7 oz.) pkg. macaroni rings
4 hard boiled eggs, chopped
1/2 small onion, chopped fine
4 large radishes, chopped fine

1/2 green pepper, chopped fine
1 c. celery, chopped fine
3 carrots, grated
1 (8 1/2 oz.) can peas, drained

Mix together equal amounts of mayonnaise and cole slaw dressing. Pour over the ingredients; mix well. Chill overnight. Serves 8 to 10.

Betty M. Case, Hibbing, Mn.

SALAD

Put in 9x13 inch pan:
2 cans chicken rice soup, undiluted
2 pkg. lemon jello
1 can tuna
2 c. chopped celery

1 c. cream, whipped
1/2 c. chopped nuts
1 c. Miracle Whip salad dressing

Dissolve jello in hot soup; cool and refrigerate until partly set. Pour hot water over tuna in strainer; drain. Whip jello; fold in rest of ingredients. Make salad the day before so it sets well. Truly a party dish.

Helen H. Clark, Grand Forks, N.D.

SAUERKRAUT SALAD

Drain 1 large can sauerkraut; squeeze out as much liquid as possible. Add:

1 c. grated carrots	1/4 c. chopped onion
1/2 c. chopped celery	1/4 c. chopped green pepper

Dissolve 3/4 cup sugar in 1 cup vinegar; pour over sauerkraut mixture. Cover and refrigerate a few hours or overnight; stir occasionally.

Leslie Zimbrick, Minneapolis, Mn.

Similar recipes submitted by: K. Otto, Harvey, N.D., K., St. Cloud, Mn.

SEAFOAM SALAD

1 large box lime jello	1 (8 oz.) pkg. cream cheese, softened
2 c. hot pear juice	
1 large can pears	1 pt. whipping cream, whipped

Drain juice from pears; add enough water to make 2 cups. Heat to boiling; dissolve jello. Let stand until slightly thickened. Mash pears; add softened cream cheese and mix together. Whip jello until frothy; add whipped cream and pears. Mix all together; pour into molds.

Ruth Rehschuh, Minneapolis, Mn.

SEAFOOD RICE SALAD

1 (8 oz.) pkg. frozen, cooked shrimp	1/2 c. finely chopped sweet pickles
1 (6 1/2 - 7 oz.) can tuna, drained	1 1/2 c. thinly sliced celery
3 c. cool, cooked rice	1/4 c. diced pimientos
1/2 c. finely chopped onion	3 hard cooked eggs, chopped
	1 Tbsp. lemon juice
	1 c. mayonnaise

Combine all ingredients; toss lightly. Season to taste; chill. Serve on salad greens and garnish with tomato wedges, if desired. Makes 6 servings.

Ann Christensen, Litchfield, Mn.

SESAME SALAD

Dressing:

1 1/2 tsp. salt
1 Tbsp. plus 1 tsp. sugar

2 Tbsp. Japanese rice wine
  vinegar
1/2 tsp. Accent

Salad:

3 cucumbers
1/2 head lettuce, shredded
1 tsp. onion

1/4 c. celery, thinly sliced,
  diagonally
1 tsp. black sesame seeds,
  toasted

Shred lettuce; add cucumbers, celery and onion. Toss with sesame seeds. Add dressing just before serving. (Toast sesame seeds in small frying pan on top of stove for 5 minutes; no oil.)

Ginny Harwood, St. Cloud, Mn.

SEVEN-LAYER SALAD

Layers: Use 3 ounce jello packages - 1. Black cherry; 2. Cherry; 3. Lime; 4. Lemon; 5. Orange; 6. Orange-pineapple; 7. Strawberry. Have ready 1 can sweetened condensed milk.

Using a glass 9x13 inch pan, alternate layers, adding each after the former layer is firm. For layers 1, 3, 5 and 7, dissolve jello in 3/4 cup hot water; add 3/4 cup cold water. For layers 2, 4 and 6, dissolve jello in 1/2 cup hot water; add 1/2 cup cold water and 1/3 of the can of sweetened condensed milk for each. Top with Cool Whip when ready to serve.

Loretta Van Engelenhoven, Luverne, Mn.
Similar recipe submitted by: Betty M. Case, Hibbing, Mn.

SHOESTRING SALAD

1 c. celery, chopped
1 c. carrots, shredded
1 tsp. grated onion
2 hard boiled eggs, chopped

1 c. salad dressing
1 can tuna
1 (4 oz.) can shoestring
  potatoes

Mix all ingredients, except potatoes; chill several hours. Add potatoes just before serving. (Leftovers not as tasty, so eat and enjoy.)

104   Mrs. Burton Peterson, Rochester, Mn.

SHRIMP SALAD

1 lb. shrimp, cooked and
   cleaned
1 c. celery, sliced
1 can mandarin oranges

1/2 c. French dressing
1/2 c. whole walnuts
1 tsp. butter
1 tsp. garlic salt

Drop walnuts in boiling water; boil for 3 minutes. Drain. Toast walnuts in a 350° oven, with the butter and garlic salt, for 20 minutes. Combine all ingredients, except nuts, and toss lightly. Add walnuts just before serving.

Ginny Harwood, St. Cloud, Mn.

SHRIMP SALAD

1 c. celery
1 c. marinated 3 bean salad,
   drained

1 c. onion, diced
1 pkg. frozen shrimp,
   rinsed in cold water

   Sauce:

1 c. Miracle Whip
1/4 c. vinegar

2 Tbsp. sugar

Mix together sauce ingredients until smooth; add 1/2 cup milk and mix well.

Mix sauce and shrimp; pour over other ingredients. Blend together and marinate overnight. Serving: Spoon over nests of shoestring potatoes. Use enough shoestring potatoes to soak up extra sauce.

Gloria McMahon, Fargo, N.D.

$6 SALAD

4 c. broccoli buds (fresh)
1 basket cherry tomatoes,
   sliced
2 c. diced celery
1 basket sliced mushrooms

2 pkg. Good Seasons Italian
   dressing
1 3/4 c. Mozzarella cheese
1 1/2 c. water
1/3 c. vinegar

   Chill.

Cindy Roney, Minneapolis, Mn.

SIX VEGETABLE SALAD

2 c. cauliflower	2 c. shredded carrots
4 c. peas (frozen)	1/3 c. salad oil
2 c. celery, sliced	2/3 c. vinegar
1 c. radishes, sliced	1 tsp. salt
1 c. sliced green onions	3/4 c. sugar
with tops	1/8 tsp. pepper

Combine salad oil, vinegar, salt, pepper and sugar; stir till sugar is dissolved. Pour over vegetables; cover. Keep in refrigerator. Let stand 24 hours before serving. Drain before serving.

Gordy and Elaine Sneva, Brainerd, Mn.

Similar recipe submitted by: Marilyn Radakovich, Duluth, Mn.

SPINACH SALAD

1 (10 oz.) bag raw spinach	2 hard boiled eggs
10 large mushrooms	

Dressing:

2 Tbsp. Dijon mustard	2/3 c. salad oil
Salt and fresh pepper to	1/4 c. wine vinegar
taste	

Wash spinach well; remove stems. Drain on paper towel; pat dry and refrigerate. Mix dressing in small bowl. Mix mustard, salt and pepper; add oil, a few drops at a time, beating well. Mixture should be smooth. Add vinegar a little at a time. Wipe off mushrooms with a damp cloth; slice thin. Mash eggs with fork. Toss mushrooms, eggs and spinach in large salad bowl. Add dressing just before serving and toss. Use only enough dressing to coat spinach.

Bev. Jensen, Willmar, Mn.

SUNSHINE SALAD

Dissolve in 2 cups boiling water:

1 pkg. orange jello	1 pkg. lemon jello

Add:

1 1/2 c. cold water	1 (No. 2) can crushed
	pineapple, drained

2 bananas, sliced

12 big marshmallows, quartered

Pour into 9x13 inch pan; cool.

Topping:

1 egg, beaten
2 Tbsp. flour

1/2 c. sugar
1 c. pineapple juice

Cook until thick; let cool. Whip 1 cup cream or 1 small can of condensed milk; beat into topping. Spread on set jello and shred 1 cup of Cheddar cheese on top. Keep cool.

Shirley Erickson, Fargo, N.D.

SUPER SALAD

2 pkg. fresh spinach, cut or torn in halves
1 pkg. fresh mushrooms, sliced
1 head cauliflower, cut in small pieces

1 pkg. broccoli, cut in small pieces
Pecan halves (as many as you want - you may slice them if you wish)

Dressing:

1 c. mayonnaise
1 tsp. Dijon mustard

2 tsp. horseradish
1/2 c. beer

Toss just before serving. Serve corn muffins (warm) with this fresh vegetable salad.

Dode Desch, St. Paul, Mn.

STRAWBERRY SALAD

1 (13 1/2 oz.) ctn. Cool Whip
1 (2 lb.) ctn. small curd cottage cheese
1 (6 oz.) pkg. strawberry jello

1 (20 oz.) can crushed pineapple, drained
1 qt. fresh strawberries, quartered, or 1 qt. frozen strawberries, drained

Mix Cool Whip and cottage cheese together; add dry jello, then fruits. Let stand overnight. Garnish with fresh strawberries.

Karen M. Larson

STRAWBERRY DELIGHT SALAD

Mix together:

1 can strawberry pie filling

1 can Eagle Brand sweetened condensed milk

Fold in:

1 can well drained pineapple chunks

1 can drained fruit cocktail

1 can drained mandarin oranges

1 (12 oz.) ctn. Cool Whip

Refrigerate overnight before serving.

Mrs. Norma Applen, Minneapolis, Mn.

SUNSHINE SALAD

1/2 (21 oz.) can apricot pie filling

1/2 (4 1/2 oz.) ctn. Cool Whip

1/2 can Eagle Brand milk

1/4 c. lemon juice

2 (11 oz.) cans mandarin oranges, drained

1 (13 oz.) can pineapple tidbits, drained

1/2 c. miniature marshmallows

1/2 c. chopped walnuts

1/4 c. shredded cocoanut

Combine pie filling, Cool Whip, Eagle Brand milk and lemon juice; fold in remaining ingredients. Cover and chill overnight.

P.S. Double the recipe - it's that good! Bananas can also be added.

June Szymczak, Duluth, Mn.

SWEET SOUR VEGETABLE SALAD

1 pkg. mixed vegetables, cooked, drained

1/3 c. chopped onion

1/2 c. celery, cut fine

1/2 c. chopped green pepper

1 can kidney beans, drained and rinsed

Dressing: Mix -

1 Tbsp. flour

1/2 c. sugar

1/2 c. vinegar

1/2 tsp. salt

1 Tbsp. prepared mustard

Cook until thick; add to vegetables.

Esther Mungovan, Duluth, Mn.

TACO SALAD

Mix together:

1 head lettuce
1 can kidney beans, drained
1 can ripe, pitted olives, drained
1 regular size bag Fritos

1 lb. hamburger
1/2 pkg. taco seasoning
1 c. shredded Cheddar cheese

Dressing:

1 pkg. Hidden Valley dressing, made as on pkg.

1 pkg. frozen avocado dip

Place Fritos on bottom, next lettuce, beans and olives, then the hamburger mixed with taco seasoning. Sprinkle cheese over hamburger and put the dressing on top.

Liz Tuft, St. Paul, Mn.

TACO SALAD

1 1/2 lb. ground beef
1 1/2 c. diced onion

3 cloves garlic, cut fine
1 c. diced green pepper

Brown meat; in separate pan, saute onion, garlic and green pepper. Mix the two together; season with salt and 1 teaspoon chili powder. In top of double boiler, melt 1 pound Velveeta cheese. After cheese has melted, add 1 can diced jalapeno peppers and 1 large can peeled tomatoes. Cook together until well blended. Chop up 1 large head of lettuce and 2 large tomatoes; place in large bowl. When ready to serve, layer lettuce and tomatoes with Fritos (2 large bags are needed), meat mixture and top off with hot cheese mixture.

Mary Andrew, St. Paul, Mn.

TOSTADO SALAD

1 lb. lean hamburger
1 can kidney beans, drained
1 head lettuce, broken in pieces
4 tomatoes, quartered (I used more than 4)
1 c. grated Cheddar cheese

1 onion, chopped
Tabasco sauce to taste (use sparingly)
1 (8 oz.) jar Thousand Island dressing
1 (39¢) bag Doritos, crushed in bag

Brown hamburger; drain off grease. Add beans; simmer 10 minutes. Add small amount of Tabasco sauce, couple drops, and taste as it takes very little. Cool for several minutes. Mix rest of ingredients; add hamburger mixture. Cool in refrigerator. Garnish with avocado slices before serving.

Maryann Skelton, Duluth, Mn.

MOCK TOMATO ASPIC

1 pkg. raspberry or
   strawberry gelatin

1 c. boiling water
1 (16 oz.) can stewed
   tomatoes

Mix gelatin and water; cool to room temperature and mix in stewed tomatoes.

Olga Pederson, Minneapolis, Mn.

TUNA SALAD

4 (7 oz.) cans tuna, well
   drained
1 c. salad dressing
2 c. chopped celery

3/4 c. chopped pimento
1 Tbsp. salt
2 tsp. Worcestershire sauce
1/4 tsp. pepper

Blend all together. Layer dark and white bread for sandwiches or use open face buns.

Marion Round, Faribault, Mn.

CRUNCHY TUNA SALAD

2 (6 1/2 oz.) cans tuna,
   drained
4 c. frozen peas, cooked
1 c. diced celery
1 small onion, chopped
1/2 tsp. salt

2 or 4 eggs, hard boiled,
   chopped
1 c. raw cauliflower, diced
1 Tbsp. lemon juice
3/4 c. mayonnaise or salad
   dressing

Optional: To make it more yummy, add 1 can sliced water chestnuts and sliced olives.

Helene Rice, Bradenton, Fl.

TUNA CHEDDAR SALAD

1 (6 3/4 oz.) can tuna,
 packed in water,
 drained and flaked
1 small apple, chopped
1/3 c. diced sharp
 Cheddar cheese

1/4 c. chopped celery
1/4 c. mayonnaise
1/4 c. low-fat plain yogurt
1 Tbsp. finely chopped onion
1/8 tsp. salt
Dash of pepper

Combine tuna, apple, cheese and celery; toss. Add remaining ingredients. Stir with a fork until well blended. Cover; chill at least 1 hour. Serve on lettuce leaves or on bread.

Joan Wichman, Duluth, Mn.

TURKEY (CHICKEN) SALAD

1 c. chopped celery
1 c. grated carrots
1 Tbsp. grated onion

2 c. turkey, diced
1 c. Miracle Whip
1 pt. sour cream

Mix and chill. Add 1 (7 ounce) can shoestring potatoes last. For a big batch, add 2 packages Creamette rings.

Kathie Ells, Duluth, Mn.

TURKEY OR CHICKEN SALAD

3 c. diced chicken or
 turkey
2 c. diced celery
1/2 c. mayonnaise

3 Tbsp. lemon juice
1 tsp. seasoned salt
1/4 tsp. pepper

Mix all together; chill at least 1 hour. Good served with tomato slices, hard cooked eggs and ripe olives for garnish.

Dee Olson, St. Paul, Mn.

TURKEY OR CHICKEN SALAD

2 lb. turkey or chicken,
 cut in chunks
1 pkg. slivered almonds
3 c. chopped celery

3 lb. green grapes, cut in
 halves
1/2 pt. whipping cream,
 whipped

Add mayonnaise or salad dressing; mix well. Refrigerate and serve immediately after adding whipped cream and mayonnaise.

Mary Paul, Minneapolis, Mn.

24 HOUR SALAD

Cook until thick in double boiler:

3 eggs	1/4 c. pineapple juice
1 Tbsp. sugar	Juice of 1 lemon

Mix:

1 (No. 2 1/2) can pineapple tidbits, drained	1/2 c. slivered almonds
1 pt. cream, whipped	1 can drained fruit cocktail, if desired
1 1/2 lb. mini marshmallows	Some maraschino cherries, if desired

Combine sauce and other ingredients; place in serving bowl and cover. Chill for 24 hours.

Linda C. Shannon, Bloomington, Mn.

24 HOUR SALAD

Layer in order in large salad bowl:

3/4 head lettuce, broken small	1 small can water chestnuts, sliced
1/2 c. green onions, sliced	1 (8 oz.) pkg. frozen raw peas
1/2 c. celery, sliced	

Mix 2 tablespoons sugar and 2 cups Hellmann's mayonnaise well; spread over salad. Sprinkle Parmesan cheese over top. Cover; put in refrigerator 24 hours. Garnish salad with hard boiled eggs.

Florence Peine, St. Paul, Mn.

24 HOUR MACARONI RING SALAD

1 box macaroni rings, cooked	1/2 tsp. salt
Juice of 2 cans of pineapple tidbits	1 c. sugar
Juice of 1 lemon	1 large can drained fruit cocktail
2 eggs	1 small bottle cherries
2 Tbsp. flour	1 pt. whipping cream

Cook macaroni rings; drain and cool. Combine juice of pineapple tidbits (about 2 cups), juice of the lemon, eggs, flour, salt and sugar; boil until thick. Cool. Pour custard over the macaroni rings; refrigerate. The next day, add

fruit, marshmallows and whipped cream. Refrigerate.
Serves 24 generously. Keeps for 2 to 3 days.

Sigrid Johnson, Hibbing, Mn.

VEGETABLE SALAD

Cook 1 package frozen mixed vegetables 3 minutes in
salt water; drain. Add:

1 1/2 c. cauliflower
1 1/2 c. celery

1 small onion
Water chestnuts, if desired

Dressing:

1/2 c. mayonnaise
1/2 c. sour cream

1 tsp. mustard

Make the night before.

Marlys Swehla, Albert Lea, Mn.

VEGETABLE SALAD

Mix together:

4 potatoes, cooked, chopped
4 carrots, cooked, chopped
4 eggs, cooked, chopped
1 c. peas

2 Tbsp. mayonnaise (to
  taste)
2 tsp. salt (to taste)
1 Tbsp. oil
1 Tbsp. vinegar

Peg Kaufmann, Rochester, Mn.

VEGETABLE BEAN SALAD

2 c. thin sliced cabbage
2 medium carrots, shredded
2 stalks celery, thick sliced
1 small onion, thick sliced

1 (16 oz.) can red kidney
  beans, drained
1/2 tsp. salt
3/4 c. mayonnaise
4 Tbsp. French dressing

Mix all together; let set overnight. Serve the next
day. Serves 6.

M.A. Paul, Minneapolis, Mn.

VEGETABLE JELLO SALAD

1 small pkg. lemon jello
1/2 c. hot water
2 Tbsp. vinegar
1 c. cold water
1/2 c. mayonnaise

1/2 tsp. salt and pepper,
  mixed together
2 c. shredded cabbage
1 tsp. grated onion
1/2 c. grated carrots
1/4 c. chopped green pepper

Dissolve jello in hot water, then add cold water and vinegar. Cool; add mayonnaise, salt and pepper, cabbage, onion, carrots and green pepper. Pour in mold, rinsed in cold water or sprayed with Pam. Set until firm. Serves 6 to 8.

Marty Eger, South St. Paul, Mn.

LAYERED   VEGETABLE   SALAD

Layer:
1 head shredded lettuce
1/2 c. chopped celery
1/4 c. diced onion

1 regular can drained peas
1 c. shredded carrots

Top with:
2 c. Miracle Whip
1 c. whipping cream

2 Tbsp. sugar

Make the night before; cover and refrigerate. When ready to serve, toss, then top with 10 pieces crumbled, fried bacon and 1 cup grated cheese.

Jan Eschbach, Duluth, Mn.

MARINATED   VEGETABLE   SALAD

Wash, drain and prepare the following:
1 head cauliflower, broken into flowerets
1 pkg. fresh broccoli (use part of stock, too)
6 carrots, peeled and sliced

3 cucumbers, sliced with skins
1 small pkg. radishes, sliced*
Onion (as you like)
Cherry tomatoes, left whole

Prepare Good Seasons brand of Italian dressing, in which you mix oil and vinegar; do not add water. This dressing comes in a package; pour dressing over prepared vegetables and let marinate. Keeps in refrigerator for over a week. Depending upon the size of cauliflower and broccoli used, you perhaps might us 2 packages of dressing. Add salt and pepper according to your taste. Add the radishes the same day you serve the salad. Serves 16.
*The red coloring leaves the skin of the radish if left to marinate several days.

Marion Iverson, Bismarck, N.D.

POTPOURRI VEGETABLE SALAD

1 1/2 c. white vinegar
1 c. salad oil
2 c. sugar
6 tsp. salt
1/4 tsp. pepper
1 (16 oz.) can French cut
  green beans, drained
1 large onion, chopped
1 green pepper, chopped
1 (16 oz.) can bean sprouts,
  drained
1 (4 oz.) can mushroom
  pieces, drained

1 (12 oz.) can white corn,
  drained
1 (2 oz.) jar pimento,
  chopped
1 c. sliced celery
1 small head cauliflower,
  broken in small pieces
3 large raw carrots, grated
  or shredded
1 (8 oz.) can water chestnuts, sliced thin
1 (15 oz.) can garbanzo
  beans, drained

Combine vinegar, salad oil, sugar, salt and pepper; bring to a boil. Cool; pour over vegetables. Mix gently. Let stand 24 hours. Stir before serving. Serves 15.
Jane Bohline, Minneapolis, Mn.

SWEDISH VEGETABLE SALAD

1 1/2 c. carrots, cooked
  and diced
1 1/2 c. fresh cauliflower
  slices, just parboiled
1 box frozen green beans,
  parboiled
1 box frozen green peas,
  parboiled
1/2 c. chopped onion
1/2 c. chopped celery

1 c. canned artichoke
  hearts, sliced
3/4 c. sharp French
  dressing
3/4 c. mayonnaise
1/4 c. chili sauce
2 tsp. ground dry dill
1 tsp. salt
1/2 tsp. pepper
1 Tbsp. lemon juice

Marinate vegetables in French dressing for 1 hour; drain well. Mix mayonnaise, chili sauce, dill, salt, pepper and lemon juice. Stir into vegetable mixture. Chill before serving. This salad is better the second day. Serves 12.
Va Fyksen, Duluth, Mn.

"THE RADISSON" WALDORF SALAD

3 large apples, cored, diced
1/2 c. celery, diced
Juice of 1/2 lemon
1/2 c. mayonnaise

1 c. whipping cream
Sugar to taste
Walnut halves

Mix apples and celery. Add lemon juice and mayonnaise to mixture. Whip cream stiff; add sugar to your liking. Fold in apples. Serve on bed of lettuce with halves of walnuts on top. Serves 6.

Note: I am not so fond of lemon flavor, so use less than their recipe calls for. Use your own judgement there.

Bernice Fonos, Minneapolis, Mn.

WILD RICE SALAD

Bring to boil:
6 c. water   1 3/4 tsp. salt

Add 2 cups soaked wild rice (washed in colander and soaked all night in airtight container, Tupperware). Cover and turn electric stove to simmer; simmer for 25 minutes. While rice is cooking, in a cup mix:

1 medium onion, cut fine
2 Tbsp. cooking oil
2 tsp. mustard

1/2 c. mayonnaise (not salad
   dressing)
1/4 tsp. paprika

Cover and chill thoroughly; serve on lettuce leaves. Pour rice in colander and add 1/2 cup brown sugar and 1 teaspoon salt. Pour into salad bowl. Mix rice mixture well with fork to get extra moisture out; blend. Scoop in scoops on lettuce leaf and add topping. Serves 3.

Bonnie Govick, Marshall, Mn.

WILD RICE SALAD

1 (6 oz.) pkg. long grain
   and wild rice mix
1 1/2 c. mayonnaise
1/4 c. plain yogurt
1 c. sliced celery

1 c. cubed tomatoes
1/2 c. diced cucumber
1/8 tsp. seasoned salt
1/8 tsp. pepper
2 Tbsp. chopped parsley

Cook rice as directed on package, omitting the butter. Toss lightly with next 8 ingredients; cover and chill. Garnish with 1/4 cup dry roasted peanuts.

116   Sally Bartsch, Blaine, Mn.

NAN'S WINE JELLO SALAD

2 (3 oz.) pkg. raspberry
   jello
1 (13 1/2 oz.) can crushed
   pineapple (all)

1 can whole cranberry sauce
   or 2 c. homemade
   cranberry sauce
2 c. boiling water

Mix and let thicken slightly. Add 3/4 cup burgundy (Mogan David sherry) and 1/2 cup nuts; let set in refrigerator.

Maryann Skelton, Duluth, Mn.

ZESTY BEET SALAD

1 (16 oz.) can shoestring
   beets, drained (save
   juice)
1 (8 1/4 oz.) can crushed
   pineapple, drained
   (save juice)
1 (3 oz.) pkg. cherry gelatin

1 (3 oz.) pkg. raspberry
   gelatin
2 c. boiling water
Ice cubes
2 Tbsp. vinegar
1 c. diced celery
2 Tbsp. minced onion

Drain beets and pineapple, reserving juices. Combine gelatins and boiling water; add enough ice to make 2 cups liquid. Add to gelatin mixture. Add the vinegar; chill until slightly set. Next, add beets, pineapple, onion and celery. Pour into 1 1/2 quart mold; refrigerate until set.

Dressing: Combine -

1 c. mayonnaise
1 Tbsp. green pepper

1 Tbsp. onion
1 Tbsp. parsley

Add:
1/2 c. diced celery

2 Tbsp. lemon juice

Chill at least 2 hours.

Clifford H. Carlson, Saginaw, Mn.

DODE'S BLENDER DRESSING

Blend thoroughly:
1 medium onion
1 tsp. salt
1 tsp. dry mustard
1 tsp. celery salt

1 tsp. paprika
1 c. sugar
1/2 c. vinegar

Add 1 cup oil and blend again. Shake before using.
1507-82   Helen Teeuwen, Minneapolis, Mn.

'SECRET RECIPE' BLEU CHEESE SALAD DRESSING

1 c. Miracle Whip
1/3 c. Carnation milk
1 Tbsp. vinegar
1 1/2 tsp. hot mustard
1 1/2 tsp. finely chopped
   onion

1 1/2 tsp. monosodium
   glutamate
1 1/2 tsp. garlic
3/4 tsp. pepper
4 oz. Bleu cheese, crumbled

Mix together with wire whip. Store in refrigerator.
Debbie Burgum, Dickinson, N.D.

COLE SLAW DRESSING

1 c. salad oil
1 c. sugar
1/2 c. white vinegar

1 tsp. salt
1 tsp. celery seed
1 chopped onion

Mix well in quart jar; refrigerate. Tastes best after setting at least 24 hours.
Jan Farley, Sartell, Mn.
Similar recipe submitted by: Inez Wagner, Austin, Mn.

CREAMY LOW-CALORIE SALAD DRESSING

1 c. lowfat cottage cheese

1/4 c. lemon juice or vinegar
1/2 c. tomato juice

Blend all ingredients with hand beater until very smooth. Store in covered jar in refrigerator. Makes 1 3/4 cups, with 14 calories per 2 tablespoons.
Phylliss Mae Johnson, Winona, Mn.

DELICIOUS SALAD DRESSING

To 1 quart mayonnaise, add:

1 c. milk
1 tsp. Accent
1 tsp. celery salt

1/2 tsp. onion salt
1/2 tsp. garlic salt
Salt and pepper to taste
Esther Mungovan, Duluth, Mn.

FOOLPROOF DRESSING

1 c. sugar
2 tsp. mustard
2 eggs or 4 egg yolks
3/4 c. vinegar

2 tsp. salt
2 1/2 Tbsp. flour
2 c. milk

Mix dry ingredients; add eggs and beat until mixed. Add milk. Heat this slowly until it thickens. Add vinegar, which has been heated. Makes a large quart of salad dressing.

Jo-Lyn Freitag, Minneapolis, Mn.

FRENCH DRESSING

1/3 c. catsup
1/2 c. oil (salad)
1/4 c. vinegar
1/4 c. sugar
1/4 tsp. pepper

1 tsp. paprika
1 tsp. salt
1 tsp. onion juice
1 tsp. dry mustard

Combine ingredients in glass container; shake well. Store in refrigerator.

Jean Taylor, Grand Forks, N.D.

Similar recipes submitted by: Jan Farley, Sartell, Mn., Mrs. Verne Andal, St. Cloud, Mn.

FRENCH DRESSING

1 can condensed tomato soup
1/4 c. vinegar
1/2 c. salad oil
1 Tbsp. minced onion

2 Tbsp. sugar
2 tsp. dry mustard (opt.)
1 tsp. salt
1/4 tsp. pepper

Combine ingredients in quart jar; shake well before using. Makes 2 1/4 cups dressing.

Gemma Pierson, St. Cloud, Mn.

Similar recipe submitted by: Jeanne Shaver, Minneapolis, Mn.

BUNGALOW INN (CRYSTAL) FRENCH DRESSING

1 (10 oz.) can tomato soup
3/4 c. vinegar
2 Tbsp. finely ground onion
1 tsp. Worcestershire sauce
1 tsp. celery salt

1 tsp. dry mustard
1 c. Mazola oil
1 tsp. paprika
3/4 c. sugar

1507-82

Blend all ingredients in a jar and shake violently before serving. Store in refrigerator. (This is super!)

Eileen Thompson, Minneapolis, Mn.

FRENCH SALAD DRESSING

1/2 c. vinegar	2 tsp. salt
1/2 c. water	1 1/2 tsp. dry mustard
3/4 c. sugar (scant)	1 tsp. Worcestershire sauce
2 large onions	1 tsp. paprika
1 clove garlic	1 small can tomato paste

Put in blender and gradually add 1 cup salad oil or shake in quart jar.

Va Fyksen, Duluth, Mn.

FRESH VEGETABLE DRESSING

1 c. Hellmann's mayonnaise	1 Tbsp. dill seed
1 c. sour cream	1 Tbsp. dried minced onion

Mix and let set overnight. Recipe can be halved easily and is still just as good.

Helen H. Clark, Grand Forks, N.D.

FRESH FRUIT SALAD DRESSING

1 c. orange juice	1/4 tsp. salt
1/2 c. honey	2 (7 oz.) bottles 7-Up
1/2 tsp. cinnamon	

Simmer first 4 ingredients for 5 minutes; cool. Stir in chilled 7-Up. Store in jar in refrigerator and pour over fresh fruit, as needed.

Olga Pederson, Minneapolis, Mn.

HONEY FRUIT DRESSING

1/2 c. sugar	1/3 c. honey
1 tsp. dry mustard	1/3 c. vinegar
1 tsp. paprika	1 c. salad oil
1 tsp. celery seed	1 Tbsp. lemon juice
1/4 tsp. salt	

Mix with electric beater till thickened slightly; refrigerate.

Irene Callahan, Austin, Mn.

GERT'S DRESSING FOR CABBAGE

2 Tbsp. mayonnaise
1 tsp. sugar

1/2 tsp. celery seed
2 Tbsp. vinegar

Combine. Enough dressing for cabbage for 2 servings.

Helen Teeuwen, Minneapolis, Mn.

GREEN GODDESS DRESSING

1 scallion
1 bunch fresh chives
1/2 c. firmly packed parsley
   leaves
1 small clove garlic, pressed
   (optional)
8 anchovy fillets, drained
   and minced, or 2 tsp.
   anchovy paste

2 Tbsp. fresh tarragon
   leaves or 2 tsp. dried
   tarragon
2 tsp. Dijon-style mustard
1/4 c. white wine vinegar or
   tarragon vinegar
2 1/2 c. mayonnaise
1/2 c. dairy sour cream

Finely chop the scallion, chives and parsley. Combine in a mixing bowl with the remaining ingredients; mix thoroughly. (In food processor: Process scallion, cut up chives, parsley, garlic, anchovy and tarragon briefly with the steel blade. Change to the plastic blade and add remaining ingredients, processing just until well mixed.) Cover and refrigerate at least 2 hours to mellow flavors. Taste and adjust seasonings. Serve at room temperature. Makes 1 quart, about 16 servings. If any of your guests are dieting, you may want to use this low calorie dressing in place of the sweet-sour, red one.

St. Cloud, Mn.

ITALIAN DRESSING

1 Tbsp. sugar
3/4 tsp. salt
1 Tbsp. minced garlic
1 tsp. minced onion
1/4 tsp. whole tarragon
1/4 tsp. dehydrated red
   bell pepper

1/8 tsp. oregano
Pinch of ground red pepper
1/4 tsp. whole basil
3/8 c. vinegar
1/4 c. water
1 c. oil (or mayonnaise)
1/8 c. cream

Thoroughly mix together sugar, salt, garlic, onion,

tarragon, bell pepper, oregano, ground pepper and basil. Combine vinegar and water; stir in dry mixture. Slowly add oil, using mixer on slow speed, or mix by hand with a wire whip until all ingredients are completely blended. Makes about 1 3/4 cups.

St. Cloud, Mn.

OIL SALAD DRESSING

1 c. white sugar
1/2 c. vinegar
1/4 tsp. salt
1 tsp. celery seed

1 grated onion
1 tsp. mustard
1 c. oil

Beat all together; keeps well in refrigerator.

Ollie Kearney, Owatonna, Mn.

GRANDMA HOEFLING'S OIL AND VINEGAR DRESSING

1 c. oil
2 tsp. salt
1 c. vinegar (cider)

1 1/2 c. sugar
2 tsp. ground pepper

Put in quart jar; cover and shake well. Store in refrigerator. Shake before using. This is great dressing for cole slaw and three bean salad. This dressing will keep for a long time.

Gretchen Marquart, Fargo, N.D.

BLENDER MAYONNAISE

2 whole (large size) eggs
1 tsp. salt
1/2 tsp. dry mustard
Dash of Tabasco sauce

1 Tbsp. lemon juice or white wine vinegar
1 1/2 c. olive oil or half olive oil and half peanut oil

1. Place in container of blender the eggs, salt, mustard, Tabasco sauce and lemon juice. Process at high speed for only 5 seconds. 2. Remove center of blender cover and, with blender at high speed, add the oil very slowly, pouring in a teaspoon or two at a time. Continue adding the oil very slowly in a thin stream, still at high speed. 3. As the sauce thickens and emulsifies, you can add the oil more rapidly. You may also wish to scrape down the sides of the

blender once or twice when sauce thickens and before all the oil is added. 4. Spoon out of blender container and serve immediately. If making ahead and you wish to serve later, spoon into jar or bowl; cover and refrigerate. Makes about 2 cups.

Marion Round, Faribault, Mn.

FOOD PROCESSOR MAYONNAISE

1 whole (large size) egg
1 tsp. salt
1/4 tsp. freshly ground
   black pepper or 1/8 tsp.
   Tabasco sauce

1 Tbsp. white wine vinegar
   or lemon juice
1 1/2 c. olive oil, peanut oil
   or half olive oil and half
   peanut oil

1. In bowl of food processor, with metal blade in place, add the egg, salt, vinegar and pepper. Process until blended, about 2 to 3 seconds. 2. Continue processing and pour in the oil very slowly, a little at a time, especially at first. As sauce thickens and emulsifies, you may add the oil a little more rapidly. Do not overprocess. Stop machine when all oil has just been incorporated. 3. Taste mayonnaise and add additional salt, vinegar or pepper to your liking. Spoon out of food processor and serve immediately. If making ahead to serve later, spoon into jar or bowl; cover and refrigerate. Makes about 2 cups.

Marion Round, Faribault, Mn.

O DRESSING
(Low Calorie)

3/4 tsp. green pepper
3/4 tsp. onion
1/3 c. grated carrots
2 tsp. dried parsley flakes

1 tsp. sugar substitute
1 c. vinegar
1/4 tsp. tomato paste
1 c. water

Combine green pepper, onion, carrots and parsley flakes in blender. Add rest of ingredients; blend well. Shake well each time it's used. Store in tightly covered container. Each tablespoon is 7 1/2 calories.

Marion Round, Faribault, Mn.

ORANGE POPPY SEED DRESSING

1/2 c. salad oil
1/3 c. orange juice
  concentrate, thawed

2 Tbsp. honey
2 Tbsp. vinegar
1 tsp. poppy seed or celery
  seed

Combine all ingredients in a screw top jar; shake well. Serve with avocado or fruit salads. Store in refrigerator.

Leslie Zimbrick, Minneapolis, Mn.

PARMESAN SALAD DRESSING

3/4 c. salad oil
1/4 c. lemon juice
2 Tbsp. Parmesan cheese
3/4 tsp. salt

Dash of pepper
1/4 tsp. sugar
Dash of paprika
1 clove garlic, halved

Mix all in a jar; shake till well blended. Refrigerate. Discard garlic. Shake again and pour over salad.

Dee Olson, St. Paul, Mn.

POPPY SEED DRESSING

Mix and chill:
1 pt. mayonnaise
2 Tbsp. wine vinegar
1 Tbsp. lemon juice
1 Tbsp. catsup
1 Tbsp. grated onion

1/2 Tbsp. dry mustard
1 tsp. salt
1 1/4 Tbsp. sugar
2 Tbsp. poppy seed
3 dashes of Tabasco sauce

Wanda Thompson, Minneapolis, Mn.

ROQUEFORT DRESSING

2 c. real mayonnaise (not
  salad dressing)
1/4 c. white vinegar
2 Tbsp. sugar (or 2 Tbsp.
  Sugar Twin substitute)

1/2 c. sour cream
1 clove garlic (or garlic powder may be used)
1/4 lb. Blue cheese (about
  1 c. crumbled)

Mix all ingredients. Keep refrigerated. (A little milk may be added because it becomes thick after refrigerating. Also, you may use as much sour cream as mayonnaise and more Blue cheese, if desired.)

Caroline 'Cari' Bennett, Apple Valley, Mn.

ROQUEFORT DRESSING

1 pkg. cream cheese
1 pkg. Bleu or Roquefort
cheese

3 Tbsp. milk
3 Tbsp. mayonnaise

Mix at room temperature. Additional milk may be added if thinner dressing is desired.

Carol Anderson, Fargo, N.D.

FRAN'S ROQUEFORT DRESSING

2 (12 oz.) pkg. sour cream
1 large can milk
1 (48 oz.) jar Hellmann's
mayonnaise (no substitute)

1 tsp. Accent
1 tsp. white pepper
1 lb. Roquefort cheese

Beat very well. Do not use blender.

Helen Teeuwen, Minneapolis, Mn.

REISINGER'S ROQUEFORT DRESSING

1 qt. mayonnaise
1/4 lb. crumbled Blue cheese
1 small chopped onion

1/2 c. sour cream with
chives
1 tsp. lemon juice

Mix all together in large bowl; return to jar and store. Makes slightly more than a quart.

Variation: Double the cheese; add 1 cup salad dressing and entire 8 ounce carton of sour cream with chives.

Don Reisinger, St. Cloud, Mn.

RUSSIAN DRESSING

1 can tomato soup
1 c. Mazola oil
1 1/2 tsp. salt
1/4 tsp. paprika
2/3 c. vinegar

2/3 c. sugar
1 tsp. dry mustard
2 Tbsp. grated onion
2 Tbsp. green pepper

Shake well in quart jar.

M.L. Roskoski, Virginia, Mn.

SOUR CREAM DRESSING

1 c. dairy sour cream
1/4 c. mayonnaise
3 Tbsp. honey
1 Tbsp. fresh lemon juice
1/2 tsp. dill weed
1/8 tsp. vegetable seasoned
    salt

1/4 c. minced red cabbage
2 Tbsp. minced fresh celery
    leaves
1 Tbsp. minced green onion
2-3 spring fresh parsley,
    minced

Combine sour cream, mayonnaise, honey, lemon juice, dill weed and seasoned salt in medium bowl. Add vegetables; mix well. Refrigerate at least 1 hour for flavors to meld before serving. Also good as a dip for vegetables. Makes 2 cups. This spicy red dressing is a perfect contrast to salad greens.

St. Cloud, Mn.

SWEET-SOUR DRESSING

1/2 c. vinegar
1 c. oil
1 c. sugar

1 tsp. dry mustard
1/2 tsp. salt

Mix above and let set; stir every once in a while till sugar dissolves.

1 medium onion, grated   1 tsp. celery seed

When sugar is dissolved, beat with electric beater. Add onion with juice and beat some more. Store in refrigerator. (Good on vegetables, lettuce, cabbage, meat and potatoes.)

J. Pavnick, Minneapolis, Mn.

BLENDER SWEET-SOUR DRESSING

1 c. salad oil
1 c. cider vinegar
1 medium onion, chopped

3/4 c. sugar
1/3 c. ketchup
1 Tbsp. Worcestershire sauce

Measure oil, vinegar, onion, sugar, ketchup and Worcestershire sauce into blender container; blend until smooth. Refrigerate to blend flavors. Will keep for 1 week. Enough dressing to serve 15.

St. Cloud, Mn.

THOUSAND ISLAND DRESSING

1 tsp. minced onion
3 Tbsp. chili sauce
1 c. mayonnaise

1 Tbsp. chopped green
  pepper
1 tsp. chopped pimento

Mix together.

Carol Anderson, Fargo, N.D.

CALORIE-COUNTER'S TOMATO HERB DRESSING

1 c. tomato-vegetable juice
1/4 c. red wine vinegar
1/2 tsp. sugar
1/4 tsp. ground cumin
1/4 tsp. dried oregano
1/4 tsp. celery salt
1 medium clove garlic,
  pressed

1/8 tsp. freshly ground
  black pepper
Dash of Worcestershire sauce
2 tsp. cornstarch
2 Tbsp. water
2 Tbsp. minced chives
1 Tbsp. olive or vegetable
  oil

Combine tomato juice, vinegar, sugar, cumin, oregano, celery salt, garlic, pepper and Worcestershire sauce in small pan; bring to a simmer. Stir cornstarch into water until dissolved, then stir it into tomato mixture until thickened. Remove from heat; cool. Stir in chives and oil. Cool and adjust seasonings to taste. For best flavor, serve at room temperature. Makes 1 1/2 cups or 8 servings.

St. Cloud, Mn.

VINAIGRETTE DRESSING

For 1/2 cup of dressing, mix 2 tablespoons vinegar (any of the following types: Red or white wine, cider or tarragon) with 1/2 teaspoon salt and 1/2 teaspoon freshly ground black pepper. Gradually add 6 tablespoons oil, preferably olive or peanut, whisking until dressing thickens slightly. Taste for seasoning.

Helen-May Johnson, Chanhassen, Mn.

HONEY BUTTER

1 c. soft butter   1/2 c. honey

Mix all together with mixer until light and fluffy. Serve on hot toast.

Dee Olson, St. Paul, Mn.

SWEET CHERRY BUTTER

1/2 c. butter, softened   1/8 tsp. allspice
1/4 c. cherry jam   1 Tbsp. honey

Mix all together in mixer until light and fluffy. Serve on toast.

Dee Olson, St. Paul, Mn.

GLAZE FOR BAKED HAM

1 c. brown sugar   1 Tbsp. prepared mustard
1 Tbsp. flour   1 Tbsp. vinegar

Make a thick paste and put on ham 1 hour before ham is done.

Bernita Engel

JOHN'S BEEF KABOB MARINADE

1 (5 oz.) bottle soy sauce   1 tsp. ground ginger
1 medium onion, diced   1 clove garlic, sliced
1 bottle Wish-Bone Italian   1 tsp. hot sauce
  dressing   1 Tbsp. Worcestershire sauce

Use 1/2 pound meat per serving. Marinate at least 24 hours; 2-3 days even better.

Sally Bartsch, Blaine, Mn.

BEER MARINADE
(For Beef)

If you have a less expensive cut of meat, try using a marinade or sauce to enhance its flavor. A marinade will also make it more tender.

128

1 (12 oz.) can beer
1/2 c. vegetable oil
2 Tbsp. cider vinegar
1 small onion, thinly sliced

2 cloves garlic, minced
1 tsp. salt
1/2 tsp. freshly ground
  pepper

Use 1/2 cup of marinade for each pound of meat. Mix
ingredients together. Put meat in glass dish. Pour in
enough marinade to immerse meat halfway, then cover dish.
Refrigerate no longer than 24 hours. Brush both sides of
the meat with extra marinade during cooking. Keep the
marinade warm in a saucepan set over the fire.

St. Cloud, Mn.

BARBEQUE SAUCE
(For Chicken, Beef and Pork)

1/2 c. salad oil
1 1/4 c. water
2 Tbsp. chopped onion
1 clove garlic
1 1/2 tsp. sugar
1 tsp. salt
1 tsp. chili powder

1 tsp. paprika
1 tsp. pepper
1/2 tsp. dry mustard
2 Tbsp. vinegar
1 tsp. Worcestershire sauce
1 tsp. Tabasco sauce
Dash of cayenne pepper

Combine; cook 30 minutes. Can be used immediately
and refrigerates well.
We usually barbeque 2 chickens at the same time.
Select whole chickens of approximately same size, say 3 1/2
to 4 pounds. Rinse skin and clean cavity. Pin neck
opening closed. Put heaping teaspoon of salt in cavity;
skewer chickens on spit. Tie wings and legs with strong
string or twine. Brush vegetable oil over chickens and
sprinkle liberally with paprika. Insert tines; squeeze
chickens together end-to-end and tighten tines to spit.
Roast for 1 1/2 to 2 hours at about 200° to 250°. Baste with
barbeque sauce during last 1/2 hour. We prepare 6 to 8
chickens and 2 or 3 beef and pork roasts in the late fall;
place them in baking bags, freeze and reheat for mid-
winter servings. They are delicious, moist and tender as
if freshly barbequed.

Roy Bergstrom, Forest Lake, Mn.

BAR-B-Q SAUCE

1/2 c. ketchup	1/4 c. oil
1/4 c. brown sugar	2 Tbsp. dry onion flakes (or
1 tsp. dry mustard	1 tsp. onion powder)

Stir all ingredients together and brush on meat.

Judy Rieger, Grand Forks, N.D.

BAR-B-Q SAUCE

2 small bottles of ketchup	Juice of 4 lemons or 8 Tbsp.
1 small ketchup bottle of	lemon juice
water	2 Tbsp. Worcestershire sauce
1 (1 lb.) box brown sugar,	Salt, pepper, garlic salt to
less 1/2 c.	taste
1/2 c. liquid smoke	

Add a few drops Tabasco sauce. Add 2 ground onions. Simmer in slow cooker until thick.

Ellie Cox, Rochester, Mn.

BARBECUE SAUCE

2 c. catsup	2 tsp. Worcestershire sauce
1 c. brown sugar	1 tsp. horseradish
2 tsp. liquid smoke	2 Tbsp. instant minced onion

Heat on medium burner until sugar is dissolved; cool. Will keep in refrigerator for many days. Serve on meat balls, pork chops, thinly sliced beef and pork roast, etc.

Mrs. Harry Osborn, Rochester, Mn.

BLENDER AIOLI

2 whole (large size) eggs	Dash of Tabasco sauce
4 good sized cloves of	1/8 tsp. freshly ground
garlic, minced	black pepper
1 tsp. salt	1 1/2 c. olive oil or half olive
2 Tbsp. white wine vinegar	oil and half peanut oil

1. Place the eggs in container of blender. Chop garlic very fine. Sprinkle with salt and rub with flat side of knife blade to a paste. Add to blender. Add vinegar,

130

Tabasco sauce and pepper. 2. Remove center of blender cover and, with blender at high speed, add the oil very slowly, pouring in a teaspoon at a time at first. Continue adding the oil very slowly in a thin stream, still at high speed. 3. As the sauce thickens and emulsifies, you can add the oil more rapidly. Also, you may wish to scrape down the sides of the blender once or twice when sauce thickens and before all the oil is added. 4. Spoon out of blender; serve immediately. To serve later, spoon into a jar; cover and refrigerate. Makes 2 cups.

Note: Aioli is the garlic mayonnaise of Provence, France. It is excellent served with freshly steamed vegetables, served as a sauce for cooked, chilled vegetables or as a dip for fresh vegetable crudites. You can also use it as a unique sandwich spread.

Marion Round, Faribault, Mn.

CHILI SAUCE

24 large tomatoes, peeled
   and chopped
2 small red peppers
8 apples, chopped, peeled
8 onions, chopped
2 Tbsp. canning salt

2 tsp. whole cloves
2 tsp. stick cinnamon
2 tsp. ginger
6 c. white vinegar
6 c. sugar

Combine tomatoes, peppers and onions, vinegar and sugar; simmer 1 1/2 hours, stirring as needed. Add apples; simmer 1/2 hour more. Add spices and continue cooking 1/2 hour more. Pack in hot pint jars; seal and process in hot water bath 10 minutes. (This sauce can be used as a sauce for barbequed ribs.)

Jean Schwartz, Owatonna, Mn.

HOT CHOCOLATE SAUCE

1 c. sugar
3 Tbsp. flour

1/3 c. cocoa

Mix well and add 1 cup boiling water. Stir and spoon over ice cream.

Key Barck, Rochester, Mn.

CUCUMBER BASTING SAUCE
(For Chicken, Fish, Pork)

Combine:

3/4 c. peeled, diced
   cucumber
1/4 c. dairy sour cream

1/4 c. mayonnaise
1 Tbsp. sliced green onion
1 tsp. grated lemon

Baste the meat with the sauce after each time you turn it.

St. Cloud, Mn.

GERMAN HOT SAUCE FOR CABBAGE SALAD

1 Tbsp. sugar
1 Tbsp. flour
1/2 c. cream

1/2 c. vinegar
1 egg, lightly beaten

For Salad:

3-4 c. finely shredded
   cabbage

Salt and pepper to taste

Combine sugar and flour in a small heavy bottomed saucepan. Set over medium heat and slowly blend in cream, vinegar and egg, cooking and stirring constantly until mixture thickens to a sauce consistency. Makes about 1 cup sauce, enough for 3 to 4 cups finely shredded cabbage.

St. Cloud, Mn.

FRESH LINGONBERRY SAUCE

Drain berries; rinse several times with cold water. Place 12 ounces of berries and 1/2 cup water in saucepan. Simmer slowly for 15 minutes. Add 1 cup sugar and bring to a boil, stirring constantly. Remove from heat; cool and serve.

Clara O. Johnson, Chanhassen, Mn.

MUSTARD SAUCE

1/2 c. vinegar
1 c. sugar
1/4 c. prepared mustard
1/2 tsp. dry mustard

1/2 c. margarine
1 can tomato soup
3 egg yolks
Salt

Mix together and bring to a boil. Store in jar in refrigerator. (Keeps in refrigerator for a long time.) Delicious to serve on Ham Loaf.

Marian Pearson, Minneapolis, Mn.

MORNAY SAUCE

2 Tbsp. butter	1 egg yolk
2 Tbsp. flour	2 Tbsp. half & half
1 c. heated milk	2 Tbsp. grated Parmesan
Salt and white pepper	cheese
	2 Tbsp. grated Swiss cheese

Make a roux with butter and flour. Slowly add heated milk; cook and stir until thickened. Add salt and white pepper to taste. Beat together the egg yolk and half & half. Add a little sauce to egg mixture. Stir to blend, then return to saucepan and cook until heated through. Stir in cheeses; remove from heat. Makes 1 1/2 cups.

St. Cloud, Mn.

MUSTARD HAM SAUCE

1 Tbsp. flour	1/2 c. water
1 1/4 c. sugar	Scant 1/2 c. vinegar
1/4 tsp. salt	1/4 c. butter
1/2 c. prepared mustard	2 beaten egg yolks
(in jar)	

Mix the first 3 ingredients well; add mustard. Heat water and vinegar to boiling. Pour a little of the vinegar-water mixture into the mustard mixture. Keep stirring and adding until all is stirred in. Add the butter and egg yolks; bring entire mixture to a boil.

Hint: Beat egg yolks in a cup and add a tablespoon of ingredients at a time so it won't curdle. Serve hot.

Mary Jean Voss, Owatonna, Mn.

RAISIN SAUCE FOR HAM

1 c. raisins	1/2 c. sugar
2 c. water	2 Tbsp. cornstarch
2 Tbsp. vinegar	1 Tbsp. butter

Boil raisins, vinegar and sugar in water for 10 minutes. Add the cornstarch and butter; cook for a few minutes more. Serve over ham.

Bernita Engel

CROCK-POT SPAGHETTI SAUCE

1 (6 lb.) can tomato majic
1 (1 lb.) can tomato paste
2 lb. pepperoni or Italian
  sausage, ground

1/4 clove garlic
1 onion
Salt and pepper
Spices

Fry Italian sausage or pepperoni, ground; save drippings. Saute onion and garlic in oil. Mix meat drippings, onion and garlic. Pour into 6 quart crock pot. Add 1 (6 pound) can tomato majic and 1 can tomato paste. Add salt and pepper and spices (your choice - oregano, bay leaves, parsley). Cook on low heat 8-10 hours. Boil noodles; strain and drain. Pour sauce over and eat.

Mike Ferderer, Minneapolis, Mn.

ITALIAN SPAGHETTI

Sauce:

2 cans tomato paste
1 large can tomato puree
1 large can tomato juice
1/2 tsp. red pepper

2 medium or 3 small kernels
  of garlic, cut fine
About 5 Tbsp. Italian cheese
2 tsp. salt
About 1/4 c. soya sauce

Mix all together and simmer with meat balls for about 3 hours. Serve over cooked spaghetti.

Florence Wesen, St. Cloud, Mn.

PAT'S SPAGHETTI SAUCE

1 lb. ground beef

1 lb. ground pork

Brown in skillet; set aside in bowl. In same skillet, saute 1 medium onion, chopped, and 1/2 green pepper, chopped. Add:

1 large can tomatoes
1 can tomato paste

1 can mushrooms, with juice
1 tsp. anise seed

134

4 cloves crushed garlic	1 tsp. sugar
1 tsp. oregano	1/2 tsp. basil
2 bay leaves	1 Tbsp. dried parsley
Salt	1/2 tsp. red pepper flakes
Seasoned pepper	1 tsp. fennel

Bring all to a boil and turn heat to low; simmer at least 1 hour.

Helen Teeuwen, Minneapolis, Mn.

SPAGHETTI SAUCE

Use 6 to 8 quart kettle; put in 1/8 inch oil. Braise off 1-2 pounds beef neck bones slowly until well browned. Salt and pepper bones heavily. Add 3 (15 ounce) cans of tomato sauce plus 3-4 cans of water. Cook for 1 hour with:

1/4 tsp. concentrated garlic powder	2 tsp. oregano
1 tsp. paprika	1/2 tsp. sweet basil
1 tsp. crushed fennel	1 Tbsp. minced onion

Add meat balls, hard pepperoni and tomato paste (two 12 ounce cans of tomato paste with two 12 ounce cans of water). Stir frequently; taste often. Use your own judgment as to whether you need more salt and other seasonings. When boiling noodles, add salt in water and 2 teaspoons of oil. To sweeten sauce, use 2 (4 ounce) glasses of sweet wine or 3 level tablespoons of white sugar. (This is not necessary unless you prefer sauce on the sweet side.) Use own judgment for larger amounts.

Mrs. Emil Gatto, St. Paul, Mn.

SWEET AND SOUR SAUCE

1 c. brown sugar	1/2 c. catsup
1 c. vinegar (cider)	1/2 tsp. MSG
3/4 c. water	

Combine ingredients and heat to boiling. Thicken with 1/4 cup water and 1 tablespoon cornstarch.

Gretchen Marquart, Fargo, N.D.

CHOKECHERRY SYRUP

Mix 4 cups of chokecherry juice with 4 cups sugar and add 1/2 cup lemon juice and 1/2 package powdered pectin. Boil ingredients for 2 minutes; process jars of syrup 10 minutes in boiling water bath.

Helen H. Clark, Grand Forks, N.D.

** NOTES **

SOUPS
VEGETABLES

JJM

UNUSUAL HERBS

Angelica - bienniel, homegrown herb. Leaves, seeds and root used. **Bergamots** - used in these recipes are the orange scented mint and Napaka (Monarda austromonta) or mountain oregano. **Borage** - hairy annual, self seeds, leaves and flowers used, cucumber flavor. **Burdock** - root vegetable or pot herb, in Japanese produce section as "Gobo". **Burnet** - pretty leafy perennial, leaves have cucumber flavor. **Chervil** - annual, taste similar to parsley, but milder with slight anise taste. **Chia** - is the seed of a sage, high in protein. **Cilantro** - Mexican name for fresh leaf of coriander. Also called Chinese Parsley. **Chuchupate** - root of a celery flavored plant. Robust in flavor. Use sparingly. **Coltsfoot** - used in Japanese cooking, bought in cans, grows wild all over England. **Damiana** (Turnera diffusa) - aphrodisiac herb used by Aztecs in their rites. **Epasote** - Mexican herb (Chenopodium ambrosidies) used with pork and fish. **Jamica Roselle Hisbiscus** (Hisbiscus Sabdariffa) makes a pink lemonade tea. **Lemon Balm** - perennial, lemon flavored used for flavoring. **Lemon Grass** - lemon flavored grass, used in cooking and teas. **Lemon Eucalyptus** - (Eucalyptus citriodora) 30 foot tree with lemon scented leaves. **Lemon Thyme** - very fragrant, lemon scented. **Mate** - a South American tea, containing large amount of caffeine. **Mints** - orange, apple, pineapple scented, use interchangeably in any mint recipe. **Oriental Garlic** - looks like a wide leaf chive. Just leaves are used. **Perilla** - annual called "Sisho" by Japanese. Resembles purple coleus. Perilla can be used in salads. **Pineapple Sage** - pineapple fragrance, much used with fruit recipes. **Purslane** - fleshy weed common in gardens, good cooked or raw, high in Vitamin C. **Quelites** (Chenopodium album) - Indian pot herb, a variety of lambsquarters. **Saffron** - stamens of Corcus Sativus, most expensive spice in the world. **Shallots** - bulbs are small, lavender, mild onion flavor. Skirret - roots and leaves used in salad, also good cooked, green leafy plant. **Tarragon** - mild licorice taste. Do not start from seed, get divisions from nursery. **Woodruff** - courmarin scented when dry, good in wine or jelly. **Yerbanis** - (Pericon, Tagetes Lucida), marigold leaves, tarragon type flavor - Mexico.

SOPA DE AGUACATE
(Avocado Soup)

2 or 3 corn tortillas, torn
    into strips

2 large avocados, peeled
    and mashed
6 c. chicken broth

Heat the broth. Transfer it to a blender jar; add the avocado pulp and blend to smooth puree. Return the soup to the pan and heat it through gently; do not let it boil. Serve the soup immediately, garnished with tortilla squares or serve chilled.

St. Cloud, Mn.

BEER CHEESE SOUP

1 pkg. Smooth celery soup
    mix
1 pkg. Smooth leek soup mix
1/2 pkg. French onion soup
    mix

8 c. cold water
1 lb. Hickory Farms of Ohio
    sharp cold-pack Cheddar
    cheese food
1/2 can beer, room tempera-
    ture (or more to taste)

Mix soups with water and bring to a boil; reduce heat and simmer until thick, 10 minutes. Add cheese slowly, stirring constantly until melted and smooth. Add beer; heat throughly. Serves 12. (Can omit beer, if desired.)

Anne Aune, Minneapolis, Mn.

BEER CHEESE SOUP

3 stalks of celery
2 large carrots
1 medium onion
1/2 green pepper
1/3 c. butter

6 Tbsp. flour
6 c. chicken broth
14 oz. Cheez Whiz
6 oz. beer
Salt and pepper

In a heavy saucepan, melt the butter. Chop the vegetables and add, cooking until tender. Add the flour; stir into a thick paste. Slowly add the broth, stirring to mix the thickening mixture. When all the broth is added, simmer for 10 minutes. Add Cheez Whiz; stir until melted.

1507-82

Just before serving, add beer, salt and pepper to taste and heat thoroughly.

Debbie Burgum, Dickinson, N.D.

BEER CHEESE SOUP

1 1/2 gal. boiling water*
1 c. celery, chopped in
blender

1 c. onion, chopped in
blender
1 c. carrots, chopped in
blender

*Hold out a quart of the water, cool, to use while chopping in blender and to shake up the flour.
Boil for 20 minutes. Add 1 1/2 cups flour (shake up in some of saved water). Add:

3/4 c. butter
1/2 c. Velveeta cheese

8 oz. chicken base flavoring
1 (16 oz.) jar Cheez Whiz

Whip until smooth. Add 1 beer. Can be frozen; keeps well!

Ray Rieger, Grand Forks, N.D.

CHOP SOUPY

1 lb. round steak, cut in
thin strips
2 Tbsp. oil
1 1/2 c. mushrooms (4
oz. can), drained
1 1/2 c. celery, cut
diagonally
2 Tbsp. soy sauce

1 c. green pepper, cut in
strips
1/2 c. green onion (omit if
using onion soup)
1 can Campbell's beef broth
or onion soup
2 Tbsp. cornstarch
1/2 c. water

Brown beef in oil; add vegetables, soup and soy sauce. Cover; cook over low heat 20 minutes or until meat is tender. Stir now and then. Blend cornstarch and water; stir into sauce. Cook, stirring until thickened, just a few minutes. Serve over rice.

Mrs. Mel Kurvers, Chanhassen, Mn.

CHOWDER FOR ONE

1 small chopped onion,
  sauteed in 1 Tbsp.
  butter or oleo
1 rib celery, chopped
2 sprigs parsley, chopped
1/4 tsp. thyme
1 bay leaf

1 c. skim or 2% milk
1/2 c. water
1 small potato, cubed
1/4 lb. raw fish fillet
Salt and pepper may be
  added

Saute onion and parsley lightly in butter. When onion begins to sizzle a bit, add water and milk with rest of the ingredients. Simmer for about 20 minutes.

Rhea Thoms, Jamestown, N.D.

CORNED BEEF AND CABBAGE CHOWDER

1 c. thinly sliced celery
1/2 c. chopped green onions
2 cloves garlic, minced
1/4 c. margarine
3 c. chicken bouillon
2 c. shredded cabbage
1 c. thinly sliced carrot

1/4 lb. cooked corned beef,
  cut in thin shreds
  (1 1/4 c.)
1/2 tsp. salt
1/4 tsp. pepper
3 Tbsp. cornstarch
1 c. milk

Saute celery, green onions and garlic in margarine 5 minutes. Add next 6 ingredients; simmer 20 minutes. Mix cornstarch and milk until smooth; gradually stir into chowder. Stirring constantly, bring to boil and boil 1 minute. Makes 6 servings.

Jane Bohline, Minneapolis, Mn.

DON'S EGG DROP SOUP

1 can chicken broth
  (Campbell's)

1 1/2 cans of water (use
  soup can to measure)

Put above in pan; heat to boiling. As ingredients in pan are heating, add some chopped green onions, lettuce, pepper, garlic salt, MSG and about 1/2 teaspoon sesame seed oil. When broth boils, slowly pour eggs into it.

Don Billadeau, St. Cloud, Mn.

CLEAR GAZPACHO

4 c. chicken broth, chilled
4 medium tomatoes, chopped
1/2 tsp. seasoned pepper

2 Tbsp. olive oil
6-8 Tbsp. lime juice (about 3 limes)
Salt to taste

Mix all together; chill several hours. Serve with garnishes of 1 small onion, chopped, 1-2 green peppers, chopped, and 1-2 stalks celery, chopped.
Dee Olson, St. Paul, Mn.

QUICK GAZPACHO

3 c. V-8 vegetable juice
1 cucumber, thinly sliced
1/2 green pepper, chopped
1 clove garlic, minced
1 small onion, chopped

1 Tbsp. olive oil
1 Tbsp. wine vinegar or lemon juice
Dash of Tabasco sauce

Mix all together and chill at least 6 hours. Serve with more chopped vegetables as garnish.
Dee Olson, St. Paul, Mn.

HAMBURGER SOUP

Brown and crumble 1 pound hamburger; drain. Add:

3 beef bouillon cubes
6 c. hot water
2 c. (1 lb. can) tomatoes
1/2 tsp. salt (more, if desired)

1 env. onion soup mix
1 c. diced celery
1 c. sliced carrots
1/2 c. raw rice

Cook 40 minutes or put in crock pot for most of the day, stirring a couple of times.
Mrs. Burton Peterson, Rochester, Mn.

HAMBURGER SOUP

1 lb. hamburger, browned
1 c. celery
1 c. cabbage
1 large onion
1 large potato
2 carrots

5 c. hot water
5 beef bouillon cubes
1 (16 oz.) can stewed tomatoes
Salt and pepper to taste

Cook 30-60 minutes.

Vivian Brickson, Detroit Lakes, Mn.

MACKI'S SOPA DE ALBONDIGAS
(Meat Ball Soup)

1 lb. ground beef	1/2 onion, chopped
1 egg	1 fresh tomato, chopped
1/2 tsp. salt	2 medium potatoes, diced
1/2 tsp. pepper	1 carrot, sliced
1/4 c. bread crumbs	4 c. water
1 tsp. oil	1/4 c. tomato sauce

Mix ground beef, egg, salt, pepper and bread crumbs. Form into balls. Saute onion and tomato in oil until tender. Add water and tomato sauce; bring to a rolling boil. Drop meat balls into the boiling water one at a time. Add potatoes and carrots. Salt to taste. Slow boil for approximately 20 minutes or until vegetables are tender.

St. Cloud, Mn.

SOUPE A'L'OIGNON
(Onion Soup)

Soup a'l'oignon has special significance to Parisians. Parisian night clubbers find soupe a'l'oignon the perfect preventative for avoiding a hangover and to aid in the sobbering process after a night of drinking around the "pigalle" normally "les alles" is the place to go for the soup a'l'oignon.

6 onions (spicy, not sweet)	4 cubes chicken broth
1/2 lb. butter	(bouillon)
1/2 tsp. salt	4 cubes beef broth
Freshly ground black	(bouillon)
pepper	3 oz. Gruyere cheese
12 c. water	12 slices garlic toast (French
	bread)

1. Dice onions; add 1/2 pound butter and cook slowly until onions are tender and yellow. 2. Let cool for 1 hour. 3. Add pepper, salt, chicken and beef broths and water. Bring to a boil; reduce heat to simmer until mixture is golden brown in color, approximately 1 hour. 4. Take out 6 baking bowls, which shall be the serving dish. 5. To each bowl, add a layer of grated cheese. 6. Add 2 slices garlic toast to each bowl. 7. Add onion juice to each bowl. Pour over cheese and garlic toast already in bowl. 8. Add another layer of grated cheese. 9. Bake at 375° F. until

top has a golden brown color, 10-30 minutes, depending on temperature of broth. Serves 12 people.

Liz Tuft, St. Paul, Mn.

CREAM OF ONION AND POTATO SOUP

3 c. scalded milk	1 c. potato water
2 Tbsp. flour	2 Tbsp. butter
4 medium potatoes	4 onions
1 Tbsp. chopped parsley	Salt and pepper

Boil the potatoes and onions together until tender; drain. Save the water and rub the vegetables through a coarse strainer. Make a white sauce of the liquid, flour and fat; combine with the potato and onion pulp. Season with chopped parsley, salt and pepper. Beat with an egg beater and serve with croutons (toasted bread cubes).

Dena Stoddard, St. Louis Park, Mn.

FRENCH ONION SOUP

Lightly brown 2 cups sliced or diced onion in 2 tablespoons butter. Add:

1 (10 1/2 oz.) can consomme	1 tsp. salt
1/2 soup can water	

Bring to boiling and simmer for 15 minutes. Top each bowl with toasted bread cubes and sprinkle with Parmesan cheese. Serves 4.

Joan Norton, Hibbing, Mn.

FRENCH ONION SOUP

	Serves 1-2	Serves 4-6
Onions, chopped or rings	3/4 - 1 c.	3-4 c.
Butter	3 Tbsp.	1/3 c.
Beef bouillon cubes	1 1/2	6
Water	1 c.	4 c.
Worcestershire sauce	1/4 tsp.	1 tsp.
Salt	1/8 tsp.	1/2 tsp.
Pepper	Dash	4 dashes

Saute onions until tender, about 5-10 minutes. Boil

142

water in another pan. Remove from heat; add bouillon cubes, Worcestershire sauce and stir until bouillon cubes are dissolved. Add onions to broth; bring to a boil. Season with salt and pepper. Garnish each serving with croutons and Parmesan cheese. For a gourmet touch, use the following garnish:

Swiss cheese, grated
  (3/4 c. per serving)

French bread (1 slice per
  serving)

Sprinkle bottom of individual ovenproof soup bowl with cheese, about 1/4 cup. Place under broiler just until cheese begins to melt. Fill bowl with onion soup, leaving room to top with a slice of French bread and heap on the remaining 1/2 cup of grated cheese. Return to broiler until cheese topping melts.

W. Art Carlson, Lake Park, Mn.

OYSTER STEW

1 pt. oysters
Salt, pepper, paprika

4 Tbsp. butter
1 qt. milk

Put cleaned oysters, strained oyster liquor, butter and seasonings into a saucepan; simmer gently until oysters begin to curl at the edges. At the same time, heat the milk, being careful not to scorch it. Add the hot milk to the oysters and oyster liquor and serve at once.

Dena Stoddard, St. Louis Park, Mn.

GREEN PEA SOUP

2 c. stock
1 qt. green peas
1 onion
1 turnip
1 Tbsp. flour
1 qt. water

Salt, pepper and sugar to
  season
1 celery stalk
2 sprigs of mint
1 Tbsp. butter

Reserve 1/2 cup of peas; to the stock and water, add the rest of the peas, the celery stalk, onion and turnip, cut into pieces, and the mint. Stew until the mass is tender. Strain through a sieve or coarse cheesecloth. Thin with stock or water, if necessary; thicken a bit with flour and fat. Season with salt, pepper and a little sugar. Add the 1/2 cup of whole peas. Stew for a few minutes; serve.

Dena Stoddard, St. Louis Park, Mn.

SPLIT PEA SOUP

2 pkg. split peas, soaked
   overnight
1 small picnic ham (or
   1/2 larger one)
3 large carrots

2 large onions
1 bay leaf
1 bunch parsley
Water to cover generously
   (add more if necessary)

Cook above 2 hours slowly; let cool. Remove meat from bone and cube; discard all fat. Strain rest of ingredients with food mill or strainer. Simmer another hour. If too thin, thicken with a can of split pea soup. Serves 10-12.

Jean Schwartz, Owatonna, Mn.

CROCK POT POTATO SOUP

6 potatoes, peeled, cut
   in bite size
2 onions, chopped
1 carrot, pared, sliced
1 stalk celery, sliced
4 chicken bouillon cubes
   (I use George Washington)

1 Tbsp. parsley flakes
5 c. water
Salt to taste (opt.)
Pepper to taste
1/3 c. butter
1 (5.13 oz.) can evaporated
   milk

Put all ingredients, except milk and butter, in crock pot. Cover; cook slow 10-12 hours; high 3-4 hours (or simmer 1 1/2 hours on stove). Stir in last 2 ingredients the last hour or before serving. May serve topped with chives. Very good.

Note: I use less onion and 2 carrots and 2 celery stalks. So, it is easy to vary these portions according to individual.

Marion Vonesh, Grand Forks, N.D.

HAM-CHEESE POTATO SOUP

1 (10 1/2 oz.) can condensed
   cream of potato soup,
   undiluted
1 c. light cream or half &
   half

3/4 c. milk
1 c. (4 oz.) shredded
   Mozzarella cheese
1 (3 oz.) pkg. thinly sliced
   smoked ham, diced

Combine all ingredients in a medium sized saucepan. Heat over low heat, stirring constantly, until cheese is melted and soup becomes hot, about 10 minutes. Do not boil. Yield: 4 cups.

Mankato, Mn.

POTATO SOUP

Cut up potatoes, celery and onion. Grate carrots. Add green pepper. Cook all together until done. (Mash potatoes a little.) Drain; add milk, butter and salt.

Bea Aslakson, E. Grand Forks, N.D.

POTATO SOUP

Peel 1 quart of potatoes; cut them in cubes, also 1 medium sized onion. Put in kettle; cover with cold water. Boil until tender. Add 1 cup cream, pepper, salt and celery salt to season. Melt some butter in a frying pan; brown 1 cup of the bread crumbs in the butter. Serve with the soup. It's delicious!

Helen H. Clark, Grand Forks, N.D.

SAUERKRAUT SOUP

3 lb. country style spareribs (no bones in these)	1 1/2 c. finely chopped onion
	1 c. dried green split peas
10 c. cold water	1/2 lb. bacon
2 lb. sauerkraut	2 Tbsp. flour

Trim off any excess fat from the spareribs. Place the spareribs in a kettle; add 8 cups water and sauerkraut. Do not drain the juice from the sauerkraut. Bring to a boil and simmer about 45 minutes. Meanwhile, combine the split peas in 2 cups water; bring to a boil. Simmer 30 minutes or until peas are tender. Add the peas and liquid to kraut and ribs. Cut the bacon; cook. Add the onion. Drain grease; transfer bacon and onion to the soup mixture. In skillet, put the drained grease; add the flour and stir. Gradually add 1/2 cup of the soup liquid to make a paste. Add this to the soup. Soup may be served after 2 hours cooking time. It may continue to cook for 6 hours. The longer it cooks, the thicker it gets. You may have to cut the spareribs into small pieces. Yield: 12 or more servings.

Mrs. B.V. Feller, Excelsior, Mn.

TOMATO SOUP

10 lb. tomatoes
6 onions
1 bunch celery

1/2 c. brown sugar
1/4 c. salt
1 red pepper

Boil onion, celery and pepper with a little water. Mix with the tomatoes, cut up, and boil until tender. Add brown sugar, salt, 1/4 c. butter, melted, and 1/4 c. flour; boil 25 to 35 minutes more. Put in jars and seal while hot. Tomatoes are best if peeled.

Fern Groskreutz, Litchfield, Mn.

CUEBALL'S FAVORITE HOMEMADE TOMATO SOUP

Melt 1 tablespoon butter or margarine in saucepan over low heat. Add 1 tablespoon flour, 1 teaspoon salt and pepper to taste. Add 1 pint or can tomatoes and 1/2 teaspoon soda. Bring to boil; stir well to break up tomatoes. Add 6 cups milk. Turn up heat and stir constantly. Do not allow to boil. Serve piping hot. Makes 6-8 servings.

Gloria Smith, Jackson, Mn.

SOPA DE TORTILLA

12 small corn tortillas, cut into strips
6 c. chicken broth
3 chilies pastilla (or dried red chili)
Lard for frying

6 Tbsp. grated Cheddar cheese
2 medium tomatoes
1/3 medium onion, chopped
1 clove garlic
1 sprig epazote (or cilantro)

Heat lard and fry the chilies, broken into pieces; remove and let cool. In same lard, fry tortilla strips until they are well browned but not too crisp; drain them on paper toweling. Pour off all but 2 tablespoons of the lard. Blend the tomatoes, onion and garlic to a smooth sauce, then cook in the lard for about 8 minutes, until the sauce is well seasoned and has reduced somewhat. Add the sauce to the broth in the pan; bring to a boil. Add the tortilla strips to the broth; cook them for about 3 minutes. Just before serving, add the epazote or cilantro. Cook for 1 minute more. Serve each portion garnished with pieces of crumbled chili and grated cheese.

St. Cloud, Mn.

VEGETABLE SOUP

2-3 lb. beef soup bones,
  cracked
2 qt. water
4 whole peppers
1 bay leaf
2 1/2 tsp. salt
1 c. carrots, sliced

1/2 c. celery, sliced
2 c. potatoes, diced
1/4 c. onion, chopped
1 Tbsp. parsley, chopped
1 c. peas
1 (1 lb. 4 oz.) can tomatoes

In a large kettle, put beef bones, water, whole peppers, bay leaf and salt; cover and simmer over low heat for 4 hours. Add carrots, celery, potatoes, onion, parsley, peas and tomatoes; continue cooking about 45 minutes. (If you use a pressure cooker, follow directions in your instruction book.) Taste and add more salt and pepper, if needed. Makes 6 to 8 large servings.

Helen Clark, Grand Forks, N.D.

QUICK BEEF-AND-VEGETABLE SOUP

1 1/2 lb. ground beef
1 medium onion, sliced
1 (16 oz.) can stewed
  tomatoes
2 beef flavor bouillon cubes
  or env.
7 c. water

1/2 c. regular long-grain
  rice
2 tsp. salt
1/2 tsp. basil
1/4 tsp. pepper
1 (16 oz.) pkg. frozen mixed
  vegetables (broccoli,
  carrots and cauliflower)

About 45 minutes before serving: In 5 quart Dutch oven over high heat, cook ground beef and onion until all pan juices evaporate and meat is well browned, stirring frequently. Add stewed tomatoes and next 6 ingredients; heat to boiling. Reduce heat to low; cover and simmer 15 minutes, stirring occasionally. Add frozen mixed vegetables over high heat; heat to boiling. Reduce heat to low; cover and simmer 10 minutes longer or until vegetables are tender, stirring occasionally. Makes about 12 cups or 6 main dish servings.

Judy Rieger, Grand Forks, N.D.

"REALLY OLD-FASHIONED" VEGETABLE-BEEF SOUP

Brown 1 1/2 pounds beef stew meat in a heavy large pan (I use a 5 1/2 quart size) with about 2 tablespoons butter. Season with salt and pepper. Add about 6 cups of water and 2 beef bouillon cubes. Simmer at lowest setting on stove about 3 or 4 hours. Set in refrigerator overnight and fat will harden on top. Lift off fat carefully. Place pan on fire. Add 1 cup finely chopped celery (I always add a few of the leaves too; they add flavor to soups), 3/4 cup finely chopped onion, 5 peeled, sliced carrots, 1/4 cup barley and 1 can stewed tomatoes. (I have learned that other vegetables are good added if you love a good thick soup, so I add 1 diced parsnip, 1/4 or 1/2 small rutabaga, diced, and 1 or 2 small potatoes, diced.) Cook, covered, slowly till vegetables are tender, about 1 hour, then salt and pepper to taste (but go easy on the pepper; keep sampling it!). Makes a large kettle full but goes if you like good homemade soup!

Bernice Fonos, Minneapolis, Mn.

FRESH VEGETABLE SOUP

4 lb. soup bones	2 medium fresh carrots, quartered
2 qt. water	
2 Tbsp. salt	4 c. diced potatoes
6 whole black peppers	1 1/2 c. sliced fresh carrots
2 medium onions, quartered	2/3 c. sliced celery
2 sprigs fresh parsley	1 c. fresh snap beans
2 stalks celery with leaves	4 c. diced fresh tomatoes

Simmer first 8 ingredients together in a covered soup kettle, 2 hours. Remove bones and trim off meat (set aside to add to stock later). Strain stock and combine with remaining ingredients. Cover; cook until vegetables are crisp tender. Add meat. Serve hot as the main dish. Yield: 10-12 servings.

Adeline Jasken, St. Cloud, Mn.

WILD RICE SOUP

1 c. uncooked wild rice, cooked as you like it	2 cans cream of mushroom soup
1 grated onion	1 can chicken broth
1 grated carrot	4 soup cans of water
2 cans cream of chicken soup	

While cooking the wild rice, cook the onion and carrot in a small amount of water until they are tender. Add with the rest of the ingredients, rice added last. Heat together, but do not boil. You can substitute 1 cup of sauterne for 1 cup of the water added. Season with salt and pepper to taste. Serves 12.

Betty Cortright
Similar recipe submitted by: Sue Kurtz, Minneapolis, Mn.

ASPARAGUS-TOMATO SKILLET

3 slices bacon
1/4 c. sliced onion
3 Tbsp. vinegar
3 Tbsp. water
2 tsp. sugar

1/4 tsp. salt
3 c. fresh asparagus, cut in
1 inch pieces
2 medium tomatoes, cut in
eighths

Cook bacon until crisp; crumble. Add onion to skillet and cook until tender. Return bacon to skillet; add vinegar, water, salt and sugar. Bring to a boil. Add asparagus; cover and cook 15-20 minutes over low heat. Add tomatoes; cover and cook about 3 minutes.

Carolyn Brudevold, Fargo, N.D.

ARROZ

1 medium onion, minced
1 green pepper, minced
1 medium tomato, chopped

1 c. rice
2 c. hot chicken broth
2 Tbsp. olive oil

Saute onion, green pepper, tomato and rice in olive oil until onion is transparent and rice is yellow. Add broth; bring to boil. Cover; bake in 325° oven for about 20 minutes. Serves 6.

Dee Olson, St. Paul, Mn.

ASPARAGUS SUPREME

2 boxes frozen asparagus
1/4 c. butter
1/4 c. flour
2 c. milk
1/4 c. asparagus liquid

1 c. grated cheese
3 hard cooked eggs
1/2 c. corn flakes
2 Tbsp. melted butter

Cook asparagus according to directions. Remove from water; boil down to 1/4 cup liquid. Make white sauce of flour, butter, milk and asparagus liquid. When thickened, add cheese and stir until melted. Place asparagus, sliced eggs and sauce in alternate layers in buttered casserole. Crush corn flakes slightly; coat with melted butter. Sprinkle over top of casserole. Garnish around edge with one of the sliced eggs. Bake at 325° for 30 minutes. Serves 6-8.

Elynor Pederson, Minneapolis, Mn.

BAKED BEANS

1 large can pork and beans (about 2 c.)
1 lb. ground meat, cooked with diced onion (1 large at least)

1/2 bottle catsup (7 oz.)
2 Tbsp. molasses
2 Tbsp. brown sugar
2 Tbsp. Worcestershire sauce
1 tsp. salt

Bake 1 hour at 350°.

Mabel Gunner, Minneapolis, Mn.

BEANS

1 1/2 lb. hamburger, browned
1/2 onion

Chile powder to season
1/2 lb. bacon, browned

Add:
1 large (16 oz.) can pork and beans
1 small can kidney beans, drained

1 c. brown sugar
2 Tbsp. mustard
3/4 c. catsup

Put in crock pot on low heat.

Shirley Ryan, Albert Lea, Mn.

BAKED BEANS

1 1/2 lb. dry navy beans
1 medium onion, chopped
1 c. catsup
1 c. brown sugar
1 c. water

2 tsp. dry mustard
2 Tbsp. dark molasses
1 tsp. salt
1/3 lb. bacon, cut in small pieces, unfried

Parboil beans in 9 cups of water about 45 minutes; let

stand 1 hour, then drain. Mix beans and sauce together. Mix together about 3 times while cooking in a crock pot. Start on high for 2 hours, then low for about 6 hours or until done.

Marion Round, Faribault, Mn.
Similar recipe submitted by: Colleen Landwehr, St. Cloud, Mn.

BOSTON BAKED BEANS

2 c. dried pea beans,
   washed and drained
6 c. water
1/4 lb. lean salt pork
1 medium onion

1 tsp. salt
1/2 c. light molasses
1/2 tsp. dry mustard
1 Tbsp. brown sugar

Cover beans with water; bring to a boil and boil for 2 minutes. Cover pan; let stand for 1 hour, then cook until tender. Replace water to keep up level of liquid. Drain and reserve liquid. Put beans in pot. Cut through pork rind every 1/2 inch, making cuts 1 inch deep. Bury onion and pork in beans, leaving rind exposed. Mix 1 cup bean liquid and remaining ingredients; pour over beans. Add enough liquid to cover beans. Cover pot and bake in pre-heated slow oven, 300° F., for 6 to 8 hours. Uncover pot last hour. Makes 6 servings.

Helen-May Johnson, Chanhassen, Mn.

BEAN BAKE

1 (12 oz.) can red kidney
   beans, drained
1 (17 oz.) can lima beans,
   drained
1/2 c. spaghetti sauce

1 small onion, chopped
1 c. shredded Cheddar
   cheese
4-6 franks (or sausages,
   ring bologna, ham, etc.)

Mix beans, spaghetti sauce, onion and cheese in un-greased 1 1/2 quart casserole. Arrange meat on top (or slice and mix in). Bake, uncovered, 30 minutes at 375°. Also good cooked over an open fire.

Liz Tuft, St. Paul, Mn.

CALICO BEANS

Brown:

1/2 lb. hamburger

1/2 lb. bacon, cut into small pieces

Add 1 cup onion, cut fine; cook slightly. Add:

1/2 c. catsup
1 tsp. salt
1 tsp. mustard

2 Tbsp. vinegar
3/4 c. brown sugar

Add:

1 can pork and beans, undrained
1 can kidney beans, undrained

1 can lima beans or butter beans, undrained

(Use 1 pound cans.) Mix and bake 40-50 minutes at 350°, uncovered. Serves 10-12.

Anne Aune, Minneapolis, Mn.
Similar recipe submitted by: Jeanie Rose, Tracy, Mn.

CHEESY BAKED BEANS

2 (1 lb. 2 oz.) jars baked beans
1/4 c. chili sauce
2 Tbsp. brown sugar

1 Tbsp. prepared mustard
8 slices onion, about 1/4 inch thick
1 c. (4 oz.) shredded Colby cheese

Preheat oven to 350° F. Combine beans, chili sauce, brown sugar and mustard. Pour into a 1 1/2 quart rectangular baking dish. Arrange onion slices on top. Bake until hot and bubbly. Yield: 8 servings, about 1/2 cup each.

Mankato, Mn.

CREAMED GREEN BEANS WITH ONIONS

3 Tbsp. margarine or butter
2 Tbsp. flour
1 tsp. salt
1 tsp. dry mustard
1/4 tsp. pepper
1 c. half & half
2 pkg. frozen French green beans, thawed, drained

1 (20 oz.) pkg. frozen whole onions, thawed, very well drained
12 slices Borden's American process cheese
1/2 c. chopped pecans or walnuts

152

Preheat oven to 350°. In large saucepan, melt butter; stir in flour, mustard and pepper. Cook and stir over low heat until mixture is bubbly; add half & half gradually. Stir in vegetables. In 8 inch square baking dish, place 1/3 of vegetable mixture; top with 4 slices of cheese. Repeat twice, ending with cheese. Add nuts on top. Bake, uncovered, 35 minutes or until hot.

Grace Locke, St. Paul, Mn.

CREAMY GREEN BEANS

2 (9 oz.) pkg. frozen green beans
1 (5 oz.) can water chestnuts, sliced, drained
1/2 c. finely chopped onion
2 Tbsp. butter
1 tsp. sugar
1 tsp. seasoned salt
1 tsp. vinegar
1 c. sour cream

Cook beans according to package directions; heat chestnuts through. Saute onion in butter, but don't brown. Add rest of ingredients and a dash of pepper. Heat through, but don't boil.

Paula Earhart, Jackson, Mn.

Similar recipe submitted by: Margaret McKenney, Minneapolis, Mn.

EASY BAKED BEANS
(Real Good)

3 cans Bush's Great Northern beans
1/2 bottle chili sauce
1 medium onion
1 1/2 c. brown sugar, lightly packed
1/2 lb. bacon, fried and cut in pieces

Mix and bake, uncovered, at 300° for 2 hours.

Mrs. Robert Sloneker, Chisholm, Mn.

4 KINDS OF BEANS

Fry and drain 1/2 pound bacon. Brown 3 or 4 medium onions, sliced, in bacon fat; pour off fat.

1 can green beans, drained
1 can butter beans
1 can pork and beans
1 can kidney beans
3/4 c. brown sugar
1/2 bottle chili sauce

Bake at 350° for 1 hour.

Sue Hetland, Grand Forks, N.D.

FOUR BEAN CASSEROLE

1/2 - 1 lb. bacon, diced
  and browned
1 lb. hamburger, browned

1 medium onion, browned in
  hamburger

Drain grease from above; pour into casserole dish. Add:

1 medium can pork and
  beans
1 (16 oz.) can lima beans
1 (16 oz.) can kidney
  beans
1 (16 oz.) can butter beans

Dash of salt
Dash of garlic salt, if desired
1/2 c. brown sugar
1/4 c. molasses, if desired
1/2 c. ketchup

Bake at 325° for 1 1/2 hours or use crock pot and simmer all day.

Helen Martin, Fargo, N.D.

GREEN BEAN SUPREME

4 c. fresh cut green beans
  or 2 (10 oz.) pkg. frozen
  cut green beans
1/2 tsp. dill weed

1 tsp. dry mustard
1/2 lb. Velveeta cheese,
  cubed
6 slices crisply cooked bacon,
  crumbled

Cook bacon with dill weed; drain. Add mustard and cheese; mix lightly. Place in a 1 quart casserole; top with bacon. Bake at 350° for 12 to 15 minutes. Serves 6-8.

Mary Perron, Rochester, Mn.

GREEN BEANS SUPREME

4 slices bacon
2 Tbsp. bacon drippings
1/4 c. chopped onion
1 (10 1/2 oz.) can condensed
  cream of celery soup

1/3 c. milk
1 lb. fresh green beans,
  cooked and drained, or 2
  (9 oz.) pkg. frozen beans

Cook bacon until crisp; cool and crumble. Cook onion in bacon drippings until tender. Blend in soup, milk and beans; heat slowly, stirring occasionally. Place in serving dish; sprinkle bacon on top. Yields 4 servings.

Colleen Landwehr, St. Cloud, Mn.

M. LOU'S BARBEQUED LIMAS

Boil 1 pound lima beans (1 teaspoon salt) for 1 hour; drain.

Sauce: Fry -

1/4 lb. bacon
1 medium onion

1/2 c. celery

Add:

1/2 c. brown sugar
1/2 tsp. pepper
1 tsp. salt

1 can tomato soup
1 can water
1/2 c. chile sauce or catsup

Cook 15 minutes. Add 1 tablespoon butter. Bake 1 hour at 325°.

Helen Teeuwen, Minneapolis, Mn.

PONCHO'S LIMAS

2 c. dried lima beans
1 tsp. salt
1/2 lb. hamburger
1 clove garlic, crushed
1 Tbsp. chopped red pepper

2 Tbsp. shortening
1 (1 lb.) can tomatoes,
  drained (2 c.)
1 tsp. chili powder
1/2 c. grated cheese

Cover beans with water; soak overnight. Add water, if necessary, and bring to a boil slowly. Simmer, uncovered, 1 hour. Add salt the last 1/2 hour of cooking; drain, reserving 1 cup of the liquor. Brown the meat, onion, garlic and red pepper in hot shortening. Add chili powder and tomatoes, then the limas, reserved liquor and cheese. Pour into greased baking dish and bake in 350° oven for 1 hour or longer. Serves 8.

Dee Olson, St. Paul, Mn.

SMOKEY LIMA BEANS

3/4 c. light brown sugar
1/2 c. catsup
1/3 c. dark corn syrup
2-3 tsp. liquid smoke

3 large cans lima beans,
  drained
1 medium onion, diced
4 strips raw bacon on top

Combine all ingredients, bacon on top, and bake at 325° for 1 1/2 to 2 hours.

Jake Laughlin, Des Moines, Ia.

MINNEHAHA BEANS

Though cooked on top of range, these have a baked quality. Serve with baked yams and stewed tomatoes plus a light dessert of diced tofu (oriental soy bean curd) mixed with thawed, frozen strawberries.

2 c. dried navy beans,
   rinsed and picked over
6 c. water
1/2 c. butter or margarine
1 small onion, minced

1/2 c. packed brown sugar
2 Tbsp. mild molasses
1 tsp. salt
1/2 tsp. dry mustard

Soak beans in water; drain, reserving liquid. In heavy saucepan, mix well the beans, butter, onion, sugar, molasses, salt and mustard. Add enough reserved liquid barely to cover beans. Cover tightly and simmer 2 hours or until beans are tender. (Or, if desired, cook in covered pressure cooker without pressure regulator over low heat 1 hour or until tender.) For drier beans and thicker sauce, bake, uncovered, in 400° oven until most of the liquid is absorbed. Makes 3 or 4 servings.

Margaret McKenney, Minneapolis, Mn.

SOAKING AND COOKING

Cooking dried beans is easy, but it does take time. After rinsing and picking over beans, they must be soaked. Use 2 1/2 to 3 cups water or other liquid for each cup of dried beans. There are 2 methods: 1. Let beans soak in water at room temperature overnight. 2. In saucepan, bring beans and water to boil; boil 2 minutes. Remove from heat; cover and let stand 1 hour. (Some beans and legumes such as black-eyed peas, lentils and split peas do not require soaking.)

After soaking, cook beans as specified in desired recipe. Or, place in heavy saucepan; cover and simmer with soaking liquid until tender or according to suggested times (follows). A pressure cooker will save considerable time and fuel. Follow manufacturer's directions for use. Beans may also be cooked in a slow cooker 10 to 12 hours at low heat; 5 to 6 hours at high heat. Follow manufacturer's directions. (See following chart.)

SUGGESTED COOKING TIMES

Bean or Legume	Simmer in Pot On Top of Range	In Pressure Cooker At 15 Lb.	At 10 Lb.
Black-eyed peas	30 minutes	6-10 minutes	15 minutes
Lentils	30 minutes	6-10 minutes	15 minutes
Split peas	30 minutes	6-10 minutes	15 minutes
Pink beans	45 minutes	10 minutes	20 minutes
Small limas	45 minutes	10 minutes	20 minutes
Brown beans	1 - 1 1/2 hours	10-15 minutes	25-30 minutes
Chick peas	1 - 1 1/2 hours	10-15 minutes	25-30 minutes
Great Northern beans	1 - 1 1/2 hours	10-15 minutes	25-30 minutes
Large limas	1 - 1 1/2 hours	10-15 minutes	25-30 minutes
Whole peas	1 - 1 1/2 hours	10-15 minutes	25-30 minutes
Navy beans	2 hours	10 minutes	20 minutes
Pinto beans	2 hours	10 minutes	20 minutes
Black beans	2 hours	10-15 minutes	25-30 minutes
Kidney beans	2 hours	10-15 minutes	25-30 minutes
Red beans	2 hours	10-15 minutes	25-30 minutes
Soy beans	2 hours	25-30 minutes	50-60 minutes

Margaret McKenney, Minneapolis, Mn.

PINTO BEAN POT

1 lb. (2 1/2 c.) pinto beans
Water as needed
1 1/2 tsp. salt (opt.)
3 Tbsp. oil
4 oz. cut up bacon or stew
   or ribs (brown other
   meats used first)
1 small onion
1/2 clove garlic (opt.)

1/8 tsp. black pepper
2 Tbsp. molasses
1/2 tsp. Worcestershire sauce
1/2 c. catsup
1/2 c. brown sugar
3 Tbsp. vinegar
1/8 tsp. dry mustard
1 3/4 Tbsp. cornstarch
1 1/4 c. cold water

Presoak beans 4-5 hours or overnight in water to cover. Add salt and oil; bring to boil. Cover and simmer until tender; drain. Combine cornstarch and cold water; mix with remaining ingredients. Add to cooked beans. Stir carefully; cover and cook slow: Top of stove, 30-40 minutes; bake at 350° for 1 1/2 - 2 hours. I have also used crock pot. If you like more juice, add cold water or make double juice recipe. Very good.

Marion Vonesh, Grand Forks, N.D.

POT O' GOLD BEANS

4 slices of bacon
1 c. onion rings
1/2 lb. Velveeta cheese,
   cubed
1/4 c. milk

1/8 tsp. white pepper
1 (20 oz.) pkg. frozen green
   beans (French cut)
1-2 c. Kellogg's Croutettes

Fry the bacon until crisp; drain and crumble. Cook the green beans for the minimum amount of time recommended on the package; drain. Cook the onion rings in 1 tablespoon bacon fat until translucent. Add the cubed cheese, milk and pepper; continue to cook and stir over low heat until the cheese has melted. Combine the beans, bacon and cheese sauce in a buttered casserole; top with the Croutettes. Bake at 350° for 25 minutes.

Note: This dish may be prepared ahead of time and refrigerated. Do not add the Croutettes until baking time and allow extra cooking time to compensate for the chill of the dish.

Mrs. Donald Thompson (Eileen)
Minneapolis, Mn.

SWEDISH BROWN BEANS

Soak overnight 1 cup of dried brown beans in approximately 3 cups cold water, 1 teaspoon salt and 1 stick of cinnamon. In the morning, cook until done; add more water, if necessary. When done, add 1 tablespoon vinegar and 1/4 cup white sugar. Stir in 1/3 cup cornstarch, mixed with 1/2 cup cold water. Cook until clear, about 5 minutes.

Thelma Olson, St. Cloud, Mn.

SWEET AND SOUR BEANS

Simmer 20 minutes:

1/2 lb. bacon, fried not too crisp	1/2 tsp. dry mustard
4 medium onions, chopped	1/2 c. vinegar
1 tsp. garlic salt	1 c. brown sugar

Drain:

1 can kidney beans	1 can green lima beans
1 can butter beans	1 can green cut string beans

Add 2 cans pork and beans with liquid. Pour bacon mixture over beans and bake 1 hour at 350°.

Adeline Jasken, St. Cloud, Mn.

THREE BEAN CASSEROLE

1 medium can pork and beans	1/4 c. ketchup
1 medium can kidney beans	1/3 c. brown sugar
1 medium can butter beans	1 Tbsp. Worcestershire sauce
	Salt and pepper

Brown 1 pound hamburger and 5 slices of bacon, chopped. Add 1 chopped onion and 1 cup celery. Mix with remaining ingredients and bake 1/2 hour at 350°.

Liz Tuft, St. Paul, Mn.

3 BEAN CASSEROLE

1/2 lb. ground beef,
  browned with 1 medium
  onion, chopped
1 can kidney beans
1 can lima beans

1 can pork and beans
2 Tbsp. vinegar
1 Tbsp. Worcestershire sauce
1/4 c. brown sugar
1/2 c. ketchup

Mix together and bake at 350° for 1 hour.

Marilyn Radakovich, Duluth, Mn.

2 BEAN CASSEROLE

1 can green beans, drained
1 can wax beans, drained
1/2 c. fresh frozen peas

1 c. chow mein noodles
1 can cream of mushroom
  soup

Put green beans, wax beans, peas and chow mein noodles into 1 quart greased casserole. Add cream of mushroom soup; mix. Add sharp Cheddar cheese, shredded, on top. Cover and bake at 350° for 25 minutes. Remove lid and bake until cheese becomes a golden brown, about 10 minutes.

Mrs. Harold Ericksen, Minneapolis, Mn.

BROCCOLI ALMOND CASSEROLE

2 (10 oz.) pkg. frozen
  chopped broccoli
1 (10 1/2 oz.) can cream
  of mushroom soup
1 c. pure mayonnaise
2 eggs, well beaten

1 c. sharp Cheddar cheese,
  grated
1/2 c. toasted, slivered
  almonds
Salt and pepper to taste
Ritz crackers, crushed

Preheat oven to 375°. Cook broccoli according to package directions; drain well. Mix soup, mayonnaise, eggs, cheese and almonds together; add seasonings. Stir in broccoli. Cover bottom of buttered casserole with cracker crumbs; pour mixture over crackers. Add layer of crushed crackers over top. Bake about 30 minutes or until mixture is heated thoroughly. Yield: 8-10 servings.

Maryann Skelton, Duluth, Mn.

BROCCOLI BAKE

1 (10 oz.) pkg. broccoli
1 (10 oz.) pkg. frozen peas
1 can creamy chicken-
   mushroom soup

1/2 c. grated American
   cheese
1 (4 oz.) can mushrooms,
   drained
1 small jar pimento (opt.)

Place all ingredients in covered baking dish and bake at 350° for 45 minutes or until done. Stir once during baking.

Olga Pederson, Minneapolis, Mn.

BAKED BROCCOLI

2 pkg. frozen broccoli
1 small can water chestnuts

1 can cream of celery soup
1 can French fried onion
   rings

Cook broccoli; drain. Place broccoli and drained, sliced water chestnuts in alternate layers in a casserole. Top with undiluted soup. Bake at 300° for 30 minutes. A few minutes before done, sprinkle crushed onion rings over top; bake a few minutes more. Makes 4-6 servings.

G.W. Seemans, Robbinsdale, Mn.

BROCCOLI BAKED DINNER

2 pkg. frozen broccoli or
   1 (20 oz.) pkg.
1/2 lb. Velveeta American
   cheese, sliced

1 can celery soup
1/2 pkg. herb dressing
Water chestnuts, if desired

Cook broccoli 3 minutes. Spread a layer of broccoli and water chestnuts in a well buttered baking dish. Add layer of sliced cheese. Cover with undiluted soup. Moisten bread dressing with a little water. Crumble dressing over the top. Bake for 30 minutes at 350°. Serves 6-8.

Ruth Eberlein, Luverne, Mn.

BROCCOLI CASSEROLE

1 pkg. frozen chopped
broccoli, defrosted
1 1/2 c. Minute rice,
uncooked
1 can cream of mushroom
soup, plus 1/2 can water

1 small jar Cheez Whiz
1/2 c. finely chopped onion
1/2 c. finely chopped celery
Salt and pepper to taste
1 stick butter, cut into small
pieces

Mix thoroughly all ingredients. Place and flatten into a 13x9 inch greased baking dish. Bake at 350° for 30 minutes in preheated oven, uncovered.

Mary Paul, Minneapolis, Mn.

BROCCOLI CASSEROLE

1 small box long grain and
wild rice
1 bag chopped frozen
broccoli
Paprika

1 can cream of mushroom soup
1 cube chicken bouillon,
diluted in 1/3 c. hot water
Sharp Cheddar cheese,
grated (enough to cover
top of casserole generously)

Cook rice according to directions on box. Cook broccoli minimum time; drain. Mix bouillon with mushroom soup. Add 1/2 of soup to broccoli and 1/2 to rice. Put broccoli in bottom of 2 quart casserole and rice mixture on top. Add grated cheese on top; sprinkle with paprika. Cover and bake at 350° for 1 hour.

T.A. Jensen, Willmar, Mn.

BROCCOLI CHEESE DISH

2 (10 oz.) pkg. chopped
broccoli, cooked, drained
1 can cream of chicken soup
1 c. mayonnaise
2 eggs, beaten

1/2 c. Parmesan cheese
1 c. grated sharp Cheddar
cheese
Salt and pepper
Seasoned bread crumbs

Combine all ingredients, except bread crumbs; place in greased casserole. Top with bread crumbs. Bake at 350° for 45 minutes to 1 hour. Makes 6-8 servings.

Geri Running, St. Paul, Mn.

BROCCOLI OR SPINACH CHEESE PIE

6 eggs
6 Tbsp. flour
12 oz. cottage cheese with
   chives
1/4 lb. butter, cut into cubes

5 oz. Cracker Barrel sharp
   Cheddar cheese, cut into
   cubes
1 pkg. frozen broccoli or
   spinach, defrosted

In large mixing bowl, combine all ingredients; spoon into two 9 inch pie pans. Bake at 350° for 1 hour.

Marly Korn

BROCCOLI AND RICE CASSEROLE

1 (10 oz.) pkg. frozen
   chopped broccoli
1/2 c. regular rice, raw
1 stick margarine, sliced
1 c. milk

1 egg
3 or 4 (1/2 inch) slices
   Velveeta cheese
About 1 Tbsp. chopped
   onion

Cook broccoli according to directions; drain. Cook rice in 1 cup water until water is absorbed, about 15 minutes. Place thin layer of rice in bottom of buttered 2 quart casserole. Top with half of broccoli, cubed cheese and margarine. Sprinkle onion over top, then repeat layers, saving a little rice for top. Combine beaten egg with milk; pour over all. Sprinkle with pepper and bake in 350° oven, uncovered, for 30 or 40 minutes, until slightly browned.

Olga Stanley, Duluth, Mn.

BROCCOLI RICE CASSEROLE

Saute together:
1/2 c. celery
1/2 c. chopped onion

1/2 c. butter

Combine:
1 can mushroom soup
1/2 c. water

1 (8 oz.) jar Cheez Whiz

Thaw a 10 ounce package of chopped broccoli. Have ready 2 1/4 cups cooked rice. Combine all ingredients. Bake at 350° for 45 minutes.

Annette Erspamer, Duluth, Mn.

BROCCOLI AND RICE CASSEROLE

1 c. rice, cooked (regular
   or converted)
1/2 c. celery, chopped
2 pkg. broccoli, cooked
1/4 - 1/2 c. chopped onion

6 Tbsp. butter
1 can cream of chicken soup
1 small jar Cheez Whiz
Grated Parmesan cheese

Form rice into crust in large casserole. Saute onion
and celery in butter. Combine this with broccoli, soups and
Cheez Whiz. Pour over crust and sprinkle with cheese or
paprika. Bake, uncovered, at 350° for 20-30 minutes until
bubbly.

Eileen Sleeman, Virginia, Mn.

BROCCOLI DELUXE

Cook and drain 1 (10 ounce) package frozen broccoli.
Blend:

1 (10 oz.) can cream of
   chicken soup

1 Tbsp. flour

   Add:
1/2 c. sour cream
1/4 c. grated carrot

1/4 tsp. salt
1/8 tsp. pepper

Arrange broccoli in buttered casserole; pour soup mixture on top. Combine 3/4 cup dry bread crumbs with 2
tablespoons melted butter. Sprinkle on top of broccoli.
Bake, uncovered, at 350° for 30-35 minutes.

Alicia Woodford, Montevideo, Mn.

BROCCOLI ALA SAN FRANCISCO

3 bunches fresh broccoli
Melted butter
   Sauce:

Grated Parmesan cheese
   (optional)

3 Tbsp. butter
3 Tbsp. flour
Salt, cayenne pepper and
   celery salt
1 c. milk
1 Tbsp. lemon juice

3 Tbsp. orange juice
1 Tbsp. grated orange rind
1 tsp. grated lemon rind
About 1/4 c. heavy cream
About 1/3 c. blanched,
   slivered almonds

Wash broccoli; with vegetable peeler, scale away tougher bottom portions of the stems. Cook according to the Paul Mayer method. Drain broccoli thoroughly, then rinse quickly in cold water to prevent further cooking. If desired, dip broccoli in melted butter and sprinkle liberally with Parmesan cheese. Arrange on a flameproof serving dish. Prepare sauce: Melt 3 tablespoons butter in saucepan; remove pan from heat and stir in flour. Season with salt, cayenne pepper and celery salt. Add milk, blending carefully. Return to heat and stir gently until sauce boils. Add lemon juice, orange juice, orange rind and lemon rind, plus enough cream to achieve desired consistency. Spread sauce carefully over broccoli; sprinkle entire dish with blanched, slivered almonds. Place dish in 425° oven until almonds have browned and sauce is bubbling. Serves 8.

St. Cloud, Mn.

BROCCOLI SPEARS

2 (10 oz.) pkg. frozen
   broccoli spears
2 cans cream of chicken soup
3/4 c. mayonnaise
3 c. cooked chicken

1 Tbsp. lemon juice
1/2 c. cheese, grated
1/4 tsp. curry powder
2 or 3 slices cubed bread,
   sauteed in butter

Cook broccoli as directed. Arrange in bottom of casserole. Add chicken on top of broccoli. Combine soup, mayonnaise and lemon juice; pour over chicken. Sprinkle top with cheese and bread cubes. Bake 45 minutes at 350°.

Millie Perrault, Duluth, Mn.

BAKED CABBAGE

1 small-medium head of
   cabbage
1 Tbsp. sugar
2 Tbsp. flour

1 c. sweet cream
1 tsp. salt
1/4 tsp. pepper
3 slices uncooked bacon

Tear up cabbage and place in greased casserole. Mix rest of ingredients; pour over cabbage. Cover with bacon slices. (Bacon can be omitted; I have made it without and it's just as good.) Bake, covered, at 350° for 50 minutes; uncover and bake 20 minutes.

Mrs. Robert Sloneker, Chisholm, Mn.

CABBAGE MARINARA

1 lb. ground beef
1 large onion
1 c. cooked rice (optional)
1/4 tsp. thyme
1/4 tsp. oregano
1/4 tsp. garlic powder

1/4 tsp. pepper
1 tsp. salt
6 c. coarsely shredded
   cabbage (1 medium head)
2 c. tomato soup

Saute ground beef until no longer pink; add chopped onion and cook another 5 minutes. Stir in seasonings. Spread 3 cups shredded cabbage in 2 quart baking dish; cover with meat mixture and top with remaining 3 cups cabbage. Pour undiluted tomato soup over top. Cover and bake in 350° oven until cabbage is tender, 1 hour. Serves 4-6.

                    Liz Tuft, St. Paul, Mn.

SCALLOPED CABBAGE

1 small head cabbage
1 can cream of chicken soup
1/2 soup can of milk

1 c. bread crumbs
1/2 c. grated cheese

Cut cabbage in small wedges. Cook in salted water until tender; drain completely. Into greased casserole, place alternate layers of cabbage and soup-milk-cheese mixture. Top with bread crumbs; dot with butter. Bake 30 minutes at 350°.

                    Sally Bartsch, Blaine, Mn.

SKILLET CREOLE CABBAGE

1 Tbsp. butter or oleo
1/4 c. chopped onion
1/4 c. sliced celery
1/2 c. chopped green pepper

1 c. cut up tomato (1 large)
2 c. shredded cabbage
3/4 tsp. salt
1 tsp. sugar
Dash of pepper

Melt butter in 8 inch skillet; add remaining ingredients. Cover tightly and cook over high heat until steaming. Reduce heat to low; cook about 8 minutes or until tender, but not soft. Serves 2.

                    Betty M. Case, Hibbing, Mn.

SWEET 'N' SOUR CABBAGE

1 medium size cabbage
2 Tbsp. brown sugar
1/2 tsp. monosodium
   glutamate (MSG)

3 Tbsp. soy sauce
2 Tbsp. vinegar
2 Tbsp. water
3/4 c. sherry

Remove first layer of tough leaves from cabbage; cut cabbage into quarters and remove hard stems from each quarter and discard. Cut quarters crosswise from top to bottom into 1/2 inch strips. Combine sugar, MSG, soy sauce, vinegar and water for sauce; set aside. Heat wok or pan until very hot. Add 3 tablespoons of oil; heat oil. Add salt. Add cut cabbage; cook over high heat for 1 minute, stirring constantly. While stirring, add sauce mixture. Cover pan and cook for about 1 minute. Remove cover; add 3/4 cup of sherry. Stir to mix well; heat until entire mixture is hot. Serve immediately. Serves 4-6.

St. Cloud, Mn.

CABBAGE-TOMATO-CHEESE DISH

3 c. cabbage, finely
   shredded
1 1/2 c. stewed tomatoes
3/4 tsp. salt
1/2 tsp. paprika

2 tsp. brown sugar
1 c. cheese, grated
1 c. bread crumbs
1 Tbsp. butter or 2 strips
   bacon, minced

Cook cabbage for 5 minutes; drain. Cook tomatoes and seasonings together. Alternate layers of cabbage and tomatoes in a buttered casserole. Sprinkle the layers with the cheese and bread crumbs. Dot the top with butter or bacon. Bake at 325° for about 30 minutes, or until the crumbs are brown. Yield: 6 servings.

Adeline Jasken, St. Cloud, Mn.

CARROT CASSEROLE

3 c. sliced carrots
1 can cream of celery soup

1 c. cubed Velveeta cheese
1/2 c. saltine cracker crumbs

Cook carrots in water until done; drain. Add soup and cheese to carrots in a casserole. Cover with cracker crumbs; bake in a 350° oven for 45 minutes.

Mrs. Norma Applen, Minneapolis, Mn.

CARROT CASSEROLE

4 1/2 c. shredded carrots
1/2 c. mayonnaise
2 Tbsp. chopped onion
2 Tbsp. horseradish

Dash of pepper
7 saltine crackers, crushed
2 Tbsp. melted butter

Cook carrots in a little salted water 10 minutes; drain. Place in casserole; cover with mix. Sprinkle buttered crumbs and cover. Bake at 350° for 30 to 40 minutes; uncover to brown. Serves 8.

Toni Larson, Minneapolis, Mn.

GLAZED CARROTS

1/4 c. oleo
1/4 c. firmly packed light
brown sugar
1 Tbsp. lemon juice

1/4 tsp. dry mustard
1/8 tsp. salt
1 1/2 lb. pared, thinly sliced
carrots, cooked crisp
tender and drained

In a large skillet over moderate heat, melt oleo; blend in brown sugar, lemon juice, mustard and salt. Add carrots and increase heat to moderately high, about 300°. Cook, stirring constantly, until carrots are glazed, about 3-5 minutes. Makes 6 servings.

Colleen Landwehr, St. Cloud, Mn.

COMPANY CARROTS

Slice 2 packages of carrots; cook and drain. Put in a 2 quart casserole. Add 1 medium onion, sliced in rings, and 1 medium green pepper, cut in strips. Set aside. Combine in saucepan:

1 can tomato soup
1/4 c. vinegar
1/2 c. sugar

1/2 c. cooking oil
Salt and pepper

Cook 5 minutes; pour over carrot mixture. Bake 30 minutes at 350°.
Note: Can be served hot or cold.

Geri Running, St. Paul, Mn.
Similar recipe submitted by: Mary Paul, Minneapolis, Mn.

COPPER CARROTS

2 cans cooked carrots or
  2 c. sliced, cooked
  carrots
1 medium onion, chopped
1 small green pepper,
  chopped

1 can tomato soup
Scant 1/3 c. oil
1 c. sugar
3/4 c. cider vinegar
1 tsp. prepared dry mustard
1 tsp. Worcestershire sauce

Refrigerate in glass jar.

Betty Schroll, Minneapolis, Mn.

ZESTY CARROTS

6 large carrots
Salt
2 Tbsp. grated onion
2 Tbsp. horseradish

1/2 c. mayonnaise
1/4 tsp. pepper
1/4 c. cracker crumbs
2 Tbsp. melted butter

Cut carrots in circles or strips; cook 6-8 minutes in 1 inch boiling water with salt. Drain; reserve 1/4 cup cooking liquid. Put carrots in 1 1/2 quart baking dish. Combine onion, horseradish, mayonnaise, salt to taste, pepper and reserved carrot liquid. Toss crumbs with butter; sprinkle on top. Bake at 350° for 15 minutes.

Helen Teeuwen, Minneapolis, Mn.

CELERY ALMONDINE

2 Tbsp. butter
1/3 c. blanched, whole
  almonds
4 c. diagonally sliced
  celery
1 tsp. minced onion

1 chicken bouillon cube,
  crumbled
1 tsp. MSG
1/2 tsp. sugar
1/8 tsp. garlic powder
1/8 tsp. ginger

About 30 minutes before dinner, heat butter and almonds over low heat until lightly browned. Add celery and other ingredients; stir until mixed. Cover and cook, stirring occasionally, 10 minutes. Serve tender crisp.

Dee Olson, St. Paul, Mn.

EXOTIC CELERY

1 bunch celery	1/2 tsp. paprika
1/2 c. slivered almonds	1/8 tsp. pepper
1/2 c. grated cheese	1/2 c. buttered bread crumbs
2 cans cream of celery soup	

Butter 9 inch square pan. Slice celery in 1/4 inch pieces into pan; sprinkle with almonds, then the grated cheese. Mix the soup with spices; pour over all. Top with buttered bread crumbs. Bake at 375° for 45 minutes.

Olive Kallevig, Willmar, Mn.

CHINESE VEGETABLES

Cook 4 cups celery, cut diagonally, in small amount of salted water until done, but still crisp.

1 can water chestnuts, sliced thin	1 pkg. pea pods (frozen), cooked as directed on pkg.
2 Tbsp. pimento	

Place in buttered casserole; put 1 can undiluted cream of chicken soup over top. Sprinkle with salted, toasted, slivered almonds. Bake for 30 minutes at 325°.

Vivian Bergstrom, Minneapolis, Mn.

BAKED CORN

2 eggs, slightly beaten	1/2 tsp. celery salt
1 pt. corn (whole kernel or cream style)	1 c. milk
	6 Tbsp. melted butter
1 c. coarsely crumbled soda crackers	1/2 tsp. salt
	1/8 tsp. pepper

In a bowl, slightly beat the 2 eggs; add remaining ingredients and blend well. Bake in a 2 quart baking dish at 350° for 1 hour, or until knife inserted in center comes out clean.

Colleen Landwehr, St. Cloud, Mn.

CREAM STYLED FROZEN CORN

18 c. corn, cut from cob   1 tsp. sugar
1 lb. butter   1 tsp. salt
1 pt. half & half

Mix all ingredients together; bake for 1 hour in a 350° oven. Cool; put in freezer containers and freeze. Stir the corn several times during the baking.
Fern Groskreutz, Litchfield, Mn.

ESCALLOPED CORN

1 can cream style corn   2 Tbsp. melted butter
7 soda crackers, crushed   Milk to thin (1/4 - 1/2 c.)
1 egg, beaten   1/2 c. American cheese,
Salt and pepper to taste   diced

Top with crushed soda crackers. Bake in 8 inch square pan, buttered, at 350° for 1 hour or until a knife comes out clean.
Gloria Smith, Jackson, Mn.

ESCALLOPED CORN

1 egg, beaten   1 can whole kernel corn
1 c. milk   3 Tbsp. melted butter
1 c. fine, dry cracker
    crumbs

Mix in the order given. Pour into a buttered baking dish; bake in 350° oven for 45 minutes.
Dee Olson, St. Paul, Mn.

SCALLOPED CORN

1 (No. 2) can corn   1/2 c. sweet milk
3 eggs   1 Tbsp. butter
2 Tbsp. sugar   Pinch of salt

Beat the last 5 ingredients together in a buttered baking dish. Add the corn; mix together very well. Sprinkle top with crushed corn flakes or cracker crumbs. Bake at 350° until done, approximately 1 1/2 hours. Chopped green pepper and chopped onion will also add a lot of flavor.
Phyllis Granum, Moorhead, Mn.

SCALLOPED CORN

Have 1 large can creamed corn. Use same can to measure:

1 can crushed saltines	1 can grated sharp Cheddar
1 can milk	cheese

Mix together; pour into greased 2 quart casserole. Sprinkle with paprika; do not cover. Bake in a 350° oven for 50 minutes.

Mrs. Norma Applen, Minneapolis, Mn.

CRISPY FRIED EGGPLANT

Eggplant	Seasoned bread crumbs
Egg	Vegetable oil
Flour	

Peel and slice eggplant; salt both sides of each slice and place between 2 layers of paper towel for approximately 15 minutes. (This will remove excess moisture and bitterness.) When slices are dry, dip in flour, then egg (beaten and mixed with a little water), then seasoned bread crumbs. Fry in vegetable oil until crisp. Delicious in pocket bread sandwiches with tomato sauce, or layered with Mozzarella and Parmesan cheeses and tomato sauce and baked for 30 minutes at 350° for eggplant Parmesan or plain as vegetable side dish.

Pat Carlson, Minneapolis, Mn.

HOMINY HOT DISH

1 can hominy, drained and rinsed	1 can tomato soup
	1 can red kidney beans

Fry 1 small bunch celery, 3 medium onions and 1/4 pound bacon. Saute 1 pound hamburger, dash of red pepper, salt and black pepper. Put in casserole and bake 1 hour at 350°.

Kris Riley, South St. Paul, Mn.

SCALLOPED MUSHROOMS

1 lb. mushrooms, washed, drained and sliced
2 c. soft French bread crumbs
1/2 c. butter, melted
Salt and pepper
1/3 c. dry white wine

Place about 1/3 of the mushrooms in a buttered 1 1/2 quart baking dish; cover with 1/3 of the bread crumbs and drizzle on 1/3 of the butter. Salt and pepper the layer, then add another layer of the mushrooms, crumbs, butter, salt and pepper. Make third layer; pour wine over all. Cover and bake in 325° oven for 35 minutes.

Dee Olson, St. Paul, Mn.

FRENCH FRIED ONIONS

Mix well:
1 c. flour
1/4 tsp. salt
1 beaten egg
1 c. milk
2 tsp. oil

Dip onion rings (large onions work best) in batter; fry in hot oil. Drain well.

Jean Schwartz, Owatonna, Mn.

SIERRA ONION TARTS

1 stick pie crust mix
1 Tbsp. butter or margarine
1 onion, chopped
1 c. grated Monterey Jack cheese
3 eggs, separated
1 c. sour cream
1/4 tsp. salt
1/4 tsp. pepper
1/2 tsp. paprika
1/4 c. grated Parmesan cheese
2 Tbsp. minced parsley

Preheat oven to 450°. Prepare pie crust stick according to package directions; divide into 5 portions. On a lightly floured board, roll out each pie crust portion into a 5 inch round. Fit rounds into 5 baking cups. Flute edges; prick with a fork. Bake 8 minutes or until golden. Meanwhile, in a small saucepan, melt butter or margarine. Add onion; cook until tender. Divide onion and Monterey Jack cheese into tart shells. In a small bowl, beat together egg yolks, sour cream, salt, pepper and paprika. Spoon egg mixture into shells. Lower oven temperature to 325°; bake tarts 20 minutes. In a medium bowl, beat egg whites until stiff, but not dry. Remove tarts from oven; spoon egg whites over tarts and sprinkle with Parmesan cheese. Bake 10 minutes longer. Sprinkle with parsley. Serve immediately. Makes 5 servings.

Bernita Engel, Minneapolis, Mn.

YORKSHIRE ONIONS

3 large sweet onions
3 Tbsp. butter
2 c. sifted flour
3 tsp. baking powder

1 tsp. salt
1 tsp. sugar
1 slightly beaten egg
1 1/2 c. milk

Peel and slice onions; saute in butter about 5 minutes. Cool. Mix and sift dry ingredients. Combine egg and milk; mix quickly to make a soft dough. Stir in onions and any butter in the skillet. Turn into a greased square pan, 8x8 inches. Bake at 350° for about 50 minutes.

Dee Olson, St. Paul, Mn.

PEAS EN CASSEROLE

2 (10 oz.) pkg. frozen
   green peas
1/2 c. bread crumbs

1 can cream of celery soup,
   undiluted
4 Tbsp. butter

Break up blocks of frozen peas in shallow 2 quart casserole. Pour soup over peas. Saute bread crumbs in butter; sprinkle over top. Bake at 400° for about 45 minutes. Serves 6.

Olive Kallevig, Willmar, Mn.

SWEET PEA CASSEROLE

1 (16 oz.) can tiny peas,
   drained
1 can cream of mushroom
   soup

1 chopped medium onion
1 (8 oz.) can water
   chestnuts, sliced
1 (8 oz.) can pimento

Mix above together. Mix 2 cups Pepperidge Farm dressing mix and 1 cup melted margarine or butter; spread over above mixture. Bake at 350° for about 20 minutes or until bubbly.

Mary Jean Voss, Owatonna, Mn.

AU GRATIN POTATOES

1 can Cheddar cheese soup
1/2 c. milk
1 small chopped onion
2 Tbsp. butter

4 c. raw, sliced potatoes
1/2 tsp. salt
1 dash of paprika

Blend soup, milk and salt in greased 1 1/2 quart casserole. Arrange sliced potatoes and onion alternately in soup mixture. Dot with butter; sprinkle with paprika. Cover and bake for 1 1/2 hours at 350°. Uncover and bake 20 minutes.

Jolaine Farley, Sartell, Mn.

POTATO CASSEROLE

1/2 c. milk
3 eggs
1/2 tsp. salt
Pepper

1 c. sharp cheese, grated
2 Tbsp. butter
1 medium onion, grated
3 medium potatoes, grated

Grate potatoes, cheese and onion. Beat eggs with a fork; mix all together. Grease baking dish. Bake in moderate oven, 375°, for 1 hour and 15 minutes. Serves 6.

Fern Raddant, Minneapolis, Mn.

CHEESE SCALLOPED POTATOES

6-8 medium potatoes, peeled
1 medium onion, peeled and
  chopped fine
1 tsp. salt
1/4 tsp. black pepper

3 c. milk
3 Tbsp. flour
3 Tbsp. butter
3/4 c. American or Cheddar
  cheese, diced (I use more)

Slice potatoes into 1/8 inch rounds; layer in buttered 2 quart baking dish with onion, salt and pepper. Melt butter and stir in flour. Add milk, stirring constantly, over low heat until thick. Stir in cheese. When cheese is nearly melted, pour sauce over potatoes. Cover; bake in 350° oven for 1 hour. Remove lid and continue to bake 30 minutes more until golden crust forms on top. Makes 4 to 6 servings.

Mrs. D.H. Richardson, St. Paul, Mn.

GRILLED CHEESY POTATO BACON BAKE

3 large potatoes, peeled
5 slices bacon, fried crisp, crumbled
1 large onion, sliced

2 c. sharp American cheese, cubed
1/2 c. butter

Slice potatoes on foil; sprinkle with salt and pepper. Add bacon, onion and cheese; dot with butter. Grill or bake in oven 1 hour.

Irene Faber, St. Paul, Mn.

CREAM POTATO PUFF

1 (8 oz.) pkg. cream cheese
4 c. hot, mashed potatoes
1 egg, beaten

1/3 c. finely chopped onion
1 tsp. salt
Dash of pepper

Combine softened cream cheese and potatoes; mix until well blended. Add remaining ingredients; mix until well blended. Place in 1 1/2 quart casserole. Bake 45 minutes at 350°.

Maryann Skelton, Duluth, Mn.

POTATO DUMPLINGS

Beat 4 eggs with 1 cup instant potatoes or 2 cups mashed potatoes. Add:

2 c. flour
1 Tbsp. baking powder

1/2 c. milk

Let set for 20 minutes. Put dumplings on top of ribs and sauerkraut that have boiled for 1 hour.

K., St. Cloud, Mn.

HASH BROWNS DELUXE

Place 2 pounds frozen hash browns (4 sections) in cake pan or low casserole (do not double deck). Bring to boil:

3 c. half & half
1 tsp. salt

1 stick margarine or butter

Pour over hash browns. Sprinkle over this 1/2 cup Parmesan cheese. Bake at 350° for 1 hour.

Mrs. Robert Sloneker, Chisholm, Mn.

DELUXE HASH BROWNS

1 (2 lb.) pkg. hash browns
1 small container sour
  cream
1 medium onion, chopped
Salt and pepper to taste

Green pepper, chopped
  (optional)
1 can cream of chicken soup
1 can cream of mushroom
  soup

Bake at 325° for 1 1/2 to 2 hours; uncover last 1/2 hour.

Emogene Homan, Minneapolis, Mn.

DELUXE POTATO BAKE

1 (2 lb.) pkg. frozen hash
  browns, thawed
1/2 pt. sour cream
1/2 c. chopped onion

1/2 c. shredded cheese
1 can cream of chicken or
  mushroom soup
Salt and pepper

Line 8x12 inch pan with potatoes; cover with remaining ingredients. Top with crushed corn flakes, which have been mixed with 1 stick of oleo. Bake for 45 minutes in 350° oven.

Esther Mungovan, Duluth, Mn.

POTATO HOTDISH

4 medium size potatoes,
  sliced 1/4 inch thick,
  boiled in salt water 10-15
  minutes, drained
1 can mushroom soup

1 can vegetable beef soup
1 can mushrooms, drained
1 lb. hamburger, browned
  together with 1 small
  onion

Mix all ingredients together. Bake 1 hour at 300°.

Liz Tuft, St. Paul, Mn.

MISSISSIPPI POTATOES

8 c. potatoes, cooked and
  diced
1 c. mayonnaise
1 tsp. salt
1/2 tsp. pepper

1 lb. processed American
  cheese, diced
1/2 c. chopped onion
4-6 slices bacon, fried
1/2 c. olives (green or
  black)

1507-82

Toss potatoes with mayonnaise, salt, pepper, diced cheese and onion. Place mixture in a greased 9x13 inch pan. Sprinkle with crumbled bacon and olives. Bake at 325° for 1 hour. Makes 8-10 servings. Can be made ahead and frozen.

St. Cloud, Mn.

ONIONED POTATOES

6 medium baking potatoes
1/2 c. soft butter or oleo
1 env. onion soup mix

Scrub potatoes; do not peel. Cut each in 3 or 4 lengthwise slices. Blend butter and soup mix; spread on slices, then reassemble potato. Wrap each in foil, overlapping ends. Bake until done, turning once. Can be put on top of grill or on coals 45 to 60 minutes.

Minneapolis, Mn.

OVEN FRIED POTATOES

8 large unpeeled baking potatoes, each cut in 8 wedges
1/2 c. oil
2 1/2 Tbsp. Parmesan cheese

1 1/2 tsp. salt
3/4 tsp. garlic powder
1/2 tsp. paprika
1/2 tsp. pepper

Arrange wedges, peel side down, in 2 shallow baking pans. Mix remaining ingredients; brush over potatoes. Bake in 375° oven for 45 minutes.

Mrs. Norma Applen, Minneapolis, Mn.

PARTY POTATOES

Peel number of potatoes needed and put in ice water. Grind with a coarse blade of food grinder into ice water. Wash off all starch. Use clean water several times; cold water always. Layer with onion (chopped), celery (diced), salt, pepper and pimento. Scald enough milk to cover the potatoes; add lots of butter. Pour over potatoes. Bake at 250° for at least 3 hours. The last 1/2 hour of baking, top with grated cheese.

Dee Olson, St. Paul, Mn.

178

PARTY POTATOES

8-10 potatoes
1 (8 oz.) pkg. cream cheese

1/2 c. sour cream
Salt and pepper to taste
Paprika

Cook potatoes until soft; peel and mash. Beat softened cream cheese and sour cream until well blended. Add the hot potatoes; beat until light and fluffy. Salt and pepper to taste. You may add a few tablespoons of butter at this time. Spoon mixture into buttered 1 1/2 quart casserole; sprinkle with paprika. Wrap well and refrigerate until ready to heat. Place in 350° oven for 30 minutes.

Virginia Anderson, Crystal, Mn.
Similar recipe submitted by: Ruth Roemeling, Luverne, Mn.

PIZZA POTATOES

1 pkg. scalloped potato mix
  (Betty Crocker or other)
1 (16 oz.) can tomatoes
1 1/2 c. water

1/4 tsp. oregano leaves
4 oz. sliced pepperoni
4 oz. shredded Mozzarella
  cheese

Place potatoes and seasoning packet in greased 2 quart casserole. Heat water, tomatoes and oregano to boiling; mix in with potatoes. Arrange pepperoni on top; sprinkle with cheese. Bake, uncovered, in 400° oven for 30 to 35 minutes.

Olga M. Stanley, Duluth, Mn.

SCALLOPED POTATOES SUPREME

2 qt. sliced potatoes
1/4 c. minced onion
1/8 tsp. pepper
1 can mushroom soup

1/4 c. chopped green pepper
2 tsp. salt
1 c. milk

Alternate layers of potatoes, pepper and onion in a greased dish. Season each layer with salt and pepper. Mix soup and milk; pour over potatoes. Bake at 350° for 1 hour.

Liz Tuft, St. Paul, Mn.

SCALLOPED POTATOES

6 medium size potatoes
1 onion
2 Tbsp. flour
1 tsp. salt

1/8 tsp. pepper
3 Tbsp. butter
3 c. whole milk or half & half

Peel potatoes and onion; slice both in thin slices. Pour boiling water over potatoes and onion; let stand 2 minutes, then drain. Place in alternate layers with seasoned flour and butter in a buttered 2 quart baking dish. Pour milk over contents and bake, covered, at 350° for 30 minutes. Remove cover and continue baking until potatoes are tender and a light, firm crust has formed. The onion may be left out and thin slices of ham may be added. Makes 6 servings.
Alicia Woodford, Montevideo, Mn.

SYNTT NA MAI POTATOES

2 qt. diced potatoes
1 lb. butter, sliced
1 chicken bouillon cube

1 can Franco-American
    chicken gravy
1/2 c. boiling water

Put the potatoes and the butter in a 9x13 inch glass cake pan; bake at 350° for an hour, stirring now and then. Combine gravy and bouillon cube with the boiling water, stirring to dissolve bouillon cube. Pour over potatoes. Bake another hour or until done. Serves 6 to 8.
St. Cloud, Mn.

TWICE BAKED POTATOES

2 Tbsp. melted butter
Salt and pepper
1 Tbsp. cream
Paprika

1/3 c. cream
1 large egg
2 Tbsp. grated cheese

Heat butter and 1/3 cup cream until hot. Scoop out 4 or 5 baked potatoes; beat with electric mixer. Add heated butter, cream, salt and pepper. Beat egg till thick; add to potato mixture. May make in the morning and cover and refrigerate. Before baking, put in 1 tablespoon cream on top of each; sprinkle with paprika and cheese. Bake at 450° for 15 minutes.
Joan Norton, Hibbing, Mn.

TATORS

Boil 8 medium potatoes only 25 minutes until barely soft; cool and cube. Mix together:

1 can celery soup
1/4 c. or less melted butter
  or margarine
1 pt. sour cream

1 1/2 c. grated Cheddar
  cheese
1/4 c. or 2 green onions,
  chopped fine

Combine with potatoes in buttered casserole; add dash of salt and pepper. Cover with 3/4 cup crushed corn flakes, mixed with 3 tablespoons melted butter. Bake at 350° for 45 minutes.

Mrs. Robert L. Benson, Stillwater, Mn.

VALLEY SPUD SUPREME

8 medium baked potatoes
1/2 lb. midget Longhorn
  style Colby cheese (2 c.
  grated)

1 1/2 c. cream
Salt and pepper
Onion salt

Bake potatoes for 1 hour in 350° oven; cool completely (may be done the day before). Remove skins from the potatoes. Grate 4 potatoes into an 8x8 or 9x9 inch pan. Season with salt and pepper and a generous amount of onion salt. Sprinkle 1 cup of grated cheese over the grated potatoes. Grate the remaining 4 potatoes over the cheese; season with salt, pepper and onion salt again. Add another cup of grated cheese. Before baking, pour the cream over them and bake 40-45 minutes in moderate oven until bubbly on top and a light golden brown. Serves 8. This may be prepared ahead of time, except for the cream, and refrigerated until baking time. Ideal for company and also a good way to make use of leftover baked potatoes.

Judy Rieger, Grand Forks, N.D.

SAUERKRAUT

Rinse 1 package or 1 large jar of kraut with cold water (about 1 quart). Add:

1/4 c. white sugar
1 Tbsp. caraway seed

1/8 c. pearl barley

Cook and add to meat or whatever.

Ollie Kearney, Owatonna, Mn.

SAUERKRAUT

Use 5 pounds of cabbage; finely shred cabbage.
Sprinkle 3 1/2 tablespoons salt over cabbage; mix well.
Let stand 30 to 60 minutes to wilt slightly. Pack firmly into
jars, leaving a 2 inch head space. Fill with cold water,
leaving 1/2 inch head space. Adjust lids, screwing band
tight. Place jars on jelly roll pan to catch brine that over-
flows during fermentation and curing. Keep cabbage
covered with brine. If necessary, open jars and add more
brine, made by dissolving 1 1/2 tablespoons salt in 1 quart
water. Sauerkraut is cured and ready to can in 6 to 8
weeks. Clean rims of jars, replacing lids, if necessary.
Screw bands tight. Set jars in water bath canner filled
with cold water; water should extend 2 inches above jars.
Bring water slowly to boiling. Process kraut in pints or
quarts 30 minutes. Makes 7 pints.

Mary Perron, Rochester, Mn.

MOTHER'S HOMEMADE SAUERKRAUT
(Very Easy)

12 c. water (be sure to use hard water)
1 c. white vinegar

3/4 c. coarse cannery salt
Onions
Caraway seed

Bring water, white vinegar and salt to boil; pour over
shredded kraut, which has been packed in quart jars with
1 slice onion and 1 teaspoon caraway seed. Seal.
Note: Use a wooden spoon to pack down the cabbage
in quart jars. Use about a bushel of cabbage.

Mrs. B.V. Feller, Excelsior, Mn.

SAUERKRAUT HOT DISH

Drain 2 large cans kraut; save 1/2 of juice. Dice and
fry 1 pound bacon; save drippings. Dice very fine 1/3 cup
onion; put over kraut in greased casserole. Put on bacon
and drippings. In saucepan, put juice, 1/3 cup sugar, 1/2
cup tomato paste and 1/3 cup butter; heat until melted.
Pour over other ingredients. Dice about 5 slices of bread;
put on top, just enough to cover. Do not stir up. Bake 1
hour at 375°.

Joyce Meyer, Minneapolis, Mn.

BAKED SPINACH

2 pkg. frozen chopped
   spinach
1 small onion, minced, or
   1/2 tsp. dry onion
1 tsp. salt

1 c. sour cream
1 c. diced, cooked celery
1 c. soft bread crumbs
2 eggs, slightly beaten
3/4 c. cheese cracker
   crumbs

Cook and drain spinach. Mix with remaining ingredients, except cracker crumbs. Put in buttered casserole; top with crumbs. Bake at 375° for 20-25 minutes. May prepare in morning and bake in the evening.

Pearl Paulsrud, Montevideo, Mn.

SPINACH PIE

1 medium egg, boiled,
   finely chopped
1 pkg. frozen chopped
   spinach or 1 lb. fresh
   spinach, chopped
1/4 c. olive oil
1/2 lb. Feta cheese

1/2 filo leaf pastry
6 oz. cottage cheese (small
   curd)
3 eggs, beaten
1/2 c. butter or margarine
1/4 c. bread crumbs

Saute the onion in olive oil for 5 minutes; add well drained spinach. Simmer with onion over low heat. Stir occasionally until most of the moisture evaporates. In a separate dish, crumble Feta cheese into small pieces; add cottage cheese and blend well. Add beaten eggs; mix well. Toss bread crumbs into the spinach mixture; add egg and cheese mixture. Stir until well blended. In buttered pan, place 10 layers of filo leaves, each one buttered. Spread spinach mixture over all. Top with 10 filo leaves, each one buttered. Bake 30 minutes or until browned on top in 350° oven. You can increase cheese to taste.

Mary Paul, Minneapolis, Mn.

STUFFED SQUASH

Select 1 fresh medium sized squash; clean out all seeds and peel. Dip in hot water for a few seconds.

Filling: Fry a few slices of onion in fat until brown; add 1/2 pound ground meat and fry lightly. Take 1/2 cup rice; boil until soft. Add to meat; salt and pepper to taste.

Stuff into prepared squash and put in pan. Cover with butter or lard; bake until soft. Cut into slices and serve.

Clara G. Gabriel, Bismarck, N.D.

CHERRY TOMATOES IN BUTTER

1 1/2 c. cherry tomatoes
2 tsp. butter

Salt and pepper to taste

Cut tomatoes in halves. Heat quickly, uncovered, in butter, shaking pan until heated through. Season with salt and pepper and serve. Serves 2.

Dee Olson, St. Paul, Mn.

TOMATOES WITH DILL SAUCE

4 large tomatoes
1/2 c. dairy sour cream
1/4 c. mayonnaise
2 Tbsp. chopped onion

1 tsp. snipped fresh dill weed or 1/4 tsp. dried dill weed
1/4 tsp. salt

Combine all ingredients, except tomatoes; chill. Cut tomatoes in halves. Season with salt and pepper; dot with oleo. Broil, cut side up, about 5 minutes. Spoon sour cream mixture over hot tomatoes just before serving.

Carolyn Brudevold, Fargo, N.D.

HERBED TOMATOES

6 tomatoes, peeled and quartered
1 tsp. salt
1/4 tsp. black pepper
1/4 tsp. thyme

1/4 tsp. marjoram or 1/2 tsp. of one of the other
1/4 c. chopped parsley
2/3 c. salad oil
1/4 c. tarragon vinegar

Mix together and let stand at least 1 hour before serving. Keeps well in refrigerator.

Mary Lou Roskoski, Virginia, Mn.

SOUTHERN STEWED TOMATOES

10 tomatoes
1 small onion, chopped
1 Tbsp. sugar
1 tsp. salt
1 1/8 tsp. pepper
2 tsp. Worcestershire sauce

Simmer until most of liquid is gone. Add 1 Shredded Wheat biscuit or 2 tablespoons corn flakes. Stir and add 1 tablespoon butter.

K., St. Cloud, Mn.

SUNDAY COMPANY CASSEROLE

1 pkg. frozen peas, cooked and drained
1 can bean sprouts, drained
2 (4 oz.) cans mushroom pieces
1 can sliced water chestnuts, drained
1 can cream of mushroom soup
1/2 lb. grated Cheddar cheese
1 can French fried onion rings

Put peas, bean sprouts, mushrooms and water chestnuts in a 9 inch casserole. Mix some of the mushroom liquid into the soup; heat. Add to casserole; mix. Sprinkle cheese over top. Cover and bake in a 350° oven for 30 minutes. Remove from oven and place onion rings over the top. Bake, uncovered, for 15 minutes longer. Makes 4 to 6 servings.

Dorothy Savig, Minneapolis, Mn.

VEGETABLE CASSEROLE

1 (No. 2) can green beans
1 (No. 2) can whole onions
1 medium can mushrooms
1 can cream of mushroom soup
Cheddar cheese

Add about 1/2 cup liquid from mushrooms to soup; heat. Add grated cheese; blend well. Add beans, onions and mushrooms. Salt and pepper to taste. Pour into buttered casserole. Top with buttered crumbs. Bake 45 minutes at 350°. May use 2 cans beans, if needed.

Mrs. William (Liz) Voss, Virginia, Mn.

VEGETABLE CASSEROLE

1 pkg. frozen broccoli   1 pkg. frozen cauliflower

    Mix above as package directs.

1 can green French style   Frozen tater tots
  beans, drained

    Mix above all together; put in 9x13 inch glass pan.
Mix together 1 can mushroom soup and 1/2 can milk; pour
above mixture over vegetables and sprinkle 1/2 can fried
onions on top. Sprinkle a few pieces of cheese on top 5
minutes before done. Bake at 350° for 1/2 hour.
                            Mary Jo Conneran, Fargo, N.D.

VEGETABLE CASSEROLE

1 pkg. Brussels sprouts   1 pkg. cauliflower
1 pkg. broccoli

    Mix 1 large jar Cheez Whiz and 1 can mushroom soup.
Bake at 350° for 45 minutes.
                            Liz Tuft, St. Paul, Mn.

MIXED VEGETABLE CASSEROLE

3 boxes frozen cauliflower   2 cans mushrooms, drained
1 box frozen French style   1/2 c. milk
  green beans   1 c. soda cracker crumbs
1 box frozen carrots

    Mix all together; put slivered almonds on top. Bake
at 350° for 1 1/2 hours.
                        Joan Norton, Hibbing, Mn.

VEGETABLE DELIGHT

1 head cauliflower, washed   1 (2 oz.) jar chopped
  and trimmed   pimento, drained
1 bunch broccoli, washed   1 c. mayonnaise
  and trimmed   1 (8 oz.) ctn. or 1 c. dairy
2 green onions, finely   sour cream
  chopped   1 Tbsp. garlic juice (I don't
                           use)

Salt and pepper to taste

1 (10 oz.) pkg. frozen
peas (optional)

Cut cauliflower and broccoli into bite size pieces; add onion and pimento. Mix mayonnaise, sour cream, garlic juice, salt and pepper. Combine dressing with raw vegetables; add peas, if wanted. Refrigerate and allow flavors to blend. Serves 12-16. I usually prepare the night before.

Marion Round, Faribault, Mn.

HONEY ORANGE VEGETABLES

Cook 1 cup frozen mixed vegetables in small amount of salted water until tender. Drain; add:

2 Tbsp. butter
1 Tbsp. honey

2 Tbsp. orange juice
1 tsp. grated orange rind

Simmer 2 or 3 minutes. (Children will eat their vegetables when prepared this way.)

Leslie Zimbrick, Minneapolis, Mn.

VEGETABLE PIE

1 (10 oz.) pkg. frozen
chopped broccoli, drained
well
1/2 c. chopped onion
1/2 c. chopped green pepper
1 1/2 c. milk

1 c. (4 oz.) shredded
Cheddar cheese
3/4 c. Bisquick baking mix
3 eggs
1 tsp. salt
1/4 tsp. pepper

Mix broccoli, onion, green pepper and cheese in 9 inch pie plate. Beat remaining ingredients until smooth. Pour over top of vegetables. Bake until golden brown at 400° for 35 to 40 minutes. Use knife test for doneness.

Lila Houser, Aitken, Mn.

POTLUCK VEGETABLE

1 (17 oz.) can whole kernel
corn
1 (10 oz.) pkg. cauliflower,
cooked and drained

1 (10 oz.) pkg. broccoli,
cooked and drained
1 (4 oz.) can sliced
mushrooms

1 (17 oz.) can cream style corn
2 Tbsp. butter
2 c. shredded Cheddar cheese
1 1/2 c. soft bread crumbs

Combine cream style corn, cheese and soup; fold in drained vegetables. Put into 12x7x2 inch pan. Top with bread crumbs and butter. Bake at 375° for 30-35 minutes or until hot.

Sally Bartsch, Blaine, Mn.

BAKED VEGETABLE SALAD

1 can mushroom soup
1 can bean sprouts
1 box frozen French cut green beans, cooked
1/2 onion, diced
1 can mushrooms
1 can water chestnuts, sliced thin
1 can French fried onions

Drain all vegetables; add soup and diced onion. Line baking dish with 1/2 of French fried onions, crumbled. Add vegetable mixture; cover with remaining French fried onions. Bake, uncovered, 35 minutes in 350° oven.

Grace Locke, St. Paul, Mn.

VEGETABLE CASSEROLE

1 can drained asparagus
1 1/2 c. sliced carrots and 1 medium sliced onion, cooked in juice from asparagus
1 can sliced water chestnuts
1 can drained green beans
Cheese sauce

Put 1/2 the vegetables in bottom of greased casserole, then 1/2 of cheese sauce. Repeat with vegetables and rest of cheese sauce. Cover with buttered crumbs. Bake at 350° until hot, 20 to 30 minutes.
Cheese Sauce: Use cream of cheese soup or white sauce with 1 cup grated cheese.

Jan Eschbach, Duluth, Mn.

PEACH YAM BAKE

1/2 c. packed brown sugar
3 Tbsp. flour
1/2 tsp. nutmeg
2 Tbsp. margarine
1/2 c. chopped pecans

2 (17 oz.) cans yams,
  drained
1 (16 oz.) can peach slices,
  drained
1 1/2 c. mini marshmallows

Combine sugar, flour and nutmeg. Cut in margarine until mixture resembles coarse crumbs; add nuts. Arrange yams and peaches in 1 1/2 quart casserole; sprinkle with sugar mixture. Bake at 350° for 35 minutes. Sprinkle with marshmallows; broil until lightly browned. Makes 6 servings.

Mary Ann Dinius, Coon Rapids, Mn.

VEGETARIAN CASSEROLE

1 stalk celery, chopped
1 medium onion, chopped
1 small green pepper,
  chopped
2 Tbsp. cooking oil
2 c. noodles, cooked and
  drained
1 1/2 c. (6 oz.) shredded
  Monterey Jack cheese
  (frozen mix)
1/2 c. milk

1 c. broccoli cuts, cooked
  and drained (sub. tater
  tots)
3/4 tsp. salt
1/3 tsp. pepper
1/4 c. fine, dry bread
  crumbs
2 Tbsp. shredded Cheddar
  cheese
1 Tbsp. wheat germ
1 Tbsp. butter or margarine,
  melted

Cook celery, onion and green pepper in hot oil till tender but not brown; stir in noodles, Monterey Jack cheese, broccoli, milk, salt and pepper. Turn into an ungreased 1 1/2 quart casserole. Bake, covered, in 350° oven for 15 minutes. Combine bread crumbs, Cheddar cheese, wheat germ and butter or margarine; sprinkle around edge of casserole. Bake, uncovered, 10 minutes more. Makes 4 servings. (This recipe idea also lends itself well to carrots or zucchini, too.)

Nance Martin, Ramsey, Mn.

ZUCCHINI CASSEROLE

4 c. zucchini, precooked
and sliced
1 can cream of chicken soup
(or use 1 can cream of
mushroom)
1 c. grated carrots

1/2 lb. hamburger, browned
and drained
1 (4 oz.) can mushrooms
1 small onion, diced
1/2 c. Parmesan cheese
1/2 c. sour cream

Mix all together. Put in casserole; top with 2 cups
seasoned bread crumbs. Bake in 350° oven for 1/2 hour.

Mrs. B.V. Feller, Excelsior, Mn.

ZUCCHINI CASSEROLE

Prepare 1 package chicken flavored Stove Top
dressing; set aside. Cook 6 cups grated zucchini and 1 cup
grated carrots for 5 minutes in a little water. Add 1/4 cup
chopped onion; drain well. Mix in 1 can cream of chicken
soup and 1 cup of dairy sour cream. Grease large casserole; put 1/2 of dressing and 1/2 of zucchini, then remaining dressing and top with zucchini. Bake, uncovered,
for 30 minutes at 350°.

Jo Lyn Freitag, Minneapolis, Mn.

DODE'S ZUCCHINI CASSEROLE

4 c. zucchini, sliced 1/4
inch thick
1 c. carrots, shredded
1 medium onion, chopped

1/4 lb. butter or margarine
1 can cream of chicken soup
1 c. seasoned croutons
1 c. sour cream

Boil zucchini until tender. Meanwhile, saute carrots
and onion in butter until limp. Add soup and sour cream;
mix. Add 3/4 cup of the croutons and the zucchini, stirring gently. Pour into greased casserole. Put remaining
croutons in another tablespoon of butter; heat until coated.
Sprinkle over top of casserole. Bake at 350° for 20-25
minutes.

Helen Teeuwen, Minneapolis, Mn.

ZUCCHINI CREOLE

In a skillet, saute 1 thinly sliced onion and 1 clove of garlic in 1/4 cup cooking oil. Add:

2 lb. sliced zucchini   1 chopped green pepper
4 cut up tomatoes

Add salt and pepper to taste; cook until tender. Sprinkle minced parsley and Parmesan cheese before serving. Serve over rice.

Colleen Fahey, Grand Forks, Mn.

ZUCCHINI PIZZA PIE

5 slices firm white bread
3 Tbsp. butter or margarine
1 lb. zucchini, sliced
1 onion, sliced
1/2 tsp. salt
1/2 tsp. thyme
1/2 tsp. basil

1/8 tsp. pepper
1 c. ripe pitted olives, cut
   into wedges
1 (10 1/2 oz.) can pizza
   sauce
1 (6 oz.) pkg. sliced
   Mozzarella cheese

Preheat oven to 375°. Spread bread slices with 1 tablespoon of the butter or margarine; cut diagonally into halves. Line bottom and sides of a 9 inch pie plate with bread halves. In medium saucepan, melt remaining butter or margarine. Add zucchini and onion; cook just until tender. Sprinkle with salt, thyme, basil and pepper. Add olives; toss to blend. Layer half the vegetable mixture, pizza sauce and Mozzarella cheese over bread shell in pan. Repeat with remaining ingredients. Bake 25 minutes or until toast points and cheese are golden. Makes 6 servings.

Bernita Engel, Minneapolis, Mn.

ZUCCHINI SOUFFLE

2 lb. zucchini (2 1/2 c.
   cooked, mashed with
   water out of vegetables)
2 eggs, beaten
1 grated medium size onion
1 c. milk

1 c. cracker crumbs (about
   30 soda crackers)
1/2 tsp. salt
1/4 tsp. pepper
1/4 tsp. mace
1/4 tsp. curry powder
1 c. grated Cheddar cheese

Prepare zucchini as before and drain again. Add remaining ingredients; mix well. Bake in greased casserole at 350° for 40 minutes.

Grayce Funke, Minneapolis, Mn.

ZUCCHINI SQUASH

3 medium zucchini
1/2 tsp. salt
1/8 tsp. pepper
1 Tbsp. butter or oleo

1 large onion, chopped
1 (8 oz.) can tomato sauce
1 (4 oz.) can sliced
  mushrooms

Wash squash; cut into cubes. Combine everything; simmer slowly until squash has a glossy look, 15 minutes. Serve. Makes 3 to 4 servings.

Mary Paul, Minneapolis, Mn.

RICE CASSEROLE

1 1/2 c. raw rice
1 small onion, browned in
  butter
4 c. water

2 chicken or beef bouillon
  cubes
1/2 tsp. salt
1 can mushrooms

Cover and bake at 300° for 1 to 1 1/2 hours. Stir once in a while.

Lila Houser, Aitkin, Mn.

CURRIED RICE

Saute 1 cup chopped onion in 3 tablespoons butter for 3-4 minutes. Add 1/2 teaspoon salt, 1/2 teaspoon curry powder and 1 cup uncooked rice; cook for 3 minutes. Add 1 can consomme and 1/2 cup water; cook on low, covered, for 30 minutes.

Joan Billadeau, St. Cloud, Mn.

GOLDEN RICE

1 c. converted rice
3 medium carrots (1/2 lb.),
  peeled and shredded
3 green onions, sliced
2 Tbsp. butter or margarine

1/2 tsp. salt
1/4 c. toasted, slivered
  almonds, peanuts or
  sunflower nuts
1/2 tsp. dill weed

192

Cook rice according to package directions, omitting butter, 20 minutes. At the point of removing pan from heat, add carrots, green onions, butter and salt; stir. Cover and continue to cook over low heat until water is absorbed and carrots are just tender, about 5 minutes. Stir in nuts and dill. Serves 6.

St. Cloud, Mn.

GREEN RICE

Saute in 1 stick butter:

1/2 c. celery	1/4 c. onion

Add:

1 frozen pkg. broccoli	1 c. Minute rice
1/2 c. cubed Colby cheese	1 can cream of mushroom soup

Mix and bake for 45 minutes at 350°.

Cindy Roney, Cottage Grove, Mn.

ORIENTAL (CURRY) RICE

2 c. water	1 c. rice
1/2 lb. bacon	1 large slice of liver
1 medium onion	1/2 c. mushrooms, sliced (opt.)
Salt	
Chicken bouillon granules	Pepper
	Curry powder

Heat water to boiling; add enough chicken bouillon to make it taste like chicken stock. Do not add salt to water. Add rice; bring to boil. Set aside, or put on low heat so rice will steam done, or use instant rice. Chop bacon, liver and onion in small pieces; slice mushrooms. Saute all together in skillet until bacon and onion are done. Drain off grease; add meat mixture to rice when rice is done. Salt and pepper to taste; add curry powder, being careful not to put in too much. This dish is excellent as a replacement for potatoes or stuffing.

Sandra Norris, Minneapolis, Mn.

WILD RICE CASSEROLE

1 c. wild rice, uncooked	1/2 c. white wine (optional)
1 chopped onion	2 Tbsp. butter
3 stalks chopped celery	1 qt. chicken broth
1 tsp. seasoned salt	Salt and pepper to taste

Combine all ingredients; place in casserole. Bake, covered, at 325° for 2 hours. May be prepared in advance. Freezes well.

Lovise Lorenz, St. Paul, Mn.

WILD RICE AND ALMONDS

1/2 c. wild rice, rinsed in cold water	2 tsp. butter
1 1/4 c. chicken broth	1/4 c. slivered almonds
	Salt, if needed

Combine rice, broth, butter and almonds in a saucepan. Bring to a boil; simmer, covered, for about 45 minutes or until rice is tender but not mushy. Taste and salt, if necessary. Add more butter when serving if you'd like. This is good as a side dish with chicken.

Alicia Woodford, Montevideo, Mn.

WILD RICE CASSEROLE

1 c. wild rice, washed	1/2 c. sliced almonds
1/2 c. butter	2 cans mushrooms
2 Tbsp. green pepper	3 c. chicken broth, bring to
2 Tbsp. onion	boil
1 clove garlic	Salt and pepper to taste

Saute everything, except broth, in butter until onion turns yellow; add chicken broth. Place in casserole. Bake for 1 1/2 hours at 325°.

Ginny Harwood, St. Cloud, Mn.

WILD RICE CASSEROLE

1 c. wild rice, washed 2 or 3 times, cooked (may also be soaked overnight instead)	1 lb. ground beef
	1/2 lb. bacon, cut in small pieces
	1 onion, chopped

3 ribs celery, chopped
1 green pepper, chopped
   (optional)
1 can chicken noodle soup

1 can cream of mushroom
   soup
1 can water
1 can stewed tomatoes

Fry bacon; remove from pan. If a lot of grease, drain some out. Fry beef, onion, celery and green pepper. Add soups, water, tomatoes and bacon; simmer slowly, about 1/2 hour. Add rice and bake 45 minutes at 350° in covered casserole. Can add strips of fried bacon on top, if desired, before baking.

Mary Lou Roskoski, Virginia, Mn.

WILD RICE CASSEROLE

1 lb. pork sausage, browned
1 lb. ground beef, browned
1 onion, chopped
2 c. celery, chopped
1 green pepper, chopped
1 can pimento
2 cans mushrooms
1/2 tsp. salt

2 cans mushroom soup
1 pkg. Uncle Ben's wild rice
   and long grain rice with
   seasonings, plus extra
   1/4 c. wild rice, cooked
   together as directed on
   pkg.
1 Tbsp. soy sauce

Mix everything together and bake* 1 1/4 - 1 1/2 hours at 325° to 350°. Makes a 3 quart casserole.
   *I usually bake some of it for immediate use and freeze the rest of it.

Marian Pearson, Minneapolis, Mn.

WILD RICE HOT DISH

1/2 c. wild rice
1/2 c. rice
4 Tbsp. butter
1 c. chicken rice soup
   (plus extra chicken)

1 tsp. salt
1/2 c. chopped parsley
1 3/4 c. water
Sliced almonds

Bake 1 hour at 350°. Heat can of mushroom soup; thin with cream. Instead of chicken, you can use cream of celery soup and tuna. Add a little more liquid. Can use crock pot on low all day. Serves 4.

Thelma Olson, St. Cloud, Mn.

WILD RICE HOT DISH

Pour 4 cups boiling water over 1 cup wild rice; cover and let stand 30 minutes. Drain. Brown 2 pounds ground beef. Mix together:

1 can cream of mushroom
  soup
1 can cream of celery soup
1 can cream of chicken soup
1 (6 oz.) can mushrooms,
  sliced
1 medium onion, chopped
1 medium green pepper,
  sliced

Browned ground beef
1/2 tsp. garlic salt
1/2 tsp. paprika
1/2 tsp. celery salt
3 Tbsp. soy sauce
1 can bean sprouts, drained
1 can water chestnuts, sliced
1 tsp. salt

Mix with rice. Pour into 9x13 inch pan; top with buttered crumbs and Parmesan cheese. Bake 1 hour at 350°.

Arlene Carlson, Lake Park, Mn.

WILD RICE HOT DISH

Boil 1/2 cup white rice and 1/2 cup wild rice 20 minutes; drain. Brown and drain:

1 1/2 lb. hamburger
1/2 chopped onion

1 stalk chopped celery

Add 1 can cream of mushroom soup and 1 can cream of chicken soup. Bake in casserole 1 hour at 375°. Serves 8.

Freida Paro, Crystal, Mn.

WILD RICE HOT DISH

1 c. wild rice
2 c. diced celery
2 large onions, chopped
2 or 3 Tbsp. soy sauce
1 can cream of mushroom
  soup

1 lb. hamburger, browned,
  or 1 cooked chicken, diced
1 can cream of chicken soup
1 can cold water
1/2 c. mushrooms, diced

Wash rice in warm water; let stand in water 3-4 hours or overnight. Drain. Saute celery, onion and hamburger. Add soy sauce, then soup and water. Stir in rice, mushrooms and chicken (if used instead of hamburger). Place in buttered casserole. Bake at 325° for 1 1/2 hours. Don't add any salt.

Maryann Skelton, Duluth, Mn.

196

WILD RICE HOT DISH

2 c. wild rice
1/2 lb. bacon
1 medium onion, diced
1 basket mushrooms, sliced
1 can cream of chicken soup

1 can water chestnuts, sliced
1 can cream of celery soup
Chicken bouillon cubes
Slivered almonds, if desired

Swell rice by favorite method. Fry bacon; crumble. Saute onion and mushrooms. Mix all together. Add some water. Bake at 350° for 2 hours or more. Keep very moist while cooking with chicken bouillon.

Jean Hoffman, Duluth, Mn.

WILD RICE HOT DISH

Soak 3/4 cup wild rice all night (change water 3 times) in covered Tupperware. You should have 1 1/2 cups wild rice.

2 1/2 c. shredded raw
   carrots (5 from store)
5 pieces browned bacon
   strips

1/2 tsp. salt
1/4 tsp. sweet basil
   (Durkee's)
1/2 c. chopped onion

Place in Dutch oven or 1 1/2 pint dish, covered. Add onion, finely chopped. Add rice and carrots; stir and add:

1 egg, lightly beaten
1 1/4 c. light cream

3/4 tsp. salt
1 Tbsp. butter

Butter the baking dish. Put in mixture; cover with liquid. Dot with butter. Cover; set in electric oven to preheat 5 minutes at 350°, then bake 35 minutes.

Bonnie Sovick, Marshall, Mn.

WILD RICE HOT DISH

1 c. wild rice
2 cans cream of chicken soup
1 can chicken broth
1 tsp. salt
2 c. cubed chicken
1 c. mushrooms

1/4 c. diced pimento
1/2 c. diced green pepper
1/2 c. sliced almonds (save
   some for top)
1 can water chestnuts, sliced

This may need a bit more broth. Bake in casserole at 350° for 30-40 minutes.

Va Fyksen, Duluth, Mn.

UNCLE BEN'S LONG GRAIN AND
WILD RICE CASSEROLE

2 pkg. Uncle Ben's long
   grain and wild rice
1 lb. bacon
2 lb. ground beef
2 c. diced green pepper
1 c. diced onion

2 c. diced celery
3 (4 oz.) cans mushrooms
3 cans cream of mushroom
   soup
Salt and pepper to taste
2 c. soda cracker crumbs
   (optional)

Preheat oven to 350°. In a large frying pan, place bacon, that has been cut into 1 inch bits. When partially cooked, add ground beef, green pepper, onion and celery. Cover; cook until ground beef is browned, stirring often. Drain and set aside. In a large kettle, prepare 2 boxes of long grain and wild rice according to the directions on the box. When rice is done, add the ground beef mixture, mushrooms and the cream of mushroom soup. Mix well; pour into a 9x12 inch cake pan. The mixture can be topped with soda cracker crumbs, if desired. Bake for 30 minutes.

Marcia Theisen, Duluth, Mn.

WILD RICE STUFFING

1 c. bread crumbs
1 chopped onion
4 c. boiled wild rice
1 c. broth

1/2 tsp. sage
1/2 tsp. salt
1/4 tsp. pepper

Mix well.

Debra Tollefson, Fargo, N.D.

WILD RICE SOUP

1/4 - 1/2 lb. bacon, diced,
   and 2-3 Tbsp. chopped
   onion, fried together
1 can cream of potato soup
1 can cream of chicken soup

1 1/2 c. milk or more
1 c. diced Velveeta cheese
1/4 - 1/3 c. wild rice, boiled
   until fluffy

Heat soups and milk. Add cheese; stir until melted. Add bacon and onion, which have been fried, and cooked wild rice.

Dorothea Olson

198

CHEESE
EGGS

HOW TO COOK A HUSBAND.—A recipe for cooking husbands "tender and good". A good many husbands are utterly spoiled by mismanagement. Some women go about it as if their husbands were bladders and blow them up. Others keep them constantly in hot water. Others let them freeze by their carelessness and indifference. Some keep them in a stew by irritating words and ways. Others roast them. Some keep them in pickle all their lives. It cannot be supposed that any good husband will be tender or good managed in this way, but they are really delicious when properly treated. In selecting your husband you should not be guided by the silvery appearance, as in mackerel, nor by the golden tint, as if you wanted salmon. Be sure and select him yourself, as tastes differ. Do not go to the market for him, as the best are always brought to your door. It is far better to have none unless you will patiently learn how to cook him. A preserving kettle of the finest porcelain is best, but if you have nothing but an earthenware pipkin it will do with care. See that the linen in which you wrap him is nicely washed and mended, with the required number of buttons and strings sewed on. Tie him in the kettle with a strong silk cord called comfort, as the one called duty is apt to be weak. They are apt to fly out of the kettle and be burned and crusty on the edges, since, like crabs and lobsters, you have to cook them while alive. Make a clear, steady fire out of love, neatness and cheerfulness. Set him as near this as seems to agree with him. If he sputters and fizzes, do not be anxious. (Some husbands do this until quite done.) Add a little sugar in the form of what the confectioners call kisses; but no vinegar or pepper on any account. A little spice improves them, but it must be used with judgment. Do not stick any sharp instrument into him to see if he is becoming tender. Stir him gently, watch the while lest he lie too flat and close to the kettle and so become useless. You cannot fail to know when he is done. If thus treated you will find him very digestible, agreeing nicely with you and the children, and he will keep as long as you want, unless you become careless and set him in too cold a place.
—A.K.P., Reading, Pa.

This "recipe" was published in a 1907 cookbook.

CHEESE BURGUNDY CASSEROLE

1 lb. ground beef	Salt and pepper to taste
1/3 c. chopped onion	1 c. sifted flour
1 (10 1/2 oz.) can tomato	1 1/2 tsp. double-acting
soup	baking powder
1/4 c. dry red wine	1/4 tsp. salt (for biscuits)
1 c. peas, undrained	2 Tbsp. lard
8 (3/4 inch) cubes American	1/3 c. plus 1 Tbsp. milk
or Cheddar cheese	

Brown ground beef and onion in skillet; drain off fat. Add the tomato soup, wine, peas, salt and pepper. Place mixture in 1 1/2 quart casserole. Sift together the flour, baking powder and salt into a mixing bowl; cut in the lard until the particles are fine. Add the milk and stir until dough clings together. Knead on lightly floured surface 12 times. Divide into 8 pieces. Mold the dough around cheese cubes; place on casserole. Bake at 425° for 25 to 30 minutes until deep golden brown. Serves 4 to 6.

St. Cloud, Mn.

CHEESE POUF
(Double for big pan)

8 slices white bread	1 tsp. salt
1 (8 oz.) pkg. Old English	1/2 tsp. pepper
cheese slices	3/4 tsp. dry mustard
1/4 c. melted butter	2 c. milk
3 eggs	

1. At least 4 hours before serving time, trim crusts from bread; cut in 1 inch squares. Cut cheese slices into bit size pieces. 2. In greased shallow casserole, alternate layers of bread and cheese; pour melted butter over top. 3. Beat eggs well; stir in salt, pepper, mustard and milk. Combine thoroughly, then pour over ingredients in casserole. Cover and refrigerate. 4. One hour before serving, bake, covered, at 350° for 30 minutes. Bake, uncovered, for 30 minutes until top is golden brown and puffy.

Katie Johnson, Duluth, Mn.

MACARONI SURPRISE

1 box macaroni, cooked
1 can Spam
1 c. milk (evaporated)
1 c. grated cheese
1/4 c. melted butter
3 eggs, separated

1/2 small onion
1/2 tsp. salt
1/4 tsp. pepper
1 jar pimento
1 green pepper

Grind onion, Spam and green pepper. Mix with macaroni, salt, egg yolk, melted butter and milk. Lastly, fold in stiffly beaten egg whites. Turn into buttered casserole. Sprinkle top with grated cheese. Bake at 350° for 1 hour. Serve with cream of mushroom soup, heated.

Evelyn Swing, Anoka, Mn.

MACARONI AND CHEESE

1 (7 oz.) pkg. elbow
   macaroni
1 (11 oz.) can cheese soup
1 soup can of milk
1 (8 oz.) ctn. sour cream
1 tsp. salt

Dash of pepper
1 (8 oz.) pkg. shredded
   Cheddar cheese
1/4 tsp. prepared mustard
2 tsp. minced onion

Cook macaroni according to package directions; drain. Combine remaining ingredients; fold in macaroni and spoon into greased casserole. Bake in 350° oven for 30 minutes, covered, and 15 minutes, uncovered. Serves 6-8.

Colleen Landwehr, St. Cloud, Mn.

SO-EASY MACARONI AND CHEESE

1 1/2 Tbsp. butter or
   margarine

1 c. uncooked elbow macaroni
1 c. (4 oz.) grated cheese
2 c. milk

Melt butter in oblong baking dish in oven (while it preheats). Pour in macaroni; season with salt and pepper. Stir until butter coats macaroni thoroughly. Sprinkle cheese over macaroni. Pour on milk until macaroni is covered; use all the milk. Bake at 325° for 45 to 55 minutes. Serves 4.

D. Klosterman, Anoka, Mn.

SAVORY CHEESE/ONION PIE

Basic Shortcrust Pastry for
    one 10 inch pie (see
    page 642)
10 oz. cheese (half Swiss,
    half Switzerland
    Gruyere, or in
    proportion desired)

2 Tbsp. flour
2 large onions
4 Tbsp. butter
1 tsp. chopped basil
2 large firm tomatoes, sliced
2 large eggs
3/4 c. cream

Prepare the Shortcrust Pastry as directed; line a 10 inch pie dish and chill it. Grate all cheese; toss it with the flour. Melt butter in large skillet; slice the onions and saute them very gently in the butter until they begin to turn golden, about 1/2 hour. Spread about 1/3 of the cheese over the bottom of the pie dish, then spread the onions over it. In the butter that is left in the pan, heat the tomato slices with the chopped basil for a minute or two. Arrange the tomato slices over the onions, then cover with the remaining cheese. Beat the eggs with the cream; pour it over the cheese. If you like nutmeg, sprinkle over the top. Bake for about 35-40 minutes or until top browns nicely. Serve hot, in wedges.

Joan Billadeau, St. Cloud, Mn.

CHEESE PASTA IN A POT

2 lb. lean ground beef
2 medium onions, chopped
1 garlic clove, crushed
1 (14 oz.) jar spaghetti
    sauce (comes in 16 oz.)
1 (1 lb.) can stewed tomatoes
1 (3 oz.) can sliced
    mushrooms

8 oz. shell macaroni
1 1/2 pt. dairy sour cream
1 (1/2 lb.) pkg. sliced
    Provolone cheese (can use
    Swiss)
1 (1/2 lb.) pkg. Mozzarella
    cheese

Brown meat; drain off fat. Add onion, garlic, sauce, tomatoes and mushrooms; mix well. Simmer 20 minutes. Cook shells. Pour half the shells in deep casserole. Cover with half the sauce; spread half the sour cream over sauce. Top with half the cheese; repeat. Cover casserole. Bake at 350° for 35-40 minutes. Remove cover; continue to bake until cheese melts. Serves 8.

Georgine Isakson, Fargo, N.D.

BRUNCH

Slice bread; remove crusts and line bottom of greased 8x12 inch cake pan. Place thick slice of American cheese on bread. Place ham slice on cheese. Top with matching bread slices. Beat 4 eggs and 2 1/2 cups milk; add 1 teaspoon salt. Pour over bread; let stand 8 to 18 hours (overnight). Bake at 350° for 45 minutes. Heat can of mushroom soup and can of mushrooms together. Pour over serving. Serve with fruit cup and blueberry muffins.

Katie Johnson, Duluth, Mn.

HAM AND EGG BRUNCH
(Early Lunch)

First Layer: Put 7 slices day old bread, cubed, in greased 9x11 inch baking dish. Second Layer: Add 1 pound precooked ham or Spam, cubed. Third Layer: Add 1/2 pound sharp Cheddar or Monterey Jack cheeses or a combination of both, cubed. Fourth Layer: Beat slightly 3 eggs, 2 cups milk and 1/4 teaspoon dry mustard.

Cover; refrigerate overnight. Bake, uncovered, at 325° for 1 hour. Let stand 5 minutes before cutting. This is very good.

Mrs. Kermit A. Haugen, Clarkfield, Mn.

SUNDAY MORNING BRUNCH

16 slices of bread, crusts removed

8 slices Cheddar cheese
8 slices precooked ham

Grease 9x13 inch pan; lay 8 slices of bread on bottom layer, ham and cheese. Top with remaining bread. Beat 6 eggs, 3 cups milk, 1/2 teaspoon salt and 1/2 teaspoon dry mustard; pour over bread, ham and cheese. Sprinkle with crushed corn flakes. Melt 1/2 cup butter; pour over all. Fry 10 slices of bacon; crumble and sprinkle on top. Bake 1 hour at 350°. (Prepare the day ahead.) Serves 8-10 people.

Marion Round, Faribault, Mn.

EGG CASSEROLE

6 eggs   1 tsp. salt
2 c. milk   1/4 tsp. onion powder (opt.)

Beat eggs slightly; add milk and salt.

2 c. seasoned croutons   1/2 lb. bacon, fried and
4 oz. grated Cheddar cheese   crumbled

Grease 8x8 inch pan (double 9x13 inch pan). Add:
1. Croutons; 2. Bacon; 3. Cheese. Pour egg mixture on
top. Bake for 1 hour at 350°.

Phyllis Christenson, Brooklyn Center, Mn.

BRUNCH EGG CASSEROLE

In bottom of greased 10x6 inch baking dish, combine
2 cups plain croutons and 4 ounces (1 cup) shredded
natural cheese. Combine:

4 slightly beaten eggs   1/2 tsp. prepared mustard
2 c. milk   1/8 tsp. onion powder
1/2 tsp. salt   Dash of pepper

Mix till blended. Pour over croutons in casserole.
Cook 4 slices bacon till crisp; drain and crumble. Sprinkle
over top of casserole and bake at 325° for 55 to 60 minutes.
Garnish with bacon curls, if desired. Serves 6.

G.W. Seemans, Robbinsdale, Mn.

EASTER MORN CASSEROLE

1/4 c. butter or margarine   2 tsp. parsley flakes
1/4 c. flour   1 c. cooked wide noodles
1 Tbsp. prepared mustard   2-3 c. cubed ham
1/8 tsp. pepper   6 hard cooked eggs
1/2 tsp. salt   1/3 c. bread crumbs
2 c. milk   1 tsp. paprika
1 c. grated Cheddar cheese

Melt butter; add flour, mustard, salt and pepper.
Gradually stir in milk, until it boils; add cheese, parsley,
noodles and ham. Pour into greased 3 quart casserole.
Press quartered eggs into mixture; sprinkle top with
crumbs. Bake at 350° for 30 minutes.

Mabel Marka, St. Paul, Mn.

BREAKFAST AND LUNCH DISH

Place 6 slices of buttered bread, crusts removed, in a 9x13 inch pan. Spread over bread 3 cups ground ham (may use Spam); top with sliced cheese (American or Old English). Dice 6 slices bread, buttered, crusts removed. Sprinkle over cheese. Beat 5 eggs; add 2 1/2 cups milk, salt and pepper; beat together. Pour over bread and ham. Drizzle with 1/3 cup melted butter; sprinkle with paprika. Cover and refrigerate 24 hours. Bake 1 hour at 350°. Let stand 10 minutes before serving.

Katie Johnson, Duluth, Mn.

DEVILED EGGS ON RICE

6 hard boiled eggs	Pepper and salt to taste
Mayonnaise to taste	1 c. shrimp
Prepared mustard to taste	1 c. cooked mushrooms

Cut eggs in halves crosswise; remove yolks. Mash yolks; mix with mayonnaise, mustard, salt and pepper. Refill egg whites; place in greased casserole with shrimp and mushrooms. Cover with Cheese Sauce and bake at 350° for 10 minutes.

Cheese Sauce:

2 Tbsp. butter	1 c. milk
2 Tbsp. flour	1/2 c. cheese, cut up

Make white sauce; add cheese till melted. Serve on fluffy rice. Serves 6.

Toni Larson, Minneapolis, Mn.

EGG DISH FOR BREAKFAST

Beat 18 eggs; add 1 cup half & half cream. Scramble lightly. Put in greased casserole (9x13 inch pan). Pour over top:

1 can cream of mushroom soup	1 pkg. shredded cheese (Cheddar)
2 cans mushrooms	1/4 lb. fried bacon bits

Bake 25-30 minutes if warm or 40 minutes if cold. (Can be made the night before.) Bake in 350° oven. Serves 12.

Katie Johnson, Duluth, Mn.

EGG FOO YONG

Sauce:

2 Tbsp. soy sauce
1 tsp. cornstarch
1 tsp. sugar

1 tsp. vinegar
3/4 tsp. salt
1/2 c. cold water

Eggs:

1 c. drained, canned bean
sprouts
2/3 c. thinly sliced onions,
chopped
6 eggs

1 c. cleaned, cooked or
canned shrimp, coarsely
cut up (or chopped
leftover roast pork)
2 Tbsp. bacon fat or salad
oil

About 50 minutes before supper, make sauce: In saucepan, combine soy sauce, cornstarch, sugar, vinegar and salt; stir in water. Cook over low heat until thickened.

Combine bean sprouts with onion and shrimp. Then, with fork, beat eggs; add bean sprouts mixture. In hot fat in skillet, fry, as pancake, about 1/4 cup mixture at a time, turning once. Keep hot until all mixture is cooked. Arrange on hot platter; cover with heated sauce. I like these with hot fluffy rice. Makes 3 or 4 servings. Use about 350° electric fry pan; it shouldn't cook too fast. (I suggest cut down soy sauce; we found 2 tablespoons salty tasting.)

Jim Tuft, St. Paul, Mn.

CHOPPED EGG MOLD

1 doz. hard cooked eggs
1/2 c. melted butter or
margarine
1 1/2 tsp. salt

2 Tbsp. prepared mustard
1 small onion, grated
1/2 c. mayonnaise
1 Tbsp. cream

Chop eggs finely. Add butter, salt, mustard, onion and mayonnaise, thinned with cream; mix well. Season further, if desired. Turn into a 1 quart mold or individual molds and chill overnight. Approximate yield: 8 portions.

Quick Trick Chopping: Cut hard cooked eggs in halves lengthwise; place on waxed paper covered chopping board. Using sharp knife with a pointed blade, place a finger on point, and holding firmly in position, chop lightly. Swivel knife in semi-circle back and forth until eggs are finely cut. Turn the chopped eggs from wax paper into a bowl; blend together with other ingredients.

Dena Stoddard, St. Louis Park, Mn.

EGGS LORRAINE

2 tsp. butter
2/3 c. (about 3 oz.)
   shredded Cheddar cheese

8 eggs
8 link sausages, cooked and
   drained
1/2 c. whipping cream

Spread butter in 8x8x2 inch baking dish. Sprinkle 1/3 cup cheese over butter. Break eggs onto cheese and pierce yolks, but do not stir. Place sausages over eggs. Pour cream over. Sprinkle with remaining cheese. Bake at 350° for 20-30 minutes. Makes 4-6 servings. Can be made a day early and refrigerated.

Mary Paul, Minneapolis, Mn.

SCRAMBLED EGG CASSEROLE

18 eggs
1 c. plus 2 Tbsp. half &
   half
3 Tbsp. butter
1 can cream of mushroom
   soup

2 (3 oz.) jars mushrooms,
   drained
5 oz. shredded Cheddar
   cheese
1 - 1 1/2 c. diced ham

Beat eggs and half & half together; scramble in butter in frying pan. Put eggs in 3 quart shallow casserole. Pour on soup, mushrooms and cheese; top with ham. Bake at 250° for 45 to 60 minutes. Serves 10-12. Can be made ahead and refrigerated before baking. Bake 1 1/2 hours. Can be held in oven an additional 30 to 45 minutes without becoming tough. Very versatile recipe. Serve with a fresh fruit cup and homemade rolls for a delicious brunch.

Eloise Hoff, Preston, Mn.

FANCY EGG SCRAMBLE

1 c. diced ham or bacon
3 Tbsp. margarine
1 (3 oz.) can mushrooms or
   8 oz. fresh mushrooms
1/8 tsp. paprika

2 1/2 c. bread crumbs
1/4 c. chopped green onions
12 eggs, beaten
4 tsp. melted butter

Cheese Sauce:

2 Tbsp. butter
1/2 tsp. salt, pepper
1 c. shredded cheese

2 Tbsp. flour
2 c. milk

Make cheese sauce. Melt butter; add flour, salt and pepper. Slowly add milk; cook over slow heat until bubbly. Add cheese; cover and set aside. In large skillet, heat meat or lightly fried bacon and onion in 3 tablespoons margarine until tender. Add eggs, stirring until just barely set, not dry. Fold eggs and drained mushrooms into cheese sauce. Turn into greased baking dish. Combine remaining ingredients; sprinkle on top. This may be prepared and refrigerated, covered, overnight. Let stand at room temperature 30 minutes. Bake, uncovered, for 30 minutes at 350°. Cut in squares to serve. Makes 8-12 servings.

Martha Fjelstad, Minneapolis, Mn.

EGG-VEGETABLE BAKE

Cut round circle out of each slice of 12 slices of white bread; save circles for top. Break rest of slices into small pieces in bottom of 9x13 inch buttered pan. Layer 1 (10 ounce) package of chopped broccoli (frozen can be used), 2 cups diced ham and 12 ounces grated Cheddar cheese over bread. Arrange bread rounds on top; pour the egg mixture over all. Let set in refrigerator overnight.

Egg Mixture: Mix well in blender -

3 1/2 c. milk	1/2 tsp. salt
6 eggs	1/4 tsp. dry mustard
2 Tbsp. minced onion	Dash of pepper

Bake 1 1/2 hours at 325°. Let set 15 minutes before serving. Serves 12.

Colleen Grapentin, St. Cloud, Mn.

QUICHE
(Make the night before)

Line 9x13 inch pan with 8 slices bread. Beat 1 dozen eggs and 4 cups milk; heat this up so it thickens a bit. Saute 1 large onion and 1 green pepper together. Fry 1 pound bacon; drain. Grate 1 cup cheese of your choice. Drain 2 small cans of mushrooms. Pour egg mixture over bread; layer onion, green pepper, bacon, cheese and mushrooms. Let set in refrigerator overnight. The next morning, bake in 300°-325° oven for 45 minutes to 1 hour. Let stand a while before you cut.

Colleen Fahey, Grand Forks, N.D.

BAKED OMELET

6 well beaten eggs
3/4 c. milk
1/2 c. green pepper
1/4 c. chopped green onions

1 can Spam or ham, cubed
1/2 c. cracker crumbs (6)
1 c. grated or cubed cheese

Mix and bake at 325° for 30-40 minutes or until set; cut in squares. Serve with a sauce made of:

1 can mushroom soup
1/2 c. milk
1 tsp. horseradish

1 jar diced pimento
1 jar drained, sliced
  mushrooms

Heat through and ladle over omelet.

Ann Christensen, Litchfield, Mn.

BRUNCH HAM AND EGGS

Blend:
1/2 c. mayonnaise
1/4 c. flour

1/2 tsp. salt

Add 1 1/2 cups hot milk; cook until thick and smooth. Add 1/4 pound cubed American cheese, 1/2 cup chopped onion, 1 jar drained, diced pimento. Cook until cheese melts, then add 4 quartered, hard boiled eggs, 1 jar sliced mushrooms and 1 large can Spam or ham, diced. Serve over toasted English muffins or Holland rusks. For a luncheon, you can substitute shrimp for the ham and add 1 can shrimp and 1 small can peas. Serve in warm patty shells.

Ann Christensen, Litchfield, Mn.

OVERNIGHT BREAKFAST

1 1/2 lb. pork links or
  patties, browned
12 eggs, lightly beaten

8 oz. grated Cheddar cheese
1/2 pt. whipping cream
Mushrooms, drained (opt.)

Put eggs in well greased 9x13 inch pan; salt and pepper. Sprinkle in half the cheese. Pour in whipping cream; sprinkle in mushrooms. Add meat. Sprinkle in rest of cheese. Do not stir. Refrigerate 10 or more hours. Bake at 350° for 50-60 minutes.

Geri Running, St. Paul, Mn.

BASIC QUICHE

It's up to you to decide which cheese you'd like to mix or match with which vegetable or meat. Whichever you choose, use no more than 1 1/2 cups total. Then, pick the appropriate seasoning.

1 (9 inch) pie shell*
1/2 - 1 c. shredded cheese
1/2 - 1 c. chopped, cooked
   and drained meat,
   seafood, poultry or
   vegetable

6 eggs
1 c. half & half or milk
1/2 tsp. herb or other
   seasoning
1/2 tsp. salt

Sprinkle cheese and meat into pie shell. Beat together remaining ingredients until well blended. Pour over cheese and meat. Bake in preheated 375° F. oven until knife inserted near center comes out clean, 30 to 40 minutes. Let stand 5 minutes before serving. Makes 6 servings.

Quick Quiche Combinations:

Swiss Cheese with: Corned beef, onion, dry mustard; chicken or turkey, green onions with tops, poultry seasoning; ham, caraway seed or dry mustard; potatoes, pimiento, dill weed.

Cheddar cheese with: Tuna, tarragon or dry mustard; green beans, toasted, slivered almonds, garlic powder; carrots, walnuts, marjoram or nutmeg; ground beef, mushrooms, onion salt; peas, onion, rosemary.

Muenster or Brick cheese with: Spinach, bacon, onion; broccoli, oregano; cauliflower, dry mustard; shrimp, dill weed; pork sausage, onion.

Marion Round, Faribault, Mn.

QUICHE FOR BRUNCH

3 eggs
1/2 c. Bisquick
1/3 c. melted butter
1 1/2 c. milk

1/4 tsp. salt
1 c. shredded cheese (Swiss,
   American, etc.)
1/2 c. bacon, ham or
   sausage

Brown bacon, cut in 1 inch pieces, or sausage, broken up, or cut up ham; ham need not be browned. Take everything but cheese and meat and put in blender for a few seconds. Pour into 9 inch greased Pyrex pan; sprinkle meat and cheese on top and press gently down into batter with spoon until meat and cheese are covered. Bake 45 minutes at 350°; let stand 10 minutes. Can add onion, green pepper and mushrooms, if desired.

Helen Martin, Fargo, N.D.

QUICHE LORRAINE

1 (9 inch) baked pastry
  shell
1/2 lb. bacon
1 c. shredded Cheddar
  cheese

1/3 c. finely chopped onion
1/2 c. light cream
3 eggs
3/4 tsp. salt
1/4 tsp. sugar
1/8 tsp. pepper

Place bacon slices between layers of paper towels in 12x7 inch baking dish; microwave for 8-9 minutes until crisp. Cool and crumble into baked pastry. Top bacon with cheese and onion. Pour cream into 1 cup glass measure. Microwave 1 - 1 1/2 minutes or until hot. In small bowl, beat eggs and seasonings; slowly blend in heated cream. Pour over ingredients in shell. Microwave on Defrost for 26-28 minutes or until knife comes out clean. Let stand 5 minutes before serving. Makes 5-6 servings or 10-12 appetizers.

CRUSTLESS QUICHE LORRAINE

7-10 slices bacon, cooked
  and crumbled
1 c. shredded Swiss or
  Gruyere cheese
1/3 c. Parmesan cheese
1/3 c. onion, minced

1 (13 oz.) can evaporated
  milk or 1 3/4 c. half & half
4 large eggs
1/8 tsp. pepper
1/2 tsp. salt
1/8 tsp. cayenne pepper

Sprinkle bacon, Swiss cheese and onion into 9 inch glass pie plate or quiche dish. In a large mixing bowl, beat Parmesan cheese, eggs and remaining ingredients with rotary beater, until well blended. Pour over bacon mixture. Microwave at 80% for 9 to 11 minutes, or until knife inserted near center comes out clean. Turn once or twice during cooking time. Let stand 10 minutes before cutting.

Marlene Barton, Grand Forks, N.D.

MINI QUICHES

2 (3 oz.) pkg. cream cheese
1 c. margarine
Finely minced chives
4-8 eggs*
1 3/4 - 3 1/2 c. light cream*
1-2 tsp. salt

Dash of white pepper and
    cayenne pepper
2 c. flour
1/2 lb. Brick or Monterey
    Jack cheese, shredded

*Eight eggs and 3 1/2 cups cream are enough for two 9x13 inch pans.

Day before serving: Combine the cream cheese, margarine and flour in medium size bowl; form into a ball. Flatten slightly and chill 1 hour or more (1-2 days is O.K.). When well chilled, roll out on floured surface; cut into small rounds to fit in tiny muffin tins. This amount of dough will make 72 small shells, 48 larger ones, or 9x13 inch pan. Fit dough into as many tins as you have. Cover remaining dough; return to refrigerator until ready to use. In each shell, sprinkle a small amount of shredded cheese and a few minced chives. Make filling by beating the eggs well, then adding the cream and spices to the eggs, blending thoroughly. Spoon this mixture into the shells, filling each about 2/3 full. Bake the quiches in a 400° oven for 15 to 20 minutes or until puffed and golden. Cool quiches slightly; remove from tins and cool completely. Wrap in foil and refrigerate until ready to use. Repeat procedure until all dough and filling are used up. To serve: Place quiches on a cookie sheet and reheat in a 350° oven for about 15 minutes or until nice and hot. May be frozen and reheated, allowing an extra 10 minutes; do not thaw first. You can add small pieces of shrimp, ham or bacon with the cheese and chives, if desired.

Virginia Anderson, Crystal, Mn.

BERNIE'S SUPER SOUFFLE

6-8 slices buttered bread,
    cut in halves
1 lb. bacon, cut up, fried
1 (10 oz.) pkg. Schweigert's
    Smokies (or pork links),
    cut in 1/2 inch pieces

10 eggs, beaten, combined
    with 3 1/2 c. milk
2 c. American cheese, grated
1 (8 oz.) pkg. Monterey
    Jack cheese, grated
1 (8 oz.) pkg. Cheddar
    cheese, grated

Place bread in bottom of a greased 13x9 inch pan. Sprinkle bacon and Smokies over bread; add cheese. Pour

the eggs and milk mixture over all. Refrigerate overnight,
then bake in 350° oven for 1 hour; let it set for 5 minutes
before serving. Mushrooms, green peppers and onions may
be added if you like. Or, just use 2 cheeses such as
Cheddar and American or Monterey Jack and American.

Mrs. B.V. Feller, Excelsior, Mn.

BREAKFAST SOUFFLE

14 slices white bread   3 c. milk
Ham or bacon   1/2 tsp. dry mustard
1 lb. grated cheese   1/2 tsp. salt
8 eggs

Fill greased 9x13 inch pan with bread; cover with
slices of ham or crumbled, fried bacon, then grated cheese.
Beat eggs; add milk, mustard and salt. Pour over bread,
meat and cheese; cover and refrigerate overnight. Mix 2
cups crushed cereal flakes and 1/2 cup melted butter;
sprinkle over top. Bake 45 minutes at 350°.

Jan Eschbach, Duluth, Mn.

TEA EGGS

8 eggs   3 whole star anise
3 Tbsp. black tea leaves   1 Tbsp. salt
1 cinnamon stick   Preserved ginger

Boil eggs in water to cover for 10 minutes; drain and
let stand in cold water until cool. With the back of a spoon,
gently crack shells all over to achieve a spider-web effect,
but do not peel. Place eggs, in one layer, in a saucepan
with tea leaves, cinnamon stick, star anise and salt. Cover
with water; cook over low heat 1 hour. Remove from heat;
let cool in tea water. Shell and serve whole or halved with
preserved ginger.

St. Cloud, Mn.

TEXAS EGGS

Season and scramble 12 eggs. Put in glass 9x13 inch
pan. Top with chopped green pepper, sliced green onions
and sliced mushrooms. Cover with heated, undiluted mushroom soup; cover with grated cheese. This can then be refrigerated overnight and baked the next morning. Bake
1 1/4 hours at 325°.

Ann Christensen, Litchfield, Mn.

MEAT
POULTRY
SEAFOOD

MEAT ROASTING GUIDE

Cut	Weight in Pounds	Approx. Time (Hours) (325° oven)	Internal Temperature
BEEF			
Standing Rib Roast[1] (10-inch ribs)	4	1¾	140° (rare)
[1] If using shorter cut (8-inch) ribs, allow 30 min. longer		2	160° (medium)
		2½	170° (well done)
	8	2½	140° (rare)
		3	160° (medium)
		4½	170° (well done)
Rolled Ribs	4	2	140° (rare)
		2½	160° (medium)
		3	170° (well done)
	6	3	140° (rare)
		3¼	160° (medium)
		4	170° (well done)
Rolled rump[2]	5	2¼	140° (rare)
		3	160° (medium)
		3¼	170° (well done)
Sirloin tip[2]	3	1½	140° (rare)
[2] Roast only if high quality.		2	160° (medium)
Otherwise, braise.		2¼	170° (well done)
LAMB			
Leg	6	3	175° (medium)
		3½	180° (well done)
	8	4	175° (medium)
		4½	180° (well done)
VEAL			
Leg (piece)	5	2½ to 3	170° (well done)
Shoulder	6	3½	170° (well done)
Rolled Shoulder	3 to 5	3 to 3½	170° (well done)

POULTRY ROASTING GUIDE

Type of Poultry	Ready-To-Cook Weight	Oven Temperature	Approx. Total Roasting Time
TURKEY	6 to 8 lbs.	325°	2½ to 3 hrs.
	8 to 12 lbs.	325°	3 to 3½ hrs.
	12 to 16 lbs.	325°	3½ to 4 hrs.
	16 to 20 lbs.	325°	4 to 4½ hrs.
	20 to 24 lbs.	300°	5 to 6 hrs.
CHICKEN (Unstuffed)	2 to 2½ lbs.	400°	1 to 1½ hrs.
	2½ to 4 lbs.	400°	1½ to 2½ hrs.
	4 to 8 lbs.	325°	3 to 5 hrs.
DUCK (Unstuffed)	3 to 5 lbs.	325°	2½ to 3 hrs.

NOTE: Small chickens are roasted at 400° so that they brown well in the short cooking time. They may also be done at 325° but will take longer and will not be as brown. Increase cooking time 15 to 20 minutes for stuffed chicken and duck.

PEKING BEEF

Cut slits at random in a 3 to 5 pound beef roast (any cut). Insert slivers of garlic or onions or both down into the slits. Pour 1 cup vinegar over the meat, making sure it runs down into the slits where the garlic or onions have been placed. Refrigerate for 24-48 hours. After marinating, place in a big, heavy pot (iron, if possible) and brown in oil until nearly burned on all sides. Pour 2 cups of strong black coffee over the meat. Add 2 cups of water; cover. Simmer on top of the stove for 4-6 hours. Season 20 minutes before serving time. Will melt in your mouth and very tasty. The juice makes very good gravy.

Phyllis Granum, Moorhead, Mn.

NEW CHINA INN CHINESE BEEF WITH BEANS

1/4 c. vegetable oil
1 lb. sliced beef tenderloin or other tender beef strips
2 garlic cloves, minced
1/2 tsp. salt
1 lb. fresh green beans

1 large sweet onion, cut into 8 to 10 wedges
1/2 c. chicken broth
1 tsp. cornstarch
1 tsp. Chinese bead molasses, oyster sauce or Kitchen Bouquet for color

Pour 2 tablespoons of the oil into a very hot wok and quickly stir-fry the beef strips with the garlic and salt. Remove beef strips; add remaining oil to wok. Heat to frying temperature, then separately stir-fry green beans and onion, a few at a time, oil-blanching quickly in a minute. When all green beans and onion are oil-blanched, drain excess oil and return beef, beans and onion to wok; add chicken stock, in which the cornstarch and molasses have been stirred. Cook, turning food carefully, only until juices thicken and coat food. Serve to 4.

St. Cloud, Mn.

MARY LOU'S CROCK POT BEEF

Beef (either chunked or
   roast)
10 1/2 oz. beef consomme
1/2 c. wine

1/4 c. flour
1/4 c. bread crumbs
Salt and pepper

    Mushrooms make a nice addition if added towards end
of cooking period (8 to 10 hours on low). Serve over
noodles.

                Helen Teeuwen, Minneapolis, Mn.

MONGOLIAN BEEF

1 lb. flank steak, shredded
1 egg white
1/2 tsp. salt
1 Tbsp. cornstarch
2-4 c. oil for deep frying

1/2 c. bamboo shoots,
   shredded
1 c. scallions (green parts
   only), cut into 1 inch
   pieces

    Sauce:

1 Tbsp. sherry
2 Tbsp. Hoisin sauce
2 Tbsp. soy sauce
2 Tbsp. chicken stock

1/2 tsp. sugar
1 tsp. cornstarch
1/2 tsp. chili paste with
   garlic

    Combine beef, egg white, salt and 1 tablespoon corn-
starch; mix well with hand. Heat oil for deep frying. Deep
fry beef 30 seconds; drain. Add 2 tablespoons of oil to a
hot wok; stir-fry bamboo shoots and scallions 1 minute.
Combine sherry, Hoisin sauce, soy sauce, chicken stock,
sugar, cornstarch and chili paste in a bowl. Add to vegetables in wok; bring to a boil. Add beef. Stir-fry quickly
until all ingredients are thoroughly heated. Serves 2-4.

                St. Cloud, Mn.

NEW CHINA INN TOMATO PEPPER BEEF

1 lb. sliced beef tenderloin
1 1/4 tsp. black bean sauce
2 garlic cloves, finely
   minced
1/2 tsp. salt
2 Tbsp. oil
1 green pepper, cut into 1/2
   inch lengthwise strips

2 medium size sweet onions,
   cut into eighths lengthwise
2 tomatoes, cut into eighths
1/2 c. chicken bouillon
1 tsp. cornstarch
1/2 tsp. Chinese bead
   molasses, or Kitchen Bouquet, for color, if desired

Sear the beef with the black bean sauce, garlic and salt in the oil in a hot wok. Remove the beef; add the green pepper and onions and stir-fry until the vegetables are just beginning to get tender. Add the beef and tomatoes; stir in the chicken stock, thickened with cornstarch and Chinese molasses. Stir just until the sauce thickens and coats the foods. Serves 4.

St. Cloud, Mn.

BONELESS BRISKET

3-4 lb. brisket
3 medium onions, sliced
1 (12 oz.) bottle of beer
1 Tbsp. brown sugar

1 clove garlic, minced
1/4 tsp. thyme
6 whole peppercorns
1 bay leaf
Salt and pepper

Trim fat from meat; salt and pepper to taste. Place brisket in a large brown and bag (or crock pot); cover meat with sliced onions. Mix all other ingredients; pour over meat. Bake in 350° oven for 3 1/2 to 4 hours. If gravy is desired, skim excess fat from juices. Remove bay leaf and thicken with flour/water paste.

Irene L. Moe, Fargo, N.D.

MOCK FILET MIGNON

1 1/2 lb. hamburger
1 c. cooked rice
1/2 c. onion, chopped
1 clove garlic, chopped
  (optional)

2 Tbsp. Worcestershire
  sauce
1 1/2 tsp. salt
1 1/4 tsp. pepper
Canned mushrooms

Mix together; form patties and wrap with bacon. Secure with toothpicks. Broil till done; turn once.

Rhea Layne, Sauk Rapids, Mn.

ROAST BEEF AU VIN

1 (3 lb.) sirloin tip roast
Salt and pepper to taste
Strip of suet

3/4 c. blackberry wine
4 Tbsp. flour

Season roast with salt and pepper. Place roast on

1507-82

aluminum foil; place suet on top of roast. Fold foil over roast; seal top and one end of foil. Pour wine in open end; seal. Place on baking sheet. Bake at 325° to desired doneness. Drain roast drippings from foil package. Mix 1/2 cup water, 4 tablespoons flour and 2 cups roast drippings in large skillet. Cook over low heat until thickened, stirring well. Pour remaining drippings into thickened mixture gradually, stirring constantly. Cook over low heat to desired gravy consistency. Serve gravy with roast.

Stella Bliss, Minneapolis, Mn.

ROAST BEEF BARBECUE

5-6 lb. roast	2 Tbsp. Worcestershire sauce
Small bottle of catsup	2 medium onions, diced
Small bottle of chili sauce	1 bay leaf
6 Tbsp. mustard	4 Tbsp. brown sugar
1 Tbsp. vinegar	1/2 green pepper, diced

Mix all ingredients; pour over roast. Cook 7 hours in slow cooker or 225° oven in covered roaster. Slice meat; skim off grease. Return meat to sauce. Serve over buns.

Mrs. Gary L. Hagen, Princeton, Mn.

FORGOTTEN BEEF ROAST

Place roast on sheet of heavy aluminum foil; sprinkle with minced onion and pour a can of undiluted cream of celery soup or cream of mushroom soup or golden mushroom soup over the roast. Seal the edges of the foil tightly and place in a 300° F. oven for about 1 hour per pound of meat. (Four pounds would be 4 hours.) This roast makes its own gravy.

Lorraine H. Follrath, Anoka, Mn.

OVERNIGHT BEST EVER BEEF ROAST

Put a 6 pound sirloin tip beef roast in roasting pan. Pour over it 2 jars Heinz mushroom gravy and 2 packages Lipton dry onion soup mix, 1 cup Wish-Bone Italian dressing and 2 cans mushrooms. Roast at 350° for 3 hours. Remove the meat from drippings; cool slightly and cover well. Put in refrigerator. Put the drippings in a bowl and also put in refrigerator. Next day, slice the beef. Put it in a large casserole. Skim the fat off the top of drippings and pour over the meat. Reheat for 1 hour in 350° oven.

Joan Norton, Hibbing, Mn.

POT ROAST WITH POTATO PANCAKES

Guy Evans Springer started at Murray's in 1938 as a fry cook when it was in a different location. He began cooking in Denver, Colorado in 1920. Then he deserted the kitchen and started growing things to cook in one on a farm in the Dakotas. In 1930 he arrived in Minneapolis to resume his cooking career. Steaks are his most frequent order, but one of his specialties is pot roast with potato pancakes.

6 lb. choice beef round	1 tsp. grated onion
Salt and pepper	Salt
Flour	Chopped parsley
Beef stock	4 eggs
Celery, carrots, onions	1 Tbsp. flour
2 or 3 large potatoes, grated	

Season beef with salt and pepper; flour well and brown on all sides. Add beef stock; simmer about 3 hours or until tender. Add celery, carrots and onions about an hour before roast is done. Mix the rest of the ingredients together for the pancakes. Fry cakes in hot oil or lard.

Dena Stoddard, St. Louis Park, Mn.

TENDER ROAST

3-4 lb. roast	1 pkg. Lipton onion soup
1 can of beer	mix

Place roast in a 9x13 inch pan; pour onion soup mix and beer over roast. Cover with foil. Bake at 325° until desired doneness. Liquid makes excellent gravy.

Lynn Cooch, Minneapolis, Mn.

BEEF STEAK PIE

1 lb. round steak, cut in
   1 inch cubes
3 Tbsp. fat
3 small onions, thinly sliced
3 Tbsp. flour
1 1/2 tsp. salt
1/4 tsp. pepper
Dash of thyme
Dash of garlic salt
2 c. water
3 medium potatoes, pared and
   sliced

Dredge meat in flour; cook in 3 tablespoons fat in skillet about 15 minutes, browning all sides. Add onions; cook about 10 minutes, until golden brown. Put in 2 quart baking dish. Sprinkle with 3 tablespoons flour and seasonings; pour water over top. Cover and bake at 350° for 45 minutes to 1 hour; remove from oven. Increase temperature to 425°. Place potatoes on top. Sprinkle with salt and a little paprika. Bake 30 minutes longer, till potatoes are tender. Uncover the last few minutes to brown. Makes 4 to 6 servings.

Bernice Fonos, Minneapolis, Mn.

ROLLED BEEF STEAKS

8 medium size minute steaks
3/4 c. celery, chopped fine
1 medium onion, chopped
   fine
1/2 c. cracker crumbs
2 1/2 Tbsp. oleo (or butter)
2 Tbsp. bacon grease
3 Tbsp. Parmesan cheese
2 tsp. beef bouillon, dissolved in water
Garlic powder to taste
Salt and pepper to taste

Flatten steaks (do not break); season with salt, pepper and garlic powder on both sides. Saute onion and celery in oleo (or butter) until soft. Put in bowl; add salt, pepper, garlic powder, cracker crumbs and Parmesan cheese until mixture stays together. (Oleo from onions and celery will make this mixture stay together.) Spoon onto steaks and roll up; tie with string. Brown in bacon grease and bake in oven about 45 minutes to 1 hour, until tender. Keep basting with beef bouillon and water so they do not dry out. (I saute another onion and serve over them.)

Pat Hornung, St. Paul, Mn.

CHICKEN FRIED ROUND STEAK

1 1/2 lb. round steak, 1/2 inch thick	2/3 c. fine cracker crumbs
1 beaten egg	1/4 c. salad oil
1 Tbsp. milk	Salt and pepper

Pound round steak thoroughly; cut in serving pieces. Blend egg and milk. Dip meat in egg mixture, then in crumbs. Slowly brown meat in hot oil, turning once. Season with salt and pepper. Cover; cook over low heat 30 to 40 minutes or until tender.

Helen H. Clark, Grand Forks, N.D.

STEAKS CUJO

4 Tbsp. butter or margarine	1 medium green pepper, cut into strips
4 beef loin steaks (about 3/4 inch thick)	1 medium clove garlic, minced
1/4 lb. mushrooms, sliced	1/4 c. shredded carrot
1 c. green onions, cut into 1 inch pieces	1/4 c. light rum
1/3 c. beef broth	Chopped parsley

In skillet, melt 2 tablespoons butter. Add steaks and cook to desired doneness, turning once. Remove to serving platter; keep warm. Season with salt and pepper. Add remaining 2 tablespoons butter to pan. Brown mushrooms. Add onion, green pepper and garlic. Cook until vegetables are tender. Add beef broth and carrot; remove from heat. Add rum. Spoon mixture over steaks. Garnish with parsley. Makes 4 servings.

St. Cloud, Mn.

GOOD ROUND STEAK

Lay round steak on cookie sheet lined with foil. Pour over steak, mixed together:

1 (5 oz.) bottle A.1. steak sauce	1 pkg. dry onion soup mix
	1 can mushroom soup

Cover with foil; cook 3 hours at 325°.

Jeanie Rose, Tracy, Mn.

HE-MAN STEAK

3 lb. sirloin steak, 1 1/2 -
  2 inches thick
1 (12 oz.) can beer
1/2 c. chili sauce or catsup
1/2 c. salad oil
2 Tbsp. soy sauce
1 Tbsp. mustard

1/2 tsp. Tabasco sauce
1 medium onion, chopped
2 cloves garlic, minced
1 1/2 tsp. salt
1/2 tsp. pepper
1/2 tsp. liquid smoke

Combine all ingredients, except steak; simmer 10-15 minutes. Brush both sides of steak with sauce; grill 4 inches from medium hot coals for 10-12 minutes. Turn; baste with extra sauce and broil 8-10 minutes. Serve with remaining sauce. Makes 6-8 servings.

Colleen Landwehr, St. Cloud, Mn.

PEPPER STEAK

1-2 lb. round steak, sliced
  thin (cut while still
  frozen)
1 medium onion, cubed
2 small bell peppers, cubed
1 large can whole tomatoes,
  cut in halves (save juice
  for thinning if needed)

2 c. sliced, fresh
  mushrooms
2 cloves of garlic, grated
  fine or pressed
Salt and pepper
1/3 c. soy sauce
1 c. beef bouillon
2 or 3 Tbsp. cornstarch

Prepare vegetables and meat. Cook meat in skillet with 2 tablespoons oil on medium heat with garlic, salt and pepper. Cook until just done, about 10 minutes. Put in bowl; set aside. In skillet, cook mushrooms with 2 tablespoons margarine about 10 minutes. Add onion and bell pepper; cook 10 minutes. Add tomatoes, bouillon and mixture of soy sauce and cornstarch; stir until thick. Add meat; stir until mixed and simmer for 15 minutes. Serve with rice.

Arlene Lindgren, Princeton, Mn.

CHINESE LANTERN GREEN PEPPER STEAK
WITH TOMATO

4 tsp. peanut oil
1/3 tsp. salt
1 Tbsp. cooking wine

8 oz. beef tenderloin or flank
  steak, sliced in very thin
  1 inch strips

Pinch of sugar
1 tsp. oyster sauce
2/3 c. water
3 large green peppers, cut
into 8 pieces each,
blanched

2 large ripe tomatoes, cut
into 6 triangular pieces
1 Tbsp. cornstarch, mixed
with 2 Tbsp. water

Have all ingredients measured and ready before you begin cooking. In Chinese wok or electric fry pan, mix oil and salt; heat until very hot. Add sliced beef and stir-fry until beef is browned, less than 1 minute. Add wine, sugar, oyster sauce, water, green peppers and tomatoes; cover and bring to boil. Again, this takes less than 1 minute. Heat must remain on high during cooking. If cooked too long, green peppers lose their crunch and tomatoes turn mushy. Stir in cornstarch-water paste and stir until thickened. Serves 3.

Variation: Add finely diced onion and ground black beans with green pepper.

St. Cloud, Mn.

BARBECUED ROUND STEAK

2 lb. round steak, 3/4 inch
thick

2 Tbsp. seasoned flour
2 Tbsp. shortening

Pound flour into steak and brown in shortening.

1 can tomato soup
1/3 c. chopped onion
1/3 c. chopped celery
1 clove garlic, minced
2 Tbsp. brown sugar

2 Tbsp. Worcestershire
sauce
2 Tbsp. lemon juice
2 tsp. prepared mustard
4 drops of Tabasco sauce

Blend together above ingredients; pour sauce over steak. Cover; cook over low heat about 1 1/2 hours. Baste now and then.

Joan Lewis, Minneapolis, Mn.

SCOTTY'S CROCK POT ROUND STEAK

Cut round steak in serving pieces; dip in flour and season with salt and pepper. Brown. Layer in crock pot with 1 package dry onion soup mix. Slice and add 3 or 4 onions. Add 1 cup water and 1 tablespoon Kitchen Bouquet. Add a little water to pan meat was browned in and add these drippings. Cook 5 hours on low. Just before serving, remove meat and add 1 cup sour cream. (Can use sour cream mix.)

Helen Teeuwen, Minneapolis, Mn.

PARSLEY STEAK ROLL

1 can mushroom pieces
1 diced onion
3 Tbsp. Parmesan cheese
Salt and pepper to taste

Dry parsley flakes
1 large round steak
1 Tbsp. cornstarch
1 can beef broth

Place mushrooms, onion, cheese, salt, pepper and parsley over steak; roll into large roll. Serve with string or heavy thread. Brown in fat on all sides in ovenproof fry pan; drain off excess fat. Stir cornstarch in small amount of broth. Add remaining broth; pour over steak. Cover; bake at 350° for 1 hour. Serves 6 to 8.

Stella Bliss, Minneapolis, Mn.

SALISBURY STEAK

2 c. cooked rice (I use
   instant)
1 lb. ground beef

1/2 lb. ground pork (I use
   sausage)
Salt and pepper
1 egg, beaten

Combine all ingredients; mix well. Shape into 6 to 9 patties. Bake in 350° oven for 20 minutes. To prepare onion soup sauce, add 2 1/2 cups hot water to a package of onion soup mix; cook 10 minutes. Add 2 tablespoons of flour to 1/2 cup water; blend well. Add to soup mix; let thicken. Pour soup mixture over steaks; bake them another 20 minutes. If desired, you can leave out the ground pork and make the meat patties from 2 pounds of ground beef.

Mrs. D.H. Richardson, St. Paul, Mn.

SWISS BLISS

1/2 tsp. oleo
2 lb. chuck steak, cut in
   1 inch thick slices
1 env. onion soup mix
1/4 tsp. salt

1/2 lb. mushrooms, sliced
1/2 green pepper, sliced
1 (1 lb.) can tomatoes,
   drained (reserve liquid),
   chopped

222

Pepper   1 Tbsp. A.1. steak sauce
1/2 c. tomato juice   1 Tbsp. cornstarch

In center of large sheet of heavy duty foil, spread the oleo. Arrange meat on foil. Sprinkle with soup mix, mushrooms, green pepper and tomatoes. Season with salt and pepper. Mix juice, A.1. sauce and cornstarch; pour over meat and vegetables. Double-fold edges of foil to seal well. Bake 2 hours at 350°. Sprinkle with parsley before serving.

Carolyn Brudevold, Fargo, N.D.

BURGER BUNDLES

1 lb. ground beef   1 Tbsp. ketchup
1/3 c. milk   2 tsp. Worcestershire sauce

Mix and pat out into 5 circles. Make Stove Top stuffing according to package; put dressing in middle of patty. Bring hamburger up around stuffing; place in baking dish. Pour 1 can cream of mushroom soup, thinned a little, around bundles. Bake 1 hour at 350°.

Cathy Rudolph, Grand Rapids, Mn.

CASSEROLE

1 1/2 lb. ground beef   1 can mushrooms
1 medium onion   1 lb. shredded Mozzarella
2 (15 oz.) cans pizza sauce   cheese
2 cans Cheddar cheese soup   1 (10 oz.) bag noodles

Cook noodles as directed on package; divide into two 9x13 inch greased cake pans. Brown ground beef with chopped onion. Add pizza sauce, cheese soups, mushrooms and 1/2 pound of Mozzarella cheese. Simmer until cheese is melted. Pour over cooked noodles in pan; mix. Spread evenly in pan and bake 45 minutes. Add 1/2 pound of Mozzarella cheese the last 10 minutes. Also can be done in crock pot; keep it on low.

Adeline Hortsch, St. Cloud, Mn.

CASSEROLE

1 lb. hamburger
1 chopped onion
1 pkg. macaroni rings, cooked
1 can cream style corn

1 can chicken noodle soup
1/2 green pepper, chopped fine
1 tsp. salt
Pepper to taste

Brown meat and onion together. Add other ingredients; mix well. Place in casserole; sprinkle top with crushed potato chips. Bake 1 hour in a 350° oven.

Liz Tuft, St. Paul, Mn.

CASSEROLE QUICKIE

1 lb. hamburger, browned
1 layer sliced raw carrots
1 layer sliced raw onions
1 layer sliced raw potatoes
1/4 c. Minute rice, uncooked

1 can cream of mushroom soup
1 can cream of chicken soup
1 c. milk
Salt and pepper

Place alternate layers of potatoes, carrots, onion, rice and hamburger in a 2 quart casserole. Mix soups together with milk; pour over layers. Bake at 325° for 60-75 minutes.

Maxine Olsen, Duluth, Mn.

ALL IN ONE CASSEROLE

2 medium potatoes, diced   1 c. whole kernel corn

Sprinkle with salt and pepper; pour over 1/2 can of cream of tomato soup, diluted as directed on can. Add:

1 small-medium onion, chopped

2 Tbsp. chopped green pepper
1 lb. uncooked hamburger

Sprinkle with salt and pepper and pour over the rest of the tomato soup. One small can of kidney beans may be added to the top of this. Bake at 350° for 1 1/2 hours, covered; uncover and bake for 1/2 hour longer.

Ruth Koepke, Silver Bay, Mn.

BORSCH-STYLE CASSEROLE

2 lb. beef short ribs,
  cut up
1 Tbsp. cooking oil
2 c. sliced carrots
1 c. sliced celery
1 c. sliced onion
1 1/2 c. turnip strips (opt.)
4 c. water

1 (6 oz.) can tomato paste
1 Tbsp. salt
1/4 tsp. pepper
1 c. water
1 Tbsp. sugar
1 Tbsp. vinegar
1 small head cabbage, cut in
  wedges
Dairy sour cream

In 4 1/2 quart roaster, brown ribs in oil; drain off fat. Add carrots, turnips, celery and onion. Blend together the 4 cups water, tomato paste, salt and pepper; pour over vegetables in roaster. Cover; bake at 350° for 2 hours. Skim off fat. Combine remaining 1 cup water, sugar and vinegar; add to meat mixture. Add cabbage wedges atop mixture, pushing partially into liquid. Cover and continue baking 1 1/2 hours more. Pass sour cream to spoon atop each.

Mrs. Gary L. Hagen, Princeton, Mn.

"SO GOOD CABBAGE CASSEROLE"

Shred 1 head of cabbage coarsely. Saute 1 pound of hamburger and 1 medium sized chopped onion in butter until heated through, not browned. Season to taste. (I drain about half of the grease.) In bottom of casserole, put 1 layer of cabbage; spread meat mixture over it and finish with the rest of the cabbage. Pour over all 1 can of condensed tomato soup. Cover casserole and bake at 325° for 1 1/2 hours, or until cabbage is tender.

Diane Kitch, Duluth, Mn.

CABBAGE-HAMBURGER CASSEROLE

1 head of cabbage,
  shredded or chopped

1 lb. hamburger
1 can tomato soup

Layer hamburger and cabbage in a casserole; pour the soup on top (no water). Cover and bake in 350° oven for 1 hour, until cabbage is soft.

Bonnie Sovick, Ortenville, Mn.

CHEESEBURGER CASSEROLE

1 lb. hamburger
1/4 c. chopped onion
3/4 tsp. salt
Pepper
1/8 c. ketchup

1 (8 oz.) can tomato sauce
1 (8 oz.) pkg. American
cheese slices
1 can refrigerator biscuits

Lightly brown beef and onion; drain. Add salt, pepper, ketchup and tomato sauce; heat thoroughly. Turn into a 1 1/2 quart casserole. Top with cheese, then with biscuits. Bake in hot oven, 425°, until biscuits are golden brown. Makes about 6 servings.

Rhea Layne, Sauk Rapids, Mn.

CHIPPED BEEF CASSEROLE

6 c. water
1 1/2 tsp. salt
1 tsp. oil
1 c. uncooked macaroni
1/2 c. finely chopped onion
1 (10 3/4 oz.) can condensed
cream of mushroom soup
1 Tbsp. water

1 (2 1/2 oz.) pkg. dried or
smoked beef, cut into thin
strips
1/4 c. milk
1 small tomato, sliced
1/2 c. shredded Cheddar
cheese

The night before, combine water, salt and oil in 2 quart glass bowl; cover with plate. Microwave on High for 11 to 13 minutes or until water boils; add macaroni. Microwave on High, uncovered, for 7 to 8 minutes or until macaroni is just about tender; drain. Combine onion and water in 1 1/2 quart glass casserole; cover with casserole lid. Microwave on High for 2 to 2 1/2 minutes or until just about tender. Add soup, beef, milk and macaroni; mix well. Cover and refrigerate up to 2 days. To serve, microwave on High, covered, 7 to 8 minutes or until hot, stirring once. Top with tomato slices and cheese. Microwave on High, uncovered, 2 1/2 to 3 minutes, or until cheese is melted. Makes 4 or 5 servings. If serving casserole immediately, decrease baking time to 5 or 6 minutes before adding cheese and tomatoes. Casserole can be frozen up to 2 months. Thaw in refrigerator before heating.

St. Cloud, Mn.

TASTY DRIED BEEF CASSEROLE

2 Tbsp. butter or margarine
2 Tbsp. finely chopped
   onion
1 (2 1/2 oz.) jar dried beef
1 can condensed cream of
   chicken soup

3/4 soup can of milk
1/4 tsp. pepper
4 oz. macaroni, uncooked
1/2 c. shredded sharp
   Cheddar cheese

Melt butter in saucepan; add onion and cook until tender, about 5 minutes. Cut dried beef with scissors into small pieces. Add to onion mixture; continue cooking until beef is lightly browned. Stir in soup, milk and pepper; bring to a boil. Cook macaroni as directed on package, using unsalted water; drain. Rinse with cold water; drain again. Combine macaroni with sauce; pour into 1 1/2 quart casserole; sprinkle with cheese. Bake, uncovered, at 350° for 20 to 30 minutes. Yields 6 to 8 servings.

Bessie Wilke, Detroit Lakes, Mn.

EASY HOT DISH CASSEROLE

1 1/2 lb. hamburger
1 (8 oz.) pkg. egg noodles,
   uncooked
1 can mushroom soup
1 can chicken gumbo soup

1 can vegetable soup
1 1/2 cans water
3 medium carrots, shredded
1/2 c. celery, finely
   chopped
1 c. potato chips

Butter baking dish or small roaster. Crumble raw hamburger on bottom; add uncooked noodles and soup, diluted with water. Season with salt and pepper. Add carrots and celery; mix well. Bake at 350° for 45 minutes. Do not stir while baking. Crush potato chips over top and bake 15 minutes more.

Norma Berglund, Two Harbors, Mn.

FOR THE CROWD CASSEROLE

1 1/2 lb. ground beef
1 c. chopped onion
1 (12 oz.) can corn, drained
1 can cream of mushroom
   soup
1 can cream of chicken soup

1 c. dairy sour cream
1/4 c. chopped pimento
3/4 tsp. salt
1/4 tsp. pepper
1 c. buttered bread crumbs
3 c. noodles, cooked

Brown meat; add onion. Cook till tender, but not brown. Add corn, soups, sour cream, pimento, salt and pepper; mix well. Stir in noodles; pour into casserole. Sprinkle crumbs over top. Bake at 350° for 30 minutes or until hot. Serves 8-10.

Marlys Swehla, Albert Lea, Mn.

GOLDEN BEEF CASSEROLE

1 lb. lean ground beef
1/4 c. diced onion
1/4 c. diced green pepper
3/4 tsp. salt
1/8 tsp. pepper

1 (10 1/2 oz.) can cream of
   mushroom soup, undiluted
1 c. shredded Cheddar
   cheese
2 (12 oz.) cans whole kernel
   corn, drained

Brown beef, onion and green pepper in small amount of melted shortening in large heavy frying pan. Mix in remaining ingredients; spoon into greased 1 3/4 quart casserole. Bake in preheated moderate oven, 350°, for about 40 minutes. Yield: 4 to 6 servings.

Dode Desch, St. Paul, Mn.

GRAVY-MEAT CASSEROLE

1 lb. ground beef
1/2 c. bread crumbs (dry)
2 Tbsp. chopped onion
1/8 tsp. pepper

1/4 lb. pork sausage
1/3 c. evaporated milk
1 tsp. chili powder

Combine and mix well. Shape meat balls (drop by teaspoon and brown on a cookie sheet, 15x10 inches with edge in oven). Place in casserole (9x13 inch pan works well, too). Heat until steaming:

1 can cream of mushroom
   soup
1 can cream of celery soup

1 c. evaporated milk
1/2 c. water

Pour over meat balls. Top with baking powder biscuits or refrigerator rolls. Fifteen biscuits is about the right amount for a 9x13 inch pan. Bake at 350° for 30 minutes.

Bessie Wilke, Detroit Lakes, Mn.

GROUND BEEF CASSEROLE

1 lb. ground beef, browned
1 c. rice, uncooked
1/2 c. celery
1 small onion, chopped

1 can cream of mushroom
 soup
1 can cream of chicken soup
1 soup can of water
1 tsp. soy sauce

Bake in 350° oven for about 2 hours. Serves 6.
Inez Hagen, Duluth, Mn.
Similar recipe submitted by: Jane Paulson, Virginia, Mn.

HAMBURGER CASSEROLE FOR ONE

1/4 lb. ground beef (lean
 hamburger or ground
 turkey can be used)
1/2 chopped onion
1/2 tomato or 6 cherry
 tomatoes
1/2 green pepper

1/2 celery rib
1/2 tsp. basil leaves
1 (5-6 inch long) zucchini,
 thinly sliced
Garlic powder (optional)
Salt and pepper (optional)

Saute meat and onion together; don't add fat, just
stir until some fat has melted. Add chopped tomatoes; stir.
Add chopped green pepper and celery; stir. Add seasonings; cover and simmer 5 minutes. Add sliced zucchini and
simmer a few more minutes.
Rhea Thoms, Jamestown, N.D.

HAMBURGER CASSEROLE

1 lb. hamburger
1 medium onion, diced
1 can mushrooms, drained
1 small can corn Niblets,
 drained

1/2 pkg. egg noodles
1-2 cans cream of mushroom
 soup with 3/4 can of milk
1 can onion rings

Brown hamburger and onion together; drain fat off.
Set aside. Boil egg noodles as directed on package; drain.
In 2 quart casserole, add hamburger, onion, mushrooms,
corn and egg noodles; mix. Take 1 can of cream of mushroom soup; dilute with 3/4 can of milk. Heat on stove on
low temperature until soup and milk are mixed well. Add to
hamburger mixture; mix well. If mixture looks dry, add

second can of mushroom soup, as mixture gets dry when baking. Add can of onion rings to top. Cover and bake at 350° for 1 - 1 1/2 hours. Check and mix occasionally.

JoAnne Andresen, Duluth, Mn.

HAMBURGER MACARONI CASSEROLE

2 Tbsp. fat
1/2 c. chopped onion
1 lb. ground beef (or 3/4 lb. ground beef and 1/4 lb. pork sausage meat)
3 1/2 c. cooked or canned tomatoes (one No. 2 1/2 can)
1 c. diced celery
1/2 c. cut up green pepper

2 tsp. salt
1/4 tsp. celery salt or seasoned salt
1/8 tsp. pepper
1 tsp. Worcestershire sauce
1/4 tsp. chili powder
1 (8 oz.) pkg. elbow macaroni, cooked, rinsed and drained
Chopped parsley
Grated cheese

Preheat fry pan to 300°; add fat. When melted, add onion; fry, stirring until just beginning to brown. Add meat. Place cover in Spatter Shield position. Turn dial to 400°; fry, stirring frequently until browned; spoon off excess fat. Add tomatoes, celery, green pepper and seasonings. Bring to boil; cover. Close vent; simmer about 25 minutes. Add cooked macaroni; simmer 10 minutes longer, stirring occasionally. Sprinkle with chopped parsley and cheese. Serve directly from fry pan. Serves 6.

Note: Sauce may be cooked separately and poured over hot, cooked spaghetti or macaroni. Also, 1 minced clove of garlic and 1 cup sliced mushrooms may be sauteed with onion, or 4 ounce can of mushrooms may be added with tomatoes. Recipe may be increased, if desired, by 1/2 amount of all ingredients.

Temperature: 400° to brown; about 220° to finish.
Time: 35 minutes.

Margaret McKenney, Minneapolis, Mn.

ITALIAN CASSEROLE

1/2 lb. bacon
1 medium onion
3 c. spaghetti, broken
1 (1 lb.) can tomatoes

1 (6 oz.) can tomato sauce
1 can spinach, drained
Parmesan cheese

Dice bacon and 1 medium onion; fry until slightly crisp. Boil broken spaghetti; drain. Spray casserole with Pam or no stick. Pour cooked spaghetti in casserole; add vegetable and crisp bacon. Mix well; sprinkle the top generously with Parmesan cheese. Bake at 400° for 35 minutes.

Mary Jones, Spirit Lake, Ia.

CASSEROLE ITALIANO

1 lb. ground beef
1/3 c. chopped onion
1 medium glove garlic or
   1/2 tsp. garlic salt
1 tsp. oregano
1/2 tsp. salt

1 can tomato soup
1/3 c. water
1 c. shredded American
   cheese
2 c. cooked wide noodles

Brown beef with onion, garlic and seasoning. Combine in 1 1/2 quart casserole with soup, water, noodles and cheese. Bake in 350° oven for 30 to 45 minutes.

Becky Anderson, Duluth, Mn.

JACKPOT CASSEROLE

1 lb. hamburger, browned
   with 1/4 c. onion
1 can tomato soup
1 1/2 c. water
Salt and pepper

1/2 (8 oz.) pkg. noodles,
   cooked
1 (No. 2) can creamed corn
1 c. American cheese,
   grated

Bake at 350° for 45 minutes.

Anne Aune, Minneapolis, Mn.

MEAL-IN-ONE CASSEROLE

1 1/2 lb. ground beef
1/2 c. chopped onion
1 (10 oz.) pkg. frozen
   mixed vegetables
1 1/2 c. sliced, cooked
   carrots
1 (10 oz.) can cream of
   mushroom soup

1 (10 oz.) can tomato soup
1/4 c. water
1/4 tsp. salt
1/4 tsp. pepper
4 c. hot, mashed potatoes
1/2 c. grated Cheddar
   cheese

Brown beef and onion; drain off fat. Cook mixed vegetables according to package directions; drain. Add mixed vegetables, carrots, soup, water, salt and pepper to meat. Pour mixture into 12x8 inch baking pan. Spoon mashed potatoes in 3 lines, across top of casserole. Sprinkle cheese over potatoes. Bake, uncovered, in 350° oven for 30 minutes. Serves 6.

Dorothy Savig, Minneapolis, Mn.

MEXICAN FIESTA CASSEROLE

1 lb. ground beef
1 c. dairy sour cream
2/3 c. mayonnaise or salad
 dressing
1 c. (4 oz.) shredded sharp
 Cheddar cheese

2 Tbsp. chopped onion
2 c. Bisquick
1/2 c. cold water
2-3 medium tomatoes, thinly
 sliced
3/4 c. chopped green pepper

Heat oven to 375°. 1. Cook and stir ground beef until brown; drain and set aside. 2. Mix sour cream, mayonnaise, cheese and onion; set aside. 3. Stir Bisquick and water to a soft dough. 4. Pat dough in greased oblong pan, 13x9x2 inches, pressing dough 1/2 inch up side of pan. 5. Layer ground beef, tomatoes and green pepper; spoon sour cream mixture over top. Bake 25-30 minutes until brown. Makes 8-10 servings.

Anne Aune, Minneapolis, Mn.

POLISH CASSEROLE

Brown 1 pound ground beef; add 1 can carrots, drained, or cooked fresh carrots. Add 1 can mushroom soup, diluted with 1/2 can water. Mix together in casserole and top with tater tots. Bake at 350° for 45 minutes. Can add corn or green beans. Serves 5 or 6.

Marge Pye, St. Paul, Mn.

POTATO GROUND BEEF CASSEROLE

Line 1/3 of well greased casserole with sliced raw potatoes; cover with layer of parboiled celery, onion and green pepper (1/2 cup of each). Add 1 pound of browned, seasoned ground beef. Pour over all this 1 can of tomato soup. Bake 1 hour in 375° oven.

Goldie Mikish, Staples, Mn.

REUBEN CASSEROLE
(Meal-in-One)

1 jar sauerkraut
1/3 c. Thousand Island
  dressing

1 can Spam or other
  lunch meat
1 pkg. sliced Swiss cheese
6 slices pumpernickel bread

Mix slightly drained kraut and dressing; put in glass cake pan and top with sliced meat. Bake 15 minutes in 350° oven. Top with cheese and bread, brushed with butter. Return to oven 10 minutes more or until bread gets crusty.

Helen Teeuwen, Minneapolis, Mn.

ST. BARNABAS 5 SOUP CASSEROLE

2 lb. ground beef
1 can cream of mushroom
  soup
1 can cream of chicken soup
1 can beef with barley soup

2 onions, chopped
1 can cream of celery soup
1 can chicken with rice soup
1 pkg. chow mein noodles

Brown ground beef and onions together; add soups. Just before baking, add 2/3 package of chow mein noodles. Mix well; add remaining noodles to top. Bake at 350° for 45 minutes.

Virginia Miller, Anoka, Mn.

THREE BEAN CASSEROLE

1 lb. ground beef
1/2 lb. bacon, cut up
1 c. chopped onion
1 c. catsup
1/2 c. brown sugar
1 1/2 Tbsp. vinegar

1 tsp. mustard
1 can kidney beans
1 can lima beans or butter
  beans
1 can pork and beans

Brown lightly the first 3 ingredients. Mix the rest in order given. Bake in slow oven, 325° to 350°, for 1 1/2 hours. Serves many. Use Dutch oven or large casserole.

Mary Ann Ohman, Fargo, N.D.

KERRIE'S FAVORITE KASSEROLE

Prepare 1 package noodles Romanoff according to package directions. Brown 1 1/2 pounds hamburger, lean, with 1 tablespoon chopped onion. Mix prepared noodles Romanoff and meat with:

1 can cream of mushroom soup	1 small jar pimento, chopped
1/2 c. milk	3 slices white bread, dried and cubed

Put in large covered casserole and bake at 350° for 45 minutes. Remove from oven; top with 1/2 pound sharp Cheddar cheese, cubed, and return to oven for an additional 10 minutes until cheese melts and bubbles. (Do not cover after cheese is added.)

Kerrie C. Applen
Mrs. Norma Applen, Minneapolis, Mn.

CHILI

2 lb. ground beef	1 large onion

Saute onion and ground beef. Add:

3 (8 oz.) cans Hunt's tomato sauce	2 tsp. paprika
1 qt. whole tomatoes	1 tsp. garlic powder
3 tsp. salt	1/4 tsp. pepper
4 tsp. chili powder	Dash of red pepper
2 tsp. cumin	1 bay leaf

Simmer 1 hour, then add 3 (16 ounce) cans kidney beans, drained. Heat until heated through, then simmer another 30 minutes.

Alicia Woodford, Montevideo, Mn.
Similar recipe submitted by: Gerri Ruprecht, St. Cloud, Mn.

LORIE'S CHILI

1 medium onion	2 small cans tomato sauce
1 small green pepper	1 small can tomato paste
3 lb. hamburger	1 Tbsp. salt
1 pt. tomatoes	2 Tbsp. chili powder

Last 5 minutes, add 1 can chili beans.

Sally Bartsch, Blaine, Mn.

MAMA'S HOMEMADE CHILI

1 lb. ground beef
2 cans kidney beans
1 (42 oz.) can tomato juice
   or V-8 juice

2 ribs celery, cut in small
   pieces
2 small potatoes, cut in small
   pieces
1 pkg. chili seasoning

Brown ground beef in Dutch oven or large kettle. Drain; add tomato juice, celery and potatoes. Cook on low heat till mixture starts to boil. Turn to simmer; add chili seasoning and kidney beans. Cook on simmer until potatoes and celery are tender. Serve plain with crackers or over rice.

Mary Paul, Minneapolis, Mn.

CHILE CON CARNE

1 can kidney beans
1 can tomato soup
1 lb. ground beef
   (hamburger)
1 Tbsp. shortening

1 tsp. salt
1/8 tsp. pepper
1/4 tsp. chili powder (or as
   you like)
2 Tbsp. chopped onion

Melt shortening in a pan; add onion and beef. Stir until well mixed. Cover and cook until onion and beef are well browned; stir. Add beans and soup; season. Cook for 1/2 hour; stir occasionally.

Mrs. Verne Andal, St. Cloud, Mn.
Similar recipes submitted by: Colleen Landwehr, St. Cloud, Mn., Dena Stoddard, St. Louis Park, Mn.

VEG CHILI

2 lb. hamburger
1/2 lb. sausage
2 cans kidney beans
1 large can tomatoes

3 large onions
4 large potatoes
Salt and pepper to taste
Chili powder to taste

Fry hamburger and sausage with onions until brown. Put this into a kettle; add rest of ingredients. Add 1 box of macaroni, 1 can peas and 1 can carrots. Cook slowly until thick and done. Even better warmed up the next day.

Mildred Wills, Austin, Mn.

CHUCK WAGON SKILLET

1 lb. ground beef
2 c. uncooked medium
  noodles
2 c. (8 oz.) cubed Cheddar
  cheese
1 c. chopped celery

1/2 c. sliced ripe olives
1 (16 oz.) can stewed
  tomatoes
1/2 c. water
1 tsp. salt
1 tsp. instant minced onion

In a large covered skillet, brown beef. Add noodles, cheese, celery, olives, tomatoes, water, salt and onion. Cover; simmer 25 to 30 minutes. Yield: 6 servings.
Mankato, Mn.

HAMBURGER BISCUIT BAKE

1 lb. ground beef
1/4 c. chopped onion
4 oz. (1 c.) sharp American
  cheese, shredded (can
  use Velveeta cheese)

1/4 c. mayonnaise
2 Tbsp. snipped parsley
1 1/2 c. biscuit mix
1/2 c. milk

Vegetable Sauce*:

1 can cream of mushroom or
  cream of chicken soup

1/3 c. milk
1 small can of peas or mixed
  vegetables, drained

Cook beef and onion till meat is browned; drain excess fat. Stir in cheese, mayonnaise and parsley. Combine biscuit mix and milk; stir till moistened. Turn out onto floured surface; knead 8 to 10 times. Divide in half; roll into two 8 inch circles. Press one circle into well greased round cake dish. Spread meat mixture over biscuit; top with second biscuit. Bake at 375° for 20 to 25 minutes. Cut wedges and serve with Vegetable Sauce. While casserole is baking, mix all ingredients under *Vegetable Sauce in saucepan and heat. Serves 6.
Kathy Wakefield, Duluth, Mn.

HAMBURGER JUMBLE

1 lb. ground beef
2 c. uncooked noodles
1 c. pared, sliced, raw
  carrots

2 c. shredded cabbage
1 (1 lb.) can or 2 c. of
  home canned tomatoes
1 can cream of celery soup

1 c. water   1/2 tsp. salt
1 tsp. instant minced onion

Shape ground beef into a large patty in a large skillet; brown 5 minutes on each side, then break up into small chunks. Spoon meat chunks into 8 cup casserole, discarding excess fat. Stir noodles, cabbage, carrots, tomatoes, soup, water, instant onion and salt into skillet; blend well. Spoon into casserole; <u>cover</u>. Bake in 350° oven for 40 to 50 minutes, until noodles and vegetables are tender. Serves 6.

Bernice Fonos, Minneapolis, Mn.

HOT DAGO'S

Meat Mixture:

2 lb. hamburger	1/3 c. cracker crumbs
1 lb. sausage mixture	1/4 tsp. black pepper
(Italian)	3 eggs
3 Tbsp. salt	1/4 c. Parmesan cheese
3/4 tsp. red pepper	

Mix together really well. Form into patties; brown.

Sauce Mixture:

1 large can tomato puree	2 tsp. basil
1 can water (puree can)	1/4 tsp. oregano
1 small can tomato paste	2 tsp. salt
	1/4 tsp. red pepper

Stir together and pour over patties; cook slowly 1 - 1 1/2 hours. To serve: Have slice of garlic bread, patty and sauce with some Parmesan cheese on top. Serves 8-10.

Jim Tuft, St. Paul, Mn.

HOTDISH

1/2 c. chopped onion	2 Tbsp. butter
1 1/2 lb. hamburger	1 1/4 c. sour cream
1 can cream of chicken soup	1 pkg. noodles, cooked
1 can cream of mushroom	1 tsp. salt
soup	1 tsp. pepper
1 can whole kernel corn	1 c. crushed potato chips

Brown onion in butter; add hamburger and brown.

1507-82

Combine rest of ingredients, except potato chips; blend well. Put in a buttered casserole. Top with crushed chips and bake at 350° for 1 hour. Serves 8 to 10.

Jackie Jaenisch, Windom, Mn.

"HOT DISH"

7 c. Rice Krispies
2 c. (2 cans) chicken rice
  soup

1 can cream of chicken soup
1 lb. hamburger
1 medium onion

Brown hamburger and onion; add rest of ingredients. Bake at 350° for 1/2 hour.

Mary Paul, Minneapolis, Mn.

BARLEY HOT DISH

3/4 c. quick cooking barley
1 lb. ground beef
1 onion, minced
2 Tbsp. shortening
1 can cream of mushroom
  soup
1 can peas (use liquid)

1 can tomatoes or soup
2 c. celery
1 chopped green pepper
2 Tbsp. sugar
1 1/2 tsp. salt
Pepper

Bake at 325° for 2 hours.

G.W. Seemans, Robbinsdale, Mn.

BEAN HOTDISH

1 lb. ground beef
1 large can B&M beans
1 chopped onion

1 bottle (or less) chili sauce
1 green pepper
Salt and pepper

Chop onion and green pepper; brown with hamburger. Add other ingredients and pour into casserole. Bake about 1 hour at 325°.

Mary Jean Voss, Owatonna, Mn.

BUSY DAY HOT DISH

1 medium onion, chopped
1 can tomato soup
1/2 green pepper, chopped
1/2 lb. cheese
1 Tbsp. Worcestershire
   sauce
1 (16 oz.) can cream style
   corn
8 oz. spaghetti, cooked and
   drained
1/2 lb. hamburger
Small bottle of stuffed olives

Fry onion, pepper and hamburger; add rest of ingredients and cook 5 minutes. Turn into buttered 2 quart casserole; put cheese on top. Bake 1/2 hour in 350° oven.

Clifford H. Carlson, Saginaw, Mn.

CABBAGE-HAMBURGER HOT DISH

In skillet, melt 3 tablespoons butter or margarine. Add 1 medium chopped onion; brown the onion. Add 1/2 pound hamburger; heat through to remove the pink color. Add 3/4 teaspoon salt and sprinkle of pepper. Put 3 cups coarsely sliced cabbage in the bottom of a well greased baking dish; add browned meat and onion. Add 3 more cups shredded cabbage. Pour 1 can undiluted tomato soup over the top of the mixture. Cover; bake in 350° oven for 1 hour or until cabbage is done.

Marcy Brown, Minneapolis, Mn.

CHINESE NOODLE HOT DISH

1 lb. hamburger, browned
1 onion, chopped
1/2 green pepper, chopped
5 stalks celery, chopped
1 can cream of mushroom
   soup
1 can tomato soup
1 can chop suey noodles

Mix the above ingredients all together; bake for 1 hour at 325°.

Ruth Koepke, Silver Bay, Mn.

CHOW MEIN-RICE HOT DISH

Let 1 cup uncooked rice stand in 4 cups boiling water; add 2 teaspoons chicken bouillon. Brown 1 pound chow mein meat and 1 pound ground turkey; add 2 large onions, chopped, and 1/2 rib chopped celery. Fry all together.

Add:

6 Tbsp. soy sauce   1 can cream of mushroom
1 can cream of chicken soup   soup

In casserole, add all ingredients and bake 1 1/2 hours at 350°. Last 15 minutes, cover with chow mein noodles and cashews. One can mushrooms and 1 can water chestnuts can be added before baking. Uncle Ben's rice seems to work best.

Mary Paul, Minneapolis, Mn.

CRINKLE POTATO HOT DISH

1 lb. hamburger   1/4 c. green pepper
1 chopped onion   1 can French style green
1 pkg. Ore-Ida crinkle   beans
   cottage fries   1 can cream of celery soup,
5 or 6 slices American cheese   diluted with 1/3 c. milk

Brown hamburger and chopped onion until red is gone from meat. In a 9x13 inch pan, layer meat and onion mixture, then green pepper, beans and potatoes. Top with cheese slices; pour soup over all. Bake 45 minutes at 350°. Let stand 15 minutes before serving.

Sigrid Johnson, Hibbing, Mn.

DEMONSETTE HOT DISH

1 lb. ground beef, browned   1/2 bag fine egg noodles,
   well   slightly undercooked,
1 large can whole tomatoes,   drained
   chopped   Salt and pepper to taste
1/4 c. minced onion   Red pepper to taste (less
3/4 c. finely chopped celery   than 1/8 tsp.)
3/4 c. finely chopped green   2 Tbsp. oil or shortening
   pepper

Boil onion, celery and green pepper until tender in 1/4 cup water. Combine all ingredients. Bake at 350° for 35-50 minutes.

Sherry Schneider, Grand Forks, N.D.

GRANDMA'S HOT DISH

1 lb. ground beef
1 medium onion
1 c. celery
1 can cream style corn

1 can chicken rice soup
1 pkg. cooked macaroni
  rings

Fry beef and onion until brown. Mix all ingredients and bake 45 minutes at 350°. Serves about 4. I always double the recipe.

Maryann Skelton, Duluth, Mn.

HAMBURGER CRUNCH HOT DISH

Brown:
2 lb. ground beef

2 medium onions

Simmer 10 minutes:
2 c. chopped celery
1/2 green pepper
1 Tbsp. sugar
1 can chopped water
  chestnuts

3 tsp. soy sauce
2 c. hot water
1 can cream of chicken soup
1 can mushroom soup
1 c. uncooked rice

Mix well and put in greased casserole. Bake at 325° for 90 minutes. You may use 3 cups chopped turkey or chicken instead of beef.

Char Reno, Duluth, Mn.

HAMBURGER HOT DISH

To 1 pound hamburger, add onion and 1 egg. Form into meat balls; brown. Dilute 2 cans soup (1 cream of mushroom and 1 cream of celery). Place browned meat balls in baking dish. Mix soups and heat; pour over meat balls. Make a biscuit dough (follow recipe on Bisquick box). Roll out and spread with a cupful of shredded cheese; sprinkle with chili powder. Roll up like cinnamon rolls. Cut and place biscuits on mixture in baking dish. Bake at 350° until biscuits are nicely browned. This makes quite a large amount.

Olga Pederson, Minneapolis, Mn.

HAMBURGER HOT DISH

1 1/2 or 2 lb. hamburger,
  uncooked
1 large onion, chopped
1 1/2 c. chopped celery
1/2 c. margarine

1/2 c. water
1 box croutettes
1 can cream of celery soup
2 cans cream of chicken soup

Lay uncooked, broken up hamburger in 9x13 inch pan. Season slightly. Saute onion and celery in margarine. Pour onion, celery and margarine over croutettes. Add 1/2 cup water; mix well. Pour this mixture over hamburger. Mix the soups together; pour over the croutettes. Bake, uncovered, at 350° for 1 hour. Let set 15 minutes before cutting. Yield: 10 servings.

Jeanette Guzek, Grand Forks, N.D.

"HAMBURGER HOT DISH"

Brown together in large pan:
1 lb. hamburger   1 onion, cut up

Add 1 teaspoon salt and 1/4 teaspoon pepper. Cut up 4 stalks celery; add to hamburger and onion.

1 large can tomatoes (do
  not drain)

1 can Campbell's chicken rice
  soup
1 can water

Add to hamburger and onion; let boil. Add 1 1/2 cups egg noodles; let simmer 1/2 hour. Serves 4.
Note: This can be made on top of the stove or in the oven. Bake at 400° for 1 hour.

Delores Foucault, Saginaw, Mn.

EASY HAMBURGER HOT DISH

1 1/2 lb. ground beef
1 onion
1 c. celery, chopped
1 pkg. frozen or canned
  mixed vegetables

1 can cream of mushroom
  soup
1 can chicken rice soup
1 can chow mein noodles

Brown beef and onion together. Add to other ingredients. Put chow mein noodles on top. Bake in casserole in medium oven, 350°, for 1 1/2 hours.

Lorraine Rieger, Minneapolis, Mn.

HAMBURGER MACARONI HOT DISH

2 lb. hamburger
2 (16 oz.) cans mixed
vegetables
1 (10 1/2 oz.) can cream of
chicken soup

1 medium size onion, diced
1 small box shell macaroni
1 (2 lb.) bag tater tots
1 (10 1/2 oz.) can cream of
mushroom soup

Cook macaroni; drain and place in 9x13 inch pan. Brown the hamburger and onion. Save liquid of 1 can mixed vegetables; add to the cream soups. Combine all ingredients, except tater tots, in baking pan. Place tater tots on top of hot dish; bake in 350° oven for 45 to 60 minutes until the hamburger-macaroni mixture is bubbly and the tater tots are golden brown.

Lorraine Rieger, Minneapolis, Mn.

HAMBURGER NOODLE HOT DISH

1 lb. hamburger
1 c. onion, chopped
1 c. celery, chopped
1 (8 oz.) pkg. noodles

2 cans cream of mushroom
soup
2 cans cream of chicken soup
1/2 can tomato soup
1 c. green pepper, sliced

Cook the hamburger, onion and celery together in a frying pan. Add the cooked noodles, soups and green pepper (optional). Mix the ingredients together and bake at 325° for 1 1/2 hours.

Lorraine Rieger, Minneapolis, Mn.

HAMBURGER AND VEGETABLE HOT DISH

6 medium raw potatoes,
sliced
1/2 c. uncooked rice
1 lb. beef hamburger,
browned
1 layer of onions

1 layer of raw carrots
2 c. water
1 can cream of chicken soup
1 Tbsp. salt
1 Tbsp. sugar

Place in large casserole in order given. Bake 1 1/2 hours at 350°. Serves 12.

Mary Fingalson, Detroit Lakes, Mn.

PARTY HOT DISH

1 box Creamettes
1 lb. ground beef
1 small green pepper,
    chopped
1 small onion, chopped
2 Tbsp. butter
1 can cream style corn

1 c. chopped celery
1 c. tomato juice
1 can tomato soup
1 can chicken rice soup
2 tsp. salt and pepper
Crushed corn flakes

Cook Creamettes until tender in salted water. Brown beef, onion and green pepper in butter. Add remaining ingredients, except corn flakes. Simmer 10 minutes. Place in greased 2 1/2 quart casserole. Add Creamettes; stir. Sprinkle with corn flakes and dot with butter. Bake at 350° for 30 minutes.

Bessie Wilke, Detroit Lakes, Mn.

POTATO HOT DISH

4-5 c. sliced potatoes
1 lb. ground beef, browned

2 small cans vegetable beef
    soup

Place half of sliced raw potatoes in baking dish. Put half of ground beef and half of soup. Put another layer of potatoes and remainder of meat and soup on top. Cover and bake for 1 1/2 - 2 hours at 350°.

Eileen Durham, Brainerd, Mn.

RICE KRISPIES HOT DISH

1 1/2 lb. ground beef
1 small onion, diced
2 ribs of celery, diced

2 cans chicken rice soup
1 can cream of chicken soup
5 or 6 c. Rice Krispies

Saute beef; drain excess fat. Saute onion and celery in remaining fat. Mix all together with soups and celery in large bowl. Pour into 2 quart casserole. Bake 45 to 50 minutes at 350°.

Clifford H. Carlson, Saginaw, Mn.

SAUERKRAUT HOT DISH

1 lb. hamburger
3 strips of bacon
1 small onion, chopped
1 can kraut

1 c. raw rice
2 c. water
1 1/2 tsp. salt

Brown hamburger, onion and chopped bacon; add rice, sauerkraut, water and 1 teaspoon salt. Stir to mix all ingredients, thoroughly. Cook in heavy kettle over low heat. Stir often and add more water as it cooks away. Cook until rice is tender, about 1/2 hour. If you wish, you may add more salt and pepper to taste.

Goldie Mikish, Staples, Mn.

WILD RICE HOT DISH

1 c. wild rice, cooked
1 c. brown rice, cooked
1 can crabmeat
1 can shrimp
1 1/2 c. celery, cut up

1 medium onion, cut up
2 cans mushrooms
1 small jar pimento, cut up
1 green pepper, cut up
2 cans mushroom soup

Bake in 2 1/2 quart casserole, buttered, for 1 1/2 hours at 350°. For sauce, thin 2 cans mushroom soup with a little milk.

Gladys Turk, Duluth, Mn.

SUE'S WILD RICE HOT DISH

Brown 2 pounds hamburger, no seasonings; drain. Prepare 1 package "Minute" long grain 'n wild rice product, according to package. Add 2 cans cream of mushroom soup. Mix all together. Bake 1 hour at 350°.

Jackie Reisinger, St. Cloud, Mn.

MEAT BALLS

In 3 pound portions, spread over large area, salt and pepper to your pleasure. Sprinkle 3/4 pound bread crumbs, 1/4 pound dry, chopped onion (do not soak onion). If fresh parsley is available, cut 1/2 cup and sprinkle over top. Add 1/2 teaspoon dry sweet basil, 1/4 pound Parmesan cheese and 1/4 teaspoon concentrated garlic powder.

Add 6-8 large eggs; mix thoroughly and taste raw. This will tell what is lacking. It may be salt. Make normal size meat balls and boil in water before putting in sauce. (If mixture is too dry, add milk.)

Mrs. Emil Gatto, St. Paul, Mn.

Similar recipe submitted by: Florence Wesen, St. Cloud, Mn.

MEAT BALLS

2 lb. lean hamburger (or extra lean)	1 pkg. Lipton onion soup mix
1/2 c. bread crumbs	Salt and pepper to taste

Mix together and roll into little balls the size of walnuts. Brown under broiler, 15 to 20 minutes.

Sauce:

1/2 c. apple jelly	1 small bottle ketchup (I use Heinz)

Simmer the above and add meat balls; simmer till ready to serve.

Gerri Ruprecht, St. Cloud, Mn.

CASSEROLE MEAT BALLS

1 lb. hamburger	3 slices bread crumbs, soaked in milk
1 egg	Salt and pepper
1 onion, diced	

Beat with electric mixer until fluffy. Form into balls; stuff with desired amount of cheese. Place in casserole dish and top with cream of mushroom soup and shredded cheese. Bake 40 minutes at 350°.

Jeanie Rose, Tracy, Mn.

CHAFING DISH MEAT BALLS

1 1/2 lb. ground chuck	1/2 c. milk
1/2 c. crushed, dried bread crumbs	1/4 c. shortening
	2 c. canned tomato juice
1 tsp. salt	2 Tbsp. flour
1/4 tsp. pepper	3/4 c. bottled barbeque sauce
1 egg, slightly beaten	1/4 c. water

1 (1 lb. 4 1/2 oz.) can   Stuffed olives
  pineapple chunks, drained

Early on day of serving, toss together with a fork in a bowl the ground chuck, bread crumbs, salt, pepper, eggs and milk until well blended. Shape this mixture into 3/4 inch balls. Place in shallow pan, 12x8x2 inches, with shortening; refrigerate. In saucepan, combine tomato juice and flour until smooth. Add barbeque sauce and water; blend. Set aside. About 1 1/2 hours before serving, heat oven to 350° and bake meat balls 30 minutes. Drain off excess fat from browned meat balls; pour on tomato sauce and bake 45 minutes. To serve, spoon meat balls into chafing dish. Place pineapple chunks and olives here and there. Spoon sauce over all. Makes 48 meat balls.
Donna Hoff, Fargo, N.D.

CHEDDAR MEAT BALLS

1 lb. ground beef   1/4 tsp. salt
1/4 c. fine, dry bread   1 can Cheddar cheese soup
  crumbs   1/2 c. water
1/4 c. finely chopped onion   2 Tbsp. chopped parsley
1 egg, slightly beaten

Mix beef, bread crumbs, onion, egg and salt; shape into about 16 (or a few more) meat balls. In skillet, brown meat balls (use shortening, if needed); pour off fat. Stir in soup, water and parsley. Cover and cook over low heat for 20 minutes or until done; stir occasionally. Makes about 3 1/2 cups. Very good served right over mashed potatoes, or just plain boiled potatoes, because of it's gravy.
Bernice Fonos, Minneapolis, Mn.

IRENE'S STUFFED MEAT BALLS

1 lb. ground chuck   1/3 c. canned milk
Salt and pepper to taste   (evaporated)

Combine this and divide in fourths for patties; pat flat. Use Pepperidge Farm dressing or croutons (about 1/4 cup per serving of meat) and wrap the meat around dressing. Bring to a boil 1 can golden mushroom soup, 2 teaspoons Worcestershire sauce and 1 tablespoon catsup. Put meat balls in pan; pour over sauce. Bake 1 hour at 350°. Serves 4.
1507-82   Liz Tuft, St. Paul, Mn.   247

NORWEGIAN MEAT BALLS

1 lb. ground beef
1 lb. ground pork
2 1/2 tsp. ginger
1/2 tsp. allspice
Salt and pepper

1 onion, grated
1 c. bread crumbs
1/2 c. cream or milk
1 egg

Combine all ingredients; roll into balls the size of walnuts. Fry in hot fat until brown. Add a small amount of water and milk; cook until ready to serve. Makes 6 to 8 servings.

Bernice Fonos, Minneapolis, Mn.

ROWE'S EASY MEAT BALLS

1 1/2 lb. hamburger
2 cans Franco-American
  beef gravy

2 c. Kellogg's Croutettes,
  soaked in 1 c. milk for 10
  minutes

Using 1 tablespoon of meat mixture, form into balls. Place with edges touching in a 9x13 inch pan. Pour over the beef gravy. Bake at 350° for 35 minutes. Stir once to brown.

Helen Teeuwen, Minneapolis, Mn.

SWEET AND SOUR MEAT BALLS

1 c. cubed bread
1 c. milk
1/3 c. finely chopped onion
1 1/2 lb. ground beef
1/2 lb. ground pork
1 egg

1 tsp. pepper
1 tsp. salt
2 (12 oz.) bottles chili sauce
1 (10 oz.) jar grape jelly
1 c. sour cream (optional)

Soak bread cubes in milk. Combine with meat, onion, egg, salt and pepper. In large saucepan, combine chili sauce, 1 cup water and grape jelly. Heat to simmering. Shape meat mixture into balls the size of walnuts. Drop into hot sauce and simmer gently 1 hour. Skim off excess fat. Stir in 1 cup sour cream, if desired.

Ellie Cox, Rochester, Mn.

MEAT BALLS AND VEGETABLES

1 c. diced celery
1 c. diced carrots

2 c. water

Parboil the above and cool; save water. Combine:

1 lb. ground beef
1 1/2 c. bread crumbs
1 egg
2/3 c. milk

2 Tbsp. grated onion
1 Tbsp. parsley, minced
1 tsp. salt
1/2 tsp. pepper

Form into balls and brown in 2 tablespoons shortening; drain and arrange in casserole. Dilute 1 can tomato soup with 1 can water. Mix with vegetables and cooking liquid; pour over meat balls. Bake at 350° for 1 hour.

Marie Holmberg, Duluth, Mn.

MEAT LOAF
(Easy and Very Good)

2 lb. ground beef
2 eggs
1 1/2 c. bread crumbs
  (3 1/2 slices)

1 c. warm water
3/4 c. catsup
1 tsp. Accent
1 pkg. Lipton onion soup

Mix all together. Bake at 350° for 1 hour.

Mrs. Kermit A. Haugen, Clarksfield, Mn.

CURRIED MEAT LOAF

6 oz. ground meat (beef,
  lamb or veal)
1/4 tsp. grated lemon rind
1/2 tsp. curry powder
4 Tbsp. minced onion
2 Tbsp. minced parsley
1/4 tsp. salt or to taste

2 Tbsp. raisins
1/4 small head red cabbage,
  coarsely chopped
1/2 small apple, cored and
  sliced 1/8 inch thick
Juice of 1/2 lemon

Mix together ground meat, grated lemon rind, curry powder, onion, parsley and salt; shape into single patty 1 inch thick. Brown in pan over medium heat. In a bowl, toss shredded cabbage, apple and raisins with lemon juice; add to pan with meat. Cover and steam over low heat about 5 to 10 minutes until cabbage is tender, crisped and meat is done to taste. If meat is desired rare, remove from pan when browned on both sides and continue cooking cabbage a few minutes more. Serve with parslied noodles. Serves 1.

Rhea Thoms, Jamestown, N.D.

FAMILY BEST BEEF LOAF

2 lb. ground beef	2 medium onions, chopped
1 (8 oz.) can tomato sauce	3/4 c. finely crushed cracker
1 egg	crumbs
1 Tbsp. Worcestershire	1 tsp. salt
sauce	1/4 tsp. pepper
1/3 c. chopped green pepper	1/4 c. catsup

Combine ground beef, tomato sauce, egg, Worcestershire sauce, green pepper, onions, cracker crumbs, salt and pepper. Mix lightly, but thoroughly. Shape meat mixture into a loaf, about 9x4x3 inches; place on a rack in an open roasting pan. Bake at 350° for 1 hour and 15 minutes. Pour catsup over top of beef loaf and continue baking 10 to 15 minutes or until done. Makes 6-8 servings.

Bernice Fonos, Minneapolis, Mn.

PARTY HAMBURGER LOAF

1/4 c. bread crumbs	1/4 tsp. pepper
1/2 c. milk	3 Tbsp. catsup
1 lb. ground beef	1 (12 oz.) can sweet potatoes
2 Tbsp. catsup	1 can drained pineapple
1 onion, chopped	chunks
1 tsp. salt	1 large apple, in wedges
Small marshmallows	Brown sugar

Soak bread crumbs in milk; add to meat with first catsup, onion, salt and pepper. Shape into loaf; put in center of shallow baking pan. Bake at 375° for 40 minutes. Remove from oven and top meat with second catsup. Put potatoes, pineapple chunks, apple wedges and marshmallows around meat; sprinkle with brown sugar. Bake about 20 minutes longer.

Maxine Olsen, Duluth, Mn.

ROLLED UP MEAT LOAF

Mix together:

1 lb. ground beef	1 Tbsp. catsup
1 egg	1 tsp. Worcestershire sauce
1/4 c. chopped onion	1/2 tsp. salt
1/4 c. dry bread crumbs or cracker crumbs	1/4 tsp. pepper

Pat mixture out on waxed paper into a rectangle about 1/2 inch thick. Top with 6 to 8 thin slices of dried beef. Sprinkle with 1 cup Cheddar or Swiss cheese; top with small can of sliced mushrooms. Roll up carefully so meat loaf looks like a jelly roll. Place seam side down in pan. Bake in preheated oven, 350°, for 45 minutes to 1 hour. May put catsup or barbecue sauce on top for last 15 minutes of baking. Makes 6 to 8 servings.

Betty Drier, Rochester, Mn.

STUFFED MEAT LOAF

2 lb. hamburger (lean)	1 can bouillon, poured over top
3 eggs	1 Tbsp. oregano
4 slices of bread	1/4 tsp. garlic
1/2 c. Parmesan cheese	1/2 tsp. basil

Mix all ingredients together, except bouillon, in a large bowl. Place on a bread board; pat out to a rectangle.

Stuffing: Grate any type of cheese you have on hand. Use leftover salami, pepperoni or ham, cut up, and place both cheese and meat in the middle. Potatoes and vegetables may also be used. Roll hamburger up like a jelly roll; seal ends. Place seam side down in a loaf pan. Pour bouillon over meat loaf. Bake at 350° for 1 1/4 to 1 1/2 hours.

Lynn Cooch, Minneapolis, Mn.

SUSAN'S MEAT LOAF

2 c. fresh bread crumbs	2 lb. ground chuck
3/4 c. minced onion	2 Tbsp. bottled horseradish
1/4 c. minced green pepper (optional)	2 1/2 tsp. salt
	1 tsp. dry mustard
2 eggs	1/4 c. milk
1/4 c. catsup	1/2 c. catsup

1507-82

With fork, slightly beat eggs. Lightly mix in chuck, then crumbs, onion and green pepper. Add horseradish and next 4 ingredients. Combine lightly, but thoroughly. Shape meat in oval loaf. Place in shallow baking dish. Spread top with the 1/2 cup catsup. Bake 50 minutes at 400°, or bake a little longer at lower temperature.

Betty Babich, Virginia, Mn.

TASTY MEAT LOAF

Oven: Combine -

1 1/2 lb. ground beef	2 Tbsp. chopped onion
1 c. herb stuffing	2 eggs
(Pepperidge Farm)	1 tsp. salt
1 c. milk	1/8 tsp. pepper

Mix all together and put in a covered casserole. Bake at 350° for 1 hour.

Microwave: Or, you can put in a covered 2 quart baking dish and put in microwave on Roast for 20-25 minutes. Let stand, covered, for 5 minutes before serving.

Loretta VanEngelenhoven, Luverne, Mn.

VENISON AND PORK MEAT LOAF

2 lb. ground venison	1 tsp. powdered mustard
1 lb. ground pork	2 eggs, well beaten
1/4 c. minced onion	1 tsp. salt
1/2 c. horseradish	1/8 tsp. fresh pepper

Grease sides of casserole and put 1/2 cup ketchup on the bottom. Bake at 350° for 1 hour or until done.

Marion Round, Faribault, Mn.

MEAT POTATO HOT DISH

Sliced potatoes, as for	1 medium onion, chopped
scallop	2 c. celery, cut up
1 1/2 lb. raw beef	2 cans beef-barley soup
(round steak)	1 can mushrooms

Lay 2 layers of potatoes, onion and celery, then the raw beef and more potatoes. Mix the soup in a bowl with 1/2 can water; pour over potatoes. Salt and pepper. Bake in a covered 2 1/2 quart casserole at 350° for 2 hours.

Gladys Turk, Duluth, Mn.

MINNESOTA HOT DISH

Season 1 pound ground beef with salt and pepper; brown. Put in bottom of casserole and cover with the following in order given:

1 c. chopped onion   Diced raw potatoes to cover
1 c. chopped celery

Sprinkle 1 tablespoon flour over above. Add 1 can mushroom soup and 1 can tomato soup. Pour milk over all, sufficient to cover. Bake at 350° until potatoes are tender, about 1 1/2 hours.

Marian Pearson, Minneapolis, Mn.

HAMBURGER PILAFF

1 lb. ground beef   2 tsp. prepared mustard
1 chopped onion   1/2 tsp. salt
1 can chicken gumbo soup   Pepper
1/2 can water   2 Tbsp. ketchup

Brown beef and onion. Add remaining ingredients; simmer for 30 minutes. Serve hot over rice. Makes 4 to 6 servings.

Phyllis Christenson, Brooklyn Center, Mn.

POOR BOY FILLETS

5 slices bacon   1 (2 oz.) can mushroom
1 lb. lean ground beef   stems and pieces, drained
Lemon pepper   3 Tbsp. finely chopped
1/4 c. grated Parmesan   pimiento-stuffed olives
  cheese   2 Tbsp. finely chopped
2 Tbsp. finely chopped onion   green pepper (optional)

In a skillet, partially cook bacon; drain on paper toweling. Pat ground beef on waxed paper to a 12 x 7 1/2 x 1/4 inch rectangle*. Sprinkle lightly with salt and lemon pepper; top with Parmesan cheese. Combine mushrooms, olives, onion and green pepper; sprinkle evenly over meat. Roll up jelly roll fashion, starting from the short end. Cut into 1 1/2 inch slices. Wrap edge of each slice with a strip of partially cooked bacon, securing with wooden picks. Grill over medium coals 8 minutes. Turn and grill 8 minutes more. Makes 5. (See following.)

1507-82 253

*After preliminary shaping, you can lay another piece of waxed paper and use the rolling pin.

After making the 'jelly roll', I left it wrapped in the waxed paper and set it in the freezer for 5-10 minutes before cutting.

Roger Farley, Sartell, Mn.

PORCUPINES

1 1/2 lb. hamburger   Onion
1 1/2 c. raw rice   Salt and pepper
2 eggs

Mix well and form into meat balls. Drop in mixture in pressure cooker of 1 big can tomato soup and 1 big can of water. Cook 10 minutes.

K., St. Cloud, Mn.

PROCUS
(Sweet/Sour Cabbage Rolls)

1 head cabbage   2 cans tomato soup
1 1/2 lb. hamburger   Sugar to taste
1 c. chopped onion   Lemon juice to taste
1 c. bread crumbs   Salt and pepper to taste
2 eggs

Boil cabbage; separate leaves. Cook until tender enough to roll. Mix hamburger, onion, bread crumbs and eggs; add enough water to moisten bread crumbs. Mix together, then add sugar, lemon juice, salt and pepper to taste. Roll meat mixture in cabbage leaves; layer in pan. Add 2 cans tomato soup and enough water to cover. Add lemon juice and sugar to taste. Bring to boil. Lower heat; simmer until tender, approximately a couple of hours.

Carol Salokar, Brook Park, Mn.

RICE-A-RONA

1 1/2 c. rice, uncooked   1 can bouillon soup (beef
1/3 c. Parmesan cheese   consomme)
   (in the can)   1 (8 oz.) can mushrooms with
1 c. (can) onion soup   liquid
                                1 stick margarine

Use large casserole at 350° for 1 hour. Mix all ingredients in the casserole. Stir 3 times during baking time. Serves 6.

Mary Jones, Spirit Lake, Ia.

BEEF-ZUCCHINI ITALIENNE

3 Tbsp. butter
3 Tbsp. flour
3/4 lb. ground steak
1 large (20 oz.) can
 tomatoes, chopped
1/2 green pepper, chopped

2 green onions with tops,
 chopped
1/2 tsp. basil
1 bay leaf, crushed
Salt and pepper to taste
5 or 6 small zucchini
1 c. grated cheese (opt.)

Melt butter; blend in flour. Add all other ingredients, except zucchini and cheese. Cook slowly for 8 minutes, breaking up meat well. Slice zucchini thin; do not peel. Parboil 2 or 3 minutes; drain well. Arrange zucchini in shallow buttered casserole; pour meat sauce over it. Add cheese. Bake in 350° oven for 30 minutes. Serves 4.

Irene L. Moe, Fargo, N.D.

BEEF-POTATO BOATS

1 lb. lean ground beef
1/2 c. chopped onion
1/4 c. chopped green pepper
1/4 c. chopped celery
1 tsp. salt
1/4 tsp. nutmeg

1/8 tsp. pepper
1 (8 oz.) can Hunt's tomato
 sauce
4 medium potatoes, baked
1 c. shredded Cheddar
 cheese

Brown beef, onion, pepper and celery in skillet; drain fat. Add seasoning and Hunt's sauce. Cut potatoes in halves lengthwise; scoop out and reserve shells. Mash potatoes; combine with meat mixture. Fill shells; place in baking pan. Sprinkle cheese on top. Bake 15 minutes at 400° F. Makes 4 servings.

K., St. Cloud, Mn.

MASHED POTATO PIE
("Just Like Mom Used to Make")

Cook potatoes and mash with milk and butter. Brown hamburger and onion in separate skillet. Pour hamburger into pie pan; spread mashed potatoes like frosting. Place in 350° oven for 1/2 hour or until light brown.

Optional: Can be eaten with catsup.

Dave Fahey, Grand Forks, N.D.

DINNER-IN-A-DISH

4 Tbsp. shortening	2 eggs
1 medium onion	2 c. whole kernel corn
2 green peppers, sliced	4 medium potatoes
1 lb. hamburger	1/2 c. dry bread crumbs
1 1/2 tsp. salt	1/4 tsp. pepper

Put shortening in skillet; lightly fry pepper and onion for 3 minutes. Add seasonings; remove from fire. Let stand 5 minutes; stir in eggs and mix well. Put 1 cup of corn in casserole, then half of meat mixture and a layer of sliced tomatoes. Repeat layers; cover with crumbs. Dot with bits of butter. Bake in moderate oven, 375°, for 1 hour.

Stella Bliss, Minneapolis, Mn.

MEAL-IN-A-DISH

1 1/2 lb. hamburger	Salt and pepper
1 medium onion, chopped	

Brown above ingredients; put in bottom of small roaster, then add 1 can tomato soup and 1 can of water. Mix all together. Cook 1 package frozen peas until nearly done; drain and put on top of hamburger mixture. Slice raw potatoes and put over mixture. Fill the roaster nearly full. Spread 1 can of cream of mushroom soup over potatoes. Bake, covered, at 350° for 1/2 hour. Uncover and bake until potatoes are tender.

Mary Jo Conneran, Fargo, N.D.

1 - 1 1/2 lb. ground beef
1 large pkg. frozen mixed
  vegetables

1 small onion, chopped
1 can cream of chicken soup
1 pkg. frozen tater tots

Crumble raw hamburger in bottom of greased casserole or baking pan. Add chopped onion, then frozen vegetables. Cover with soup; top with tater tots. Bake in 350° oven for 1 hour. Cream of mushroom or cream of celery soup may be substituted.

Olga M. Stanley, Duluth, Mn.

SARMA
(Stuffed Cabbage Leaves)

1 large head of cabbage
1/2 lb. ground pork
1/2 lb. ground beef
1 1/2 tsp. salt
1/4 tsp. pepper
1/2 c. uncooked rice
Garlic (to suit taste)
2 eggs

3 onions, diced
1 Tbsp. butter
1/4 tsp. pepper
1 c. water
3 Tbsp. sugar
1 (20 oz.) can tomatoes
Juice of 1 lemon (2 Tbsp.)

Freeze cabbage head for a day or two, then unthaw completely, or, remove core from cabbage; place in boiling water. Remove from heat and let stand 20 minutes. After you have wilted cabbage using either of these methods, pull leaves apart gently and trim thick center vein. Brown onions Dutch oven in the butter. Add 1/4 teaspoon pepper, water and sugar. Mix in tomatoes, lemon juice and 1 teaspoon salt; sim ner for 30 minutes. Combine pork and beef with salt, pepper, rice and garlic; add eggs. Mix very well Place approximately 1 tablespoon of meat mixture on each cabbage leaf; roll up by bringing opposite sides together over meat. Overlap and roll. (Toothpicks can be used to hold together, but be sure they are removed when people start to eat.) Place cabbage rolls in heated sauce, seam side down; cover and simmer 1 hour. Can also be placed in oven and baked at 350° for 1 1/2 hours. Check while baking and add a small amount of water, if needed. Serves 6 to 8.

R. Mielke, Chisholm, Mn.

SOUPER GOOD 'N EASY

2 lb. ground beef
1 (7 oz.) box croutettes
1 can cream of chicken soup
1 can cream of mushroom soup
1 can cream of celery soup

Crumble ground beef in bottom of greased 9x13 inch pan. Cover with croutettes. Combine the soups (no water) and spread over croutettes. Bake in 350° oven for 1 1/2 hours, uncovered.

Olga Stanley, Duluth, Mn.

Similar recipe submitted by: Mrs. Norma Applen, Minneapolis, Mn.

SPICEY BBQ

1 lb. hamburger
1/2 c. chopped onion
1 1/2 Tbsp. Worcestershire sauce
1 Tbsp. vinegar
1 Tbsp. sugar
1 1/2 tsp. pepper (that's right)
1 can tomato soup
1/4 c. ketchup

Brown hamburger and onion; drain. Add rest of ingredients.

Mrs. Robert Sloneker, Chisholm, Mn.

BEEFY MACARONI SKILLET

1 1/2 lb. ground beef
1 medium onion, chopped
1 (28 oz.) can tomatoes
1 c. water
1 (8 oz.) box Creamettes, parboiled
1/2 lb. shredded Cheddar cheese
1 (2 oz.) jar chopped pimento olives, drained
1 tsp. salt
1/4 tsp. pepper

Brown ground beef and onion; add the rest of the ingredients. Cook on top of stove in large skillet. Boil for 10 minutes. Simmer till done, 25 minutes. Add noodles the last 5 minutes.

Marilyn Radakovich, Duluth, Mn.

MOCK STEAK

2 tsp. Worcestershire sauce
1 tsp. salt
Few grains of pepper
1/2 c. ketchup
2 lb. hamburger

1 c. bread crumbs
1/4 c. chopped onion
3 c. mashed potatoes
Button mushrooms
2 c. green peas

Combine Worcestershire sauce, salt, pepper and ketchup; blend with meat, crumbs and onion. Heat plank in a moderate oven, 350° F.; grease well. Shape meat mixture on plank to resemble a T-bone steak. Bake at 350° F. for 45 minutes. Spoon border of mashed potatoes around meat; garnish with a few mushrooms. Return to hot oven, 450° F., to brown potatoes. Add hot peas. Approximate yield: 6 servings.

Dena Stoddard, St. Louis Park, Mn.

GOLFER'S STEW

1 can onion soup
1 can cream of mushroom
soup

2 lb. stew meat, cut up into
bite size pieces

Put all ingredients together in casserole dish; do not dilute soup. Cover; bake at 250° for 3 hours. Serve over rice or noodles. Serves 4-6.

Minneapolis, Mn.

HUNGARIAN GOULASH

1/2 c. butter (must use
butter)
1-2 lb. beef, cubed
2 c. water
2 tsp. Worcestershire sauce

2 c. chopped onions
3 Tbsp. flour
1/2 c. ketchup
Egg noodles
Salt and pepper

Brown onions in butter; add cubed meat and brown. Make a paste of flour and some of the water. Add to meat mixture, then the remaining ingredients; simmer for 2 1/2 hours.

Note: Any leftover beef, pork, veal may be used. Adjust cooking time according to precooked or uncooked meat.

Lynn Cooch, Minneapolis, Mn.

HUNGARIAN GOULASH

1 1/2 lb. beef, cut in cubes
1/2 lb. pork, cut in cubes
1/2 lb. veal, cut in cubes
2 bunches of celery, cut
   in chunks
2 large onions, sliced

1 can pimento and juice
1 qt. tomatoes
1 pkg. noodles (wide)
Salt
Chili powder (optional)

Cook at least 3 hours. Serves 8 plus.
Luella Horsman

ELEPHANT STEW

1 medium size elephant
3 rabbits (optional)

Salt to taste
Pepper to taste

Cut elephant into bite size pieces; add brown gravy to cover. Cook over kerosene fire for about 4 weeks at 485°. If more than 3,800 people are expected, 3 rabbits may be needed, but do this only in case of emergency. Most people do not like hare in their soup. Yield: 3,800 servings.
Joan Lewis, Minneapolis, Mn.

IRISH MULLIGAN STEW

2 lb. rather bony boiling
   meat
1 c. dry navy beans
3 tsp. salt
Water to cover
1 pt. canned tomatoes

2 c. diced, raw carrots
2 c. diced, raw potatoes
4 large onions, quartered
1 lb. cabbage, cut in chunks
1/2 tsp. black pepper
Cornstarch to thicken

Cook meat, beans, salt and water in rather heavy kettle, bringing them to rapid boil and then easing to slow boil. Cook for 3 hours. If necessary, add water to keep meat covered. Remove bone and tissue, but return meat to juice. To this, add remaining ingredients, except cornstarch. Cook until vegetables are well done and thicken with cornstarch. Makes 4 to 6 servings. Serve with fresh homemade crusty rolls, cole slaw, green tea or milk.
Dena Stoddard, St. Louis Park, Mn.

NEVER FAIL STEW

1 1/2 lb. stew meat	1 bay leaf
3 carrots	4 medium potatoes
2 tsp. salt	1 stalk celery
3 onions	1/2 tsp. pepper
2 cans water	1 can mushroom soup

Preheat oven to 275°. In heavy skillet, heat a little bacon grease or Crisco; brown meat in hot grease. Add soup and water, then vegetables, which have been peeled and cut into chunks, and finally, all other ingredients. If needed, add additional water during cooking. Bake, covered, for 5 hours. Serves 4. Flour meat before browning. More carrots, spuds and onions can be added. Very good to put in oven before church; it's ready when you return. Good!

Mrs. Kermit A. Haugen, Clarkfield, Mn.

PRESIDENT EISENHOWER'S*
OLD FASHIONED BEEF STEW

4 lb. sirloin tip or top round, cut in 1 1/2 inch cubes	Pinch of cayenne pepper
	2 medium cloves of garlic, halved
1/3 c. shortening or butter	12 small Irish potatoes, halved
3 (10 1/2 oz.) cans condensed bouillon	12 small onions
3 cans water	1 bunch carrots, cut in 1 inch pieces
4 peppercorns	
2 bay leaves	4 medium tomatoes, peeled and cut in eighths
6 whole cloves	
1 tsp. thyme	Flour

Brown beef cubes in shortening; add bouillon and water. Simmer, covered, until meat is tender, 1 1/2 to 2 hours. Add bouquet garni (peppercorns, bay leaves, cloves, thyme, cayenne pepper and garlic, tied loosely in cheesecloth or clean, thin white cloth) and vegetables. Cover; simmer until vegetables are tender, 30 to 45 minutes. Remove bouquet garni bag; drain off liquid. Thicken with beef roux made by combining 2 tablespoons each of flour, water and stew stock for each cup of liquid. Blend; add to liquid. Cook, stirring constantly, until thickened. Pour over stew and simmer a few minutes longer. Yield: 12 servings. Recipe may be increased according to number of servings desired.

*This is President Eisenhower's very own recipe.

Helen-May Johnson, Chanhassen, Mn.

PORK AND APPLE STEW

6 shoulder pork chops
3 onions, sliced thin
4 tsp. brown sugar

4 cooking apples, peeled,
  cored and sliced
Salt and pepper to taste

Trim chops of fat, then cut fat in thin strips; set aside. In large casserole, layer half of the onions and apples. Sprinkle with 2 teaspoons of brown sugar. Add pork chops in a single layer. Layer with remaining onions and apples and the fat; sprinkle with remaining sugar, salt and pepper. Cover and bake in 350° oven for 1 1/2 hours or until meat is tender. Makes 3-6 servings.

Bonnie Sovick, Ortonville, Mn.

QUICKIE STEW

1 pkg. frozen Ore-Ida
  stew vegetables
1 lb. stew meat

1 can tomato soup
1 can cream of mushroom
  soup

In a crock pot on low, put stew meat, vegetables on top and both soups. Cook on low for 8 hours. Serves 4.

K. Ells, Duluth, Mn.

"SIX HOUR STEW"

Mix in large bowl:
2 lb. stew meat
6 cubed carrots
6 cubed potatoes
1 can whole onions and juice

1 can cut string beans and
  juice
1/2 c. tapioca
Season to taste

Bake in buttered 13x9 inch cake pan, covered with aluminum foil, for 6 hours at 275°.

Diane Kitch, Duluth, Mn.

WASHDAY PORK STEW

1 1/2 lb. pork stew meat
  or pork steak, cut into
  1 inch cubes
3 medium carrots, cut into
  3/4 inch pieces

3 medium potatoes, cut into
  1 inch cubes
2 ribs celery, sliced
1 (10 oz.) pkg. frozen lima
  beans

1 medium onion, chopped
1 (10 oz.) can tomato soup
1/2 c. water
2 Tbsp. quick cooking
  tapioca
1 tsp. salt
1/2 tsp. dried basil,
  crushed
1/4 tsp. garlic powder
1/4 tsp. cayenne pepper

Mix together; put into Dutch oven. Cover; bake 2 to 2 1/2 hours at 325°, or simmer on top of stove. Also, great for crock pot.

Millie Monte, Chisholm, Mn.

STIR-FRY, USA

3 Tbsp. vegetable oil
2 medium-large peeled
  potatoes, sliced thin
1/2 tsp. salt
2 carrots, sliced thin (opt.)
1 large onion, cut into 8
  wedges
1/4 tsp. salt
2 c. cut green beans
1 lb. lean ground beef
1/2 c. chicken broth
1 tsp. cornstarch
1/2 - 1 tsp. Kitchen
  Bouquet, black bean
  sauce or beef extract

Add the oil to a hot wok or large skillet. When oil is heated almost to smoking point, add potatoes and stir-fry quickly, working with about 1/3 of the potatoes at a time and cooking until they begin to brown around edges. Sprinkle lightly with salt. Stir-fry carrots and onion separately, adding a little more oil if needed and sprinkling each vegetable lightly with salt. Remove each when just tender and set aside. Stir-fry green beans, cooking only about 2 minutes so beans remain tender-crisp. Remove and set aside. Break the ground beef into small pieces into hot wok. Quickly stir-fry meat until it loses its red color. Drain excess fat from wok or skillet and add all the other prepared vegetables, stirring to mix. Stir a tablespoon of the chicken broth into the cornstarch, then blend this into the remaining chicken broth with the Kitchen Bouquet. Stir this into the meat and vegetables. Cook and stir gently until the juices thicken. Serves 4 to 6.

St. Cloud, Mn.

BEEF STROGANOFF

2 lb. cubed sirloin steak,
  rolled in flour, browned
1 medium onion, chopped
Dash of garlic salt
1 (4 oz.) can mushroom
  pieces and juice
1 can beef consomme

2 (8 oz.) cans tomato sauce
1/2 c. cooking sherry
1 Tbsp. Worcestershire sauce
1 tsp. salt
1 tsp. pepper
1 c. sour cream

Mix all together; put in casserole. Cover and bake 2 hours or until tender at 350°. Stir occasionally. Thicken more if necessary. Serve on rice or noodles. Serves 8.

> Dorothy Savig, Minneapolis, Mn.
Similar recipe submitted by: Lila Houser, Aitkin, Mn.

BEEF STROGANOFF

1 1/2 - 2 lb. hamburger
1 medium onion, chopped

1/2 tsp. pepper
1 1/2 tsp. salt

Brown above in oil. Add 4 to 5 tablespoons flour; stir and cook 5 minutes. Add:

1 c. sliced mushrooms
1 can cream of mushroom
  soup

1/3 soup can hot water with
  beef bouillon cube
  dissolved

Cook 10 minutes, uncovered. Before serving, add 12 ounces sour cream and heat through. Serve over Minute rice or noodles.

> Barb Discher, Bismarck, N.D.

HAMBURGER STROGANOFF

1 lb. hamburger
1 medium onion, chopped
1/4 c. butter
2 Tbsp. flour
1 tsp. salt
1 tsp. garlic salt

1/4 tsp. pepper
1 (4 oz.) can mushrooms
  (stems and pieces),
  drained
1 can cream of chicken soup
1 c. sour cream
2 or 3 c. hot egg noodles

Cook hamburger and onion in butter. Stir in flour, salt, garlic salt, pepper and mushrooms. Cook, stirring constantly, 5 minutes. Stir in soup; heat to boiling, stirring constantly; reduce heat. Simmer, uncovered, for 10 minutes. Stir in sour cream; heat through. Serve over hot noodles.

Jackie Jaenisch, Windom, Mn.

LAZY DAY STROGANOFF

1 env. Lipton onion soup
1 can cream of celery soup
1/3 can water
1 can cream of mushroom soup
2 lb. stew meat or cubed round steak

Mix ingredients together; put in crock pot and cook all day, or bake in oven at 275° for 3 to 4 hours. Stir in 1/2 cup of sour cream just before serving. Serve over wet or dry noodles or rice.

Eloise Hoff, Preston, Mn.

WAYNE'S STROGANOFF

1/2 c. Crisco and 1 lb. round steak, cubed and rolled in flour, browned
1 can beef broth
1 can mushroom soup
1 (4 1/2 oz.) jar mushrooms
1 large onion, sauteed in 1/4 lb. butter
1 tsp. salt
1 Tbsp. Worcestershire sauce
1 ctn. sour cream

Combine all ingredients and simmer at least 1/2 hour before serving.

Debra Tollefson, Fargo, N.D.

STUFFED BURGER BUNDLES

1 c. herb seasoned stuffing mix
1/3 c. evaporated milk
1 lb. ground beef
1 (10 1/2 oz.) can condensed cream of mushroom soup
2 tsp. Worcestershire sauce
1 Tbsp. catsup

Prepare stuffing according to package directions. Combine evaporated milk and meat; divide in 5 patties. On waxed paper, pat each to 6 inch circle. Put 1/4 cup stuffing in center of each; draw meat over stuffing. Seal; place in 1 1/2 quart casserole. Combine remaining ingredients; pour over meat. Bake, uncovered, at 350° for 45 minutes. Makes 5 servings.

Mrs. D.H. Richardson, St. Paul, Mn.

TAGLIARINI

2 lb. ground beef
2 small onions, chopped
2 cloves of garlic, minced
2 Tbsp. bacon grease
Pinch of oregano
Dash of cumin
Dash of marjoram
1 Tbsp. chili powder
1 tsp. salt
Dash of pepper

Seedless raisins
1/2 c. red wine
1 (8 oz.) can tomato sauce
1 (No. 303) can creamed corn
1 (4 1/2 oz.) can chopped
   olives
1 (2 oz.) can mushrooms
1 (1 lb.) pkg. noodles,
   cooked
1 c. grated cheese

Brown meat, onions and garlic in bacon grease. Mix all ingredients in casserole, except cheese. Sprinkle cheese on top and bake in covered dish for 1 hour in 300° oven.

Variations: Chopped green pepper, whole corn instead of creamed corn, whole pitted olives instead of chopped, fresh mushrooms, and a few dashes of Worcestershire sauce. Make a little more sauce. Blend 1/2 cheese in mixture.

Florence Swanson, Minneapolis, Mn.

STIR FRIED PORK AND CABBAGE

About 1 1/2 lb. lean pork
   steak, cut in strips
1/4 c. soy sauce
1 1/2 c. onion, sliced

1 tsp. sugar
3 Tbsp. oil
5 c. cabbage, cut in strips
Salt to taste

Toss meat strips in soy sauce; let stand a few minutes. Heat 1 tablespoon oil in heavy skillet or wok until very hot. Stir pork until brown, 3-4 minutes. Strain over bowl, saving juices. Wipe pan clean. Heat remaining oil; add onion. Cook until barely soft. Add cabbage; sprinkle with salt. Cook until wilted, stirring often. Add sugar and pan juices; cook until crisp-tender. Add pork strips; cook until heated through. Makes 4-5 servings.

Martha Fjelstad, Minneapolis, Mn.

SWEET AND SOUR PORK

2 Tbsp. corn oil
1 lb. boneless pork, cut
   in 1 inch cubes
1 (20 oz.) can pineapple
   chunks

1/2 c. Karo light corn syrup
1/4 c. cider vinegar
2 Tbsp. catsup
2 Tbsp. soy sauce
1 clove garlic, crushed

| 1/2 c. green pepper, cut | 2 Tbsp. cornstarch |
| into 1 inch sq. | 2 Tbsp. water |

Heat oil over medium heat; add pork and brown. Add next 6 ingredients; bring to a boil. Reduce heat; simmer, uncovered, stirring occasionally, 10 minutes or until pork is tender. Add pepper. Mix cornstarch and water; stir into mixture. Stirring constantly, bring to boil; boil 1 minute. Serve on rice. Serves 4.

Marcia Theisen, Duluth, Mn.
Similar recipe submitted by: Anne Aune, Minneapolis, Mn.

APPLE GLAZED PORK CHOPS

1/4 c. flour	2 Tbsp. brown sugar
1/2 tsp. salt	2 Tbsp. flour
1/4 tsp. garlic powder	1 1/2 c. apple juice
1/2 tsp. dry mustard	2 apples, peeled and sliced
1/8 tsp. pepper	1/3 c. raisins
2 lb. pork chops	1/2 tsp. cinnamon
2 Tbsp. margarine or butter	

Combine 1/4 cup flour, salt, mustard, pepper and garlic powder. Coat pork chops; brown in margarine. Remove chops; stir 2 tablespoons flour and brown sugar into drippings to make thick paste. Gradually stir in apple juice; cook and stir until thickened. Place chops in 2 quart casserole. Arrange apple slices and raisins over pork chops; cover with apple juice mixture. Sprinkle with cinnamon. Cover and bake at 350° for 1 hour. Makes 4 servings.

Dorothy Duffy, Minneapolis, Mn.

BAKED PORK CHOP CASSEROLE

4 pork chops (1/2 inch thick)	1 1/2 tsp. salt
2 Tbsp. fat or cooking oil	1/8 tsp. pepper
1/4 c. diced onion	3 medium potatoes, peeled
1 (10 3/4 oz.) can condensed	and sliced
cream of celery soup	1 lb. cabbage, shredded
1/2 c. milk	1/4 c. flour

Brown chops in fat in skillet. When brown, remove chops. Add onion, soup, milk, salt and pepper to fat in

1507-82

pan; blend and set aside. Alternate potato and cabbage layers in 2 quart casserole. Sprinkle each potato and cabbage layer with a little flour. Pour a portion of the soup sauce over each layer. Place chops on top of potato/cabbage layers. Pour a little remaining sauce on chops. Bake, covered, 1 1/4 hours in 350° oven or until potatoes and cabbage test done.

Betty Schroll, Minneapolis, Mn.

BAKED CHOPS WITH SOUR CHERRIES

4 thick pork loin chops
Salt and pepper to taste
1 c. rice

1 (No. 2) can sour red
  cherries
Grated rind of 1/2 lemon
Dash of cinnamon

Season chops with salt and pepper; brown on both sides. Place rice in casserole; pour cherries and juice over rice. Sprinkle sugar, lemon peel and cinnamon over cherries. Arrange chops on top; cover. Bake for 1 hour and 15 minutes at 350°. Makes 4 servings.

Stella Bliss, Minneapolis, Mn.

CHINESE PORK CHOPS

4 pork chops
1/2 tsp. sugar
1 1/2 c. hot water
1/2 c. sliced celery
1 large onion, sliced

1/2 lb. whole green beans
2 c. sliced cabbage
1 Tbsp. cornstarch
2 Tbsp. cold water
3 Tbsp. soy sauce

Sprinkle sugar over bottom of skillet. As soon as sugar has browned, place chops in pan and brown on both sides. Add onion and hot water; cover and simmer for 30 minutes. Add celery and beans; cook 5 minutes. Add cabbage; cook 5 minutes more. Thicken with cornstarch, water and soy sauce mixture. Serve with additional soy sauce. If you use fresh beans, you will have to increase cooking time. All vegetables should be fork tender.

Dorothy Bowe, Duluth, Mn.

2 HOUR BARBECUE PORK CHOPS

5 or 6 pork chops, plus
    4 Tbsp. oil
1/2 c. catsup
1/2 tsp. chili powder
1 tsp. dry mustard
1 Tbsp. sugar

1 c. water
2 Tbsp. vinegar
1 1/2 tsp. Worcestershire
    sauce
1 Tbsp. brown sugar
1/8 c. chopped dried onion

Sprinkle chops with black pepper. Brown chops in oil. Get roaster and place chops in; bring other ingredients to boil on top of stove. Bake 2 hours at 325°. Remove cover last 1/2 hour; baste every 15 minutes.

Bonnie J. Sovick, Marshall, Mn.

PORK CHOPS EN CASSEROLE

4 thick pork chops
2 tomatoes, sliced
1 large onion, sliced
1 green pepper, chopped
1/4 tsp. thyme

1/4 tsp. sage
Salt and pepper to taste
2/3 c. uncooked rice
1 c. chicken broth

Brown chops; place in buttered casserole. Arrange vegetables on top of chops; sprinkle on spices. Heat broth with 1/3 cup white wine; sprinkle rice over casserole. Pour broth over all. Bake until liquid is gone in a 350° oven, about 45 minutes.

Dee Olson, St. Paul, Mn.

FRUITED PORK CHOPS FOR THE GRILL

6-8 pork chops (1 - 1 1/2
    inches thick)

    Fruit Sauce:

Salt and pepper

2 c. thinly sliced nectarines
    or peaches
2 Tbsp. lime juice
1 c. apple juice

1 Tbsp. brown sugar
1 Tbsp. cornstarch
1/2 tsp. cinnamon
1 c. fresh blueberries

To make sauce: Put the nectarines and lime and apple juices in a small saucepan. Combine brown sugar, cornstarch and cinnamon; slowly stir into fruit and juices. Cook over low heat until juices thicken slightly. Use juices to baste chops as they cook, keeping sauce warm in small container set on grill rack.

Place chops on grill rack set 5 to 7 inches over hot coals; cook about 10 minutes on each side. Season with salt and pepper; brush with Fruit Sauce. Continue cooking, occasionally turning and brushing with Fruit Sauce, another 10 to 15 minutes, or until chops are no longer pink near bone. Just before serving, add blueberries to Fruit Sauce and serve with grilled chops. Serves 6 to 8.

St. Cloud, Mn.

PORK CHOPS HAWAIIAN

4 pork chops	1/2 c. ketchup
1 can beef broth	1 Tbsp. vinegar
1/2 c. pineapple tidbits	1 Tbsp. brown sugar
1/2 c. green pepper	

In skillet, brown pork chops; pour off fat. Add remaining ingredients. Cover; simmer 45 minutes. Stir now and then. Mix 2 tablespoons water and 1 tablespoon cornstarch; stir into sauce. Cook and stir till thickened. Serve with rice. Serves 4.

Gladys Orutt, Minneapolis, Mn.

PEANUT BUTTER PORK CHOPS

Now and then we come across a recipe that sounds a bit different. This is obviously one of them. Before you wrinkle up your nose, you should try this unusual dish. You may agree that perhaps they should be called "Her Majesty's Imperial Pork Chops"! But, they're not. They're humbly known as 'Peanut Butter Pork Chops'.

Trim fat from 4 to 6 (3/4 inch thick) pork chops. Heat fat in skillet or electric fry pan. When there is 2 tablespoons melted fat, remove trimmings. Sprinkle chops with seasoned salt. Brown chops over high heat. Remove chops from skillet; drain excess fat, leaving 1 tablespoon fat in skillet. Blend in skillet fat 1 envelope dry mushroom soup mix and 1/3 cup smooth peanut butter. Gradually add 2 cups water and 1 teaspoon Kitchen Bouquet. Stir until smooth; bring to a boil. Reduce heat; add pork chops, 1 medium onion, sliced, and 1/2 green pepper, cut in strips. Cover; simmer (don't boil) for 1 hour or until done. Spoon off any excess fat. Gravy forms while chops cook tender.

Caution: They may be habit forming!

270   Jordy and Boyd Uppman, Minneapolis, Mn.

PORK CHOPS ROBERTO

2 lb. pork chops	Salt and pepper
2 Tbsp. butter	1 tsp. prepared mustard
1 c. beef stock	1/2 c. white wine
Flour	

Dry chops; dredge with flour and brown. Add beef stock, gradually; cover and cook slowly for 25 minutes. Add mustard to wine; pour over chops and simmer 10 minutes.

Mary J. Sward, New Hope, Mn.

PORK CORDON BLEU

4 pork butterfly chops, cut 1/4 inch thick	2 slices American cheese, cut in halves
4 slices ham, cut 1/8 inch thick	1/4 c. brandy
4 slices bacon	Salt and pepper to taste
	Cooked rice (optional)

Place 1 ham slice on each pork chop; roll chop with ham inside. Wrap with slice of bacon. Place on grill over low to medium heat for about 45 minutes to 1 hour, turning meat every 10 minutes. After the meat is tender, place 1/2 slice of cheese on top of each meat roll; continue cooking just long enough to begin melting the cheese. Do not brown the cheese. Place on steak plate; pour 1/4 cup brandy over meat rolls. Light with a long match just before serving. If desired, serve on cooked white or wild rice. Makes 4 servings.

SWEET SOUR PORK CUBES

1/2 lb. pork tenderloin	1 1/2 tsp. soy sauce
3 Tbsp. flour	1/2 tsp. MSG
1/4 c. sliced green pepper	Dash of pepper
1 ring of pineapple	2 tsp. cornstarch
1/4 c. sliced carrots	3 Tbsp. water
1/2 tsp. salt	1/4 c. vinegar
1 clove of crushed garlic	1/2 c. water
5 Tbsp. sugar	

Cut pork into 1 inch cubes; roll in flour. Deep fry. Pork floats when done. Boil green pepper for 3 minutes;

drain. Slice pineapple into 1 inch pieces. Using high flame, heat a well greased frying pan. Add salt and garlic. Add the 1/2 cup water, vinegar, soy sauce, sugar, MSG and pepper; bring to a boil. Mix cornstarch and 3 tablespoons water; add to the boiling mixture. Cook and stir for 1/2 minute. Add green pepper, carrots, pineapple and cooked pork cubes; cook for 1/2 minute more.

Dee Olson, St. Paul, Mn.

TANGY PORK CUTLETS

2 c. Kellogg's Rice Krispies
  cereal, crushed to fine
  crumbs
1 egg
3 Tbsp. lemon juice or
  water
1/4 c. flour

1/2 tsp. salt
1/4 tsp. pepper
1 lb. pork cutlets, 1/4 - 1/2
  inch thick
1/4 c. margarine or butter
4 thin lemon slices (optional)

1. Place crushed Rice Krispies in shallow dish or pan; set aside. 2. In a second shallow dish or pan, beat egg and lemon juice until foamy. 3. In a third shallow dish or pan, stir together flour, salt and pepper. Dip cutlets in flour mixture, then dip in egg mixture. Coat with crushed cereal. 4. Melt margarine in large fry pan over low heat. Increase heat to medium. Brown cutlets in melted margarine on both sides. Reduce heat to low. Cover; cook about 20 minutes or until cutlets are tender. Garnish with lemon slices, if desired. Yield: 4 servings.

Marion Round, Faribault, Mn.

TORGERSON ROLLED PORK LOIN

1 (5-6 lb.) boneless, rolled
  and tied pork loin roast
1 c. ketchup
1/3 c. bourbon
1/4 c. molasses
1/4 c. cider vinegar

1 Tbsp. Worcestershire sauce
2 Tbsp. soy sauce
1 Tbsp. lemon juice
1/2 tsp. dry mustard
1/4 tsp. pepper
2 cloves of garlic, crushed

Several hours before cooking the roast, combine ketchup, bourbon, molasses, vinegar, Worcestershire sauce, soy sauce, lemon juice, mustard, pepper and garlic. Let sauce stand to blend. To cook roast, insert rotisserie rod lengthwise through center of roast; balance roast and secure with rotisserie prongs. Insert meat thermometer at angle so tip is in center of roast but not touching rod. Place roast on rotisserie. Close grill lid. After 2 to 2 1/2 hours of cooking or when thermometer registers 130° to 135°; continue cooking, brushing roast with sauce frequently. When meat thermometer registers 165° to 170°. Remove roast from grill and let stand 10 to 15 minutes before carving. Serves 8 to 10.

St. Cloud, Mn.

SAVORY PORK STEAKS

4 pork blade steaks, cut
  1/2 - 3/4 inch thick
2 Tbsp. shortening
1 tsp. salt
1/4 tsp. pepper
1 (10 1/2 oz.) can condensed
  beef broth
2 medium onions, sliced

2-3 medium potatoes, pared
  and quartered
3-4 carrots, pared and
  quartered
1 tsp. dried basil, crushed
2 Tbsp. all-purpose flour
Snipped parsley (optional)

In skillet, brown steaks on both sides in shortening. Pour off drippings. Season with salt and pepper. Reserve 1/4 cup of broth; pour remaining broth into skillet. Add onions, potatoes and carrots; sprinkle with basil. Cover and simmer for 45 to 60 minutes or until meat and vegetables are tender. Remove meat and vegetables to warm serving platter. To make gravy, measure pan juices and add water to make 1 cup. Thoroughly combine flour and reserved broth. Add to pan juices in skillet; cook, stirring constantly, until mixture thickens and bubbles. Serve gravy over meat and vegetables; sprinkle with parsley, if desired. Makes 4 servings.

St. Cloud, Mn.

BARBECUED RIBS

Sauce: Mix together -

1 c. catsup
1 heaping c. brown sugar

1/2 c. water
1 env. Lipton's onion soup
  mix

Grease roaster or line with foil. Arrange ribs in single layer. Spoon sauce over meat; cover and bake about an hour at 350°. Add more sauce and bake, covered, another hour or until done.

Alicia Woodford, Montevideo, Mn.

BARBECUED STYLE RIBS

5 lb. spareribs
1 lemon, unpeeled

1 onion, thinly sliced

Take ribs; cover with water and 1/4 cup liquid smoke. Boil for about 30 minutes. Place ribs in shallow roasting pan; pour 3 cups of sauce over ribs. Bake 1 1/2 hours at 350° or until tender. Baste every 20 minutes, adding remaining sauce as needed. Makes 6 servings.

Barbecue Sauce:

2 Tbsp. sugar
1 Tbsp. salt
1/4 tsp. pepper
2 1/4 tsp. chili powder
1 1/2 tsp. curry powder
1/4 tsp. garlic salt

1 Tbsp. grated lemon peel
6 Tbsp. Worcestershire sauce
2 1/4 c. ketchup
3 3/4 c. water
2 dashes Tabasco sauce
2 Tbsp. liquid smoke

To make sauce, combine ingredients, blending well. Bring to a boil; briskly simmer, uncovered, over medium heat for 20 minutes or until reduced to 4 cups.

Stella Bliss, Minneapolis, Mn.

LILLIAN'S BARBECUED SPARERIBS

3 lb. spareribs

1 c. water

Steam spareribs 55 minutes, or until tender in the 1 cup water. Remove from steamer; place side by side on the broiler pan. Broil 20 minutes on each side, with 2 applications of barbecue sauce to each side. These may be baked if preferred, in the oven about 1 1/2 hours at 350°, basting often.

Barbecue Sauce:

1 c. catsup
1 c. water
4 tsp. dry mustard
6 tsp. smoked salt*
1 Tbsp. Worcestershire
sauce

1 tsp. garlic salt or 1 tsp.
chopped garlic
1/2 tsp. red pepper (more,
if desired)
1 Tbsp. vinegar

*If you can't get smoked salt, smoked liquid will do.
Helen-May Johnson, Chanhassen, Mn.

274

PAT'S FARM STYLE RIBS

1 pkg. 4-6 "country style
  ribs"
1 (8 oz.) can tomato sauce
  with onions
1 c. chicken broth
2 Tbsp. brown sugar
2 Tbsp. vinegar

1 tsp. Worcestershire sauce
1 tsp. salt
1 tsp. dry mustard
1 (1 lb.) can whole potatoes,
  drained
1 (1 lb.) can Italian style
  green beans

In Dutch oven or deep kettle, combine all but potatoes and beans. Simmer, covered, 1 to 1 1/2 hours until meat is tender. (Meat can now be refrigerated, if desired.) Skim fat, if necessary. Add potatoes and beans; simmer until heated through. Serves 2.

Helen Teeuwen, Minneapolis, Mn.

FESTIVE PORK ROAST

1 pkg. dry onion soup mix
1 (4 lb.) pork roast
1 tsp. garlic powder
1/2 c. milk
1/4 c. diced mushrooms

1 tsp. butter
2 Tbsp. flour
Dash of salt
Pepper to taste

Line roasting pan with heavy duty foil, leaving enough foil to cover top of roast. Sprinkle onion soup mix on bottom of pan. Place roast over soup mix. Sprinkle top of roast with garlic powder. Combine milk, mushrooms and butter in saucepan. Cook over low heat until butter is melted. Add small amount of hot mixture to flour. Return to saucepan, stirring constantly, until thickened. Season. Pour over roast. Cover with foil. Bake at 350° for about 2 hours or until done. Makes 6 servings.

Stella Bliss, Minneapolis, Mn.

CORN DRESSING FOR PORK CHOPS

Brown 6-8 chops; place on cookie sheet. Generously cover each chop with Corn Dressing:

1 can cream style corn
1 c. bread crumbs
2 tsp. chopped green pepper
A little pepper

1 Tbsp. finely chopped
  onion
1 tsp. salt
2 Tbsp. melted oleo

Bake at 350° for 1 hour.

1507-82   Alice Holman, Grand Forks, N.D.   275

RICE AND PORK CASSEROLE

4 pork chops
1 c. uncooked rice
1 can mushroom soup

1 can water
1 can milk

Brown chops; place in baking dish. Add rest of ingredients; cover and bake 1 1/2 hours at 350°. As rice cooks, more water may need to be added.

Jo Lyn Freitag, Minneapolis, Mn.

WILD RICE AND PORK CHOPS

1 c. wild rice

1/4 c. butter or margarine

Wash rice. Saute:

1 small onion
2 stalks celery, chopped
1/4 diced green pepper

1 small can mushrooms
1/2 c. almonds

Add rice and 4 cups chicken broth. Brown 8 pork chops; put in roaster pan. Top with a 1/2 inch thick slice of onion on each chop and 1 thick slice of tomato on top of onion. Pour rice mixture over all chops; bake for 2 hours at 250°.

Vivian Bergstrom, Forest Lake, Mn.

PEACH AND SAUSAGE BAKE

2 c. Bisquick mix
1 (16 oz.) can peach slices

1 (8 oz.) pkg. brown and
serve sausages

Prepare mix according to directions, using 1 cup milk. Turn batter into a greased 9x13 inch pan. Drain peaches, reserving 1/2 cup juice; set aside. Slice sausages, crosswise. Arrange peaches and sausages on batter. Bake at 350° for 30 minutes or until toothpick comes out clean. Must cover and refrigerate overnight. Reheat at 350° for 20 minutes before serving. Serve with the following warm peach syrup:

1/4 c. sugar
3/4 c. maple syrup

1 Tbsp. cornstarch
1 Tbsp. margarine

Combine sugar and cornstarch in saucepan with the peach juice; cook and stir until thick and bubbly. Stir in maple syrup and margarine until the margarine is melted.

276 Mrs. Gary L. Hagen, Princeton, Mn.

BREAKFAST SKILLET

1/2 lb. seasoned pork
   sausage
2 Tbsp. chopped onion
2 c. cooked, cubed potatoes

6 eggs
1 tsp. salt
Dash of pepper
1 c. shredded Cheddar
   cheese

Brown pork sausage and onion; drain well. Add potatoes. Cook and stir 5 minutes. Beat eggs with salt and pepper; stir into meat mixture. Cook and stir over medium heat until eggs are almost set. Sprinkle with cheese; cover and cook over low heat about 2 minutes.

Pam Doyea, Fargo, N.D.

TOAD IN THE HOLE

Have 1 pound pork sausage links or 1 pound bulk sausage, made into link shapes. Pat the above in a shallow ovenproof dish, about 12x8x2 inches high, in preheated 425° oven for 5-10 minutes while you make the Yorkshire Batter.

Batter:

1 c. plain flour
1/4 tsp. salt
2 eggs, beaten

1 1/4 c. milk
Pepper to taste

Mix dry ingredients smooth with half the milk. Stir in remaining milk and beaten eggs; beat vigorously. Pour over the hot pan of sausages; bake a further 40-45 minutes or until risen, brown and crisp. For a gourmet touch, add a few mushrooms and tiny tomatoes when you pour in the batter.

Juliet Lindblad, Coon Rapids, Mn.

VERA AND MARGE'S BROCCOLI AND HAM AU GRATIN

1 small jar chopped pimento
1 medium chopped onion
1 Tbsp. butter
1 can cheese soup
1 (6 oz.) roll sharp Cheddar
   cheese

1/2 tsp. garlic powder
1 (8 oz.) can mushrooms
3 c. hot, cooked rice
1 pkg. frozen chopped
   broccoli, cooked, drained
3 c. diced, cooked ham

Cook onion in butter until clear; add soup, cheese and garlic powder. Cook over low heat until cheese melts. Drain mushrooms (add the liquid to mixture gradually); add the rest of the ingredients. Turn into greased casserole. Bake 30 minutes at 350°. Top with can of French fried onions; bake 5 minutes. Serves 10 people.

Charlotte Bailey, St. Paul, Mn.

HAM AND BROCCOLI BAKE

1 (10 oz.) pkg. frozen, chopped broccoli
12 slices white bread, crust removed
1 c. shredded Cheddar cheese
2 c. cooked, diced ham
2 tsp. finely chopped onion
6 eggs, slightly beaten
3 1/2 c. milk
1/2 tsp. salt
1/2 tsp. dry mustard

Grease 13x9 inch baking dish. Partially cook broccoli; drain. Cut each slice of bread with a doughnut cutter. Fit the scraps and the crusts into greased dish. Layer cheese, broccoli and ham over bread scraps; sprinkle with onion. Arrange "doughnuts" on top. Combine remaining ingredients; pour over bread. Cover; refrigerate at least 6 hours. Bake, uncovered, at 325° for 1 hour. Let stand 10 minutes before cutting. Cut so each piece has a "doughnut" on top. Makes 12 servings and has become a tradition for our Christmas brunch.

Alice Nelson, Minneapolis, Mn.

HAM AND CHEESE DELIGHT

1/2 c. finely chopped onion
1 Tbsp. butter
2 c. finely cubed, cooked ham
2/3 c. finely crushed crax crumbs (about 15)
3 slightly beaten eggs
1 c. shredded sharp processed American or Cheddar cheese
1 1/2 c. milk
Dash of pepper
Mushrooms (optional)

Saute onion in butter. Mix ingredients all together; put in a 9x9 inch greased pan. Insert knife to test if done. Bake at 350° for 45-50 minutes. Make night before and refrigerate. Serves 6. Doubled in a 9x12 inch pan. Good for breakfast or brunch.

Teresa Cupkie, Owatonna, Mn.

HAM AND CHEESE DELIGHT

1/2 c. finely chopped onion
    and 1 Tbsp. butter,
    sauteed
2 c. finely cubed ham
3 slightly beaten eggs
2/3 c. finely crushed crax
    crumbs (about 15)

1 c. shredded sharp
    processed American or
    Cheddar cheese
1 1/2 c. milk
1 can mushrooms (optional)
Dash of pepper

Bake in 10 x 6 x 1 1/2 inch dish at 350° for 45-50 minutes. Double for 9x12 inch dish. Make the night before and refrigerate. Insert knife to test if done.

Marion Round, Faribault, Mn.

HAM LOAF

1 lb. ham

1 1/2 lb. pork steak

Grind together; add:

2 eggs, beaten
1 c. milk

1 c. bread crumbs
Very little salt and pepper

Bake 3 hours at 325°. Last hour, baste with sauce:

1 1/2 c. brown sugar
1/2 c. vinegar

1/2 c. water
1 Tbsp. dry mustard

Cook 5 minutes. Make the loaf the day before; cut while cold and reheat. I drain the grease from ham loaf, then pour sauce over and finish baking the last hour. I double this and bake in an angel food loaf pan. Very good.

Harriet Haggard, Anoka, Mn.

LAYERED HAM LOAF

2 or 3 potatoes, boiled
    and riced or sliced
Salt and pepper to your
    liking
1 c. cubed, cooked ham

1/2 c. whipping cream,
    whipped
1/2 c. shredded sharp
    Cheddar cheese
1 1/2 tsp. prepared
    horseradish

Heat oven to 350° F. Place riced potatoes in a well buttered loaf pan. Layer the cubed ham over the potatoes.

Lightly sprinkle with salt and pepper. Blend the whipped cream with the cheese and horseradish; spread over ham. Bake for 30 minutes or until hot and bubbly. Good for brunch.

Elaine L. Rolerat, East Grand Forks, Mn.

HAM MOUSSE

1 env. Knox gelatine	1/2 c. celery
1/4 c. cold water	1/4 c. green pepper
1 c. Miracle Whip	1 tsp. grated onion
2 c. chopped, cooked ham	1/2 c. whipped cream

Sprinkle gelatine over cold water in saucepan over low heat; stir until dissolved. Gradually add to Miracle Whip. Stir until smooth; chill until slightly thickened. Stir in ham, celery, green pepper and onion. Fold in whipped cream. Pour into 1 quart mold; chill until firm. Unmold. Garnish with watercress and deviled eggs around edge.

Arlene Carlson, Lake Park, Mn.

HAM-POTATO CASSEROLE

1 (12 oz.) pkg. hash brown potatoes, thawed enough to break apart	2 c. plus chopped, smoked ham
1 1/2 c. (about 6 oz.) shredded Cheddar cheese	1/2 c. sliced green onions with tops
1 c. milk, plus 1/4 c. water	1 tsp. salt
	1 tsp. dry mustard
	5 eggs, beaten

Heat oven to 350°. Mix all ingredients in bowl; pour into ungreased baking dish. Sprinkle with paprika. (I use 9x9 inch pan.) Bake until knife in center comes out clear, 40-45 minutes.

Bev. Jensen, Willmar, Mn.

ELEGANT HAM ROLLS

2 (10 oz.) pkg. frozen broccoli spears	1 can mushroom soup
8 slices Swiss cheese	1/2 c. sour cream
8 slices ham (thin)	1 tsp. prepared mustard

Cook broccoli according to directions; cool slightly. Place cheese slices on ham slices. Divide broccoli 8 ways. Place 1 portion on ham and cheese stack; roll up securely and place in large shallow baking dish, seam side down. Blend soup, sour cream and mustard; pour over ham rolls. Bake, uncovered, at 350° for 20 minutes. Serves 4 (2 each).

Mary Boe, Minneapolis, Mn.
Similar recipe submitted by: Pearl Mohn, Montevideo, Mn.

HAM ROULADE

Batter:

5 eggs, separated	3/4 c. flour
1/2 tsp. cream of tartar	2 tsp. baking powder
2 Tbsp. sugar	1 tsp. salt
1/4 c. water	1 tsp. parsley flakes

Grease bottom of 15x10 inch jelly roll pan; line with waxed paper and grease again. Beat egg whites with cream of tartar in large mixer bowl at high speed until soft peaks form. Gradually add sugar; continue beating until stiff, but not dry. Combine remaining ingredients in small mixer bowl; mix at low speed just until blended. By hand, fold egg yolk mixture into egg whites. Spread in pan. Bake in 400° oven for 10-12 minutes. Invert onto wire rack; remove waxed paper. Spread with Filling. Start with 10 inch side; roll up jelly roll fashion.

Filling:

1 large can mushrooms (stems and pieces), cut in small pieces, sauteed in 2 Tbsp. butter	2 c. diced ham (fine)
	3 oz. cream cheese
	1 Tbsp. horseradish
	1 1/2 c. sour cream

Sauce:

1 can cream of mushroom soup	1 c. diced ham
	1 c. button mushrooms

May be refrigerated overnight or frozen. Keep smiling! Makes 8-10 servings. (Have used this for many brunches and shower brunches.)

Mrs. Carl Granrud, Montevideo, Mn.

HOT BAKED HAM SALAD

3 c. diced, cooked ham
1 c. diced celery
1/2 c. chopped stuffed olives
2 hard cooked eggs, chopped
2 tsp. onion

2 Tbsp. lemon juice
2 tsp. mustard
Dash of pepper
3/4 c. mayonnaise
1 c. crushed potato chips

Combine all ingredients, except potato chips; put into 8x8 inch baking dish. Sprinkle with potato chips. Bake in 400° oven for 20 to 25 minutes.

Stella Bliss, Minneapolis, Mn.

MUSHROOM-HAM ESCALLOPED POTATOES

1 c. cream
1/2 c. shredded American
   cheese
2 Tbsp. pimento
1/2 tsp. salt

2/3 c. milk (regular or
   evaporated)
4 c. potatoes
1 1/2 c. cubed ham

Put into casserole. Bake at 350° for 50 to 60 minutes. Top with 2 tablespoons pimento and 1/4 cup cheese. Return to oven 6 to 8 minutes.

Marion Round, Faribault, Mn.

SOUR CREAM SCALLOPED POTATOES AND HAM

2 slices smoked ham
8 medium potatoes
1 can cream of mushroom
   soup
1 c. sour cream

1 tsp. salt
1 c. sliced onion
Dash of pepper
1 c. shredded Cheddar
   cheese

Slice potatoes. Combine soup, sour cream, salt and pepper. In greased 3 quart casserole, alternate layers of ham, potatoes and onion with sour cream mixture. Top with cheese; cover loosely with foil. Bake at 350° for 2 1/2 hours.

Sally Bartsch, Blaine, Mn.

HAM SOUFFLE

1 1/2 c. ring macaroni
2 1/4 c. grated sharp
  Cheddar cheese
1 tsp. chopped onion
1 tsp. chopped green
  pepper
1 1/2 c. ground, boiled ham

3/4 c. chopped almonds
1 1/2 small cans pimiento
1 1/2 c. half & half cream
  and milk
5 eggs, slightly beaten
Butter
Salt and pepper to taste

Cook macaroni; rinse in cold water. Drain; add remaining ingredients. Bake at 350° for 35-40 minutes in 9x13 inch pan. Serve in squares with hot cream of mushroom soup as sauce. May be slightly diluted.

Pearl Mohn, Montevideo, Mn.

HAM STRATA

12 slices white bread
  (frozen)
3/4 lb. sharp American
  cheese
1 (10 oz.) pkg. chopped
  broccoli, cooked, drained
2 c. diced, cooked ham

2 1/2 - 3 c. milk
2 Tbsp. minced onion
1/2 tsp. salt
1/4 tsp. dry mustard
6 slightly beaten eggs
1 c. shredded Cheddar
  cheese

Using doughnut cutter, make 12 doughnuts and holes in slices of frozen bread (these are to be reserved for the top). Using the scraps and crusts, line the bottom of a 13x9 inch pan. Over the top of the bread pieces, layer the American cheese, broccoli, ham and onion. Arrange the doughnuts and holes in a decorative manner on top. Combine remaining ingredients, except Cheddar cheese; pour over. Refrigerate overnight. Bake at 350°, uncovered, for 60 minutes. Add cheese and bake 5 minutes. Let stand 10 minutes before serving. This is excellent. The extra fuss is well worth it!

Debbie Burgum, Dickinson, N.D.

HAM ROLLS

2 (10 oz.) pkg. frozen
  broccoli spears
8 slices Swiss or American
  cheese

8 slices of ham
1 can cream of mushroom
  soup
1/2 c. sour cream
1 tsp. prepared mustard

Cook broccoli; cool. Place slice of cheese on ham slice. Divide broccoli; place on cheese. Roll up securely. Place seam side down in pan. Blend soup, sour cream and mustard; pour sauce over ham rolls. Bake, uncovered, at 350° for 20 minutes or a little longer. Serves 4.

Pearl Mohn, Montevideo, Mn.

Similar recipe by: Mary Boe, Minneapolis, Mn.

VEAL ALL-IN-ONE

2 medium onions, sliced	1 1/2 tsp. salt
4 Tbsp. butter or margarine	1 bay leaf
4 Tbsp. flour	1/4 tsp. sugar
1 can beef bouillon	3 c. cubed, cooked veal
1 c. canned tomatoes	6 medium potatoes, cubed

Cook onions in butter or margarine until soft; remove from heat. Blend in flour; add bouillon slowly, stirring until smooth. Add tomatoes and seasonings and cook, stirring constantly, until sauce boils and thickens. Place meat and potatoes in greased 3 quart casserole; pour on hot sauce. Bake, uncovered, in a moderate oven, 350° F., for 45 minutes. Garnish with parsley. Serves 6.

Dena Stoddard, St. Louis Park, Mn.

CHALBER BALLELI
(Veal Balls)

2 1/2 lb. veal, ground	1 tsp. salt
1/2 lb. pork, ground	1/2 tsp. pepper
4 eggs	6 slices toasted bread, finely
1 c. light cream	crumbled
1/4 c. milk	6 Tbsp. butter or margarine
1/4 c. finely chopped onion	1 Tbsp. flour
1/4 tsp. nutmeg	1 c. milk

Mix veal and pork with eggs and cream, diluted with milk; stir in onion. Season with nutmeg, salt and pepper. Crumble toast to make fine crumbs; mix in thoroughly. Form meat mixture into balls about the size of an egg; brown in butter. Turn balls and fat into casserole; cover. Place in moderate oven, 350° F., for 30 minutes. Uncover and let veal balls brown, about 10 minutes. Place balls on platter; keep aside in warm place. Combine flour and juice in bottom of casserole in a skillet; brown slightly. Add cup of milk or

water and stir until slightly thickened. Pour gravy over
veal balls or serve in separate bowl. Yield: 6 portions.
Dena Stoddard, St. Louis Park, Mn.

VEAL CHOPS ROMA

6 veal chops
1 medium clove of garlic,
  minced
1/2 tsp. oregano, crushed
3 Tbsp. butter or margarine

1 can condensed tomato soup
1/2 c. sliced onion
1 c. green pepper strips
1/2 c. sliced ripe olives

In fry pan, brown chops; cook garlic with oregano in
butter. Add soup and onion. Cover; cook over low heat
30 minutes. Add pepper and olives; cook 15 minutes more
until done. Stir occasionally. Makes 4 servings.
Stella Bliss, Minneapolis, Mn.

VEAL PARMIGIANA

12 veal cutlets, pounded thin
2 eggs, well beaten
1/2 tsp. pepper
1/2 tsp. salt
1 1/2 c. bread crumbs

6 Tbsp. Parmesan cheese
1/2 c. butter
2 (8 oz.) cans tomato sauce
12 slices Mozzarella cheese

Dip the veal in the beaten eggs, to which salt and
pepper have been added. Roll in the combined bread
crumbs and Parmesan cheese. Refrigerate for 1/2 hour.
Saute in butter until golden brown; place in a shallow
baking dish. Pour tomato sauce over all; top with slices of
Mozzarella cheese. Sprinkle with additional Parmesan
cheese. Bake at 350° for 1/2 hour. Serves 6 to 8.
St. Cloud, Mn.

VEAL PICCATA

3 slices veal leg steak,
  separated into scallops
  and pounded thin
1/4 c. flour
3 Tbsp. plus 1/8 lb. butter
1/8 c. olive oil

1 Tbsp. lemon juice
1 clove garlic, minced
1 Tbsp. capers
1/2 c. dry white wine
3 Tbsp. chopped fresh
  parsley
Salt and pepper

Dip veal scallops in flour; shake off excess. Brown in a mixture of 3 tablespoons butter and olive oil, a few pieces at a time. Remove to baking dish. Melt 1/8 pound butter and when it cools slightly, add lemon juice, garlic, capers, wine, parsley, salt and pepper to taste. Simmer 5 minutes, stirring, then cool and pour over veal. Refrigerate 3 to 4 hours before baking. Bake 30 minutes at 350°. Serves 4-6.

St. Cloud, Mn.

VEAL SCALLOPINE

8 Tbsp. butter or margarine
3/4 lb. mushrooms, sliced
1 small onion, finely
  chopped
4 green peppers, sliced thin
1 clove garlic, peeled
2/3 c. dry white wine

3 c. coarsely chopped,
  peeled tomatoes
3/4 tsp. plus 1/2 tsp. salt
1/4 tsp. dried tarragon
12 (1 1/2 lb.) thin veal
  scallops
1/8 tsp. pepper

In 5 tablespoons butter, saute mushrooms until golden. Add onion, green pepper and garlic; cook until onion is translucent. Add tomatoes, wine, 3/4 teaspoon salt and tarragon; stir well. Reduce heat and simmer, covered, for 30 minutes, stirring occasionally. Wipe veal with damp cloth; sprinkle with 1/2 teaspoon salt and pepper. Heat remaining 3 tablespoons butter in another skillet. Add veal, a few pieces at a time; cook until lightly browned on both sides. Remove and keep warm. Return veal to skillet. Remove garlic from sauce; pour over veal. Simmer, covered, for 5 minutes. Serves 6.

St. Cloud, Mn.

CHOP SUEY

3 lb. boneless pork or 3 lb.
  ground lean pork
6 Tbsp. vegetable oil
1/2 tsp. salt
1/2 tsp. pepper
3 medium size onions
8 celery stalks
1/4 c. soy sauce

2 (15 3/4 oz.) cans chicken
  or beef broth
1 (1 lb.) can bean sprouts,
  drained
4 Tbsp. cornstarch
1/2 c. water
Hot rice
Chinese noodles

Cut pork into 1/4 inch cubes; heat oil in large saucepan. Add pork cubes or ground pork, salt and pepper.

Cook over medium heat for 5 minutes, stirring frequently. Cut each onion into 6 wedges; cut celery into 1 inch pieces. Heat chicken or beef broth; add to meat with onion wedges, celery pieces and soy sauce, mixing well. Cook over low heat, stirring occasionally, for 15 minutes. Add drained bean sprouts and cook 3 minutes longer. Mix cornstarch with water; add to the saucepan. Stir until thickened; cook 2 minutes longer. Serve hot over rice and Chinese noodles. Makes 12 servings.

Georgine Isakson, Fargo, N.D.

AMERICAN CHOP SUEY

1 lb. ground beef
1/2 lb. seasoned pork
  sausage
1 onion, chopped
3/4 c. celery

1 c. catsup
1 qt. tomatoes
3/4 lb. spaghetti, broken
  small and cooked

In Dutch oven, brown and drain ground beef and pork sausage. Add onion and celery; cook until partially soft. Add remaining ingredients; season with salt, pepper and garlic salt to taste. Simmer slowly several hours.

Pam Doyea, Fargo, N.D.

MOCK CHOP SUEY

1 1/2 lb. ground beef
2 c. boiling water
2 c. celery
1/3 c. soy sauce

1 can cream of mushroom
  soup
1 medium onion
1 c. uncooked regular rice

Combine and bake at 350° for 1 hour. Stir after 30 minutes.

Barbara Lueck, Duluth, Mn.

CHOW MEIN

Brown together:
2 Tbsp. butter
1 small onion, chopped

1 1/2 c. celery
1 c. mushrooms

Simmer for 15 minutes. Add:

4 Tbsp. soy sauce

1 tsp. salt

1507-82

1 1/2 c. cooked chicken, 1 tsp. sugar
  browned hamburger or 1 can bean sprouts
  pork sausage 1 can water chestnuts

Cook until celery is tender. Add 1 1/2 tablespoons cornstarch in 3 tablespoons water; cook until thick. Serve with chow mein noodles and cooked rice.

Gemma Pierson, St. Cloud, Mn.

CHOW MEIN

Brown 1 pound cubes of pork, beef or veal. Sprinkle with 1/2 teaspoon salt. Add 1 cup water. Cover pan; simmer for 30 minutes. Add more water, if necessary. Add 3 cups sliced celery and 2 chopped onions; cook about 1/2 hour. Add 1 can bean sprouts, drained; cook 5 minutes. Add 2 tablespoons molasses, 1 teaspoon soy sauce, 3 tablespoons cornstarch, mixed in 2/3 cup water, and season to taste. Mix together. Add 1 can water chestnuts, sliced, and 1 can mushrooms (or you can use fresh ones, but put them in a little sooner so they cook about 10 minutes). Heat through and let get real bubbly. Makes 4 or 5 servings. You can buy Durkee's chop suey sauce mix in any store where the dry package mixes are and use for added flavor and color. Serve over chow mein noodles or rice.

Jim Tuft, St. Paul, Mn.

EASY CHOW MEIN

1 (1 lb.) pkg. frozen 2 Tbsp. vegetable oil
  Oriental vegetables 2 Tbsp. cornstarch
1 lb. chopped or ground 2 Tbsp. soy sauce
  meat (pork, veal, 1 c. water, boiling
  turkey or beef) Bouillon (optional)
1 small onion Almonds

Cook vegetables until almost done. Meanwhile, saute meat and onion until done. Make gravy of the oil, cornstarch and hot water, to which you add the bouillon, if desired. Cook, stirring constantly, until thickened. Pour over meat and vegetables; heat. Serve with chow mein noodles or rice.

D. Klosterman, Anoka, Mn.

CHOW MEIN HOT DISH

1 1/2 lb. hamburger
1 medium onion
1 can tomato soup
2-3 c. celery, cut

1 can mushroom soup
1 can mushrooms
1/4 c. soy sauce

Brown meat and onion. Bring celery to a boil in 2 cups of water; save liquid. Use 1 cup of liquid from cooking celery. Stir all ingredients together. Put in baking dish; cover with chow mein noodles. Bake 1 hour at 350°.

K., St. Cloud, Mn.

MOCK CHOW MEIN HOT DISH

1 lb. hamburger
1 can chicken rice soup

1 can green beans

Brown meat; drain fat and add seasonings. Add soup and beans; simmer. Serve over white or brown rice. Top with chow mein noodles.

Anne Aune, Minneapolis, Mn.

OVEN CHOW MEIN

1 lb. ground beef
1 large or 2 small bunches
  celery, chopped
2 onions, chopped

2 Tbsp. soy sauce
1/2 c. raw rice
2 cans mushroom soup
2 c. water

Brown meat, then mix all together. Bake 45 minutes at 350°. Stir and bake 45 minutes more.

Myrtle Bohline, Gamaliel, Ar.

Similar recipes submitted by: Mary Jane Schmitz, Wadena, Mn., Bea Aslakson, E. Grand Forks, Mn.

CREOLE JAMBALAYA

1 lb. smoked pork sausage
  or ham, cut in 1/2 inch
  cubes
1 c. chopped green pepper
1 c. chopped onion

1 clove garlic, crushed
1 Tbsp. flour
1 (28 oz.) can (3 1/2 c.)
  tomatoes
2 1/2 c. water

2 Tbsp. chopped parsley	1/2 tsp. thyme
2 c. uncooked rice	1/4 tsp. red pepper
2 Tbsp. Worcestershire	1 lb. peeled, deveined raw
sauce	shrimp
2 tsp. salt	

Cook sausage in a large skillet about 5 minutes. (If ham is used, add 1 tablespoon shortening.) Drain off all but 2 tablespoons pan drippings. Add green pepper, onion and garlic; cook until tender. Blend in flour; brown slowly, stirring often. Stir in tomatoes, water and parsley; bring to a boil. Add remaining ingredients, except shrimp. Return to a boil; cover. Reduce heat and simmer 20 minutes. Add shrimp; cook 10 minutes longer. Fluff lightly with a fork. Makes 8 servings.

Ann Christensen, Litchfield, Mn.

CRISPY HOT DOGS

Remove crust from square bread. Melt butter and mix with catsup. Roll hot dogs in bread; secure with toothpick. Spread butter and catsup on outside of bread. Place on cookie sheet in 350° oven until brown and crisp.

Mary Perron, Rochester, Mn.

HOBO DINNER

1 hamburger patty	2 slices of potato
2 slices of onion	2 slices of carrot

Layer on piece of tinfoil. Bake at 350° for 1 hour.

Kris Riley, So. St. Paul, Mn.

BEEF JERKY

Choose any lean cut of meat; venison, flank, brisket or round steak work well. Slice very thin. Slicing is easiest if it is partially frozen. Remove every bit of the fat because it will become rancid if left on. Cut the meat into long, narrow strips, with the grain. Cut not more than 1/4 inch thick. Seasonings for 1 pound of meat:

1 tsp. salt	1/4 tsp. garlic powder
1/4 tsp. pepper	1/4 tsp. Worcestershire sauce
1/2 tsp. onion powder	1 drop Tabasco sauce

290

Stir these together in a medium bowl with a little water to dissolve them. Lay in the sliced meat; add just enough water to cover it. Put a dish on top of the meat to keep the meat submerged. Refrigerate overnight. When you are ready to cook the meat, drain the liquid and pat the long slices dry with paper towels. Lay the strips directly on the oven rack, close together, but not overlapping. Bake as low as possible, 150°, with oven door slightly ajar to allow for circulation. You may want to place foil on the oven bottom to catch drips. Bake till the meat is very dark and dry and cracks sharply, but does not break when bent. It will take from 3 to 6 hours depending on the thickness of the meat. After it cools completely, pack in airtight container. You may also want to try other spices, such as oregano, basil or thyme. Or, you can brush on soy sauce or liquid smoke, mixed with water.

Mary Jean Voss, Owatonna, Mn.

LAMB RIBS
(I Used Chicken)

Saute 3/4 pound lamb ribs per person, after trimming off fat. Add 1 sliced onion and 1 clove of chopped garlic. Sprinkle 1/4 to 1/2 teaspoon curry powder over meat; sprinkle a dash of cinnamon, a pinch of thyme and salt. Add 3/4 cup water, 1-2 tablespoons raisins and 1 teaspoon of honey. Cover and bake in 400° oven for 45 minutes. Remove cover and brown. Serve over rice.

Rhea Thoms, Jamestown, N.D.

BAKED LIVER WITH ONIONS

6 slices bacon
6 medium onions, sliced
1 1/2 lb. beef, lamb or
    pork liver, sliced

1/2 c. flour
1 1/2 tsp. salt
1 c. onion soup

Fry bacon until crisp; remove from pan and save. Cook onions in half of bacon fat until soft and yellow; place in shallow casserole or baking dish. Coat liver slices with flour, mixed with salt. Brown on both sides in remaining fat, then add to casserole. Pour in onion soup. Cover and bake in a moderate oven, 350° F., for 1 hour. Top with bacon strips; return to oven, uncovered, long enough to crisp bacon. Garnish with parsley and onion rings.

Dena Stoddard, St. Louis Park, Mn.

PICNIC SALAMI

In large bowl, mix:

4 lb. ground beef
1/4 c. curing salt
2 Tbsp. liquid smoke

1 1/2 tsp. garlic powder
1 1/2 tsp. ground pepper

Cover and chill 24 hours. Divide mix in 4 parts; shape each into logs. Wrap tight in a 12x18 inch piece of nylon net and tie ends with string or bag twists. Place on broiler pan with rack; bake 4 hours in 225° oven. Remove from oven and take off net. Pat rolls with paper towels. Cool slightly and wrap in foil; refrigerate or freeze. Makes about 3 pounds.

Myrtle Bohline, Gamaliel, Ar.

SPAM LOAF

Grind:

1/4 lb. American cheese
1 can Spam

4 small onions, if desired
1/2 green pepper

Mix together:

1 1/2 c. soda cracker
   crumbs
1 1/2 c. milk

4 eggs, beaten
1/4 c. softened butter

Combine the two mixtures. Cook 1 package ring macaroni; add to the first two mixtures. Bake in a 9x13 inch pan at 350° for 1 hour. Cut in squares and serve with sauce, made of chicken, celery or mushroom soup, which has been diluted with 1/2 cup milk. This hot dish may be frozen.

Georgine Isakson, Fargo, N.D.

SUMMER SAUSAGE

2 lb. hamburger
2 Tbsp. Morton's Tender
   Quick
1 tsp. black pepper

1 c. cold water
2 Tbsp. liquid smoke
1 tsp. onion salt

Mix all together well; let stand in refrigerator 24 hours. Roll into 2 or 3 rolls and wrap in foil. Poke holes in bottom; place on rack in broiler pan. Bake 1 1/2 hours at 325°. Let cool; rewrap in foil. Put in plastic bag; freeze for future use. (See following note.)

Note: For variety, you may add 1 teaspoon mustard, 1 teaspoon hickory salt, sausage and poultry seasoning.

Ruth Rehschuh, Minneapolis, Mn.

SQUAW DISH
(Camping Supper)

6 eggs, beaten slightly
  with fork
1 can cream style corn
6 slices bacon, cut in pieces

1 (4 oz.) can mushrooms
1 small onion
Salt and pepper to taste

When campfire is low, fry bacon in iron skillet; add cut up onion and mushrooms. Add corn. When hot, add eggs. A small amount of green pepper may also be added.

Helen Teeuwen, Minneapolis, Mn.

SKILLET SUPPER

1 lb. bulk sausage
1 large onion, chopped
1 green pepper, chopped
1 (14 oz.) can tomatoes
1/2 c. water

2 c. uncooked macaroni
1 tsp. salt
2 Tbsp. sugar
2 tsp. chile powder
2 c. sour cream

Brown sausage in skillet; pour off fat as it collects. Stir in remaining ingredients, except sour cream. Bring to a boil; cover and simmer 20-25 minutes. Stir often. Blend in sour cream; serve.

Dee Olson, St. Paul, Mn.

TETRAZZINI SUPPER

14 oz. elbow spaghetti
  (4 c.)
2 Tbsp. salad oil
2 (10 1/2 oz.) cans
  condensed cream of
  mushroom soup
2 (10 1/2 oz.) cans
  condensed cream of
  chicken soup

1 1/2 c. milk or 1 1/4 c.
  milk plus 1/4 c. sherry
4 c. cubed, cooked turkey
  or chicken
1 c. cubed, cooked ham
1/2 c. chopped green pepper
1 c. halved, pitted ripe
  olives
1 c. grated Parmesan cheese
1 c. slivered almonds

Cook spaghetti as directed on package; drain. Pour oil over spaghetti; toss. In each of two ungreased 2 quart casseroles, mix 1 can mushroom soup, 1 can chicken soup and 3/4 cup milk. Stir in half the turkey, ham, spaghetti, green pepper and olives. Sprinkle 1/2 cup cheese over each casserole. Heat oven to 375°. Bake, uncovered, 20 minutes. Sprinkle 1/2 cup almonds over each casserole; bake 10 minutes longer. Makes 12 servings.

Lovise Lorenz, St. Paul, Mn.

FETTUCCINI

4 oz. fettuccini noodles,
  cooked and drained
3/4 c. butter or margarine
1 (10 oz.) pkg. frozen
  spinach, chopped*
1 beaten egg
1/2 c. dairy sour cream
1/4 c. milk

2 Tbsp. grated Parmesan
  cheese
2 tsp. minced dry onion
1/2 tsp. salt
Dash of pepper
2 c. shredded Monterey Jack
  cheese

Mix together all the above. Bake at 350° for 15 minutes, uncovered, and 15 minutes, covered. Makes 4-6 servings.

*I use fresh when available and cook just slightly.

Donna Chapp, St. Paul, Mn.

BAKED LASAGNE

1 1/2 lb. ground beef
1/2 lb. ground lean pork
1 c. chopped onion
1 clove garlic, crushed
1 (1 lb. 12 oz.) can tomatoes
1 (15 oz.) can tomato sauce
1 1/2 Tbsp. parsley flakes
1 1/2 Tbsp. sugar
1 tsp. salt
1 tsp. crushed basil leaves
1/2 c. grated Parmesan
  cheese

1 (2 lb.) ctn. creamed (large
  curd) cottage cheese
1 Tbsp. parsley flakes
1 tsp. salt
1 tsp. crushed oregano leaves
8 oz. lasagne noodles, cooked
  and well drained
3/4 lb. Mozzarella cheese,
  shredded
1/2 c. grated Parmesan
  cheese

Cook ground beef, ground pork, onion and garlic in heavy Dutch oven or roaster until meat is browned and onion is tender; drain off excess fat. Add tomatoes and break up with a fork. Stir in tomato sauce, 1 1/2 tablespoons parsley flakes, the sugar, 1 teaspoon salt and the basil; simmer, uncovered, 1 hour, or until mixture is as thick as a good spaghetti sauce. Heat oven to 350°. Mix cottage cheese, 1/2 cup Parmesan cheese, 1 tablespoon parsley flakes, 1 teaspoon salt and the oregano. In oblong baking dish, 13 1/2 x 9 x 2 inches, layer half each of noodles, sauce, Mozzarella cheese and cottage cheese mixture. Repeat; reserve enough sauce for a thin top layer. Spread sauce over top; sprinkle with 1/2 cup Parmesan cheese. Bake, uncovered, 45 to 55 minutes, or until cheese is bubbly in center. Let stand 15 minutes after removing from oven (sets). Cut in squares. Makes 8 to 10 servings.

Mary Jean Voss, Owatonna, Mn.

Similar recipe submitted by: Maryann Skelton, Duluth, Mn.

EASY LASAGNE

1 lb. ground beef
2 cloves of garlic, minced
1 can tomato paste
1 (16 oz.) can whole
    tomatoes
1 tsp. salt

3/4 tsp. pepper
1/2 tsp. oregano
1 (8 oz.) pkg. lasagne
    noodles
1 1/4 c. cut up Swiss cheese
1 (12 oz.) ctn. cottage
    cheese

Brown beef and garlic in small amount of fat; add tomato paste, tomatoes, salt, pepper and oregano. Cover and cook 20 minutes. Cook noodles as directed. Heat oven to 350°. Using 11 1/2 x 7 1/2 x 1 1/2 inch baking dish, alternate layers of meat sauce, noodles and cheese. Bake 20 minutes. Serve with grated Parmesan cheese sprinkled on top.

Mary Paul, Minneapolis, Mn.

SKINNY LASAGNE

1/2 lb. lean ground beef
1 clove garlic, minced
1/2 c. chopped onion
1/2 c. chopped celery
2 (1 lb.) cans stewed
    tomatoes, drained
1/4 c. catsup

1/4 c. chopped parsley
1 tsp. salt
1/2 tsp. basil
1/2 tsp. oregano
2 c. low fat cottage cheese
1 egg, beaten
6 lasagne noodles, cooked

1507-82

1 c. grated Mozzarella
  cheese
Paprika

1 Tbsp. grated Parmesan
  cheese
Mixed Italian herbs

Saute beef until lightly browned; add garlic, onion, celery and tomatoes. Cook, stirring, 10 minutes. Add catsup, parsley, salt, basil and oregano; simmer about 20 minutes. Mix cottage cheese and egg. Place 2 noodles in bottom of shallow baking dish, 10x6x2 inches. Spoon half the cheese mixture on noodles; top with 1/3 of the beef mixture. Repeat layers as follows: Noodles, cheese mixture and meat sauce, noodles, then sauce. Spread Mozzarella cheese on top; sprinkle with Parmesan cheese. Sprinkle with mixed herbs. Bake in a 350° oven for about 35-40 minutes. Let stand about 10 minutes before cutting. Serves 6; 270 calories per serving.

Mary Jean Voss, Owatonna, Mn.

ITALIAN CRAZY LASAGNE

1 pkg. Kraft's tangy
  Italian style spaghetti
  dinner
2 lb. ground beef

Salt
Onion
6 oz. Mozzarella cheese,
  shredded
1 c. cottage cheese

Prepare dinner as directed on package. Brown the ground beef and onion. Stir in the sauce and salt to taste. Place in a 9x13 inch pan in layers. Bake at 350° for 30 minutes.

Florence Wesen, St. Cloud, Mn.

LASAGNE FLORENTINE CASSEROLE

1 pkg. frozen chopped
  spinach, cooked, drained
1 lb. ground beef
1 (15 oz.) can tomato sauce
1 tsp. sugar
1/2 tsp. salt
1/4 tsp. garlic powder
1/4 tsp. black pepper

1 (8 oz.) pkg. egg noodles,
  cooked
1/2 c. Cheddar cheese,
  grated
3 Tbsp. milk
2 c. cottage cheese
1 (3 oz.) pkg. cream cheese,
  cubed
1 small onion, cut in eighths

Grease a 7x11x2 inch pan. Brown the ground beef.

Add seasonings, tomato sauce and cooked noodles; remove from heat and stir to combine. Combine milk and 1/2 cup of the cottage cheese; whip or blenderize until smooth. Add the remaining cottage cheese; whip or blenderize. Add the cubed cream cheese; repeat until smooth. Chop onion and add; if blenderizing, add onion and blenderize until onion is finely chopped. Spoon 1/2 the noodle mixture into bottom of baking dish. Spoon on 1/2 the cottage cheese mixture; lay on spinach. Top with remaining noodle mixture. Cover with foil; bake for 40 minutes at 350°. Uncover and spread with remaining cottage cheese mixture. Sprinkle with grated Cheddar cheese. Return to oven until cheese melts, about 10 minutes. Makes 4-5 servings.

D. Klosterman, Anoka, Mn.

SAUSAGE LASAGNE WRAPS

Cook and drain 6 lasagne noodles. Divide 1 pound Hillshire Farm sausage into 6 pieces; split lengthwise and stuff with 1/2 slice Mozzarella cheese. Wrap each piece in a noodle. Place in baking dish and cover with 1 (16 ounce) jar Ragu cooking Italian sauce. Bake at 350° for 30 minutes.

Gladys Turk, Duluth, Mn.

ITALIAN MEAT PIE

Form pie crust in round pan with crescent rolls. Brown hamburger in separate pan; add onion, green pepper, Italian seasoning and chili pepper. Drain off grease, then add 1 can tomato paste. Stir; pour into pie crust. Top with shredded Mozzarella cheese. Serve with hot sauce: Heat 1 can tomato paste with Italian seasoning. Serve with above meat pie. (Bake at 375° for 30 minutes.)

Anne Aune, Minneapolis, Mn.

BREAKFAST PIZZA

1. Place 1 package crescent roll dough in 9x13 inch ungreased pan. 2. Sprinkle with 2 to 3 cups shredded Monterey Jack and Cheddar cheeses. 3. Brown 1 package maple flavored sausage; cut up and sprinkle over cheese (regular sausage will work). 4. Mix 6 eggs, 1 cup milk, salt and pepper; pour over sausage. 5. Bake in 400° oven for 25-30 minutes.

Cathy Rudolph, Grand Rapids, Mn.

PIZZA CASSEROLE

12 oz. enriched wide
  noodles
1 1/2 lb. ground beef
2 tsp. salt

3 c. any kind of pizza sauce
2 c. shredded Mozzarella or
  American cheese

Cook noodles in salted water 2 to 3 minutes. Brown meat; drain excess fat. Add pizza sauce, salt and pepper; stir to blend. Make layers of noodles, sauce and cheese. Bake at 350° for 15 to 25 minutes.

Marian Nelson, Dickinson, N.D.
Similar recipe submitted by: K., St. Cloud, Mn.

EASY DEEP DISH PIZZA

3 c. Bisquick baking mix
3/4 c. water
1 lb. ground beef
1/2 c. chopped onion
1/2 tsp. salt
2 cloves garlic, crushed
1 tsp. Italian seasoning

1 can (or 15 oz.) tomato
  sauce
1 (4 1/2 oz.) jar sliced
  mushrooms, drained
1/2 c. chopped green pepper
2 c. (about 8 oz.) shredded
  Mozzarella cheese

Heat oven to 425°. Lightly grease jelly roll pan. Mix baking mix and water until soft dough forms; gently smooth dough into ball on floured surface. Knead 20 times. Pat dough on bottom and up sides of pan with floured hands. Pinch edges, forming 3/4 inch rim. Cook and stir ground beef, onion, salt and garlic until beef is browned; drain. Mix tomato sauce and seasoning; spread evenly over dough. Spoon beef mixture evenly over sauce. Top with mushrooms, green pepper and cheese. Bake until crust is golden brown, about 20 minutes. Serves 8.

Ina Veal, Bismarck, N.D.

PIZZA HOT DISH

2 lb. hamburger, browned
  and drained
1 c. sliced pepperoni (reserve some for top)
1 (10 1/2 oz.) can pizza
  sauce

Chopped onion
Salt and pepper
Red pepper
1 tsp. oregano
1/2 tsp. garlic salt
1 (15 oz.) can tomato sauce

Mix previous ingredients together. Cook 8 ounces egg noodles; drain. Add 1 cup milk and 1 1/2 cups shredded Mozzarella cheese. Combine with meat mixture in 9x12 inch pan. Top with reserved pepperoni and 1/2 cup Mozzarella cheese. Bake at 350° for 45 minutes. Serves 12.

For variety, try 1 pound hamburger and 1 pound Italian sausage.

Ella Fennessy, Duluth, Mn.

Similar recipes submitted by: Karen Moe, Duluth, Mn., Liz Tuft, St. Paul, Mn., Betty Olson, St. Paul, Mn.

MEAT-ZA PIZZA

In large bowl, mix the following ingredients thoroughly:

1/4 c. Campbell's tomato
  soup
1 1/2 lb. ground beef
1/4 c. fine, dry bread
  crumbs
1/4 c. minced onion

1 egg, slightly beaten
1 tsp. salt
1 medium clove of garlic,
  minced, if desired
1/8 tsp. oregano, crushed

Place one square of foil on a cookie sheet. Put ground beef mixture on foil; pat out till 1/2 inch thick with stand-up rim. Turn up edge of foil to catch drippings; spread rest of tomato soup over meat. Top with 3 slices of Mozzarella process cheese. Sprinkle more oregano over it and add anchovies or mushrooms. Bake at 450° F., for 15 minutes or till done.

Alice Corrigan, Windom, Mn.

PIZZA SPANISH RICE

2 lb. ground beef
1/2 lb. bacon, cut into 1
  inch pieces
1 large onion
2 c. green pepper
2 c. celery
1 can Contadina pizza sauce

2 (10 oz.) cans tomato soup
2 pkg. shredded Mozzarella
  cheese
3 c. dry Minute rice
Salt and pepper to taste
Onion powder to taste
Garlic powder to taste

In a large frying pan, place bacon; brown slightly. Add ground beef, onion, green pepper, celery and seasonings. Cover and cook until ground beef is browned, stirring often; set aside. In a large kettle, make Minute rice according to directions on box. Add ground beef mixture, pizza sauce and tomato soup; mix well. Put in 9x12 inch cake pan and bake at 375° for 20 minutes. Reduce heat to 350°; top mixture with cheese and bake for another 15 minutes or until cheese melts without turning brown.

Marcia Theisen, Duluth, Mn.

UPSIDE DOWN PIZZA

Brown 2 pounds hamburger; add salt, pepper, onion, crushed garlic (2 cloves), 1 1/2 teaspoons oregano and 1 jar spaghetti sauce. Add 1 (4 ounce) can mushrooms, pepperoni, green pepper, sausage, black olives or anything else you like. Put above mixture into a 9x13 inch pan. Cover with 2 packages Mozzarella cheese; use whole slices to cover pan.

Top Layer: Mix together in a bowl -

2 eggs
1 c. milk
1 Tbsp. oil

1 c. flour
1/2 tsp. salt

Pour over meat and spaghetti sauce; sprinkle Parmesan cheese over all. Bake at 375° for 40 to 50 minutes.

Laverne M. Akerstrom, Duluth, Mn.

SPAGHETTI

4 qt. tomatoes, cut up
4 small cans tomato paste
Garlic powder to taste

1/2 - 1 Tbsp. Italian
  seasoning
Red pepper to taste

Simmer 3-4 hours.

Meat Balls:

2-3 lb. hamburger
Cracker crumbs
2-3 eggs
Onion

Italian seasoning
Garlic powder
Red pepper
Salt and pepper

Brown meat balls; cook in sauce.

Geri Running, St. Paul, Mn.

FRITTATA DI SPAGHETTI

1/2 (1 lb.) pkg. spaghetti
3 Tbsp. butter for the
   spaghetti, plus 1 Tbsp.
   for cooking the frittata
1/3 c. freshly grated
   Parmesan cheese
2 Tbsp. chopped parsley

3 eggs
Salt
Freshly ground black
   pepper
11-12 inch skillet or saute
   pan
Tomato sauce

1. Cook the spaghetti in at least 3 quarts salted, boiling water until very firm to the bite. It should be a bit more al dente, more underdone, than usual because it will undergo further cooking. 2. Drain and toss the spaghetti in a bowl together with 3 tablespoons butter, the grated cheese and the parsley. Allow the spaghetti to cool off some. 3. Break the eggs into a deep dish or small bowl and lightly beat them together with salt and pepper. 4. Add the beaten eggs to the spaghetti; mix thoroughly. 5. Put 1 tablespoon butter into the pan; turn on the heat to medium. When the butter foam begins to subside, put in the spaghetti, spreading to an even thickness over the entire bottom of the pan. 6. Cook for 3 to 4 minutes without touching the pan; tilt the pan slightly, bringing its edge closer to the center of the heat source. After about 1 1/2 minutes, always keeping the pan very slightly tilted and its edge near the center of the burner, rotate the pan a shade less than a full quarter turn. Cook another minute or so; continue turning and cooking until you have come around full circle. This procedure is necessary in order to cook the frittata evenly; otherwise, it will be overcooked in the middle and undercooked at the edges. To see if it is cooked properly, lift up an edge of the frittata with a spatula and make sure that the underside has formed a nice golden crust. 7. Take a round platter at least as large as the pan; place it upside down over the pan, then turn the pan over, letting the frittata plop onto the dish. Slide the frittata back into the pan, with its uncooked side facing the bottom. Repeat the cooking procedure described in step 6 until the second side of the frittata has also formed a fine, golden crust. 8. Transfer to a cutting board and cut into wedges. Like nearly all frittatas, it may be served hot, lukewarm or at room temperature. Serve with tomato sauce and more grated Parmesan cheese, if desired. For 6 persons; 63 cents for each serving.

Nance Martin, Ramsey, Mn.

ITALIAN SPAGHETTI

1/3 c. olive oil
3 bay leaves
1 medium onion, chopped fine
2 buttons of garlic
1 pinch of thyme
1 large can tomatoes

1 large can tomato sauce
1 regular can tomato soup
Salt and pepper to taste
1/4 tsp. oregano
12 whole black peppers
1/4 Tbsp. spaghetti
seasoning

Brown onion and garlic in oil; add spices and all tomato soup, sauce and tomatoes. If this is too thick, add a little water. Simmer 2 hours; add meat balls the last 1/2 hour.

Meat Balls: Mix -

1 lb. ground beef
2 eggs

1 c. bread crumbs

Add:
Salt and pepper to taste
Garlic salt to taste

About 3/4 c. water

Shape into balls and fry in oil; add to spaghetti sauce the last 1/2 hour of cooking. Have crushed red pepper and Parmesan cheese on the table for those who want it.
Vivian Johnson, Fargo, N.D.

BURRITOS

1 pkg. flour tortillas
1 can chili without beans
1 can Cheddar cheese soup
1 (4 oz.) can chopped green
chili peppers

Colby cheese, grated
2 lb. ground beef
Diced onion, if desired
1 can tomato sauce with bits
2 tsp. cumin
1 tsp. red pepper

Mix green pepper, onion, chili and cheese soup in a saucepan; heat. Fry ground beef until browned; drain. Put enough of the chili mix in with the beef to moisten. Place meat mixture inside tortilla; sprinkle with some grated Colby cheese and roll up. Place in baking pan. Cover with rest of chili mix and some grated Colby cheese. Heat in oven, 350°, until cheese is soft. Serve with a sauce made from the tomato sauce, cumin and red pepper.
Mary Ann Ohman, Fargo, N.D.
Similar recipe submitted by: Pam Doyea, Fargo, N.D.

BURRITO PIE

1/4 c. salad oil
4 (8 inch) flour tortillas
1/2 lb. ground beef
1 medium onion, diced
1 small garlic clove, minced
1 (4 oz.) can chopped green
   chilies, drained (I use 1/2
   can)
1 (8 oz.) can refried beans

1/3 c. hot taco sauce
1/4 tsp. salt
1/2 lb. Monterey Jack
   cheese, shredded (2 c.)
1 c. shredded lettuce
1 medium tomato, diced
5 large pitted ripe olives,
   sliced

About 1 hour before serving: In 10 inch skillet over medium heat, in hot salad oil, fry 1 tortilla at a time, about 30 seconds on each side until lightly browned and blistered. With tongs, remove tortilla to paper towels to drain. Discard any remaining oil. Preheat oven to 350°. In same skillet over high, cook ground beef, onion and garlic until all pan juices evaporate and meat is well browned, stirring occasionally. Remove from heat; stir in green chilies, refried beans, taco sauce and salt. In 9 inch pie plate, place 1 tortilla; top with 1/4 of bean mixture and 1/4 of cheese. Repeat 3 times. Bake pie 30 minutes or until heated through. Sprinkle pie with shredded lettuce, diced tomato and olives. Makes 4 main dish servings.

Judy Rieger, Grand Forks, N.D.

QUICK ENCHILADAS

1 (7 oz.) bag tortilla chips
1 can cream of mushroom
  soup

1 c. sour cream
1 (4 oz.) can diced green
   chilies
1/2 c. chopped green onions

Mix and spread in 9x13 inch pan. Cover with 3 cups grated cheese. Bake at 400° for 15 minutes.

Fran Basch, White Bear Lake, Mn.

TACOS

1 lb. ground beef
1/2 c. chopped onion
1 (8 oz.) can tomato sauce

1 tsp. chili powder
3/4 tsp. salt
1/2 tsp. garlic powder

Brown beef in skillet, stirring until crumbly. Drain

off excess fat. Stir in remaining ingredients; simmer, covered, for 10 minutes. Warm up taco shells in 250° oven for 5 minutes. Serve with chopped tomatoes, shredded lettuce and grated cheese.

Mary Jean Voss, Owatonna, Mn.

TACOS

2 1/2 lb. ground beef
2 medium onions, chopped
   small
2 pkg. taco mix
1 small jalapeno pepper,
   chopped fine

1 c. water
1 pkg. soft taco shells (flour
   tortillas)
Grated Cheddar cheese to
   taste

Brown ground beef, onions and jalapeno pepper together. Add taco mix and water; cook about 10 minutes or until fairly dry. Spoon onto taco shells and use toothpicks to hold together. Fry in small amount of oil until heated through; open about 5 minutes before serving and add cheese. Continue cooking on low heat until cheese is melted. Serve with chopped lettuce, tomatoes and taco sauce on top. Yummy!

Pat Hornung, St. Paul, Mn.

CRUSTY CRESCENT TACO SQUARES

1 lb. ground beef
1/2 c. chopped onion
1 (1.31 oz.) env. taco
   seasoning mix
1 (16 oz.) can refried beans
1 (8 oz.) can tomato sauce
2 (8 oz.) cans Pillsbury
   refrigerated quick
   crescent dinner rolls

1 Tbsp. oil
1/3 c. corn meal
4 oz. (1 c.) shredded
   Cheddar cheese
4 oz. (1 c.) shredded
   Monterey Jack cheese
2 c. shredded lettuce
1 c. chopped tomatoes
Taco sauce

Heat oven to 375° F. Brown meat and onion; drain. Stir in taco seasoning mix, beans and tomato sauce; simmer 5 minutes. Unroll dough into 4 long rectangles. Place in ungreased 15x10 inch jelly roll pan; press over bottom and 1 inch up sides to form crust. Brush dough with oil; sprinkle with corn meal. Spoon hot meat mixture over crust. Bake at 375° F. for 25 to 30 minutes or until crust is golden brown; sprinkle with cheese. Return to oven until cheese is melted, about 1 to 2 minutes. Cut into squares. Top with lettuce, tomatoes and taco sauce, as desired. Makes 8 servings.

Liz Tuft, St. Paul, Mn.

TAMALE PIE

Brown:
1 lb. ground beef	1 rib celery
1 onion	

Add:
1 (12 oz.) can tomato paste	1 tsp. chili powder
1 can whole kernel corn	Dash of red pepper
1 green pepper, diced	1/2 tsp. oregano
1 tsp. salt	

Mix the above and place in buttered 2 quart casserole or cast iron pan. Top with 1/2 cup grated Cheddar cheese. Mix together:

1 c. corn meal	1/8 c. sugar
1 c. flour	1 c. milk
4 tsp. baking powder	1/8 c. vegetable oil
1/2 tsp. salt	

Spoon on top of cheese. Bake at 350° for 40 minutes.

Lila Houser, Aitkin, Mn.

CEDRIC ADAMS' SAGE DRESSING

3 small loaves day old bread, torn into small bits	Sage enough to taste, but not enough to gag (use 1 level tsp. sage)
1 medium size onion, chopped fine	Salt just enough to season (don't oversalt)
1 lb. butter, melted*	

First, get a large pan. Mix bread, onion, sage and salt together well; toss like for a salad. Pour over melted butter; mix well and that's it.

*The secret, says Cedric, is to use butter (not margarine).

Note: A 1 pound loaf makes 8 cups (2 quarts) of loosely packed crumbs.

Helen-May Johnson, Chanhassen, Mn.

MOTHER'S DRESSING

1 lb. stale bread
1 tsp. salt
1/4 tsp. pepper
2 Tbsp. poultry seasoning
1/2 c. shortening, melted
1 tsp. sage

1/4 tsp. minced onion
1 c. chopped celery
2 apples
2 eggs
1 c. milk

Mix together and bake.

Marie Capen, Duluth, Mn.

MRS. GELINEAU'S TURKEY DRESSING

In a large bowl, cube a 1 1/2 pound loaf of white bread; let this dry out for several days. Brown 1 pound of bulk pork sausage with 2 cups chopped celery and 1 cup chopped onion. Boil the neck and gizzard with a little salt and pepper, onion and celery tops in 5 cups water; boil until tender. Strain; add this liquid to bread cubes. Use about 4 cups of the liquid. Add the browned meat mixture and 1 teaspoon salt, 1 teaspoon pepper and 3 teaspoons sage. Stuff turkey loosely and bake in a normal manner.

Joan Norton, Hibbing, Mn.

STUFFING

1 pkg. dry onion soup
1 can cream of celery soup
1 can cream of chicken soup
2 eggs

Celery, partially precooked
1 lb. pork sausage, seasoned, browned and drained

Mix all above ingredients with plain bread cubes (2 bags). Can also use broth from gizzards, etc. Add enough broth to moisten. Bake till done.

Mary Jean Voss, Owatonna, Mn.

DRESSING FOR TURKEY

Use blender and grind the turkey gizzard, liver and onion; fry in 2 sticks of margarine. Put 1 tablespoon salt, 1/2 teaspoon pepper, 1 teaspoon sage, 2 teaspoons poultry seasoning, either flaked or fresh celery, 2 eggs, 2 cups milk, 1/8 teaspoon (dash) of garlic powder into blender;

mix well. Add to the mixture in the margarine; heat. Add 10 slices bread, torn up, and 1/2 package of a seasoned dressing mix. Stir until well mixed, adding more milk, if necessary. Stuff the bird. (Sometimes I also add a little chicken base flavoring to mixture in blender.)

Ray Rieger, Grand Forks, N.D.

CHICKEN ALMOND
(Favorite of Victor, Nicollet hotel)

1 lb. chicken, boned and diced	1 handful Chinese pea pods (optional)
1/2 c. mushrooms, sliced	2 c. chicken broth
1/2 c. bamboo shoots, sliced very thin	1 Tbsp. cornstarch
1/2 c. sliced water chestnuts	1 tsp. salt
2 c. diced celery	Rice
	Whole almonds

Saute the diced chicken in peanut oil over medium heat about 10 minutes until lightly browned. Add vegetables and salt; saute for another 5 minutes. Add chicken broth; cover and simmer an additional 5 minutes. Thicken sauce with cornstarch; serve with steaming mounds of rice. Sprinkle handful of whole almonds on top of each serving. Serves 4 people.

Dena Stoddard, St. Louis Park, Mn.

BAKED CHICKEN BREAST

Cut 3 chicken breasts in halves (6 pieces); skin and brown in butter or oil. Place in foil lined pan, enough to cover top also. Season with salt and pepper. Add to the browning pan the following and bring to boil:

1 c. chopped celery	1/4 c. cooking sherry
1 can golden mushroom soup	1/2 c. chopped onion
1/2 c. chicken broth (bouillon cube)	1/2 c. mayonnaise

Pour over breasts; sprinkle with paprika. Cover; bake in slow oven, 275°-300°, for 3 hours. For more gravy, add 1 more can of soup and more broth. Serve with mashed potatoes or rice.

Colleen Grapentin, St. Cloud, Mn.

BARBECUE CHICKEN

Cut 1 frying chicken in serving pieces. Combine 1 cup ketchup with 1 (16 ounce) bottle or can of Coke in kettle. Put cut up chicken in and boil slowly until chicken is tender and it will be coated with sauce.

Fern Graskieutz, Litchfield, Mn.

HONEY BARBECUED CHICKEN

1 (8 oz.) can tomato sauce
1/4 c. cooking oil
1/2 c. orange juice
1/4 c. vinegar
1/2 tsp. dried oregano, crushed

1 tsp. salt
6 peppercorns
1 clove of garlic, minced
1 chicken, cut up
Honey Mustard Glaze

In large jar, combine all ingredients, except chicken and glaze. Cover and shake vigorously to blend. In shallow dish, pour mixture over chicken; cover and marinate for 2 hours at room temperature or overnight in refrigerator, turning occasionally. Drain, reserving marinade. Grill chicken over medium coals for 45-50 minutes, brushing with marinade and turning frequently. Just before serving, brush with Honey Mustard Glaze. Serves 6.

Glaze: Mix well 1/4 cup honey and 1 1/2 teaspoons dry mustard.

Diane Haan, Bismarck, N.D.

BREAST OF CHICKEN ON RICE

1 can cream of mushroom soup
1 soup can of milk
3/4 c. uncooked regular rice
1 (4 oz.) can mushroom stems and pieces

1 (1 1/2 oz.) env. Lipton onion soup mix
4-6 chicken breasts, split in halves
Salt and pepper to taste

Mix mushroom soup with milk; reserve 1/2 cup of mixture. Mix remaining soup mixture with rice, mushrooms (including liquid) and half of the onion soup mix. Pour into 9x13 inch pan. Place chicken breasts on top. Pour reserved soup mixture over chicken breasts; sprinkle with remaining onion soup mix. Cover; bake 1 hour in 350° oven. Uncover and bake 15 minutes longer.

Gerri Ruprecht, St. Cloud, Mn.

FRIED "CRACKERED" CHICKEN

Roll skinned chicken pieces as follows and in this order: 1. Flour (salt and pepper, if desired); 2. Eggs, beaten; 3. Soda crackers, crushed fine. Fry in oil, high temperature, until brown on one side. Reduce heat; turn pieces over. Cover pan; fry until chicken is soft and well done, 10-12 minutes.

Netta Capetz, St. Paul, Mn.

CHICKEN DELICIOUS

Cook 1 large chicken until tender; remove meat from bones and dice. Let the broth cool; remove fat until you have 1 cup. If there is not enough fat to make 1 cup, add butter. Add 6 well beaten eggs to broth and enough milk to make 2 quarts. Heat the fat and add 1 cup flour to it; blend well. Add liquid and cook until thick; let cool. Butter a large baking dish. Make dressing of bread, giblets, onion and sage (or your favorite dressing recipe). Put layer of dressing on bottom; pat smooth, then layer of sauce, layer of chicken, layer of sauce. Spread rest of dressing on top and bake until brown. Serve with rest of sauce. Serves 15 to 20.

Mary Perron, Rochester, Mn.

CHICKEN CONFETTI

4-5 lb. broiler-fryer chicken, cut up	1 (6 oz.) can tomato paste
1 tsp. salt	2 Tbsp. snipped parsley
1/8 tsp. pepper	2 tsp. salt
1/4 c. salad oil	1 tsp. basil
1/2 c. chopped onion	1/4 tsp. pepper
1 clove garlic, minced	7 or 8 oz. spaghetti, cooked and drained
2 (16 oz.) cans tomatoes	Grated Parmesan cheese
1 (8 oz.) can tomato sauce	

Wash chicken pieces; pat dry. Season with 1 teaspoon salt and 1/8 teaspoon pepper. In large skillet or Dutch oven, brown chicken in oil; remove chicken. Pour off all but 3 tablespoons fat. Add onion and garlic; cook and stir until onion is tender. Stir in chicken and remaining ingredients, except spaghetti and cheese. Cover tightly; cook chicken slowly 1 to 1 1/2 hours, or until tender, stirring occasionally and adding water, if necessary. Skim off excess fat. Serve on spaghetti; sprinkle with Parmesan cheese. Makes 4 to 6 servings. Serve with Dilled Zucchini (below), garlic bread and spumoni ice cream.

Dilled Zucchini: Cut 2 unpared medium zucchini lengthwise in halves. Cook, covered, in 1 inch boiling, salted water 12 to 15 minutes or until tender; drain. Brush with melted butter and sprinkle with dill weed. Makes 4 servings.

Marion Round, Faribault, Mn.

EASY OVEN FRIED CHICKEN

Cut chicken into serving pieces. Melt 1 stick butter or margarine in cake pan or other shallow baking pan. Add 2 tablespoons paprika. Put chicken in pan; turn to coat. Salt and pepper. Bake at 350° for 1 hour. Gets brown and crisp; don't have to turn while baking.

Mary Perron, Rochester, Mn.

ITALIAN STYLE OVEN FRIED CHICKEN

Cut up and wash 3 pounds chicken. Drip dry or wipe dry with paper towel. Combine the following 6 ingredients:

1 1/2 c. dry bread crumbs
3/4 c. grated Parmesan
   cheese
1/2 c. chopped parsley

1 clove garlic, minced
2 tsp. salt
1/4 tsp. pepper

Melt 1 cup butter; roll chicken in melted butter, then roll in crumb mixture. Arrange in shallow pan without over-lapping. Drizzle with remaining butter and crumbs. Bake 1 hour at 375° F. Turn chicken one time while baking.

Donna VanderVorst, Bismarck, N.D.

FOOLPROOF CHICKEN

1 can cream of celery soup
1 can cream of chicken soup
1 pkg. onion soup mix
1 c. rice

1 soup can white wine (or
   water)
3 chicken breasts, skinned,
   split (can use other parts)

Mix soups, wine and rice in ovenproof casserole; let stand several hours. Arrange chicken on top of mixture. Cover; place in oven for 1 hour. After 1 hour, remove cover. Stir and cook another hour, uncovered.

K., St. Cloud, Mn.

HOT CHICKEN AND WALNUTS

3 or 4 boned chicken breasts
1 c. rice
Salt
1 Tbsp. butter
3 Tbsp. soy sauce
2 Tbsp. cornstarch
2 Tbsp. dry red wine
Pinch of sugar
1/2 tsp. salt

1/2 - 1 tsp. crushed red
  pepper
2 c. your favorite vegetables
  (green pepper, zucchini,
  broccoli, whatever is in
  season)
5 scallions
2 Tbsp. peanut oil
1 c. chopped walnuts

Put 2 cups of water on to boil for the rice, adding a little salt and butter. While the water is coming to a boil, take out the thawed chicken breasts. Chop the breasts into bite sized pieces; set aside. Mix soy sauce with cornstarch. Add to this the wine, sugar, 1/2 teaspoon salt and 1/2 to 1 teaspoon crushed red pepper (depending on your taste); set aside. Chop into bite sized pieces your favorite vegetables. Chop scallions into 1 inch pieces; set aside. Back to the rice: Stir 1 cup of rice into the boiling water; turn the flame down to a simmer. Cover; simmer for 20 minutes or until the water is absorbed. Add 2 tablespoons of peanut oil to a wok or deep frying pan. Turn heat to medium (never to high, since the oil burns easily). Stir-fry green vegetables and scallions for 2 minutes or until crisp-tender. Remove from pan. Stir-fry chopped walnuts until golden, about 1 minute. Remove from pan. If necessary, add another tablespoon of oil. Add half the chicken. Stir-fry 3 minutes until translucent. Remove and stir-fry the rest of the chicken. When second batch is also translucent, return first batch of chicken to wok. Stir soy sauce mixture so that ingredients are well combined. Push the chicken to the sides of the pan; add the soy sauce mixture. Blend chicken with sauce; cook for 2 minutes or until mixture is bubbly. Add vegetables and walnuts. Stir-fry 1 more minute until all is heated through. Pour over rice.

St. Cloud, Mn.

"CHICKEN JULIENNE"

2 boned chicken breasts
1/2 c. butter
1/2 c. flour (or as needed)
2 Tbsp. lemon juice

Salt and white pepper to
  taste
1 c. heavy cream
1/4 - 1/3 c. Parmesan cheese
Paprika

1507-82

311

Preheat oven to 400°. Cut chicken into rather large strips, 4 to each 1/2 breast. Melt butter in a shallow pan; dredge chicken with flour, then butter. Place in ovenproof pan, one layer only. Sprinkle lemon juice over and salt and pepper. Pour cream over, then cheese. Sprinkle with paprika. Bake for 20 minutes. Serve with rice pilaf.

Julaine Burbach, Winona, Mn.

BRUCE'S MARINATED CHICKEN

Cut chicken in serving pieces; marinate in any wine for at least 1 hour, longer if possible. Put on grill; salt and pepper. Baste with barbeque sauce the last 15 minutes.

Bruce Perron, Faribault, Mn.

COUNTRY-STYLE CHICKEN KIEV

2/3 c. butter
1/2 c. dry bread crumbs
2 Tbsp. grated Parmesan
    cheese
1 tsp. basil
1 tsp. oregano leaves
1/2 tsp. garlic salt

2 chicken breasts, split
    (about 1 1/2 lb.)
1/4 c. dry white wine
1/4 c. chopped green onion
1/4 c. chopped parsley
1/4 tsp. salt

Preheat oven to 375°. Melt butter. On waxed paper, combine crumbs, cheese and spices; dip chicken in butter, then roll in crumbs. Place skin side up in ungreased 9 inch dish. Bake for 50 to 60 minutes, or until golden brown and tender. Meanwhile, add wine, onion and parsley to remaining butter (about 1/2 cup). When chicken is golden brown, pour sauce around and over. Return to oven for 3 to 5 minutes more, just until sauce is hot. Serve with sauce spooned over. Serves 4.

Alice Nelson, Minneapolis, Mn.

OLIVE-CHICKEN BAKE

Make a broth with 2 tablespoons margarine, 2 tablespoons flour and 1 can beef consomme. Add:

4 oz. cut stuffed olives
1/2 lb. fresh mushrooms,
    sliced

1/3 c. dry sherry
2 medium tomatoes, skinned
    and cut

Simmer 10 minutes; pour over boned and browned chicken breasts. Bake, uncovered, for 1 hour at 350°.
Ginny Harwood, St. Cloud, Mn.

ORANGE CHICKEN

3-4 lb. chicken
Salt and pepper
2 cloves garlic, crushed
2 medium oranges, peeled and sliced (reserve the rinds)
1/2 c. orange juice

1/4 c. soy sauce
1 tsp. grated fresh ginger root
1/2 tsp. allspice, ground
1 Tbsp. brown sugar
Arrowroot (about 1 1/2 Tbsp.), added to some cold water

Presoak pot, top and bottom, in water for 15 minutes. Wash chicken, inside and out, under running cold water. Rub inside of chicken with salt, pepper and pressed garlic. Stuff with orange slices, peeled. Place chicken in pot, breast up. Grate orange rind; sprinkle over chicken. Mix and add orange juice, soy sauce, ginger, allspice and brown sugar.

In conventional oven: Place covered pot in cold oven. Turn temperature to 480°; cook for 90 minutes. Ten minutes before done, remove from oven. Pour liquid into saucepan. Return the pot, uncovered, to oven for final 10 minutes to brown the chicken. Meanwhile, bring sauce to a boil and thicken with arrowroot. You may want to add a bit of brown sugar to the sauce, to taste. Serves 4.

In microwave oven: Variable Power Ovens - Microwave 15 minutes on full power, then 20 to 30 minutes on 50% of full power.

Note: Do not forget to immerse the pot for 10 to 15 minutes in cold water. You may thicken the sauce in the pot (after removing the chicken to carve) by microwaving the drippings plus arrowroot for 2 minutes on full power.
St. Cloud, Mn.

OVEN BARBECUED CHICKEN WINGS

3 lb. chicken wings
Salt and pepper to taste
2 Tbsp. oil
1 c. honey

1/2 c. soy sauce
1/2 clove garlic, chopped
2 Tbsp. catsup

1507-82

Preheat oven to 375°. Cut off small wing tips of each chicken wing and discard. Cut remaining wing into 2 parts. Sprinkle with salt, pepper and oil; set aside. Combine honey, soy sauce, garlic and catsup; pour over chicken pieces. Make one layer of coated chicken pieces in a baking dish. Bake 1 hour or until chicken pieces are thoroughly coated and the sauce is caramelized. If chicken starts to burn, reduce heat.

Stella Bliss, Minneapolis, Mn.

QUICK 'N EASY CHICKEN

1 (2-3 lb.) chicken, cut in pieces

1 c. (8 oz. bottle) Western salad dressing
1 pkg. onion soup and dip mix

Arrange chicken in a roaster or cake pan. Mix dressing and soup mix thoroughly; pour over chicken. Bake at 350° for 2 hours.

Jean Taylor, Grand Forks, N.D.

SPICY CHICKEN WITH SPINACH

1/2 c. dry sherry
1/4 c. soy sauce
1 Tbsp. cornstarch
1 whole chicken breast, skinned, boned, cubed
6 Tbsp. peanut oil
3 large cloves garlic, chopped
1 inch piece fresh ginger root, chopped
1 lb. bean curd (tofu), cubed
3 scallions, chopped

1 medium zucchini, sliced
1/2 (8 1/2 oz.) can sliced water chestnuts, drained
1/3 can (8 1/2 oz.) bamboo shoots, drained
1 Tbsp. Kochee Chang Sauce (see following note)
1/3 c. chicken broth or stock
1/3 lb. fresh spinach, washed and dried
Hot cooked rice or chow mein noodles

Combine sherry, soy sauce and cornstarch in medium sized bowl; add chicken and marinate at least 15 minutes. Drain chicken, reserving marinade. In wok or large skillet, heat 3 tablespoons of the oil. Add chicken with half each of garlic and ginger. Stir-fry until chicken becomes opaque. Remove chicken; keep warm. Add remaining garlic and ginger and half the scallions; stir-fry about 3 minutes. Add zucchini, water chestnuts, bamboo shoots, Kochee Chang Sauce and chicken broth. Reduce heat; stir-fry until zucchini is tender-crisp. Return chicken and reserved marinade to wok; add spinach. Raise heat and stir-fry until sauce thickens and spinach just starts to wilt. Serve over bed of rice or chow mein noodles; sprinkle with remaining scallions.

Note: If you cannot get Kochee Chang sauce, substitute 3 teaspoons Hoisin sauce, 1 teaspoon hot pepper flakes, 1 teaspoon sesame seeds and 1 teaspoon sesame oil.

St. Cloud, Mn.

CRISPY CHICKEN SUPREME

4 c. Kellogg's Rice Krispies
  cereal, crushed to 2 c.
1 tsp. paprika
1 egg
3/4 c. milk
3/4 c. all-purpose flour
1 1/2 tsp. salt

1/4 tsp. pepper
1 tsp. poultry seasoning
3 lb. frying chicken pieces,
  washed, patted dry
3 Tbsp. margarine or butter, melted (optional)

1. Place crushed Rice Krispies cereal in shallow dish or pan. Stir in paprika; set aside. 2. In a second shallow dish or pan, beat egg and milk slightly. Add flour, salt, pepper and poultry seasoning. Mix until smooth. Dip chicken in batter; coat with crushed cereal. Place in single layer, skin side up, in well greased or foil lined shallow baking pan. Drizzle with melted margarine. 3. Bake at 350° F. for about 1 hour or until chicken is tender. Do not cover pan or turn chicken while baking. Yield: 6 servings.

Marion Round, Faribault, Mn.

CHICKEN WAIKIKI BEACH

Ideal for outdoor or indoor entertaining, this tempting sweet-and-pungent recipe comes from our newest state, Hawaii. If desired, garnish the platter with fresh lemon leaves, available at florists' shops, and serve with a tossed green salad and your favorite dressing.

2 whole chicken legs and 2
  whole chicken breasts
1/2 c. flour

1/3 c. salad oil or
  shortening
1 tsp. salt
1/4 tsp. pepper

Sauce:

1 (1 lb. 4 oz.) can sliced
   pineapple
1 c. sugar
2 Tbsp. cornstarch
3/4 c. cider vinegar

1 Tbsp. soy sauce
1/4 tsp. ginger
1 chicken bouillon cube
1 large green pepper, cut
   crosswise in 1/4 inch
   circles

1. Wash chicken; pat dry with paper towels. Coat chicken with flour. 2. Heat oil in large skillet. Add chicken, a few pieces at a time; brown on all sides. Remove as browned to shallow roasting pan, arranging pieces skin side up. Sprinkle with salt and pepper. 3. Meanwhile, preheat oven to 350° F. 4. Make sauce: Drain pineapple, pouring syrup into 2 cup measure. Add water to make 1 1/4 cups. 5. In medium saucepan, combine sugar, cornstarch, pineapple syrup, vinegar, soy sauce, ginger and bouillon cube; bring to boiling, stirring constantly. Boil 2 minutes. Pour over chicken. 6. Bake, uncovered, 30 minutes. Add pineapple slices and green pepper. Bake 30 minutes longer, or until chicken is tender. Serve with fluffy white rice. Makes 4 servings.

Blanche Masica, Minneapolis, Mn.

FRICASSEE DE VOLAILLE AU VERMOUTH
(Chicken Fricassee with White Vermouth Sauce)

1 (3 1/2 lb.) ready-to-cook
   chicken, cut into serving
   pieces
Salt and pepper to taste
2 Tbsp. butter
1/2 c. coarsely chopped
   onion
1 clove garlic, finely
   chopped
2 Tbsp. flour
3/4 c. dry white vermouth

1 1/4 c. chicken broth
1 bay leaf
2 sprigs fresh thyme or 1/2
   tsp. dried
1 c. carrots, cut into fine,
   julienne strips, about 2
   inches long
1 1/2 c. loosely packed leeks,
   cut into fine, julienne
   strips, about 3 inches long
1/2 c. heavy cream

Sprinkle the chicken with salt and pepper to taste. Heat the butter in a skillet; add the chicken pieces, skin side down. Cook over moderate heat about 1 minute without browning. Scatter the onion over all; cook 30 seconds. Add the garlic; stir it around. Cook the chicken about 4 minutes, turning the pieces often in the butter. Sprinkle the flour over all, turning the pieces so that they are evenly coated. Add the vermouth, chicken broth, bay leaf and thyme. Cover; cook over moderate heat about 20 minutes. Meanwhile, bring 2 batches of water to a boil for the carrots and leeks. Drop the carrots into one batch; the leeks in the other. Let the carrots simmer about 1 minute; drain. Let the leeks simmer about 4 minutes; drain. When the chicken has cooked for a total of 30 minutes (start to finish), add the cream, carrots and leeks. Let simmer about 2 minutes. Serve with rice.

St. Cloud, Mn.

POULET PROVENCAL

1 (2 1/2 - 3 lb.) chicken	4 cloves fresh garlic, peeled
1 tsp. salt	and cut in halves
1 tsp. freshly ground pepper	1/4 tsp. rosemary
1 tsp. butter	1/2 tsp. basil
2 Tbsp. olive oil	1/4 tsp. thyme

Season the cavity of the bird with about half the salt, all the pepper and all the butter. In a baking pan just large enough to hold the bird, pour in half the oil; add the garlic. Place the bird in the pan; sprinkle the bird with remaining salt, rosemary, basil, thyme and remaining olive oil. Roast in a 425° oven for 1 hour, basting frequently. (May also be cooked in a covered charcoal grill, basting often until bird is tender and meat separates easily from the bones.) Remove from pan; cut in serving pieces. Serve hot or cold. Serves 4.

For a 9 to 12 pound turkey, multiply ingredients by 4 and roast for 4 hours at 375°.

St. Cloud, Mn.

CHICKEN AND BROCCOLI BAKE

2 pkg. plain broccoli spears, thawed, drained	1 can cream of mushroom soup
3-4 lb. chicken, cooked and boned	1 can water chestnuts, drained and sliced
Velveeta cheese	1 can French fried onion rings
1/2 c. mayonnaise	

Place thawed and drained broccoli in a well greased 9x12 inch pan. Cut the chicken in large pieces; spread over broccoli. Place 1/8 inch slices of cheese over entire pan. Mix soup with mayonnaise; spread over cheese. Sprinkle water chestnuts on top. Bake 40 minutes at 350°, then remove from oven and cover with onion rings. Bake 15 to 20 minutes longer.

Lovise Lorenz, St. Paul, Mn.

CHICKEN BROCCOLI CASSEROLE

2 whole chicken breasts, cooked
2 pkg. frozen broccoli
1 c. mayonnaise
2 cans cream of chicken soup

1 Tbsp. lemon juice
4 Tbsp. butter
1 c. dry bread crumbs
1 c. shredded mild Cheddar cheese

Cook broccoli according to package directions; drain and place in buttered 3 quart casserole. Cut chicken into pieces; put in a layer over broccoli. Mix together the mayonnaise, soup and lemon juice; pour over chicken and broccoli. Sprinkle cheese over soup mixture. Melt butter; mix with bread crumbs. Sprinkle over cheese. Bake, uncovered, at 350° for about 30 minutes or until bubbly. Serve over hot rice. Makes 6-8 servings.

Alicia Woodford, Montevideo, Mn.

CHICKEN AND BROCCOLI

6 whole chicken breasts

2-3 pkg. frozen broccoli

Mix together:
2 cans Cheddar cheese soup
1 can cream of chicken soup

3 c. Hellmann's mayonnaise
1 1/2 tsp. curry powder

Mix 1 1/2 cups bread crumbs with 3 tablespoons melted butter and 2 cups shredded Cheddar cheese. Boil chicken 1 hour; thaw broccoli. Layer in 9x13 inch pan; dot with butter. Pour soup mixture on top and sprinkle with cheese and bread crumbs. Bake, covered, at 350° for 1/2 hour and 300° for 1/2 hour.

Renee Andreasen, Duluth, Mn.

318

CHICKEN BROCCOLI RICE CASSEROLE

4 c. cooked chicken, cut up
  in pieces
1/2 c. white rice
1 Tbsp. chopped onion
1 can cream of chicken soup
2 Tbsp. butter

1/2 c. grated Velveeta
  cheese
1/2 c. wild rice
1 pkg. cooked broccoli
1 can mushroom soup

Saute onion in butter. Add cooked rice, soups and cheese, salt and pepper and cut up chicken. Alternate broccoli with chicken mixture in a greased casserole. Cover; bake for 30 minutes at 325°.

Annette Erspamer, Duluth, Mn.

CHICKEN CASSEROLE

2 c. cooked chicken, cut
  in cubes
2 cans cream of chicken soup
4 tsp. diced onion
1 c. rice, cooked
1 c. mayonnaise

1 c. slivered almonds
6 hard boiled eggs, sliced
2 c. celery, cut fine
1 c. water chestnuts, sliced
2 Tbsp. lemon juice
Crushed potato chips to top

Bake at 350° for 1 hour.

Gladys Turk, Duluth, Mn.

CHICKEN CASSEROLE

2 1/2 - 3 c. boned chicken
4 c. chicken broth
2 c. dried bread crumbs
2 Tbsp. chopped pimento
2 Tbsp. chopped green
  pepper
2 Tbsp. grated onion
1 can cream of mushroom
  soup

1 can cream of chicken soup
2 beaten eggs
3/4 c. chopped celery
1 tsp. salt
1/4 tsp. pepper
3/4 c. Uncle Ben's long
  grain rice, cooked in 2 c.
  of broth for 2 minutes

Cover; let set for 10 minutes until rice takes up all liquid. Mix all ingredients, except 1 cup of bread crumbs, together; put in 9x13 inch buttered pan. Top with bread crumbs. Bake at 350° for 1 to 1 1/4 hours or until set. Cut and serve with Mushroom Sauce (follows). Serves 15.

Mushroom Sauce:

1 can mushroom soup   1 small can mushrooms
1/2 c. sour cream   Paprika and pepper

Heat and spoon over each serving.
Eloise Hoff, Preston, Mn.

CHICKEN CASSEROLE

3/4 c. brown and wild   1 c. mushrooms
   rice, mixed   3 lb. chicken, cut in pieces
Slivered almonds to top

Pour the following over:

1 large can condensed milk   1/4 c. sherry wine
1 can cream of chicken soup 1 pkg. Lipton's dry onion
Juice from mushrooms   soup

Cover and bake 2 hours at 350° in 9x13 inch pan.
Uncover and bake 1/2 hour more.
G.W. Seemans, Robbinsdale, Mn.

CHICKEN CASSEROLE

Stewed chicken, cut up   Water chestnuts, drained
Cream of chicken soup to   and sliced
   moisten   Triscuits, crushed
Asparagus, drained   Salt and pepper

Line baking pan with crushed crackers. Combine
other ingredients; pour over crackers. Put crushed
crackers on top. Bake 1 hour at 350°.
Anne Aune, Minneapolis, Mn.

CHICKEN CASSEROLE

1/4 lb. sliced fresh mush- 1 c. milk
   rooms or 1 (4 oz.) can 1 c. chicken broth
1 Tbsp. butter   2 beaten eggs
3 c. cut up chicken   2 Tbsp. minced onion
3 c. soft bread cubes   Salt and pepper

Saute mushrooms in butter. Mix all and place in
greased 2 quart casserole. Set in pan with 1 inch of water.

Bake 1 1/2 hours at 350°. Serve with Almond Sauce: Melt 2 tablespoons butter; add 2 tablespoons flour. Cook on low heat until bubbly. Take off heat; add 1 cup chicken broth. Bring to boil; boil for 1 minute. Add 1/4 cup slivered almonds. Pour over casserole.

Jan Eschbach, Duluth, Mn.

CHICKEN CASSEROLE

4 c. cooked chicken (you may also use turkey)
2 1/3 c. chopped almonds
1 tsp. salt
1 c. grated Cheddar cheese
4 hard cooked eggs, sliced
1 1/2 c. crushed potato chips
2 Tbsp. lemon juice
3/4 c. mayonnaise
1/2 soup can of sherry or white wine (you may use milk in place of wine)
1/2 tsp. Accent
2 c. chopped celery
2 pimentos, cut up
1 can cream of chicken soup, diluted with wine or milk

Combine all ingredients, except the potato chips, almonds and grated cheese (put on top when you bake it). Let this stand overnight in refrigerator. Bake next day at 400° for 45 minutes or until bubbly. Serves 8.

Mrs. B.V. Feller, Excelsior, Mn.

UNCLE BEN'S CHICKEN CASSEROLE

1 (6 oz.) box Uncle Ben's long grain and wild rice
2 c. hot water
1 fryer chicken, cut up, or thighs
Salt and pepper
1 (10 oz.) can cream of mushroom soup
1/2 c. milk
1/2 c. slivered almonds, if desired
1 Tbsp. butter or margarine

Combine contents of box and water in 2 1/2 quart casserole. Salt and pepper chicken to taste. Arrange chicken on top of rice mixture. Bake, covered, 1 1/4 hours at 375° or until done (chicken). Combine soup and milk. Saute almonds in butter or margarine. When casserole is done, pour soup mixture over casserole. Sprinkle top with almonds, if desired. Return to oven, uncovered, and bake until soup is bubbly. Serves 4-6.

Vi Geving, Duluth, Mn.
Similar recipe submitted by: Evelyn Swing, Anoka, Mn.

GOURMET CHICKEN CASSEROLE

1 pkg. Uncle Ben's wild
   rice mix (do not use
   seasoning in pkg.)
1/4 c. brown rice
1 can cream of mushroom
   soup
1 can cream of chicken soup
1 can cream of celery soup
1/2 c. milk

1/4 c. melted butter
1/2 c. sherry wine
1 (3 oz.) pkg. shaved
   almonds
1 (3 oz.) pkg. grated
   Parmesan cheese
10 chicken breasts, boned
   and halved

Grease large pan; put in raw rice. Mix the soups together with melted butter. Mix the milk and sherry wine; pour small amount of it on top of rice. Place chicken pieces on rice; add remaining liquid. Sprinkle almonds and cheese on top. Bake in 275° oven, uncovered, for 2 1/2 hours. Do not touch during baking. Serves 8-10.

Teresa Cupkie, Owatonna, Mn.

CHICKEN RICE CASSEROLE

8 chicken breasts
1 can cream of mushroom
   soup
1 can cream of chicken soup
1 Tbsp. minced onion
1 c. uncooked rice (not
   Minute rice)
1 tsp. salt

1/2 tsp. pepper
1/2 c. diced celery
1/2 c. chopped green pepper
1 small jar pimento, chopped
1 small can water chestnuts,
   chopped
1 Tbsp. butter

Butter 9x13 inch pan. Mix rice, undiluted soup, pepper, onion, celery, pimento and chestnuts; pour into pan. Place chicken breasts on top; dab with butter, salt and pepper. Bake in a 350° oven for 1 1/2 - 2 hours.

Mrs. Norma Applen, Minneapolis, Mn.

DELECTABLE CHICKEN CASSEROLE

6 whole chicken breasts,
   boned and halved
10 slices bacon
1 lb. fresh mushrooms, sliced
1 can cream of chicken soup

1 can cream of mushroom soup
1/2 c. sour cream
White pepper
Parsley
1 can water chestnuts, sliced

Cut 6 slices of bacon in halves; fry until translucent to remove some of the fat. Remove from the pan; fry the remaining slices until crisp. Remove from the pan; drain and crumble. Set aside. Pour off most of the bacon fat; reserve about 2 tablespoons and fry the mushroom slices in it, about 5-10 minutes, until they are beginning to brown. Sprinkle the chicken breast halves lightly with white pepper, then wrap each piece with 1/2 slice of the partially cooked bacon, securing with a toothpick. Place them in a large, oblong buttered baking dish. Rinse and drain the water chestnuts; combine them with the soups, sour cream and the mushrooms. Pour this mixture over the chicken. Cover the dish tightly with foil; bake in a 325° oven for 2 hours. Garnish with the reserved crumbled bacon and chopped fresh parsley before serving. Good served with a mixture of wild and white rice.

Eileen Thompson, Minneapolis, Mn.

MEXICAN CASSEROLE

4 chicken breasts or 1 whole
   chicken
1 (8 oz.) pkg. Doritos
1 can tomatoes
1 can cream of mushroom
   soup
1 can cream of chicken soup

1 Tbsp. green chilies
1 medium onion, chopped
1 small can mushrooms,
   drained
1 1/2 c. grated Cheddar
   cheese
4-6 drops hot sauce
   (Tabasco)

Boil or microwave chicken; cool and remove from bone. Cut into 1 inch pieces. Heat tomatoes, soups, onion, chilies and mushrooms. Add hot sauce; stir well. In casserole, put layers of crumbled Doritos, layer of chicken; cover with half of soup mixture and half of cheese; repeat layers. Refrigerate for 24 hours. Bake at 300° for 1 hour. Serves 6.

Liz Tuft, St. Paul, Mn.

CREAMY CHICKEN CHOP SUEY

1 (10 1/2 oz.) can condensed
   cream of celery soup
1 c. milk
3 Tbsp. soy sauce
1 1/2 tsp. instant minced
   onion

3 c. chopped, cooked
   chicken
1 (1 lb.) can bean sprouts,
   drained
1/2 c. dairy sour cream
2 Tbsp. chopped parsley

In a large skillet, gradually add milk to soup. Add soy sauce, onion, chicken and bean sprouts. Simmer 5 to 10 minutes. Stir in sour cream and parsley. Serve over rice and top with chopped cashew nuts, if desired.
Mankato, Mn.

CHICKEN DIVAN

1 can cream of chicken soup
1-2 Tbsp. milk
1/2 c. sour cream
3 Tbsp. cooking sherry
  (optional)
Garlic salt
3 tsp. butter

2 pkg. frozen broccoli,
  cooked, or fresh broccoli
2 double chicken breasts,
  cooked, broken into bite
  size pieces
1/2 c. slivered almonds
1/4 lb. sharp cheese, grated

Combine soup, milk, sour cream, sherry and garlic salt, stirring until smooth. Place vegetables in bottom of casserole; cover with chicken. Pour soup mixture over this. Dot with butter; sprinkle almonds over entire mixture. Top with cheese. Bake at 350° until mixture bubbles. Makes 4-6 servings.
Kathie Ells, Duluth, Mn.

CHICKEN ENCHILADA

1 can cream of chicken soup
1/2 c. sour cream
1/2 c. diced green chilies

1/2 c. chopped green onions
1/2 c. grated Longhorn
  cheese
1/2 c. grated Jack cheese

Mix all together (and save out 1/2 cup). Cook and shred 3 cups chicken. Add all together (except for 1/2 cup). Spoon onto 4 large tortillas; fold and roll. Place in buttered 9x13 inch pan. Add 1/4 cup milk to the 1/2 cup mixture; pour over top. Sprinkle grated cheese on top. Bake at 375° for 30-40 minutes. Serves 6.
Fran Basch, White Bear Lake, Mn.

CHICKEN HOT DISH

1 chicken, fried, skinned,
removed from bone
3/4 c. brown rice, cooked
until almost tender
1 medium-large green
pepper, chopped

1 medium onion, chopped
2 c. celery, chopped fine
1/2 pkg. slivered almonds
1 can mushrooms
Crushed potato chips

Drain the fat from pan in which chicken was fried, then add a small amount of water to loosen the drippings. Mix all but the chips. Put into a greased casserole dish. Cover with crushed chips. Bake at 350° for 1/2 - 1 hour.

Dee Olson, St. Paul, Mn.

CHICKEN HOT DISH

1 can chicken and rice soup
1 can cream of mushroom
soup
1 (3 oz.) can chow mein
noodles

1 (5 oz.) can boned or
chunk chicken (white
meat - Swanson's)
1 (6 oz.) can evaporated
milk

Mix and bake 45 minutes at 350°.

Florence Wesen, St. Cloud, Mn.

CHICKEN HOT DISH

1 c. cooked chicken
1 can cream of chicken soup
1 can cream of mushroom
soup
1 small can mushroom
buttons

Pimento, as desired
2 c. chow mein noodles in
can
1/2 green pepper
1 c. whole cashews
1 small can evaporated milk

Mix all together. Bake at 275° for 2 hours.

Marion Round, Faribault, Mn.

CHICKEN HOT DISH

1 can cream of mushroom
soup
1 can cream of chicken soup
1 can Carnation milk

1 can chow mein noodles
1 c. cooked, chopped celery
2 c. chopped, cooked
chicken
1/2 c. slivered almonds

Mix well; put in buttered casserole. Bake in water for 1 1/2 hours at 275°. Remove water; bake for 1/2 hour at 325°.

Marilyn Radakovich, Duluth, Mn.

CHICKEN HOT DISH

4 c. seasoned croutons or more

1 c. butter, melted

Mix croutons and butter together; press half of mixture into 9x13 inch pan.

2 cans cream of celery soup
1 can of milk
3 or 4 c. diced chicken or turkey

1 box frozen peas
1 small jar of pimientos
Pepper to taste

Mix all together; pour over croutons mixture and top with remaining crumbs. Bake at 350° for 1 hour. Serves 12.

Elizabeth Redmond, Long Prairie, Mn.

CHICKEN AND RICE HOT DISH

1 c. rice
1 can cream of mushroom soup
1 can cream of chicken soup

1 c. diced celery
1 1/2 c. diced chicken, cooked
1 small can mushrooms or more, if desired

Soak rice the night before; drain next A.M. Mix all ingredients. Bake; use moisture from broth chicken was cooked in.

Evelyn Swing, Anoka, Mn.

CHICKEN POT PIE

1 c. onion, diced
1 c. celery, diced
1 c. carrots, diced
1/2 c. oleo
1 c. half & half cream

2 c. chicken broth
Dash of salt and pepper
1/2 c. flour
4 c. chicken, diced

Saute vegetables in butter. Stir in flour, then half & half and chicken broth. Add chicken; stir. Put in pan; cover with crust (follows). Bake at 375° for 1 hour.

326

Pie Crust:

3 c. flour

1 c. lard

1 tsp. salt

1 Tbsp. vinegar

1 egg

3 Tbsp. water

Wanda Thompson, Minneapolis, Mn.

BAKED CHICKEN SALAD

2 c. cooked chicken,
chopped large

2 c. chopped celery

1/2 c. toasted almond
slivers

2 Tbsp. chopped pimento

1/3 c. chopped green pepper

3 Tbsp. chopped green onion

1/2 tsp. salt

2 Tbsp. lemon juice

1/2 c. mayonnaise (real)

1/3 c. grated Swiss cheese

2 c. crushed potato chips

Blend all but the chips and cheese in a large bowl. Top with the cheese, then the chips. Bake in 350° oven until heated through, about 25 minutes.

Dee Olson, St. Paul, Mn.

CHICKEN OR TURKEY SOUFFLE

4 c. chicken or turkey

2 small cans mushrooms

1/4 c. butter

1 can water chestnuts,
drained and sliced

1/2 c. mayonnaise

9 slices Cheddar cheese

4 eggs

2 c. milk

1 tsp. salt

1/4 tsp. pepper

1 can mushroom soup

1 can celery soup

1 jar pimentos, cut up

2 c. bread crumbs*

Butter 9x13 inch pan; cover bottom with slices of bread, with crusts removed. Top with chicken or turkey; sprinkle on mushrooms after cooking them in butter for 5 minutes. Sprinkle on chestnuts; spread on mayonnaise. Cover with cheese slices. Combine milk, eggs, salt and pepper, then pour over cheese. Mix soups; spread over all. Cover with foil; place in refrigerator overnight. Remove foil; sprinkle on bread crumbs 15 minutes before taking from oven. Souffle firms up after it has been out of oven a few minutes. Bake 1 1/2 hours at 325°. Serves 12.

*Crumbs may be omitted.

Mrs. Joe Kelso, Sun City, Az.

CHICKEN AND STUFFING

2 c. diced chicken
1/2 pkg. stuffing
1/2 c. chopped onion
1/2 c. chopped celery
1/2 c. chopped green pepper
1/2 c. mayonnaise
1 can cream of mushroom soup
3/4 tsp. salt
2 eggs, beaten
1 1/2 c. milk
1/2 c. shredded Cheddar
cheese

Place 1/2 of stuffing into 8x8 inch pan. Top with chicken, onion, celery, green pepper and mayonnaise, mixed together. Spread remaining stuffing over mixture. Combine eggs and milk; pour over all. Cover and chill overnight. Next day, spoon soup over top. Bake, uncovered, at 325° for 50 minutes. Sprinkle cheese over top.

Renee Andreasen, Duluth, Mn.

CHICKEN WITH VEGETABLES

1/4 c. cornstarch
1/2 tsp. ground ginger
2 chicken breasts, skinned, boned, cut into 1 inch cubes
1/4 c. corn oil
1 c. zucchini strips
1 c. thinly sliced carrots
2 Tbsp. sliced green onion
1 clove garlic, minced or pressed
1/4 c. soy sauce
2 c. finely shredded iceberg lettuce
1 c. diagonally sliced celery
Hot rice

In shallow dish, stir together cornstarch and ginger. Coat chicken with cornstarch mixture. In large skillet or wok, heat corn oil over medium-high heat. Add chicken, stirring occasionally; cook 5 to 8 minutes or until browned. Add zucchini, carrots, celery, green onion and garlic. Stir in soy sauce. Cover; reduce heat and cook 5 minutes or until vegetables are tender-crisp. Lightly toss chicken vegetable mixture with lettuce. Serve over rice. Makes 4 servings.

Marion Round, Faribault, Mn.

CHICKEN AND WILD RICE

1 3/4 c. wild rice
2 cans cream of mushroom soup
3 c. boiling water
2 cans mushrooms
1 1/2 pkg. Lipton onion soup mix

Soak rice overnight in 3 cups hot tap water; rinse in cold water. Drain. Add 3 cups boiling water. Mix in soup and mushrooms. Pour into 9x13 inch pan. Place raw chicken, cut in pieces (or legs and breasts), on top of rice. Sprinkle with soup mix; cover well. Bake at 350° for 1 1/2 - 2 hours. Serves 6.

R. Martinson, Duluth, Mn.

Similar recipe submitted by: Mary Jo Conneran, Fargo, N.D.

WILD RICE BAKED CHICKEN

2/3 c. uncooked wild rice	2 tsp. chicken bouillon
4 celery stalks, sliced (2 c.)	granules or 2 bouillon
1 medium green pepper,	cubes
diced (1 c.)	2 whole chicken breasts,
1 1/3 c. water	halved and skinned
1 tsp. salt	Soy sauce

In bowl, thoroughly wash wild rice in warm tap water; drain in strainer. In buttered 2 quart casserole or baking dish, mix wild rice, celery, green pepper, water, chicken bouillon and salt. Place chicken on top of rice mixture; brush with soy sauce. Cover dish; bake in preheated 350° oven for 1 1/2 hours, or until rice is tender. Garnish with celery leaves. Serves 4.

Note: Can use a whole, cut up chicken instead of just the breasts, if desired.

Kady O'Connell, Duluth, Mn.

CHICKEN WIGGLE FOR 20 PEOPLE

Season to taste:

1 1/2 lb. cubed pork	1 1/2 lb. cubed veal

Brown about 1 hour on low heat. Add 1 green pepper, onion and 1 1/2 cups diced celery; saute about 1/2 hour. Use 1 small can pimento and 1 can mushrooms, cut up. Add 1 package cooked noodles, 3 cans cream of chicken soup, 2 cans mushroom soup and a little celery seed. Put in buttered baking dish. Sprinkle with grated cheese and bake 3/4 hour.

Mrs. Virgil Schrupp (Vivian)
Montevideo, Mn.

CLUB DAY CHICKEN AND DRESSING

1 (8 oz.) pkg. seasoned
    bread stuffing
1 stick oleo/margarine,
    melted
1 c. water
2 1/2 c. cooked, diced
    chicken or turkey
1/2 c. chopped onion
1/2 c. chopped celery
1/2 c. mayonnaise

1/4 c. chopped green onion
    (chop onion and greens -
    the whole thing)
3/4 tsp. salt
2 eggs
1 1/2 c. milk
1 can condensed cream of
    mushroom soup (or may
    use leftover gravy)
Grated cheese for topping

Mix package of stuffing with melted oleo and water; toss lightly to blend. Place half of mixture in buttered 9x13 inch pan, or buttered casserole dish. Mix chicken, onion, onion greens (chives), celery, mayonnaise and salt; spread over stuffing mixture. Top with remaining bread mixture. Beat eggs slightly; add to milk. Pour evenly over mixture. Cover with foil; refrigerate overnight. Take out 1 hour before baking. Spread with mushroom soup. Bake, uncovered, for 40 minutes at 325°. Sprinkle top with grated cheese. Return to oven for 10 minutes. Serves 8-10.

Liz Tuft, St. Paul, Mn.

COLD NOODLES WITH CHICKEN AND PEANUTS

Dressing:

1/4 c. water
3 Tbsp. sesame seed paste
    (tahini) or peanut butter
3 Tbsp. peanut oil or other
    vegetable oil

3 Tbsp. red rice vinegar or
    red wine vinegar
1 tsp. sugar
3 Tbsp. light soy sauce
1 Tbsp. Oriental sesame oil

Salad:

1 lb. fresh egg noodles,
    parboiled, chilled 2 hours
1 c. cooked, shredded
    chicken

1/2 c. chopped, roasted
    peanuts
2 Tbsp. toasted sesame seeds
1/4 c. minced green onions or
    chives

Combine dressing ingredients; blend well and set aside. Place chilled noodles on serving dish. Top with chicken, peanuts, sesame seeds and green onions or chives. Drizzle dressing over salad and serve to 4.

St. Cloud, Mn.

CORNISH GAME HENS AND RICE

1 c. raw rice
1 can cream of chicken soup

1 env. Italian salad dressing
  mix
3 Cornish game hens

Spread rice in 3 quart shallow dish; bake at 370° for 15 minutes, stirring every 5 minutes, till brown. Combine the dressing mix with 2 1/2 cups boiling water and the soup; stir into the rice. Cut the hens in halves lengthwise; season with salt and pepper. Place hens cut side down on top of rice. Cover dish and bake at 350° for 1 hour. Uncover; bake 30 minutes longer until rice and hens are tender.

Joan Norton, Hibbing, Mn.

STUFFED GAME HENS

4 (1 lb.) Cornish game hens
Salt and pepper
4 Tbsp. slivered almonds
4 Tbsp. finely chopped onion
2/3 c. uncooked long grain
  rice
6 Tbsp. butter or margarine

2 c. water
2 chicken bouillon cubes
2 tsp. lemon juice
1 tsp. salt
2 (3 oz.) cans chopped
  mushrooms, drained

Season game hens inside and out with salt and pepper. In small saucepan, cook almonds, onion and rice in butter for 5-10 minutes, stirring frequently. Add water, bouillon cubes, lemon juice and salt. Bring mixture to boil, stirring to dissolve cubes. Reduce heat; cover and cook slowly about 20-25 minutes, or until liquid is absorbed and rice is fluffy. Stir in drained mushrooms. Lightly stuff birds with rice mixture. Place breast up on rack in shallow baking pan; brush with butter. Roast, uncovered, in hot oven, 400°, for 30 minutes. Uncover; roast 1 hour longer or till drumstick can be twisted easily in socket. Brush with butter again the last 15 minutes. Makes 4 servings.

Becky Carlson, Fargo, N.D.

HONEYED DUCK

1 duck
2 tsp. salt
1 tsp. ground ginger
1 tsp. crushed basil

1/2 tsp. pepper
3/4 c. honey
1/4 c. butter
1 tsp. grated orange peel

3 Tbsp. orange juice
2 tsp. lemon juice
1/8 tsp. dry mustard

1 unpeeled orange, cut into
1/2 inch slices
1/2 tsp. cornstarch

Wash duck; drain and pat dry. Combine salt, ginger, basil and pepper; rub half of mixture inside the duck. Combine honey, butter, orange peel and juice, lemon juice and mustard in saucepan; heat, stirring, until butter melts. Rub inside of duck with 2 to 3 tablespoons of honey mixture. Place orange slices in duck cavity; pour 4 to 5 tablespoons of honey mixture into cavity. Truss duck; rub remaining salt mixture over outside of bird. Place on large piece of heavy duty foil; cover with remaining honey mixture. Wrap duck; place in shallow baking pan. Roast at 325° F. for 1 3/4 hours. Unwrap; baste with drippings. Bake 20 to 25 minutes longer, or until tender and brown. Place duck on hot platter to keep warm. Combine cornstarch with a little cold water; stir into drippings. Cook and stir until bubbly. Serve sauce over duck. Makes 2 servings.

Marion Round, Faribault, Mn.

ROAST DUCK WITH PARSLEY BUTTER

3 ducks
1 1/2 tsp. salt
1/4 tsp. pepper
1 1/2 apples, pared, cored

3 small onions, peeled
6 whole cloves
1/2 c. cranberries
6 slices of salt pork

Wash ducks; drain and wipe dry. Sprinkle with salt and pepper. Stick 2 cloves in each onion. Place 1/2 apple, 1 onion and a few cranberries in the cavity of each duck; truss. Place in roaster. Lay 2 slices of salt pork on breast of each duck. Roast, uncovered, at 500° F. for 1/2 hour. Reduce heat to 350° F.; roast 3/4 to 1 hour longer, or until tender. Discard stuffings before serving. Serve with boiled rice, moistened with Parsley Butter. Makes 6 servings.

Parsley Butter: Cream 1/2 cup butter until light; add 1/2 teaspoon salt, dash of pepper, 1/2 teaspoon chopped parsley and 3/4 tablespoon lemon juice, very slowly, beating until well blended. Serve atop hot, cooked rice.

Marion Round, Faribault, Mn.

ROAST GOOSE

1 (12-14 lb.) ready-to-
  cook goose
1 lemon, quartered
1 Tbsp. salt
1/2 tsp. pepper

4 c. pared, quartered
  apples
4 c. dried prunes, pitted
2 c. boiling water
4 red apples

Wash goose thoroughly; dry. Rub inside and out with lemon quarters. Combine salt and pepper; rub over inner and outer surfaces. Stuff neck and body cavities with alternate spoonfuls of quartered apples and prunes; truss and secure. Place bird, breast side up; in shallow roasting pan. Prick surface of goose with sharp pronged fork. Roast at 450° F. for 20 minutes. Reduce heat to 325° F. and continue roasting approximately 4 1/2 to 5 hours, or until bird tests done. After 1 hour, pour off grease and baste bird with boiling water. Continue to baste with hot water every hour. Prick red apples well; place in roasting pan for last 40 minutes of cooking. Use to garnish serving platter. Yield: About 8 to 10 portions.

Dena Stoddard, St. Louis Park, Mn.

QUAIL WITH ALL-GAME DRESSING

4 quail
Salt and pepper
1/3 c. finely chopped onion
1/3 c. finely chopped celery
1/2 c. melted butter

1 c. dry bread crumbs
1/4 tsp. poultry seasoning
1/4 tsp. dried savory
1/8 tsp. crushed rosemary
1/4 c. beef broth
1/2 beaten egg

Wash quail; drain and pat dry. Cook onion and celery in 1/4 cup melted butter until tender, but not brown. Combine vegetables with bread crumbs and seasonings; toss lightly. Add beef broth and egg; toss lightly until well moistened. Lightly spoon stuffing into cavity of each bird. Place birds breast up in a buttered baking pan. Brush with melted butter; sprinkle with salt and pepper. Roast, uncovered, at 350° F. for 45 minutes to 1 hour, or until birds are tender. Baste often with melted butter. Makes 4 servings.

Marion Round, Faribault, Mn.

PUFFED TURKEY BAKE

1 (10 1/2 oz.) can condensed cream of mushroom soup
1/3 c. water
2 c. cubed, cooked turkey
1 1/2 c. seasoned bread stuffing mix
1 (8 oz.) can French style green beans, drained
4 eggs, separated
1 (3 oz.) can French fried onion rings

Combine mushroom soup and water in 1 1/2 quart casserole. Add turkey, stuffing mix and green beans in layers. Beat egg whites until stiff. Beat egg yolks until light, then fold into egg whites; pile over top of casserole. Bake at 300° for 40 minutes. Sprinkle with onion rings. Bake 5 minutes longer. Serves 6 to 8.

Liz Tuft, St. Paul, Mn.

SWISS TURKEY-HAM BAKE

1/2 c. onion, chopped
2 Tbsp. butter or margarine
3 Tbsp. flour
1/2 tsp. salt
1/4 tsp. pepper
1 (3 oz.) can sliced mushrooms
1 c. light cream
2 Tbsp. dry sherry
2 c. cubed turkey
1 c. cubed ham
1 (5 oz.) can water chestnuts, sliced
1/2 c. Swiss cheese, shredded
1 1/2 c. soft bread crumbs
3 Tbsp. butter or margarine, melted

Saute onion in the 2 tablespoons of butter. Add flour, seasoning and cream to make sauce. Add mushrooms and sherry; mix with other ingredients. Bake at 350° for approximately 30 minutes.

Kim Kazmierczak, Duluth, Mn.

TURKEY/CHICKEN BROCCOLI CASSEROLE

1 (10 oz.) pkg. cooked, drained broccoli
Chicken or turkey, sliced or pieces, cooked
1 can cream of celery soup
1/3 c. milk
1/2 - 1 c. shredded cheese

Place cooked, drained broccoli in a layer in 1 1/2 to 2 quart casserole. Add 1 layer of cooked turkey or chicken (slices or pieces). Combine 1 can of uncooked cream of celery soup and 1/3 cup milk. Pour over first 2 layers. Spread 1/2 to 1 cup shredded cheese on top. Bake at 450° for approximately 15-20 minutes, covered or uncovered.

Karen Moe, Duluth, Mn.

GOBBLE-UP CASSEROLE

6 c. cooked turkey (or chicken)
1 c. celery, diced
1/2 small onion, chopped fine
3 c. bread crumbs
1/2 c. butter or margarine

1 tsp. salt
1/4 tsp. baking powder
1/2 tsp. pepper
1 tsp. poultry seasoning
1 egg, beaten
3/4 c. milk
1 can cream of chicken soup

Place turkey in 9x13 inch lightly greased pan. Saute bread crumbs, celery and onion in butter. Add salt, baking powder, pepper and poultry seasoning. Stir in egg and milk. Spoon over turkey; spread soup over top. Bake, uncovered, in 350° oven for 1 hour.

Mrs. Norma Applen, Minneapolis, Mn.

AFTER THANKSGIVING CASSEROLE

1 can cream of celery soup
1 c. milk
1 c. grated Swiss cheese
1 Tbsp. instant minced onion
1/2 tsp. sage

1/2 tsp. salt
1 c. uncooked noodles
1-2 c. turkey, chopped
2 hard cooked eggs, sliced
2 Tbsp. chopped pimento

In a buttered 1 1/2 quart casserole dish, stir soup to make a creamy consistency. Add all other ingredients; stir gently. Store, covered, overnight, all day or at least 3 to 4 hours in the refrigerator. Just before baking, stir once more. Bake, uncovered, at 350° for 1 hour. Makes 4 to 6 servings.

Beverly Fox, Fargo, N.D.

TURKEY CASSEROLE

Mix together:
3 cans cream of mushroom soup

3 cans cream of chicken soup
2 cans Cheddar cheese soup

Add:

9 c. chopped, cooked turkey
9 c. diced celery
1/2 c. chopped onion

6 c. chow mein noodles
2 cans water chestnuts, chopped

Mix and bake at 350° for 50 minutes. The last 10 minutes, add 1 1/2 cups chopped cashews.

Mary Geurs, Crystal, Mn.

EASY TURKEY CURRY

1/4 c. chopped onion
1/4 c. chopped green pepper
1 can cream of mushroom soup

1/4 c. milk
1 c. sour cream
1/2 tsp. curry powder
1 1/2 c. cooked turkey

Cook onion and pepper in 1 tablespoon butter. Add soup and milk; blend well and heat. Stir in sour cream and curry powder. Add meat. Serve on hot rice.

Mrs. Burton Peterson, Rochester, Mn.

TURKEY HOT DISH

2 c. cut up turkey, already cooked
2 c. cut up celery
1 c. toasted bread crumbs
1 c. almonds

1 c. salad dressing
2 tsp. grated onion
2 Tbsp. lemon juice
1/2 tsp. salt

Topping:

1/2 c. grated cheese

1 c. potato chips or Ritz crackers, crushed

Mix all ingredients together, then put grated cheese over all, then crushed chips or crushed crackers. Bake at 450° for 15 minutes or until it bubbles. Tuna can be substituted for turkey.

Mary Paul, Minneapolis, Mn.

IMPOSSIBLE TURKEY PIE

2 c. cut up cooked turkey (or chicken)
1 (4 1/2 oz.) jar sliced mushrooms, drained
1/2 c. sliced green onions
1/2 tsp. salt
1 c. shredded natural Swiss cheese
1 1/2 c. milk
3/4 c. Bisquick baking mix
3 eggs

Heat oven to 400°. Grease pie plate, 10 x 1 1/2 inches. Sprinkle turkey, mushrooms, onions, salt and cheese in pie plate. Beat remaining ingredients until smooth, 15 seconds in blender on high, or 1 minute with hand beater; pour into plate. Bake until knife inserted between center and edge comes out clean, 30 to 35 minutes. Cool 5 minutes. Makes 6 to 8 servings.

Laverne M. Akerstrom, Duluth, Mn.

TUR-KEY-ROLE

4 c. cooked turkey, cubed (or chicken)
2 (10 oz.) cans chow mein noodles
2 c. diced celery
1 can cream of celery soup
1/2 c. onion, diced fine
1 pkg. frozen peas, slightly thawed
1 small jar pimento, diced
3 c. milk, heated
1 Tbsp. salad oil
1 (10 oz.) can sliced mushrooms

Combine turkey, noodles, celery, soup, onion, peas and pimento. Add heated milk. Saute mushrooms in oil; add to turkey mixture and blend well. Pour mixture into two 1 1/2 quart lightly greased casseroles. Bake in 350° oven for 1 to 1 1/2 hours.

Mrs. Norma Applen, Minneapolis, Mn.

HOT TURKEY SALAD

6 slices white bread, cubed
2 c. diced, cooked turkey
1/2 c. minced onion
1/2 c. minced celery
1/2 c. mayonnaise
3/4 tsp. salt
2 eggs, slightly beaten
1 1/2 c. milk
1 can cream of mushroom soup
1/2 c. grated sharp cheese
1/2 tsp. pepper

Combine turkey, vegetables, mayonnaise and seasonings; spoon over bread in pan. Top with bread cubes.

(I save some to put on next day when cheese is sprinkled on.) Combine eggs and milk; pour over all. Chill at least 1 hour or overnight. Spoon soup over top. Bake at 325° for 45 minutes. Sprinkle cheese over top; bake 15 minutes longer. Yield: 8 servings. Double recipe for 9x13x2 inch pan.

Maryann W. Skelton, Duluth, Mn.

TURKEY OR CHICKEN SQUARES

3 c. chicken or turkey, cut up
1 c. cooked rice
2 c. soft bread crumbs
1/3 c. cut up celery

4 eggs, beaten
1/4 tsp. sage
2 c. gravy or 1 can cream of chicken soup, mixed with 1/3 c. water

Bake at 350° for 1 hour in 7x11 inch dish.

Marlys Swehla, Albert Lea, Mn.
Similar recipe submitted by: Gladys Turk, Duluth, Mn.

TURKEY SUPREME

2 c. diced turkey
2 c. diced celery
1/4 c. diced green pepper
1 medium onion, diced

1/2 c. uncooked regular rice
1 can cream of chicken soup
1 can cream of mushroom soup
1 soup can of water

Mix all together. Bake in lightly greased casserole for 2 hours at 350°, uncovered.

Debbie Burgum, Dickinson, N.D.

CHILIED TURKEY THIGHS

4 (about 1/2 lb.) turkey thighs
1/2 c. bottled chili sauce
1/2 c. apple juice

1 Tbsp. lemon juice
1 tsp. sugar
1/2 tsp. chili powder

Rinse turkey thighs and pat dry with paper towel. Combine chili sauce, apple juice, lemon juice, sugar and chili powder. Grill turkey thighs on rack set about 6 inches above hot coals for 30 minutes, turning once or twice and rotating over hottest coals. Continue cooking thighs, basting frequently with chili sauce mixture, another 30 minutes, or until the meat, when slit near the bone, is no longer pink. Serves 4.

St. Cloud, Mn.

POACHED BASS FOR TWO

Have ready 1 pound (6) bass fillets.

Court Bouillon:

1 large onion, studded with
  4 cloves
2 stalks celery, cut in
  chunks
2 carrots, cut in rounds
3 bay leaves
5 whole black peppers

1 tsp. salt
6 Tbsp. lemon juice
1 c. dry white wine
2 sprigs of parsley
1/2 green pepper, sliced
  into rings
1 qt. plus 1 c. water

For the court bouillon, gently simmer the vegetables (and fish trimmings, if you wish) in the water for about 20 minutes. Add half the wine after 10 minutes and the other half about 5 minutes later. Wipe the fish dry with a paper towel. Completely wrap 2 fillets in a piece of cheesecloth. Submerge the fish completely in the liquid. Cover and simmer about 3 minutes; turn the fish and simmer another 2 minutes. Small fillets should take about 5 minutes. If the fish flakes easily, it's done. When fish is done, remove; drain momentarily and remove the cheesecloth. Repeat with remaining fillets. Serves 2-4. The court bouillon can be strained and kept in the freezer for later use.

This recipe can also be done in the oven, using the same court bouillon recipe. Cover the fillets with cheesecloth. Place the fish in a greased baking pan. Pour the boiling hot liquid over the fish; cover and place in a 425° oven. Oven poaching time is slightly longer, 6 to 8 minutes. A delicious variation using commercial soups also uses the poaching technique with wine.

St. Cloud, Mn.

QUICK 'N EASY BASS

1 lb. (6 fillets) bass
1 can cream of shrimp soup
1 can cream of celery soup

1 1/2 soup cans of milk
1/2 c. dry white wine

Gradually mix the condensed soups and milk; stir continuously until thoroughly mixed. Heat liquid to a simmer. Add the wine; bring to a simmer. Add the fillets, watching to ensure fish doesn't stick to pan. Cook 3 minutes on one side. Flip the fillets carefully; cook 2 more minutes. Fish is done when it flakes easily with a fork. Serve with rice and use cooking liquid as a gravy. Serves 2-4. To prepare in the oven, simmer the fish in the previous poaching liquid in a 400° oven for about 15 minutes.

St. Cloud, Mn.

BAKED COD
(Torsk)

2/3 c. melted butter
1/4 c. ReaLemon juice
1/2 c. flour
1 1/2 tsp. salt
1/2 tsp. white pepper

2 lb. boneless, skinned, trimmed cod fillets
Paprika (about 1 tsp.)
Chopped parsley and lemon slices for garnish

Combine melted butter and lemon juice. Combine flour, salt and white pepper. Cut cod fillets into 6 equal portions. Dip cod portions in lemon butter; coat cod portions with seasoned flour. Place in shallow baking pan. Pour remaining lemon butter over fish. Sprinkle lightly with paprika. Bake in preheated 350° oven for 30 minutes or until fish flakes easily. Garnish each serving with chopped parsley and a thin slice of lemon. Serves 6.

Betty Cortright, Minneapolis, Mn.

ESCALLOPED CRAB

1 c. rich medium white sauce

3 Tbsp. sherry

Add:
Minced onion
Green pepper

Lemon juice
Seasoning

Pour over flaked crab in greased casserole. Top with buttered crumbs. Bake at 400° for 25 minutes.

Helen Teeuwen, Minneapolis, Mn.

MOCK CRAB CASSEROLE

1 lb. fish fillets (flounder or other white fish)
2 Tbsp. butter or margarine
1 c. chicken broth
3 c. cooked rice
3/4 c. chopped onion
3/4 c. chopped celery
1/2 c. chopped green pepper

2 Tbsp. dehydrated parsley flakes
1 c. crumbled corn bread (or soft bread crumbs)
2 eggs, slightly beaten
1 tsp. salt
1 tsp. poultry seasoning
1/4 tsp. pepper

340

Simmer fish in seasoned water to cover for 10 minutes or until fish flakes easily. Drain; cool and flake. Melt butter in chicken broth. Combine all ingredients; mix well. Turn into a lightly greased shallow casserole. Cover; bake at 350° for 30 minutes. Remove cover and bake for 15 minutes more. Serve with tartar sauce. Makes 6 servings.

Ann Christensen, Litchfield, Mn.

CRAB SUPPER PIE
(A Cousin of the Famous Quiche)

1 c. (4 oz.) shredded natural Swiss cheese
1 unbaked (9 inch) pastry shell
1 (7 1/2 oz.) can crabmeat, drained and flaked
2 green onions, sliced (with tops)

3 beaten eggs
1 c. light cream
1/2 tsp. salt
1/2 tsp. grated lemon peel
1/4 tsp. dry mustard
Dash of mace
1/4 c. sliced almonds

Sprinkle cheese evenly over bottom of pastry shell. Top with crabmeat; sprinkle with green onions. Combine eggs, cream, salt, lemon peel, dry mustard and mace; pour over crabmeat. Top with sliced almonds. Bake in a slow oven, 325°, for about 45 minutes or till set. Remove from oven; let stand 10 minutes before serving. Makes 6 servings. Nice for brunch or a bridge lunch.

Mrs. Carl Granrud, Montevideo, Mn.

ELEGANT AND EASY

There comes a time in every woman's life when she must prepare for a luncheon...two or three tables of bridge, the garden club, the Mother's Club, the choir. This is the answer! Twenty servings, easily done, and so delicious you fear they'll ask for seconds. Choose your own accompaniments although we might suggest a green salad of tender leaves and a garnish of crisp croutons.

2 c. cooked wild rice
1 c. cooked white rice
1 c. crabmeat, flaked
1 1/2 c. chopped celery
1 green pepper, chopped
Butter

1 medium onion, chopped
1 small can pimento, chopped
3 cans mushroom soup
1 c. shrimp, broken
1 lb. fresh mushrooms or 1 large can mushrooms

Combine first 7 ingredients; add 1 1/2 cans mushroom soup and 1/2 cup shrimp. Place mixture in baking dish. Bake at 350° for 1 1/2 hours.

Sauce: Brown mushrooms in small amount of butter. Add remaining 1 1/2 cans of mushroom soup and remaining 1/2 cup of shrimp; heat through. Serve crab and rice mixture with the hot mushroom sauce. Yield: About 20 servings.

Lovise Lorenz, St. Paul, Mn.

BROCCOLI-STUFFED FISH FILLETS

1 c. finely chopped onion	6 fillets of fresh flounder or
2 Tbsp. butter or margarine	other white fish (about
1 (10 oz.) pkg. frozen	1 1/2 lb.)
chopped broccoli, cooked	2 Tbsp. lemon juice
and drained	1/2 c. water
1/2 c. dry bread crumbs	1 c. grated Cheddar cheese
1/4 tsp. thyme	2 Tbsp. dry white wine
1 (10 3/4 oz.) can condensed	3 c. cooked rice
cream of mushroom soup	2 Tbsp. diced pimiento

Saute 1/2 cup onion in 1 tablespoon butter until tender. Stir in broccoli, bread crumbs and thyme; set aside. Season fillets with salt and pepper; sprinkle with lemon juice. Place about 1/4 cup broccoli mixture on each fillet. Roll up; secure with a toothpick. Place in a greased baking dish. Bake at 350° for 15 minutes. Blend soup, water, cheese and wine. Heat; pour over fish rolls. Bake 20 minutes longer. Meanwhile, saute remaining onion in rest of butter until golden; stir in rice and pimiento. Heat thoroughly. Serve stuffed fillets with sauce and mounds of pimiento rice. Makes 6 servings.

Ann Christensen, Litchfield, Mn.

CRUNCHY FISH FILLETS

2 lb. fish fillets (fresh	1/8 tsp. pepper
or frozen)	1 Tbsp. dried parsley flakes
3 c. Kellogg's Rice Krispies	1/2 c. margarine or butter,
cereal, crushed to 1 1/2 c.	melted
1/2 tsp. salt	

1. If frozen fish is used, thaw; rinse and pat dry. Set aside. 2. Place crushed Rice Krispies cereal in shallow

dish or pan. Stir in salt, pepper and parsley flakes; set aside. 3. Pour margarine into a second shallow dish or pan. Dip fish fillets in margarine; coat with cereal mixture. Place in single layer in well greased or foil lined shallow baking pan. 4. Bake at 375° F. for about 25 minutes or until fish flakes easily when tested with a fork. Do not cover pan or turn fish while baking. Yield: 6 servings.

Marion Round, Faribault, Mn.

OVEN FRIED FISH FILLETS

1 lb. sole or flounder fish
  or any other fish fillets
1/4 c. mayonnaise
Bread crumbs

Paprika
1/2 tsp. salt
1/4 tsp. pepper
Lemon wedges

Thinly coat fish fillets with mayonnaise; dredge in bread crumbs. Arrange in a 13x9x2 inch baking pan. Sprinkle with paprika, salt and pepper. Bake at 450° for about 12 minutes or until fish flakes easily when tested with fork. Garnish with lemon wedges. Can also use corn flake crumbs.

Mary Jean Voss, Owatonna, Mn.

FROG LEGS

8 oz. olive oil
3 frog legs
1 egg
1/2 c. milk
Flour as needed
1 tsp. parsley flakes

8 oz. chablis or other dry
  white wine
2 oz. butter
1 tsp. garlic powder
1 Tbsp. lemon juice

Heat olive oil in 10 inch skillet over moderate heat. Dip frog legs in a mixture of egg and milk; roll in flour. Brown in oil until golden brown, 5 to 7 minutes on each side. Remove frog legs and olive oil. Into the skillet, put the wine, parsley, butter, garlic powder and lemon juice; simmer until mixture reduces by 1/4. Add frog legs and simmer another 3 minutes. Serve topped with some of the sauce. Serves 1.

St. Cloud, Mn.

GUMBO A LA CREOLE

1 1/2 c. chopped onions
3 Tbsp. vegetable oil
1/4 c. flour
5 c. fish stock
1 (28 oz.) can tomatoes
1 (10 oz.) pkg. frozen sliced
  okra
2 tsp. salt
2 tsp. lemon pepper
1/4 tsp. cayenne pepper
1/4 tsp. black pepper
1 Tbsp. gumbo file

Bouquet garni*
8 oz. cubed boneless fish
  (flounder, red snapper,
  etc.)
8 oz. peeled, deveined raw
  shrimp
8 oz. crab fingers or
  crabmeat
2 doz. or 3 c. shucked oys-
  oysters, drained (reserve
  liquid)
6 c. hot, cooked rice

Saute onions in oil until well browned; add flour and cook, stirring constantly, until a deep brown color is obtained. Stir in fish stock, tomatoes, liquid from oysters, okra and seasonings. Cook, covered, about 30 minutes. Add fish, shrimp, crab fingers and oysters. Continue cooking about 10 minutes or until shrimp turn pink and oysters begin to curl. Remove bouquet garni. Just before serving, add gumbo file. Never let gumbo boil after file is added. Serve in shallow bowls with rice. Makes 12 servings.

*Bouquet garni is a small bunch of herbs such as marjoram, savory, basil, thyme, sage, rosemary and oregano tied together in a cheesecloth bag, or a prepared mix may be purchased.

Ann Christensen, Litchfield, Mn.

HALIBUT STEAKS

1 (12 oz.) pkg. halibut
  steaks, thawed
2/3 c. thinly sliced onion
1 (4 oz.) can sliced
  mushrooms, drained
1/3 c. chopped tomatoes

1/3 c. chopped green pepper
1/4 c. melted butter
1 Tbsp. lemon juice
Salt and pepper to taste
1/3 c. grated Cheddar cheese

Cut steak into serving size pieces. Arrange onion on bottom of well greased shallow pan; place fish on top of onion. Combine mushrooms, tomatoes and green pepper; sprinkle vegetable mixture over fish. Combine lemon juice and melted butter; pour over vegetables. Sprinkle fish with salt and pepper. Bake at 350° for 25-30 minutes or until fish flakes when tested with a fork. Sprinkle cheese over vegetables. Return to oven 3-4 minutes or until cheese is melted. Serve immediately.

Suzie Brainard, Minneapolis, Mn.

CHINESE DRAGON'S LOBSTER SOONG

2 Tbsp. cooking oil
1 tsp. salt
1/2 lb. lobster meat, cut
  into small chunks
About 1/4 c. minced,
  uncooked pork
1 clove garlic, chopped
1/2 shot cooking sherry
1/2 c. sliced mushrooms
1/2 c. sliced water chestnuts
1/2 c. diced bamboo shoots
1/2 c. green peas

Small handful of diced fresh
  pea pods
1 can chicken broth
1/2 tsp. monosodium
  glutamate
1 tsp. oyster sauce
1/2 tsp. sesame oil
Dash of white pepper
3 tsp. cornstarch, mixed
  with a little water
2 eggs

Heat wok to frying temperature; put in cooking oil. Add salt. Fry the lobster chunks and minced pork with a little bit of chopped garlic clove. Add cooking sherry. Fry for 30 seconds, then add mushrooms, water chestnuts, bamboo shoots, peas and pea pods. Cook ingredients, covered, with chicken broth for 5 minutes. Stir in monosodium glutamate, oyster sauce, sesame oil and white pepper. Thicken with cornstarch and water mixture; bring to boil. Beat eggs; spread on top of boiling ingredients. Allow to cook for 1 minute. Serves 6.

St. Cloud, Mn.

LUTEFISH PUDDING

2 c. cooked lutefish, flaked
1/2 c. rice
1 tsp. salt
1 c. water

1 c. milk
2 eggs
2 Tbsp. butter

Cook the rice in the water with the salt until done. Beat the eggs; add the milk. Pour over the rice, lutefish and butter. Put in buttered baking dish; bake until done.

Easy recipe for lutefish: Use similar size pieces of lutefish to be layered in a glass baking dish. Cover them closely with aluminum foil. Bake at 350° for 40 minutes. Drain water during cooking.

Jerry Brinster, Bismarck, N.D.

NEPTUNE'S BOUNTY

1 lb. frozen sole fillets
6 oz. frozen cooked shrimp
1/3 c. white wine

1 (10 oz.) can cream of
  shrimp soup
3/4 c. shredded Swiss cheese

Thaw fish fillets until they can be separated, about 12 hours in the refrigerator. Place the fillets in the bottom of a buttered baking dish, about 7x11 inches. Sprinkle the frozen shrimp over the sole. Combine the soup and white wine; spread the mixture over the fish. Spread the Swiss cheese on top. Bake in a 325° oven until the sole just becomes opaque and flakes easily with a fork, about 25 minutes. Do not overcook. Serve with rice.

Eileen Thompson, Minneapolis, Mn.

CREOLE NORTHERN

1 c. sliced onion
1 c. sliced celery
2 cloves garlic, chopped
1 (1 lb.) can tomatoes
1 bay leaf
1/2 c. water

4-5 slices of lemon
1-2 Tbsp. butter
Salt and pepper to taste
Tabasco sauce, to taste
1 1/2 - 2 lb. Northern fillets
Hot cooked rice, for 4

Simmer the onion, celery, garlic, tomatoes, bay leaf and water with the lemon slices and butter until celery and onion are soft. Add salt, pepper and Tabasco sauce to mixture. Place the fish fillets in this sauce; simmer gently until the fish flakes easily. Serve fish with sauce over rice to 4.

St. Cloud, Mn.

MILDRED'S OYSTER CASSEROLE

Grease casserole. Roll soda crackers for crumbs. Wash 1 pint fresh oysters. Put a layer of crumbs in casserole, layer half of the oysters, salt, pepper, butter, another layer of crumbs, rest of oysters, salt, pepper and butter; top with crumbs. Put in oven; pour milk over it. Use a knife to be sure milk gets to the bottom. Bake until heated through. Can be made the day before, except, add the milk when you put it in the oven.

Helen Teeuwen, Minneapolis, Mn.

PACA BARRON'S PAELLA
(Pä-ā-ya)

Mixture 1: Fry 4-5 strips of bacon, cut in small pieces, with 1 large onion, chopped. Cook until onion is tender. Add 1 cup fresh or frozen shrimp (any size); steam about 2 minutes. Put above mixture into a large baking dish.

Mixture 2: Fry 2 strips of bacon, cut in small pieces, about medium. Add 2 slices of sandwich ham, cut in small pieces. Add:

1 small can sliced mushrooms, drained	2 small jars pimento (water and all), cut in small pieces
1 small can peas, drained	
20 stuffed olives, sliced	1 strip sour pickle, cut in tiny pieces

Add mixture 2 to the mixture 1 in baking dish. Cut fryer (as much as you want) into small pieces or use legs, thighs and breast. Skin and fry to brown only. Boil 2 cups rice (long grain) with chopped parsley or green onion tops and 3-4 threads of saffron. Use about 4 cups water; boil only until about half tender. Drain; mix with vegetables and put chicken into rice. Add 1 small can clams (optional). Bake about 300° for about 35-45 minutes. Be sure to cover baking dish. Can be refrigerated and reheated later. Be sure to salt and pepper to taste.

Marlys Wendorf, Deer Creek, Mn.

SNAPPER POACH

Lay red snapper fillets in baking dish; cover with grapefruit juice. Poach in 350° oven for 10 minutes. Saute chopped hazelnuts (1/2 cup) and green onion tops (1/4 cup) in 2 tablespoons butter. Spread this over fish and bake an additional 5 minutes.

Mrs. Norma Applen, Minneapolis, Mn.

SALMON LOAF

1 large can salmon	2 Tbsp. melted butter
1/2 c. cracker crumbs	1 Tbsp. chopped parsley
2 eggs	1 c. grated Monterey Jack cheese
1/4 c. milk	
Pepper	2 Tbsp. grated onion

Bake at 375° for 40 minutes.

K. Ells, Duluth, Mn.

SALMON OLIVE RICE CASSEROLE

1/2 c. sliced celery
1/2 small onion, chopped
2 Tbsp. butter
1 (10 3/4 oz.) can condensed
   cream of celery soup
1 1/2 c. water

1/3 c. sliced green olives
1 tsp. lemon juice
1 1/2 c. instant rice
1 (15 1/2 oz.) can salmon,
   drained
3 slices of cheese

In large skillet, brown celery and onion in butter till soft. Add soup and water; bring to a boil. Stir often. Add olives and lemon juice. Pour 1/2 of sauce into lightly greased 1 1/2 quart casserole. In separate layers, add rice and salmon. Cover and bake at 375° for 10 minutes. Remove from oven; stir well. Cut each cheese slice into 4 triangles and arrange around edge of casserole. Cover; bake 10 minutes longer. Garnish center with whole green olives.
Dolores Foucault, Saginaw, Mn.

SALMON PORCUPINES

1 tall can pink salmon
1/2 c. uncooked white rice
1/2 c. grated raw carrots
3 Tbsp. minced onion
1 egg

1/2 tsp. salt
Sprinkle of pepper
1 can cream of mushroom soup
1/2 c. water

Mix together everything except soup and water; form into 6 large balls. Place in 2 quart baking dish. Combine soup and water; heat, then pour over balls. Bake 1 hour in 350° oven. Don't put too close together as they expand. Cover until the last 15 minutes.
Maryann Skelton, Duluth, Mn.

SALMON ROMANOFF
(A protein-packed entree with poppy seeds for crunch.)

1 (8 oz.) pkg. medium
   egg noodles
1 Tbsp. butter or margarine
1/2 c. chopped onion
1 (7 3/4 oz.) can salmon,
   drained and flaked

1 1/4 c. sour cream
1 c. cottage cheese
1/4 c. milk
2 tsp. poppy seed
3/4 tsp. salt
Dash of hot pepper sauce

Cook noodles according to package directions; drain

and set aside. Preheat oven to 350° F. In medium saucepan, melt butter or margarine. Add onion; saute 3 to 5 minutes until soft. Remove from heat; add remaining ingredients, except noodles. Stir to combine. Fold in noodles until well mixed. Spoon into a 1 1/2 quart casserole. Bake, covered, for 30 to 35 minutes until hot. Makes 6 servings, about 370 calories each.

Elizabeth Redmond, Long Prairie, Mn.

SALMON SURPRISE

1 can salmon	1 c. mashed potatoes
1 c. cream sauce	

Place salmon in colander; wash under running water. Break into small pieces. Mix thoroughly with hot cream sauce; put in a greased casserole. Cover with mashed potatoes; bake until the potatoes are browned.

K., St. Cloud, Mn.

SEAFOOD AND RICE SUPREME

1/2 c. chopped onion	1 (6 1/2 oz.) can fresh or
1 c. chopped celery	frozen crabmeat
1/2 c. chopped green pepper	1 c. mayonnaise
2 Tbsp. water	1 tsp. Worcestershire sauce
2 c. cooked rice	1 tsp. salt
12 oz. peeled, deveined raw	1/4 tsp. pepper
shrimp	3/4 c. buttered rice cereal,
	crushed

Cook onion, celery and green pepper in water until tender. Add rice, shrimp, crabmeat, mayonnaise and seasonings; mix well. Turn into a buttered shallow casserole or individual sea shells. Top with buttered rice cereal. Bake at 375° for 25 minutes. Makes 6 servings.

Ann Christensen, Litchfield, Mn.

BATTER-FRIED SHRIMP

1 lb. uncooked shrimp	1/2 tsp. salt
1 egg	1/2 c. unsifted flour
1/2 c. milk	Dash of Tabasco sauce

Rinse and drain shrimp well. Heat 1 to 1 1/2 inches of

oil in a frying pan or saucepan to 375°. In a mixing bowl, beat together egg and milk. Beat in flour, salt and Tabasco sauce until smooth. Dip shrimp in batter, draining off excess; fry shrimp until golden brown and crisp, 3 to 4 minutes. Drain slightly on paper towel. Serve hot with tartar sauce or cocktail sauce. Makes 4 servings.

St. Cloud, Mn.

QUICK SHRIMP CHOW MEIN

1 1/2 c. diagonally sliced celery
1 c. sliced onion
1 large green pepper, cut in slivers
12 oz. peeled, deveined raw shrimp
2 Tbsp. vegetable oil
3 Tbsp. soy sauce
1 (16 oz.) can fancy mixed Chinese vegetables
1 (10 3/4 oz.) can condensed cream of chicken soup
1/4 tsp. pepper
1/3 c. sliced pimientos
3 c. hot, cooked rice
1 (3 oz.) can rice noodles or chow mein noodles

Saute celery, onion, green pepper and shrimp in oil until vegetables are tender crisp and shrimp are pink. Add Chinese vegetables, soup, soy sauce, pepper and pimientos; heat thoroughly. Serve over beds of fluffy rice; sprinkle with noodles. Makes 6 servings.

Ann Christensen, Litchfield, Mn.

SHRIMP CANTONESE WITH RICE

3 c. cooked rice
12 oz. peeled, deveined raw shrimp, halved lengthwise
2 Tbsp. butter, margarine or vegetable oil
2 c. diagonally sliced celery
2 c. sliced onions
1 qt. (8 oz.) fresh spinach leaves
1 (16 oz.) can fancy mixed Chinese vegetables
1/4 tsp. pepper
1/4 c. soy sauce
1 1/4 c. chicken broth
2 Tbsp. cornstarch

While rice is cooking, saute shrimp in butter, using a large skillet, for 1 minute or until shrimp turn pink. Add celery and onions; cook, stirring, 2 minutes. Add spinach and Chinese vegetables, which have been rinsed and drained. Cover; cook 1 minute. Blend pepper, soy sauce, chicken broth and cornstarch; stir into shrimp-vegetable mixture. Cook, stirring, until sauce is clear and thickened, about 2 minutes. Serve over beds of fluffy rice. Makes 6 servings.

Ann Christensen, Litchfield, Mn.

350

SHRIMP AND EGGPLANT CASSEROLE

1 c. chopped onion
1 c. chopped green pepper
1 c. chopped celery
4 c. peeled, diced eggplant
  (about 1 lb.)
2 cloves garlic, crushed
2 Tbsp. butter or margarine
2 c. cooked rice
2 tsp. salt

12 oz. peeled, deveined raw
  shrimp, sliced in halves
  lengthwise
1 Tbsp. Worcestershire
  sauce
1/2 tsp. pepper
1/2 tsp. thyme
3/4 c. mayonnaise
1 c. buttered soft bread
  crumbs

Saute onion, green pepper, celery, eggplant and garlic in butter until vegetables are tender crisp. Stir in remaining ingredients, except bread crumbs. Turn mixture into a lightly greased shallow 2 quart casserole. Top with bread crumbs. Bake at 350° for 45 minutes. Makes 6 servings.

Ann Christensen, Litchfield, Mn.

SHRIMP FRIED RICE

1/4 c. butter
2 c. cooked or 2 cans
  cleaned shrimp
1 1/4 tsp. salt
1/2 tsp. pepper
2 eggs, beaten

5 c. cooked rice
3 Tbsp. soy sauce
3 green onions, chopped
1/4 c. sliced mushrooms
1/4 c. water chestnuts
1 c. bean sprouts

Melt butter in fry pan; add shrimp and seasonings until lightly browned. Add beaten eggs; stir until well mixed. Add rice until golden. Add rest of ingredients; heat thoroughly.

Mary Perron, Rochester, Mn.

SHRIMP AND LOBSTER SAUCE

1 lb. frozen, shelled
  and deveined shrimp
1/2 c. pork or veal
2 cloves garlic, crushed
3 Tbsp. oil
1 Tbsp. sherry
1 Tbsp. soy sauce
1/2 tsp. salt

1/2 tsp. sugar
1/2 c. chicken broth
1/4 c. water
1 Tbsp. cornstarch
2 eggs, slightly beaten
2 stalks green onions, cut
  in 2 inch lengths

1507-82

351

1. Thaw frozen shrimp; cut lengthwise. 2. Cut pork or veal in small cubes. 3. Add garlic to oil in large skillet; heat 1 minute and remove garlic. 4. Stir in pork, sherry, soy sauce, salt and sugar. Cook 2 minutes; stir constantly. Add shrimp; stir till pink. Add broth and water. 5. Combine cornstarch with 1 tablespoon water; add to skillet. Bring to boil and cook till thick; remove from heat. 6. Pour in eggs and stir till mixed. Sprinkle with onions. Serve over rice.

Bette Thistle, Minneapolis, Mn.

SHRIMP LOUISIANE CASSEROLE

1 c. chopped onion	3 c. cooked rice
3/4 c. chopped green pepper	1 Tbsp. chopped parsley
1 clove garlic, minced	1 1/2 Tbsp. lemon juice
2 Tbsp. butter or margarine	1 1/2 tsp. salt
1 lb. peeled, deveined raw	1/4 tsp. black pepper
shrimp or crawfish tails	1/4 tsp. red pepper
1 (10 3/4 oz.) can condensed	2 slices white bread
cream of mushroom soup	1/2 c. milk

Saute onion, green pepper and garlic in butter until tender crisp. Add shrimp; continue cooking 3 minutes longer. Stir in soup, rice, parsley, lemon juice and seasonings. Add bread, which has been soaked in milk; mix well. Spoon into a buttered shallow 2 quart casserole. Sprinkle with paprika. Bake at 350° for 30 minutes. Makes 6 servings.

Ann Christensen, Litchfield, Mn.

SHRIMP AND RICE ROCKEFELLER

1 c. chopped onion	3 c. cooked rice
2 Tbsp. butter or margarine	1 (8 oz.) can water chest-
12 oz. peeled, deveined raw	nuts, drained and sliced
shrimp, cut in halves	2 (10 oz.) pkg. frozen
lengthwise	chopped spinach, cooked
1 (10 3/4 oz.) can condensed	and drained
cream of mushroom soup	1 Tbsp. lemon juice
1 c. grated Swiss cheese	1/4 c. grated Parmesan
1/4 c. sherry	cheese
	Salt and pepper to taste

Saute onion in butter until tender but not brown. Add

shrimp; continue cooking until slightly pink, about 2 minutes. Stir in soup, Swiss cheese and sherry; heat until soup is warm. Add rice, water chestnuts, spinach, lemon juice and 2 tablespoons Parmesan cheese. Season to taste. Turn into a greased shallow 2 quart casserole; sprinkle with remaining Parmesan cheese. Bake, uncovered, at 350° for 25 minutes, or until hot and bubbly. Makes 6 to 8 servings.

Ann Christensen, Litchfield, Mn.

BAKED STUFFED SHRIMP

30 large shrimp	1 tsp. salt
3 Tbsp. oleo	Dash of pepper
1/4 c. minced onion	1 egg, beaten
1 green pepper, chopped	2 Tbsp. melted oleo
1 c. bread crumbs	

Shell and devein 6 shrimp; set the rest aside. Chop 6 shrimp in 3 tablespoons oleo for 2 minutes or until pink. Remove and chop finely. Add onion and green pepper to skillet; cook 3 or 4 minutes, stirring often. Remove from heat. Stir in crumbs, chopped shrimp, salt and pepper; blend in eggs. Shell reserved shrimp, leaving tails on. Place shrimp, back down, on board. Make a slit along underside of each shrimp with knife, but do not cut through. Remove vein. Mound stuffing mixture in hollow of each shrimp; bring tail over shrimp. Arrange shrimp, tails up, in greased, shallow baking dish. (Dish may now be covered and refrigerated, if desired.) Drizzle shrimp with melted oleo. Bake at 400° for 10 minutes.

Carolyn Brudevold, Fargo, N.D.

CHICKEN SHRIMP SUPREME

1/4 c. (1/2 stick) butter	1/2 c. light cream or half & half
1/2 lb. sliced fresh mushrooms	1 c. (4 oz.) shredded Cheddar cheese
2 Tbsp. sliced green onions	2 c. cut up, cooked chicken
2 (10 1/2 oz.) cans condensed cream of chicken soup	2 c. cooked shrimp
1/2 c. sherry	2 Tbsp. chopped parsley
	Hot, buttered rice

In 3 quart saucepan, melt butter; add mushrooms and

onion and saute 5 minutes. Add soup; gradually stir in
sherry and cream. Add cheese; heat over low heat, stirring occasionally, until cheese is melted. Add shrimp and
chicken; heat to serving temperature (do not boil). Just
before serving, stir in parsley. Serve over rice. Yield:
8 servings.

Mankato, Mn.

TORSK
(Cod)

Torsk is a very popular Minnesota specialty and without a doubt has earned its way onto our tables by rewarding
us with some excellent eating. It is a high quality source of
protein and supplies minerals such as iron, iodine, calcium,
phosphorus, copper and potassium. It is low in fat...but it
can be sauced luxuriously if you are not calorie counting.

Allow 4-6 ounces per person. The usual method of
preparation is poaching in small amount of water. Serve
with drawn butter.

To poach: For 2 pounds torsk, add just enough water
in skillet or pan to barely cover. Add 1 teaspoon salt, 1
bay leaf, a few slices of onion, 1 slice of lemon and 1/2 cup
dry white wine. Bring to a boil; cover and simmer until
fish flakes with fork, 10-12 minutes. Remove carefully with
slotted spoon. For a cream sauce, add cream to broth and
thicken with a little flour and water.

To bake: Place serving portions in shallow buttered
baking pan; sprinkle with salt and pepper. Cover; bake in
325° oven until fish flakes easily with fork, 20-30 minutes.
Do not overcook! Serve with drawn butter or cream sauce.

Betty Cortright, Minneapolis, Mn.

BAKED TORSK

Torsk   Kellogg's corn flake crumbs
Butter or margarine

Preheat oven to 400°. Bake about 20 minutes or until
fish flakes. Cut thawed and cleaned torsk into serving
sized pieces, about 2 inches square. Melt margarine or butter in a small pan. Turn torsk in fat to cover all sides; roll
in Kellogg's corn flake crumbs. Put onto greased baking
pan; sprinkle with salt and pepper and bake.

Harriet C. Kurek, Minneapolis, Mn.

354

DEEP SEA DELIGHT

1 (6 oz.) pkg. noodles
1 small can mushrooms
1 (10 oz.) can asparagus
1 small green pepper,
  chopped

1 can tuna fish
1 can mushroom soup, to
  which liquid from
  mushrooms and asparagus
  has been added
1/2 - 1 c. grated cheese

Cook noodles; add mushroom soup, mushrooms, green
pepper and tuna, 1/2 of the asparagus and 1/2 of the
grated cheese. Put into a greased casserole. Add rest of
the asparagus and cheese on top. Bake 45 minutes at 350°.
Jo-Lyn Freitag, Minneapolis, Mn.

TUNA CASSEROLE

1 can cheese soup
1/2 c. milk
2 c. cooked rice

1 can tuna
1/4 c. chopped parsley
1 can mushrooms

Combine all ingredients; pour into 1 1/2 quart casserole. Top with 3/4 cup corn flake crumbs, mixed with 2
tablespoons melted butter. Bake in 425° oven for about 15
minutes. Serves 6-8.
Inez Hagen, Duluth, Mn.

GINNY'S EASY TUNA CASSEROLE

Melt 2 tablespoons butter in baking dish. Add some
chopped green pepper; saute. Add 1 can Cheddar cheese
soup; stir in 3/4 can milk and 2 tablespoons minced onion.
Stir in 1 can sliced carrots (I like the small carrots in glass
jar), 1 can potatoes, quartered, and 2 cans tuna (1 may be
used). Top with 1 package of unrolled crescent rolls.
Sprinkle top with grated Cheddar cheese. Bake 15 minutes
at 400°.

Ginny Harwood, St. Cloud, Mn.

TUNA-CASHEW CASSEROLE
(The chopped nuts give it a crispy texture.)

3/4 c. elbow macaroni,
  cooked and drained
1 c. sour cream

1/4 tsp. ground oregano
2 (about 7 oz.) cans tuna,
  drained

1/2 c. sliced ripe olives
1 (4 oz.) can sliced
  mushrooms, drained
1/4 c. chopped green pepper
1/2 c. chopped cashew nuts

1 1/2 tsp. seasoned salt
1/4 tsp. pepper
1 c. grated sharp Cheddar
  cheese

Mix well all ingredients, except cheese; put in shallow 1 1/2 quart baking dish. Sprinkle with cheese. Bake in moderate oven, 350° F., for about 25 minutes. Serves 4-6.

Margaret McKenny, Minneapolis, Mn.

TUNA CHOW MEIN
(Use tuna packed in vegetable oil; cook it in the oil.)

2 (about 7 oz.) cans tuna,
1 medium onion, sliced
1 c. diagonally sliced celery
1 (1 lb.) can bean sprouts
1/8 tsp. pepper

1 (8 oz.) can water chestnuts
1/3 c. cornstarch
1/4 c. soy sauce
2 (3 oz.) cans chow mein
  noodles

Drain oil from tuna into a large saucepan; add onion and celery to oil and cook, stirring, 2 or 3 minutes. Drain liquid from sprouts and chestnuts; add enough water to make 4 cups. Thinly slice chestnuts. Add liquid to saucepan with sprouts, chestnuts and pepper. Bring to boil; stir in cornstarch, blended with soy sauce and a little water. Cook, stirring, until thick. Add tuna; heat. Serve on noodles. Serves 6.

Margaret McKenny, Minneapolis, Mn.

TUNA CHOW MEIN CASSEROLE

Mix together 1 can mushroom soup and 1 can beef consomme; heat. Mix in:

1 regular size can tuna
1/4 c. slivered almonds
1 c. Chinese chow mein
  noodles

1/2 c. diced celery
1 c. bean sprouts
2 Tbsp. minced onion
Salt and pepper

Place in greased 1 1/2 quart casserole. Bake at 350° for 30 minutes.

Mary Perron, Rochester, Mn.

TUNA-CHOW MEIN CASSEROLE

1 c. chopped celery
1/4 c. chopped onion
1/4 c. chopped green pepper
1 Tbsp. butter
1 can cream of mushroom
   soup, thinned with 1/4 c.
   milk and 1/4 c. water

1 (6 1/2 or 7 oz.) can tuna
1 1/3 c. chow mein noodles
3/4 c. (4 oz.) salted cashew
   nuts
1/4 tsp. monosodium
   glutamate
1/4 tsp. pepper
1 Tbsp. soy sauce

Heat oven to 350°. Saute celery, onion and green pepper in butter. Mix thinned soup, tuna, 1 cup of the noodles, cashews and seasonings; pour into buttered 1 1/2 quart casserole. Sprinkle with remaining 1/3 cup chow mein noodles. Bake 35 minutes.

                 Kerrie C. Applen, Minneapolis, Mn.

TUNA CROQUETTES

2 c. firm mashed potatoes
2 cans tuna, drained

1 egg, beaten
2 tsp. prepared mustard

Mix and form; roll into crumbs. Place on buttered baking sheet. Bake at 450° for 15 minutes. Makes 9 or 10.

                 G.W. Seemans, Robbinsdale, Mn.

CREAMED TUNA DIVAN

1 (6 or 7 oz.) can light
   chunk tuna
1 (10 1/2 oz.) can cream of
   mushroom, cream of
   chicken or cream of celery
   soup
1/2 c. milk

1 (10 oz.) pkg. frozen
   broccoli, thawed, or 1
   bunch fresh broccoli,
   blanched
1/2 c. dry bread crumbs
1 Tbsp. soft butter or
   margarine

Thoroughly drain tuna; break up with a fork into large chunks. Mix soup with milk; stir until completely smooth. Fold in tuna. Arrange thawed or blanched broccoli in an ovenproof serving dish. Top with tuna mixture and crumbs; dot with butter. Bake at 350° for 25 or 30 minutes, until sauce is bubbly and bread crumbs are nicely browned. Serves 2.
    Note: Cooked chicken or turkey may be substituted for tuna.

                 Blanche B. Masica, Minneapolis, Mn.

TUNA HOT DISH

1 can mushroom soup
1 can chunk tuna, drained

1 soup can of milk
1 c. chow mein noodles

Mix; put in a greased 7x11 inch pan. Put in real hot oven, 500°, until it begins to bubble. Place under broiler and brown; watch it very closely as it takes only a few minutes. Serve over chow mein noodles immediately.

Mary Fingalson, Detroit Lakes, Mn.

TUNA ITALIAN

1/2 c. chopped onion
1 can cream of mushroom
  soup
2/3 c. evaporated milk
1 (6 oz.) can tuna, drained
1/2 c. sliced ripe olives

1 (4 oz.) can mushrooms,
  drained and sliced
2 tsp. lemon juice
3 c. egg noodles
1/3 c. grated mild Cheddar
  cheese

Saute onion in butter; add soup and milk. Heat and stir until hot and smooth. Stir in lemon juice. Combine cooked noodles, tuna, mushrooms and olives in buttered 3 quart casserole. Add soup mixture; sprinkle cheese on top. Bake at 350° for 30 minutes.

Alicia Woodford, Montevideo, Mn.

TUNA ORIENTAL NOODLE SUPPER

1 1/2 c. sliced celery
2/3 c. chopped onion
1/2 c. chopped green pepper
2 Tbsp. margarine
3/4 c. mayonnaise
1 Tbsp. prepared mustard

1 Tbsp. chopped pimento
3/4 c. milk
1 (6 1/2 oz.) can tuna
1/2 tsp. salt
1/4 tsp. pepper
1 can chow mein noodles

Cook and stir celery, onion and green pepper in butter until crisp and tender. Mix mayonnaise, mustard, pimento and milk until smooth. Stir in tuna, salt and pepper. Stir in celery mixture. Keep warm. Serve over noodles.

Alice Lee, Phoenix, Az.

358

TUNA ON A SHOESTRING

1 c. grated raw carrots
1 c. chopped celery
1/4 c. chopped onion

3/4 - 1 c. mayonnaise
1 (4 oz.) can tuna

Add 1 (4 ounce) can shoestring potatoes just before serving.

Florence Swanson, Minneapolis, Mn.

TUNA PATTIES

3/4 c. cooked rice
1 (7 oz.) can solid pack (or
chunk style) tuna
1 egg
1 Tbsp. chopped parsley

3/4 tsp. salt
1/8 tsp. pepper
2 Tbsp. chopped onion
1/4 c. flour
2 Tbsp. salad oil or melted
fat

Combine all ingredients, except flour and oil; shape into 6 patties. Dredge with flour. Fry at medium heat until browned, about 5 minutes on each side. Serve with chili sauce or ketchup.

Harriett C. Kurek, Minneapolis, Mn.

TUNA AND RICE CASSEROLE

Cook 3/4 cup rice; drain. Add tuna, a little chopped onion and green pepper. Add 1/4 cup milk and 1 can cream of mushroom or cream of celery soup. Bake for 30 minutes at 325° or 350°.

Elsa Ditty, St. Cloud, Mn.

TUNA TIMBALES

2 eggs, beaten
2 c. flaked tuna fish
1/2 tsp. salt
1/8 tsp. pepper
1/4 tsp. celery salt
1 tsp. paprika

1 tsp. Worcestershire sauce
1 Tbsp. lemon juice
1 1/2 c. milk
1 c. Quaker or Mother's oats
(quick or old fashioned),
uncooked

Combine all ingredients thoroughly; place in 6 greased custard cups or greased loaf pan (glass preferred). Bake in a moderate oven, 350° F., for 50 minutes to 1 hour, or until set. Makes 6 servings. Calories per serving: 275.

Dena Stoddard, St. Louis Park, Mn.

SCOTTY'S TUNA PATTIES

1 (family size) can tuna
1 large potato, grated
1/4 c. chopped onion

3 or 4 crackers, crumbled,
  or 2 Tbsp. flour
1 egg
Salt and pepper to taste

Mix all ingredients together; form into large patties. Fry in small amount of oil; brown on both sides.

Helen Teeuwen, Minneapolis, Mn.

HOT TUNA SANDWICHES

Butter 9x13 inch pan. Butter 6 slices of white bread, crusts removed, and lay in pan. Cover each with a slice of cheese. Sprinkle 2 cans of drained tuna over top of bread. Cover with 6 slices of bread, crusts removed. Beat 4 eggs; add 3 cups milk, 1/4 teaspoon salt and pepper. Pour over top of bread; let stand in refrigerator overnight. Bake at 300° for 1 hour.

Ruth Rehschuh, Minneapolis, Mn.

BREADS
COFFEE CAKES
ROLLS
SANDWICHES

EQUIVALENT CHART

3 tsp.	1 tbsp.
2 tbsp.	1/8 c.
4 tbsp.	1/4 c.
8 tbsp.	1/2 c.
16 tbsp.	1 c.
5 tbsp. + 1 tsp.	1/3 c.
12 tbsp.	3/4 c.
4 oz.	1/2 c.
8 oz.	1 c.
16 oz.	1 lb.
1 oz.	2 tbsp. fat or liquid
2 c.	1 pt.
3½ c. unsifted whole wheat flour	1 lb.
8 to 10 egg whites	1 c.
12 to 14 egg yolks	1 c.
1 c. unwhipped cream	2 c. whipped
1 lb. shredded American cheese	4 c.
¼ lb. crumbled blue cheese	1 c.
1 lemon	3 tbsp. juice
1 orange	1/3 c. juice
1 lb. unshelled walnuts	1½ to 1¾ c. shelled
2 pt.	1 qt.
1 qt.	4 c.
5/8 c.	1/2 c. + 2 tbsp.
7/8 c.	3/4 c. + 2 tbsp.
1 jigger	1 1/2 fl. oz. (3 tbsp.)
2 c. fat	1 lb.
1 lb. butter	2 c. or 4 sticks
2 c. sugar	1 lb.
2 2/3 c. powdered sugar	1 lb.
2 2/3 c. brown sugar	1 lb.
4 c. sifted flour	1 lb.
4½ c. cake flour	1 lb.
4 oz. (1 to 1¼ c.) uncooked macaroni	2¼ c. cooked
7 oz. spaghetti	4 c. cooked
4 oz. (1½ to 2 c.) uncooked noodles	2 c. cooked
28 saltine crackers	1 c. crumbs
4 slices bread	1 c. crumbs
14 square graham crackers	1 c. crumbs
22 vanilla wafers	1 c. crumbs

SUBSTITUTIONS FOR A MISSING INGREDIENT

1 square **chocolate** (1 ounce) = 3 or 4 tablespoons cocoa plus ½ tablespoon fat.
1 tablespoon **cornstarch** (for thickening) = 2 tablespoons flour.
1 cup sifted **all-purpose flour** = 1 cup plus 2 tablespoons sifted cake flour
1 cup sifted **cake flour** = 1 cup minus 2 tablespoons sifted all-purpose flour
1 teaspoon **baking powder** = ¼ teaspoon baking soda plus ½ teaspoon cream of tartar.
1 cup **sour milk** = 1 cup sweet milk into which 1 tablespoon vinegar or lemon juice has been stirred; or 1 cup buttermilk (let stand for 5 minutes).
1 cup **sweet milk** = 1 cup sour milk or buttermilk plus ½ teaspoon baking soda.
¾ cup **cracker crumbs** = 1 cup bread crumbs.
1 cup **cream, sour, heavy** = 1/3 cup butter and 2/3 cups milk in any sour milk recipe
1 teaspoon **dried herbs** = 1 tablespoon fresh herbs.
½ cup **evaporated milk** and ½ cup **water** or 1 cup **reconstituted nonfat dry milk** and 1 tablespoon **butter** = 1 cup whole milk.
1 package **active dry yeast** = 1 cake compressed yeast.
1 tablespoon **instant minced onion, rehydrated** = 1 small fresh onion.
1 tablespoon **prepared mustard** = 1 teaspoon dry mustard.
1/8 teaspoon **garlic powder** = 1 small pressed clove of garlic.
1 lb. **whole dates** = 1½ c. pitted and cut.
3 medium **bananas** = 1 c. mashed
3 c. **dry corn flakes** = 1 c. crushed
10 **miniature marshmallows** = 1 large marshmallow

GENERAL OVEN CHART

Very slow oven	250° to 300° F.
Slow oven	300° to 325° F.
Moderate oven	325° to 375° F.
Medium hot oven	375° to 400° F.
Hot oven	400° to 450° F.
Very hot oven	450° to 500° F.

CONTENTS OF CANS

Of the different sizes of cans used by commercial canners, the most common are:

Size	Average Contents
8-oz.	1 cup
picnic	1¼ cups
No. 300	1¾ cups
No. 1 tall	2 cups
No. 303	2 cups
No. 2	2½ cups
No. 2½	3½ cups
No. 3	4 cups
No. 10	12 to 13 cups

APPLE CHERRY BREAD

6 Tbsp. oleo	2 c. flour
2/3 c. sugar	1 tsp. baking powder
2 eggs	1/2 tsp. soda
1 tsp. grated lemon peel	1/2 tsp. salt
1 c. applesauce	1/2 c. chopped walnuts
2 Tbsp. milk	1/4 c. chopped maraschino cherries

Cream oleo and sugar until fluffy; add eggs one at a time, beating after each addition. Add grated lemon peel. Combine applesauce and milk. Sift together flour, baking powder, soda and salt. Add alternately with applesauce mixture to creamed mixture. Stir in walnuts and cherries. Pour into a greased 8 1/2 x 4 1/2 inch loaf dish. Bake in moderate oven, 350° F., for about 35 minutes or until done; cool.

Colleen Landwehr, St. Cloud, Mn.

DUTCH APPLE BREAD

1/2 c. margarine	1 tsp. soda
1 c. sugar	1/3 c. milk
2 eggs	1 c. peeled, chopped apples
2 c. flour	1/2 c. chopped nuts (opt.)
1/2 tsp. salt	

Grease 9x5 inch loaf pan. Cream margarine and sugar; add eggs and beat. Combine flour, salt and soda; add alternately with milk. Fold in chopped apples. Bake 55 minutes at 350°.

Norma Haugerud, Montevideo, Mn.

APPLE CINNAMON SWIRL LOAF

Dissolve 1 package active dry yeast in 1 1/2 cups warm water. Add 1 beaten egg, 1 package (one layer) white cake mix and 1 teaspoon salt; beat till smooth. Add 3 1/2 to 3 3/4 cups flour; knead till smooth and elastic. Place in greased bowl; let rise till double in a covered bowl, about 1 1/2 hours. Punch down; divide in two. Cover and let rest for 10 minutes. In the meantime, prepare

2 1/2 cups chopped apples. Add 1/3 cup sugar, 1/3 cup chopped pecans and 2 teaspoons cinnamon. Melt 4 tablespoons butter; set aside. Prepare each half of dough in the following manner. Roll to 12x8 inch rectangle. Brush surface with melted butter; spread apple mixture over dough. Roll from short end; seal sides and ends. Place in 8x4x2 inch pans, which have been greased. Brush with butter. Cover; let rise till double, about an hour. Bake in 375° oven for 30 to 35 minutes. Cool. Makes 2 loaves.

Esther Mungovan, Duluth, Mn.

APRICOT NUT BREAD

1/2 c. snipped, dried apricots	3/4 c. sugar
	1/4 tsp. salt
1 c. broken walnuts	1 tsp. baking powder
2 1/4 c. Bisquick	1 egg
1 c. rolled oats	1 1/4 c. milk

Mix Bisquick, oats, sugar, salt and baking powder. Stir in nuts and fruit. In a small bowl, beat egg well, then beat in milk. Stir milk into dry ingredients; beat for 30 seconds. Turn into greased and floured loaf pan. Bake 1 hour at 350°; cool 10 minutes, then turn out on rack and cool thoroughly. Wrap in Saran Wrap to mellow overnight.

Dee Olson, St. Paul, Mn.

ALL-BRAN BANANA NUT BREAD

Cream well:

1/3 c. shortening	3/4 c. sugar

Mix well:

1 large egg	1 1/2 c. mashed bananas
1 c. All-Bran	

Add:

1 1/2 c. flour	1/2 tsp. soda
1/2 tsp. salt	1 tsp. vanilla
2 tsp. baking powder	Nuts, to taste

Bake at 350° for 60 or 70 minutes.

Martie Athey, Osage, Mn.

BANANA BRAN BREAD

1 c. sugar
1/2 c. margarine

2 eggs

Beat well and add:

1/4 c. milk
1 c. Bran Buds

3 large bananas, mashed well

Sift and stir in:

2 c. flour
1 tsp. salt

1 tsp. soda
1/2 c. chopped walnuts

Bake in greased loaf pan for 45 minutes to 1 hour. This makes 2 small loaves or 1 very large one.

Liz Tuft, St. Paul, Mn.

BANANA BREAD

1 c. sugar
1/2 c. shortening
2 eggs
3 large bananas, mashed

2 1/2 c. flour
1 tsp. soda
1/4 tsp. salt
1/2 c. chopped nuts

Cream sugar and shortening. Add beaten eggs; stir until smooth. Add bananas; add dry ingredients. Stir in nuts. Bake 1 hour at 350° (little longer usually).

Emogene Homan, Minneapolis, Mn.

BANANA BREAD

Cream 3/4 cup butter or margarine. Add 1 1/2 cups sugar gradually; cream well. Blend in 1 1/2 cups (3-4) mashed bananas, 2 eggs and 1 teaspoon vanilla. Sift together 2 cups flour, 1 teaspoon salt and 1 teaspoon soda. Add alternately 1/2 cup buttermilk or sour milk, blending just until well combined. Fold in 1/2 cup walnuts, if desired. Pour into 9x5 inch greased loaf pan. Bake in 350° oven for 1 1/2 hours.

Bea Juliot, Wyoming, Mn.

BISHOP'S BREAD

2 c. flour
1 tsp. baking powder
1 tsp. salt
1/2 c. margarine
1 1/2 c. sugar
6 beaten eggs

1 tsp. vanilla
2 lb. dates, cut in pieces
1 lb. walnuts, chopped
1 lb. Brazil nuts, chopped
2 (8 oz.) jars maraschino
   cherries, chopped

Cream margarine, sugar, eggs and vanilla. Add flour, baking powder and salt. Add dates, nuts and cherries. Bake 1 hour in a 350° oven. Place a pan of water in the oven while baking bread. This will make five 1 pound loaves. Grease the pans lightly before filling 1/2 to 3/4 full.

Mrs. Norma Applen, Minneapolis, Mn.

BUTTER BRICKLE BREAD

Mix together:
1 small pkg. vanilla instant
   pudding
1 pkg. butter brickle cake
   mix

4 eggs
1/2 c. oil
1 c. water

Add 1/4 cup poppy seeds. Grease 2 loaf pans. Bake at 325° for 45 minutes.

Topping: Whip together -

1 stick butter
2-3 Tbsp. powdered sugar

3 oz. cream cheese

Virginia Miller, Anoka, Mn.

GARLIC BUBBLE BREAD

1 loaf frozen white bread
   dough
1/4 c. butter or margarine,
   melted

1 egg, beaten
1 tsp. dried parsley flakes
1/4 tsp. salt
1/2 tsp. garlic powder

Thaw dough. Mix together the melted butter, egg, parsley flakes, salt and garlic powder. Cut off pieces of dough the size of walnut. Dip in butter mixture and place pieces in well greased loaf pan. Cover; let rise until doubled in size. Bake in moderately hot oven, 375°, for 30 minutes or until done. Cool in pan on wire rack about 10 minutes. Remove from pan; continue cooling. Makes 1 loaf. Can also make 1 dozen cloverleaf rolls in muffin tins. Bake about 20 minutes.

Marty Eger, South St. Paul, Mn.

BLUEBERRY GINGERBREAD

1/2 c. cooking oil	1 tsp. cinnamon
1 c. sugar	1/2 tsp. nutmeg
1/2 tsp. salt	1 tsp. baking soda
3 Tbsp. molasses	1 c. fresh or frozen
1 egg	blueberries
2 c. flour	1 c. buttermilk
1/2 tsp. ginger	2 Tbsp. sugar

Beat together oil, sugar, salt and molasses. Beat in egg. Combine flour, spices and baking soda; dredge blueberries with 2 tablespoons of flour mixture. Add remaining flour mixture to first mixture alternately with buttermilk, beating after each addition. Stir in blueberries. Pour into greased and floured 12 x 7 1/2 x 2 inch pan. Sprinkle top with 2 tablespoons sugar. Bake at 350° for 35-40 minutes.

Sally Bartsch, Blaine, Mn.

QUICK CHEDDAR BREAD

3 1/3 c. all-purpose biscuit mix	2 c. (8 oz.) shredded sharp natural Cheddar cheese
2 eggs	1 1/4 c. milk

Grease and flour bottom and sides of loaf pan. Combine biscuit mix and cheese in large mixing bowl. Break eggs into small bowl; beat slightly with fork to blend yolks and whites. Add to large bowl with milk. Stir with wooden spoon just until dry ingredients are moistened. Pour batter into prepared loaf pan. Bake at 350° for 35 minutes. Remove immediately from pan and serve warm.

Phylliss Mae Johnson, Winona, Mn.

CHEESE BREAD

Dissolve 1 package yeast in 1/4 cup lukewarm water.
Combine:

2 Tbsp. shortening	1 tsp. salt
1 Tbsp. sugar	

Scald 3/4 cup milk. Cool; add yeast and 2 1/4 cups
flour. Knead 3-5 minutes; let rise 1 1/2 hours. Press onto
greased cookie sheet; let rise 45 minutes. Combine 1 egg
and 5 tablespoons milk. Have 1/2 pound grated cheese of
your choice and 3/4 cup chopped onion ready, also 1 1/2
teaspoons caraway, sesame or poppy seed. Put milk and
egg mixture on top, then seed and last the grated cheese.
Bake at 425° for 15-20 minutes.

Martha Fjelstad, Minneapolis, Mn.

CHERRY NUT BREAD

1/2 c. shortening	1/2 c. milk
1 1/2 c. sugar	1/2 c. chopped nuts
3 beaten eggs	16 cherries, cut up
2 1/2 c. flour	Pinch of salt
2 tsp. baking powder	1 tsp. vanilla
1/4 c. cherry juice	

Cream shortening and sugar; add beaten eggs. Sift
flour and baking powder; add alternately to the first mixture with the cherry juice and milk. Add rest of ingredients; put into 2 small greased loaf pans. Bake at 350° for
up to 1 1/2 hours or until done.

Mary Jean Voss, Owatonna, Mn.
Similar recipe submitted by: Mary Paul, Minneapolis, Mn.

CHRISTMAS BREAD

3 c. milk	1/2 c. butter
2 tsp. salt	2 eggs, well beaten
3/4 c. sugar	2 cakes yeast, added to
8 1/2 c. flour	cooled milk

Scald milk; cool. Add yeast; set aside. Cream sugar,
butter and eggs. Add milk, yeast and 4 cups flour; mix
into the other 4 1/2 cups flour 1 1/2 cups candied pineapple,
diced, and candied cherries, sliced, 3/4 cup raisins, 1 1/2
teaspoons cardamon and candied orange, if desired.

Esther Beatty, Duluth, Mn.

CHOC-CHIP BANANA BREAD

1 c. sugar	1 1/2 tsp. soda
1/2 c. Crisco	1/2 tsp. salt
2 eggs	10 Tbsp. sour milk
3 c. flour	3 mashed bananas

Mix the above together. Take 1 tablespoon flour; mix in 1/2 cup chocolate chips. Fold flour and chips into above mixture. Grease and flour 2 loaf pans. Bake at 325° for 1 hour.

Jan Ferry, Golden Valley, Mn.

CINNAMON SWIRL ORANGE BREAD

1 cake yeast	1 Tbsp. orange peel
1/4 c. water	3/4 c. orange juice
1 c. milk, scalded	6 1/2 - 7 c. flour
1/2 c. sugar	1 egg, beaten
1/4 c. shortening	1/2 c. sugar
1 1/2 tsp. salt	1 Tbsp. cinnamon

Frosting:

1 c. powdered sugar	4 Tbsp. orange juice
1 tsp. orange peel	

Let rise twice; divide dough into 2 rolls, each in rectangle. Combine sugar and cinnamon; spread over dough. Roll; seal edge. Place sealed edge down in greased loaf pan. Let rise. Bake at 350° for 30 minutes. Frost with powdered sugar frosting.

Mary Perron, Rochester, Mn.

CORN BREAD

1 c. corn meal	1 tsp. salt
1 c. flour	4 tsp. baking powder
1/4 c. sugar	

Sift all together. Make hole in center; add 1 large egg and 5 tablespoons melted Crisco. Pour in well oiled pan or muffin tins. Bake at 375° for 20 minutes or until done.

Ava S. Day, St. Paul, Mn.

NEW CRANBERRY NUT BREAD
(Just a pinch of imagination and Bisquick)

You'll like the fresh tangy flavor of cranberries and orange in this tasty nut bread. And, it's so easy!

3/4 c. sugar
1 egg
1 1/4 c. orange juice
1 Tbsp. grated orange rind

3 c. Bisquick
3/4 c. chopped nuts
1 c. chopped cranberries
(fresh or frozen; if frozen, do not thaw)

Heat oven to 350° (moderate). Mix sugar, egg, orange juice, rind and Bisquick. Beat vigorously 30 seconds. Batter may still be lumpy. Stir in nuts and cranberries; pour into well greased loaf pan, 9x5x3 inches. Bake 55 to 60 minutes, or until toothpick stuck into center comes out clean. Crack in top is typical. Remove from baking pan. Cool before slicing.

To bake in cans: Heat oven to 350°. Divide batter among three well greased No. 2 cans or five well greased soup cans. Fill slightly more than half full. Bake No. 2 cans 45 to 50 minutes; soup cans about 40 minutes.

Dena Stoddard, St. Louis Park, Mn.

CRACKED WHEAT BREAD

2 c. boiling water
2 c. cracked wheat
1/2 c. powdered milk
1/2 c. brown sugar
2 Tbsp. margarine

1/2 Tbsp. salt
2 pkg. dry yeast
1/2 c. warm water
5 - 5 1/2 c. white flour

Combine cracked wheat, brown sugar, powdered milk, margarine and salt. Pour boiling water over all; stir well. Cool to lukewarm. Meanwhile, soften yeast in warm water. Combine when first mixture is cool. Gradually beat in 4 cups flour. Turn out on floured surface; knead in enough of the remaining flour to make a stiff dough. Knead 8-10 minutes. Place in greased bowl, turning to grease all surfaces of dough. Cover; let rise until double, about 1 1/2 hours. Knead down and shape into 2 loaves. Place in greased loaf pans. Let rise until double. Bake at 375° for about 30-35 minutes.

Liz Tuft, St. Paul, Mn.

WHOLE WHEAT HONEY BREAD

2 pkg. dry yeast
1 Tbsp. sugar
1 c. warm water
1 Tbsp. salt
1/2 c. honey

1/2 c. cooking oil
2 c. water
4 c. whole wheat flour
4-5 c. white flour

In large bowl, combine yeast, sugar and warm water. Stir; let stand 15 minutes. Add salt, honey, oil and water; stir. Add the flours gradually; knead for 10 minutes. Cover; let rise about 2 hours or until double in size. Knead again; divide into 3 loaves. Place in well greased loaf pans; let rise. Bake 25-30 minutes at 350°.

Alicia Woodford, Montevideo, Mn.

DATE NUT BREAD

2 c. sweet milk
2 c. graham flour
2 c. white flour
1 c. brown sugar
4 tsp. baking powder

2 eggs
1 tsp. salt
1 c. nuts
1 c. dates

Beat the eggs; add sugar. Mix the dry ingredients, including the nuts and dates. Alternating, add liquid and dry ingredients to eggs and sugar mixture. Put into greased and floured pans; let stand 15 minutes. Bake at 375° F. for 55 minutes; test for doneness. Amount: 2 small loaves. (Fifty years ago I entered this recipe in a Red and White grocery store contest and won a $5.00 gift certificate.)

Helen-May Johnson, Chanhassen, Mn.

FLAT BREAD

4 c. white flour
2 c. yellow corn meal
1/2 c. Crisco

1 tsp. salt
2 tsp. sugar

Add about 3 cups warm water; mix all together. Roll thin. Bake on grill at about 350°, then put into 350° oven to crisp it.

Lydia Skaret, Austin, Mn.

GARLIC BREAD

1 c. butter or margarine   1/4 tsp. dill weed
1/4 tsp. oregano   1 tsp. garlic powder

Mix well; spread on sliced French bread, both sides of slice and on top of loaf. Sprinkle with Romano cheese and parsley flakes. Wrap loaf in foil, leaving top open. Bake at 400° for 10 minutes.

Eloise Hoff, Preston, Mn.

QUICK GINGERBREAD

Sift together into large bowl:
2 1/4 c. sifted all-purpose   1 tsp. soda
   flour   1/2 tsp. salt
1 tsp. ginger   1/2 tsp. baking powder
1 1/2 tsp. cinnamon

Add:
1/2 c. shortening (soft)   3/4 c. milk (sweet or sour)
1/3 c. sugar   1 c. molasses
2 eggs, unbeaten

Beat only until blended, about 2 1/2 minutes. Pour into greased 9x13 inch pan. Bake at 350° for 45 minutes.

Eileen Durham, Brainerd, Mn.

HAWAIIAN BREAD

3 1/2 c. crushed pineapple   1 1/2 c. sugar
   and juice   4 c. flour
3 c. (or 10 oz.) coconut   2 tsp. salt
4 eggs, beaten till light   2 tsp. soda

Combine pineapple, coconut, eggs and sugar; mix well. Sift flour, salt and soda; add. Bake 1/2 hour. Makes 3 loaves. (Bake at 325°.)

K., St. Cloud, Mn.

HOBO BREAD

Soak overnight:
2 c. raisins   4 tsp. soda
2 c. boiling water

Combine:

2 c. sugar
1/3 c. oil
Salt

4 c. flour
Chopped nuts

Add raisin mixture. Bake in three greased and floured 1 pound coffee cans. Bake in 350° oven for 1 - 1 1/2 hours.

Esther Mungovan, Duluth, Mn.

KNOKKELROD

1 pkg. Dromedary corn muffin mix
1 c. graham or whole wheat flour
1 c. white flour

1 tsp. salt
2 Tbsp. sugar
1/2 tsp. soda
3 Tbsp. shortening

Mix the above together as you would a pie crust. Add 1 cup buttermilk. Roll out thin; cut into pieces and bake on a cookie sheet at 350° or less for 8 to 10 minutes.

Donna Hoff, Fargo, N.D.

LEMON LOAF BREAD

3/4 c. margarine
1 1/2 c. sugar
3 eggs
2 1/4 c. flour
1/4 tsp. salt

1/4 tsp. soda
3/4 c. buttermilk
Grated rind of lemon
3/4 c. chopped nuts

Glaze:

Juice of 2 lemons

3/4 c. sugar

Preheat oven to moderately slow, 325°. Grease and flour 9x5x3 inch (2 quart size) loaf pan. Cream margarine and sugar; beat in eggs. Sift dry ingredients; add to batter alternately with milk. Mix well. Stir in grated rind and nuts. Pour into pan and bake about 1 hour or until tester comes out clean. Cool 15 minutes. While bread is cooling, mix lemon juice and sugar. Remove from pan; place on rack. Pierce top with tester or toothpick in several places and spoon glaze over top. Allow to cool before slicing. Makes 1 large loaf or can divide to 2 small.

Marion Vonesh, Grand Forks, N.D.

GARLIC MONKEY BREAD

1 loaf frozen bread dough
1/4 c. melted butter

1 large clove garlic, pressed
1/4 tsp. salt
1 tsp. dried parsley

Cut partially thawed bread dough into 20 or 30 small pieces. Mix remaining ingredients; dip the pieces of dough into the mixture. Put pieces of dough into a round tube pan; let rise until doubled in bulk. Bake in 375° oven for 25-30 minutes. Serve hot.

Dee Olson, St. Paul, Mn.

LIPTON ONION BUTTER BREAD

1 env. Lipton onion soup mix
1 (1 lb.) loaf Italian bread

1/2 lb. butter or margarine

Blend onion soup mix thoroughly with softened butter or margarine. Makes 1 1/4 cups onion butter. Preheat oven to 375°. Slice bread diagonally without cutting through lower crust. Generously spread onion butter between slices; wrap in foil, partially open at top. Bake 15-20 minutes.

Betty Babich, Virginia, Mn.

MANDARIN ORANGE NUT BREAD

Mix in order:
4 eggs, slightly beaten
1 1/2 c. sugar
2 1/2 c. flour
2 tsp. salt
2 tsp. baking soda

1 1/2 c. quick oats
2 small (11 oz.) cans man-
    darin oranges with juice
1 (3 oz.) pkg. orange jello
1 c. walnuts, floured (will
    not sink)

Pour into 2 greased pans (bread size). Bake at 325° for 1 hour. Hard to mix, but don't give up. Batter gets juicy at end of mixing.

Terry Sandulak, Altoona, Wi.

RAE'S ORANGE BREAD

Chop rind of 1 orange; put into a saucepan with 1 cup sugar and 1/3 cup water. Boil 15 minutes. Cool and add 1 cup milk and 1 egg. Add 3 cups flour, mixed with 4 teaspoons baking powder and 1/4 teaspoon salt. Stir just until moistened. Pour into loaf pan, greased and floured. Bake 1 hour in 350° oven.

Dee Olson, St. Paul, Mn.

MONKEY BREAD

1. Cut each biscuit (3 or 4 cans of any Pillsbury country buttermilk biscuits) into 4 pieces. 2. Mix 3/4 cup white sugar and 1 teaspoon cinnamon; put into plastic bag. 3. Add pieces of biscuit into bag; shake well, enough to coat biscuits. Place into a Bundt pan. 4. Take leftover sugar from bag; place into cup and add enough brown sugar to make 1 full cup. Place into pan with 1 stick of margarine. Bring this to a boil, then pour over biscuits. Bake in 350° oven for 25-30 minutes (right away).

Catherine Selfors, Minot, N.D.

FRENCH ONION BREAD

Soften 2 cakes yeast in 1/2 cup water (or 2 packages dry yeast, softened in 1/2 cup very warm, not hot water). Combine 2 tablespoons Crisco and 1 1/2 cups hot water in large bowl; stir to melt the shortening. Stir in:

3 Tbsp. sugar   1 pkg. dry onion soup
2 tsp. salt

Cool to lukewarm. Add the softened yeast. Add gradually 5 1/2 to 6 cups sifted flour to form a stiff dough. Knead on floured surface until smooth and satiny, about 5 minutes. Let rise in warm place, 85° to 90°, until light and doubled in size, about 1 1/2 hours. Punch down; let rise again for 1/2 hour. Divide dough into 2 parts; shape into loaves and place in 2 greased pans. Cover and let rise in warm place until light and doubled in size, about 1 hour. Bake at 375° for 35 to 40 minutes.

Rhea Layne, Sauk Rapids, Mn.

ORANGE-DATE BREAD

2 c. sugar
1 c. shortening
4 eggs
2 tsp. vanilla
1 1/2 c. buttermilk
4 c. flour

1 tsp. soda
1 tsp. salt
1 lb. orange candy slices,
 cut in pieces
1 lb. dates, cut in pieces
1 c. chopped nuts

Sift 1 cup flour over the orange and date pieces. Mix sugar and shortening until creamy; beat in eggs and vanilla. Add flour, soda and salt alternately with buttermilk. Fold in fruit and nuts. Bake in 2 large or 3 small greased bread pans in 325° oven for 60-70 minutes.

Mrs. Norma Applen, Minneapolis, Mn.

ORANGE MARMALADE NUT BREAD

1/2 c. (1 stick) margarine
1/2 c. packed brown sugar
2 eggs
1 (10 oz.) jar orange
 marmalade
2 3/4 c. flour

2 tsp. baking powder
1 tsp. salt
1/2 tsp. baking soda
1/2 c. pure 100% unsweetened
 pasteurized orange juice
1/2 c. chopped nuts

Grease and flour bottom and sides of loaf pan. In large mixing bowl, cream margarine and sugar until light and fluffy. Add eggs, one at a time, mixing well after each addition; blend in marmalade. Combine flour, baking powder, salt and baking soda in medium mixing bowl. Add flour mixture to large bowl alternately with orange juice. Mix well after each addition; stir in nuts. Spoon batter into greased pan. Bake at 325° for 1 hour and 20 minutes or until wooden pick inserted in center of loaf comes out clean. Remove from oven; cool 10 minutes on wire cooling rack. Remove bread from pan and cool on wire cooling rack.

Phylliss Mae Johnson, Winona, Mn.

ORANGE SLICE BREAD

1 c. orange slices, chopped
 fine
1 Tbsp. sugar
1/4 c. butter
1/2 c. sugar

1 egg
1 banana, mashed
2 1/2 c. flour
2 tsp. baking powder
1/2 tsp. salt

1/2 c. chopped nuts   1/2 tsp. soda
1 c. milk

Mix chopped orange slices and sugar. Cream butter and sugar; add egg and banana. Mix well. Sift dry ingredients; alternately add milk and dry ingredients to creamed mixture. Add nuts and orange slices. Pour into greased and floured bread pan. Bake in 350° oven for 65 minutes or till done.

Mary Jean Voss, Owatonna, Mn.

PEANUT BUTTER BREAD

2 c. flour   1 c. peanut butter
1/3 c. sugar   1 c. milk
2 tsp. baking powder   1 well beaten egg
1 tsp. salt

Sift together dry ingredients; add peanut butter, blending with a fork. Stir in milk and egg; mix well. Spoon into a 9x5 inch lightly greased loaf pan. Allow to rise in a warm place 20 minutes. Bake in a 350° oven for 50 minutes.

Mrs. Norma Applen, Minneapolis, Mn.

PEPPERONI BREAD

4 c. water (warm)   1/4 c. oil
2 pkg. yeast   2 Tbsp. salt
1/2 c. sugar

Stir all together and add 10 cups flour (may need a little more). Knead a lot, then round dough into ball and grease. Put in bowl to rise; cover with towel. Let rise 1/2 hour. Punch down; let rise 1 1/2 hours or until double. Divide into 4 (3 if large pans) pieces. Roll out as for cinnamon rolls. Spread with beaten egg. Sprinkle Romano or Parmesan cheese over entire piece, then chopped pepperoni and sprinkle with pepper. Roll up; put loaf in greased bread pan. Let rise about 1 hour. Bake at 375° for 40-45 minutes. After baking, brush with butter. Very good toasted, too.

R. Johansen, Angora, Mn.

PINEAPPLE BREAD

1 beaten egg
1/3 c. milk
1/3 c. melted margarine or
  salad oil
3 c. flour
3/4 tsp. salt

1 (9 oz.) can (1 c.) crushed
  pineapple
1 c. chopped nuts
1 c. chopped dates
3/4 c. sugar
1/4 tsp. soda
3 tsp. baking powder

Combine first 6 ingredients. Sift together dry ingredients; add to first mixture. Stir till just moistened. Bake in greased 9x5x3 inch pans at 350° for 50 minutes or until done. Cool; remove from pans. In smaller pans, check at 30 minutes.

Mary Paul, Minneapolis, Mn.

PRUNE BREAD

1 c. sugar
1 1/2 c. flour
1 tsp. soda
1/2 tsp. salt

1 egg
2 Tbsp. cooking oil
1/2 c. milk
1/2 c. chopped walnuts
1 jar baby food prunes

Combine all ingredients; mix well. Pour into loaf pan. Bake at 350° for 1 hour.

Stella Bliss, Minneapolis, Mn.

DARK PUMPERNICKEL BREAD

3 pkg. dry yeast
1 1/2 c. warm water
1/2 c. dark molasses
1 Tbsp. plus 1 tsp. salt
2 Tbsp. caraway seeds

2 Tbsp. shortening
2 3/4 c. rye flour
1/4 c. cocoa
2 1/2 c. white flour
Corn meal

Dissolve yeast in warm water in large mixing bowl. Stir in molasses, salt, caraway seed, shortening, rye flour and cocoa; beat until smooth. Stir in enough flour to make dough easy to handle. Turn dough onto lightly floured surface. Cover; let rest for 10 to 15 minutes. Knead until smooth, 5 to 10 minutes. Place in greased bowl; turn greased side up. Cover; let rise in warm place until double, 1 hour. Punch down dough; round up and let rise until double, 40 minutes. Grease baking sheet; sprinkle with corn meal. Punch down dough; divide in half. Shape into round loaves on baking sheet. Let rise 1 hour. Bake at 375° for 30 to 35 minutes. Cool on wire rack.

Lila Houser, Aitken, Mn.

PUMPKIN BREAD

Beat 4 eggs well. Add one at a time:

1 c. pumpkin   1 c. water
1 c. oil   3 c. white sugar

Sift together:
3 c. flour   1 tsp. nutmeg
1/2 tsp. baking powder   1 tsp. cinnamon
2 tsp. soda

Add to first ingredients. Pour into two 9x5 inch loaf pans, greased. Bake in 350° oven for 1 hour or until done.

Arnita Rieger, Minneapolis, Mn.

Similar recipe submitted by: Joan and Margaret McKinney, Minneapolis, Mn.

PULL APART BREAD

2 loaves frozen bread   1 c. sugar
1 stick margarine, melted,   1 tsp. cinnamon
    mixed with 1/2 c. dark   Chopped nuts
    syrup

Mix last 3 items together. Thaw bread; cut into 3 long sections, then into small squares or make them round. Dip into margarine mixture, then into sugar mixture. Put into greased Bundt pan; let rise 1 hour. Bake at 350° for 1/2 hour. Cool an hour.

Mrs. Gary L. Hagen, Princeton, Mn.

RHUBARB BREAD

1 1/2 c. brown sugar   1 tsp. salt
2/3 c. oil   1 tsp. soda
1 beaten egg   2 1/2 c. flour
1 c. buttermilk   1 1/2 c. diced rhubarb
1 tsp. vanilla   1/2 c. chopped nuts

1507-82

Mix together. Brush on topping of 1/2 cup white sugar and 4 tablespoons butter before baking. Bake at 350° for 45 minutes. Makes 2 loaf pans.

Ruth Lee, Detroit Lakes, Mn.

Similar recipe submitted by: Ardis Peterson, Rochester, Mn.

SOUR CREAM HERB BREAD

3 1/4 c. flour	2 pkg. yeast
1/4 c. sugar	1 tsp. salt
1/2 tsp. celery seed	1/2 tsp. dill seed
1/2 tsp. grated orange peel	1 c. sour cream
1/2 c. hot tap water	3 Tbsp. butter
1 egg	Sesame seeds

Blend 2 cups flour with next 10 ingredients; beat 2 minutes at medium speed. By hand, stir in remaining 1 1/2 cups flour. Cover; let rise until doubled, 45-60 minutes. Grease 1 1/2 or 2 quart round casserole or two 8x4 inch loaf pans. Stir batter vigorously; pour into greased pan. Cover; let rise until doubled, 30-45 minutes. Bake 35-40 minutes or until golden brown in 350° oven. Remove from casserole immediately; brush with butter and sprinkle with sesame seeds.

Bonnie Sovick, Ortonville, Mn.

STRAWBERRY NUT BREAD

2 (10 oz.) pkg. frozen sliced strawberries	3 c. flour
	1 Tbsp. cinnamon
4 eggs	1 tsp. baking soda
1 c. cooking oil	1 tsp. salt
2 c. sugar	1 1/4 c. chopped nuts

Defrost strawberries. Beat eggs in a bowl until fluffy. Add oil, sugar and strawberries. Sift together flour, cinnamon, soda and salt into mixing bowl. Add strawberry mixture; mix well. Stir in nuts. Pour into two greased and floured 9 1/2 x 5 x 3 inch loaf pans. Bake in 350° F. oven for 1 hour and 10 minutes or until done. Cool in pans for 10 minutes, then on racks. Slice when cool, chilled easiest. Serve with whipped cream, cheese or butter.

Sharon Wilson, Park Rapids, Mn.

Similar recipe submitted by: Sally Bartsch, Blaine, Mn.

3 C BREAD

2 1/2 c. flour
1 c. sugar
1 tsp. baking powder
1 tsp. baking soda
1/2 tsp. salt
1/2 tsp. mace
3 beaten eggs

1/2 c. cooking oil
1/2 c. milk
2 c. (4-6) shredded carrots
1 (3 oz.) can (1 1/3 c.)
  flaked cocoanut
1/2 c. maraschino cherries,
  chopped and drained

In mixing bowl, stir together flour, sugar, baking powder, soda, salt and mace. Combine eggs, oil and milk. Add to dry ingredients; mix well. Stir in remaining ingredients. Pour into three greased 21 ounce pie filling cans (or 3 small pans). Bake in 350° oven for 1 to 1 1/4 hours. Cool in pans or cans for 10 minutes; remove. Cool completely on rack; wrap and store overnight before slicing. Makes 3 loaves or bake in one 9x5x3 inch pan for 45 to 60 minutes, then proceed as before.

Berniece Wicklund

TRAMP BREAD

In the evening, pour 2 1/2 cups boiling water over 2 cups raisins; add 4 teaspoons soda. Let stand overnight. In the morning, in a large bowl, mix:

1 c. white sugar
1 c. brown sugar
4 Tbsp. cooking oil

1/2 tsp. salt
4 c. flour

Mix well. Grease thoroughly three 1 pound coffee cans. Fill half full and bake in 350° oven for 70 minutes; cool. Remove from cans; slice thin. Butter and serve.

Mrs. Norma Applen, Minneapolis, Mn.

ZUCCHINI BREAD

1 c. brown sugar
1 c. white sugar

1 c. oil
3 eggs

Cream and add 2 cups grated zucchini. Sift 3 cups flour, 2 teaspoons cinnamon, 1 teaspoon baking soda and 1/2 teaspoon salt. Add nuts; mix well. Pour into 2 greased loaf pans. Bake at 350° for 60 minutes.

Esther Beatty, Duluth, Mn.

APPLE MUFFINS WITH CRUNCH TOPPING

2 c. sifted flour	3 Tbsp. shortening
1 tsp. baking powder	1 egg
1/2 tsp. salt	3/4 c. buttermilk
1/2 tsp. soda	1 c. peeled, finely chopped
1/2 c. sugar	apple

Cream shortening and sugar. Combine egg, then buttermilk alternately. Mix until flour is dampened. Fold in apples. Fill muffin tins 1/2 full; sprinkle tops with topping, pressing it lightly in batter. Bake at 375° for 25 minutes.

Topping:

1/3 c. brown sugar	1/3 c. chopped nuts
1/2 tsp. cinnamon	

Mary Fingalson, Detroit Lakes, Mn.

BLUEBERRY MUFFINS

1/4 c. melted butter	1 egg
2/3 c. brown sugar	1/3 c. milk
1 c. flour	1/4 tsp. salt
1 tsp. baking powder	1/2 c. frozen blueberries
1/2 tsp. cinnamon	

Stir sugar, butter, eggs and milk together. Stir in dry ingredients; fold in blueberries. Bake 24 minutes at 350°.

K., St. Cloud, Mn.

CHEDDAR-ALMOND MUFFINS

1/3 c. chopped, slivered	1 Tbsp. baking powder
almonds	1 tsp. salt
2 Tbsp. butter, melted	3/4 c. (3 oz.) shredded
1 tsp. Worcestershire sauce	Cheddar cheese
1/2 tsp. garlic salt	1 c. milk
1 3/4 c. flour	1 egg, beaten
1/4 c. sugar	3 Tbsp. butter, melted

Combine almonds, butter and seasonings. Combine flour, sugar, baking powder and salt; stir in cheese. Add combined milk, egg and butter; stir just until dry ingredients are moistened. Fill buttered muffin pans. Sprinkle

1 teaspoon almond mixture on top; press into batter. Bake in a preheated 400° oven for 20 to 25 minutes or until wooden pick inserted in center comes out clean. Serve warm. Yield: 12 muffins. Variations -

Parmesan Muffins: Substitute 1/3 cup grated Parmesan cheese for Cheddar cheese.

Cinnamon-Apple Muffins: Omit almond topping. Increase sugar to 1/3 cup. Add 3/4 cup chopped apple with liquid ingredients. Sprinkle muffins with combined cinnamon and sugar.

Pineapple Muffins: Omit almond topping. Add 1/2 cup drained, crushed pineapple with liquid ingredients.

Mankato, Mn.

FIVE STAR BLUEBERRY MUFFINS

1/4 c. butter or margarine, softened	1/4 tsp. vanilla
	1 3/4 c. plus 1 Tbsp. flour
1/2 c. sugar	2 1/2 tsp. baking powder
1 egg	1/2 tsp. salt
3/4 c. milk	1 c. blueberries

Cream butter and sugar until light and fluffy; beat in egg, then milk and vanilla. Beat until nearly smooth. In small bowl, stir together 1 3/4 cups flour, baking powder and salt. Add to milk mixture; stir until moist. Batter will be lumpy. Toss berries with remaining 1 tablespoon flour; fold into batter. Spoon into greased tins. Bake in preheated oven at 425° for 25 minutes, or until evenly browned.

Note: While muffins are still hot, brush them with butter and dip in sugar.

Cathy Farah, Minneapolis, Mn.

GINGERBREAD MUFFINS

1/4 c. soft margarine	1/2 tsp. soda
1/4 c. molasses	1 tsp. cinnamon
1 egg	1/2 tsp. ginger
1 1/4 c. flour	1/4 tsp. cloves
1/2 tsp. salt	1/2 c. hot water
1/2 tsp. baking powder	Raisins

Preheat oven to 350°. Blend margarine and sugar till fluffy. Blend in molasses and egg; beat. Add dry

ingredients to creamed mixture alternately with hot water.
Add raisins. Spoon batter into muffin tins, filling 2/3 full.
Bake 12-15 minutes.

Karen Ireland, Montevideo, Mn.

GRAHAM CRACKER MUFFINS

1/2 c. oleo	32 graham crackers, crushed
1 c. sugar	2 tsp. baking powder
2 egg yolks	1/2 c. nuts
1 c. milk	Vanilla
	2 egg whites, beaten stiff

Add egg yolks to creamed shortening and sugar. Add
crushed graham crackers and milk alternately to mixture.
Put baking powder in small amount of crackers; add last
with chopped walnuts. Fold in beaten egg whites. Bake
18-20 minutes in 350° oven, using cupcake papers. Drain
1 cup crushed pineapple; add 3/4 cup sugar and boil.
Place a small amount on each baked muffin.

Eva Anderson, Duluth, Mn.

OATMEAL MUFFINS

2 Tbsp. sugar	2 c. Bisquick
1 egg	3/4 c. rolled oats
3/4 c. milk	

Heat oven to 400°. Mix all ingredients until blended.
Beat vigorously 30 seconds. Fill well greased muffin cups
2/3 full. Bake 15 minutes. Makes 12 muffins.

Kerrie C. Applen
Mrs. Norma Applen, Minneapolis, Mn.

OAT-RAISIN MUFFINS
(Low Sugar)

1 c. quick cooking oats	1 c. all-purpose flour
1/2 c. raisins	3 tsp. baking powder
2/3 c. skim milk	1/2 tsp. salt
1/3 c. frozen apple juice	1 large egg, slightly beaten
concentrate	1/4 c. vegetable oil

Stir together oats, raisins, milk and juice concentrate;

let stand 1 hour. Stir together flour, baking powder and salt. Stir egg and oil into oat mixture. Add flour mixture and quickly stir with a fork just until moistened; mixture should be lumpy. Spoon into greased muffin tin or paper lined cups. Bake in a preheated 400° oven until golden brown, 15-20 minutes. Serve hot. Makes 12 muffins.

Mary Lou Sebesta, Rochester, Mn.

CRUNCHY TOPPED RHUBARB MUFFINS

1 1/2 c. brown sugar, packed	3 c. flour
1 c. oil	1 tsp. soda
2 eggs	1 tsp. salt
1 c. buttermilk	3/4 c. chopped nuts
2 tsp. vanilla	2 c. finely sliced rhubarb

Topping:

1/2 c. brown sugar	1/2 c. chopped nuts
2 tsp. cinnamon	

Combine sugar, oil, eggs, milk and vanilla in mixing bowl; mix well. Sift flour, soda and salt together. Stir into liquid mixture. Blend in nuts and rhubarb. Spoon into muffin tins and sprinkle with topping. Bake at 325° for 25 to 30 minutes. Makes 24 or more big muffins.

Bev. Jensen, Willmar, Mn.

SOUR CREAM NUT MUFFINS

1/2 c. butter	1 1/2 c. dairy sour cream
1 1/2 c. granulated sugar	2 3/4 c. flour
1/2 tsp. salt	Nutmeg, sugar and nuts for topping
4 eggs, well beaten	
1 tsp. soda	

Mix butter, sugar and salt until light. Add eggs, soda, sour cream and flour; mix thoroughly. Pour into greased muffin tins and sprinkle with some nutmeg, sugar and nuts. Bake in very hot oven, 450°, for 15 minutes. Makes 20 muffins.

Elaine Berry, Crystal, Mn.

SURPRISE MUFFINS

1 egg	1/2 tsp. salt
1/2 c. milk	2 tsp. baking powder
1/4 c. salad oil	1 1/2 c. flour

Beat egg; stir in milk and oil. Add remaining ingredients; mix just until moistened. Batter will be lumpy. Fill muffin cups 1/2 full; drop 1 teaspoon jelly or jam, then add more batter. Bake at 400° for 20 to 25 minutes.

Phyllis Mathe, St. Paul, Mn.

CORN FRITTERS

1 1/2 c. flour	2 eggs
2 1/2 tsp. baking powder	1/4 c. milk
1 tsp. salt	1 c. cream style corn
2 tsp. sugar (optional)	

Mix together. Drop by teaspoonfuls in hot grease and deep fry.

Anne Aune, Minneapolis, Mn.

NEBRASKA CORN FRITTERS

1 1/2 c. whole kernel corn, drained	Dash of pepper
	1 tsp. sugar
2 eggs	3 Tbsp. all-purpose flour
1/2 tsp. salt	Butter or margarine

Mix ingredients together. Heat 2 tablespoons butter in a large skillet. Drop batter by double tablespoon to make small oval cakes. Cook over medium heat for 5 minutes, or until browned on both sides; turn only once. Add more butter or margarine if necessary to keep corn fritters from sticking. Makes 4 servings.

Helen-May Johnson, Chanhassen, Mn.

"CREPES" - FRYING PAN SIZE

4 eggs, beaten	1 c. milk
3/4 c. flour	Pinch of salt

Mix in order given, thin batter (lumps don't matter - I

use electric mixer). Pour about 1/4 cup of batter into greased fry pan; fry until brown, high temperature, and turn over with knife or pancake turner. Makes about 5 pan size crepes. Add any filling. Recipe may be doubled.

Netta Capetz, St. Paul, Mn.

FRENCH TOAST

8 slices firm, dry white
   bread (preferably
   homemade)
2 eggs
Pinch of salt
2/3 c. milk

1/2 tsp. vanilla
4-6 Tbsp. butter
Maple syrup* or 2 tsp.
   cinnamon, mixed with
   1/4 c. sugar (for serving)

Beat the eggs until well mixed; stir in the salt, milk and vanilla. Dip half the slices of bread in the egg mixture, turning them so they are soaked on both sides. Heat half the butter in a skillet; fry the soaked bread until browned. Turn and brown on the other side. Keep the slices hot while soaking and frying the remaining bread in the same way.

*Serve the toast with maple syrup or cinnamon sugar.

Helen-May Johnson, Chanhassen, Mn.

PUFFY FRENCH TOAST

Batter:

1 c. milk
2 eggs

1 1/2 c. pancake mix

Have ready 8 day-old bread slices (no crusts) and 1 cup shortening. In medium bowl, beat milk, eggs and mix until just combined. Cut each bread slice in half diagonally. Dip bread in batter; let stand 1 minute. Slowly heat shortening in heavy skillet. Saute bread slices 2 at a time until golden brown and puffy, about 3 minutes on each side. Drain on paper towels.

Grayce Funke, Minneapolis, Mn.

APPLE PANCAKES

2 1/4 c. buttermilk
2 c. flour
3 eggs
1 tsp. baking powder
1/2 tsp. salt

1 tsp. soda
2 Tbsp. sugar
2 medium sized apples, thinly
  sliced

Beat eggs; add sugar, salt and milk. Add sifted dry ingredients (flour, baking powder and soda). Add thinly sliced apples. Bake on hot griddle. Serve with butter and syrup or jam. A dab of whipped cream is also very good if you want to splurge.

Helen-May Johnson, Chanhassen, Mn.

OATMEAL PANCAKES

1 c. flour
1 c. quick oatmeal
2 tsp. baking powder
1/2 tsp. soda
1 tsp. salt

2 eggs
1 1/2 c. buttermilk
1/4 c. salad oil or melted
  margarine

Place dry ingredients in a medium sized bowl. Add eggs, oil and buttermilk; stir until blended.

Mrs. Robert Benson, Stillwater, Mn.

POTATO PANCAKES

2 c. coarsely grated potatoes
1 egg
3 Tbsp. flour

Salt and pepper
Onion juice
Milk

Grate potato into cold water; drain. Add well beaten egg, salt, pepper and onion juice to taste. Add flour and milk to make a stiff batter. A large spoonful of batter makes a good sized cake. Bake on grill in hot fat until brown and crisp.

Helen-May Johnson, Chanhassen, Mn.

POTATO PANCAKES

2 c. grated raw potatoes
1/2 tsp. salt
1 Tbsp. flour

Pepper to taste
2 egg yolks, beaten
3 egg whites, beaten

Beat egg yolks, then add other ingredients, except egg whites. Fold in beaten egg whites last. Fry in shortening or oil as desired.

Emmy Thielmann, Minneapolis, Mn.

SWEDISH OVEN PANCAKE

Beat:
6 eggs
1 tsp. salt
1/2 c. sugar

3/4 c. flour
2 1/2 c. milk, added slowly
while beating

Place butter, the size of an egg, in a 9x12 inch pan to melt. Pour butter into batter, then pour batter into buttered pan. Bake 1/2 hour in 400° oven.

June Paulson, Virginia, Mn.

BULK PANCAKE FLOUR

8 c. whole wheat flour
1/2 c. sugar
2 1/2 Tbsp. baking powder

4 tsp. soda
4 tsp. salt

Combine and store in airtight container. To make pancakes, mix 1 cup milk or buttermilk, 1 cup mix, 1 egg and 2 tablespoons oil. Makes 6 pancakes.

Helen Teeuwen, Minneapolis, Mn.

MARYLAND CREAM WAFFLES

2 c. sifted flour
4 tsp. baking powder
1/2 tsp. salt
2 Tbsp. sugar

2 eggs, separated
1 3/4 c. milk
1/2 c. melted butter

Mix and sift flour, sugar, baking powder and salt. Beat egg yolks. Blend beaten egg yolks with milk; add to flour mixture. Beat until free of lumps. Add melted butter; beat until light and fluffy. Last, fold in beaten egg whites. (The sugar makes them crisp and the butter brown.)

Helen-May Johnson, Chanhassen, Mn.

WYOMING WAFFLES

Mix:

1 1/2 c. flour	1 1/2 tsp. baking powder
1 1/2 tsp. salt	1 Tbsp. sugar
2 egg yolks	Buttermilk to mix well
Sweet milk to thin	

Add 6 tablespoons melted Crisco. Beat egg whites and fold in.

Ava S. Day, St. Paul, Mn.

BLITZ-KUCHEN
(Coffee Cake)

The following recipe is from a 1915 cookbook put together by students from Fountain City, Wisconsin, High School to raise money. It is collected from the parents of one of the students and is still used.

4 eggs, plus their weight in sugar and 1/2 their weight in flour	1/2 tsp. baking powder
	Cinnamon
	Nutmeg

Bake in pan; sprinkle chopped nuts on top. When baked, sprinkle with sugar and cinnamon.

Mr. Hubert Funke, Grayce Funke
Minneapolis, Mn.

COFFEE CAKE

1 c. sugar	2 c. flour, sifted with 2 tsp.
1/2 c. shortening	baking powder
2 well beaten eggs	Pinch of salt
1 c. milk	

Cream sugar and shortening; add beaten eggs. Add flour alternately with milk.

Topping:

3/4 c. brown sugar 1/4 c. butter
4 Tbsp. flour 1/2 tsp. cinnamon

Bake in 9x13 inch pan at 350° for 30 minutes.
Leona Kellerman, Roseau, Mn.

ALMOND COFFEE CAKE

1/2 c. butter 1 Tbsp. water
1 c. flour

Mix like pie crust; divide in 2 parts. Roll or pat on cookie sheet in 2 strips, about 1/4 inch thick.

Topping:

1/2 c. butter 3 eggs
1 c. water Almond flavoring
1 c. flour

Combine butter and water in saucepan; bring to boil. Remove from heat; add flour all at once, stirring rapidly. Add eggs one at a time; mix well (like cream puffs). Add flavoring and mix. Spread mixture on top of unbaked pie crust mixture. Bake at 400° for 45 minutes without peeking. Cool and frost with a mixture of 1 cup powdered sugar, 1 tablespoon butter, few drops of cream and almond extract. Frost; sprinkle with slivered almonds. Cut into bars. Preparation and baking time: 1 hour and 20 minutes.
Eloise Hoff, Preston, Mn.

CRUNCHY APRICOT COFFEE CAKE

2 c. Kellogg's Rice Krispies cereal, crushed to measure 1 c.
3 Tbsp. sugar
1/8 tsp. ground ginger
1/4 c. margarine or butter, softened
1 1/2 c. all-purpose flour

2 tsp. baking powder
1/2 tsp. salt
1/4 c. margarine or butter, softened
3/4 c. sugar
1 egg
1 (17 oz.) can California apricot halves, drained, reserving 1/2 c. syrup

1. Combine first 4 ingredients, mixing until crumbly.

Set aside for topping. Stir together flour, baking powder and salt; set aside. 2. In small mixing bowl, beat remaining margarine and sugar until well blended. Add egg; beat well. Stir in the 1/2 cup apricot syrup. Add flour mixture, mixing well. Spread in greased 8x8x2 inch baking pan. Chop apricots; spoon about 3/4 cup evenly over batter. Sprinkle with cereal topping and remaining apricots. 3. Bake in oven at 350° F. for about 45 minutes or until cake begins to pull away from sides of pan. Serve warm. Yield: 9 servings.

Marion Round, Faribault, Mn.

TRUE BLUEBERRY COFFEE CAKE

1/2 c. butter or shortening	4 c. flour
1 1/2 c. sugar	1/2 tsp. salt
1 tsp. vanilla	5 tsp. baking powder
2 eggs	1 can blueberry fruit filling
1 1/2 c. milk	

Cream butter until soft. Beat in sugar until light; blend in vanilla. Beat eggs slightly with milk. Sift flour, salt and baking powder; blend in milk mixture and flour mixture. Turn batter into two buttered pans, 9x9x2 inches. Spread half of blueberry filling over each cake. Sprinkle each with topping.

Topping: Mix until crumbly -

1 c. sugar	1/2 tsp. cinnamon
2/3 c. flour	1/2 c. butter

Bake 30 minutes at 375°.

'Cari' Caroline M. Bennett, Apple Valley, Mn.

CHERRY COFFEE CAKE

Cream:
1 c. butter	1 1/4 c. sugar

Add:
4 eggs, one at a time	1 1/2 tsp. baking powder
1 tsp. vanilla	3 c. flour
1/2 tsp. salt	

Put 2/3 of batter into 10x15 inch pan. Spread 1 can of cherry pie filling over, then drop the rest of the dough over the top. Bake at 350° F. for 30 minutes or until done.

Glaze:

1 c. powdered sugar   2 Tbsp. milk
1 Tbsp. melted butter

Mix well and drizzle over the top.

Kathryn Otto, Harvey, N.D.

CHOCOLATE SWIRL COFFEE CAKE

1/3 c. flaked coconut   1/4 c. sugar
1/4 c. chopped nuts   1 egg
1/4 c. sugar   3/4 c. milk
3 Tbsp. melted butter   1/3 c. semi-sweet chocolate
2 c. Bisquick or buttermilk   chips
    baking mix

Heat oven to 400°. Grease square pan, 8x8x2 inches.
Stir together coconut, nuts, 1/4 cup sugar and 1 tablespoon melted butter; set aside. Mix baking mix, 1/4 cup
sugar, remaining melted butter, egg and milk. Beat vigorously 1/2 minute; pour in pan. Spoon chocolate chips
over batter; with knife, cut through batter. Sprinkle coconut mixture over top. Bake 20 to 25 minutes.

Liz Tuft, St. Paul, Mn.

CINNAMON APPLE COFFEE CAKE

1 yellow cake mix   1/2 c. chopped nuts
1 pkg. instant vanilla   1/2 c. sugar
    pudding   2 tsp. cinnamon
4 eggs   3 medium apples, peeled,
1 c. sour cream   cored and sliced
1/2 c. salad oil

Combine cake mix, pudding mix, cream, eggs and
salad oil; beat with electric mixer for 5 minutes. Combine
nuts, sugar and cinnamon. Pour 1/2 of mix into greased
10 inch tube or Bundt pan. Arrange 1/2 of apple slices
over batter; sprinkle with 1/2 of sugar, cinnamon and nut
mixture. Repeat. Bake at 350° for 1 hour. Serve with
Rum Sauce:

1/2 c. butter   1/2 c. cream

Bring to boil; add 1 teaspoon rum flavoring. Serve
warm.

Carolyn Anderson, Fargo, N.D.

DANISH COFFEE CAKE

4 c. flour
1/2 c. sugar
1 c. lard
3 Tbsp. butter
1 tsp. salt

1 c. milk
1 cake yeast (or 2 pkg.)
1/2 c. lukewarm water
3 eggs

Mix flour, sugar, lard, butter and salt (as for pie crust). Scald milk; cool. Dissolve yeast in the water; add eggs, beaten. Add to flour mixture. Keep in refrigerator overnight; the batter is quite thin. In the morning, roll out thin; fill with any kind of pie filling or make your own. Lap the sides hanging over the pan to the center of the cake. Grease and sprinkle with sugar. Let rise 1 hour and bake 20 minutes in 375° oven. Makes 6 or 8 inch pie tins.

Goldie Mikish, Staples, Mn.

DANISH COFFEE CAKE

1 pkg. dry yeast
1/4 c. warm water
4 c. flour
1 Tbsp. sugar
1 tsp. salt

1 c. chilled butter or
  margarine
1 c. milk, scalded
3 slightly beaten egg yolks

Almond Filling:

1/4 c. soft butter

1 c. packed brown sugar

Cream until smooth and fluffy. Add 1/2 cup almond paste; mix until smooth.

Coffee Cake: Soften yeast in water. Sift dry ingredients in bowl and mix like pie crust until mixture is like corn meal and the size of peas. Mix cooled milk and egg yolks; add with yeast to flour, stirring to make soft dough. Cover and chill a few hours in refrigerator or overnight. Divide dough in 4 parts. Roll to 12x9 inches and about 1/8 inch thick. Spread filling on; roll up. Put on cookie sheet; shape like crescent. Do the same with the rest of the dough. Makes 4 crescents. Let rise an hour or two and bake 20 minutes at 375°. (I usually frost with a small amount of powdered frosting and a few chopped nuts.)

Mrs. Robert Benson, Stillwater, Mn.

EASY COFFEE CAKE

4 eggs, well beaten   1 c. sugar
1 c. cooking oil   2 c. flour
1 1/2 tsp. baking powder   1 can apple pie filling

Combine first 5 ingredients; mix well. Spread 1/2 of the dough in large pan, 9x13 inches. Spoon on the pie filling; top with remaining dough. Cover the top with a butter, cinnamon, sugar and flour crumb topping. Bake at 350° for 30-45 minutes.

Betty Goebel, Williston, N.D.

HEATH BRUNCH COFFEE CAKE

1/4 lb. butter   1 c. buttermilk
2 c. flour   1 tsp. soda
1 c. brown sugar   1 egg
1/2 c. white sugar   1 tsp. vanilla

Topping:

6 Heath Bars or 1 (5 oz.)   1/4 c. pecans or almonds
  box miniatures

Blend the flour, butter and the sugars; take out 1/2 cup of the mixture. To the rest, add the buttermilk, soda, egg and vanilla; blend well. Pour into a greased and floured 10x14x2 inch cake pan.

Topping: Crush Heath Bars finely with 1/4 cup pecans or almonds; add to the 1/2 cup of mixture. Sprinkle over the top of the batter. Bake in a 350° oven for 30 minutes.

Helen-May Johnson, Chanhassen, Mn.

GLAZED HUNGARIAN COFFEE CAKE

1 pkg. yeast roll mix   1/3 c. melted butter
1 c. sugar   1/2 c. chopped nuts
1 tsp. cinnamon   1/3 c. syrup (light or dark)

Prepare roll mix as directed. When double in bulk, punch down. Mix together sugar and cinnamon; sprinkle about 1/3 of sugar mixture evenly in well greased 10 inch tube pan. Cut dough into pieces the size of walnut. Shape in ball; dip in melted butter and arrange in pan so they touch. Use about 1/2 of dough for bottom layer. When bottom is covered, sprinkle with 1/2 of nuts, then sprinkle with 1/2 of remaining sugar. Top with second layer of balls and sprinkle with rest of nuts and sugar. Let rise in warm place about 45 minutes. Just before putting in oven, drizzle syrup over balls. Bake at 350° for 60 minutes or until well browned. Invert and remove immediately.

Mrs. Neva Kost, Fairmont, Mn.

PEACH COFFEE CAKE

3/4 c. flour
1 tsp. baking powder
1/2 tsp. salt
3 Tbsp. margarine

3 1/2 oz. dry vanilla pudding
  (not instant)
1/2 c. milk
1 egg

Combine in mixer bowl; beat 2 minutes. Pour into 9 inch round greased pan. Place 15 ounces canned sliced peaches, well drained (reserve juice) over batter.

1 (8 oz.) pkg. cream
  cheese, softened

1/2 c. sugar
3 Tbsp. reserved juice

Combine in bowl; beat 2 minutes. Spoon to within 1 inch of edge of batter. Combine 1 tablespoon sugar and 1/2 teaspoon cinnamon; sprinkle over cream cheese filling. Bake at 350° for 30-35 minutes.

Fern Groskreutz, Litchfield, Mn.

PISTACHIO COFFEE CAKE

1 pkg. yellow cake mix
1 pkg. pistachio instant
  pudding mix

4 eggs
1 c. water
2/3 c. oil

Beat all together for 10 minutes.

Topping:

1/2 c. sugar
1 tsp. cinnamon

1/2 c. chopped nuts

Grease well a Bundt pan. Put 1/3 of topping in pan; swish around, then alternate the batter and topping, ending with the batter. Bake in a 325° oven for 1 hour. Cool for 10 minutes and remove from pan.

Joan Norton, Hibbing, Mn.

POTECA COFFEE CAKE

2 pkg. dry yeast	1/4 tsp. salt
1/3 c. warm water	3 Tbsp. sugar
1/2 c. scalded milk	3 egg yolks, beaten
3/4 c. butter or margarine	2 1/2 - 2 3/4 c. flour

Dissolve yeast in warm water. Scald milk; add butter to melt. Add salt and sugar; set aside to cool. Beat egg yolks; stir into milk mixture. Pour into large mixing bowl; gradually add flour and yeast mixture, beating well. Cover and refrigerate overnight. This dough will be very sticky.

Filling:

2 c. nuts, ground	1/2 c. milk
2 Tbsp. brown sugar	3/4 c. sugar
2 Tbsp. honey	3 egg whites, stiffly beaten
1/2 tsp. cinnamon	8 dates, cut up

Combine nuts, brown sugar, honey, cinnamon, milk and dates; cook to a paste. Cool this mixture. Beat egg whites until stiff, gradually adding 3/4 cup sugar. Fold in the filling paste. Roll 1/2 of the dough on cloth to a 20x20 inch square on a well floured board. Spread 1/2 of the filling over the dough; roll up as a jelly roll. Put this into a greased angel food cake pan. Roll other 1/2 of dough and proceed in the same method. Place the second roll directly on top of the first roll in the pan. There are 2 layers, but the cake becomes one during the baking. Bake at 350° for 1 hour. Sprinkle top with powdered sugar or a glaze made with 3/4 cup of confectioners sugar, 2 tablespoons frozen orange juice and 1 teaspoon water. Blend well; drizzle over top of cake. Cool before removing from pan.

Mary Pintar, Gilbert, Mn.

Similar recipes submitted by: Mrs. William (Liz) Voss, Virginia, Mn., Mary Lou Roskoski, Virginia, Mn.

RUSSIAN COFFEE CAKE

1 c. oil	2 c. flour
1 c. sugar	1 can favorite pie filling
1 egg	1/2 c. sugar
1 tsp. baking powder	1 tsp. cinnamon
1 tsp. salt	

Mix together oil, sugar, eggs, baking powder, salt

and flour. Pour 1/2 of this batter in a 9x13 inch pan.
Spread the pie filling over; add rest of the batter. Combine
1/2 cup sugar with the cinnamon; sprinkle on top. Bake at
325° for 1 hour. Can frost with 1 cup powdered sugar, 1/4
cup water and 1 teaspoon vanilla. Combine and drizzle
over the cake.

Marilyn McPhee, St. Cloud, Mn.

SWEDISH KRINGLE

1 c. flour   1/2 c. butter
1 Tbsp. water

Mix as for pie crust. Pat on cookie sheet in ovals 3
inches wide. Put 1 cup water in saucepan with 1/2 cup butter; heat to boiling point. As mixture is removed from heat,
add 1 cup flour; stir until smooth. Stir in 3 eggs, one at a
time; beat well after each addition. Add 1/2 teaspoon almond extract. Spread on first mixture. Bake 1 hour at
350°. Cool and frost with 1 cup powdered sugar, 1/2 teaspoon almond extract and enough cream to make a spreading
consistency.

Betty Olson, St. Paul, Mn.
Similar recipe submitted by: Winnie Johnson, St.
Paul, Mn.

ORANGE DROPS

2 eggs   1/2 c. cream
1/2 c. sugar   1/4 tsp. salt
Rind of 1 orange   2 1/4 c. flour
1/3 c. orange juice   2 1/2 tsp. baking powder

Drop from teaspoon in deep, hot fat; fry until golden
brown.

Mary Fingalson, Detroit Lakes, Mn.

PEANUTY TEA RING

1 can refrigerator biscuits   1 c. finely chopped peanuts
1/4 c. melted butter or   1/2 c. powdered sugar
  margarine   1 Tbsp. water

Separate biscuits; dip both sides in melted butter,

then in peanuts, coating well. Arrange overlapping circle on greased baking sheet. Bake at 425° for 10 to 15 minutes or until golden brown. Mix powdered sugar and water. Drizzle over hot tea ring. Serve warm.

Stella Bliss, Minneapolis, Mn.

STRUDEL

4 c. flour	1 egg
1 tsp. salt	Warm water to make soft
1 tsp. baking powder	dough

Knead until smooth. Divide dough in 3 portions; roll into 9 inch circle. Cover with hot fat or oil; let rest about 2 hours. Stretch each piece of the dough as thin as possible. Roll up very loosely; place on a skillet that has cubed potatoes in it with onions, salt, pepper and 1/2 cup cream. Add enough water to barely cover potatoes. Cook 1/2 hour or until you hear that they are frying. Do not uncover during cooking.

Variation: You can brown and cook 1 pint sauerkraut very carefully; add 1 cup cubed ham. Cool thoroughly and spread on Strudel before rolling up.

F. Schwartzbauer, Bismarck, N.D.

APRICOT STREUDEL

2 c. flour   2 sticks margarine

Mix with pastry blender; add 1 cup sour cream and mix. Make into 2 balls; refrigerate overnight. Next day, roll out and spread with about 1/2 (12 ounce) jar of apricot jam, thin. Add 4 maraschino cherries, cut in fourths (16 pieces), nuts, golden raisins and coconut. Roll up like jelly roll; put several slits on top. Bake on teflon cookie sheet at 350° for about 1/2 hour or till golden brown. Do the same thing with other ball. Put 2 streudels on cookie sheet. Put powdered sugar on top when serving.

Jake Laughlin, Des Moines, Ia.

BAKING POWDER BISCUITS
(Supreme)

2 c. flour
1/2 tsp. salt
4 tsp. baking powder
2 tsp. sugar

1/2 tsp. cream of tartar
1/2 c. shortening
2/3 c. milk

Sift dry ingredients; cut in shortening. Add milk. Knead lightly on floured board; roll to 1/2 inch thickness. Bake 12 minutes at 450°. Yield: 1 dozen biscuits.

Eva Anderson, Duluth, Mn.

BISCUITS SUPREME

2 c. flour
1/2 tsp. salt
4 tsp. baking powder
1/2 tsp. cream of tartar

2 tsp. sugar
1/2 c. shortening
2/3 c. milk

Sift flour, salt, baking powder, cream of tartar and sugar; cut in shortening until mixture resembles coarse crumbs. Add milk all at once; stir just until dough follows fork around bowl. Pat or roll 1/2 inch thick; cut with biscuit cutter. Bake on ungreased cookie sheet in hot oven, 450°, for 10-12 minutes. These are best served warm, and may also be used as a base for creamed foods. Yield: 16 medium sized biscuits.

Donna Hoff, Fargo, N.D.

BISCUITS

2 c. flour
1/2 tsp. salt
5 Tbsp. Crisco

3 tsp. baking powder
1 tsp. sugar
3/4 c. milk

Handle lightly; pat out. When cutting, curl the tail into next biscuit so that none is leftover to handle the second time. Bake at 375° for 20 minutes or until brown.

Ava S. Day, St. Paul, Mn.

CRISPY ONION BISCUITS

1 (8 oz.) pkg. refrigerated
  buttermilk biscuits
1/2 c. butter or margarine,
  softened

1 (1 3/8 oz.) env. onion
  soup mix

Preheat oven to 450°. Place biscuits in an 8 inch round pan. In a small bowl, cream together butter or margarine and soup mix; spread over biscuits. Bake 15-20 minutes or until golden. Makes 10.

Bernita Engel, Minneapolis, Mn.

BUNS

1 1/2 c. sugar
1 c. salad oil
1 pkg. Fleischmann's yeast

2 eggs
1 tsp. salt
5 c. water

Mix this like you would bread dough. Let rise and knead down twice. Shape; let rise again and bake.

Clara G. Gabriel, Bismarck, N.D.

CINNAMON CRISPS

Dissolve 1 cake yeast in 1/2 cup water; set aside. Mix and sift together:

2 c. flour
4 tsp. sugar

1/2 tsp. salt

Add 1/2 cup lard; cut in as for pie crust. Add 1 egg, beaten, and yeast; stir well. Let rise; roll. Cut as for cinnamon rolls. Take each roll; roll out in cinnamon and sugar; let rise. Bake 20 minutes at 350°. Remove from pan at once as they stick. Roll as thin as you want and bake as crisp as you like.

Bessie Wilke, Detroit Lakes, Mn.

ICEBOX BUNS

Cool to lukewarm:
1 c. boiling water
1/4 c. sugar

1/2 tsp. salt
1 Tbsp. shortening

1507-82

Soften 1 cake yeast in 1/8 cup lukewarm water; add 1/2 teaspoon sugar, 1 beaten egg and 2 cups flour. Beat well; add 2 more cups flour. Let rise 3 hours. Shape and let rise again. Bake in 375° oven for 15 to 20 minutes.

Lydia Skaret, Austin, Mn.

EYE-OPENING STICKY BUNS

2 loaves frozen white
  bread dough
1/2 c. margarine
1 tsp. cinnamon
1 c. brown sugar

1 (6 oz.) pkg. vanilla or
  butterscotch pudding mix
  (regular, not instant)
2 Tbsp. milk

Thaw bread dough, but do not let it rise. Break it off in walnut size pieces. Put half of the dough balls in the bottom of a well greased Bundt pan. Melt margarine; add the rest of the ingredients. Mix well. Pour caramel mixture over the dough; place a second layer of dough balls on top. Let rolls rise for 3 hours. Bake at 350° for 30 minutes. Flip out of the pan immediately.

Betty Cortright

POPOVERS

Beat together until smooth:
1 c. sifted flour
1/2 tsp. salt

1 c. milk
2 eggs, slightly beaten

Fill well greased glass cups half full. Start in cold oven, 425°, for 35 to 45 minutes.

Arlene Carlson, Lake Park, Mn.

Similar recipe submitted by: Helen-May Johnson, Chanhassen, Mn.

HEIDELBERG POPOVERS

These popovers were renowned for their flavor as well as their size. Properly made, the popovers should be larger than a grapefruit. It is very important never to open the oven door and to watch the timing exactly.

6 eggs, slightly beaten
1 c. milk
1/4 c. salad oil

1/2 tsp. salt
1 c. flour

400

Blend eggs, milk and oil by hand or at the slow speed in electric mixer. Add flour and salt; mix at medium speed until smooth. Preheat oven to 450°. Heat cast iron pop-over pans or cast iron cupcake pans, then coat cups with oil. Fill every other cup 3/4 full of batter. Bake in a 450° oven for 30 minutes, then reduce heat to 300° and bake 15 minutes. Makes 10-12 popovers.

Note: Gas and electric ovens may vary with regards to heat, so if you have an oven with a glass door, you can watch how the popovers brown. I mixed these popovers with a wire whisk by hand and I used oven Pyrex custard cups (10 ounce size). I also oiled without heating first. They turned out great. I put some in a cast iron pan and they stuck. To prevent sticking, cast iron pans should be seasoned between use.

Helen May Johnson, Chanhassen, Mn.

ROLLS

1 1/2 c. milk

1/4 lb. oleo, heated with milk

Add to warm milk:
3/4 c. sugar
1/2 tsp. salt

2 yeast cakes

Beat 4 eggs; add to milk and rest of ingredients. Six cups flour makes a soft dough, just so you can handle. Let rise, then cut pieces and make into rolls. Let rise. Bake at 375° for 15 minutes or until light brown.

Vi Geving, Duluth, Mn.

OVERNIGHT BUNS OR ROLLS

2 c. warm water
1 c. sugar
1/2 c. shortening or lard
1 pkg. active dry yeast

1/4 c. warm water
2 eggs, beaten
8 c. flour
1 tsp. salt

Mix dough in early afternoon. Combine water, sugar, salt and lard in saucepan; bring to boil, then let cool. Dissolve yeast in warm water with a pinch of sugar. Into the cooled liquid, mix dissolved yeast, beaten eggs and 4 cups flour. Blend at low speed on electric mixer; beat until smooth. Add remaining flour. Place in a greased bowl;

let rise 4 to 5 hours. Punch down. Let rise 2 to 3 hours and shape into buns or rolls. Place on greased baking pans; don't place too close together. Cover each pan with plastic wrap; let rise overnight. Bake at 350° for 15 to 20 minutes. Makes 4 dozen buns.

Marion Standring, Big Lake, Mn.

CARAMEL ROLLS

Syrup:

6 c. brown sugar	12 Tbsp. corn syrup
3 Tbsp. vinegar	3/4 c. oleo, melted
12 Tbsp. water	1 tsp. vanilla

Boil for 1 minute; cool to lukewarm. Pour in pans and put cut rolls on top.

Buns: Dissolve 4 packages of yeast in 1 cup lukewarm water. Mix together:

7 c. warm water	2 Tbsp. salt
1 c. dry milk	2 sticks oleo
1 1/2 c. sugar	

Combine above with yeast mixture; add enough sifted flour to make soft dough, but not sticky, 17 to 19 cups. Let rise 1 hour; punch down. Let rise again at least till double. Form rolls; cut. Put on caramel. Let rise to double. Bake at 375° for 20 minutes or till brown. Makes 8 dozen rolls. Freeze really well.

Marian Nelson, Dickinson, N.D.

ONE HOUR ROLLS

2 c. scalded milk	7 c. flour, measured after
1/2 c. sugar	sifting
2 tsp. salt	4 Tbsp. butter
3 cakes compressed yeast	2 eggs, unbeaten

Dissolve yeast and sugar; add to milk when lukewarm. Add salt, eggs, flour and butter. Let rise 35 minutes; make into rolls. Let rise 25 minutes and bake in moderate oven. Very good.

Helen H. Clark, Grand Forks, N.D.

PEANUT BUTTER SWEET ROLLS

In large bowl, mix well together:

2 c. flour	3/4 c. sugar
1 Tbsp. salt	2 pkg. dry yeast

Heat to 120°:

2 c. milk	1/2 c. butter

Have 3 eggs, beaten, room temperature, ready. Mix
heated milk/butter mixture with dry ingredients; beat well
until smooth and lump free. Add eggs; beat well. Add
flour until hard to stir, then turn dough onto floured board
and knead in enough flour until dough is soft and satiny.
Cover; let rise until double in bulk. Punch down; let rise
again until almost double. In the meantime, soften peanut
butter in small saucepan until it spreads easily. Roll out
dough, after it has been divided in several parts, in a rectangle. Spread peanut butter generously on dough.
Sprinkle cinnamon/sugar mixture on top. Roll up like for
cinnamon rolls; slice and place on greased pan. Let rise
until double. Bake at 375° for about 15-20 minutes until
light brown. When cool, frost with powdered sugar icing.
Peanut butter may be added to icing, if desired.

Bernie Reveland, Rochester, Mn.

POPPY SEED ROLLS

1 1/2 c. milk	2 cakes quick yeast
2 Tbsp. sugar	4 c. sifted flour
1 tsp. salt	2 Tbsp. melted butter
6 Tbsp. shortening	Celery salt or seed or poppy seeds

Mix milk, sugar, salt and shortening; melt on stove.
Let cool till lukewarm. Add yeast, then 1/2 of the flour.
Mix until blended, then add rest of the flour. Put in a
greased bowl; let rise for 30 minutes. Empty out on a
floured board; divide into 2 halves. Roll till 1/4 inch thick.
Melt butter. Cut dough into wedges; start to roll by the
largest part. Put on a cookie sheet or pan; let rise. Dip
in melted butter and dip in a bowl of either poppy seed,
celery seed or celery salt. Bake at 450° for 12 minutes.

Virginia Miller, Anoka, Mn.

ALMOND RUSKS

Beat:
3 eggs   1 c. oil
1 c. sugar

Add:
3 1/2 c. sifted flour   1 c. diced almonds
1 1/2 tsp. baking powder   2 tsp. almond extract
1 tsp. salt

Mix and roll in three narrow rolls, about 2 1/2 inches wide and 1 inch high. Place on baking sheet, greased. Bake 30-35 minutes at 350°. Slice into 1/4 inch slices; lay on cookie sheet and return to oven to brown, about 15 minutes. Makes about 6 dozen.

Mrs. Carl Granrud, Montevideo, Mn.

GARLIC STICKS

In a saucepan, melt 2 tablespoons butter. Add 3/4 teaspoon garlic salt and 1 teaspoon parsley flakes. Cut Pillsbury packaged buttermilk biscuits in halves. With hands, roll each half of biscuit into a 6 inch stick. Put on cookie sheet; brush with melted mixture and bake in 400° preheated oven for 8 minutes. Use more than the 3/4 teaspoon of garlic salt, if desired.

Joan Norton, Hibbing, Mn.

SOFT BREAD STICKS

3 Tbsp. margarine   1 egg white, slightly beaten
1 (8 oz.) can biscuits   Sesame seeds

Preheat oven to 450°. Melt butter in cake pan; remove from oven. Roll or stretch biscuits into long strips. Place in pan and brush with egg white. Sprinkle with sesame seeds. Bake 10 minutes or until golden brown.

Joan Dinius, Coon Rapids, Mn.

ORANGE TOAST

1 1/4 c. oleo
1 1/2 c. sugar
3 eggs
Grated rind and juice of
  1 orange

1 tsp. vanilla
4 1/2 c. flour
1 tsp. soda
1 tsp. cream
1 c. nuts (optional)

Mix and shape into 3 loaves. Put on a greased cooky sheet; dough will be sticky. Refrigerate overnight. Bake at 350° for 30 minutes. Cool and slice. Toast in a 300° oven on 2 cooky sheets.

Esther Mungovan, Duluth, Mn.

FILLED LUNCHEON ROLLS

1 (3 oz.) can chopped,
  broiled mushrooms
3 hard cooked eggs
1 Tbsp. minced parsley
1 tsp. grated onion
1 c. grated American cheese

1/2 c. chili sauce
1/2 tsp. salt
1/8 tsp. pepper
8 hamburger rolls
Melted butter

Drain mushrooms, reserving broth for use in soup or gravy. Chop hard cooked eggs; add mushrooms, parsley, onion, cheese, chili sauce, salt and pepper. Mix thoroughly. Cut tops off rolls. Scoop out centers; fill with the mushroom-egg mixture. Replace tops; brush with melted butter. Place on baking sheet; bake in moderate oven, 350° F., until thoroughly heated, about 25 minutes. Makes 4 generous servings.

Dena Stoddard, St. Louis Park, Mn.

MINI PIZZA MUFFINS

1 can tomato soup
2 tsp. oregano
1 small clove garlic, minced

4 English muffins, split and
  toasted
4 slices Mozzarella cheese,
  cut in halves

In saucepan, combine soup, garlic and oregano; heat to blend flavors. Spread on muffins; top with cheese. Broil until cheese melts. Makes 8 mini pizzas.

Joan Norton, Hibbing, Mn.

BARBEQUE HAMBURGER PATTIES

2 Tbsp. butter
1/2 medium onion, diced
2 Tbsp. vinegar
2 Tbsp. brown sugar
4 Tbsp. lemon juice

1 c. ketchup
1/2 Tbsp. mustard
1/2 c. water
2 Tbsp. Worcestershire sauce

Pour uncooked sauce over 2 pounds of hamburger made into patties and layered in 9x13 inch cake pan. Bake in 350° oven for 1 hour. Turn patties over after the first 30 minutes. Serve in hamburger buns. Make before hand; freeze and just heat.

Joan Norton, Hibbing, Mn.

BEEF BARBEQUED

3 lb. lean boneless stew
  meat
2 Tbsp. Worcestershire
  sauce
2 Tbsp. brown sugar

3 Tbsp. vinegar or lemon
  juice
1/2 c. water
1 c. catsup
1 Tbsp. onion

Cover meat with water; cook 4 1/2 hours. Pull meat apart while cooking with fork. Add sauce; simmer about 1 hour. Use on hamburger buns. Very good.

Patricia Larson, Grafton, N.D.

BAR-B-QUE BEEF ROAST SANDWICHES

4 lb. chuck roast
10 whole cloves

4 c. water

Cook roast till tender, about 3 hours on top of stove. Remove from pan and, while hot, take fork and shred up roast. Put roast in sauce and reheat. If not juicy enough, add some of liquid from the roasting pan.

Sauce: In saucepan, put -

1 (14 oz.) bottle ketchup
1 medium onion, chopped
1 tsp. dry mustard

1 medium green pepper,
  chopped
2 Tbsp. vinegar

Simmer all together for 1/2 hour. Serve on hamburger buns. Makes about 16.

Joan Norton, Hibbing, Mn.

CEDRIC ADAM SANDWICH

Butter 9x12 inch pan. Cut crusts off 6 slices of bread; lay in pan. Cover bread with grated Parmesan cheese. Add layers of sliced ham, chicken and turkey. Butter 5 more slices of bread; lay on top of meat. Beat 4 whole eggs; add 3 cups milk and 1/2 teaspoon salt. Pour over the bread. Bake 1 hour at 300°.

Sauce:

1 can cream of mushroom
  soup

1 c. milk
3 hard boiled eggs

Add chopped onion and green pepper to taste. Cook like a white sauce. Serve over sandwich.

Mary Lou Sebesta, Rochester, Mn.

MONTE CRISTO SANDWICH

Sandwich:

1 Tbsp. soft butter or
  margarine
1/2 tsp. prepared mustard
3 slices of white bread

3 thin slices of turkey
3 thin slices of ham
Shortening or oil for deep
  frying

Batter:

2 eggs, separated
2 Tbsp. milk

Dash of salt and pepper
Tart jelly

In small bowl, blend together butter and mustard; spread on bread, buttering one slice on both sides. Arrange turkey on one slice of bread; top with bread slice, buttered on both sides. Top with ham and third slice of bread; secure sandwich with wooden picks. In saucepan or deep fat fryer, heat shortening, about 2 inches deep, to 400° F. over medium-high flame or at 400° F. on controlled burner. Beat egg whites until stiff peaks form. In medium bowl, beat egg yolks, milk, salt and pepper; gently fold in egg whites. Dip sandwich into batter, coating thoroughly. Fry in hot fat until golden, about 1 minute on each side. Drain on absorbent paper. Slice diagonally. Serve with tart jelly. Makes 1 sandwich.

Blanche B. Masica, Minneapolis, Mn.

OVEN-BAKED HAM SANDWICHES

Mix:

1/4 c. soft butter	1 tsp. poppy seed
1 Tbsp. horseradish	2 Tbsp. minced onion
1 Tbsp. mustard	

Spread on 8 buttered buns (both sides). Put thinly sliced ham and 1 slice of Swiss cheese in each bun. Wrap in foil; bake at 300° for 1/2 hour or until cheese is melted.

Sally Bartsch, Blaine, Mn.

RHODE'S PIZZA BREAD

Thaw 1 loaf of Rhode's white bread; let rise slightly. Roll bread out as for cinnamon rolls in a rectangle. Beat 2 eggs till frothy; spread over the bread. Spread the bread with 2 cups of grated Mozzarella cheese and then sprinkle with 1/4 cup Romano cheese. Cut 1 long stick of pepperoni into thin slices, then cut each slice into fourths. Put the pepperoni on top of cheese; roll very tightly. Seal edges and ends well. Place on cookie sheet; let set for about 1 hour. Bake in oven at 350° for 35 minutes. Remove from oven; spread with butter. Can freeze and reheat when needed.

Joan Norton, Hibbing, Mn.

PIZZA BUNS

Brown and cool:

1 lb. hamburger	Garlic, oregano and salt
1 onion	

Add:

1 c. diced Velveeta cheese	1 (8 oz.) can tomato sauce
1/2 c. stuffed olives	

Spoon mixture into hamburger buns; wrap in foil. Bake 20 minutes at 400°. Two and one-half pounds make 26 buns.

Peggy Nevers, Minneapolis, Mn.

PIZZA BURGERS

2 lb. hamburger, browned
2 cans Spam or Prem
2 cans Chef-Boy-Ar-Dee
  spaghetti sauce with
  mushrooms

1/2 lb. Colby cheese
1 Tbsp. oregano
1 Tbsp. sage

Grind Spam and cheese; mix well with hamburger and spaghetti sauce with spices added. Spread on hamburger buns. Bake at 400° for about 15-20 minutes.

Maryann Skelton, Duluth, Mn.

PIZZA BURGERS

1 can Spam
1 (4 or 8 oz.) pkg. shredded
  Cheddar cheese

1 can chili without beans
Dash of garlic salt

Grind or grate the Spam; add the rest of the ingredients. Use as much cheese as you like. Spread mixture on halved buns and place under broiler; watch closely. When bubbly, remove from oven. Delicious and quick.

Karen Ireland, Montevideo, Mn.

PICNIC PIZZA LOAVES

1 lb. ground beef
1 (8 oz.) can (1 c.) pizza
  sauce
1/2 tsp. dried oregano,
  crushed
1 c. (4 oz.) pimento stuffed
  green olives
1/2 c. chopped onion
1/2 tsp. salt

1 c. (4 oz.) Muenster or
  Mozzarella cheese,
  shredded
1 loaf French bread, halved
  lengthwise
Mushrooms, black olives and
  green pepper, chopped
  (all in desired amounts)

Brown beef and onion; add pizza sauce, salt and oregano. Place each loaf half, crust side down, on prepared pieces of foil large enough to wrap sandwiches. Spread 1/2 of meat mixture over each loaf; layer the olives, pepper and mushrooms. Sprinkle with cheese. Wrap loaves in foil, folding to seal edges. Heat over low coals 15 minutes or till heated through. Loaves can also be heated in a 350° oven for 25-30 minutes. This can be frozen and heated or reheated later.

Diane Haan, Bismarck, N.D.

1507-82

RIBBON SANDWICH LOAF

2 (2 lb.) sandwich loaves, sliced lengthwise by bakery into 1/2 slices*
7 (8 oz.) pkg. cream cheese
1 small jar stuffed olives
1 small pkg. walnuts, chopped
1 small can crushed pineapple
1 can Spam, ground
1 jar pickle relish
1 green pepper
7 eggs, boiled and chopped
1 can tuna
2 c. cooked chicken or turkey, chopped fine or ground
1 jar dried beef, shredded fine
1/2 c. chopped celery
1/2 c. chopped onion
1/4 c. chopped parsley
Mayonnaise, as needed
Miracle Whip as needed

Each filling mixed separately in a bowl: Tuna, Miracle Whip and 1/4 cup chopped onion; Chopped Spam, Miracle Whip, 1/2 jar pickle relish; Chopped Chicken, mayonnaise, celery and parsley; Chopped Eggs, 1/2 jar pickle relish, mayonnaise, 1/4 teaspoon salt; 2 packages Cream Cheese, drained crushed pineapple, 1/4 cup nuts; 1 package Cream Cheese, dried beef, 1/4 cup chopped green pepper; 1 package Cream Cheese, 1/2 bottle olives, chopped, 1 tablespoon chopped onion.

Alternate each loaf with white and wheat slices. Spread fillings as follows: Loaf 1 - Tuna, egg, cheese-olive, chicken; loaf 2 - Spam, cheese-pineapple, egg, tuna; loaf 3 - Chicken, cheese-dried beef, Spam, cheese-pineapple. Soften rest of cheese and frost top and sides. Decorate with green pepper rings, nuts, parsley or olives leftover. Refrigerate overnight. Slice and serve. Makes 3

*Crusts are not used, but can be used for stuffing or snacking.

Jean Schwartz, Owatonna, Mn.

SLOPPY JOES

2 1/2 lb. ground beef
1 onion, chopped up
Salt and pepper to taste
1 (8 oz.) can tomato sauce
1 can tomato soup
1/4 c. catsup
2 Tbsp. Worcestershire sauce
3 c. chopped celery

Brown meat until done. Simmer celery and onion until done in shortening. Add all the other ingredients to meat, celery and onion. Simmer 1 hour. Very good.

Mary Paul, Minneapolis, Mn.

410

GLORIA'S SLOPPY JOES

1 1/2 lb. hamburger
Small onion or 1 Tbsp.
   dried onion
2 Tbsp. brown sugar
1 tsp. prepared mustard

2 Tbsp. vinegar
1 c. catsup
1/4 c. water
A little Worcestershire sauce

Brown hamburger and onion. Add other ingredients; let simmer 30 to 45 minutes.

Gloria Smith, Jackson, Mn.

SPAM SANDWICH SPREAD

5 boiled eggs, chopped fine
1 can Spam, grated well
Onion, grated fine

Pickles, grated fine
Salt and pepper

Add mayonnaise, mustard and a little milk. Mix all together well; add Salad Supreme. Serve on small buns. Makes enough for 2 dozen buns.

Mary Jo Conneran, Fargo, N.D.

TACO BURGERS

Brown 1 pound ground beef. Add:

1 (16 oz.) can tomatoes
1 tsp. chili powder
1 tsp. Worcestershire sauce

3/4 tsp. salt
1/2 tsp. sugar
1/4 tsp. dry mustard

Simmer 20 minutes. Serve on toasted hamburger buns with 2 cups shredded lettuce, 1 cup shredded American cheese (4 ounces). Makes 8.

Irene Faber, St. Paul, Mn.

TAVERN BURGERS

2 lb. hamburger
1/2 pt. water
1/2 tsp. chili powder
1 tsp. salt

2 Tbsp. horseradish mustard
1 tsp. pepper
1 large onion
3/4 c. catsup

Cook chili powder, water, salt, pepper, onion and catsup for 7 minutes. Add hamburger and mustard; cook 1/2 hour. Very good.

Goldie Mikish, Staples, Mn.

PENNSYLVANIA DUTCH CORN MEAL MUSH

1 c. yellow corn meal
1 Tbsp. flour
1 tsp. salt

1 c. cold water
4 c. boiling water

Combine corn meal, flour and salt; add cold water and stir into a paste. Add boiling water slowly; cook for 30 minutes on top of stove, stirring frequently, or for 3 to 4 hours in double boiler. Pour into a bread pan to mold. Chill; slice and fry slowly until brown. Serve with syrup.

Irene Wall, Little Falls, Mn.

DANISH EBLESKIVER*
(Buttermilk Recipe)
*(Or Aebleskiver....Apple Pancake Balls)

2 c. buttermilk
2 c. flour
3 eggs
1 tsp. baking powder

1/2 tsp. salt
1 tsp. soda
2 Tbsp. sugar
Applesauce

Beat egg yolks; add sugar, salt and milk, then flour, soda and baking powder, which have been sifted together. Last, fold in stiffly beaten egg whites. Place small amount of fat in each depression of Ebleskiver iron and fill 2/3 full of batter. Place a small teaspoon of applesauce on top of dough batter, then barely cover applesauce with a few drops of dough. Cook until bubbly; carefully turn over with a fork and finish baking on other side. (I find a heavy knitting needle is easier in turning over apple ball.) Serve with butter, maple syrup, jam or brown sugar.

Note: Avoid spilling applesauce in cups, as this will cause the iron to stick.

Clara O. Johnson, Chanhassen, Mn.

RICH DOUGHNUTS

4 egg yolks or 2 whole eggs
1 c. white sugar
2 Tbsp. soft butter
3/4 c. buttermilk
3 1/2 c. sifted all-purpose
    flour

2 tsp. baking powder
1 tsp. baking soda
1/2 tsp. salt
1/4 tsp. ground nutmeg
1/4 tsp. ground cinnamon
Shortening for frying

Beat eggs well; beat in sugar and shortening. Stir in buttermilk. Sift together remaining ingredients; work them into batter. Chill dough at least 2 hours. Roll out 1/3 inch thick; cut with floured doughnut cutter. Drop in heavy saucepan or deep-fat fryer in 3 inches of shortening. (Note: Use thermometer and heat accordingly.) Drain on absorbent paper. Dust with confectioners sugar.

Bev. Jensen, Willmar, Mn.

KNEPFLA DOUGH

Combine:

3 c. flour
2 eggs
1 slice bread with crust
  removed

Enough water to make a
  medium stiff dough
4 medium potatoes, cubed
2 tsp. baking powder
1 tsp. salt

Mix dough well; let rest for an hour before using. Bring potatoes and enough water to cover potatoes and knepfla to a boil in large kettle. Cut dough into small bits (the size of a peanut) into the boiling water; boil about 5 minutes. Drain well; top with the following:

2 slices bread, finely
  crumbled

1/2 c. butter, melted

Brown this mixture in frying pan; pour over drained knepfla and potatoes. Serve with sauerkraut, or, any type of soup stock can be used in the boiling stage and can be served as a soup.

Frances Schwartzbauer, Bismarck, N.D.

DUMPLINGS
(For Fricassee of Chicken)

1 1/2 c. sifted flour,
  sifted twice before
  measuring
2 tsp. baking powder

1 tsp. salt
1 Tbsp. shortening
3/4 c. milk

Combine flour, baking powder and salt. Work in shortening like for pie crust. Add milk and mix; drop by spoonfuls. Makes 12 dumplings.

Helen-May Johnson, Chanhassen, Mn.

KASE KNEPFLA
(Cottage Cheese Buttons)

3 eggs   3 c. flour (about)
1/2 c. milk

Mix above ingredients. Add flour until the dough is softer than noodle dough, so that the dough can easily be folded over. Roll out on floured board; cut into 4 inch squares. Place desired filling in center. Seal edges by pressing opposite corners together to enclose filling. Drop into 3 quarts of boiling water until they rise to the surface, then boil for a few minutes longer; should be about 15 minutes. Drain. Prepare a mixture of browned bread crumbs with butter or shortening and mix with drained knepfla in large bowl. Serve.

*One cup of sour cream can be mixed with the butter and bread crumbs to make a richer, tastier topping.

Filling:

1 pt. dry curd cottage   Pinch of salt and pepper
    cheese   1 green onion or chives
1 egg

Mix; put 1 heaping teaspoonful on each square.

F. Schwartzbauer, Bismarck, N.D.

SCHLITZ KUECHLA

1 c. sugar   3 eggs
1 tsp. baking powder   1 tsp. soda
1/2 c. cream   1 c. milk or buttermilk

Beat above ingredients well; add enough flour to make a soft dough, soft enough to handle without being sticky. Roll to 3/4 inch thickness; cut into squares or oblong pieces then cut slit in center (some people pulled the ends through; others fry them as is). Deep fry in shortening or oil till golden brown.

Frances Schwartzbauer, Bismarck, N.D.

BEGINNERS' LEFSE

3 c. riced potatoes   3/4 c. unsifted flour
2 Tbsp. butter, melted   1/2 tsp. salt

Use riced potatoes so you are sure there are no lumps. Combine potatoes, butter, salt; set aside to cool. Add the

414

flour when you are ready to roll. Roll as thin as possible.
Bake on hot pancake or lefse griddle; turn only once.
Your kids will love you!

Donna Hoff, Fargo, N.D.

HOMEMADE NOODLES

Mix together:

2/3 c. flour	1 tsp. salt
1 egg	

Knead on board or brown paper. Cover with cloth for
20 minutes, then roll like jelly roll. Cut, then let dry.
Boil in salt water (like other noodles).

Marion Round, Faribault, Mn.

STIRRUM

3 eggs, beaten	3 tsp. baking powder
1/2 c. sugar	2 c. flour
1/2 tsp. salt	

Add enough milk to make a thin batter (like pancake
dough). Melt 1/4 pound butter in pan on medium heat.
Pour all the batter into pan at once. Stir occasionally until
all dough has been cooked. This is very delicious with
lettuce that has been mixed with cream.

Frances Schwartzbauer, Bismarck, N.D.

Similar recipe submitted by: Judy Rieger, Grand
Forks, N.D.

TEMPURA BATTER

3/4 c. flour	1/2 tsp. baking powder
1/4 c. cornstarch	1/4 tsp. soda

Add 1 cup water; beat well, then add 1 egg and beat
again. Good for fish and onion rings. If you have some
batter left, it can be frozen. No salt in this batter.

Gloria Smith, Jackson, Mn.

TEMPURA
(French Fry Batter)

1 1/2 c. flour	Dash of MSG
1 1/2 tsp. salt	1 Tbsp. cornstarch
3 tsp. sugar	1 1/2 c. water
1 1/4 tsp. baking powder	2 drops yellow food color

Combine ingredients in bowl; gradually add water and food color. Mix well. Dip fish, vegetables, chicken, etc. and deep fry. Delicious! Try this with dill pickles, cauliflower, onions, etc.

Mary Perron, Rochester, Mn.

** NOTES **

CAKES
COOKIES
BARS

HANDY CHART OF KITCHEN MATH
(Size of Pans and Baking Dishes)

Cooking need never become a crisis, when you use our handy charts. Need a 4 or 6-cup baking dish? Will your fancy mold be the right size for the recipe? See below for the answers.

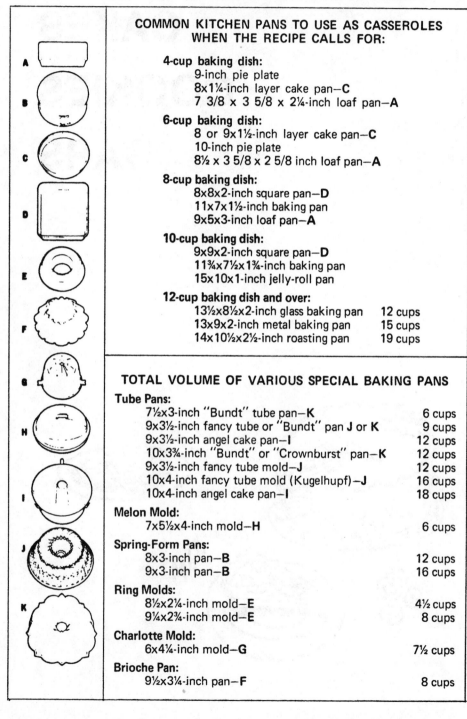

COMMON KITCHEN PANS TO USE AS CASSEROLES WHEN THE RECIPE CALLS FOR:

4-cup baking dish:
- 9-inch pie plate
- 8x1¼-inch layer cake pan—**C**
- 7 3/8 x 3 5/8 x 2¼-inch loaf pan—**A**

6-cup baking dish:
- 8 or 9x1½-inch layer cake pan—**C**
- 10-inch pie plate
- 8½ x 3 5/8 x 2 5/8 inch loaf pan—**A**

8-cup baking dish:
- 8x8x2-inch square pan—**D**
- 11x7x1½-inch baking pan
- 9x5x3-inch loaf pan—**A**

10-cup baking dish:
- 9x9x2-inch square pan—**D**
- 11¾x7½x1¾-inch baking pan
- 15x10x1-inch jelly-roll pan

12-cup baking dish and over:

13½x8½x2-inch glass baking pan	12 cups
13x9x2-inch metal baking pan	15 cups
14x10½x2½-inch roasting pan	19 cups

TOTAL VOLUME OF VARIOUS SPECIAL BAKING PANS

Tube Pans:

7½x3-inch "Bundt" tube pan—**K**	6 cups
9x3½-inch fancy tube or "Bundt" pan **J** or **K**	9 cups
9x3½-inch angel cake pan—**I**	12 cups
10x3¾-inch "Bundt" or "Crownburst" pan—**K**	12 cups
9x3½-inch fancy tube mold—**J**	12 cups
10x4-inch fancy tube mold (Kugelhupf)—**J**	16 cups
10x4-inch angel cake pan—**I**	18 cups

Melon Mold:

7x5½x4-inch mold—**H**	6 cups

Spring-Form Pans:

8x3-inch pan—**B**	12 cups
9x3-inch pan—**B**	16 cups

Ring Molds:

8½x2¼-inch mold—**E**	4½ cups
9¼x2¾-inch mold—**E**	8 cups

Charlotte Mold:

6x4¼-inch mold—**G**	7½ cups

Brioche Pan:

9½x3¼-inch pan—**F**	8 cups

ALMOND CAKE

1 c. butter or margarine	2 1/4 c. flour
1 c. sugar	2 tsp. baking powder
3 eggs	1/2 tsp. salt
1 can Solo almond filling	1/4 c. milk

Cream butter and sugar; add eggs, one at a time, mixing thoroughly. Add filling; mix well. Sift flour, baking powder and salt together; add alternately with milk to creamed mixture. Pour into greased and floured tube pan. Bake at 350° for 50 minutes or until done. Cool in pan. Remove from pan and drizzle with glaze over top of cake, if desired.

Glaze:

1 c. powdered sugar	1/4 tsp. almond flavoring
2 Tbsp. cream	

M.L. Roskoski, Virginia, Mn.

ALMOND SHERRY CAKE

1 pkg. yellow cake mix	1 (3 5/8 oz.) pkg. instant
4 large eggs	vanilla pudding mix
3/4 c. Christian Brother's	Streusel Filling
cream sherry	Sherry Glaze
3/4 c. vegetable oil	1/4 c. Blue Diamond sliced
1/2 tsp. nutmeg	almonds, toasted

Grease and flour a 10 inch Bundt pan; set aside. In large bowl, combine cake mix, eggs, sherry, oil, pudding mix and nutmeg; mix at low speed 1 minute, scraping bowl constantly. Mix at medium speed for 3 minutes, scraping bowl occasionally. Pour half of batter into prepared pan. Sprinkle evenly with Streusel Filling. Pour in remaining cake batter. Bake at 350° for 45-50 minutes; cool 15 minutes. Unmold from pan; cool completely. Brush with Sherry Glaze and garnish with almonds.

Streusel Filling:

1/3 c. packed brown sugar	3 Tbsp. firm butter or
1/4 c. flour	margarine
	1/2 tsp. cinnamon

Mix together until crumbly; stir in 3/4 cup toasted almonds.

Sherry Glaze: Stir together 2 cups sifted powdered sugar, 1/3 cup melted butter and 1 tablespoon Christian Brother's cream sherry. Stir in 1 to 2 teaspoons hot water until glaze is of desired consistency. Serves 10-12.

Liz Tuft, St. Paul, Mn.

MOCK ANGEL FOOD CAKE

2 c. cake flour	1/4 tsp. salt
2 c. sugar	

Sift together and add 1 cup boiling water; let cool. Beat 5 egg whites with 1/2 teaspoon cream of tartar until foamy, then add 2 teaspoons baking powder and beat until stiff. Fold in cooled mixture; put in 9x13 inch ungreased pan. Bake at 350° for 35 minutes.

Creamy Nut Frosting: Combine 2 1/2 tablespoons cake flour with 1/2 cup milk; cook until thick, then cool. Cream:

1/2 c. sugar	1/4 tsp. salt
1/2 c. Crisco	

Add cooled mixture, 1 cup powdered sugar and 1/2 teaspoon vanilla; beat. (Add nuts - optional.)

Gloria Smith, Jackson, Mn.

APPLE CAKE

Cream:

1/2 c. butter	2 c. sugar

Add 2 eggs; beat well. Stir in 4 cups sliced apples and 1 cup chopped nuts. Add:

2 c. flour	1 1/2 tsp. soda
1 tsp. cinnamon	1/2 tsp. salt

Bake at 325° for 50 minutes in 9x13 inch pan. Combine 1 scant cup of brown sugar, 1/4 cup butter and 2 tablespoons flour; sprinkle on top of batter. Serve with whipped cream or butter sauce.

Gloria Smith, Jackson, Mn.

FRESH APPLE CAKE

1/2 c. butter	2 1/4 c. flour
1 c. sugar	2 tsp. soda
1/2 c. brown sugar	1 tsp. cinnamon
1 c. sour milk or buttermilk	1/2 tsp. nutmeg
2 eggs	1/2 tsp. salt
	2 apples, chopped fine

Cream butter and sugars; add milk and eggs. Sift dry ingredients together; add to first mixture. Add apples. Place in greased 9x13 inch pan. Sprinkle topping on batter and gently press into dough.

Topping:

1/2 c. sugar	1/4 c. brown sugar
3/4 c. nuts	1/2 tsp. cinnamon

Bake 40 minutes at 375°.

Anne Aune, Minneapolis, Mn.

Similar recipe submitted by: Sue Hetland, Grand Forks, N.D.

GERMAN APPLE CAKE

3 eggs	1/2 tsp. salt
1 tsp. vanilla	2 c. sugar
1 tsp. soda	2 tsp. cinnamon
1 c. chopped walnuts	4 c. sliced apples (about 5
1 c. cooking oil	medium)
2 c. flour	

Beat the eggs and oil together until thick. Add sugar, vanilla, flour, cinnamon, soda, salt and walnuts; blend thoroughly. Slice the apples; spread on bottom of greased 9x13 inch pan. Drop batter over apples. Bake 1 hour in moderate oven, 350°. After cake is cool, frost by mixing a Cream Cheese Frosting:

1 (8 oz.) pkg. cream cheese	4 Tbsp. melted butter
2 tsp. vanilla	2 c. powdered sugar
1 Tbsp. lemon juice	

Spread frosting on cake.

Lorraine Rieger, Minneapolis, Mn.

APPLE HARVEST CAKE

2 eggs, beaten
2 c. sugar
1 1/2 c. oil
3 c. flour
1 tsp. soda

1 tsp. salt
1 tsp. cinnamon
3 c. finely chopped apples, peeled
1 c. chopped nuts

Combine eggs, sugar and oil; beat well. Add flour, soda, salt and cinnamon; mix by hand until dry ingredients are moistened. Stir in apples and nuts. Bake at 350° in layer pans or 8x8 inch pans for 35-40 minutes; 13x9 inch pan for 1 hour.

Cream Cheese Icing: Soften 2 (3 ounce) packages cream cheese with 3 tablespoons milk or cream. Gradually add 1 1/2 cups powdered sugar. Stir in 3 teaspoons grated lemon peel or 2 teaspoons vanilla or 1 teaspoon cinnamon.

Mary Paul, Minneapolis, Mn.

APPLE-NUT CAKE

Beat together:

1 c. sugar
1 egg

1/2 c. oleo

Sift:

1 c. flour
1 tsp. soda
1 tsp. cinnamon

1/2 tsp. nutmeg
1/4 tsp. salt

Add to above mixture. Stir into rest of ingredients:

2 apples, peeled and chopped fine (about 1 c.)   1/2 c. chopped nuts

Bake in 11x7 inch pan at 350° for 35-40 minutes. When ready to serve, top each piece with Cool Whip or whipped cream; pour warm sauce over all.

Sauce:

1/2 c. cream
1/2 c. brown sugar

1/2 c. white sugar
1/2 c. oleo

Boil for 5 minutes. May be refrigerated. Warm before serving.

Carolyn Brudevold, Fargo, N.D.

APPLE-OVER GINGER CAKE

1/2 c. margarine
1/4 c. firmly packed brown sugar
1 1/2 c. (2 medium) apples, sliced
1 1/2 c. flour
3/4 c. sugar
1 1/2 tsp. ground ginger

2 tsp. baking powder
1 tsp. cinnamon
1/2 tsp. salt
1/2 c. water
1/3 c. light molasses
1/3 c. oil
2 eggs
1/4 c. chopped walnuts

Melt margarine in 9 inch round baking dish; sprinkle with brown sugar. Arrange apple slices and walnut halves in pan. Stir together dry ingredients. Blend in 1/4 cup water, molasses and oil; beat 2 minutes at medium speed of electric mixer. Add remaining water and eggs; beat 2 minutes. Stir in chopped walnuts. Pour batter evenly over apples. Bake at 350° for 35 to 40 minutes, or until done. Immediately loosen edges and invert onto serving plate. Serve warm or cold.

Mary Fingalson, Detroit Lakes, Mn.

RAW APPLE CAKE

1/2 c. margarine or butter
2 c. sugar
2 eggs
2 c. flour
1 tsp. cinnamon
2 tsp. soda

1/2 tsp. salt
4 c. raw apples, chopped fine
1/2 c. chopped nuts (opt.)
1 tsp. vanilla

Topping:

1/2 c. butter, melted
1 c. brown sugar

6 Tbsp. flour

Combine butter and sugar; add beaten eggs. Sift dry ingredients together; add alternately with the chopped apples and nuts. Put in greased 9x13 inch pan. Cover with the topping before baking. The topping will not spread, but should be put on as evenly as possible. Bake 50 minutes at 350°.

Lorraine Rieger, Minneapolis, Mn.

RAW APPLE CAKE

2 c. sugar
1 c. shortening (part
  margarine)
2 c. chopped, raw apples
4 eggs, beaten
1 c. cold coffee
3 c. flour
1 1/2 tsp. soda

1 1/2 tsp. cinnamon
1/2 tsp. nutmeg
1/2 tsp. cloves
1/2 tsp. salt
1 tsp. vanilla
1 c. chopped nutmeats
1/2 c. raisins

Sift together flour, soda, salt and spices; sift 3 times. Cream shortening and sugar well; add beaten eggs. Add chopped apples; beat alternately with flour mixture and coffee, added in small amounts. Beat to blend well. Add vanilla; stir in nuts and raisins. Spread dough evenly in large size cake pan, at least 13x9 inches. Bake at 350° for 50 minutes, or until center tests done with toothpick. Cool; frost with Praline Frosting. (I use two 9x13 inch pans and bake 30 to 40 minutes.)

Sharon Wilson, Park Rapids, Mn.

AUTUMN APPLE CAKE

1 c. raisins or currants
3 c. flour
2 tsp. baking soda
1 tsp. salt
1 tsp. cinnamon
1/2 tsp. nutmeg
1 1/2 c. oil

1 c. granulated sugar
1 c. firmly packed brown
  sugar
4 eggs
1 tsp. vanilla
3 c. thickly sliced, pared
  apples
1 c. chopped pecans

Soak raisins or currants in water for about 1 hour. Sift together flour, baking soda, salt, cinnamon and nutmeg. In a large bowl, with electric mixer, beat oil and sugar until well blended. Add eggs one at a time, beating well after each. Add vanilla, then gradually beat in flour mixture. Fold raisins into batter along with apples and pecans. Preheat oven to 350°. Spoon batter into a tube pan, that has been greased; bake for 1 1/2 hours. Remove and cool on a wire rack.

Lynn Cooch, Minneapolis, Mn.

JEANETTE'S APPLESAUCE CAKE

1/2 c. butter	2 c. bread flour
1 c. sugar	1 tsp. soda
1 egg, beaten lightly	1 tsp. cinnamon
1 c. dates or raisins	1/2 tsp. cloves
1 c. currants or nuts	1 c. strained applesauce

Cream butter; add sugar gradually. Add egg, fruit and nuts. Add the flour, sifted with the soda and spices; add applesauce. Bake in greased tube pan at 325° for 1 hour.

Helen Teeuwen, Minneapolis, Mn.
Similar recipe submitted by: Dena Stoddard, Minneapolis, Mn.

BANANA CAKE

1/2 c. less 1 Tbsp. shortening	1 1/2 c. sugar
	2 eggs

Mix thoroughly; add 1 cup (2 large) mashed bananas. Mix together:

2 c. flour	1 tsp. baking powder
1 tsp. soda	1/2 tsp. salt

Add to first mixture alternately with 3/4 cup sour milk. Bake in two 8 inch round cake tins, greased, at 350° for about 25 minutes; or 9x9 inch loaf for 50 minutes.

Frosting:

1 c. sugar	1/2 tsp. cream of tartar
2 unbeaten egg whites	1 tsp. vanilla
1/4 tsp. salt	2 Tbsp. water

Place all ingredients in double boiler; beat over low heat for 4 minutes. Frosting should stand in peaks when done.

Mrs. H. Erickson, Minneapolis, Mn.

BETTY'S TORTE

3 egg whites	16 crushed soda crackers
1/4 tsp. cream of tartar	1/4 c. chopped nuts
1 c. sugar	1 tsp. vanilla

Beat whites until foamy; add cream of tartar. Beat

until stiff; gradually beat in 1 cup sugar. Fold in crackers, nuts and vanilla. Bake in 9 inch pan at 325° for 30 to 40 minutes. Cool; spread with the following topping:

1 c. cream, whipped   1 c. well drained, crushed
                                                             pineapple

Chill before serving.
                                        Beverly Fox, Fargo, N.D.

BLACK MAGIC CAKE

1 3/4 c. flour   2 eggs
2 c. sugar   1 c. strong coffee
3/4 c. cocoa   1 c. sour milk
2 tsp. soda   1/2 c. oil
1 tsp. baking powder   1 tsp. vanilla
1 tsp. salt

Combine dry ingredients; add liquids. Beat at medium speed 2 minutes (thin batter). Bake in greased 9x13 inch pan or two 9 inch layer pans at 350° for 35-40 minutes for oblong or 30-35 minutes for layers.
                                        Marge Pye, St. Paul, Mn.

BUTTERCUP CAKE

2 1/4 c. sifted cake flour   1 tsp. vanilla
1 1/2 c. sugar   3/4 tsp. other flavoring (1/4
1 tsp. baking powder   tsp. each almond, lemon
1/2 tsp. soda   and orange)
1 tsp. salt   1/3 - 1/2 c. unbeaten eggs
1/2 c. shortening   (2 medium)
1 c. buttermilk or sour milk

Sift together in bowl the flour, sugar, baking powder, soda and salt. Add shortening, milk and flavoring; beat at medium speed for 2 minutes. Add unbeaten eggs; beat for 2 more minutes. Bake in 2 layer tins or a 9x13 inch pan. Frost with any frosting.
                                   Mary Fingalson, Detroit Lakes, Mn.

CARROT CAKE

3 c. flour
2 c. sugar
1 c. coconut
2 1/2 tsp. soda
2 1/2 tsp. cinnamon
1 tsp. salt
1 1/4 c. cooking oil

2 c. (4 medium) shredded
carrots
2 tsp. vanilla extract
1 tsp. grated orange peel
1 (11 oz.) can undrained
mandarin oranges
3 eggs

In large bowl, blend all ingredients; beat 2 minutes at high speed. Pour into greased pan. Bake 45-55 minutes until toothpick inserted comes out clean.

Frosting:

1 (8 oz.) pkg. Philadelphia
cream cheese
2 Tbsp. melted butter

1 tsp. vanilla extract
3 c. powdered sugar
1/2 - 1 c. chopped nuts
(optional)

Blend frosting ingredients; beat until smooth. Spread over cake; sprinkle with nuts.

Ellie Cox, Rochester, Mn.

CARROT-PINEAPPLE CAKE

3 1/4 c. sifted flour
2 tsp. baking powder
1 tsp. baking soda
1/2 tsp. salt
2 tsp. cinnamon
1 tsp. nutmeg
2 c. sugar

3 eggs
1 1/2 c. salad oil
1 tsp. vanilla
2 c. finely shredded carrots
1 c. (8 1/2 oz. can) crushed
pineapple, undrained

Sift together flour, baking powder, soda, salt and spices; set aside. In mixing bowl, combine sugar, eggs, oil and vanilla; beat well with mixer. Stir in carrots and pineapple, mixing well. Blend in flour mixture. Pour into greased and floured 10 inch tube pan. Bake in 350° oven for 60 to 70 minutes, or until cake tests done. Cool in pan 10 minutes, then loosen edges and turn out on rack to cool thoroughly. Frost as desired, or sprinkle with powdered sugar before serving. One cake makes 12 servings.

Mrs. Lydia Rieger, Harvey, N.D.

CHAMPAGNE CAKE

1 Jiffy cake mix (white)
2/3 (8 oz.) pkg. cream
  cheese, softened
1 large ctn. Cool Whip

2 (13 oz.) cans crushed
  pineapple, drained
1 pkg. instant vanilla
  pudding

First Layer: Prepare Jiffy cake according to directions; bake in greased, floured 9x13 inch cake pan for about 15 minutes at 350°. Second Layer: Beat cream cheese with 1/2 or more of Cool Whip; spread on cake. Third Layer: Spread drained pineapple on top. Fourth Layer: Prepare instant pudding; spread on top of pineapple. Fifth Layer: Spread remainder of Cool Whip. Keep refrigerated.

Dorothy Savig, Minneapolis, Mn.

CHERRY PINEAPPLE CAKE

1 can cherry pie mix
1 can crushed pineapple

1 Duncan Hines yellow butter
  cake mix
1 can coconut
2 sticks melted butter

Using a 9x13 inch buttered cake pan, layer in order given. Bake at 325° for 40 minutes or until coconut is brown.

Ruth Roemeling, Luverne, Mn.

CHOCOLATE CAKE

Cream:
1/2 c. butter
1/8 tsp. salt

1 c. sugar

Blend and add 1/2 cup cocoa in 1/3 cup cold water. Add 2 1/2 cups cake flour alternately with 1 cup cold water. Add 1 teaspoon vanilla. Fold in 3 egg whites (beat stiff), to which has been added 3/4 cup sugar. Last, add 1 1/3 teaspoons soda, dissolved in 1 tablespoon boiling water. Bake at 350° in 9x13 inch pan.

Mary Fingalson, Detroit Lakes, Mn.

CHOCOLATE APPLESAUCE CAKE

1/2 c. shortening
1 1/2 c. sugar
2 eggs
1 (16 oz.) can applesauce
1 (6 oz.) pkg. chocolate
  chips

3/4 c. chopped nuts
1 tsp. cinnamon
2 Tbsp. cocoa
2 c. flour
1 1/2 tsp. soda
1/2 tsp. salt

Combine shortening, sugar and eggs. Add sifted dry ingredients alternately with applesauce. Mix in 1/3 of the chocolate chips. Combine 2 tablespoons sugar with chopped nuts and remaining chocolate chips; sprinkle on top before baking. Bake at 350° for 40 minutes, or until tests done, in 9x13 inch pan.

BEST EVER CHOCOLATE CAKE

Stir:
2 c. flour
2 c. sugar
2 tsp. soda

2 tsp. baking powder
1/2 tsp. salt
4 heaping Tbsp. cocoa

Add 1 cup salad oil and 1 cup hot water. Stir until lumps are gone. Add 1 more cup of hot water; stir. Add 2 beaten eggs and 2 teaspoons vanilla; stir. Bake at 350° for 40 minutes in 9x13 inch pan. Don't use electric mixer!
Sue Hetland, Grand Forks, N.D.

CHOCOLATE FRUIT CAKE

1 c. white sugar
1 c. brown sugar
1 c. shortening
1 egg
1 c. sour milk
3 sq. chocolate, melted
1/2 c. white sugar

4 c. flour
2 tsp. soda
3/4 tsp. salt
1 tsp. cinnamon
1/2 tsp. allspice
1/2 tsp. cloves

Add raisins, dates, nuts and candied fruit. Bake in 2 loaf pans at 325° for about 1 hour.
Gemma Pierson, St. Cloud, Mn.

GRANDMA'S CHOCOLATE CHIP CAKE

1 3/4 c. boiling water
1 c. uncooked quick oats
1 c. lightly packed brown
  sugar
1 c. granulated sugar
1/2 c. margarine
2 large eggs

1 3/4 c. flour
1 tsp. soda
1 Tbsp. cocoa
1/2 tsp. salt
1 (12 oz.) pkg. chocolate
  chips
3/4 c. walnuts

Pour boiling water over margarine and oatmeal; let stand for 10 minutes. Stir until margarine melts. Add sugar and eggs; mix well. Add flour, soda, salt and cocoa as you continue mixing. Stir in 1/2 package of chocolate chips. Pour into greased 9x13 inch pan. Sprinkle chopped walnuts and remaining chocolate chips on top. Bake in 350° oven for 30-40 minutes; cake is done when toothpick inserted in the center comes out clean. Keeps well in refrigerator or can be frozen. Serve with whipped cream or ice cream as a delicious dessert. Can be baked in a 10x15 inch pan as bars at 350° for approximately 20 minutes.

Marian Pearson, Minneapolis, Mn.

CHOCOLATE MAYONNAISE CAKE

Mix together:
1 c. mayonnaise or Miracle
  Whip

1 c. sugar
1 c. water (cold)

Sift together:
2 c. flour
4 Tbsp. cocoa

2 tsp. soda

Add 1 teaspoon vanilla. Bake at 350° for 30-40 minutes in 13x9 inch pan. For cupcakes, add a little more flour.

Sharon Wilson, Park Rapids, Mn.

OLD FASHIONED CHOCOLATE CAKE

2 c. flour
2 c. sugar
3/4 c. cocoa

2 tsp. soda
1 tsp. salt

Mix; add 2 eggs, 1/2 cup oil and 1 cup milk. Mix and blend in 1 cup boiling water. Bake 35-40 minutes at 350°. Frost when cool.

Key Barck, Rochester, Mn.

CHOCOLATE PISTACHIO CAKE

Combine in large mixing bowl:

1 pkg. white or yellow
  cake mix
1 pkg. pudding mix

1/2 c. orange juice
1/2 c. water
4 eggs
1/2 c. oil

Blend to moisten, then beat 2 minutes at medium speed of electric mixer, scraping bowl occasionally. Pour about 3/4 of batter into well greased, floured Bundt pan or 10 inch tube pan. Add 3/4 cup chocolate flavored syrup to remaining batter; mix well. Pour over batter in pan. Bake at 350° F. for about 1 hour, or until done. Cool in pan on wire rack 10 minutes. Remove from pan; cool on wire rack. Sprinkle with confectioners sugar.

Margaret McKenney, Minneapolis, Mn.

CHOCOLATE RUM CAKE

1 chocolate cake mix
1 pkg. chocolate instant
  pudding
4 eggs

1/2 c. dark rum
1/2 c. cold water
1/2 c. Wesson oil
1/2 c. slivered almonds

Filling: (Makes 4 cups)

1 pt. heavy cream
1/3 c. cocoa
1/2 c. confectioners sugar

1 tsp. vanilla
1/2 c. Bacardi dark rum

Combine all cake ingredients together in large bowl; blend well. Beat at medium 2 minutes. Turn into two greased and floured 9 inch layer cake pans. Bake 30 minutes or until done; do not underbake. Cool in pans 10 minutes. Remove from pans; finish cooling on racks. While baking, make filling: Combine first 4 ingredients; beat until stiff. Fold in rum; keep chilled. When cake is cooled, slice layers in halves horizontally. Stack layers, putting 1 cup filling between layers and on top; none on side. Serve. (Bake at 350°.)

Mary Paul, Minneapolis, Mn.

DEEP CHOCOLATE UPSIDE DOWN CAKE

1 pkg. Duncan Hines deep
   chocolate Deluxe cake mix
1/2 c. (1 stick) butter or
   margarine
1/4 c. water

1 c. brown sugar
1 c. chopped nuts
1 1/3 c. (3 1/2 oz. can)
   flaked coconut
Whipped cream, if desired

Melt butter in a 13x9x2 inch pan. Add water, then brown sugar. Mix in nuts and coconut; spread evenly in pan. Mix cake at medium speed for 2 minutes as directed on the label. Pour batter over mixture in pan. Bake at 350° for about 40 minutes, until cake springs back when touched lightly. Let stand 5 minutes for topping to begin to set. Turn upside down onto a large platter or a cooky sheet. Serve with whipped cream. Makes 12 to 14 servings.

When baking at high altitudes, use flour, water and baking temperature given on package side panel.

Lorraine Rieger, Minneapolis, Mn.

CINNAMON CAKE

The following recipe is taken from a 1915 cookbook prepared by the students of Fountain City, Wisconsin high school.

Yolks of 2 eggs
1 1/2 c. sugar
3/4 c. milk

1/2 c. butter
1 1/2 c. flour (or more)
2 tsp. baking powder

After this preparation is put in the pan, sprinkle powdered sugar, cinnamon and walnut meats over the top. Bake in a quick oven.

Grayce Funke, Minneapolis, Mn.

CINNAMON CAKE

3/4 c. sugar
1 egg
1 tsp. butter
2 c. flour

2 tsp. baking powder
Pinch of salt
1 c. milk

Topping:

1/4 lb. butter
3/4 lb. dark brown sugar

Cinnamon
Butter

Cream sugar, butter and egg. Sift flour, salt and

baking powder together. Gradually add sifted ingredients and milk to batter, stirring constantly. Pour into 9x13 inch ungreased pan. On top, spread brown sugar; sprinkle generously with cinnamon. Dot closely with butter. Bake 25 minutes at 350°. Serve warm.

Mrs. Lydia Rieger, Harvey, N.D.

CINNAMON BUNDT CAKE

Mix together at high speed for 8 minutes:

1 pkg. yellow cake mix
1 pkg. vanilla instant
  pudding
3/4 c. Wesson oil
3/4 c. water

4 eggs
1 tsp. vanilla
1 tsp. imitation butter
  flavoring (optional)

Grease Bundt pan well with pastry brush. Sprinkle 1 cup nuts in pan; spread around. Nuts will cling to grease. Place 1/3 of batter in pan; sprinkle with cinnamon and sugar mixture. Place another 1/3 of mixture in pan; sprinkle with cinnamon and sugar. Place remaining 1/3 of batter in pan. Bake at 350° for 1 hour or more.

Anne Aune, Minneapolis, Mn.

CINNAMON CHOCOLATE CHIP CAKE
(Bundt)

1 pkg. yellow cake mix
1 pkg. instant vanilla
  pudding

4 eggs, beaten
1/2 c. oil
1 (8 oz.) ctn. sour cream

Beat 5-7 minutes. Mix:

1/2 c. sugar
6 oz. chocolate chips

2 tsp. cocoa
1 tsp. cinnamon

Grease Bundt pan or angel food pan; layer 1/3 cinnamon mix, 1/2 cake mix, 1/3 cinnamon mix, 1/2 cake mix and 1/3 cinnamon mix. Bake at 350° for 50-60 minutes.

Liz Tuft, St. Paul, Mn.

CRANBERRY CAKE
(Cut recipe in half for muffins)

3 Tbsp. butter, creamed
   with 1 c. sugar
1/2 c. evaporated milk
1/2 c. water
2 c. flour

3 tsp. baking powder
1 tsp. salt
4 c. (one 16 oz. pkg.) raw
   cranberries

Combine. Bake in 9x13 inch pan at 375° for 30 minutes. Serve with warm sauce.

Sauce:

1/2 lb. butter
2 c. sugar

1 c. evaporated milk
Vanilla

Anne Aune, Minneapolis, Mn.

CREME DE MENTHE CAKE

Mix 1 box of Duncan Hines white cake mix per instructions on box. Add 3 tablespoons green creme de menthe; mix. Bake per instructions on box; cool. Frost with Hershey's fudge topping (heat slightly so it will spread easily); let set for 1 hour. Top with 1 (8 ounce) carton Cool Whip, to which 3 to 5 tablespoons of creme de menthe has been added. Refrigerate.

Mavis Ann Hjielberg, St. Paul, Mn.
Similar recipe submitted by: Gloria Smith, Jackson, Mn.

CRUMBLE CAKE

2 c. brown sugar
2 c. flour
3/4 c. shortening

1 tsp. baking powder
1 c. chopped walnuts

Mix well; take out 1 cup for top of cake.

1 egg
1 c. sour milk

1/2 tsp. soda

Mix well; add to first mixture. Cover with the cup you left out. Bake at 350° for 40 minutes.

Mrs. Mel Kurvers, Chanhassen, Mn.

DELIGHTFUL CAKE OR BARS

Mix together in bowl:

1 yellow cake mix
4 eggs
1/2 c. oil

1 can mandarin oranges
(juice, too)

Beat 2 to 3 minutes with electric mixer. Bake cake in 9x13 inch pan for 35-40 minutes at 350°; bars in 10x15 inch pan for 20 minutes at 350°. Frost when cool with:

1 small pkg. instant vanilla
  pudding

1 (15 oz.) can crushed
  pineapple, juice and all

Cook until thick. Fold in 1/4 teaspoon lemon flavor and 9 ounces Cool Whip topping.

Ruth Eberlein, Luverne, Mn.

DEVILS FOOD CAKE

1 c. white sugar
1/2 c. shortening
2 eggs
2/3 c. milk
1 tsp. vanilla
1 2/3 c. flour

1/2 tsp. salt
1 tsp. soda
1 tsp. baking powder
1/2 c. cocoa, mixed with hot
  water to make thin paste

Add paste last. Bake at 350° until done.

Broiled on Frosting:

1 c. brown sugar
6 Tbsp. butter
1 c. chopped nuts

1/4 c. evaporated milk or
  cream
1 c. coconut

Spread on cooled cake; put under broiler until brown and bubbly, about 3 to 5 minutes.

Gemma Pierson, St. Cloud, Mn.

DIABETIC CAKE

1/2 c. dates
3/4 c. raisins

1 c. water

Boil together for 5 minutes. Add 1 stick of margarine. Mix together:

2 eggs
1 tsp. soda

1 tsp. vanilla
1/4 tsp. salt

1 c. flour   1 chopped apple
1/2 c. nuts

    Add fruit mix. Bake in 9x9 inch pan at 350° for 25 to
30 minutes, well greased pan.
Patricia Larson, Grafton, N.D.

DUMP CAKE

    In a large bowl, dump:

2 c. flour	1 can cherry pie filling
2 c. sugar	2 tsp. soda
2 eggs	1 c. nuts (optional)
1/2 c. oil	1 tsp. cinnamon
1 tsp. salt	1 tsp. vanilla

    Mix well; don't beat. Bake in a greased and floured
Bundt pan for 45-60 minutes in 350° oven. Remove from
pan; cool and drizzle with powdered sugar frosting.
Lois M. Brice, Omaha, Ne.

EMERGENCY CAKE WITH BROILED ICING

1 3/4 c. cake flour	1/3 c. shortening
1 c. sugar	2/3 c. milk (not too cold)
1/4 tsp. salt	1 egg
2 1/2 tsp. baking powder	1 tsp. flavoring

    Sift flour once before measuring. Sift flour, sugar,
salt and baking powder together. Measure milk into cup
and fill with softened shortening. Add these with unbeaten
egg to flour mixture; add flavoring. Beat well 2 or 3 minutes. Pour into greased and floured 8x8 inch pan. Bake
about 25 minutes at 350°.

    Broiled Icing:

3 Tbsp. melted butter	2 Tbsp. cream
5 Tbsp. brown sugar	1/2 c. shredded coconut

    Mix all together and spread on cake while still warm.
Place very low under broiler; broil until brown.
Mary Fingalson, Detroit Lakes, Mn.

FORGOTTEN CAKE

Preheat oven to 450°. Beat:

6 egg whites	1/2 tsp. cream of tartar
1 tsp. vanilla	Pinch of salt

When stiff, add 1 1/2 cups sugar very slowly; continue beating. Pack in Pyrex dish, 12x8 inches. Butter bottom of dish only. Place in preheated oven; turn off heat. Do not open oven until cold.

Lemon Custard for Meringue: Beat 6 egg yolks until very thick. Add 3/4 cup sugar, gradually; beat. Add 5 tablespoons lemon juice and 2 teaspoons rind. Cook in double boiler until thick. When cold, fold in 1 cup cream, whipped. Smooth over cooled meringue and let stand overnight before serving. Must be refrigerated.

Suzie Brainard, Minneapolis, Mn.

FRUIT CAKE

3 c. applesauce	2 c. sugar (brown or white -
1 c. shortening (Crisco,	I use brown)
margarine or butter)	

Boil above mixture 5 minutes; let stand overnight. Mix with the following ingredients:

4 1/2 c. flour	1/2 tsp. cloves
4 tsp. soda	1 lb. dates
1 tsp. nutmeg	1 lb. raisins
2 1/2 tsp. cinnamon	1/4 lb. nuts
1 tsp. salt	Candied fruit, as desired

Bake for 2 hours at 250°.

Mildred Sjastrom

FRUIT COCKTAIL CAKE

2 c. flour	2 tsp. soda
1 1/2 c. sugar	1 (No. 303) can fruit cocktail

Combine dry ingredients; add fruit cocktail. Beat well until fruit and dry ingredients are well blended. Bake in greased, floured 13x9x2 inch pan at 300° for 1 hour.

Icing:

1 stick oleo
1 c. sugar
1 tsp. vanilla

1/2 c. condensed milk
1 c. cocoanut
1/2 c. chopped nuts

Cook oleo, milk and sugar about 2 minutes. Add vanilla; remove from heat; add cocoanut and nuts. Run knife around edge of cake to loosen from the sides; also punch a few holes with a toothpick in cake so that the icing will seep into and around the edge. Ice while warm. (Stays moist for a long time if it stays around long.)

M.J. Nelson, Minneapolis, Mn.

Similar recipe submitted by: Eileen Rekowski, St. Cloud, Mn.

FRUIT COCKTAIL UPSIDE DOWN CAKE

1 pkg. Duncan Hines lemon
   supreme Deluxe cake mix
1/2 c. (1 stick) butter or
   margarine

1 c. brown sugar
1 (1 lb. 12 oz.) can fruit
   cocktail, drained
Whipped cream, if desired

Melt butter in a 13x9x2 inch pan; sprinkle brown sugar evenly in pan. Drain fruit cocktail; arrange fruit in sugar mixture. Mix cake as directed on the label; spread batter over fruit. Bake at 350° for about 45 to 50 minutes, until cake tests done with a toothpick. Let stand 5 minutes for topping to begin to set. Turn upside down onto a large platter or a cooky sheet. Serve pieces of cake, topped with whipped cream. Makes 12 to 16 servings.

When baking at high altitudes, use flour, water and baking temperature given on package side panel.

Lorraine Rieger, Minneapolis, Mn.

GERMAN CHOCOLATE CAKE

1 pkg. white cake mix
2 eggs
1 c. milk

1 c. water
1 pkg. instant chocolate
   pudding

Combine ingredients; prepare as directed on cake package.

Frosting:

1 c. evaporated milk
1 c. sugar

3 egg yolks
1/4 lb. butter or margarine

436

1 tsp. vanilla   1 1/2 c. coconut
1 c. pecans

Combine milk, sugar, egg yolks and vanilla; cook 10 minutes. Add pecans and coconut; spread on cake.

Marlys Swehla, Albert Lea, Mn.

GRANDMA'S FRENCH CAKE

1 box Pillsbury Plus   1 (13 oz.) can crushed
    lemon cake mix   pineapple (in its own
1/3 c. oil   juice, not syrup), drained
3 eggs   1/2 c. coconut (flaked)

Add pineapple juice. Beat about 3 minutes at medium speed. Bake in greased and floured 9x13 inch loaf tin for about 42 minutes or until cake leaves side of pan at 350°.

Mrs. H. Erickson, Minneapolis, Mn.

HEATH BAR CAKE

Mix:
1/4 lb. oleo   1/2 c. white sugar
1 c. brown sugar   2 c. flour

Take out 1/2 cup of this mixture. To the rest, add:

1 egg   1/2 tsp. salt
1 c. buttermilk   1 tsp. vanilla
1 tsp. soda

Pour this batter into a 9x13 inch greased, floured pan. Sprinkle over the batter the 1/2 cup of crumbs. Crush 6 Heath bars; sprinkle over the crumbs. Bake 30 minutes in 350° oven.

Gordy and Elaine Sneva, Brainerd, Mn.

HIDDEN TREASURE CUPCAKES

Filling:

1 (8 oz.) pkg. cream cheese   Pinch of salt
1 egg plus 1 egg yolk   1 (16 oz.) pkg. chocolate
1/2 c. sugar   chips

Combine ingredients and set aside.

Cake Batter:

1 1/2 c. flour
1 c. sugar
1/4 c. cocoa
3/4 tsp. soda
1/2 tsp. salt
3/4 c. water

1/3 c. salad oil
1 egg white
1 Tbsp. vinegar
Granulated sugar
Chopped nuts

For batter, combine first 5 ingredients in a bowl. Combine remaining ingredients, adding all at once to dry ingredients; mix well. Fill 24 paper lined muffin cups 1/3 full of cake batter. Top each with heaping teaspoonful of filling. Sprinkle with sugar and chopped nuts. Bake in a 350° oven for 30 to 35 minutes.

Dorothy Savig, Minneapolis, Mn.

LAZY DAISY CAKE

Beat 4 eggs lightly. Add 2 cups sugar; beat well. Add 2 cups cake flour, sifted with 2 teaspoons baking powder. Heat 1 cup milk to boiling point; add 2 tablespoons butter. Remove from heat; pour into first part of cake. Add 1 teaspoon vanilla. Bake at 350° for 30 minutes, or until done.

Icing:

6 Tbsp. melted butter
4 Tbsp. sweet cream

10 Tbsp. brown sugar
1 c. coconut or nuts or both

Spread over cake; put back into oven to brown. Use 9x13 inch pan. Icing is put on immediately when cake is removed from oven.

Ruth Rehschuh, Minneapolis, Mn.

LEMON LIME CAKE

1 box lemon cake mix
1 box lime gelatin
4 eggs
3/4 c. salad oil

3/4 c. water
Grated rind of 2 lemons
1/3 c. lemon juice
2 c. powdered sugar, sifted

Place first 5 ingredients in mixing bowl; beat for 4 minutes. Place in 9x13 inch pan. Bake at 350° for 40 minutes. Mix grated lemon rind and lemon juice with powdered sugar. Remove cake from oven; prick with fork 1 inch apart. Pour glaze over top. Serve plain or with whipped cream.

Stella Bliss, Minneapolis, Mn.

LEMON PUDDING CAKE

2 eggs, separated
1 tsp. grated lemon peel
1/4 c. lemon juice
2/3 c. milk

1 c. sugar
1/4 c. all-purpose flour
1/4 tsp. salt

Preheat oven to moderate temperature, 350°. Beat egg whites until stiff peaks form; beat egg yolks. Beat in lemon peel, juice and milk. Beat in remaining ingredients until smooth. Fold into beaten egg whites. Pour into 1 quart casserole; place in pan of hot water, 1 inch deep. Bake 45-50 minutes. Serve warm or cool and with whipped cream, if desired. Makes 6 servings.

Helen H. Clark, Grand Forks, N.D.

MALTED MILK CAKE

1 egg, beaten
1 c. sour cream (dairy)
1 tsp. vanilla
1 c. flour

1 1/2 c. malted milk powder
1/2 tsp. salt
1 tsp. soda

Stir eggs, sour cream and vanilla together. Sift dry ingredients together; add to first mixture. Pour into 8 inch square pan (no sugar). Bake at 350° for 25 minutes.

J. Pavnick, Minneapolis, Mn.

MANDARIN ORANGE CAKE

1 pkg. yellow cake mix
4 eggs

1/2 c. oil
1 can mandarin oranges and juice

Beat well with mixer; pour into greased and floured 9x13 inch pan. Bake at 350° for 30-35 minutes.

Frosting:

1 (15 oz.) can crushed pineapple, and juice

1 pkg. vanilla instant pudding (dry)

Fold 8 ounces Cool Whip into above. Frost cake. Store in refrigerator. Better if made the day before.

Cathy Rudolph, Grand Rapids, Mn.

Similar recipe submitted by: Grace Locke, St. Paul, Mn.

GRANNY PETERSEN'S MIDNIGHT CAKE

2 c. raisins   2 1/2 c. water

Bring water and raisins to a boil; let boil for 10 minutes. Add 1/2 cup margarine; remove from stove and let margarine melt. Meanwhile, mix:

2 c. sugar   1 tsp. soda
1 tsp. cinnamon   1 tsp. cloves
3 Tbsp. cocoa   1 tsp. nutmeg

Add first mixture to second mixture. Blend into above mixtures 1 teaspoon vanilla and 3 cups flour. When blended, add 1 cup liquid (sour cream, or add a few drops vinegar to half & half to sour). Grease and flour 13x9 inch pan. Bake at 350° for 1 hour. Cool and frost with Frosting for Midnight Cake.

Frosting for Midnight Cake:

1 c. sugar   6 tsp. cream
1 egg   3 Tbsp. cocoa

Mix together in saucepan; heat over low heat till it comes to boil, stirring constantly. Boil 2 minutes. Remove from heat; add 1 tablespoon butter and 1 teaspoon vanilla. Stir until thick enough to spread; will thicken as it cools. Frost Midnight Cake.

Jeanne Shaver, Minneapolis, Mn.

MOUNTAIN CAKE

6 egg yolks, beaten   1 c. nuts
1 c. white sugar   3/4 c. cream of wheat
1 c. brown sugar   1/2 tsp. baking powder
1 c. dry bread crumbs, cut   6 egg whites
    fine (I use rolling pin)

Mix above ingredients together; mix it well. It will be a stiff paste; add the 6 beaten egg whites last. Mix. Pour in greased 9x13 inch cake pan. Bake 30 minutes at 350°.
To prepare: Crumble the cake with your fingers or a fork and use whipped cream or Cool Whip. Rotate layers of crumbs, layer of whipped cream, etc. Repeat with layers until it's shaped like a mountain. Garnish with cream on top, nuts and maraschino cherries. Very good. Better to make it the day before. Keeps several days in refrigerator.

Patricia Larson, Grafton, N.D.

OATMEAL CAKE

Mix all on stove in a 3 quart pan. After mixing, bake at 350° for 25 minutes in 9x13 inch pan. Bring to a boil:

1 c. quick oatmeal	1 1/2 c. water

Add:

1 c. brown sugar	1 tsp. salt
1 c. white sugar	1 tsp. soda
1/2 c. margarine	1 1/3 c. flour
2 eggs	1 tsp. vanilla
2 tsp. cinnamon	

Topping:

2/3 c. melted margarine	1/2 c. milk
1 1/3 c. brown sugar	1 c. oatmeal

Will be runny. Pour on top of cake, after baking. Broil until crispy and tinged brown.

Linda Hamann, Minneapolis, Mn.

OATMEAL BANANA CUPCAKES

Mix together:

1/2 c. sugar	2 eggs
1/2 c. margarine	

Add:

3 bananas, mashed (equals 1 c.)	3/4 c. honey

Sift together:

1 1/2 c. flour	1 tsp. soda
1 tsp. baking powder	1/2 tsp. salt

Add to above. Add 1 cup quick cooking rolled oats and 1 teaspoon vanilla; mix oats in by hand. Fill paper cupcakes 2/3 full. Makes 24. Shake powdered sugar on top. Bake at 350° for 18 to 20 minutes.

Marion Round, Faribault, Mn.

ORANGE DATE CAKE

1 c. brown sugar
3/4 c. shortening
2 eggs, beaten
5 Tbsp. milk
1 tsp. soda
1 3/4 c. flour
Pinch of salt

1 tsp. vanilla
1/2 lb. dates
1/2 c. sugar
1 c. water
2 Tbsp. flour and 20 orange
   slices of candy

Mix first 7 ingredients; pour half in greased 9x13 inch pan. Boil dates, sugar and water; thicken with 2 tablespoons flour. Cool. Pour date mixture over batter in cake pan; slice the 20 orange candies on top. Add rest of batter and bake 45 minutes in 350° oven; cool. Cut in small squares and powder with powdered sugar. Very good.

Goldie Mikish, Staples, Mn.

PICNIC CAKE

1 c. sugar
1/2 c. shortening
2 eggs
1 1/2 c. flour
Heaping Tbsp. of cocoa

1/2 tsp. salt
1 tsp. soda
1 1/2 c. hot water
1 c. finely chopped dates

Add dates to hot water; let stand till cool. Add soda to the mixture. Cream sugar, shortening and eggs. Put date mixture into this. Add cocoa, flour and sugar. Pour into floured, greased pan, 9x13 inches. Sprinkle topping over cake.

Topping:

Scant 1/2 c. sugar
1/2 pkg. chocolate chips

1/2 c. nuts or pecan halves

Bake at 350° for 25 minutes.

Ollie Kearney, Rochester, Mn.

PIE CAKE

1/4 c. oil
1 pkg. white or yellow
   cake mix (dry)

1/2 c. water
2 eggs
1 can pie filling (any fruit
   flavor)

In 9x13 inch pan, swirl oil. Put in dry cake mix. Make a well; add eggs and water. With a rubber spatula, mix well and spread smooth. Drizzle filling over top; swirl in. If using for a coffee cake, sprinkle with cinnamon-sugar before baking. If you want it for a dessert, leave off sugar. Bake at 350° for 30-40 minutes, or until light brown. Serve topped with whipped cream.

Ann Christensen, Litchfield, Mn.

PINA COLADA CAKE

1/3 c. Bacardi dark rum	4 eggs
1 small pkg. coconut cream instant pudding mix	1/2 c. water
	1/4 c. oil
1 pkg. white cake mix	1 c. flaked coconut

Blend all ingredients, except coconut, in large mixer bowl; beat 4 minutes at medium speed of electric mixer. Pour into two greased and floured 9 inch layer pans. Bake at 350° for 25 to 30 minutes or until cake springs back when lightly pressed. Do not underbake. Cool in pan 15 minutes; remove and cool on racks. Fill and frost; sprinkle with coconut. Chill. Refrigerate leftover cake.

Pina Colada Frosting: Combine in bowl -

1 (8 oz.) can crushed pineapple, in juice	1 small pkg. coconut cream instant pudding mix
	1/3 c. Bacardi dark rum

Beat until well blended. Fold in 1 (9 ounce) container whipped topping, thawed.

Grace Locke, St. Paul, Mn.

QUICK PINEAPPLE CAKE

2 c. flour	Pinch of salt
1 1/2 c. sugar	1 (No. 2) can pineapple with juice
2 tsp. soda	

Stir all together; pour into greased and floured 9x13 inch pan.

1/2 c. nuts, chopped	1/2 c. brown sugar

Sprinkle over cake. Bake in 350° oven for 30 minutes. Pour glaze over hot cake (follows).

Glaze:

3/4 c. sugar   1 small can evaporated milk
1/2 c. oleo

Boil ingredients together 10 minutes; pour over cake.
Dee Olson, St. Paul, Mn.

PINEAPPLE UP-SIDE-DOWN CAKE

1/2 c. butter, melted   1 c. brown sugar
1 small can pineapple rings,   1/3 c. maraschino cherries
  drained (save)

Spread evenly over bottom of round Up-Side-Down
pan. Lay a complete wheel of pineapple in center of pan.
Put cherry in center and place 1/2 wheels in a circle around
center wheel; place cherries around. Make the following
batter:

3 egg yolks, beaten   1 c. flour
1 c. sugar   1 tsp. baking powder
5 Tbsp. pineapple juice   3 egg whites, stiffly beaten

Into beaten egg yolks, add sugar and pineapple juice.
Sift in flour and baking powder; fold into stiffly beaten egg
whites. Pour over fruit. Bake at 350° for 45 minutes to 1
hour. Invert immediately.
Lorraine Rieger, Minneapolis, Mn.

PISTACHIO CREME CAKE

1 pkg. Betty Crocker sour   3 eggs, slightly beaten
  cream cake mix   1 c. salad oil
1 pkg. pistachio instant   1 c. charged or regular water
  pudding mix   1/2 c. chopped nuts

Beat for 4 minutes; put in greased pan, 9x13 inches.
Bake for 30 to 40 minutes in 350° oven.

Frosting:

1 pkg. instant pistachio   1 env. Dream Whip or 1 (9
  pudding   oz.) container Cool Whip

If using Dream Whip, add 1 1/2 cups milk; beat until
thick. If using Cool Whip, defrost and whip 1/2 cup milk
with Cool Whip. Spread on cool cake; sprinkle with chopped
nuts and cocoanut.
Esther Mungovan, Duluth, Mn.

POOR MAN'S CAKE

2 c. sugar
1 c. shortening
2 c. water
2 c. raisins
2 tsp. cinnamon

1/4 tsp. ground cloves
1 tsp. soda
1 tsp. salt
3 c. flour
1 c. chopped walnuts

Combine first 4 ingredients in a saucepan; bring almost to a boil. Simmer 15-20 minutes, until raisins are soft. Put aside until cool. Mix flour and spices; add thoroughly cooled raisin mixture. Pour into a greased and floured 13x9x2 inch pan. Bake at 350° until cake springs back at the touch, about 35-40 minutes. A cream frosting may be used. Keeps well for shipment overseas if made in a coffee can and not frosted.

Georgine Isakson, Fargo, N.D.
Similar recipe submitted by: Mary Fingalson, Detroit Lakes, Mn.

POPPY SEED CAKE

1 pkg. yellow cake mix
4 eggs
1/2 c. salad oil

1 pkg. coconut cream instant
    pudding mix
1 c. hot water
1/4 c. poppy seeds

Mix all ingredients together. Bake for 50 minutes at 350°.

Blanche B. Masica, Minneapolis, Mn.
Similar recipe submitted by: Evelyn Swing, Anoka, Mn.

POUND CAKE

1/2 lb. butter and 1/2 c.
    Crisco, creamed with
    3 c. sugar
5 eggs, added one at a time

3 c. cake flour
1/2 tsp. baking powder
Pinch of salt
1 c. milk

Alternate flour mixture and milk to butter and sugar mixture. Add 1 teaspoon vanilla. Bake 1 1/2 hours at 325°.

Elizabeth Redmond, Long Prairie, Mn.

ELVIS PRESLEY'S CAKE DELUXE

2 c. brown sugar   1/4 c. margarine
1/4 c. butter   1 c. oatmeal (quick cooking)

Pour 1 cup of boiling water over the above; let stand 2 minutes. Sift together:

1 c. flour   1 tsp. cinnamon
1/2 tsp. allspice   1 tsp. soda
1/2 tsp. salt

Add 1/2 cup chopped dates and 1/2 cup chopped nuts to first mixture; stir well. Mix dry ingredients together; add to first mixture a little at a time. Mix thoroughly until all is mixed together. Pour into a slightly greased 10x10 inch cake pan. Sprinkle top of cake with an additional 1/4 cup chopped nuts. Bake 40 minutes in a 350° oven.

Mrs. Norma Applen, Minneapolis, Mn.

PRUNE CAKE AND TOPPING

2 c. flour   2 c. sugar
1 tsp. soda   1 c. oil
1 tsp. salt   1 c. buttermilk
1 tsp. cinnamon   1 tsp. vanilla
1/2 tsp. allspice   1 c. cooked, chopped prunes
1 tsp. nutmeg   1 c. chopped nuts

Sift dry ingredients; add sugar, milk, eggs, oil and vanilla. Beat until smooth. Stir in nuts and prunes. Bake 45 minutes at 350° in 9x13 inch pan.

Topping:

1 c. sugar   1 c. buttermilk
1 tsp. soda   1/2 c. butter

Bring to boil. Poke cake full of holes with a fork. Spoon topping on hot cake until all is used up.

Mary Pintar, Gilbert, Mn.

*   *   *   *   *

DESSERTS
"Desserts from the south,
North, east and west
Though left 'til the last
Are often the best."
Helen-May Johnson

446

PUMPKIN CAKE ROLL

Beat 3 eggs on high speed for 5 minutes. Gradually beat in 1 cup white sugar. Stir in 2/3 cup pumpkin and 1 teaspoon lemon juice. Stir together:

3/4 c. flour	1 tsp. ginger
1/2 tsp. baking powder	1/2 tsp. salt
2 tsp. cinnamon	1/2 tsp. nutmeg

Fold in pumpkin; spread in jelly roll pan. Top with 1 cup very fine nuts. Bake at 375° for 15 minutes. Turn out on towel and sprinkle with powdered sugar. Starting at narrow end, roll towel and cake together; cool. Unroll; fill with:

1 c. powdered sugar	4 Tbsp. butter
6 oz. cream cheese	1/2 tsp. vanilla

Beat till smooth. Spread on cake and reroll. Chill before serving. Cut in slices as for jelly roll.

Joan Norton, Hibbing, Mn.

GILDED PUMPKIN CAKE

2 c. flour	1/2 c. butter or margarine
1 tsp. baking powder	(or 1/4 c. each)
1 tsp. baking soda	1 c. sugar
1 tsp. grated lemon peel	2 eggs
1/2 tsp. salt	3/4 c. sour cream
1/2 c. packed brown sugar	1 c. pureed pumpkin (fresh
2 tsp. cinnamon	cooked or canned)
1 tsp. allspice	1 tsp. vanilla
1/2 c. chopped walnuts	Rum glaze (optional)
	(recipe follows)

Stir together flour, baking powder, soda, lemon peel and salt; set aside. Stir together brown sugar, cinnamon, allspice and walnuts; set aside. In large bowl of mixer, cream butter and sugar until fluffy. Beat in eggs one at a time until mixture is very light. At low speed of mixer or with rubber scraper, stir in flour mixture alternately with sour cream and pumpkin. Stir in vanilla. Spoon about 1/3 of the batter into greased, floured 9 or 10 inch fluted or plain tube pan. Sprinkle with 1/3 of the brown sugar mixture. Repeat layers twice. Bake in preheated 350° oven for 40 to 60 minutes or until pick inserted halfway between tube and side of pan comes out clean. Cool cake in pan on rack 10 minutes, then invert on rack. While cake is still warm, drizzle lightly with Rum Glaze. Makes 16 servings.

Rum Glaze: Mix 1 1/4 cups confectioners sugar and 1 tablespoon light rum with 1 tablespoon water until smooth.

Margaret McKenney, Minneapolis, Mn.

PUMPKIN PECAN CAKE

1 spice cake mix	3 eggs
1 c. canned pumpkin	1 tsp. cinnamon
1/2 c. cooking oil	1/2 c. water
1 pkg. vanilla instant pudding mix	1/2 c. chopped pecans

Combine first 7 ingredients; beat at medium speed for 5 minutes. Fold in nuts. Pour into greased and floured Bundt pan. Bake at 350° for 40-45 minutes. Cool, then remove. Serve with whipped cream.

Grayce Funke, Minneapolis, Mn.

RAISIN CAKE

1 c. white sugar	2 c. flour
1/2 c. shortening	2 tsp. soda
2 eggs	

Mix these ingredients; it will be real thick. Add 1 can raisin pie filling, 1 teaspoon vanilla and 1/2 cup walnuts. Bake 40-45 minutes in 9x13 inch pan in 350° oven.

Frosting: Boil -

1 c. brown sugar	4 Tbsp. cream
4 Tbsp. butter	

Bring to full boil. Add about 1 3/4 cups powdered sugar and 1/2 teaspoon vanilla.

Mrs. Harry Osborn, Rochester, Mn.

Similar recipe submitted by: Mrs. Norma Applen, Minneapolis, Mn.

AMAZIN RAISIN CAKE

3 c. flour
2 c. sugar
1 c. real mayonnaise
1/2 c. milk
2 eggs
2 tsp. soda
1 1/2 tsp. cinnamon

1/2 tsp. ground nutmeg
1/2 tsp. salt
1/4 tsp. ground cloves
3 c. chopped, peeled apples
1 c. raisins
1 c. walnuts

Grease and flour two 9 inch round baking pans. In large bowl, mixing at low speed, beat the first 10 ingredients for 10 minutes. Batter will be very thick. Stir in apples, raisins and walnuts. Bake at 350° for 45 minutes; test for doneness. Frost with Cream Cheese Frosting.

Lila Houser, Aitkin, Mn.

RASPBERRY CAKE

3 eggs
1 c. sugar
1/4 tsp. salt
1 c. dairy sour cream

1 tsp. soda
1 3/4 c. flour
1 - 1 1/2 pt. raspberries, washed, well drained

Beat the eggs, sour cream, 1/2 cup of the sugar, soda and salt together. Add flour; beat well again. Pour batter into a well greased 9x13 inch pan. Spread the well drained berries on top of batter; sprinkle rest of sugar on top. Bake at 350° for 30 minutes. Whipped cream or ice cream may be used over top. Can be reheated.

Joan Norton, Hibbing, Mn.

ROBERT REDFORD CAKE

1 c. flour
1/2 c. butter
1 c. chopped pecans
1 (8 oz.) pkg. cream cheese, softened (do not buy softened)
1 c. powdered sugar

1 (8 oz.) ctn. frozen whipped topping
1 large pkg. instant vanilla pudding
1 large pkg. instant chocolate pudding)
3 c. milk
1 small Hershey's bar

1. Mix flour, butter and pecans until crumbly. 2. Press into 9x13 inch pan. Bake at 350° for 15-20 minutes; let cool. 3. Make mixture of cream cheese, powdered sugar and 1/2 of whipped topping. Whip together with

fork. Spread on cooled crust. 4. Mix puddings with milk until smooth and thickened; spread over cream cheese mixture. Spread on rest of whipped topping. 5. Sprinkle with grated Hershey's bar. Refrigerate until served.

Dorothy Savig, Minneapolis, Mn.

RHUBARB CAKE

1/2 c. shortening	2 c. flour
1 1/2 c. sugar	1 tsp. soda
1 egg, unbeaten	1/2 tsp. salt (optional)
1 tsp. vanilla	1 c. sour milk or buttermilk

Cream 1/2 cup shortening and sugar; add egg and vanilla. Add flour, soda, salt and milk; fold in rhubarb. Sprinkle 1/4 cup sugar and 1 teaspoon cinnamon on top. Bake 45 minutes at 350° in 9x13 inch pan.

Marion Vonesh, Grand Forks, N.D.

RICH AND GOOEY CAKE

Cut 1/4 pound soft oleo or butter into a yellow cake mix. Add 2 eggs; mix well. Spread into greased 9x13 inch pan. Cream 1 (8 ounce) package cream cheese and 1 pound powdered sugar. Add 1 teaspoon vanilla and 2 slightly beaten eggs; pour over batter. Bake at 350° for 35 to 40 minutes. Do not frost.

Esther Stevens, Council Bluffs, Ia.

RHUBARB CAKE

1 1/2 c. brown sugar	1 c. sour milk
1/2 c. shortening	2 c. sifted flour
1 egg	1/2 c. or more diced rhubarb
1/4 tsp. salt	(I use 2-3 c. rhubarb)
1 tsp. soda	1 tsp. vanilla

Mix in order given. Bake in greased and floured 9x13 inch pan. Sprinkle top with a mixture of 1/2 cup sugar, 1 teaspoon cinnamon and nuts. Bake at 350° for 35 to 40 minutes.

D. Klosterman, Anoka, Mn.

Similar recipes submitted by: Margaret McKenney, Minneapolis, Mn., Mary Paul, Minneapolis, Mn., Ruth Lee, Detroit Lakes, Mn., Mary Daly, St. Paul, Mn., Katie Wenninger

YUMMY RHUBARB CAKE

2 c. flour	1/2 tsp. allspice
1 1/4 c. sugar	1/4 tsp. cloves
1 tsp. soda	1 tsp. cinnamon
1 tsp. salt	

Combine dry ingredients; cut in 1/2 cup shortening as for pie crust. Add:

2 eggs	2 c. diced rhubarb
1/3 c. milk	

Place in greased pan, 9x13 inches. Mix together and sprinkle on top:

2/3 c. flour	4 Tbsp. butter
1/2 c. brown sugar	1/2 c. chopped nuts

Bake 40 minutes at 350°.

Goldie Mikish, Staples, Mn.

RHUBARB COBBLER

1 1/4 c. sugar	1/2 c. water
2 Tbsp. cornstarch	6 c. rhubarb
1/2 c. orange juice	2 Tbsp. butter

Mix dry ingredients; add orange juice and water. Cook over low heat till it boils. Add rhubarb and butter; heat together for a few minutes. Pour in 11x7x2 inch pan. Spoon Biscuit Topping on. Bake at 425° for 25 minutes.

Biscuit Topping:

1 c. flour	2 Tbsp. sugar
1 1/2 tsp. baking powder	1/2 tsp. salt

Cut in 2 tablespoons shortening and 1 tablespoon butter. Add 1/2 cup milk. Mix all together; spoon over rhubarb.

Marion Round, Faribault, Mn.

"RUM CAKE"

1 pkg. yellow cake mix	1/2 c. oil
(Duncan Hines or	1/2 c. rum
Betty Crocker)	1/2 c. water
4 eggs	1 small pkg. instant vanilla pudding

Mix all together, except rum, oil and water, which is mixed separately. Put in with the rest. Beat only 2 minutes. Place in well greased and floured Bundt pan. Bake 1 hour at 325°. Take out of oven; let stand in pan 5 minutes, then pour on hot glaze and let stand in pan 30 minutes before removing.

Hot Glaze: Boil 2 to 3 minutes -

1/4 c. water   1 c. sugar
1/4 c. rum   1 stick margarine
    V. Robbs, Minneapolis, Mn.

Similar recipes submitted by: Mary Paul, Minneapolis, Mn., Eloise Hoff, Preston, Mn.

SCRIPTURE CAKE

1/2 c. Judges 5:25 (butter)
1 c. Jeremiah 6:20 (sugar)
3 Isaiah 10:14 (eggs)
3 Tbsp. I Samuel 14:25
 (honey)
1/2 tsp. Leviticus 2:13 (salt)
2 c. I Kings 4:22 (flour)
1/2 c. Judges 4:19 (milk)

2 tsp. Amos 4:5 (baking
 powder)
2 tsp. II Chronicles 9:9 (1
 each, cinnamon, nutmeg)
1 c. Nahum 3:12 (figs,
 chopped)
1 c. Numbers 17:8 (sliced
 almonds)
1 c. I Samuel 30:12 (raisins)

Cream butter and sugar; add honey and beaten yolks. Add remaining dry ingredients, mixed together, alternately with milk. Stir in fruit and nuts. Fold in beaten egg whites last. Bake at 325° for about 45 minutes in a 9x13 inch pan. Serve with whipped cream topping.
    Georgine Isakson, Fargo, N.D.

SHERRY BUNDT CAKE

1 yellow cake mix   3/4 c. sherry
3/4 c. oil   4 eggs

Mix first 3 ingredients, then add eggs one at a time. Bake in large Bundt pan, greased and floured, for 1 hour at 325° (low rack).
    M. Paul, Minneapolis, Mn.
Similar recipe submitted by: Diane Haan, Bismarck, N.D.

SNICKER BAR CAKE

Mix 1 package German sweet chocolate cake mix according to directions. Pour half the batter into a greased 9x13 inch pan. Bake 20 minutes at 350°. Melt 30 Kraft caramels with 1 stick margarine and 1 tablespoon milk over low heat. Pour over top of baked cake. Spread 3/4 cup chocolate chips over caramel topping, then sprinkle with 1 cup chopped nuts. Spread rest of batter over this mixture; bake 10 to 20 minutes, testing with finger for doneness. Serve with ice cream or whipped cream. It's delicious served warm.

Ruth Roemeling, Luverne, Mn.

SNO-BALL CAKE

Bake 1 white cake mix in two 8 inch layer pans; cut layers in halves with thread to make 4 layers.

Frosting:

8 oz. sour cream	14 oz. coconut
13 oz. Cool Whip	1 c. white sugar

Combine sour cream, Cool Whip and sugar; beat well. Add coconut. Frost cake and trim as desired. Refrigerate for 2 days before serving so the flavor goes throughout.

Judy Raye, Fargo, N.D.

SOUTHERN PICKLING PIG CAKE

Mix in mixer:

1 yellow cake mix	1/4 c. water
1 small can mandarin oranges plus 1/2 of juice	4 eggs
1/2 orange or 1/2 c. orange juice	1/2 c. oil
	1/2 c. coconut

Pour into three 9 inch cake pans. Bake at 325° for 25 minutes.

Frosting:

1 (9 oz.) ctn. Cool Whip	1 (15 oz.) can crushed
1 pkg. vanilla pudding	pineapple in juice

Mix and spread on cake. Sprinkle on coconut. Refrigerate for 2 days. "It's delicious, believe me."

Winnie Johnson, St. Paul, Mn.

SOUTHERN YAMMY CAKE

3 c. sifted cake flour
3 tsp. baking powder
1 tsp. ground cinnamon
1 tsp. ground ginger
1 tsp. ground nutmeg
2 c., less 2 Tbsp., vegetable oil
1 c. firmly packed dark brown sugar

1 1/2 c. granulated sugar
5 eggs, separated
5 Tbsp. very hot water
2 Tbsp. bourbon (optional)
1 c. finely chopped pecans
2 1/2 c. grated fresh yams (about 2 medium)
1/2 tsp. salt
1 tsp. cream of tartar

1. Grease and lightly flour a 10x4 inch angel food cake pan. Sift flour, baking powder, cinnamon, ginger and nutmeg onto wax paper. 2. Combine oil, granulated sugar and brown sugar in a large mixing bowl; beat with electric mixer until smooth. Beat in egg yolks, one at a time, then the hot water. Beat mixture for 3 minutes at high speed until smooth and creamy. 3. Stir in 1/4 of the flour at a time, then the bourbon (optional). Blend in the pecans and yams until well mixed. Batter will be heavy. 4. Beat the egg whites with the salt and cream of tartar in a small bowl until soft peaks form. Stir 1/4 of the egg white mixture into the cake batter, then carefully fold in the remainder until streaks of egg white disappear. Spoon batter into the prepared pan. 5. Bake in a moderate oven, 350°, for 1 hour and 15 minutes until top springs back when lightly pressed with fingertips. Cool in pan on a wire rack for 20 minutes; remove from pan to cool completely.

Note: This cake can also be baked in a 9x13 inch loaf pan.

Mrs. Harold E. Erickson, Minneapolis, Mn.

GRANDMA'S SPICE CAKE

1 c. white sugar
1/2 c. shortening
2 eggs
1/2 c. molasses
2 1/4 c. flour
1 tsp. cinnamon

1/2 tsp. salt
1/2 tsp. nutmeg
1/2 tsp. allspice or ginger
1 tsp. soda in 1 c. hot water

Raisins may be added. Bake at 350° until done.

Gemma Pierson, St. Cloud, Mn.

SPONGE CAKE

1 1/2 c. sifted flour
1 tsp. baking powder
1/2 tsp. salt
6 egg yolks
1 1/2 c. sugar

1/3 c. cold water
2 tsp. vanilla
1 tsp. lemon flavoring
6 egg whites
1/2 tsp. cream of tartar

Sift flour, baking powder and salt together; set aside. Beat egg yolks in large bowl until thick, then beat in sugar gradually. Add dry ingredients alternately with water and flavoring. In large bowl, beat egg whites and cream of tartar until stiff. Gently fold egg yolk mixture into beaten whites. Pour into ungreased angel food pan. Bake at 325° for 60 to 65 minutes; invert to cool.

Lorraine Rieger, Minneapolis, Mn.
Similar recipe submitted by: Vi Geving, Duluth, Mn.

DELUXE STRAWBERRY CAKE

1 pkg. strawberry cake mix
(white or yellow can be used)
1 (3 oz.) pkg. strawberry gelatin
1/2 tsp. salt

3/4 box frozen sliced strawberries, thawed
4 eggs
2 Tbsp. flour
1/2 c. water
3/4 c. cooking oil

Mix together cake mix, gelatin, flour, salt, eggs, oil and water; beat at medium speed on mixer for 2 minutes. Add strawberries, including syrup; beat 1 minute. Put in greased, floured pan and bake at 350° until done, 35 to 40 minutes.

Strawberry Butter Frosting:

1/2 c. butter
1/2 tsp. vanilla
1 (1 lb.) box powdered sugar

1/4 box frozen sliced strawberries, thawed

Beat butter in mixer until smooth; add sugar alternately with berries, including syrup (may have to watch so that it doesn't get too thin). Beat until smooth; add vanilla. If frosting seems too thick, thin with a small amount of milk. (Leftover icing keeps well in refrigerator.)

M.J. Nelson, Minneapolis, Mn.
Similar recipe submitted by: Gloria Smith, Jackson, Mn.

STRAWBERRY PRESERVE PARTY CAKE

Sift together:

3 c. flour	1 tsp. baking powder
1 tsp. salt	3 Tbsp. cocoa
1 tsp. soda	1 tsp. cinnamon

Cream together till light and fluffy 2/3 cup Crisco and 1 1/2 cups sugar; add 3 eggs, one at a time. Add 1 cup strawberry preserves and beat 2 minutes. Add dry ingredients with 1 cup sour milk. Fold in 1/2 cup chopped pecans. Cool and frost with Creamy Frosting.

K., St. Cloud, Mn.

SUPER WHITE COCOANUT CAKE

Bake any white cake mix per directions on box. When baked, remove from oven and poke holes in top of cake with straw the size of pencil. Heat (do not boil):

1 c. milk	1 tsp. vanilla
1/2 c. white sugar	

Pour over cake while warm. Cool above, then frost with 1 large container of Cool Whip. Top with cocoanut and refrigerate. Moist and delicious.

Dorothy S. James, Excelsior, Mn.

TORTEN CAKE
(Two Layers)

Roll 25 graham crackers fine. Mix with 3 teaspoons baking powder and 1/2 cup flour. Cream 1 tablespoon butter and 1 cup sugar. Mix 3 egg yolks, beaten, to a cream. Add 1 cup milk; stir well. Add 1 teaspoon vanilla and 3 egg whites, beaten until stiff. Add 1 cup cocoanut; fold in. Spoon into floured baking tins. Bake 40 minutes in a slow oven.

Filling and Frosting:

1 1/2 Tbsp. butter	1 1/2 c. powdered sugar

Cream and add 1/2 tablespoon cocoa and 3 tablespoons strong black coffee (cold). Cream until smooth. Add more coffee when necessary.

Charlotte Bailey, St. Paul, Mn.

TWINKIE CAKE

1 yellow or chocolate cake mix	1 c. water
	1/3 c. oil
1 pkg. vanilla or chocolate instant pudding	3 eggs
	1/2 tsp. salt

Or, use 1 pudding cake mix and follow directions on box.

Pour batter in wax paper lined 9x13 inch cake pan. Bake at 350° for 35-40 minutes. When cake is cool, remove from pan; slice lengthwise with thread. Spread filling between layers and sprinkle top with powdered sugar.

Filling:

5 Tbsp. flour	1/2 c. Crisco
1 c. water	2 tsp. vanilla
1 c. sugar	1/2 c. oleo

Combine flour and water; cook until thick. Cool in refrigerator. Combine sugar, oleo, Crisco and vanilla; beat until thick and fluffy. Add cooled mixture; beat again until fluffy and spread on cake.

Myrtle Bohline, Gamaliel, Ar.

TYROLEAN HARD CAKE

2 1/2 c. all-purpose flour	1 tsp. vanilla extract
1 c. plus 1 Tbsp. sugar	1/2 c. butter, softened
2 tsp. baking powder	1 1/2 c. finely chopped
1 tsp. salt	walnuts
2 tsp. almond extract	2 eggs

In large bowl, combine flour, 1 cup sugar, baking powder and salt; stir together well. Add extracts, butter, nuts and eggs; stir with wooden spoon until well mixed. Grease a 9 or 10 inch round cake pan. Preheat oven to 350° F. Roll dough into 1 inch balls; arrange in circular pattern to fill pan. Sprinkle 1 tablespoon sugar on top. Bake 50 minutes or until lightly browned on top. Makes 5 to 6 dozen, about 65 calories each.

Anne Aune, Minneapolis, Mn.

WACKY CAKE

3 c. flour
2 c. sugar
1 tsp. salt

2 tsp. soda
1/2 c. cocoa

Sift into ungreased cake pan, 9x13 inches. Pour over all:

2 Tbsp. vinegar
2/3 c. oil

1 tsp. vanilla
2 c. cold water

Stir until smooth. Bake at 350° for 35-40 minutes.
Mary Paul, Minneapolis, Mn.

YELLOW LOAF CAKE

1 pkg. yellow cake mix
  (no pudding in mix)
1 pkg. instant vanilla
  pudding

3/4 c. Crisco oil
3/4 c. water
4 eggs

Put all in mixer; beat 8 minutes. Add 1 teaspoon vanilla and 1 teaspoon butter extract. Put in 2 bread loaf pans. Mix 1/4 cup sugar and 2 teaspoons cinnamon; sprinkle over top. Swirl through batter with a knife to make marble effect. Bake at 350°.
Mary Fingalson, Detroit Lakes, Mn.

ZUCCHINI CHOCOLATE CAKE

1/2 c. oleo
1/2 c. oil
2 eggs
1 tsp. vanilla
1 tsp. cinnamon
1/2 c. sour milk

2 c. shredded zucchini
1 3/4 c. sugar
2 1/2 c. flour
4 Tbsp. cocoa
1 tsp. soda
1 tsp. salt

Mix together. Bake at 325° for 45 minutes in 9x13 inch greased and floured pan. Frost with:

1 c. sugar
5 Tbsp. butter

1/3 c. milk

Bring to boil 1 minute; add 1/2 cup chocolate chips.
Betty Olson, St. Paul, Mn.
Similar recipe submitted by: Margaret McKenney, Minneapolis, Mn.

CHEESE CAKE

2 lb. dry cottage cheese	2 Tbsp. flour
1 c. sugar	1 tsp. vanilla
1 1/2 tsp. salt	

Mash the above until fine like corn meal. Add 4 large eggs; beat until creamy. Mix in 1 pint whipping cream or regular cream. Take 30 graham crackers (Sunshine's best) and 1/4 pound melted butter. Roll crackers with rolling pin; add melted butter. Line bottom of 8x10 or 9x13 inch pan with half of this mixture. Put cottage cheese mixture on crust; top with remaining cracker mixture. Bake at 350° for 1 hour until firm.

Mary Paul, Minneapolis, Mn.

CHEESE CAKE

8 oz. cream cheese, room temperature	1/3 c. reconstituted lemon juice
1 can sweetened condensed milk	1 tsp. vanilla

Whip cream cheese until fluffy; add milk. Blend until smooth. Put vanilla in lemon juice; add to cream cheese mixture. Put in graham cracker crust; chill. Add your favorite canned fruit pie filling.

Jackie Jaenisch, Windom, Mn.

BUSY DAY CHEESECAKE

1 (8 oz.) pkg. cream cheese	2 c. whole milk
1 pkg. Jell-O lemon instant pudding	1 (8 inch) graham cracker crust

Stir cream cheese until very soft; blend in 1/2 cup milk. Add remaining milk and the pudding mix. Beat slowly with egg beater just until well mixed, about 1 minute; do not overbeat. Pour at once into graham cracker crust; chill 1 hour. Spread blueberry or cherry pie filling on top. Serves 8. Store in refrigerator.

Helen Martin, Fargo, N.D.

CREAMY BAKED CHEESECAKE

1/4 c. margarine, melted
1 c. graham cracker crumbs
1/4 c. sugar
2 (8 oz.) pkg. softened
   cream cheese
3 eggs

1 (14 oz.) can sweetened
   condensed milk
1/4 tsp. salt
1/4 c. lemon juice
1 (8 oz.) container sour
   cream (optional)

Preheat oven to 300°. Combine margarine, crumbs and sugar; pat firmly on bottom of buttered 9 inch spring form pan (or 8 inch square cake pan). In large mixer bowl, beat cheese until fluffy. Beat in condensed milk, eggs and salt until smooth. Stir in lemon juice; pour mixture into prepared pan. Bake 50-55 minutes or until cake springs back when lightly touched. Cool to room temperature; chill. If using sour cream, spread on top of cheesecake. Top with fruit, if desired. Keep refrigerated.

Joan Dinius, Coon Rapids, Mn.

FROZEN CHEESE CAKE

Cream together 1 (8 ounce) package Philadelphia cream cheese, at room temperature, and 1 cup sugar. Add 3 egg yolks; beat well. Add 1 cup cream, whipped. Fold in 3 beaten egg whites and vanilla. Crush 20 graham crackers; mix with 4 teaspoons melted oleo. Put part of cracker mixture in 8x8 inch pan; add cream mixture, then rest of cracker mixture. Freeze at least 24 hours. Prepare Currant-Raspberry Junket as on package; put on top of frozen mixture when serving.

Olive Kallevig, Willmar, Mn.

FRUIT IN CRUST CHEESE CAKE PIE

9 Inch Pie Shell:

1 c. flour
2/3 c. brown sugar
1/2 c. butter

1 c. quick cooking oatmeal
1/2 tsp. baking powder

Mix until crumbly; reserve 1 cup crumbs. Pat remainder on bottom and sides of ungreased pie pan. Spread 10-12 ounces of any fruit preserves over unbaked crust. Sprinkle 1 cup reserved crumbs over preserves. Bake at 350° for 20-25 minutes; cool.

460

1/2 c. powdered sugar
1 1/2 tsp. vanilla
2 Tbsp. milk

1 (3 oz.) pkg. cream cheese, softened

Blend in small mixer bowl until smooth. Fold 2 cups sweetened whipped cream or cream substitute into cream cheese mixture. Spoon into baked crust. Store in refrigerator.

Ellie Cox, Rochester, Mn.

LEMON CHEESE CAKE

Stir 8 ounces cream cheese until soft. Blend in 1/2 cup milk until smooth. Add 1 1/2 cups milk and 1 package instant lemon pudding mix. Beat slowly with rotary beater 1 minute. Pour at once into 9 inch crumb crust; chill.

Helen Teeuwen, Minneapolis, Mn.

PINEAPPLE CHEESE CAKE

2 c. graham cracker crumbs
1/4 c. sugar

1/2 c. melted butter
1 tsp. cinnamon

Combine all ingredients. Line pan; reserve 3/4 cup for topping. Chill crust.

3 egg yolks, beaten
1/4 tsp. salt

1/2 c. sugar
1/2 c. pineapple syrup

Cook together until thick; add 2 tablespoons unflavored gelatin, softened in 1/2 cup cold water.

1/2 c. diced pineapple
3 Tbsp. lemon juice

2 c. cottage cheese

Cool to room temperature; fold in 3 stiffly beaten eggs and 1 cup whipped cream. Pour into crust and top with crumbs, cherries and pieces of pineapple.

Mrs. Emma Buhl, Minneapolis, Mn.

CHEESE CAKE DESSERT

1 pkg. lemon jello

1 c. hot water

Dissolve and chill until jellied, then whip. Whip 8 ounces Philadelphia cream cheese and 1 cup sugar. Add to whipped jello mix. Whip 1 (13 ounce) can chilled (24 hours)

Carnation milk; add to previous mixture. Pour over graham cracker crust; chill thoroughly. Add pie cherries to top.

Vivian Brickson, Detroit Lakes, Mn.

BUTTERSCOTCH FILLING

1/2 c. brown sugar	1/4 tsp. salt
1/4 c. cornstarch	1/2 c. water

Cook, stirring constantly, until mixture thickens and boils; boil and stir 1 minute. Blend in 1 tablespoon butter; cool. Spread Butterscotch Filling to within 1/2 inch of edge of cake. Sprinkle 1/2 cup finely chopped nuts over filling.

K., St. Cloud, Mn.

CREAM FILLING FOR CUPCAKES
(50 Cupcakes)

3/4 c. scalded milk, cooled	1 1/2 tsp. vanilla
1 c. sugar	1/2 c. Spry or Crisco
1 egg white	1/2 c. butter

Scald milk; cool. Cream butter and shortening. Add sugar; cream together. Add egg white and vanilla; beat till smooth. Add milk, 1/2 tablespoon at a time; beat. (Be sure not to add more.) Use large tip of cake decorator and fill cupcakes, then frost.

Eileen Rekowski, St. Cloud, Mn.

FROSTING

1/3 c. butter	3 Tbsp. caramel topping
2 c. powdered sugar	2 Tbsp. milk

Beat until smooth. Frost bars while still warm.

Rosie Schudar, Fargo, N.D.

ANGEL CAKE FROSTING

Juice of 2 oranges	Pinch of salt
1/2 c. sugar	Grated rind of 1/2 orange
1/2 Tbsp. flour	1 pt. whipping cream
2 egg yolks	

Beat eggs; add sugar, flour, salt, orange juice and rind. Cook over hot water until thickened; cool. Whip cream, then fold in the cooked mixture. Spread over angel cake.

Dee Olson, St. Paul, Mn.

BEAT AND SERVE

1 egg white, unbeaten　　　　1 tsp. vanilla
3/4 c. sugar　　　　　　　　1/4 c. boiling water
1/4 tsp. cream of tartar

Mix first 4 ingredients in small, deep mixing bowl; add boiling water. Beat until it forms stiff peaks. Makes enough for 8 inch layer cake.

Suzie Brainard, Minneapolis, Mn.

QUICK BUTTERSCOTCH FROSTING

1 c. brown sugar　　　　　　1/4 tsp. salt
5 Tbsp. butter　　　　　　　1/4 c. milk

Combine brown sugar, butter and salt in saucepan; bring to a boil, stirring constantly. Add milk; cook slowly 3 minutes. Cool; add 1/2 teaspoon vanilla and 1 1/2 cups powdered sugar. Beat well; spread on bars or cake.

Rosalee Wendelbo, Grafton, N.D.

CHOCOLATE FROSTING
(Never Fail)

1 c. sugar　　　　　　　　　4 Tbsp. butter
2 sq. Baker's chocolate　　　8 Tbsp. cream

Bring to boil. Take off and let cool. Stir after cool until ready to spread.

Sharon Wilson, Park Rapids, Mn.

EASY CHOCOLATE FROSTING

Boil 1 minute:
1/3 c. butter　　　　　　　　1 1/2 c. sugar
6 Tbsp. milk

Remove from heat; add 1 (6 ounce) package chocolate chips and spread.

1507-82　　　　Vivian Brickson, Detroit Lakes, Mn.

EASY CHOCOLATE FROSTING

4 sq. Baker's unsweetened chocolate*
1/4 c. butter or margarine*
1/8 tsp. salt

1 lb. unsifted confectioners sugar
1/2 c. milk
1 tsp. vanilla

*Or, use 4 packets Baker's Redi-Blend and melt the butter.

Melt chocolate and butter over hot water. Combine sugar, salt, milk and vanilla. Stir in chocolate mixture. Let stand, stirring occasionally, until thick. Makes 2 1/2 cups or enough for tops and sides of two or three 9 inch layers.

Margaret McKenney, Minneapolis, Mn.

GOOD CHOCOLATE FROSTING

Mix together:
2 1/2 c. powdered sugar
1/2 c. cocoa (or 3 sq. chocolate)

1/4 c. hot water
1 egg, slightly beaten
1 1/2 tsp. vanilla

Add 1 stick oleo, 1 tablespoon at a time.

Mary Anne Zachman, Bemidji, Mn.

CUSTARD FROSTING FOR ANGEL FOOD CAKE

Bake angel food cake; when cool, slice in half as to layer.

Custard Frosting: Mix -

1 env. Knox gelatine

1/4 c. cold water

Mix:
2 egg yolks
1/2 c. sugar

3/4 c. milk
1 tsp. cornstarch

Cook and stir constantly so mixture doesn't burn. Add jello mixture while egg mixture is still hot, then cool. Whip 1/2 pint of whipping cream, flavored with sugar and vanilla, then add egg and jello mixture; blend very well. Frost bottom half of angel food cake, then the rest. Sprinkle with coconut.

Lila Houser, Aitkin, Mn.

FAVORITE FROSTING

1/3 c. milk
1/2 c. margarine
1/2 c. Crisco
1 c. sugar

1 egg
1 tsp. vanilla
Pinch of salt

In medium size mixer, cream margarine, Crisco and sugar. Add egg, vanilla and salt. Heat milk to warm; add to above mixture. Beat at high speed about 10 minutes. This frosting looks like whipped cream.

Sue Hetland, Grand Forks, N.D.

FUDGE FROSTING

1/4 c. cocoa
1/4 c. butter

1/4 c. milk
1 c. sugar

Boil 1 minute; add 1 teaspoon vanilla. Do not beat until cool. If too thin, add powdered sugar to thicken. (Great on brownies.) Very good.

Mary Perron, Rochester, Mn.

Similar recipes submitted by: Pearl Paulsrud, Montevideo, Mn., Anne Aune, Minneapolis, Mn.

GOOD AND EASY FROSTING

1 1/2 c. brown sugar
2 Tbsp. butter

1/3 c. milk

Boil in saucepan for 1 minute; remove from heat. Add 3 ounces (1/2 small package) chocolate chips. Beat until chips are melted and mixture starts to thicken.

K., St. Cloud, Mn.

GOOD FROSTING FOR BROWNIES

1 1/2 c. powdered sugar
1/2 c. cream

1/3 c. butter
1 1/2 tsp. vanilla

Mix the above; boil to soft ball stage. Cool; beat until smooth. Spread on brownies. When frosting is firm, dribble on 1 1/2 squares chocolate, melted with 1/2 teaspoon shortening.

Pearl Paulsrud, Montevideo, Mn.

INSTANT 7 MINUTE FROSTING

1 c. sugar
Dash of cream of tartar

1/2 c. boiling water
1 egg white, put in last

Mix in electric mixer until it stands in peaks. Add 1 teaspoon vanilla.

Janet Henry, Minneapolis, Mn.

JELLO FROSTING

Boil together for 3 to 4 minutes:

1/2 c. sugar

1 small can crushed pineapple

Dissolve 1 package red jello in 1/2 cup cold water. Add this to the hot mixture; stir well. When cool and thick, add about 1 pint cream, whipped very stiff. Extra coloring may be added. Use on angel food cake. Cut cake into 3 layers; put frosting between layers and cover cake. Refrigerate.

Gemma Pierson, St. Cloud, Mn.

MARSHMALLOW FROSTING

3/4 c. sugar
3 Tbsp. water
1 egg white

1/8 tsp. cream of tartar
6 marshmallows, cut up
Vanilla flavoring

Place sugar, water, egg white and cream of tartar in double boiler over water. Cook, boiling constantly, with rotary beater until it stands in peaks. Remove from heat; add marshmallows and vanilla. Stir until cool enough to hold its shape.

Ina Veal, Bismarck, N.D.
Similar recipe submitted by: Gemma Pierson, St. Cloud, Mn.

PRALINE FROSTING

3/4 c. brown sugar, packed
6 Tbsp. butter or margarine
1/2 c. heavy cream
1/2 tsp. salt

1 1/2 c. sifted powdered
sugar
1/2 c. pecans or walnuts,
chopped

Combine brown sugar, butter, cream and salt in a small saucepan; boil together about 5 minutes or until well blended. Remove from heat; stir in powdered sugar and vanilla. Beat until spreading consistency. Add nuts just before spreading carefully on cake.

Sharon Wilson, Park Rapids, Mn.

MOM'S WALNUT FROSTING

3/4 c. sugar	3 eggs
2 heaping Tbsp. flour	1/2 pt. half & half

Blend in double boiler or heavy saucepan in that order. Cook until thick, stirring constantly. Add 1 teaspoon vanilla and 1 cup crushed walnuts (oil from walnuts will turn frosting a darker color). Cool. Excellent on chocolate, white or yellow cake.

Thalia Fox, Willmar, Mn.

ALMOND BARK CLUSTERS

Melt 1 (2 pound) package butterscotch or vanilla almond bark. Add:

2 c. Rice Krispies	2 c. Spanish salted peanuts
2 c. Cap'n Krunch	2 c. small marshmallows

Marion Round, Faribault, Mn.

ALMOND ROCA COOKIES

1/2 c. sugar	1/2 tsp. salt
1/2 c. brown sugar	1 (6 oz.) pkg. chocolate
1 c. real butter	chips
1 egg yolk	Chopped almonds
1 c. flour	

Mix sugars, butter and egg yolk; add flour and salt. Flatten mixture in a cookie sheet, very thin. Bake 20-25 minutes in 325° oven. As soon as pan is removed from oven, sprinkle chocolate chips over crust to form frosting. Spread them out when they soften. Sprinkle chopped almonds over chocolate. Cut into squares while still warm. Almond extract (1/4 - 1/2 teaspoon) may be added to dough for a stronger almond flavor, if desired.

Dee Olson, St. Paul, Mn.

ANISE COOKIES

1 c. margarine
2 c. brown sugar
2 eggs, well beaten
1 Tbsp. anise seed

1 c. pecans, chopped fine
3 1/2 c. flour
2 1/2 tsp. baking powder
1/4 tsp. salt

Cream shortening until very light; add sugar gradually. Beat in eggs well. Add nuts and anise seed. Sift dry ingredients together; add gradually to mixture. Wrap in wax paper; chill 2 hours. Bake 10 to 12 minutes in 350° oven.

V. Robbs, Minneapolis, Mn.

APPLESAUCE COOKIES

1/2 c. shortening
1 egg
1/2 tsp. salt
1 c. brown sugar
1/2 tsp. soda
1 c. seedless raisins

1/2 tsp. nutmeg
2 c. flour
2 tsp. baking powder
1 tsp. cinnamon
1/2 c. applesauce

Cream together shortening and sugar; add egg. Beat well; add raisins. Sift together flour, salt, baking powder, soda, nutmeg and cinnamon. Add alternately with applesauce to creamed mixture. Drop by teaspoon. Bake in hot oven, 400° or 350°, for 12 to 15 minutes.

Vi Geving, Duluth, Mn.

BANANA OATMEAL COOKIES

2 c. sifted enriched flour
1 tsp. cinnamon
1/4 tsp. nutmeg
1 1/2 tsp. salt
1 tsp. baking powder
1/4 tsp. soda
1 c. sugar

1 c. shortening (soft)
1 c. mashed bananas (2-3)
2 eggs
2 c. Quaker or Mother's oats
  (quick or old fashioned),
  uncooked

Sift together flour, spices, salt, baking powder, soda and sugar; add shortening, mashed bananas and eggs. Beat until smooth, about 2 minutes; fold in rolled oats. Drop by teaspoons on a well greased cooky sheet. Bake in a moderate oven, 375° F., for 10 to 12 minutes. Makes 4 dozen cookies; 90 calories per cooky.

Dena Stoddard, St. Louis Park, Mn.

BROWN COOKIES

3/4 c. shortening	2 c. flour
1 c. white sugar	Pinch of salt
1 egg, beaten	1 tsp. ginger
4 Tbsp. molasses	1 tsp. cloves
2 tsp. soda	1 tsp. cinnamon

Roll in balls; dip in sugar. Bake in 350° oven for 10-12 minutes.

Gerri Ruprecht, St. Cloud, Mn.

BROWN SUGAR DROP COOKIES

1 c. shortening	3 1/2 c. sifted flour
2 c. brown sugar	1 tsp. salt
2 eggs	1 tsp. soda
1 c. sour milk or buttermilk	1 tsp. vanilla

May add dates, nuts, coconut or chips, as desired. Combine shortening, sugar and eggs; beat. Add remainder, then chill 1 hour. Drop by teaspoon. Bake at 375° for 8-10 minutes.

Norma Haugerud, Montevideo, Mn.

BUMPY CRUNCHY COOKIES

3/4 c. shortening	1/2 tsp. soda
3/4 c. packed brown sugar	1 c. grated carrots
1 egg	1 (6 oz.) pkg. chocolate
1/2 c. apple juice	chips
1 tsp. vanilla	2 c. oatmeal
1 c. flour	1 1/2 c. Rice Krispies
1 tsp. salt	1/2 c. chopped nuts

Beat sugar and shortening; add egg, apple juice and vanilla. Beat until smooth. Sift flour, salt and soda; add to sugar mixture. Stir in remaining ingredients. Spoon 2 teaspoons of dough on cookie sheet; flatten with spoon to make a circle. Bake 15 minutes in a 350° oven. Drizzle frosting on top:

1 c. powdered sugar	1/2 tsp. vanilla
2 Tbsp. water	

Mrs. Norma Applen, Minneapolis, Mn.

CAN'T BELIEVE IT'S A COOKIE

Mix:

1 c. sugar   1 egg
1 c. peanut butter

Drop on cookie sheet, with a chocolate star on top. Bake at 350° for 8-10 minutes. Makes 30 cookies.

Adeline Jasken, St. Cloud, Mn.

CARAMEL BALLS

1 pkg. Kraft caramels   1 pkg. large marshmallows
1/2 can Eagle Brand milk   Rice Krispies
1/4 lb. butter or margarine

Melt caramels, Eagle Brand and butter in double boiler. Dip marshmallows in caramel sauce and roll in Rice Krispies.

Ina Veal, Bismarck, N.D.

CARAMEL SPRITZ COOKIES

2 1/4 c. flour   1/4 tsp. salt
1 c. margarine   1/2 c. brown sugar
1 unbeaten egg   1 tsp. maple flavoring

Mix and put through cookie press. Bake at 375° until brown. Put together in sandwich style with Hershey's bars.

Bev. Jensen, Willmar, Mn.

CARAMELITES

Melt 35 caramels and 3 tablespoons cream over double boiler. Add:

1 c. corn flakes   1 c. Rice Krispies
1 c. coconut   1 c. nuts

Spread; press in 9x13 inch pan immediately.

Marion Round, Faribault, Mn.

CASHEW COOKIES

1/2 c. butter	1 3/4 c. salted cashews
1 c. brown sugar	3/4 tsp. soda
1 egg	3/4 tsp. baking powder
1/2 tsp. vanilla	2 c. flour
1/3 c. sour cream	3/4 tsp. salt

Cream butter and sugar until fluffy. Beat in egg and vanilla. Add dry ingredients alternately with sour cream; mix well. Carefully fold in nuts. Drop by teaspoonfuls onto greased cookie sheet. Bake at 400° for 10 minutes. Cool and frost.

Frosting: Brown 1/2 cup butter. Remove from heat and add 3 tablespoons cream and 1/2 teaspoon vanilla. Stir in 2 cups powdered sugar.

Dena Stoddard, St. Louis Park, Mn.

Similar recipe submitted by: Esther Mungovan, Duluth, Mn.

CASSEROLE COOKIES

2 eggs	1 tsp. vanilla
1 c. sugar	1/4 tsp. almond extract or
1 c. chopped dates	1/2 tsp. black walnut
1 c. coconut	extract
1 c. chopped walnuts	Confectioners sugar
	Candied cherries, if desired

Beat eggs in buttered 2 quart casserole; add granulated sugar and mix well. Add dates, coconut, nuts, vanilla and extract. Bake 30 to 35 minutes in moderate oven, 350°. Stir 4 or 5 times while baking. Let cool; stir occasionally. When cold, form into small balls. Roll in confectioners sugar; flatten out. Add 1/2 of a candied cherry for decoration, if desired. Makes about 5 dozen cookies.

Marion Poteete, Mound, Mn.

Similar recipe submitted by: Dena Stoddard, St. Louis Park, Mn.

COCONUT DATE BALLS

1/2 lb. dates, chopped	1 tsp. vanilla
1 beaten egg	1/2 c. chopped nuts
1 c. sugar	1 1/2 c. Rice Krispies
1/4 c. butter	Coconut

Cook dates, egg, sugar and butter until thick. Remove and cool slightly. Add vanilla, nuts and Rice Krispies. When cool enough to handle, form into balls; roll in coconut. Makes 36 balls.

Rosalee Wendelbo, Grafton, N.D.

CHEESE CAKE COOKIES

Use tiny muffin tins. Butter tins well or you can use liners; sprinkle bottom of tins with finely crushed graham crackers. Beat 3 egg whites until stiff; set aside. Mix:

3 egg yolks
2 (8 oz.) pkg. cream cheese
3/4 c. sugar

Mix in egg whites. Fill tins with mixture. Bake 15 minutes at 350°; will fall in the middle.

Frosting: Mix -

3/4 c. sour cream
2 1/2 Tbsp sugar
1 tsp. vanilla

Frost muffins. Put in oven for 5 minutes. Cool completely before removing from tins.

Anne Aune, Minneapolis, Mn.

CHERRY BONBONS

Cream 1 cup oleo with 3 cups powdered sugar; add:

1 tsp. almond extract
2 Tbsp. Carnation milk
3 c. flaked coconut

Drain 1 large jar maraschino cherries very well. Wrap 1 teaspoon batter around cherry; roll in graham cracker crumbs. Store in refrigerator.

Joan Norton, Hibbing, Mn.

CHERRY CHIP COOKIES

3/4 c. shortening
1 c. brown sugar, firmly
  packed
1 egg
1 tsp. vanilla
2 c. flour
1 tsp. baking powder
1/2 tsp. salt
1/2 c. (24) maraschino
  cherries, chopped
1/2 c. shredded coconut
1 (6 oz.) pkg. chocolate
  chips

472

Cream shortening and sugar; blend in egg and vanilla. Sift flour, baking powder and salt; add gradually, blending well. Stir in cherries, coconut and chocolate chips. Drop from teaspoon onto ungreased cookie sheet. Bake at 350° for 10-12 minutes. Makes 5 dozen cookies.

Sally Fuchs, Minneapolis, Mn.

CHERRY HUMPS

3/4 c. confectioners sugar
1/2 c. butter, softened
1 sq. pre-melted chocolate
1 1/2 c. sifted flour
1/4 tsp. salt
1/4 tsp. vanilla

1 oz. cherry juice
1 (10 oz.) jar maraschino
  cherries, drained and
  blotted dry on paper
  towel

Mix sugar, butter and chocolate; add remaining ingredients, except cherries. Add enough juice to make soft, but not sticky ball. Place a maraschino cherry in 1 tablespoon of dough; form into ball, completely covering cherry. Place on ungreased cookie sheet. Bake 10 minutes in 350° oven. Let set for 3 minutes before removing to cooling rack. Ice with a frosting of confectioners sugar, diluted with cherry juice. Yield: 2 1/2 dozen.

Dena Stoddard, St. Louis Park, Mn.

CHERRY WINKS

2/3 c. shortening
2 beaten eggs
1 tsp. vanilla
1 tsp. baking powder
1/2 tsp. salt
1 c. nuts

1 c. sugar
3 Tbsp. milk
2 c. flour
1/2 tsp. soda
1 c. dates
3 c. crushed Wheaties or
  corn flakes

Cream shortening and sugar; add eggs. Stir in milk and vanilla. Sift dry ingredients and add. Add dates and nuts. Roll small piece of dough in crumbs. Top each with a piece of cherry. Bake at 375°.

K., St. Cloud, Mn.

CHOCOLATE BUTTONS

Cream:
2 sticks (1/2 lb.) oleo   1 c. sugar

Add:
2 sq. chocolate   1 tsp. vanilla
2 egg yolks

Add:
2 c. flour   1/2 c. chopped nuts (opt.)
1/2 tsp. salt

Mix well; form into balls (about the size of walnut). Bake on ungreased cookie sheet for 10-12 minutes in 350° oven.

Mary Anne Zachman, Bemidji, Mn.

CHOCOLATE COVERED PEANUT COOKIE

1 1/2 c. flour   1/4 c. brown sugar
1/4 tsp. salt   1 egg
1/2 tsp. soda   1/2 c. butter
1 tsp. vanilla   1 c. chocolate covered
1/2 c. sugar   peanuts
1 c. coconut

Combine all ingredients; mix well. Fold in coconut and chocolate covered peanuts. Drop from teaspoon on ungreased cookie sheet. Bake in 350° oven for 10-12 minutes, until light brown.

Florence Peine, St. Paul, Mn.

CHOCOLATE DROP COOKIES

1/2 c. shortening   2 c. flour
1 c. brown sugar   1/2 tsp. salt
1 egg   1/2 tsp. soda
2 sq. melted chocolate   3/4 c. milk
1 tsp. vanilla   1/2 c. nuts

Cream shortening and sugar together. Add beaten egg; beat well. Add melted chocolate, milk, vanilla and sifted dry ingredients; beat together. Add nuts. Drop on greased, floured cookie sheet. Bake at 400°. Use pan of

boiling water in bottom of oven to keep cookies moist.
Frost with chocolate frosting.

Bev. Jensen, Willmar, Mn.
Similar recipe submitted by: K., St. Cloud, Mn.

CHOCOLATE DROP COOKIES

1 1/2 c. brown sugar or
  1 c. white sugar
1/2 c. melted butter
1 egg, well beaten
2/3 c. sweet milk
1 tsp. baking powder

1/2 c. cocoa or 1 1/2 sq.
  chocolate
1 tsp. salt
2 1/2 c. flour
Vanilla
Raisins, nuts or chocolate
  chips (optional)

Mix all ingredients; drop by teaspoon on greased cookie sheet. Bake and frost with a chocolate frosting.

Mary Fingalson, Detroit Lakes, Mn.

CHOCOLATE OATMEAL COOKIES

Cream together:
1/2 c. butter

1 1/4 c. sugar

Add:
3/8 c. cream

1 egg

Add and mix well:

2 1/2 c. oatmeal
2/3 c. flour
1/2 tsp. baking powder
5 Tbsp. cocoa

1/2 tsp. salt
1 1/2 tsp. vanilla
1 c. chopped walnuts

Drop by teaspoon onto greased cooky sheet. Bake at 350° for 8-10 minutes until done.

Ruth Rehschuh, Minneapolis, Mn.

CHOCOLATE SUNDAE COOKIES

1 (6 oz.) pkg. chocolate
  chips, melted
1/3 c. brown sugar
1 egg
1/2 c. shortening
1 1/2 c. sifted flour
2 Tbsp. milk

1/2 tsp. soda
1/2 tsp. salt
18 large marshmallows
1/4 c. maraschino juice
1/2 c. chopped maraschino
  cherries
1/2 c. chopped nuts

1507-82

Cream shortening, sugar and eggs; add melted chocolate chips. Sift together flour, salt and soda; add alternately with maraschino juice and milk to first mixture. Fold in chopped cherries and nuts. Drop by teaspoon on ungreased cookie sheet. Bake at 350° for 12 minutes. Cut 18 marshmallows in halves; place cut side on hot cookie. Cool. Frost with favorite chocolate frosting.

Ina Veal, Bismarck, N.D.

CHOCOLATE WALNUT COOKIES

1/2 c. shortening	1 tsp. vanilla
1 c. brown sugar	1 1/4 c. sifted flour
1 egg	1/4 tsp. soda
2 sq. unsweetened chocolate	1/4 tsp. salt
1/2 c. sour or buttermilk	1 c. chopped nuts

Cream and mix in order. Drop cookies by spoonful on ungreased pan. Bake 10-14 minutes at 350°. Frost and top with more nuts. Also good without frosting.

K., St. Cloud, Mn.

CINNAMON STARS

1/3 c. egg whites (about 2)	2 Tbsp. flour
1 1/4 c. sugar	2 Tbsp. sugar
1 1/2 c. unblanched almonds, ground	1 c. powdered sugar, sifted before measuring
1 1/2 Tbsp. cinnamon	

In a small bowl of mixer, let egg whites warm to room temperature. With electric mixer at medium speed, beat egg whites just until soft peaks form when beater is slowly raised. Gradually add 1 1/4 cups sugar, 2 tablespoons at a time; beat well after each addition. Continue to beat until egg whites are very thick and glossy, stiff peaks form. (Takes about 10 minutes.) In medium bowl, combine almonds and cinnamon. Stir in egg white mixture; combine well. Refrigerate, covered, overnight. To roll out, mix 2 tablespoons flour with 2 tablespoons sugar; sprinkle on pastry cloth. Roll out dough 1/2 at a time to 1/4 inch thick using 3 inch star cutter; cut out 12 cookies. Place 1 inch apart on greased cookie sheets. Let stand, uncovered, at room temperature 2 hours. Bake in 300° oven for 20 minutes. Remove from oven. Mix powdered sugar with 2 tablespoons water; brush frosting on cookies. Bake 5 minutes more. Cool slightly; remove onto wire racks.

Dee Olson, St. Paul, Mn.

COCONUT-APRICOT BALLS

1/2 c. butter, softened
1 large pkg. Philadelphia
  cream cheese
1/2 c. Carnation instant
  dry milk

3 c. powdered sugar
1/2 large pkg. flake coconut
1/2 tsp. vanilla
1/2 tsp. almond extract
1 c. finely cut, dried
  apricots

Mix butter and cheese until smooth. Add dry milk and sugar; add vanilla, almond extract and coconut. Mix well; more powdered sugar may be needed to make this stiff. Mix in apricots. Drop by teaspoon into additional flaked coconut; roll into walnut sized balls. Store in covered container. These freeze well.

Mrs. Norma Applen, Minneapolis, Mn.

COCOANUT COOKIES

Mix well:
1/2 lb. butter or margarine

1 lb. powdered sugar

Add:
1 can Borden's sweet milk
1 tsp. vanilla

1 large pkg. cocoanut
1/2 c. chopped nuts (opt.)

Refrigerate overnight. Make in small balls; put a toothpick in each and put in freezer on cookie sheet. Melt 1 slab of paraffin wax with 1 large package of chocolate chips. Roll balls in chocolate; refrigerate till cold. I add pineapple or cherry flavoring to the cocoanut mixture instead of vanilla.

Millie Perrault, Duluth, Mn.

COCONUT ISLANDS

Sift together:
2 c. flour
1/2 tsp. soda

1/2 tsp. salt

Melt:
1/2 c. cocoa

1/4 c. hot instant coffee

Cream:
1/2 c. Crisco

1 c. brown sugar, packed

Add 1 egg and cocoa mixture. Measure 2/3 cup thick sour cream. Add sour cream alternately with the dry ingredients to creamed mixture. Stir in 1/3 cup coconut. Drop by heaping teaspoonfuls on greased baking sheets. Bake in moderate oven, 375°, for 12 to 15 minutes. Frost with chocolate frosting while warm. Sprinkle top with coconut. Store in tightly covered container.

Phylliss Mae Johnson, Winona, Mn.

CORN FLAKE COOKIES

Cream together:

1 c. butter	1 c. white sugar
1 c. brown sugar	

Add 2 eggs and beat. Add:

2 c. flour	1 tsp. vanilla
1 tsp. soda	2 c. oatmeal (quick)
1 1/2 tsp. baking powder	1 c. coconut
1/4 tsp. salt	2 c. corn flakes

Mix with hands; drop on greased cookie tin. Bake 12 to 15 minutes in 350° oven. Makes 5-6 dozen.

Marge Pye, St. Paul, Mn.

Similar recipes submitted by: Fran Toler, Minneapolis, Mn., Lorraine Rieger, Minneapolis, Mn.

CREAM WAFERS

1 c. soft butter	2 c. flour
1/3 c. whipping cream	Sugar

Mix butter, cream and flour thoroughly; cover and chill. Roll out about 1/3 of dough at a time on a floured, cloth covered board. (Keep rest of dough chilled until ready to roll.) Roll out 1/8 inch thick; cut into 1 1/2 inch circles. Transfer rounds with spatula to waxed paper heavily coated with sugar. Coat each side of round. Place on ungreased baking sheet. Prick with a fork about 4 times. Bake 7-9 minutes or until set, but not brown; cool. Put together in pairs with Creamy Filling. Bake at 350°. Makes 5 dozen.

Creamy Filling: Cream 1/4 cup soft butter, 3/4 cup powdered sugar and 1 teaspoon vanilla until smooth and fluffy. Tint with a few drops of food color. (Add a few drops of water if necessary for proper spreading consistency.)

Jean Taylor, Grand Forks, N.D.

478

CREME DE MENTHE BALLS

1 c. vanilla wafer crumbs	2 Tbsp. light corn syrup
3/4 c. finely chopped pecans	1/3 c. white creme de menthe
1 c. powdered sugar	Powdered sugar for coating

Mix crumbs, nuts and the 1 cup powdered sugar in medium sized bowl. Add syrup and creme de menthe. Blend well with fork to make a stiff dough. Form into small balls (rounded 1/2 teaspoonful); roll in powdered sugar. Cover loosely; chill overnight. Store in airtight container.

Dee Olson, St. Paul, Mn.

CRISP WHITE COOKIES

Mix together like pie crust:

3 c. flour	1 tsp. soda
2 tsp. cream of tartar	1 c. butter

Add 1 cup sugar and 2 eggs, beaten; mix together well. Add to above mixture. Make into balls; flatten on greased cookie sheet. Sprinkle with granulated sugar. Bake in moderate oven.

Mary Fingalson, Detroit Lakes, Mn.

DARK CHRISTMAS COOKIES

Sift together:

2 1/2 c. flour	1 1/2 tsp. cinnamon
1 tsp. soda	1 tsp. ginger
1 tsp. cream of tartar	1/4 tsp. nutmeg
1/4 tsp. salt	

Set aside. Cream together:

1 c. butter or margarine	1 1/2 c. powdered sugar

Blend in and mix well:

1/4 c. molasses	1 tsp. vanilla
1 unbeaten egg	

Add dry ingredients gradually; mix well. Chill dough. Roll out and cut with cutters. Bake at 350° for 8-10 minutes.

Grayce Funke, Minneapolis, Mn.

DATE COOKIES

1 c. soft shortening	1 tsp. vanilla
2 c. brown sugar	3 1/2 c. sifted flour
2 eggs	1 tsp. salt
1/2 c. water, sour milk	1 tsp. soda
or buttermilk	1 tsp. cinnamon

Mix together shortening, sugar and eggs; stir in liquids. Sift together and stir in dry ingredients. Drop by teaspoon onto ungreased baking sheet. Place 1/2 teaspoon Date Filling (below) on dough; top with 1/2 teaspoon of dough. Bake 10-12 minutes. Makes 5-6 dozen.

Date Filling: Cook until thick, stirring constantly -

2 c. dates, cut small	3/4 c. water
3/4 c. sugar	1/2 c. chopped nuts

Cool.

Mary Paul, Minneapolis, Mn.

DATE FILLED COOKIES

Cookies:

1 c. brown sugar	1 tsp. soda
1 c. shortening	2 c. oatmeal
1/2 c. sweet milk	2 c. flour

Cream sugar and shortening; add sweet milk. Mix well. Add flour and soda; mix, then add oatmeal and mix. Cool dough. Roll out and cut with cookie cutter (I use a "shot" glass for a more dainty cookie). Bake at 375° for 10 minutes.

Filling:

1 c. chopped dates	1/2 c. water
1 c. sugar	

Boil until thick enough to spread on cookies. Put 2 baked, cooled cookies together with filling. Fill just before serving.

Mavis Ann Hjielberg, St. Paul, Mn.

480

DATE FILLED COOKIES

Mix like pie crust:

4 c. flour	1 tsp. salt
1 tsp. baking powder	1 c. shortening

Beat and add to above mixture:

2 eggs	1/3 c. milk
1 c. white sugar	1 tsp. vanilla
1 tsp. soda	

Press together by hand; wrap in wax paper. Place in refrigerator 2 hours or overnight.

Filling:

1 lb. dates	2 Tbsp. flour
1 c. sugar	1 Tbsp. butter
2 c. water	

Cook until thick; cool before using. Roll dough. Put filling between 2 round cuts of dough; I sometimes use 1 round cut of dough, put filling on and fold over. Bake at 350°.

Rhea Layne, Sauk Rapids, Mn.

"DATE FILLED DROP COOKIES"

2 c. brown sugar	1 tsp. salt
1 c. butter	3 eggs, beaten
1 tsp. vanilla	1 tsp. soda in 1 Tbsp.
4 c. flour	boiling water

Filling:

1 lb. dates, cut up	1 1/2 c. white sugar
1 c. water	

Boil dates, sugar and water until thick. Drop small amount of dough mixture from teaspoon, then drop a bit of date mixture on top of dough and again a tiny drop of dough on top of filling. Bake in moderate oven for 10 to 12 minutes.

Betty Cortright, Minneapolis, Mn.

DATE PINWHEEL ICEBOX COOKIES

2 c. brown sugar	4 c. flour
1 c. shortening (part butter or margarine)	1 tsp. salt
	1 tsp. soda
3 eggs, beaten	1/2 tsp. cinnamon (optional)

Filling:

2 1/4 c. chopped dates	1/2 c. sugar
1 c. water	1 c. nuts

Cook dates, water and sugar until thick; add nuts and set aside to cool. Cream shortening and sugar. Add eggs and dry ingredients; mix well and chill. Roll out to 1/4 inch thickness; spread with the cooled date filling. Roll as for jelly roll. Chill several hours or overnight. Slice and bake 12 to 15 minutes in a 350° oven.

Dena Stoddard, St. Louis Park, Mn.

GIN'S DATE WALNUT COOKIES

2 c. brown sugar	2 c. cut dates
1 c. shortening	1 c. chopped walnuts
1/2 tsp. salt	3 c. flour
3 eggs	1 tsp. soda

Drop. Bake at 400°.

Helen Teeuwen, Minneapolis, Mn.

DATE AND WALNUT KISSES

4 egg whites	1 c. coarsely chopped walnuts
1 1/4 c. sugar	2 c. snipped dates

Beat eggs until stiff but not dry. Add sugar slowly, beating constantly. Fold in walnuts and dates. Drop by teaspoonfuls on greased cookie sheets. Bake in 300° oven for 25-30 minutes or until firm to touch. Makes 4 1/2 dozen.

Mary Paul, Minneapolis, Mn.

DOUBLE TREAT COOKIES

2 c. sifted flour
2 tsp. baking soda
1/2 tsp. salt
1 c. shortening
1 c. sugar
1 c. brown sugar

2 eggs
1 tsp. vanilla
1 c. peanut butter
1 c. chopped, salted
  peanuts
1 (6 oz.) pkg. chocolate
  chips

Sift together dry ingredients. Beat together next 5 ingredients until fluffy; blend in peanut butter. Add dry ingredients. Stir in peanuts and chocolate chips. Shape into small balls; place on ungreased baking sheet. Flatten with a glass dipped in sugar. Bake at 350° for 8 minutes or until brown. Makes 7 dozen.
                    Adeline Jasken, St. Cloud, Mn.

ENERGY COOKIES

1 c. raisins
1 c. dried apricots, chopped
1/2 c. nonfat dry milk
1/4 tsp. baking powder
3/4 tsp. salt
1/4 tsp. baking soda
3/4 c. whole wheat flour
  (can use regular)
1/3 c. wheat germ

1/2 c. butter or margarine
1/2 c. peanut butter
1 c. brown sugar
1 egg
1 tsp. vanilla
3 Tbsp. whole milk
1/3 c. unsalted sunflower
  seeds
1 c. uncooked oats

Sift dry milk, baking powder, baking soda and salt together; stir in flour and wheat germ. In separate bowl, cream butter and peanut butter. Add sugar; beat until fluffy. Add egg; beat well. Add vanilla. Mix dry ingredients in slowly, alternating with whole milk. Add oats and fruits. Bake at 375° for about 10 minutes on greased baking sheet. Cool 5 minutes before removing.
                    Thalia Fox, Willmar, Mn.

FILLED COOKIES

1 c. shortening
2 c. white sugar
2 eggs
1 c. milk

6 c. flour
2 tsp. soda
5 tsp. cream of tartar

Roll out thin; cut with round cookie cutter.

Filling:

2 c. ground raisins	1 c. sugar
1 c. water	3 tsp. flour

Boil filling and put between 2 cookies; flatten edges. Bake until golden brown.

Gemma Pierson, St. Cloud, Mn.

FILLED SUGAR COOKIES

1 c. sugar	1 tsp. soda
1 egg	2 tsp. cream of tartar
1/2 c. butter	Vanilla
1/2 c. rich milk or half &	Salt
half	3 1/2 c. flour

Sift dry ingredients together; mix with creamed mixture.

Filling:

1 c. chopped dates	1/2 c. sugar
1/2 c. boiling water	1 tsp. flour

Boil together until thick. Use 1 teaspoon on round cut cooky and fold over. Press edges with fork. Bake at 350°. I usually double filling recipe.

Ragna Nelson, Minneapolis, Mn.

FRUIT COOKIES

1 c. Crisco	1 tsp. soda
2 c. sugar	Pinch of salt
2 c. raisins	1 tsp. cloves
2 eggs	1 tsp. cinnamon
2 Tbsp. buttermilk	1 tsp. nutmeg
3 c. flour	

Cream Crisco and sugar. Add eggs and buttermilk; blend well. Fold in dry ingredients. Add raisins, which have been soaked in hot water and drained. Roll and cut. May also be dropped from spoon. Bake at 375° for 12 minutes.

Lorraine Pauls, Fargo, N.D.
Similar recipe submitted by: Ollie Kearney, Rochester, Mn.

484

FRYING PAN COOKIES

Melt 1/4 pound of butter in frying pan and 1 cup sugar.

1 egg, mixed in real fast   1/4 tsp. salt
1 c. chopped dates

Cook 5 minutes. Take from stove; add 2 cups Rice Krispies and 1/2 cup walnuts. Stir well. Shape into balls; roll in Angel Flake coconut.

Anne Aune, Minneapolis, Mn.
Similar recipe submitted by: Pam Doyea, Fargo, N.D.

EDNA'S FRUIT COCKTAIL COOKIES

Beat together until fluffy:
1 c. shortening   1 tsp. vanilla
1 c. brown sugar   1 tsp. cinnamon
1 c. white sugar   1 tsp. cloves
3 eggs   1/2 tsp. salt

Sift together:
4 c. flour   1 tsp. baking powder
1 tsp. soda

Add 3 cups of dry ingredients to egg mixture; beat in thoroughly.

1 c. raisins   3 c. fruit cocktail, well
1 1/2 c. chopped nuts   drained

Add to dough together with the last cup of flour. Beat in by hand. Bake at 350° for 20-25 minutes.

Carolyn Brudevold, Fargo, N.D.

GINGERSNAPS

1 1/2 c. shortening   2 tsp. cloves
2 c. sugar   2 tsp. ginger
2 beaten eggs   4 tsp. soda
1/2 tsp. salt   5 1/2 Tbsp. molasses
2 tsp. cinnamon   4 c. flour

Cream shortening and sugar; add eggs. Mix dry ingredients; add to creamed mixture with molasses. Chill dough. Make into balls; roll in sugar. Bake at 350° for 10 minutes. Makes 4 dozen.

Mary Perron, Rochester, Mn.

COUNTRY RAISIN GINGERSNAPS

3/4 c. shortening
1 c. plus 3 Tbsp. sugar
1 egg
1/4 c. molasses
1 1/2 c. raisins
2 1/4 c. flour

2 tsp. soda
1 tsp. ginger
1/2 tsp. cinnamon
1/4 tsp. cloves
1 tsp. salt
1 c. chopped walnuts

Cream shortening and sugar; add egg and beat well. Add molasses and dry ingredients, which have been mixed together. Fold in raisins and walnuts; mix well. Using a rounded teaspoon, form into balls. Dip in sugar; place on cookie sheet. Bake 10-12 minutes at 350°. Makes 3 1/2 dozen.

Jean Taylor, Grand Forks, N.D.

GINGERBREAD MEN

Combine and mix:
1/2 c. brown sugar
1/2 c. vegetable shortening
3/4 c. molasses
1 tsp. soda
1 unbeaten egg
1 tsp. cinnamon

1 tsp. salt
1 tsp. cloves
2 tsp. ginger
2 tsp. vinegar
3 - 3 1/2 c. flour

Add enough flour to stiffen the dough; chill all night. Bake at 350° until lightly browned.

Mary Jane Zachman, Bemidji, Mn.

GOLD COOKIES

1/2 c. soft shortening
1 1/2 c. sugar
4 egg yolks
2 Tbsp. milk

1 tsp. vanilla
1 1/2 c. sifted flour
1/2 tsp. baking powder
1/4 tsp. salt

Mix together thoroughly the shortening, sugar and egg yolks; stir in milk and vanilla. Sift together the flour, baking powder and salt; add to creamed mixture. Chill dough. Roll into balls the size of walnuts, then roll balls in a mixture of 3/4 cup finely chopped nuts and 2 teaspoons cinnamon-sugar mixture. Place 3 inches apart on ungreased cookie sheets. Bake at 400° for 12-15 minutes. Should be golden brown, but still soft. Makes about 5 dozen.

Joan Dinius, Coon Rapids, Mn.

HICKORY NUT MACAROONS

Taken from a 1915 cookbook prepared by the students of Fountain City, Wisconsin High School.

1 egg	1 c. sugar

Beat well; add 1 cup chopped nuts and 2 tablespoons flour. Roll in little balls. Bake 20 minutes in slow oven.

Grayce Funke, Minneapolis, Mn.

HONEY COOKIES

1 c. honey	1 tsp. soda in 1/4 c. warm
1 c. sugar	water
1 c. shortening	1 tsp. baking powder
2 eggs	1 tsp. vanilla
Flour to make a stiff dough	1 tsp. lemon extract

Roll and cut.

Mary Fingalson, Detroit Lakes, Mn.

JINGLE BELL COOKIES

Cream:

1 1/2 c. brown sugar	1 c. butter

Add 2 well beaten eggs.   Add, sifted together:

2 1/2 c. flour	1 tsp. cinnamon
1 tsp. soda	1/2 tsp. salt

Add:

1 tsp. vanilla	2 lb. dates (halves)
1 c. pecans, chopped	4 slices candied pineapple
1 c. filberts, chopped	(red and green), cut up
1 c. walnuts, chopped	

Drop by teaspoon on greased cookie sheet. Bake at 350° for 15 minutes. Makes about 10 dozen.

Jeanette Skarhus, Minneapolis, Mn.

KRINGLA

1 c. sour cream
1/2 c. sour milk
1 c. sugar
1 tsp. soda

1 tsp. vanilla
1/8 tsp. salt
3 c. flour

Mix all ingredients well, using electric mixer. Let stand in refrigerator, covered, overnight. Flour large surface and roll out (with hands) a small portion of dough until it looks like a pencil and is about 6 inches long. Place on cookie sheet; form ends so it looks like a pretzel or a figure 8. Bake at 400° for 8 to 10 minutes until slightly browned. These freeze well.

Mrs. Norma Applen, Minneapolis, Mn.

KRIS KRINGLE COOKIES

1/2 c. (1 stick) butter
1/2 c. brown sugar

1/2 c. white sugar

Cream together. Mix well:

1 egg

1/2 tsp. vanilla

Add:
3/4 c. flour
1/2 tsp. salt
1/2 tsp. soda

1 1/2 c. oatmeal
1/4 c. nutmeats

Mix well. Form into 2 long rolls about the size of a silver dollar; wrap in wax paper. When thoroughly chilled, slice about 3 to an inch and bake in 350° oven for about 10 minutes. Makes about 5 dozen.

Colleen Landwehr, St. Cloud, Mn.

LEMON SNOWDROPS

1 c. butter
1/2 c. confectioners sugar
1 tsp. lemon flavoring

2 c. sifted all-purpose flour
1/2 tsp. salt

Cream butter and sugar; add rest of ingredients and mix well. Roll 1 level teaspoon of dough in a ball; flatten slightly. Place about 1 inch apart on ungreased baking sheet. Bake until light brown, 8-10 minutes at 400°. Put together with filling and roll in confectioners sugar. Makes 5 dozen. (Filling follows.)

Lemon Butter Filling:

1 egg, slightly beaten
Grated rind of 1 lemon
2/3 c. sugar

3 Tbsp. lemon juice
1 1/2 Tbsp. softened butter

Blend all ingredients in top of double boiler, cook over hot water until thick, stirring constantly. Cool before using.

Mary Fingalson, Detroit Lakes, Mn.

LEMONADE COOKIES

1 c. butter or margarine
1 c. sugar
2 eggs
3 c. sifted flour

1 tsp. flour
1 can frozen lemonade, thawed (reserve 1/3 of lemonade)

Mix above mixture; drop on cookie sheet, ungreased. Bake at 350° for 8-10 minutes. Brush lemonade on warm cookies and sprinkle sugar on top.

Mary Jo Conneran, Fargo, N.D.

MACAROON COOKIES

1 1/2 c. coconut
1/2 c. sugar
1 tsp. almond extract

1 egg, well beaten
Maraschino cherries

Combine coconut with sugar; mix well. Add egg and almond extract; mix well. Drop walnut sized mixture onto cookie sheet; add cherry. Bake at 350° until top of cookie starts to brown lightly.

Joan Billadeau, St. Cloud, Mn.

MASSACHUSETTS COOKIES

1 c. flour
1/2 tsp. baking soda
1/2 tsp. salt
1/2 c. white sugar
1/2 c. brown sugar
1/2 c. soft butter or
  margarine

1 egg
1 tsp. water
1 tsp. vanilla
1 1/2 c. quick rolled oats
1 (6 oz.) pkg. chocolate
  chips

Sift together flour, baking soda and salt. Add

1507-82

sugars, butter (soft), egg, water and vanilla. Beat until smooth, about 2 minutes. Stir in oats and chips. Drop on greased sheets, 1 inch apart. Bake at 375° for 12 minutes. Makes 4 dozen.

Mary Paul, Minneapolis, Mn.

MELTING MOMENTS

1 c. butter	3/4 c. cornstarch
1 c. flour	1 tsp. vanilla
1/2 c. powdered sugar	1/2 tsp. almond flavor

Roll in small balls. Bake at 350°; cool and frost.

Frosting:

1 c. powdered sugar	1 Tbsp. lemon juice
2 Tbsp. melted butter	1 Tbsp. orange juice

Susie Brainard, Minneapolis, Mn.

MELTING MOMENTS

3/4 c. butter	1 tsp. vanilla
1/4 c. powdered sugar	2 c. flour

Cream butter and sugar; add vanilla and flour. Form into small balls; press down with fork. Bake at 375° for 8-10 minutes. Put 2 cookies together with powdered sugar icing.

Eva Anderson, Duluth, Mn.

MILLION DOLLAR COOKIES

1 c. shortening (part butter)	1 egg, beaten
1/2 c. white sugar	2 c. flour
1/2 c. brown sugar	1 tsp. vanilla
1/4 tsp. soda	1/2 c. chopped walnuts or
1/2 tsp. salt	pecans

Cream shortening and sugar; add egg and vanilla. Add dry ingredients and nuts; form in balls. Roll in sugar. Press flat on cookie sheet with bottom of glass, dipping in sugar for each so glass won't stick. Bake at 350° for 10-12 minutes.

Marion Poteete, Mound, Mn.

Similar recipe submitted by: Clara Omlid Peterson, Minneapolis, Mn.

MOLASSES CRINKLES

Mix thoroughly:

1 1/2 c. soft shortening	2 eggs
2 c. brown sugar, packed	1/2 c. molasses

Sift together and stir in:

4 1/2 c. sifted flour	1 tsp. cloves
4 tsp. soda	2 tsp. cinnamon
1/2 tsp. salt	1 tsp. ginger

Mix together; chill dough. Roll into balls. Dip tops in sugar; place sugared side up 3 inches apart on greased cookie sheet. Preheat oven to 375°; bake 10-12 minutes.

Mary Paul, Minneapolis, Mn.

MOLASSES FILLED COOKIES

1/2 c. soft shortening	3 tsp. baking powder
1/3 c. sugar	1/2 tsp. salt
1 egg	1 tsp. ginger
2/3 c. Brer Rabbit molasses	1/2 tsp. cinnamon
2 3/4 c. sifted flour	1 c. mincemeat

Cream shortening with sugar; add egg and molasses. Beat well. Sift together flour, baking powder, salt, ginger and cinnamon. Add flour mixture; beat well. Wrap in waxed paper; chill. Roll out 1/8 inch thick on lightly floured board. Cut dough with round cookie cutter about 2 inches in diameter. On bottom part of cookie, place about 1 teaspoon of filling, with a little of the liquid portion. Slash top of cookie to about 1/2 inch from sides. Pull back and place over bottom part and filling. Bake at 375° F. for 10 minutes. Makes 3 dozen filled cookies.

Dena Stoddard, Minneapolis, Mn.

MOLASSES SUGAR COOKIES

1/2 c. shortening	1 1/2 c. plus 2 level Tbsp.
1/2 c. white sugar	sifted flour
1 egg	1/2 tsp. soda
1/2 tsp. salt	1/2 tsp. ginger
4 Tbsp. molasses	1 tsp. cinnamon

Chill dough; roll out. Sprinkle with sugar.

Lois Krause, Thief River Falls, Mn.

"MY SECRET" COOKIES

3/4 c. margarine
3/4 c. sugar
1 egg yolk
1 tsp. vanilla

1/2 c. nuts
1 1/2 c. flour
3/4 c. crushed potato chips

Cream margarine and sugar together well. Add remaining ingredients, blending well. Shape into balls the size of a walnut; flatten with a fork. Bake at 350° for 10 minutes.

Note: I have made these cookies many times and always ask my friends to guess the "Secret Ingredient". No one has ever guessed Potato Chips!

Bernice Fonos, Minneapolis, Mn.

NUTMEG COOKIE LOGS

1 c. butter
3/4 c. sugar
1 egg, beaten
2 tsp. vanilla

2 tsp. rum flavoring
3 c. sifted flour
1 tsp. nutmeg

Cream butter; gradually add sugar, creaming well after each addition. Blend in egg, vanilla and rum flavoring. Sift together flour and nutmeg; add to butter mixture. On floured board, shape dough into long rolls, about 1/2 inch in diameter. Cut into 3 inch pieces. Place on ungreased baking sheet; bake 12 to 15 minutes in a 350° oven. Cool and frost tops and sides of cookies. Use tines of fork to mark frosting to resemble bark. Sprinkle sparingly with nutmeg.

Dena Stoddard, St. Louis Park, Mn.

SOFT OATMEAL COOKIES

1 c. margarine, melted
1 c. brown sugar
2 eggs
1/2 c. strong coffee
2 c. flour
2 c. oatmeal

1 1/2 c. raisins
1 c. nuts
1 tsp. cinnamon
1/4 tsp. nutmeg
1 tsp. soda

Cream sugar, melted margarine and spices; add beaten eggs. Add sifted flour and soda with coffee. Add raisins, oatmeal and nuts. Drop by spoonful; bake at 350° for 12-15 minutes.

Lorraine Pauls, Fargo, N.D.

OATMEAL NUT COOKIES

1 c. margarine or butter
1 c. brown sugar
1 c. white sugar
2 eggs
1 tsp. vanilla
2 c. flour

1 tsp. baking powder
1 tsp. baking soda
2 c. quick oatmeal
1 c. walnuts, chopped
1 c. flaked coconut

Cream margarine or butter with sugars. Add vanilla and eggs; mix well. Add sifted dry ingredients. Mix in oatmeal, nuts and coconut with hands. Form into 3 rolls; refrigerate 2 hours or more. Slice and bake on greased cookie sheet at 375° until golden brown.

Arlene Carlson, Lake Park, Mn.

OATMEAL ROCKS

1 c. shortening
1 c. sugar (white)
2 eggs
1 tsp. vanilla
2 c. flour
2 c. oatmeal
1 1/2 tsp. cinnamon

1/2 tsp. cloves
1/2 tsp. nutmeg
Dash of salt
1 c. nuts
1 c. coconut
1 c. boiled raisins
5 Tbsp. raisin juice with
    1 tsp. soda

Cream shortening and sugar; add eggs and vanilla. Stir in raisins and raisin juice with soda, then add dry ingredients; mix well. Drop by teaspoon on greased cookie sheet. Bake at 350° until golden brown (I have used 400° for a shorter time and they were delicious, too). Makes about 5 dozen smaller cookies or you can make them large if you wish.

Bev. Jensen, Willmar, Mn.

OATMEAL ROCK COOKIES

2 c. brown sugar
1 c. shortening
3 or 4 eggs
8 Tbsp. sour milk
2 c. flour
1 1/2 tsp. salt

1 tsp. vanilla
2 Tbsp. cinnamon
1 1/2 tsp. soda
4 c. oatmeal
1 c. nuts

Mix well; spoon onto cookie sheet. Bake at 350°. (Very good.)

Mrs. Knute Andal, Henning, Mn.

OATMEAL THINS COOKIE

1 c. shortening	1 tsp. vanilla
1 c. brown sugar	Pinch of salt
1 c. quick oatmeal	1 tsp. soda in 1/4 c. boiling
2 c. flour	water

Mix in order given. Roll into a ball; press down with a glass dipped in sugar. Bake at 350° for 10 minutes.

Lucille F. Anderson, East Grand Forks, Mn.

ONE OF MOST EVERYTHING COOKIES

1 c. white sugar	1 tsp. cream of tartar
1 c. brown sugar	1 tsp. salt
1 c. vegetable oil	1 tsp. vanilla
1 c. margarine	1 c. oatmeal
1 egg	1 c. Rice Krispies
3 1/2 c. flour	1 c. nuts
1 tsp. soda	1 c. coconut

Chill dough about 1 hour; roll in balls. Flatten with 2 fingers, dipped in sugar. Bake at 325°.

Variation by Jackie Jaenisch, Windom, Mn.: Substitute 12 ounces chocolate chips (tiny) for 1 cup nuts.

Bessie Wilke, Detroit Lakes, Mn.

ORANGE DROPS

1/2 c. butter	1 tsp. baking powder
3/4 c. sugar	1/2 tsp. salt
1 1/2 c. flour	1 egg

Cream butter and sugar; add egg. Beat well. Blend in dry ingredients. Add 3 tablespoons orange juice and 3/4 cup coconut. Drop by rounded teaspoon on baking sheet; bake at 350° for 12-15 minutes. Frost while warm.

Frosting:

1 Tbsp. orange juice	1 c. powdered sugar
1 Tbsp. water	

Lorraine Pauls, Fargo, N.D.

PEANUT BUTTER COOKIES

Cream together 1 cup sugar and 1/2 cup shortening. Add 1/2 cup peanut butter; cream some more. Add 1 egg; beat well. Add:

1 1/4 c. flour	1 tsp. vanilla
1/2 tsp. salt	2 Tbsp. milk
1 tsp. soda	

Mix well. Roll out in rectangle. Spread on 1 cup or 1 package of chocolate chips, that were melted and cooled. Roll up; put in refrigerator for only 20 minutes. If you leave it in too long, the chocolate will get too hard to slice. Bake in 350° oven for a few minutes (light brown).

Bev. Jensen, Willmar, Mn.

PEANUT BUTTER COOKIES

1 c. brown sugar	1 tsp. soda, dissolved in 2
1 c. white sugar	Tbsp. hot water
1 c. shortening	1 tsp. baking powder
2 eggs	2 c. flour
1/2 c. peanut butter	2 c. quick oatmeal

Drop by teaspoon onto cookie sheet, ungreased. Bake at 350° for 12 minutes. Makes 4 dozen large cookies.

Eileen Durham, Brainerd, Mn.

PEANUT BUTTER COOKIES

Cream:

1 c. butter	1 c. granulated sugar
1 c. peanut butter	1 c. brown sugar

Add:

2 eggs	2 tsp. soda
1 tsp. vanilla	1/2 tsp. salt
3 c. flour	

Mix well. Bake at 400° for 10 minutes.

Martie Athey, Osage, Mn.

PEANUT BUTTER COOKIES

1 c. white sugar
1 c. brown sugar
1 c. shortening
2 eggs
1 1/2 c. flour

2 tsp. soda
1/2 c. peanut butter
2 c. oatmeal
1 c. corn flakes
1/2 tsp. salt

Mix in order given; roll in balls and press flat. Bake at 350° for 8 to 10 minutes.

Lucille F. Anderson, Grand Forks, N.D.

REESE'S PEANUT BUTTER CUPS
"Temptation"

1/2 c. oleo
1/2 c. peanut butter
1/2 c. sugar
1/2 c. brown sugar
1 egg
1/2 tsp. vanilla

1 1/4 c. flour
3/4 tsp. baking soda
1/2 tsp. salt
1 (10 oz.) box of Reese's miniature chocolate covered peanut butter cups

Cream oleo, peanut butter and both sugars. Beat in eggs and vanilla. Blend in flour, salt and soda. Shape dough in 1 inch balls; place in ungreased 1 1/2 inch tart tins (fluted ones). Bake 8-10 minutes at 375° or until lightly browned. Immediately after removing cookies from oven, press a Reese's peanut butter cup into the center of each cookie, until only the top of the peanut butter cup shows. Let cool for 10 minutes, then remove from tins. Makes about 40 cookies.

Loretta Van Engelenhoven, Luverne, Mn.

PEANUT BUTTER DROPS

3 c. Rice Krispies
1 lb. 8 oz. chocolate almond bark

3 Tbsp. peanut butter
3/4 c. sunflower seeds
3/4 c. Spanish peanuts

Melt almond bark and peanut butter together; mix all together. Drop on wax paper.

Jeanette Guzak, Grand Forks, N.D.

PEANUT LOGS

Cream together:

1 c. powdered sugar   2 Tbsp. melted butter
1 c. chunky peanut butter

Add 2 cups Rice Krispies; mix well. Roll into logs. Let dry on wax paper or refrigerate. Dip in chocolate mixture of:

1/2 bar paraffin   1 (6 oz.) pkg. chocolate
                            chips
          Jean Kreutzer, Rochester, Mn.

PECAN COOKIES

2 c. ground pecans   1/3 c. strawberry preserves
2/3 c. sugar   18 maraschino cherries,
1/2 tsp. salt   halved
2 egg whites

Preheat oven to 375°. In a medium bowl, combine pecans, sugar and salt; mix well. Add egg whites; mix until well blended. Shape mixture into small balls. Place on ungreased cookie sheets. Press a small depression in center of each ball with fingertip. Using a small pointed teaspoon, place a small amount of preserves in center. Top with a cherry half. Bake 20 minutes or until done. Let cool on wire racks. Makes 3 dozen.

          Bernita Engel, Minneapolis, Mn.

PEPPERMINT CHOCOLATE PUFFS

3/4 c. butter or margarine   2 c. all-purpose flour
1/4 c. sugar   2/3 c. peppermint stick
1 egg, separated   candy, crushed finely
2 tsp. vanilla   2/3 c. sugar
2 tsp. water   Semi-sweet chocolate pieces

Cream together butter and sugar until light and fluffy. Add egg yolk, vanilla and water; stir in flour and crushed candy. Dough will be crumbly. Roll into balls, approximately 1 inch. Dip balls into slightly beaten egg white, then roll in sugar; place on greased cookie sheet. Place a chocolate piece on each ball. Bake in gas oven at 350° F. for 15 minutes. Remove from sheet immediately. Makes 4 dozen.

          Blanche B. Masica, Minneapolis, Mn.

PINEAPPLE COOKIES

1 c. shortening
1 1/2 c. sugar
1 egg
1 (8 3/4 oz.) can crushed
  pineapple, with juice

3 1/2 c. flour
1 tsp. soda
1/2 tsp. salt
1/4 tsp. nutmeg
1/2 c. chopped nuts

Mix shortening, sugar and egg; stir in pineapple. Stir together flour, soda, salt and nutmeg; blend in. Mix in nuts. Chill at least 1 hour. Drop rounded teaspoonfuls of dough about 2 inches apart on lightly greased baking sheet. Bake 8-10 minutes in 400° oven. Delicious with white frosting.

Gerri Ruprecht, St. Cloud, Mn.

Similar recipes submitted by: Mrs. Verne L. Andal, St. Cloud, Mn., Norma Haugerud, Montevideo, Mn.

PORCUPINE BALLS

37 graham crackers
1 bag small chocolate chips

1 can sweetened condensed
  milk
1 pkg. fine cocoanut

Roll graham crackers fine. Place in a bowl; add chocolate chips and milk. Mix well; form into small balls. Chill at least 2 hours. Roll into small balls, then roll in cocoanut. Store in refrigerator until firm.

Dee Olson, St. Paul, Mn.

PORCUPINES

1/2 c. white sugar
1 Tbsp. butter
1 egg

1 c. dates
1 c. walnuts
1/2 tsp. vanilla

Cream sugar and butter; add beaten egg. Add walnuts and dates, chopped fine, and vanilla. Form in balls about the size of a walnut. Roll in coconut; bake on greased cookie sheet until light brown at 350°.

Arlene Carlson, Lake Park, Mn.

PUMPKIN COOKIES

1 c. shortening	1/4 tsp. salt
1 c. sugar	1 tsp. cinnamon
1 c. pumpkin	1 tsp. vanilla
2 c. flour	1/2 c. chopped nuts
1 tsp. soda	1 c. chopped dates
1 tsp. baking powder	

Cream shortening and sugar; add pumpkin. Stir in flour, sifted with other ingredients. Add vanilla, dates and nuts. Drop from a teaspoon onto a greased cookie sheet. Bake at 350° for 8 to 10 minutes. While warm, frost with Brown Sugar Icing.

Brown Sugar Icing:

1 c. brown sugar	1 tsp. vanilla
3 Tbsp. butter	1 c. powdered sugar
3 Tbsp. milk	

Mix together; boil 1 minute and stir. Cool 10 minutes; add vanilla and powdered sugar. Frost cookies.

Marlys Swehla, Albert Lea, Mn.

PUMPKIN CHOCOLATE CHIP COOKIES

1 c. margarine	1/2 c. chocolate chips
1 c. sugar	2 c. flour
1 c. pumpkin	1 tsp. baking powder
1 egg	1 tsp. soda
1 tsp. vanilla	1 tsp. cinnamon
1/2 c. chopped nuts	1/2 tsp. salt

Mix wet ingredients in large bowl. Mix in dry ingredients, nuts and chocolate chips. Drop by teaspoons onto a greased cookie sheet. Bake in 350° oven for 10 minutes.

Dee Olson, St. Paul, Mn.

RAISIN ROCKS

Boil 5 minutes and cool:

2 c. raisins	1 1/2 c. boiling water

Cream together:

2 c. brown sugar	1 c. shortening

Add 3 eggs, beaten, and 1 teaspoon vanilla. Add:

Raisin mixture	1 tsp. salt
4 c. flour	1 1/2 tsp. cinnamon
1 tsp. soda	1/4 tsp. nutmeg
1 tsp. baking powder	1/4 tsp. allspice

Add dry ingredients gradually. Drop by teaspoon on well greased cookie sheet. Bake at 350° until light brown.

Kay Buzzell, Marshall, Mn.

RITZ CRACKER COOKIES

1 box Ritz (Hi-Ho works well also) crackers	2 lb. chocolate almond bark
1 jar creamy peanut butter	2 Tbsp. oil (can use up to 3 Tbsp. oil)

Butter cracker with peanut butter; top with second cracker. Melt chocolate almond bark and oil in top of double boiler (keep warm while working with it). Dip cracker sandwich into melted chocolate almond bark. Place on wax paper and allow to harden. Can be decorated with frosting flowers to make festive.

R. Mielke, Chisholm, Mn.
Similar recipe submitted by: J.M. Bregel, Windom, Mn.

ROCHESTER COOKIES

2 c. sugar	1/2 c. milk
1/4 c. cocoa	1/2 c. peanut butter
1/2 c. butter	(crunchy)
2 tsp. vanilla	3 c. quick cooking rolled oats

Combine sugar, cocoa, butter, vanilla and milk; cook over low heat to a rapid boil and cook 1/2 minute. Remove from heat; blend in peanut butter. Add rolled oats; beat very hard. Drop by teaspoonfuls onto waxed paper. Makes about 40 cookies.

Leslie Zimbrick, Minneapolis, Mn.

ROSETTES

2 eggs, slightly beaten
2 tsp. sugar
1/4 tsp. salt

1 c. milk
1 c. flour
1 Tbsp. lemon extract

Add sugar to slightly beaten eggs, then add milk. Sift flour before measuring, then sift together with salt. Stir into milk mixture till smooth. Add lemon flavoring. Heat fat; dip rosette iron into hot fat to heat it. Drain excess fat on paper towel, then dip hot iron into batter. Fry.

Dee Olson, St. Paul, Mn.

RUM BALLS

4 c. coarsely crushed vanilla
    wafers (one 12 oz. pkg.)
1 c. chopped nuts
3 1/2 oz. coconut

1 (14 oz.) can sweetened
    condensed milk
1/2 c. rum

Mix ingredients and chill overnight or 4 hours. Dip hands in powdered sugar; roll in balls. May be rerolled in powdered sugar before serving. Makes 6 dozen.

Jeanie Rose, Tracy, Mn.

RUM BALLS

1 1/2 c. (50) crushed
    vanilla wafers
1/4 c. dark rum

1/4 c. honey
8 oz. ground walnuts
Confectioners sugar

Combine all ingredients, except sugar; blend thoroughly. Shape into small balls, about 1 inch in diameter. Roll in sugar.

Mary Paul, Minneapolis, Mn.

RUSSIAN TEA CAKES

1 c. shortening (butter)
8 Tbsp. powdered sugar
1/2 tsp. salt
2 Tbsp. cold water

1 tsp. vanilla
1 c. pecans, ground fine
2 c. flour

Cream shortening and sugar; add other ingredients. Roll into balls. Bake in 400° oven for about 20 minutes.

1507-82

Roll in powdered sugar several times.

Emogene Homan, Minneapolis, Mn.

Similar recipe submitted by: Dena Stoddard, St. Louis Park, Mn.

RUSSIAN TEA CAKES

1 c. butter	2 1/4 c. flour
1/2 c. powdered sugar	1/4 tsp. salt
1 tsp. vanilla	3/4 c. walnuts

Cream together butter and sugar. Sift flour and salt; add. Bake in 400° oven for 8 to 10 minutes until set, but not brown. Form into 1 inch diameter balls before baking; place on ungreased sheet. When still warm after baking, roll in powdered sugar. Roll again when cool. Makes about 4 dozen.

Arnita Rieger, Minneapolis, Mn.

SALTED PEANUT COOKIES

1 c. brown sugar	2 eggs
1 c. white sugar	2 tsp. vanilla
1 c. shortening	1 tsp. soda
1 1/2 c. salted peanuts	2 c. flour
1 c. corn flakes	2 c. rolled oats

Cream sugar and shortening; add eggs, beating well. Sift flour and soda; add to creamed mixture. Lastly, add the oats, corn flakes, vanilla and peanuts in that order. Drop by tablespoon on oiled baking sheet. Bake for 12 minutes at 375°.

Mildred Nelson, St. Paul, Mn.

Similar recipe submitted by: Mary Perron, Rochester, Mn.

SAND TARTS

Cookies:

1 c. sugar	2 egg yolks
1/2 c. butter	1 1/3 c. flour

Topping:

2 egg whites	Blanched almonds, oven
Cinnamon and sugar	dried

Mix sugar, butter, egg yolks and flour. Roll dough paper thin and cut shapes. Brush with slightly beaten egg whites; sprinkle with cinnamon and sugar. Press almonds on top. Bake at 325° to 350°.

Karleen Gerth, St. Paul, Mn.

SANDWICH COOKIES

1 1/3 c. shortening	2 c. milk
1 1/2 c. sugar	4 1/2 c. flour
2 eggs	2 tsp. baking powder
2 c. Nestle's Quik chocolate mix	1 tsp. vanilla
	Pinch of salt

Cream shortening and sugar well; add eggs, Nestle's Quik and vanilla. Stir baking powder and salt into flour; add alternately with milk. Drop onto baking sheet, making quite large. Bake at 400° for 7-9 minutes. Cool and fill with filling.

Filling:

3/4 c. butter or margarine   2 c. marshmallow creme
2 c. powdered sugar, sifted

Pam Doyea, Fargo, N.D.

SCOTCH SHORTBREAD

1 c. real butter   2 c. sifted flour
3/4 c. brown sugar

Cream all together. Put into cookie press and shape cookies, or roll 1/4 inch thick and cut into squares. Bake in 400° oven for 5-8 minutes.

Dee Olson, St. Paul, Mn.

ANN'S SHORTBREADS PUFFS

1 c. shortening (half butter) 1/2 c. powdered sugar
1 c. flour   Almond flavoring
1/2 c. cornstarch

Cream shortening and sugar; add rest of ingredients. Drop by teaspoonful on cooky sheet. Bake for 1/2 hour at 275°, then at 300° for 10 minutes.

Esther Mungovan, Duluth, Mn.

BRAZIL NUT SHORTBREAD COOKIES

1 c. butter (some Spry)　　2 c. flour
1/2 c. sugar　　　　　　　1 c. Brazil nuts, sliced

Cream butter and sugar. Sift flour once; add to butter and sugar. Blend in nuts. Chill dough; shape into small balls, using your hands. Dough will be very stiff; press down. Bake on ungreased pan for 15-20 minutes at 300° F. Makes 4 1/2 to 5 dozen cookies.
Helen Evenson, Litchfield, Mn.

SNICKERDOODLES

1 c. (1/2 lb.) butter or　　2 3/4 c. white flour
　margarine　　　　　　　1 tsp. baking soda
1 1/2 c. plus 2 Tbsp. sugar　1/4 tsp. salt
2 eggs　　　　　　　　　2 tsp. cinnamon

In large mixer bowl with electric mixer at medium speed, cream butter or margarine, 1 1/2 cups sugar and eggs until light and fluffy, scraping sides of bowl. Combine flour, cream of tartar, baking soda and salt. Add to creamed mixture until well blended. Refrigerate dough for 30 minutes. Preheat oven to 375°. Combine remaining 2 tablespoons sugar and cinnamon in a flat, open barrel. Shape dough into 2 inch balls; roll in cinnamon-sugar. Bake 12 to 15 minutes.
Joan Billadeau, St. Cloud, Mn.

"SOLO" QUICK COTTAGE CHEESE COOKIES

1 c. margarine　　　　　1 c. cottage cheese
2 c. all-purpose flour

Cream the margarine and cottage cheese together. Work in the flour; mold to form a dough. Wrap in wax paper and chill 2 hours. Roll out like pie crust; cut in squares, 2 to 3 inches. Put 1 teaspoon Solo apricot pie and pastry filling in each square. Bake 15 minutes in 425° oven. When cool, dust with powdered sugar. Makes a large recipe and they can be frozen.
V. Robbs, Minneapolis, Mn.

1 c. butter	1 3/4 c. flour
3/4 c. sugar	1/2 tsp. salt
1 egg yolk	1 tsp. vanilla

Cream butter and sugar; add the egg yolk, salt and vanilla. Blend in the flour. Put in cooky press and shape cookies. Bake at 325° for 10 to 12 minutes; watch closely.

Sigrid Johnson, Hibbing, Mn.

Similar recipe submitted by: K., St. Cloud, Mn.

WHITE SUGAR COOKIES

1 c. butter	4 c. flour, sifted
1 c. shortening	2 tsp. soda
1 c. white sugar	2 tsp. cream of tartar
1 c. powdered sugar	1 tsp. salt
2 eggs	2 tsp. vanilla

Cream shortening, butter and sugars. Add eggs; beat until fluffy. Sift remaining ingredients together and add; refrigerate. Roll in balls; press down with a decorative glass, dipped in sugar. Bake at 350° for 10 minutes.

Norma Stevens, Montevideo, Mn.

Similar recipes submitted by: Norma Haugerud, Montevideo, Mn., Eileen Rekowski, St. Cloud, Mn.

E-Z SUGAR COOKIES

Sift together:

3 c. flour	1 tsp. soda
2 tsp. baking powder	1/4 tsp. nutmeg

Cream:

1 c. shortening	2 eggs, beaten
1 c. sugar	

Add:

4 Tbsp. milk	1/2 tsp. salt
1 tsp. vanilla	

Add dry ingredients; mix well. Roll out on floured board and cut in any shape with cookie cutters. Brush with milk; sprinkle with sugar. Bake in 375° oven for 8 to 10 minutes.

Mrs. Norma Applen, Minneapolis, Mn.

Similar recipe submitted by: Goldie Mikish, Staples, Mn.

DIFFERENT SUGAR COOKIES

3/4 c. butter or margarine
3/4 c. white sugar
1 egg
1 tsp. vanilla

1 1/2 c. flour
3/4 c. crushed potato chips
1/2 c. walnuts

Mix in order; roll into balls. Flatten with fork. Bake at 350° for 10-12 minutes.

G.W. Seemans, Robbinsdale, Mn.

SUGAR COOKIES

Cream:
1 c. butter or margarine   2 c. sugar

Add 2 eggs. Sift:

3 c. flour   1 tsp. salt
1 tsp. baking soda

Add 2 tablespoons vanilla and 2 cups walnuts. Bake on ungreased cookie sheet at 375°.

Arlene Carlson, Lake Park, Mn.

SUGAR COOKIES

1 c. butter or margarine
1 c. Crisco oil
2 c. sugar
2 eggs
1 tsp. vanilla

4 c. flour
1 tsp. cream of tartar
1 tsp. soda
1 tsp. salt
1 1/2 tsp. nutmeg

Cream butter and sugar; add oil and beat until smooth. Beat in eggs and vanilla. Stir in dry ingredients. Chill dough 1 hour; roll in balls and flatten with glass. Bake at 350° for 12-15 minutes.

Jo Nell Murack, Fargo, N.D.

SUGAR COOKIES

3 c. flour
1 tsp. soda
2 tsp. cream of tartar

1 c. sugar
1/2 c. butter
1/2 c. lard (I use all
          margarine)

Mix like pie crust. Add 2 beaten eggs and 1 teaspoon

vanilla. (Towards the last, I mix with my hands.) Roll thin; sprinkle with sugar. Bake at 350°.

Mrs. Robert Benson, Stillwater, Mn.

WALNUT SUGAR COOKIES

1/2 c. butter	1 c. sugar
1/2 c. Crisco	1/4 tsp. salt

Cream shortenings and sugar. Add 1 egg yolk and 1 teaspoon vanilla. Add 2 cups flour; roll into small balls. Brush with egg white. Sprinkle with sugar and press walnut half on top. Bake at 350° for about 8 minutes on lightly greased cookie sheet.

Mary Flaten, Grand Forks, N.D.

WORLD'S BEST SUGAR COOKIES

Cream together:

1 c. powdered sugar	1 c. butter
1 c. granulated sugar	

Add:

1 c. Mazola oil	1/4 tsp. salt
2 tsp. vinegar	5 c. flour
1 tsp. soda	2 eggs, beaten
1 tsp. cream of tartar	

Roll into small balls; press with fancy glass, bottom dipped in sugar. Sprinkle sugar over. Bake at 350° for 10-12 minutes. For easier handling, refrigerate overnight.

Mary Paul, Minneapolis, Mn.

SHORTBREAD

1 c. butter (not margarine)	1 c. cornstarch
1 c. confectioners sugar	2 c. flour

Cream butter and sugar; add cornstarch and flour. Work well with hands; press mixture into a small rectangular pan or a 9x9 inch square pan. Prick dough with fork all over. Bake at 375° for about 45 minutes or until golden brown. The top can be sprinkled very lightly with fine granulated sugar. Cut into small squares before cool. Eat cold.

Juliet Lindblad, Coon Rapids, Mn.

SPANISH WIND

1 c. egg whites (8-11 whites) 1 c. plus 2 Tbsp. granulated
1/4 tsp. salt sugar
1/2 tsp. cream of tartar 2 3/4 c. confectioners sugar
1 Tbsp. instant coffee 2 1/2 c. chopped walnuts
1 c. (6 oz.) chocolate chips

Combine egg whites, salt, cream of tartar and instant coffee. Whip to soft peaks. Add granulated sugar a little at a time, beating until stiff. Fold in confectioners sugar, walnuts and chocolate chips. Place teaspoonfuls on a cookie sheet, that has been lightly greased and dusted with flour. Bake 1 1/2 hours at 200°; cool on racks. Makes 85 cookies.

St. Cloud, Mn.

UNBAKED COOKIES

1/2 c. milk 2 c. sugar
1/2 c. margarine

Boil 1 minute. Add 3 cups oatmeal, 3 tablespoons cocoa, 1 teaspoon vanilla and 2/3 cup peanut butter. Drop on waxed paper and cool.

Ruth Lee, Detroit Lakes, Mn.

WAFFLE IRON COOKIES

Melt 4 squares chocolate and 1 cup butter (only butter). Add:

4 eggs 2 tsp. salt
1/2 c. sugar 2 c. flour
1 1/2 tsp. vanilla

Stir all together well; drop on ungreased waffle iron. Put cover down; bake for 1 minute only. Lift off carefully with fork.

Frosting:

1/2 c. brown sugar 1/4 c. water
1 sq. chocolate 3 Tbsp. butter
1 tsp. vanilla 1 1/2 c. powdered sugar

Combine sugar, water and chocolate; let come to a boil. Boil for 3 minutes; add butter and vanilla. Blend in sugar. May thin with cream or milk, if necessary.

Joan Norton, Hibbing, Mn.
Pat Ivey, Bismarck, N.D.

508

WHITE OVEN SCONES

4 c. flour	1 oz. sugar (about 2 Tbsp.)
1 tsp. soda	6 Tbsp. butter
2 tsp. cream of tartar	1 egg
1/2 tsp. salt	Milk to mix

Sift the flour, sugar and cream of tartar into a bowl. Add the salt and sugar; rub in the butter. Beat the egg; pour into a well in the flour mixture with enough milk to make a very soft dough. Turn onto a floured board; sprinkle with flour. Roll out or pat out to 1/2 inch thickness. Cut into rounds or triangles and bake in a pretty quick oven, about 400°, for 10 to 15 minutes. If you use buttermilk (which makes a better scone), use half the quantity of cream of tartar. Serve warm (not hot) for tea; spread with butter and/or jam.

Betty Mallon, Minneapolis, Mn.

YULE LOGS
(So Easy!)

5 Tbsp. sugar	1 tsp. vanilla
1 c. margarine (best if	1 tsp. lemon extract
1/2 butter)	2 c. flour

Mix well; form into oblong logs in waxed paper. Chill 2 hours; slice 1/4 inch thick. Bake 12 minutes at 375°, until just starting to brown at edges. While hot from oven, roll in sugar and cinnamon (3 tablespoons sugar to 1/2 teaspoon cinnamon).

Pam Doyea, Fargo, N.D.

APPLE BARS

Cream together:

1/2 c. shortening	2 eggs
1 c. sugar	

Sift together:

1 c. flour	1/2 tsp. salt
1 tsp. baking powder	1/2 tsp. soda

Add:

1 Tbsp. cocoa	1/2 tsp. cloves
1 tsp. cinnamon	1/2 tsp. nutmeg

Add to the shortening mixture; mix well. Add 1 cup oatmeal, 1 1/2 cups chopped apples and 1 cup chopped nuts. Bake in a greased 9x13 inch pan in 375° oven for 25 minutes.

Frosting:

1 (3 oz.) pkg. Philadelphia cream cheese	Vanilla
	Powdered sugar
Butter	

Esther Mungovan, Duluth, Mn.

APPLE BARS

Filling:

6 1/2 c. apples, sliced	1 tsp. cinnamon
1 c. sugar	

Crust: (Make like pie crust)

2 1/2 c. flour	1 egg yolk (save white), plus
1 tsp. salt	milk to equal 2/3 c.
1 Tbsp. sugar	1 c. lard

Divide crust in half; roll out. Put half in brownie pan. Sprinkle 2 handfuls of crushed corn flakes on bottom crust. Put in filling. Roll out top crust and put it on. Beat egg white till foamy; brush across top crust. Bake at 350° for 45 minutes. While warm, frost with powdered sugar and water.

Mary Jane Schmitz, Wadena, Mn.

RAW APPLE BARS

Beat together until light:

2 c. white sugar	2 large eggs
1 c. Mazola oil	1 tsp. vanilla

Sift and add:

2 c. flour	1 tsp. cinnamon
1 tsp. soda	1/4 tsp. salt

Add 3 cups raw, thinly sliced apples and 1 cup chopped nuts. Bake in a 9x13 inch pan for 35 minutes at 350°.

Frosting: Beat until creamy -

2 (3 oz.) pkg. Philadelphia   3 Tbsp. melted butter
   cream cheese, room   1 1/2 c. powdered sugar
   temperature

              Delina Sherette, St. Paul, Mn.

APPLE NUT SQUARES

3 eggs   1 tsp. cinnamon
1 c. sugar   1/4 tsp. salt
1 c. oil   5 tart apples, peeled, diced
2 c. flour   1 c. nuts
1 tsp. soda

    Blend eggs, sugar and oil; add sifted dry ingredients. Fold in nuts and apples. Pour in jelly roll pan and top with 1 teaspoon cinnamon and 1/4 cup sugar, mixed together. Bake at 350° for 35 minutes.
              Lorraine Pauls, Fargo, N.D.

FRESH APPLE BARS

1 3/4 c. apples (heaping)   1/4 tsp. nutmeg
1 c. sugar   1/4 tsp. allspice
1 1/2 c. all-purpose flour   1/2 c. melted butter
1 tsp. baking soda   1 egg, beaten
3/4 tsp. cinnamon   1/2 c. seedless raisins (opt.)
1/4 tsp. salt   1/2 c. chopped walnuts

    Peel and core apples; chop coarsely. Measure 1 3/4 cups into a large bowl. Add sugar; let stand 10 minutes to dissolve. Sift flour; add soda, salt and spices. Set aside. Blend butter and beaten egg into apple mixture. Add flour mixture, stirring until just blended. Fold in floured raisins and nuts. Bake in shallow 7x11 inch pan at 350° for 35 minutes or until done. Cool; frost with powdered sugar frosting or sprinkle with powdered sugar.
              Bev. Jensen, Willmar, Mn.

APPLESAUCE BARS

1/2 c. shortening   1 c. dates, chopped
1 c. sugar   1 1/2 c. applesauce
1 egg   (Musselman's)
1 c. chopped nuts   1 tsp. cinnamon

1/4 tsp. cloves
2 c. flour
1/2 tsp. baking powder

1 1/2 tsp. soda
1/4 tsp. salt
Vanilla

Cream shortening and sugar; add egg and mix well. Add rest of ingredients. Bake 25 to 30 minutes at 350° in 10x14 inch pan.

Frosting:

3 c. powdered sugar
1/3 c. soft butter or
  margarine

4 Tbsp. orange juice
A little grated orange rind

Blend sugar and butter; stir in juice until smooth. Spread on bars while a little warm.

Aster Paulsrud, Montevideo, Mn.

BANANA BARS

1/3 c. butter
1 c. sugar
1 egg
1 c. flour
1/4 tsp. baking powder

1/4 tsp. salt
1/4 c. powdered milk
1/2 c. nuts, chopped
1/4 tsp. vanilla
2 or 3 bananas, mashed

Cream butter and sugar; add egg. Sift flour, baking powder and salt; add to first mixture. Add powdered milk, nuts and vanilla. Add bananas; mix well. Bake in a lightly greased 9x13 inch pan for 30 minutes in 350° oven. When cool, frost with:

2 sq. chocolate, melted with
  2 Tbsp. butter

1 tsp. vanilla
2 c. powdered sugar
Hot coffee to thin

Mrs. Norma Applen, Minneapolis, Mn.

BROWNIES

2 eggs, well beaten
1 c. sugar
5 Tbsp. melted butter
4 Tbsp. cocoa
2/3 c. flour

1/3 c. milk
1/4 tsp. salt
1 tsp. vanilla
1 c. nutmeats

Mix in order given. Bake 30 minutes at 350°. This makes a small pan of brownies.

Frosting for Brownies:

2 1/2 Tbsp. hot milk
2 Tbsp. butter or margarine

1 c. powdered sugar
2 Tbsp. cocoa
1 tsp. vanilla

Mix well in order given. Spread right away.

Marion Iverson, Bismarck, N.D.
Similar recipe submitted by: Kathryn Otto, Harvey, N.D.

BEST-EVER BROWNIES

2 sq. unsweetened chocolate
1/2 c. (1 stick) butter or
    margarine
2 eggs
1 c. sugar

1/2 tsp. salt
1 tsp. vanilla
1/2 c. sifted flour
3/4 c. chopped nuts

Melt chocolate and butter in a small saucepan over low heat; cool. Beat eggs in small bowl; gradually beat in sugar until mixture is fluffy-thick. Stir in chocolate mixture and vanilla. Fold in flour and salt until well blended. Stir in nuts. Spread evenly in an 8x8x2 inch baking pan. Bake in moderate oven, 350°, for 30 minutes or until shiny and firm on top. Cool completely in pan on a wire rack. Makes 16.

Frosting:

1 (6 oz.) pkg. semi-sweet
    chocolate pieces

1/2 c. dairy sour cream

Melt chocolate pieces in top of double boiler over hot water; stir until smooth. Remove from heat; stir in sour cream until well blended. Spread frosting on cooled brownies.

Betty Baune, St. Paul, Mn.
Similar recipe submitted by: Fisher, St. Paul, Mn.

CALIFORNIA GOLD BARS

1 c. brown sugar, firmly
    packed
1 c. (2 sticks) butter or
    margarine
1 egg

1 tsp. vanilla
1 3/4 c. flour
1 c. chopped walnuts
1/2 c. apricot jam

Beat together sugar, butter, egg and vanilla until smooth and creamy. Stir in flour and nuts. Spoon half the batter in a greased 9 inch square pan; spread evenly. Spread jam evenly over batter; put remaining batter on. Bake at 325° for 50 minutes. Cool 10 minutes, then cut into squares.

Marion Round, Faribault, Mn.

CARAMEL BARS

1/2 c. evaporated milk	2 c. flour
1 1/2 bags Kraft caramels	2 c. oatmeal
1 1/2 c. margarine	1 tsp. soda
1 1/2 c. brown sugar	1 c. chocolate chips
	1/2 c. nuts

Melt caramels with milk. Mix shortening and sugar; add dry ingredients. Pat 1/2 of crumb mixture in 9x13 inch pan. Bake at 350° for 10 minutes, then sprinkle chocolate chips over. Put melted caramel over this. Add rest of crumb mixture; bake at 350° for 20 minutes.

Sue Hetland, Grand Forks, N.D.

CHEWY CARAMEL BARS

Mix:

3/4 c. flour	1/4 tsp. salt
1/4 tsp. soda	1/2 c. brown sugar
3/4 c. oatmeal	1/2 c. melted margarine

Bake in 9x13 inch pan at 350° for 15 minutes. Mix:

3/4 c. light syrup	1/2 c. white sugar

Bring to boil slowly; remove from burner and add 3/4 cup peanut butter. Cool; pour over crust. Slowly bring to a boil and cook 1 minute:

1/2 c. milk	1 tsp. vanilla
1/4 c. butter	1 c. chocolate chips
2 c. sugar	

Remove from burner and add.

Sue Hetland, Grand Forks, N.D.

514

CARAMELICKS

1 pkg. white cake mix
2 beaten eggs

1/2 c. vegetable oil
1 c. caramel ice cream
    topping

Combine and mix well; stir in 1 cup nuts. Bake in ungreased cookie sheet at 325° for 25 to 30 minutes.

Rosie Schudar, Fargo, N.D.

CAROB AND CREAM CHEESE BROWNIES

1 c. unsalted butter
2 c. brown sugar
2 tsp. vanilla
4 eggs
1 c. sifted carob powder

1/4 c. milk
1 1/2 c. flour
2 tsp. baking powder
1 c. walnuts
Cream Cheese Filling (below)

Cream together butter and brown sugar; add vanilla. Add eggs, one at a time, beating after each. Stir in carob powder alternately with milk. Sift together flour and baking powder, reserving 1 tablespoon. Beat into creamed mixture. Toss reserved flour with nuts; add to batter. Spread half of thick batter onto greased 15 inch rectangular pan. Cover with Cream Cheese Filling; top with remaining batter. Using a table knife, zigzag through layers to marble. Bake at 275° for 50 minutes. Makes 18 generous bars.

Variation: Use carob chips and omit walnuts.

Cream Cheese Filling:

6 oz. cream cheese
4 Tbsp. butter
1/2 c. sugar

2 eggs
2 Tbsp. flour
1 tsp. vanilla

Cream together cream cheese and butter; gradually add sugar. Blend in eggs, flour and vanilla until light and fluffy.

St. Cloud, Mn.

QUICK BROWNIES

1 pkg. chocolate cake mix
1 pkg. instant vanilla
    pudding mix

2 eggs
1 c. milk
1 c. water

Mix all ingredients together; pour into greased and floured jelly roll pan. Bake about 25 minutes in 350° oven. Frost with your favorite chocolate frosting.

Gordy and Elaine Sneva, Brainerd, Mn.

GUMDROP BARS

4 eggs
1 tsp. vanilla
2 c. light brown sugar
1/4 tsp. salt

2 c. flour
1/2 c. chopped nuts
1 c. finely chopped gumdrops
(lemon and orange)

Beat eggs until light and thick. Add sugar gradually; continue beating until thick. Add nuts, gumdrops and flour (mix all together before adding so nuts and gumdrops are coated with flour). Blend well. Spread 3/4 inch thick in greased pan, 9x12 inches. Bake 20-30 minutes at 325°.

Bessie Wilke, Detroit Lakes, Mn.

TOLL HOUSE DOUBLE CHOCOLATE BROWNIES

3/4 c. unsifted flour
1/4 measuring tsp. baking
soda
1/4 measuring tsp. salt
1/3 c. butter
3/4 c. sugar
2 eggs

2 measuring Tbsp. water
1 (12 oz.) pkg. (2 c.)
Nestle's semi-sweet real
chocolate morsels, divided
1 measuring tsp. vanilla
extract
1/2 c. chopped nuts

Preheat oven to 325° F. In small bowl, combine flour, baking soda and salt; set aside. In small saucepan, combine butter, sugar and water; bring just to a boil. Remove from heat. Add 6 ounces (1 cup) Nestle's semi-sweet real chocolate morsels and vanilla extract. Stir until morsels melt and mixture is smooth. Transfer to large bowl. Add eggs, one at a time, beating well after each addition. Gradually blend in flour mixture. Stir in remaining 1 cup Nestle's semi-sweet real chocolate morsels and nuts. Spread into greased 9 inch square baking pan. Bake at 325° F. for 30-35 minutes; cool completely. Cut into 2 1/4 inch squares. Makes 16 (2 1/4 inch) squares.

Margaret McKenney, Minneapolis, Mn.

TWO LAYER BROWNIES

First Layer:

1/2 c. oleo	3 eggs
1 1/2 c. white sugar	1 c. flour
3 Tbsp. cocoa	1 c. walnuts, cut up

Bake at 350° for 25 minutes in 9x13 inch pan. Cool before adding second layer.

Second Layer: Mix -

1 can Eagle Brand milk   2 c. coconut

Pour over baked brownies. Bake 15 minutes or until golden brown.

Frosting:

1 c. sugar	6 Tbsp. milk
6 Tbsp. oleo	

Boil 1 minute; add 1/2 cup chocolate chips. Beat until spreadable.

Florence Wesen, St. Cloud, Mn.

CEREAL GO-GO BARS

1/2 c. butter or margarine	1/4 c. orange instant
32 large or 3 c. miniature	breakfast drink
marshmallows	1 c. raisins
1/2 c. peanut butter	4 c. Cheerios cereal
1/2 c. nonfat dry milk	

Melt butter and marshmallows over low heat; stir in peanut butter until melted. Stir in milk and breakfast drink. Fold in raisins and cereal, stirring until evenly coated. Turn into buttered 9x9x2 inch pan; with buttered hands, pat evenly in pan. Cool; cut into 2 x 1 1/2 inch bars.

Leslie Zimbrick, Minneapolis, Mn

CHEERIO NUGGETS

1 c. brown sugar	1/2 tsp. soda
1/2 c. butter or margarine	6 c. Cheerios
1/4 c. white corn syrup	1 c. salted peanuts
1/2 tsp. salt	1 c. raisins

Heat oven to 250°. Grease jelly roll pan and 4 quart mixing bowl. Heat brown sugar, margarine, syrup and salt in 2 quart pan over medium heat; stir constantly until it bubbles around edge. Cook 2 minutes; remove from heat and stir in soda until foamy. Pour over cereal, peanuts and raisins in bowl; stir until well coated. Spread in pan. Bake 15 minutes. Remove from oven; let stand 10 minutes and stir.

Alice Gudnecht, Faribault, Mn.

CHERRY ALMOND BARS

2 c. sugar	1 tsp. vanilla
2 sticks margarine	1 tsp. almond extract
4 eggs, beaten 1 at a time	3 c. flour

Spread 3/4 of mixture in greased and floured jelly roll pan. Spread on 1 (regular 21 ounce) can cherry pie filling. Spoon remaining 1/4 of dough on top. Bake at 350° for 20-25 minutes.

Frosting:

1 lb. powdered sugar	1/8 tsp. salt
1/2 c. soft butter or margarine	1 tsp. almond extract

Add milk to make thin consistency. Spread over cooled bars.

Liz Tuft, St. Paul, Mn.

BLACK BOTTOM CHERRY CREAM BARS

1/3 c. butter	1/2 - 1 c. maraschino
1/2 c. sugar	cherries
2 Tbsp. cocoa	2 c. grated coconut
3/4 c. flour	3/4 c. sweetened condensed
1 egg	milk

Melt butter; add cocoa, sugar, flour and egg. Mix well; spread in greased 9x9 inch pan. Place cherries on chocolate mixture. Combine coconut and sweetened condensed milk; spoon over base. Spread to cover. Bake at 350° for 30 to 35 minutes. Frost warm. Cool; cut into squares.

Chocolate Frosting: Melt together 1/3 cup semi-sweet

chocolate pieces, 1 tablespoon butter and 1 tablespoon milk. Stir in 1/2 cup powdered sugar; beat until smooth. If necessary, thin with additional milk.

Lorraine Rieger, Minneapolis, Mn.

JOANNIE'S GOOD CHERRY BARS

Cream together:

1/2 c. oleo	1/2 c. brown sugar
1/2 c. white sugar	

Sift together:

2 c. flour	1/2 tsp. salt
1 1/2 tsp. baking powder	

Blend into creamed mixture 2 eggs with 1 teaspoon vanilla. Add flour alternately with 3/4 cup milk. Stir in:

1 c. nuts	1 c. maraschino cherries
1 c. chocolate chips	

Bake in prepared 10x15 inch pan at 350° for 25 minutes.

Frosting:

1/2 c. oleo	1 tsp. vanilla
2 c. powdered sugar	Milk as needed

Mary Anne Zachman, Bemidji, Mn.

CHOCOLATE BUTTERSCOTCH BARS

Margarine	12 oz. chocolate chips
1 1/2 c. miniature	1 c. walnuts
marshmallows	20 walnut halves (optional)
12 oz. butterscotch chips	

In a double boiler over hot, not boiling, water, melt butterscotch chips with 1 tablespoon margarine. Remove from heat; stir in chopped walnuts. Spread evenly in greased 8x8x2 inch pan. Arrange marshmallows evenly over butterscotch layer, gently pressing into surface. In same double boiler over hot, not boiling, water, melt choc olate chips with 1 tablespoon margarine; stir smooth. Spread this chocolate mixture evenly on marshmallows. Lay walnuts in soft chocolate, if desired. Cool, then refrigerate until needed.

Nancy Fechtner, Fargo, N.D.

CHOCOLATE MINT STICKS

2 eggs
1 c. sugar
1/2 c. melted margarine

2 sq. chocolate
1/2 tsp. peppermint extract

Blend all well and add 1/2 cup sifted flour and 1/2 cup nuts. Mix; bake in 9x13 inch pan at 350° for 20 minutes. Cool and frost.

Frosting:

1 1/2 c. sifted powdered
   sugar
3 Tbsp. butter

1 1/2 Tbsp. cream or milk
1/4 tsp. peppermint extract

Spread over cool bars, then melt 1 1/2 squares chocolate and 1 1/2 tablespoons butter and spread over frosting. Chill and cut into strips.

Pam Doyea, Fargo, N.D.

CHOCOLATE MACAROON BARS

1 c. butter or oleo
4 eggs
1/4 tsp. salt
1 tsp. vanilla

2 c. sugar
1/2 c. cocoa
1/2 c. chopped nuts
2 c. flour

Combine the above ingredients; put 1/2 of mixture in a 9x13 inch pan, then a layer of Macaroon Mixture, then rest of batter on top.

Macaroon Mixture:

1 pkg. Betty Crocker
   macaroon mix

3/4 c. water

Bake at 350° for about 35 minutes.

Frosting:

1/4 c. water
1 sq. Baker's chocolate

1/2 c. brown sugar
6 large marshmallows

Boil over low heat until melted. Let cool; add 1 teaspoon vanilla and sifted powdered sugar until preferred consistency.

Joan Norton, Hibbing, Mn.

CHOCOLATE-MOLASSES BARS

1/2 c. margarine
1/4 c. molasses
3/4 c. brown sugar
1 egg
1 c. flour

1/2 tsp. salt
1/2 tsp. soda
1 (6 oz.) pkg. chocolate
chips

Heat margarine and molasses. Add sugar; heat and stir until melted. Cool. Beat egg until light and fluffy. Add to mixture. Add flour, salt, soda and chips; mix well. Spread in greased 9x13 inch pan. Bake for 20 minutes in a 350° oven.

Mrs. Norma Applen, Minneapolis, Mn.

CHOCOLATE-PEANUT BUTTER BARS
(For a Scrumptious Holiday Treat!)

1/2 c. light corn syrup
1/4 c. brown sugar, packed
1/8 tsp. salt
1 c. peanut butter

3 c. Cheerios cereal
1 (6 oz.) pkg. semi-sweet
chocolate pieces
1 tsp. vanilla

Butter square pan, 9x9x2 inches. In large saucepan, heat corn syrup, sugar and salt to boiling. Stir in peanut butter; remove from heat. Stir in cereal, chocolate pieces and vanilla until well coated. Turn into pan; pat mixture evenly with buttered back of spoon or hands. Refrigerate until firm, at least 1 hour. Cut into bars, about 2 1/4 x 1 1/2 inches. Makes 2 dozen.

Margaret McKenney, Minneapolis, Mn.

CHOCOLATE REVEL BARS

Cream:
1 c. shortening
2 eggs

2 c. brown sugar
2 tsp. vanilla

Add:
2 1/2 c. sifted flour
1 tsp. salt

1 tsp. soda

Filling: Melt over double boiler -

1 (6 oz.) pkg. chocolate
chips
1 c. Eagle Brand milk

2 Tbsp. butter or oleo
2 tsp. vanilla

Spread 2/3 of first mixture into bottom of pan. Pour filling on top; sprinkle rest of oatmeal mixture on top. Bake 25 minutes at 350° in 9x13 inch pan.

Linda Hamann, Minneapolis, Mn.

SARAH'S COCOANUT BARS
(Very Good)

2 c. brown sugar, packed	2 c. flour (use presifted;
1/2 c. oleo or butter	don't sift)
2 eggs (3 if small)	Pinch of salt
2 tsp. vanilla	3/4 c. cocoanut (any kind)
2 tsp. baking powder	1/2 c. nuts (if you wish)

Melt butter slowly; add sugar and stir. Melt slowly. Add remaining mixture in order given. Pour into greased 9x13 inch pan (flour also). Bake 25 minutes at 350°; cut while warm.

Caution: Do not bake too long; can test with fork, 25 minutes should be long enough, otherwise bars get dry.

Mrs. Kermit A. Haugen, Clarkfield, Mn.

COCONUT WAFERS

1 c. flour	1/2 c. butter
3 Tbsp. brown sugar	

Mix and pat in pan. Bake 10 minutes at 350°.

2 eggs, beaten	1/2 tsp. vanilla
1 1/2 c. brown sugar	1/2 tsp. salt
3 Tbsp. (heaping) flour	1/2 c. coconut
1/2 tsp. baking powder	1/2 c. chopped nuts

Mix; spread over top of first mixture. Bake 1/2 hour.

Kay Buzzell, Marshall, Mn.

CRUNCHIE MUNCHIES

Cream:

1/4 c. butter	2 eggs
3/4 c. sugar	1 1/2 tsp. vanilla

Add:

1 c. wheat germ	1/2 tsp. baking powder
1/2 c. dry milk	1/4 tsp. salt

Mix this real well; add 1 cup chopped walnuts.
Spread in greased 8 inch pan. Bake at 350° for 35-40 minutes. Cool in pan, then cut. Makes about 2 dozen.

Jo-Lyn Freitag, Minneapolis, Mn.

DATE AND CHOCOLATE CHIP BARS

1 c. dates, cut up

1 1/4 c. boiling water

1 tsp. soda

Let mixture cool. Mix:

2 eggs	2 c. flour
3/4 c. oleo	1 tsp. baking powder
1 c. brown sugar	1/4 tsp. salt

Add date mixture; put in cookie sheet. Sprinkle over bars 12 ounces chocolate chips and 1 cup nuts. Bake at 375° for 30 minutes.

Alice Bauman, St. Paul, Mn.

SAUCEPAN DATE-NUT BARS

1/2 c. butter or margarine	1 tsp. vanilla
2/3 c. packed brown sugar	1/2 c. chopped nuts
2 Tbsp. water	1 c. flour
1 c. chopped dates	1 1/4 tsp. baking powder
1 egg, slightly beaten	

Melt butter in saucepan; remove from heat. Add sugar and water; blend well. Stir in dates, egg, vanilla and nuts. Combine flour with baking powder; stir into first mixture. Pour into greased 9 inch square pan. Bake at 350° for about 30 minutes. (I usually double recipe and bake in 9x13 inch pan or jelly roll pan.)

Ruth Eberlein, Luverne, Mn.

DELICIOUS SOUTHWESTERN BARS

3/4 c. margarine	1 1/2 c. flaked coconut
1 pkg. German chocolate cake mix	1 c. chopped pecans
3 c. miniature marshmallows	1 (14 oz.) can sweetened condensed milk
1 (6 oz.) pkg. butterscotch chips	

Preheat oven to 350°. In oven, melt margarine in 15 x 10 1/2 x 1 inch pan. Tilt pan so the margarine covers the bottom. Sprinkle the dry cake mix in the pan. Layer marshmallows, butterscotch chips, coconut and nuts over cake mix in order given. Pour condensed milk evenly over the top. Bake 25 minutes or until brown.

Mildred Nelson, St. Paul, Mn.

DREAM BARS

Pastry:

1 c. sifted flour   3 Tbsp. confectioners sugar
1/2 c. butter

Mix well; put into 9x13 inch pan. Bake until brown at 350°.

Filling:

2 eggs   1 c. walnuts, chopped (not
1 1/2 c. brown sugar   fine)
2 Tbsp. flour   1 (8 or 9 oz.) bottle red
1/2 tsp. baking powder   cherries
1/2 tsp. salt   1 (8 or 9 oz.) bottle green
1 c. flaked coconut   cherries
                                1 tsp. vanilla

Reserve 1/4 cup each of walnuts, coconut and cherries for frosting. Beat eggs; add brown sugar. Add vanilla and flour, that has been sifted with baking powder and salt. Add 3/4 cup nuts, coconut and both colored cherries. Spread over baked layer of pastry; return to oven for 25 minutes. Cool and frost with:

1 1/2 c. sifted confectioners   1-2 Tbsp. grated orange rind
    sugar   Orange juice
2 Tbsp. melted butter

Mix all ingredients, adding enough orange juice to make it the right consistency to spread. (You can add red cherry juice to make it a beautiful pink color.) Sprinkle reserved nuts, coconut and cherries on frosting. Frost only when cool.

This is a long recipe but well worth the trouble for Christmas time. It's very caloric! It's delicious and gorgeous to look at!!

Margo Schmidt, Minneapolis, Mn.

DREAM BARS

1/2 c. butter   1 c. flour
1/2 c. brown sugar

Mix together; pat in bottom of pan. Bake at 350° until light brown, 15 minutes.

Topping:

2 eggs, well beaten   1 1/2 c. coconut
1 c. brown sugar   1/2 c. nuts
1 tsp. baking powder   1 tsp. vanilla
2 Tbsp. flour   Pinch of salt

Pour over bottom layer; bake about 20 minutes at 350°. Do not overbake. No frosting needed. Peanuts can be substituted for walnuts.

Adeline Hortsch, St. Cloud, Mn.

EASY BARS

1 chocolate cake mix   1 can cherry pie filling

Spread on jelly roll pan. Bake at 350° for 20 minutes. Melt 1 (12 ounce) package chocolate chips; pour over top, if desired.

Marion Round, Faribault, Mn.

FRUIT BARS

2 c. seedless raisins, rinsed   1 c. chopped walnuts
   with hot water, drained   1/2 c. orange or pineapple
1 1/2 c. chopped, candied   juice
   mixed fruit   2 tsp. vanilla

Combine and let stand. Cream together:

1 c. butter or margarine   1 c. brown sugar, firmly
1 c. white sugar   packed
2 beaten eggs

Sift together:
4 1/2 c. flour   2 tsp. baking powder
2 tsp. ground cinnamon   1 tsp. baking soda

Mix all together; let stand 1 1/2 hours or overnight. Put in greased 15 1/2 x 10 1/2 x 1 inch pan. Bake at 400° for 15 to 20 minutes. Makes 4 dozen bars.

1507-82   Marion Round, Faribault, Mn.

FRUIT COCKTAIL BARS

2 eggs
1 1/2 c. sugar
2 1/4 c. flour

1 can fruit cocktail (do not drain)
1 1/2 tsp. soda

Beat eggs and sugar; add fruit, flour mixture and vanilla. Beat at medium speed. Put in jelly roll pan. Sprinkle 1/2 cup nuts and 1 1/3 cups coconut on top. While hot, drizzle with glaze. Bake at 350° for 25 or 30 minutes.

Glaze:

3/4 c. sugar
1/2 c. butter

1/4 c. evaporated milk
1/2 tsp. vanilla

Combine sugar and milk; boil 2 minutes. Add butter; cool.

Lucille F. Anderson, East Grand Forks, Mn.

FUDGE SQUARES

2 c. sugar
1/2 c. melted butter or
  margarine
4 eggs
3 sq. melted chocolate
1/2 tsp. salt

1/2 c. milk
1 1/3 c. flour
1 tsp. vanilla
3/4 - 1 c. nuts
2 tsp. baking powder

Melt butter and chocolate together in large pan. Add sugar, then eggs. Add rest of ingredients alternately. Bake 20 to 25 minutes in 350° oven or until toothpick comes out clean. Frost with Mocha Icing.

Marie Capen, Duluth, Mn.

FUDGE SCOTCH SQUARES

Preheat oven to 350° F. Blend together:

1 1/2 c. graham cracker
  crumbs
1 can Borden's Eagle Brand
  sweetened condensed milk
  (not evaporated)

1 pkg. semi-sweet chocolate
  chips
1 pkg. butterscotch chips
1 c. chopped walnuts

Mix well; press mixture into a very well greased 9 inch square pan. Bake at 350° for 30-35 minutes. Cool for 45 minutes; cut into 1 1/2 inch squares. Makes 35.

Colleen Landwehr, St. Cloud, Mn.

GERMAN FUDGE WONDERBARS

1/4 c. butter or margarine
1 c. firmly packed brown
  sugar
1 c. chopped nuts
1 c. flaked coconut
1/2 c. evaporated milk

1 (8 oz.) pkg. cream
  cheese, softened
1 egg
1 2/3 c. fudge frosting mix
1 roll chocolate chip slice
  and bake cookies

Line a 13x9 inch pan with foil. Melt butter in pan. In large mixing bowl, blend cream cheese and egg. Measure 1 2/3 cups dry frosting mix by spooning into cup and leveling off. Gradually add dry frosting mix until well blended. Spread cheese mixture over mixture in pan. Slice cookie dough into 1/4 inch slices; arrange slices over top of cream cheese mixture. Bake in 350° oven for 35 to 40 minutes until golden brown. Immediately invert on cookie sheet to remove from pan. Chill before cutting into bars. Makes 36 bars.

Elaine Aaberg, Minneapolis, Mn.

GOORI CHEWIES

2/3 c. oleo
1 c. brown sugar

1/2 c. white syrup
4 c. oatmeal

Mix above ingredients; press into pan. Bake 15 minutes at 350°. Melt together 1 1/4 cups chocolate chips and 2/3 cup peanut butter. Spread on top while hot. Keep in refrigerator. (Use 9x13 inch pan.)

Judy Raye, Fargo, N.D.

GRANOLA BARS

3 1/2 c. oatmeal
1 c. raisins
1 c. chopped nuts
2/3 c. butter, melted
1/2 c. brown sugar

1/3 c. honey or syrup
1 egg, beaten
1/2 tsp. vanilla
1/2 tsp. salt

Toast oats in 350° oven for 15 to 20 minutes, stirring often. Combine with remaining ingredients; mix well. Press into well greased 15 1/2 x 10 1/2 inch pan. Bake at 350° for about 20 minutes. Cool and cut into bars.

Mary Flaten, Grand Forks, N.D.

GRANDMA'S RAISIN BARS

1 c. raisins	1/2 tsp. nutmeg
2 c. water	1/2 tsp. cloves
1/2 c. butter	1/2 tsp. cinnamon
1 c. sugar	1/2 tsp. salt
1 3/4 c. flour	1/2 c. nuts, if desired
1 tsp. soda	

Boil raisins and water for 10 minutes. Add butter; let cool. Sift dry ingredients; stir in well. Pour into jelly roll pan; bake for 25 minutes at 350°. Cool completely. Frost with powdered sugar frosting or any desired frosting.

Pat Wentz, Grand Forks, N.D.

HEATH BARS OR COFFEE CAKE

2 c. flour	2 c. brown sugar
1/4 tsp. salt	1/3 c. butter

Combine into fine crumbs; remove 1 cup of crumbs for top. To balance of crumbs, add:

1 egg	1 c. milk
1 1/2 tsp. vanilla	1 tsp. soda

Pour into greased 9x13 inch pan. Crush 6 chilled Heath candy bars. Sprinkle batter with crumbs, crushed candy and chopped nuts. Bake 25-30 minutes in a 350° oven.

Vivian Brickson, Detroit Lakes, Mn.

HELLO DOLLY BARS

In 8x11 inch pan, melt (in oven) 1/2 cup butter. Put on in this order:

1 c. crushed grahams	1 c. chocolate chips
1 c. coconut	1 c. chopped nuts

Pour over the top 1 can Borden's sweetened condensed milk. Bake at 350° for 25 minutes. Do not overbake.

Joyce Meyer, Minneapolis, Mn.

HERSHEY'S HAWAIIAN HULAS

3/4 c. butter
1 1/2 c. sugar
3 eggs
1 tsp. vanilla
1 1/4 c. flour
1 tsp. baking powder

1/2 tsp. salt
1/2 tsp. cinnamon
1 c. crushed pineapple,
  drained
2 blocks (2 oz.) baking
  chocolate, melted
  (Hershey's)

Cream butter and sugar; add eggs, one at a time, beating until light. Add vanilla, sifted flour, baking powder, salt and cinnamon; add gradually to creamed mixture. In another bowl, combine 1 cup of batter with the pineapple. Add chocolate and chopped nuts to the remaining batter. Spread 1 1/2 cups chocolate mixture in a greased 13x9x2 inch pan. Cover with pineapple mixture. Drop remaining cake mixture by spoonfuls on white mixture, spreading carefully. Bake at 350° for 40 minutes. Cool and spread with the following frosting. Yield: 36 squares.

Hershey's Quick Chocolate Frosting:

4 Tbsp. butter
4 blocks (4 oz.) chocolate
  (Hershey's)
1/3 c. hot milk

3 c. sifted confectioners
  sugar
1 tsp. vanilla
1/2 tsp. salt

1. Melt butter and chocolate in double boiler; stir until blended. 2. Stir hot milk into sugar; beat till smooth. 3. Stir in vanilla, salt and chocolate mixture; beat until smooth and thickened, about 5 minutes.

Harriett Haggard, Anoka, Mn.

HIP PADDLERS

1 can Eagle Brand milk
1 (6 oz.) pkg. chocolate
  chips
2 Tbsp. butter
1 tsp. vanilla
1/2 c. butter, melted
1 c. brown sugar

1 egg
1 1/4 c. flour
1/2 tsp. vanilla
1/2 tsp. soda
1 1/2 c. oatmeal
1/4 tsp. salt
Walnuts

Melt the 2 tablespoons butter, chocolate chips and evaporated milk over hot water; add vanilla. Combine butter, egg and vanilla with dry ingredients; press into bottom of 9x13 inch pan. Save some for the top. Pour chocolate mixture over this. Put remaining mixture on top of filling. Sprinkle with walnuts. Bake at 350° for 25 minutes.

Marlene Barton, Grand Forks, N.D.

JANNA'S GOOD BARS

1 pkg. colored miniature marshmallows
1 (6 oz.) pkg. chocolate chips
1 (6 oz.) pkg. butterscotch chips
1/2 c. peanut butter
1 small can (about 1 c.) peanuts

Butter a 9x13 inch pan. Melt chips and peanut butter in double boiler. Put marshmallows in pan, then add peanuts. Pour melted mixture over all. Lift a little with fork to let mixture through. Keep in refrigerator.

Pearl Paulsrud, Montevideo, Mn.

JIM JAM BARS

Cream:
1 c. butter   1 c. sugar

Add:
2 egg yolks, beaten   1 c. chopped nuts
1 tsp. vanilla   1/2 c. raspberry or
2 c. flour   strawberry jam

Divide in half. Press half in 9x9 inch buttered pan; spread jam over. Press other half over jam. Bake in 325° oven for 1 hour.

Esther Mungovan, Duluth, Mn.

LEMON BARS

Crust: Combine as for pie crust -

1 c. flour   3 tsp. sugar
1/2 c. oleo   1/2 c. chopped nuts

Spread in 9x13 inch pan; press down. Bake for 10 minutes in 375° oven; cool.

First Layer: Soften 1 (8 ounce) package Philadelphia cream cheese at room temperature. Combine with 1 cup powdered sugar. Beat till creamy. Fold in 1 cup Cool Whip. Spread over cooled crust.

Second Layer: Combine 2 packages lemon instant pudding with 2 cups milk; beat for 2 minutes, till thick. Spread over first layer. Top with rest of Cool Whip. Refrigerate, till served. (Buy the 9 ounce container of Cool Whip.) Prepare the night before.

Esther Mungovan, Duluth, Mn.

LEMON CHEESE BARS

1 pkg. yellow cake mix	1 egg
1 egg	1 Tbsp. ReaLemon juice
1/3 c. oil	1 (8 oz.) pkg. cream
1/3 c. sugar	cheese, softened

Mix dry cake mix with egg and oil until crumbly; reserve 1 cup. Pat remaining crumbs in a 9x13 inch ungreased cake pan. Bake 15 minutes at 350°. Beat cream cheese, egg, lemon juice and sugar until light and smooth. Spread over baked layer. Sprinkle with remaining crumbs and bake 15 minutes longer. Calories...but good.

Jackie Jaenisch, Windom, Mn.

LEMON DREAM BARS

Cut 1/3 cup butter into 1 cup sifted flour and 2 tablespoons sugar until coarse crumbs. Press mixture into 9x9 inch ungreased pan. Bake 15 to 20 minutes in 350° oven until set, but not brown. Combine in mixing bowl:

2 beaten eggs	1/4 tsp. salt
1/2 c. brown sugar	1/8 tsp. baking powder
3/4 c. coconut	1/2 tsp. vanilla
1/2 c. chopped nuts	

Mix well; spread over baked dough. Bake 25 to 30 minutes at 350°. Frost immediately.

Frosting:

2 tsp. grated lemon rind	1 c. sifted powdered sugar
2 Tbsp. lemon juice	

Arnita Rieger, Minneapolis, Mn.
Similar recipes submitted by: Mrs. Carl Granrud, Montevideo, Mn., Mary Paul, Minneapolis, Mn.

LEMON SQUARES

2 c. flour　　　　　　　　　1 c. butter
1/2 c. powdered sugar

Mix as for pie crust; pat into large cake pan, which has been greased and floured. Bake 25 minutes in 350° oven. Combine 4 eggs, slightly beaten, with 2 cups sugar and 6 tablespoons lemon juice. Fold in 4 tablespoons flour with 1/2 teaspoon baking powder. Pour over bottom crust. Bake 25 minutes more. Sprinkle with powdered sugar.

Esther Mungovan, Duluth, Mn.

SWEDISH LEMON SQUARES

3/4 c. butter　　　　　　　　1 (3 3/4 oz.) pkg. instant
1 1/2 c. flour　　　　　　　　　lemon pudding mix

Cream butter and pudding mix until fluffy. Blend in flour; press together to make a dough. Flatten to 9 inch square on ungreased cookie sheet. Cut with sharp knife into 1 inch squares; do not separate. Bake at 325° for 15-20 minutes or until light golden brown. Cool 10 minutes. Recut squares. Roll in powdered sugar, if desired.

Marcy Brown

MAGIC COOKIE BARS

1/2 c. butter or margarine　　1 (6 oz.) pkg. semi-sweet
1 1/2 c. graham cracker　　　　chocolate morsels
　crumbs　　　　　　　　　　1 (3 1/2 oz.) can flaked
1 (14 oz.) can Eagle Brand　　　coconut
　sweetened condensed milk　1 c. chopped nuts

Preheat oven to 350° (325° for glass dish). In 13x9 inch baking pan, melt butter. Sprinkle crumbs over butter. Pour sweetened condensed milk evenly over crumbs. Top evenly with remaining ingredients; press down gently. Bake 25 to 30 minutes or until lightly browned. Cool thoroughly before cutting. Store, loosely covered, at room temperature. Makes 24 bars.

Marion Round, Faribault, Mn.

MIXED NUT BARS

1 1/2 c. flour   1/2 c. oleo
3/4 c. brown sugar

Mix and pat in greased (sides and bottom) 9x13 inch pan. Bake 10 minutes at 350°; cool a little. Mix together in saucepan:

6 oz. butterscotch chips   1/2 c. white corn syrup
2 Tbsp. oleo

Spread 2 cups or 12 ounce can of mixed nuts over baked layer. Pour the melted mixture over nuts; bake another 10 minutes.

Liz Tuft, St. Paul, Mn.

MOUNDS BARS

2 c. crushed graham   1/4 c. powdered sugar
   crackers   1/2 c. melted butter

Mix together; pat in a 9x13 inch pan. Bake at 350° for 10 minutes. Mix 1 (15 ounce) can sweetened condensed milk and 2 cups flaked coconut; spread on baked crust. Bake at 350° for 12 to 15 minutes. Melt 6 small or 1 large Hershey's bars or 1 cup chocolate chips and spread on top of bars. Cut in squares.

Marion Round, Faribault, Mn.

MY FAVORITE BARS
(These Are Delicious - Like Eating Fudge)

1. Melt in small pan 1 bar margarine (slowly) on low heat. 2. While melting, beat 3 eggs until light in color and thick. 3. Add 4 tablespoons cocoa to melted margarine. 4. Add 1 cup sugar to eggs; beat again, thoroughly. 5. Add 1/2 cup flour to beaten eggs (all-purpose); add 1/2 teaspoon salt to flour, then add chocolate mixture to egg mixture. You may add vanilla. Spread in 9x13 inch pan. Bake 20 minutes. Bars are thin. Cover with Helen Granrud's Icing:

6 Tbsp. milk   1 1/2 c. sugar
6 Tbsp. butter

Bring to full rolling boil; boil 30 seconds. Cool. Spread. It's like fudge.

Mrs. Kermit A. Haugen, Clarkfield, Mn.

NORMA'S BARS PIPESTONE '81

1 box white cake mix (I used   1 box chocolate pudding
   Deluxe with pudding in it)   (cooked kind)

Cook pudding; add dry cake mix. Spread on cookie sheet. Over the top, sprinkle:

1 pkg. chocolate chips   1 c. nuts
1 c. coconut

Bake 20 minutes at 350°. Frost hot out of oven (I would either wait 10 minutes or put a glaze on it). The gal that made this used the white ready-made frosting out of a can. Very easy, very good.

Norma Sabies, Pipestone, Mn.

NUT GOODIE BARS

1 (6 oz.) pkg. semi-sweet   1/2 c. butter or margarine
   chocolate pieces   1/4 c. milk
1 (6 oz.) pkg. butterscotch   2 Tbsp. vanilla pudding mix
   pieces   3 c. confectioners sugar,
1 c. creamy peanut butter   sifted
1 c. salted peanuts   1 tsp. maple flavoring

Melt chips and peanut butter over low heat; spread half in foil lined, greased 9x13 inch pan. Refrigerate until cool. Add peanuts to remaining melted pieces and peanut butter mixture; set aside. In saucepan, melt margarine. Stir in milk and vanilla pudding mix; bring to boil. Remove from heat; add confectioners sugar and maple flavoring. Beat until smooth. Spread on refrigerated chocolate layer. Spread remaining pieces and peanut mixture on top. Refrigerate. Makes 48 bars.

Blanche B. Masica, Minneapolis, Mn.

Similar recipes submitted by: Mary Jane Schmitz, Wadena, Mn., Elaine Aaberg, Minneapolis, Mn., Liz Tuft, St. Paul, Mn.

O' HENRY BARS

4 c. oatmeal   1 c. half butter, half
1 c. brown sugar   shortening
                                   Pinch of salt

Mix like pie crust; press into buttered cookie sheet. Bake at 300° for 30 minutes. Melt 1 large package chocolate chips and 3/4 cup chunky peanut butter. Spread this mixture over baked mixture. Cool slightly; cut in equal squares.

Marion Round, Faribault, Mn.

PEANUT BUTTER BARS

1 pkg. yellow cake mix	1/2 c. margarine
1 c. peanut butter	2 eggs

Combine cake mix, peanut butter, margarine and eggs. Stir until dough holds together. Press 2/3 of dough in 9x13 inch ungreased pan; reserve rest of dough.

Filling:

1 c. chocolate chips	1 pkg. coconut pecan
1 can Eagle Brand milk	frosting mix
2 Tbsp. margarine	

In saucepan, combine chips, milk and margarine; melt until smooth. Continue stirring for 5 minutes. Stir in frosting mix. Spread filling over dough and crumble reserved dough over filling. Bake at 350° for about 25 minutes.

Sue Hetland, Grand Forks, N.D.

PEANUT BUTTER BARS

2 sticks margarine	1 c. peanut butter
1 3/4 c. graham cracker	2 1/4 c. powdered sugar
crumbs	8 oz. Hershey's bars (chips)

Melt margarine. Add peanut butter; mix well over low fire. Add crumbs and powdered sugar; mix well. Press into 9x13 inch pan; chill for 20 minutes. Melt chocolate; spread over mixture. Cut into squares to serve.

Mary Paul, Minneapolis, Mn.

PEANUT BUTTER FINGERS

Cream:

1/2 c. butter	1/2 c. brown sugar
1/2 c. sugar	

Blend in:

1 egg	1/4 tsp. salt
1/3 c. peanut butter	1/2 tsp. vanilla
1/2 tsp. soda	

Stir in:

1 c. flour	1 c. quick oatmeal

Makes very stiff dough. Spread in 9x13 inch pan. Bake at 350° for 20-25 minutes. Sprinkle with 1 (6 ounce) package chocolate chips. Let stand 5 minutes. Combine 1/2 cup powdered sugar, 1/4 cup peanut butter and 2-4 tablespoons milk; mix well. Spread chocolate mixture evenly; drizzle with peanut butter mixture. Cool; cut into bars.

Ruth Lee, Detroit Lakes, Mn.

PEPPERMINT SQUARE COOKIES

1. Melt 1/2 cup butter or margarine. 2. Add:

1/2 c. sugar	1 tsp. vanilla
5 Tbsp. cocoa	1 egg

3. Add:

2 c. crushed graham crackers	1 c. coconut
	1/2 c. nuts, chopped

4. Spread in large cake pan; pat down. 5. Mix:

1/4 c. butter or margarine	2 Tbsp. vanilla pudding powder
3 Tbsp. milk	2 c. powdered sugar

6. Spread over first layer and let harden for 15 minutes. 7. Pour melted chocolate chips (mint flavored) or peppermint wafers over all (6 ounces). Cut into squares before refrigerating.

Margaret Hulst, Waltham, Mn.

PRAYER BARS

First Layer: Melt in double boiler -

1/2 c. butter   4 Tbsp. cocoa

Add:
1 beaten egg   1/2 c. powdered sugar
1 1/2 tsp. vanilla

Cook 1 minute; remove from heat. Mix with 2 cups crushed graham crackers, 1 cup cocoanut and 1/2 cup chopped pecans. Press into ungreased 9x13 inch cake pan. Refrigerate while second layer cooks.

Second Layer: Melt in double boiler -

1/4 c. butter   3 Tbsp. evaporated milk

Add:
1 tsp. vanilla   2 tsp. vanilla pudding mix

Cook 1 minute, stirring constantly. Remove from heat; add 2 cups powdered sugar. Spread over first layer. Return to refrigerator.

Third Layer: Melt in double boiler -

1 Tbsp. butter   12 oz. Hershey's chocolate
                                 bar (milk chocolate)

Frost. Return to refrigerator until chocolate firms up, about 15 minutes. Cut immediately or at room temperature.

Sue Gomez

PUMPKIN BARS

1 c. chopped dates   4 Tbsp. flour
1 c. chopped nuts

Mix above together and add last. Mix together:

1/2 c. oleo, melted   2 eggs
2 c. brown sugar   1 tsp. vanilla
1 1/3 c. pumpkin

Sift together:
1 c. flour   1 tsp. salt
1 tsp. baking powder   1/2 tsp. soda

1 tsp. cinnamon	1 tsp. ginger
1 tsp. nutmeg	

Add to pumpkin mixture. Add dates and nuts. Pour into 15x10 inch pan. Bake at 350° for 35-40 minutes. When cooled, frost with:

1 c. brown sugar	1 Tbsp. syrup (Karo,
1/2 c. white sugar	pancake or white)
1/3 c. milk	1/2 tsp. salt
4 Tbsp. oleo	1/2 tsp. vanilla

Bring to a boil, stirring occasionally; boil 2 minutes. Cool and beat until thick.

Carolyn Brudevold, Fargo, N.D.

PUMPKIN BARS

1 c. flour	1/2 c. brown sugar
1/2 c. oatmeal	1/2 c. butter

Combine in bowl; mix with mixer. Pat into ungreased pan. Bake at 350° for 15 minutes.

1 (1 lb.) can (2 c.) pumpkin	2 eggs
1 small can evaporated milk	3/4 c. sugar
1/4 tsp. cloves	1/2 tsp. salt
1 tsp. cinnamon	1/2 tsp. ginger

Combine; pour into crust and bake for 20 minutes at 350°.

1/2 c. brown sugar	2 Tbsp. butter
1/2 c. walnuts	

Crumble; scatter over top of pumpkin mixture and bake another 15-20 minutes (or until knife comes out clean).
(Ed. again: And still another excellent recipe! When testing for doneness in final step, it may be a little hard to tell when the pumpkin mixture is done, as the top layer forms a caramel-like topping. You don't want to bake it too long so the topping burns. You can serve these bars either hot, topped with whipped cream, or cold!)

Patricia Larson, Grafton, N.D.
Similar recipe submitted by: Kathryn Otto, Harvey, N.D.

PUMPKIN BARS

2 c. flour
2 tsp. baking powder
1 tsp. baking soda
1/4 tsp. salt
2 tsp. cinnamon
1 tsp. pumpkin pie spice

2 c. sugar
1 c. walnuts, chopped
1 c. salad oil
4 eggs
1 (16 oz.) can pumpkin

Frosting:

1 (3 oz.) pkg. cream cheese
6 Tbsp. butter
1 tsp. vanilla

2 c. powdered sugar, sifted
1 tsp. milk

Bars: Combine all ingredients for bars in large bowl; mix. Pour into lightly greased 17x11 inch pan. Bake at 350° for 20-25 minutes. When cool, top with frosting.
Frosting: Combine all ingredients for frosting; beat until smooth. Add more milk, if necessary. Makes 25 to 30 bars.

Mrs. Lydia Rieger, Harvey, N.D.

KLANK'S PUMPKIN BARS

2 c. flour
2 tsp. baking powder
1/2 tsp. salt
2 tsp. cinnamon
1 tsp. soda

4 eggs
2 c. canned pumpkin
2 c. sugar
1 c. oil
1 c. chopped nuts or raisins

Sift first 5 dry ingredients. Add oil, sugar, pumpkin and eggs; let stand 15 minutes. Beat well. Pour into greased 10x15 inch pan; bake at 350° for 25 minutes.

Bonnie Sovick, Marshall, Mn.

RASPBERRY BARS

3/4 c. margarine
1 c. packed brown sugar
1 1/2 c. flour
1 tsp. salt

1/2 tsp. soda
1 1/2 c. oatmeal
1 (10 oz.) jar raspberry
  preserves

Cream margarine and brown sugar until light and fluffy. Add flour, salt, soda and oatmeal; mix well. Press half of crumb mixture into greased 9x13 inch pan; spread with preserves. Sprinkle with remaining crumb mixture. Bake at 400° for 20-25 minutes. Cut while warm.

Joan Dinius, Coon Rapids, Mn.

RASPBERRY SQUARES

1 egg
1 c. sifted flour
1 tsp. baking powder

1/2 c. margarine
1 Tbsp. milk
8-10 Tbsp. jam (raspberry, pineapple, etc.)

Beat egg. Sift flour and baking powder; work in margarine till it's mealy. Stir in beaten egg, then milk, mixing well. Spread mixture over bottom of 8 inch square pan, ungreased. Cover with layer of jam.

Topping:

1 egg
4 Tbsp. melted margarine
1 c. white sugar

2 c. coconut
1 tsp. vanilla

Beat up egg and melt margarine. Stir sugar into beaten egg; stir in melted butter, coconut and vanilla. Spread this mixture on top of jam. Bake 30 minutes in 350° oven until golden brown. Cool and cut into squares.

Esther Beatty, Duluth, Mn.

RHUBARB BAR DESSERT

Crust:

1 c. flour
5 Tbsp. powdered sugar

1/2 c. butter

Mix and press into 8x11 inch pan. Bake 15 minutes at 350°.

Top: Beat -

2 eggs
1 1/2 c. sugar (or less if not sour rhubarb)
1/4 c. flour

3/4 tsp. baking powder
1/2 tsp. salt
2 c. rhubarb

Pour over crust and bake 35-40 minutes at 350° (total baking time is 50 minutes).

Marion Vonesh, Grand Forks, N.D.

540

SARAH'S YUMMY BARS

3/4 c. melted butter or margarine

1/3 c. evaporated milk
1 pkg. German chocolate cake mix

Mix together; put 1/2 of mixture in 9x13 inch pan. Bake for 6 minutes. Remove from oven and top with 1 package chocolate chips, 1 cup coarsely chopped nuts and 1 package Kraft caramels, melted together in double boiler with 1/3 cup evaporated milk. Spread rest of cake mixture over this. (This is easier to do if you spread blobs of dough in different places and then spread.) Bake at 350° for 15 to 20 minutes. Freezes okay. These are delicious.

Mrs. Kermit A. Haugen, Clarkfield, Mn.

S'MORE BARS

3/4 c. sugar
1 egg
1/2 c. butter
1 tsp. vanilla
1 1/2 c. flour

1 tsp. baking powder
1 tsp. salt
1 (5 3/4 oz.) pkg. milk
    chocolate candy kisses
1 c. marshmallow creme

Combine sugar, eggs, butter and vanilla; blend in dry ingredients. Beat 1 1/2 minutes at low speed. Spread 1/2 of mixture in greased 10x6 or 11x7 inch pan. Press chocolate kisses point side down into dough. Spread with marshmallow creme. Crumble remaining cookie dough over filling; smooth slightly. Bake at 350° for 25-30 minutes or until golden brown.

Sue Hetland, Grand Forks, N.D.

INDOOR S'MORES

2/3 c. white corn syrup
2 Tbsp. margarine or butter
1 (11 1/2 oz.) pkg. milk
    chocolate morsels

1 tsp. vanilla
8 c. Golden Grahams cereal
3 c. miniature marshmallows

Spray 13x9 inch baking pan with Pam vegetable cooking spray. Heat corn syrup, margarine and milk chocolate morsels to boiling in 3 quart saucepan, stirring constantly; remove from heat. Stir in vanilla. Pour over cereal in large mixing bowl; toss until completely coated with chocolate. Fold in marshmallows, 1 cup at a time.

Press mixture evenly in pan. Let stand until firm, at least 1 hour. Cut into 1 1/2 inch squares. Makes 48 squares.

Dorothy Savig, Minneapolis, Mn.

SOUR CREAM RAISIN BARS

2 c. raisins, cooked in
water, drained, cooled
1 c. brown sugar
1 c. margarine

1 3/4 c. oatmeal
1 tsp. soda
1 3/4 c. flour

Pat 1/2 of mixture into 9x13 inch pan. Bake 7 minutes at 350°. In heavy saucepan, mix 3 egg yolks, beaten, 1 1/2 cups sour cream, 1 cup sugar and 2 1/2 tablespoons cornstarch. Boil until thick; add raisins and 1 tablespoon vanilla. Pour over crust; top with remaining crumbs. Bake for 30 minutes in a 350° oven.

Vivian Brickson, Detroit Lakes, Mn.
Similar recipe submitted by: Geri Weaver, Grand Forks, N.D.

SUNFLOWER BARS

1 stick butter
1 c. peanut butter

12 oz. butterscotch chips

Melt in double boiler, then add 1 cup coconut and 10 ounces miniature marshmallows. Spread in greased 9x13 inch pan. Sprinkle 8 ounces sunflower meats on top and press down. Refrigerate until set; cut in bars.

Geri Running

SWEDISH KRINGLE

Mix like pie crust:
1 c. flour
1/2 c. margarine

1 Tbsp. water

Pat in 2 strips on cookie sheet, 3 inches wide and length of sheet. Bring to boil 1 cup water and 1/2 cup margarine. As soon as it boils, remove from heat; add 1 cup flour. Beat well. Add 3 eggs, one at a time, beating well after adding each egg. Add 1 teaspoon almond extract and spread on first dough. Bake at 350° for 55 minutes. When cool, frost with 1 1/2 cups powdered sugar, 3 tablespoons margarine, milk to soften and 1/2 teaspoon almond.

Liz Tuft, St. Paul, Mn.

TEAS BRAG

1 (No. 2) can cherry pie filling
1 (No. 2) can crushed pineapple, not drained

1 pkg. yellow cake mix
1 c. coconut
1 c. nuts
2 sticks melted margarine

Line a 9x13 inch cake pan with pie filling. Next, spread pineapple over filling, then sprinkle dry cake mix, then coconut and then nuts. Drizzle margarine over the top. Bake at 325° F. for 70 minutes. Cut and serve with Cool Whip, etc.

Mrs. Burton Peterson, Rochester, Mn.

TOFFEE BARS

1 c. butter or margarine
1 c. flake coconut
2 c. brown sugar
3/4 c. nuts (optional)
1 3/4 c. sifted flour

2 eggs
1/2 tsp. salt
1 tsp. vanilla
1 large size Hershey's bar

Mix and pour batter into a 10x16 inch baking pan. Bake at 350° for 20 to 30 minutes, or until light brown. Take from oven and place milk chocolate squares on top; spread evenly.

Sigrid Johnson, Hibbing, Mn.

TREASURE CHEST BARS

2 c. flour
1 1/2 tsp. baking powder
1/2 tsp. salt
1/2 c. brown sugar, packed
1/2 c. white sugar
1/2 c. butter
2 eggs

1 tsp. vanilla
3/4 c. milk
1 c. walnuts, chopped
1 c. maraschino cherries, drained
1 c. chocolate chips

Sift together flour, baking powder and salt. Cream together butter and sugar; add eggs and vanilla to creamed mixture. Add milk and flour alternately, then add nuts, cherries and chocolate chips. Grease one 10x15 inch pan or two 9x9 inch pans. Bake at 325° for 25-30 minutes. When cool, frost with the following frosting.

Frosting: Brown 1/4 cup butter until dark brown. Add:

2 c. powdered sugar   1/2 tsp. vanilla
2 Tbsp. milk

Arnita Rieger, Minneapolis, Mn.
Similar recipes submitted by: Colleen Grapentin, St. Cloud, Mn., Adeline Hortsch, St. Cloud, Mn.

*   *   *   *   *

COOKIES

"Oh, weary Mothers,
  rolling dough,
Don't you wish
  that food would grow?
How happy
  all the world would be,
With a cookie bush
  and a doughnut tree."
Helen-May Johnson

*   *   *   *   *

DESSERTS
PIES

A measure full of laughter for every single hour;
And several drops of humor to keep from growing sour;
A pinch or two of discipline,
And countless pats of love.
A cup of faith, blended with prayer
Drawn from the well above.
A large amount of thankfulness
And understanding, too,
Will make your living fluffy light...
The frosting's up to you.

Recipe for a Wonderful Day

1 cup friendly words
2 heaping cups understanding
2 cups milk of human kindness
4 heaping tsp. of time and patience
Pinch of personality
Dash of dry humor
The spice of life

Instructions for mixing ingredients:

Measure words carefully; Add heaping cups of understanding to milk of human kindness and sift together 3 times before using.

Make a smooth sauce, not too thick. Use generous amounts of time and patience and cook with gas on front burner. Keep temperature low, do not boil. Add a dash of dry humor, a pinch of warm personality with individual molds.

Works best when made by a good mixer.

ALMOND RING

1/2 c. zwieback crumbs
1/4 c. sugar
4 egg whites
1 c. sugar

1 2/3 c. blanched almonds,
  ground
1/2 tsp. almond extract

Combine zwieback crumbs and the 1/4 cup sugar. Sprinkle half of mixture evenly over inside of greased 1 quart ring mold; set aside. Reserve remaining crumb mixture. Beat egg whites until stiff. Add the 1 cup sugar, a small amount at a time, beating after each addition. Continue to beat until stiff peaks form. Gradually fold in almonds and almond extract. Spread mixture in prepared ring mold; sprinkle reserved crumb mixture on top. Bake at 325° F. for 30 to 35 minutes, or until light golden brown; cool. Carefully invert onto serving platter. Serve with sweetened, crushed strawberries or ice cream or both. Yield: 8 portions.

Dena Stoddard, St. Louis Park, Mn.

ANGEL FOOD CAKE DESSERT

1 angel food cake
3/4 c. sugar
2 egg yolks

1 c. milk
1/4 tsp. salt

Cook last 4 ingredients until thick (if it isn't thick, add cornstarch); add 3 ounces lemon jello. Cook to rolling boil; cool. Beat 2 egg whites until stiff; beat 1 pint whipping cream. Combine whites and whipping cream. Add 1 small can crushed pineapple to custard (drain first). Mix everything together. Cut cake in 3 layers and frost. Refrigerate overnight.

Liz Tuft, St. Paul, Mn.

ANGEL FOOD DESSERT

1 pt. cream, whipped
2 c. powdered sugar
4 egg yolks
5 Butterfinger bars, crushed

1 c. pecans, cut up (save
  1/4 c. for topping)
1 angel food cake, broken
  up

1507-82

545

Beat egg yolks; add sugar, Butterfingers and 3/4 cup nuts. Fold in whipping cream. Place 1/2 of cake, broken up in pieces, in 9x13 inch pan; cover with half the mixture, then repeat (2 layers). Sprinkle with remaining nuts. Refrigerate overnight.

Florence Wesen, St. Cloud, Mn.

DESSERT A LA QUEEN

Melt together 2/3 cup brown sugar and 1/3 cup butter. Add 2 cups Rice Krispies, crushed a bit. Add 1 cup coconut and 1/2 cup chopped nuts. Mix this and pour 2/3 on bottom of 8x12 inch pan. Soften 1/2 gallon of ice cream; spread over this layer in pan (any flavor). Top with balance of ingredients and freeze. When serving, top with fruit. Fresh peaches are yummy.

Mary Fingalson, Detroit Lakes, Mn.

APPLE CRISP

4 c. sliced apples	1 tsp. cinnamon
1 c. sugar	1/2 tsp. salt
1 Tbsp. flour	

Arrange apples in buttered 10x15 inch jelly roll pan. Sprinkle sugar, flour, cinnamon and salt over apples.

Topping:

1 c. brown sugar	1 c. oatmeal
1 1/2 c. flour	1 c. butter

Mix together until crumbly; sprinkle over apples and bake at 350° for 45 minutes.

Alicia Woodford, Montevideo, Mn.

OLD FASHION APPLE CRISP

6 c. thinly sliced, peeled apples	2 Tbsp. butter or margarine, melted
1/3 c. sugar	3/4 c. sugar
1 tsp. cinnamon	1/3 c. butter or margarine
1/2 tsp. salt	Whipped topping
1/2 c. flour	

Mix together apples, 1/3 cup sugar, cinnamon, salt and melted butter. Place in greased 8 inch square baking dish; set aside. Combine 3/4 cup sugar and flour; cut in butter until crumbly. Sprinkle over apples. Bake at 375° for about 45 minutes, or until apples are tender. Makes 8 servings.

Gloria Smith, Jackson, Mn.

CREAMY DUTCH APPLE DESSERT

1/4 c. margarine
1 1/2 c. graham cracker crumbs
1 (14 oz.) can Eagle Brand sweetened condensed milk
1 c. sour cream
1/4 c. lemon juice
1 (20 oz.) can apple pie filling
1/4 c. chopped walnuts
1/2 tsp. ground cinnamon

Preheat oven to 350°. In a shallow baking dish, 10x6 inches, melt margarine in oven. Sprinkle in crumbs; stir well. Press on bottom of dish. In medium bowl, mix together sweetened condensed milk, sour cream and lemon juice; spread evenly over crumbs. Spoon pie filling evenly over creamy layer. Bake 25 to 30 minutes or until set; cool slightly. In a small dish, mix together nuts and cinnamon; sprinkle over pie filling. May be served warm or cold. Refrigerate leftovers. Super delicious; reminds one of cheese cake!!

Alice Nelson, Minneapolis, Mn.

APPLE DESSERT

2 cans apple pie fruit filling
Spice cake mix
1/2 c. chopped nuts
2 sticks margarine, melted

Put pie filling in bottom of pan; sprinkle cake mix over filling. Sprinkle nuts over cake mix; drizzle margarine over all. Use 9x13 inch pan. Bake at 350° for 1 hour.

Mary Jo Conneran, Fargo, N.D.

APPLE DATE DESSERT

2 c. sifted all-purpose flour
1 c. sugar
1 1/2 tsp. baking soda
1 tsp. salt
1 tsp. ground cinnamon
1/2 tsp. ground allspice
2 slightly beaten eggs
1 (21 oz.) can apple pie filling
1/2 c. cooking oil
1 tsp. vanilla
1 c. chopped dates
1/4 c. chopped walnuts

Sift together flour, sugar, soda, salt, cinnamon and allspice. Combine eggs, pie filling, oil and vanilla; stir into flour mixture. Mix well; stir in dates and nuts. Pour into greased and floured 13x9x2 inch baking dish. Bake in 350° oven for 40 to 45 minutes. Cool; cut in squares. Serve with whipped cream, if desired. Makes 12 servings.

Marlys Swehla, Albert Lea, Mn.

APPLE DUMPLINGS

Make a crust of:

3 c. flour	1/2 c. or more water
1 c. shortening	1 tsp. salt

Cut into squares large enough to cover apple. Peel and pare apples. Place in center of crust square. Fill with cinnamon, sugar and butter; bring corners up and seal. Make them ahead, then roll in waxed paper and store in freezer. Place them all in plastic bag, then remove them as you want them. Make mixture of:

1 c. sugar	2 c. water
1 Tbsp. cinnamon	4 Tbsp. butter

Pour this over the apple dumplings and bake 30 minutes at 350°. Serve with cream or whipped cream.

Mrs. Neva Kost, Fairmont, Mn.

APPLESAUCE LOAF CAKE

1/4 c. shortening	1 tsp. cinnamon
1 c. sugar	1/2 tsp. nutmeg
1 1/2 c. applesauce	1/4 tsp. cloves
2 c. flour	1 c. raisins
1 tsp. soda	1/2 c. chopped nuts
1/4 tsp. salt	

Cream shortening and sugar; stir in applesauce. Sift dry ingredients together; add to applesauce mixture. Add raisins and nuts. Bake 1 hour at 350° in 9x5x4 inch loaf pan; cool. Store overnight before cutting.

Marlys Swehla, Albert Lea, Mn.

APPLE SLICES

First, peel and slice enough apples for a large pie. Sprinkle 1 to 1 1/4 cups sugar and 1 teaspoon cinnamon over apples; let stand.

Crust:

2 1/2 c. flour   1/2 tsp. salt
2 tsp. sugar

Cut in 1 cup shortening; add 2 egg yolks, plus milk to fill cup to 2/3 full. Beat. Roll out half the dough or pat it into a jelly roll pan. Spread with a light coat of egg whites. Add apples. Roll out remaining dough; place on top of apples. Spread with light coat of egg white. Bake at 400° for 35-40 minutes. Drizzle the following frosting:

1 c. powdered sugar   Thin cream or evaporated
Vanilla   milk to make a runny
                           icing

Judy Rieger, Grand Forks, N.D.

APPLE UPSIDE DOWN CAKE

1 pkg. Duncan Hines spice   1/4 c. (1/2 stick) butter or
   Deluxe cake mix   margarine
1 c. light brown sugar   Whipped cream or confec-
1 (1 lb. 4 oz.) can pie   tioners sugar, if desired
   sliced apples, drained   Maraschino cherries, if
1/2 c. chopped nuts   desired

Melt butter in a 13x9x2 inch pan. Sprinkle brown sugar evenly in pan. Arrange apple slices and nuts over sugar mixture. Mix cake as directed on the label; pour batter over fruit. Bake at 350° for 40-45 minutes, until cake tests done with a toothpick. Let stand 5 minutes for topping to begin to set. Turn upside down onto a large platter or cooky sheet. Serve warm. Just before serving, top with confectioners sugar or whipped cream and garnish with cherries.

When baking at high altitudes, use flour, water and baking temperature given on package side panel.

Lorraine Rieger, Minneapolis, Mn.

APRICOT CRISP

1 (30 oz.) can California apricot halves, drained, reserving 2 Tbsp. syrup
1 3/4 c. Rice Krispies cereal, crushed to measure 1 c.
1/3 c. all-purpose flour
1/4 tsp. salt
1/2 c. firmly packed brown sugar
1/2 tsp. ground cinnamon
1/4 tsp. ground nutmeg
1/3 c. margarine or butter, softened

1. Cut each apricot half into 2 pieces. Combine with the 2 tablespoons apricot syrup in 1 quart casserole. Combine remaining ingredients, mixing until crumbly; sprinkle over apricots. 2. Bake in oven at 350° F. for about 30 minutes or until topping is browned. Serve warm. Top with ice cream, if desired. Yield: 6 servings.

Marion Round, Faribault, Mn.

APRICOT DESSERT

Soak 1 1/2 cups dried apricots in cold water overnight. In the morning, cook them with 1 cup sugar and cook until thick; cool. Mix together:

1 c. brown sugar
1 1/2 c. flour
1 1/2 c. oatmeal
3/4 c. butter

Pat into 9x13 inch pan; reserve a few crumbs for topping. Spread apricots over crust; cover with reserved crumbs. Bake at 350° until browned.

Ruth Rehschuh, Minneapolis, Mn.

BAKED BANANAS

1/2 c. lemon juice
2 heaping Tbsp. brown sugar
2 Tbsp. unrefined sugar
1 Tbsp. fresh grated ginger
6 small, ripe bananas
Cinnamon

Set oven at 350°. Put 2 inches of water in Pyrex baking dish; stir in lemon juice. Stir in sugars and ginger. Peel bananas and slice in halves lengthwise. Put bananas in the baking dish; sprinkle with cinnamon. Bake, uncovered, for 20 minutes. Serve with whipped cream, sweetened with brown sugar and a little dark rum.

Dee Olson, St. Paul, Mn.

BANANA FLIP

To a yellow cake mix (without pudding), add:

1 pkg. banana cream instant pudding	4 eggs 1 1/2 c. milk

Put into 2 jelly roll pans, greased and floured. Bake at 350° for 15 minutes.

Filling:

1/2 c. oleo	3 Tbsp. flour
1/2 c. Crisco	1 Tbsp. banana extract
1 c. sugar	1/2 c. milk

Put all ingredients in bowl; beat 5 minutes. Spread over 1 layer and put other layer on top.

BANANAS FOSTER

2 c. brown sugar	6 oz. white rum
1/2 lb. butter	4 bananas

Heat sugar and butter until sugar melts; cook 3 minutes. Add rum; cook 2 more minutes. Add cut up bananas. Serve over ice cream.

Ellie Cox, Rochester, Mn.

BANANA SPLIT DESSERT

3 large bananas, or more	1 c. Carnation evaporated milk
1/2 gal. vanilla ice cream	1 tsp. vanilla
1 c. chopped nuts	1 pt. whipping cream, whipped
1 c. chocolate chips	
1/2 c. butter	1/3 (1 lb.) box graham crackers
2 c. powdered sugar	

Crush graham crackers; put half in bottom of each pan (use one 9x13 inch and one 9x9 inch pan). Save half for topping. Slice bananas very thin. Slice ice cream 1/2 inch thick over bananas; sprinkle with nuts, then put in freezer. Melt chocolate chips and butter; add milk and powdered sugar. Stir constantly over low heat until thickened. Add vanilla; cool. Spread over other ingredients. Add whipping cream; top with graham cracker crumbs. Refreeze with cover on.

Liz Tuft, St. Paul, Mn.
Similar recipe submitted by: Becky Carlson, Fargo, N.D.

BOYSENBERRY GRAHAM CRACKER DESSERT

15 graham crackers
1/4 c. sugar
1/4 c. melted butter
1 c. milk
1 1/2 c. boysenberries and
   juice

1/2 lb. marshmallows
1 c. whipping cream
1/2 c. nutmeats
1 Tbsp. lemon juice
2 Tbsp. cornstarch

Roll cracker crumbs fine; add melted butter. Mix; pat into flat greased pan (reserve 2 tablespoons crumbs to sprinkle on top). Melt marshmallows with milk in double boiler; cool. Add cream, which has been whipped. Place layer of marshmallow mixture in pan, then the boysenberries, which have been thickened with cornstarch, lemon juice and sugar. Add remaining marshmallow mixture; top with crumbs and nutmeats. Cherry or blueberry pie mix may be substituted for the boysenberry mixture. Very good.

Marian Gugat, St. Cloud, Mn.

BUTTERFINGER DESSERT
(This dessert is simple and delicious.)

6 regular size Butterfinger
   candy bars

1 angel food cake, baked and
   cooled

Combine:
4 egg yolks
2 c. powdered sugar

1 tsp. vanilla

Fold in 1 (12 ounce) container Cool Whip. Use 9x13 inch pan. Break up half of angel food cake; pour 1/2 of Cool Whip mixture over pieces. Crush half of Butterfingers and sprinkle on top. Make second layer same as the first. Chill overnight.

Gretchen Marquart, Fargo, N.D.

FROZEN BUTTERSCOTCH DESSERT

Melt:
1 c. butter

2 c. brown sugar

Add 4 eggs, slightly beaten; cook till thick. Add:

1 1/2 tsp. vanilla

1 c. broken walnuts

Cool. Crush 1 (7 ounce) box vanilla wafers. Spread half in bottom of 9x13 inch pan; pour over crumbs. Put Cool Whip on top; freeze until ready to serve.

552   Liz Tuft, St. Paul, Mn.

CARAMEL DELIGHT

1 1/2 c. flour
1 c. quick cooking oatmeal
1/2 c. brown sugar

1 1/2 c. chopped nuts
1 c. melted butter

Combine above ingredients; stir in 1 cup butter. Spread in thin layer on cookie sheet. Bake 15 minutes at 350° until brown; cool and crumble. Put 1/2 of crumbs in 13x9 inch pan. Spoon a 6 ounce jar of caramel topping over crumbs. Slice softened vanilla ice cream over topping (1/2 gallon). Top with remaining crumbs. Freeze until firm. Cut in squares and serve.

Liz Voss, Virginia, Mn.

INDIVIDUAL CHEESE TARTS

24 vanilla wafers
24 cupcake liners
1/2 c. sugar
1 can cherry pie filling

2 (8 oz.) pkg. cream cheese
2 eggs
2 tsp. vanilla

Beat 5 minutes at light speed. Crumble 1 wafer in each cupcake liner. Fill about 1/2 full with cream cheese filling. Bake at 350° for 15-18 minutes; cool. Top with filling, either cherry or blueberry. Keep refrigerated.

CHERRY CLAFOUTI

2 c. fresh or well drained
  canned Bing cherries
3 eggs
2/3 c. all-purpose flour

1/2 c. granulated sugar
2 c. whole milk
Vanilla sugar

Butter a 10 inch round shallow baking dish. Wash and stem cherries; no need to pit them. Arrange in single layer in baking dish. Mix the eggs, flour, sugar and milk with rotary beater or electric mixer. Pour egg mixture over cherries. Sprinkle lightly with vanilla sugar or granulated sugar; this glazes cherry tops as Clafouti bakes. Bake at 375° for about 40 minutes; custard should set and be golden. Serve warm or cold to 8.

Variation: Use cut up, ripe plums or large blackberries in place of cherries.

St. Cloud, Mn.

CHERRY DESSERT

16 graham crackers, crushed fine	1/2 c. powdered sugar
	1/2 c. butter

Mix and press into 8x8 inch pan. Beat the following and pour over the first layer:

1 (8 oz.) pkg. Philadelphia cream cheese	2 eggs
	1/2 c. white sugar

Bake 20 minutes in 350° oven; cool. Pour 1 can cherry pie mix on top; serve with whipped cream or Cool Whip.

Goldie Mikish, Staples, Mn.

Similar recipe submitted by: Mary Paul, Minneapolis, Mn.

CHERRY DESSERT

Crust (9x13 inch pan):

1/2 c. melted butter	1 c. crushed nuts
1/2 c. brown sugar	1 c. coconut
1 c. Rice Krispies	

Mix the above and place in pan. Fold 4 cups whipped cream (can use 1 package Dream Whip). Put this on top of crust and top with 1 1/2 cans cherry pie mix. Chill until ready to serve.

Virginia Miller, Anoka, Mn.

CHERRY DESSERT

2 (12 oz.) cans cherry pie filling	1 (18 1/2 oz.) pkg. yellow cake mix
1 (20 oz.) can crushed pineapple (do not drain)	1 c. (2 sticks) butter
	1 c. flaked coconut
	1 c. chopped nuts

Spread pie filling evenly on bottom of 9x13 inch pan. Layer pineapple on top of cherries. Sprinkle cake mix over pineapple. Cover with melted butter; top with coconut and nuts. Bake at 350° for 1 hour. Serve with whipped cream.

Betty Bosquez, Minneapolis, Mn.

CHERRY HOLIDAY GIFT CAKE

Cream:

8 oz. cream cheese	1 1/2 c. sugar
1 c. margarine	1 1/2 tsp. vanilla

Add:

4 eggs, one at a time	1 1/2 tsp. baking powder
2 c. flour	

Fold in 1 small jar maraschino cherries and 1/2 cup chopped pecans. Pour into a floured Bundt pan. Bake 1 hour and 20 minutes at 325°.

Loretta Van Engelenhoven, Luverne, Mn.

CHERRY O' CREAM CHEESE TORTE

9 inch crumb crust	1 tsp. vanilla
1 (5 oz.) can Eagle Brand sweetened condensed milk	1 (1 lb. 6 oz.) can prepared cherry pie filling or
1 (8 oz.) pkg. cream cheese	Cherry Glaze
1/3 c. lemon juice	

Soften cheese at room temperature; whip till fluffy. Gradually add condensed milk; continue beating until well blended. Add lemon juice and vanilla; blend well. Pour in crust; chill 2-3 hours before putting cherry filling on top.

Cherry Glaze: Blend 1/2 cup cherry juice, 2 tablespoons sugar and 2 teaspoons cornstarch. Add cherries (1/2 pound of cherries). Stir in a few drops of food coloring.

Mrs. Emma Buhl, Minneapolis, Mn.

CHERRY-PINEAPPLE CRUMBLE

1 (16 oz.) can sour pitted cherries and liquid	1 box regular white or yellow cake mix
1 (16 oz.) can crushed pineapple, and liquid	1/2 c. oleo or butter, melted
	1/2 c. chopped nuts (opt.)

Mix cherries and pineapple in 9x13 inch ungreased pan. Sprinkle dry cake mix evenly over fruit; drizzle with butter or oleo. Top with nuts. Bake at 350° for 40-45 minutes.

Jackie Reisinger, St. Cloud, Mn.

CHERRIES IN THE SNOW

6 egg whites
1 tsp. cream of tartar
1/4 tsp. salt

1 tsp. vanilla
1 1/2 c. sugar

Beat hard, till foamy. Gradually add sugar; beat very stiff. Add vanilla. Spread in buttered 9x13 inch pan. Preheat oven to 400° and turn off. Put pan of meringue into hot oven overnight for 8 hours.

Filling:

2 (3 oz.) pkg. Philadelphia
   cream cheese

1 c. sugar
1 tsp. vanilla

Whip Philadelphia cream cheese, sugar and vanilla together. Whip 1 pint whipping cream; add cream cheese mixture. Fold in 2 cups small marshmallows. Spread over meringue; chill 8 hours. When serving, put spoon of cherry pie filling on each piece. Refrigerate; don't freeze.

Mary Fingalson, Detroit Lakes, Mn.

CHERRY-JELLO DESSERT

2 pkg. cherry jello
2 c. boiling water

1 can cherry pie filling

Mix together; let set until firm. Melt 1 cup mini marshmallows and 6 tablespoons milk; let cool. Add 8 ounce container of Cool Whip. Mix, then spread over jello. Refrigerate.

Mary Jo Conneran, Fargo, N.D.

CHOCOLATE CHERRY DESSERT

Crust:

2 c. vanilla wafer crumbs

1/3 c. melted butter

Mix together; press into bottom of 9x13 inch pan. Reserve 2 tablespoons of crumbs for top.

Butter Fluff Layer:

1/2 c. butter
2 eggs

1 1/2 c. sifted powdered
   sugar

Cream butter and sugar; add eggs, one at a time, beating well after each. Spread on crust.

Chocolate Cherry Layer:

1/4 c. sugar
2 Tbsp. cocoa
1 c. whipping cream
1 c. chopped walnuts

1 banana, mashed
1/4 c. sliced maraschino
cherries

Whip cream, sugar and cocoa; fold in nuts, bananas and cherries. Pour over butter filling; sprinkle with rest of crumbs. Chill until firm.

Alicia Woodford, Montevideo, Mn.

FROZEN CHOCOLATE DESSERT

Crush 1 small package of Hydrox or Oreo cookies; pack all but 1/2 cup of crumbs in a 9x13 inch pan. In a double boiler, put:

2 c. powdered sugar
2 sq. semi-sweet chocolate
1/2 c. oleo

3 egg yolks
1/4 tsp. salt
1 tsp. vanilla

Cook until thick; cool. Add the 3 beaten egg whites. Spread over the crumbs; sprinkle with 1 cup chopped nuts. Freeze overnight before the next step. Next day, soften 2 quarts of vanilla ice cream. Into this, fold 6 Heath Bars, that have been chopped coarsely. Spread ice cream mixture on top of the frozen mixture. Sprinkle with the 1/2 cup of reserved crumbs. Put back in freezer. Freeze at least overnight. It can be kept frozen for several weeks.

Joan Norton, Hibbing, Mn.

CHOCOLATE DESSERT

In a double boiler, melt:
1/2 or 3/4 of (1/2 lb.)
   almond Hershey's candy
   bar

15 large marshmallows
1/2 c. milk

Stir until completely melted; cool. Fold into 1 cup whipping cream, whipped and sweetened. Pour into graham cracker pie crust; sprinkle some of the cracker crumbs on top. Chill several hours or overnight. Sometimes I add more almonds.

Eva Lyn Dody, Minneapolis, Mn.

CHOCOLATE DESSERT BY PHYLLIS

Melt 1 (6 ounce) package semi-sweet chocolate chips. Add 3 egg yolks, fork whipped with 1 tablespoon water. Beat 1 pint whipping cream; sweeten. Beat 3 egg whites stiff. Add chocolate mixture to whipped cream; fold in egg whites. Line 9x13 inch pan with whole graham crackers. Cover with 1/2 of chocolate mixture. Cover with another layer of graham crackers. Top with chocolate mixture and freeze.

Jackie Reisinger, St. Cloud, Mn.

CHOCOLATE FONDUE

5 (3 3/4 oz.) milk chocolate bars
1/4 c. brandy
Bananas, cut in 1 1/2 inch pieces
Strawberries
Orange sections (or mandarin oranges)
Canned pineapple chunks, drained
Stemmed maraschino cherries, well drained
1 c. heavy cream
Toasted pound cake or ladyfingers

Break chocolate into small pieces in a small saucepan or fondue pot; add cream. Place over low heat, 200°, stirring constantly till mixture is melted and smooth. Stir in brandy. Arrange fruit on platter or individual dessert plates. With fondue forks, dip fruits and cake into warm fondue. Serves 8.

Jackie Durkot

CHOCOLATE HERSHEY DESSERT

1 c. powdered sugar
1/2 c. butter
3 egg yolks
1 small can Hershey's chocolate syrup
25 marshmallows, cut fine
1 c. nuts, chopped fine
3 egg whites, beaten stiff
14 graham crackers

Cream powdered sugar and butter; add egg yolks one at a time. Add chocolate syrup, marshmallows, nuts and egg whites, beaten with a little salt. Roll crackers fine and place 1/2 of them on bottom of pan. Place the filling on top of the cracker crumbs. Place rest of crumbs over filling. Let set 24 hours. Serves 10, cut in squares. Use 9x13 inch pan.

Grayce Funke, Minneapolis, Mn.

CHOCOLATE ICEBOX CAKE

1/2 box chocolate wafers
1 c. crushed pineapple
1/2 c. butter
2 eggs

1 pt. cream
1/2 c. cut up pecans or
   walnuts
1 c. powdered sugar

Part 1: Crush chocolate wafers and line a well buttered torte pan with 1/2 of crumbs; save remaining crumbs for on top. Part 2: Whip the cream; add the drained, crushed pineapple and nuts. Spread into the torte pan. Part 3: Cream butter and powdered sugar; add the egg yolks, then the stiffly beaten egg whites, folded in. Spread in the torte pan. Put the remaining crumbs on top and set in the refrigerator for several hours. Serve plain or with whipped cream or ice cream.

Mrs. Emma Buhl, Minneapolis, Mn.

CHOCOLATE JELLY ROLL

5 eggs, separated
1 c. sugar
3/4 c. flour

1/4 c. cocoa
1/4 tsp. salt
Flavoring

Beat egg whites stiff; add 1/2 cup sugar. Beat egg yolks; add remaining sugar. Add flavoring. Fold gently into egg whites. Combine flour and salt; fold in lightly. Line jelly roll pan with wax paper. Bake at 350° for 15 minutes. This may be filled with whipped cream and miniature marshmallows. To make regular jelly roll, omit the 1/4 cup cocoa and use 1 cup flour. This may be spread with lemon filling made of: In double boiler, beat together 3 eggs, 1/4 cup lemon juice, 1 cup sugar and 2 tablespoons butter. Cook until thick.

Irene Mittelstadt, Campbell, Mn.

PEPPERMINT CHOCOLATE DESSERT

Chop 1/2 package vanilla wafers; line 9x13 inch cake pan. Melt 2 packages German's sweet Baker's chocolate. Cream 1/2 cup butter, 1 1/2 cups powdered sugar and 3 eggs. Add to melted chocolate; pour over crumbs. Whip 1 pint cream; add 1/4 cup peppermint candy, crushed. Put on top of chocolate mixture. Sprinkle top with chopped walnuts; chill overnight. Makes 20-24 servings.

Pat Ivey, Bismarck, N.D.

FROZEN CHOCOLATE PUDDING DESSERT

Prepare 2 packages chocolate instant pudding as directed on package, except use 3 cups of milk instead of the usual 4 for 2 packages. Mix with thawed 8 ounce container of Cool Whip. Pour into 10x15 inch pan, lined with graham cracker crust. Freeze till firm. Cut in squares. Keep frozen till served.

Norma Haugerud, Montevideo, Mn.

CHOCOLATE WALNUT MOUSSE

1 (6 oz.) pkg. chocolate
  chips
1/2 c. milk
2 tsp. unflavored gelatin
2 Tbsp. cold water
2 eggs, separated
1/8 tsp. salt
1/8 tsp. cream of tartar
3 Tbsp. sugar

1/4 c. Amaretto
1 1/2 c. whipping cream,
  whipped
1/2 c. chopped, toasted
  walnuts
1 sq. semi-sweet chocolate,
  melted and cooled
1/2 tsp. instant coffee
Walnut halves

Combine chocolate chips and milk in heavy pan over very low heat. Stir occasionally until chocolate melts. Soften gelatin in water. Beat egg yolks slightly. Stir in a little hot chocolate mixture, then return to pan of chocolate mixture and cook, stirring, until it thickens slightly. Do not allow to boil. Stir gelatin into the chocolate mixture until dissolved. Cool to room temperature. Beat egg whites with salt and cream of tartar until stiff; gradually beat in sugar. Stir Amaretto into chocolate mixture. Fold in beaten egg whites, 2/3 of the whipped cream and the chopped nuts. Turn into a 6 cup dish; chill overnight. Fold chocolate and coffee into remaining whipped cream; garnish top of mousse. Decorate with walnut halves.

Dee Olson, St. Paul, Mn.

CINNAMON FLUFF

Mix together:
1/2 c. Spry or Crisco (do
  not use butter or
  margarine)

2/3 c. sugar
2 eggs

Sift together:
1 1/2 c. flour

2 Tbsp. cinnamon

1 tsp. baking powder   1/2 tsp. salt
1 tsp. baking soda

Stir in alternately with 1 cup sour milk. Milk will
sour quickly if 1/2 teaspoon of vinegar is added. Pour into
greased and floured 9 inch pan. Rub together 1/2 cup
sugar, 2 tablespoons melted Spry and 1 tablespoon cinnamon; sprinkle over cake dough. Bake 45 minutes at 325°.
Serve with whipped cream.

Mrs. H. Erickson, Minneapolis, Mn.

COCONUT CREAM DESSERT

1/2 c. margarine   1 c. flour

Mix together; press into 9x13 inch pan, greased.
Bake until golden brown.

1 (8 oz.) pkg. Philadelphia   1 c. powdered sugar
   cream cheese   1 c. Cool Whip

Whip ingredients together; spread on cooled crust.
Mix together 2 small packages coconut cream pudding mix
(instant) and 2 1/2 cups milk. Pour over cream cheese
layer. Spread remaining Cool Whip on top. Can sprinkle
coconut on top and add cherry, if desired.

Grace Locke, St. Paul, Mn.
Similar recipe submitted by: Mary Paul, Minneapolis, Mn.

COCONUT ON A CLOUD

First Layer:

1 c. flour   1/4 c. chopped nuts
1/2 c. butter

Mix as pie crust; press into 9x13 inch pan. Bake
10-15 minutes at 350°.

Second Layer: Beat together and spread over crust -

1 (8 oz.) pkg. cream cheese   1 (12 oz.) ctn. Cool Whip
1 c. powdered sugar

Third Layer: Beat 2 (3 ounce) packages instant pudding (any kind) with 2 1/2 cups cold milk until thick.
Spread on cream cheese mixture.

Fourth Layer: Whip 1 package Dream Whip according

to directions.

Fifth Layer: Broil 1/2 (7 ounce) package coconut until browned; sprinkle over top.

Anne Aune, Minneapolis, Mn.

CREAM PUFFS

Mix 1 cup water and 1 stick oleo; bring to boil until oleo is melted. Add 1 cup flour; stir until thick ball. Add 4 well beaten eggs; beat until thick. Bake at 400° for 45 minutes. Bake as soon as beaten well.

Rosalee Wendelbo, Grafton, N.D.

MOCK CREOLE CREAM CHEESE

1 c. Farmer or cottage
  cheese
1 (8 oz.) pkg. cream
  cheese, softened

1 c. heavy cream
1 1/2 - 2 c. fresh fruit
4 Tbsp. sugar or honey

Blend Farmer or cottage cheese with cream cheese; mold into 4 square or block portions. Serve in 4 breakfast dishes with cream poured over. Can be topped with fresh fruit and sprinkled with sugar, if desired. Serves 4.

St. Cloud, Mn.

CRANBERRY CRUNCH

1 c. rolled oats
1/2 c. flour
1 c. brown sugar

1/2 c. butter
1 (1 lb.) can cranberry sauce

Mix and crumble first 4 ingredients; put 1/2 in 9x9 inch pan. Put on cranberry sauce. Top with rest of mixture. Bake 45 minutes at 350°.

Minneapolis, Mn.

CRANBERRY DESSERT

1 egg
1 1/2 tsp. salt
3/4 c. milk
3 tsp. baking powder

1 c. sugar
4 Tbsp. melted butter
2 c. sifted flour
1 1/2 c. whole, uncooked
  cranberries

562

Mix sugar, egg, salt and butter. Add milk, flour and baking powder. Last, stir in whole cranberries. Grease and flour a cake pan. Bake 45 minutes at 400°.

Sauce:

1/2 c. butter	1 c. sugar
1/2 c. cream	1 1/2 tsp. vanilla

Cook butter and sugar 1 minute; add cream and cook another minute. Stir in vanilla. Spoon warm sauce over cool cake and serve.

Colleen Grapentin, St. Cloud, Mn.

CRANBERRY FLUFF

1 lb. raw cranberries, ground, drained	1/2 pkg. miniature marshmallows
6 diced, unpeeled apples	3/4 - 1 c. sugar

Combine and chill overnight. Add 1 (No. 2) can crushed pineapple, drained, and 1/2 to 1 cup heavy cream, whipped.

Marion Round, Faribault, Mn.

FROZEN CRANBERRY DESSERT OR SALAD

1 can strained cranberry sauce	3/4 c. grated raw apple

Mix and put in ice cube tray or 8 inch pan.

1 c. cream, whipped	1/4 c. powdered sugar

Spread on cranberry mixture. Top with 1/2 cup chopped nuts; freeze.

Pearl Mohn, Montevideo, Mn.

CRANBERRY WHIP

2 c. water	1 c. sugar
1 c. cranberries	1/4 c. farina or cream of wheat

Boil cranberries in water; put through sieve. Place juice on stove again; add sugar and farina very slowly. Cook until it thickens; chill thoroughly. Beat until light and fluffy. Serve cold, topped with whipping cream.

1507-82   Rose V. Johnson, Virginia, Mn.

CRANBERRY WOBBLER

1 1/2 c. ground, fresh
   cranberries
1/2 c. sugar
2 (3 oz.) pkg. or 1 (6 oz.)
   pkg. Jell-O brand orange
   or lemon flavor gelatin
1/4 tsp. salt

2 c. boiling water
1 1/2 c. cold water
1 Tbsp. lemon juice
1/4 tsp. cinnamon
1/8 tsp. cloves
1 orange, sectioned, diced
1/2 c. chopped almonds

Combine cranberries and sugar; set aside. Dissolve gelatin and salt in boiling water; add cold water, lemon juice, cinnamon and cloves. Chill until thickened. Fold in cranberries, orange and nuts; spoon into 6 cup mold. Chill until firm, about 4 hours. Unmold; garnish with crisp salad greens. Makes about 6 cups or 12 servings.

          Mavis Dilts, Valley City, N.D.

BAKED CUSTARD

4 c. milk, scalded
6 eggs
1/2 c. sugar

1 tsp. vanilla
1/8 tsp. salt

Beat the eggs; add sugar. Add scalded milk slowly. Add vanilla and salt. Pour into custard cups or 1 large baking dish. Set in a pan of hot water and bake in moderate oven until a knife comes out clean. If wanted, nutmeg may be sprinkled on custards before baking. Serves about 7.

          Marie Capen, Duluth, Mn.

BAKED CUSTARD

2 egg yolks or 1 whole egg
   to each c. of milk
2 Tbsp. sugar for each
   c. of milk

1/6 tsp. salt for each c. of
   milk
1/4 tsp. flavoring for each
   c. of milk

Beat eggs slightly; add other ingredients and mix well. Pour into custard cups. Set in pan of hot water and bake at 350° for 1 hour or until knife comes out clean.

          Marge Pye, St. Paul, Mn.

DANISH PASTRY

Crust:

1 c. flour   1/2 c. soft butter

Press into 9x13 inch pan; bake at 350° for 10 minutes.

Filling:

1 c. brown sugar   1 c. coconut
1/2 c. chopped nuts   3 eggs

Bake at 350° for 20 to 25 minutes, until golden brown. Frost with powdered sugar glaze while still hot.

Bette Thistle, Minneapolis, Mn.

EASY DESSERT

Make 1 package dessert topping according to directions on package. Add:

1 can peach pie filling   1 can fruit cocktail, drained,
2 c. miniature marshmallows   or pineapple
                                    1/2 tsp. almond flavoring

Cover with coconut; chill. Can be made the day before. Keeps well for several days.

Patricia Larson, Grafton, N.D.

DREAM SQUARES

1 pkg. white cake mix   1 (21 oz.) can fruit pie
1 1/4 c. oatmeal   filling (cherry, apple,
1/2 c. butter or margarine   blueberry)
1 egg   1/2 c. chopped nuts
                                    1/4 c. brown sugar

Heat oven to 350°. Grease 13x9 inch pan. In large bowl, combine cake mix, 6 tablespoons margarine and 1 cup oatmeal; mix until crumbly. Reserve 1 cup crumbs for topping. To remaining crumbs, add 1 egg; mix well. Press into pan. Pour pie filling over crust; spread to cover. To reserved crumbs, in large bowl, add remaining 1/4 cup oatmeal, 2 tablespoons margarine, nuts and brown sugar. Beat thoroughly; sprinkle over pie filling mixture. Bake at 350° for 30-40 minutes. Serve with whipped cream. This is very easy and so delicious.

Kathy Roberts, Grand Forks, N.D.

FINGER JELLO

2 pkg. unflavored gelatin
1 (6 oz.) or 2 (3 oz.) boxes any flavor jello
2 1/2 c. water
1/4 c. or less sugar

Dissolve gelatin in 1 cup cold water; set aside. Boil 1 cup water; add jello and sugar. Bring to boil again. Remove from heat; add gelatin mixture. Stir; add 1/2 cup water. Pour into lightly greased pan; chill. Cut into squares and serve.

Wanda Thompson, Minneapolis, Mn.

BAKED FRUIT

1 large can peaches
1 large can pears
1 large can pineapple
1 large can apricots
1 small jar maraschino cherries

Drain fruit and arrange in a baking dish.

Orange Dressing for Fruit:

1/3 c. sugar
2 Tbsp. cornstarch
1/4 tsp. salt
1/2 c. light corn syrup
1 c. orange juice
Juice of 1 lemon (may be added for tartness)
2 Tbsp. orange rind (opt.)

Cook until thick and clear; add 2 tablespoons butter. Pour over fruit and bake 1/2 hour at 325°. This may be served in place of a salad.

Marian Pearson, Minneapolis, Mn.

FRESH FRUIT DESSERT

3 c. sugar
3 c. water
1 (10 oz.) pkg. frozen strawberries
Juice of 3 lemons
1 pt. strawberries
1 (20 oz.) can crushed pineapple, not drained
3 bananas
1 cantaloupe
7-Up
Blueberries

Combine sugar and water in large saucepan; bring to a boil. Add frozen strawberries, lemon and orange juice and pineapple with juice; mix well. Add bananas, cantaloupe (cut in balls) and strawberries. Pour into a 9x13 inch pan. Sprinkle blueberries over all; freeze overnight. Before serving, let stand at room temperature for 35 to 45 minutes, till slushy. Spoon into sherbet dishes. Pour 7-Up over and serve. Use any fresh fruit you choose - honeydew, nectarines, peaches, watermelon, cherries, raspberries. So good and refreshing! Serves 20.

Marion Standring, Big Lake, Mn.

FRUIT CHIFFON

1 c. boiling water	2 c. crushed ice
2 (3 oz.) pkg. fruit	1 c. canned, fresh or frozen
flavored gelatin	fruit pieces, well drained

Put boiling water and gelatin in blender container; cover and run on low until gelatin is dissolved, about 2 minutes. Add ice; cover container and run on high until ice is liquefied and container is cool to touch. Immediately pour into a bowl; let set until it begins to thicken (it doesn't take long). Fold in drained fruit. Let set 3-4 minutes or until thickened. Serve immediately or store in refrigerator. May top with whipped cream, if desired. Makes 6-8 servings. A very good and fast dessert!

Judy Rieger, Grand Forks, N.D.

FRUIT STRIPS

Cream:
1 c. butter or margarine   1 3/4 c. sugar

Add:
4 eggs, beaten until creamy   1 tsp. vanilla

Sift together and beat in 3 cups flour and 1 1/2 teaspoons baking powder. Save out 1 1/2 cups dough; spread remaining dough in 9x13 inch pan. Spread prepared pie filling over dough (Wilderness, any flavor). Spoon remaining dough over top. Sprinkle with powdered or granulated sugar. Bake about 40 minutes at 350°.

Eileen Sleeman, Virginia, Mn.

FRUIT PIZZA

Crust:

1 c. sugar	1 tsp. vanilla
1 c. butter or margarine	1 tsp. baking powder
2 1/2 c. flour	1/4 tsp. salt
1 egg	

Mix together and bake in pizza pan at 350° till done. Cool. Mix together 8 ounces very soft cream cheese, 1/2 cup powdered sugar and 1 cup Cool Whip; put on crust. On this, put fresh fruit such as strawberries, melon, raspberries, pineapple, cherries or green grapes.

Mary Paul, Minneapolis, Mn.

QUICK FRUIT TURNOVERS

2 Tbsp. sugar	2 medium peaches, peeled,
1 Tbsp. cornstarch	pitted, thinly sliced
1/4 tsp. ground cinnamon	(about 1 c.)
1 (8 oz.) pkg. refrigerator	Confectioners sugar
crescent rolls (8)	

In small bowl, stir together sugar, cornstarch and cinnamon; toss with peaches. Unroll crescent dough and separate into 4 rectangles. Seal perforations in each rectangle. Place rectangles of dough on ungreased baking sheet. Place 1/4 of the peach mixture on half of each rectangle; fold top half of rectangle over filling. Seal edges with fork; pierce tops with fork. Bake in 400° F. oven for 15 minutes or until lightly browned; cool on wire rack 10 minutes. Sprinkle with confectioners sugar. Makes 4.

Note: Nectarines, plums, apples or pears may be substituted for peaches.

Marion Round, Faribault, Mn.

FROZEN DESSERT

3 bananas, mashed	1 c. sugar
3 lemons (juice and pulp)	2 c. water
3 oranges (juice and pulp)	1 (No. 2 1/2) can crushed
	pineapple

Mix together; freeze in foil cupcake cups. Take out about 1/2 hour before serving. Garnish with a slice of strawberry.

Ruth Lee, Detroit Lakes, Mn.

FROZEN SUNDAE DESSERT

Freeze between each layer (9x13 inch pan).

First Layer:

22 crushed Oreos   1/4 c. melted oleo

Press in bottom of pan.

Second Layer: Add 1/2 gallon vanilla ice cream, softened.

Third Layer: Add 1 large jar Smucker's chocolate fudge.

Fourth Layer: Add 1/2 pint whipping cream, whipped and sweetened with granular sugar. Sprinkle cashews over top. Serve frozen.

Paula Earhart, Jackson, Mn.

HEATH BAR DESSERT

1 c. graham cracker crumbs   1 stick oleo
1 c. soda cracker crumbs

Melt and mix; put in 9x13 inch pan. Bake 10 minutes at 350°. Mix at low speed of mixer 2 (3 ounce) packages of vanilla instant pudding with only 1 cup of milk. Beat in 1 quart of softened butter pecan or toasted almond ice cream; pour over crumbs. Cover with 1 (9 ounce) carton Cool Whip. Chop 4 Heath bars; sprinkle on top. Chill overnight at least; do not freeze.

Joan Norton, Hibbing, Mn.

ICE CREAM

5 eggs, beaten well   Nuts or pineapple (opt.)
2 c. brown sugar   Enough milk to make 1 gal.
3 c. sweet cream   of ice cream (about 3 c.)
Vanilla (or maple flavoring)

Pack in ice and salt after freezing.

Suzie Brainard, Minneapolis, Mn.

OLD FASHIONED ICE CREAM

3 c. milk
3 c. cream

3 c. sugar

Combine and freeze until mushy consistency. Last, add:

Juice of 3 lemons
Juice of 3 oranges

3 small bananas, mashed

Pack in ice and salt; allow to cure, if desired. Can be eaten immediately; however, it will be softer.
Suzie Brainard, Minneapolis, Mn.

STRAWBERRY ICE CREAM

1 1/2 c. strawberry jam

2 c. buttermilk

Stir together jam and buttermilk; freeze firm. Break up mixture and whip until fluffy. Refreeze and enjoy.
Leslie Zimbrick, Minneapolis, Mn.
Similar recipe submitted by: Marion Round, Faribault, Mn.

ICE CREAM DESSERT

1 pkg. Hydrox cookies
1/2 gal. vanilla ice cream

1 jar caramel topping
1/2 pt. whipping cream

Crush cookies; put in 9x13 inch pan. Reserve some for top. Soften ice cream; spread over crumbs. Pour topping over ice cream; place in freezer for 2 hours. Whip cream; pour over frozen mixture. Top with reserved crumbs. Place in freezer until ready to serve.
Maryann Skelton, Duluth, Mn.

FROZEN SHERBET DESSERT

1 pt. whipping cream
3 Tbsp. sugar
1 pt. each lime, raspberry,
    lemon sherbet

1 tsp. vanilla
1 c. chopped nuts
1 pkg. macaroons (18 each
    of 3 inch cookies)

Crumble macaroons; whip cream. Add macaroons to cream, nuts, vanilla and sugar. Put 1/2 of this mixture in bottom of 9x12 inch pan. Spoon on sherbet, alternating flavors. Cover with remaining mixture; freeze. Cut in squares.

Mary Boe, Minneapolis, Mn.

SHERBET

1 1/4 c. orange juice
1/3 c. lemon juice
1 1/2 c. sugar

1 c. crushed pineapple
3 c. milk

Mix juices and sugar; let stand for 10 minutes. Add milk; mix well and freeze.

Lucille F. Anderson, East Grand Forks, Mn.

JIFFY   DESSERT

1 yellow Jiffy cake mix,
  baked as directed but
  in 9x13 inch pan
1 pkg. instant vanilla
  pudding

1 (8 oz.) pkg. cream
  cheese, softened
2 c. milk
1 (15 oz.) can pineapple,
  drained

Beat pudding mix, cream cheese and milk until fluffy. Spread on top of cool cake. Spread pineapple over pudding mixture. Whip 1 package (1/2 pint) of Rich Whip and spread over pineapple layer. Refrigerate 4 hours.

Pam Doyea, Fargo, N.D.

Similar recipes submitted by: Geri Running, St. Paul, Mn., Mrs. Kermit A. Haugen, Clarkfield, Mn.

LEMON   CRACKLE

Filling:

1 c. cold water
1 c. sugar
2 well beaten eggs

Juice of 2 lemons
2 Tbsp. cornstarch
1 tsp. vanilla

Mix cornstarch, sugar, salt and remaining ingredients in double boiler; cook until thick and smooth. Cool.

Crust:

1 c. brown sugar
1/2 c. butter
1/2 tsp. soda

10 soda crackers, rolled fine
1 c. flour
1 c. coconut

Cream butter and sugar and rest of ingredients. Pat 3/4 of mixture in a 12 x 6 1/2 inch pan. Pat flat in greased pan; pour in filling. Cover with rest of dry mixture. Bake 30 minutes at 350°. Serve with whipped cream.

Liz Tuft, St. Paul, Mn.

LEMON CRACKLE DESSERT

1/4 c. butter	3 eggs
1/3 c. brown sugar	1/2 c. sugar
1 1/2 c. Wheaties	1 c. whipping cream
1/3 c. chopped nuts	1 lemon

Melt butter; blend in brown sugar. Cook over low heat to crackle stage. Remove from heat; add Wheaties and nuts. Stir until well coated; cool. Beat until stiff 3 egg whites. Gradually add white sugar. Beat egg yolks until thick. Fold into egg white mixture. Mix together and beat until stiff the whipping cream and lemon; fold into egg mixture. Sprinkle half the finely crumbled nut crunch mixture in bottom of buttered 8 inch square pan. Pour in lemon filling and sprinkle remaining crunch on top. Freeze until firm. Serve in squares. Serves 9.

Elynor Pederson, Minneapolis, Mn.

FROZEN LEMON DESSERT

1 lemon cake mix	1 can Eagle Brand sweetened
1 (9 oz.) container Cool Whip	condensed milk
1 (6 oz.) can frozen lemonade	1/2 c. coconut

Bake cake; cool. Thaw lemonade. Mix Cool Whip, Eagle Brand milk and lemonade in a large bowl; stir into a pudding mixture. Break half of cake in pieces; put in bottom of 9x13 inch Tupperware pan. Cover with half of mixture, then layer with other half of cake, broken in pieces. Cover with remaining mixture. Sprinkle top with coconut; cover tightly and freeze.

Mrs. Norma Applen, Minneapolis, Mn.

LEMON LUSH

1 c. flour   1/2 c. chopped pecans
1/4 c. oleo

Blend flour and oleo; add pecans. Press in 13x9 inch pan. Bake at 350° for 15-20 minutes.

1 (8 oz.) pkg. cream cheese   9 oz. Cool Whip (use only
1 c. powdered sugar   1 c.)

Mix well together; spread on cooled crust. Mix 2 packages instant lemon pudding mix and 3 cups milk; spread over cheese mixture. Add remaining Cool Whip on top; refrigerate.

Jean Kreutzer, Rochester, Mn.

LEMON SOUFFLE

2 Tbsp. unflavored gelatin   3/4 c. sugar
4 Tbsp. water   1 c. (about 8) egg whites,
1/2 c. lemon juice   beaten until stiff
Grated rind of 4 lemons   1 c. whipping cream, beaten
                                      until stiff

Stir gelatin and water over low heat until gelatin is dissolved. Add lemon juice, rind and sugar; chill until syrupy. Fold the egg whites and whipping cream into gelatin mix. Pour into oiled individual souffle dishes. Will also fit a 1 1/2 quart souffle dish. Serve unmolded on a puddle of Raspberry Sauce (below). Makes 8 servings.

Service: Spoon glaze of Melba Sauce into bottom of wide rimmed dessert plate. Unmold the individual souffles and place in center of sauce. Garnish with fresh flower on the side.

Melba Sauce:

1 (10 oz.) pkg. frozen,   1 Tbsp. Framboise (rasp-
  sweetened raspberries   berry liqueur)

Puree the raspberries, partially frozen, in bowl of food processor. Force through sieve to remove seeds. Stir in Framboise or other favorite liqueur.

St. Cloud, Mn.

ARLENE'S MERINGUE

3 egg whites   1 c. Kraft marshmallow
Dash of salt   topping

Beat eggs until soft peaks; add marshmallow topping and salt. Beat until it holds its shape (stiff peaks). Bake at 350° for 12-15 minutes.

Gloria Smith, Jackson, Mn.

MOM'S MINT DAZZLE

Step 1: Mix -

2 c. crushed vanilla wafers   1 Tbsp. sugar
1/4 plus c. melted butter

Blend and press into a 9x13 inch pan (mix right in pan).

Step 2:

1/2 c. butter   3 eggs, slightly beaten
1 1/2 c. powdered sugar,   6 1/2 Tbsp. cocoa, sifted
   sifted

Cream butter and powdered sugar. Mix cocoa and eggs together, then add to butter and powdered sugar mixture. Beat all together until <u>very fluffy</u> (it takes a lot of beating). Add 1 teaspoon vanilla.

Step 3: Spoon this over the crumb mixture and chill in refrigerator.

Step 4: Mix 1 (10 ounce) bag of miniature marshmallows with a 9 ounce container of Cool Whip and 1 teaspoon vanilla. Spread this over the chocolate mixture.

Step 5: Crush 5 round, hard peppermint or candy canes with a hammer (leave in wrapper and put inside a plastic bag); sprinkle the crushed peppermint over the top. Keep refrigerated until ready to serve. (This freezes well.)

Barb Discher, Bismarck, N.D.

ORANGE ANGEL DELIGHT

Dissolve 1 tablespoon unflavored gelatin in 1/4 cup cold water. Add 1/4 cup hot water. Mix 1 cup orange juice with 1 cup sugar. Blend in gelatin; chill until slightly thickened, then beat. Beat 1 pint whipping cream; fold into gelatin mixture. Add 1/2 angel food cake, broken into small pieces, and 1/2 cup short cut coconut. Pour into a 13x9 inch cake tin; chill several hours or overnight. Cut as cake. Decorate with orange slices and coconut.

Alice Gudknecht, Faribault, Mn.

ORANGE DESSERT

Heat 1 1/2 cups orange juice. Dissolve 1 small package marshmallows in juice; cool. Fold in 1 cup Cool Whip; chill.

Ava S. Day, St. Paul, Mn.

PEACH BAVARIAN

1 (3 oz.) pkg. lemon flavored gelatin	1 c. hot water
2 Tbsp. sugar	1 (1 lb. 13 oz.) can Stokely's finest sliced yellow cling peaches
Dash of salt	1 c. heavy cream, whipped

Dissolve gelatin, sugar and salt in hot water. Drain peaches well. Add 1/2 cup peach liquid to gelatin mixture. Pour 1/4 cup gelatin mixture in bottom of 1 quart mold; arrange 8 peach slices in gelatin. Chill until almost firm. Chill remaining gelatin mixture until slightly thickened, then fold in whipped cream. Cut remaining peaches in halves; fold into cream mixture. Pour into mold; chill until firm. Unmold on serving plate. Garnish with mint leaves. Makes 8 servings.

K., St. Cloud, Mn.

PEACH PUDDING DESSERT

1 c. all-purpose flour	1 (16 oz.) can sliced peaches, drained
3/4 c. white sugar	1 c. packed brown sugar
2 tsp. baking powder	1/4 c. finely chopped nuts
1/4 tsp. salt	1 tsp. cinnamon
1/2 c. milk	1 c. boiling water
3 Tbsp. vegetable oil	

Heat oven to 350°. Mix flour, white sugar, baking powder and salt; beat in milk and oil until smooth. Pour into ungreased baking pan, 8x8x2 inches; arrange peaches on top. Mix brown sugar, nuts and cinnamon; sprinkle over peaches. Pour boiling water over top. Bake until

wooden pick inserted comes out clean, 60 to 70 minutes.
Serve with whipped cream, if desired.

Mary Fingalson, Detroit Lakes, Mn.

BUTTER PECAN DESSERT

45 Ritz crackers, crushed   1/2 c. melted butter

Mix above ingredients; pat into a 9x13 inch pan.
Bake 10 minutes at 350°; cool. Beat together:

2 (6 oz.) pkg. instant   1 1/2 c. milk
    butter pecan pudding

Add 1 quart softened vanilla ice cream; spread over
crust. Refrigerate for 1 hour; spread 1 (9 ounce) carton
Cool Whip on top. Sprinkle with 3 crushed Heath candy
bars. Refrigerate or freeze until ready to serve. Even
better the next day!

Mary Flaten, Grand Forks, N.D.

PECAN TARTS

1 c. margarine   6 oz. cream cheese
2 c. flour

Cream cheese and margarine; add flour. Roll into 48
small balls, about teaspoon size. Pat in tart shell pans.

Filling:

2 eggs   1 c. chopped pecans
1 1/2 c. brown sugar   Dash of salt
1/2 tsp. vanilla

Bake at 350° the first 15 minutes, then at 250° the
next 10 minutes.

Jeanette Guzek, Grand Forks, N.D.

PEPPERMINT DELIGHT

2 c. flour   2 Tbsp. powdered sugar
1/2 lb. butter or oleo   1/2 tsp. salt

Mix like crumbs; pat lightly in 9x13 inch pan. Bake
at 325° for 25 minutes or until light brown; cool.

1 pkg. miniature
   marshmallows
1 pkg. Swedish dry mints
   (Brach's), crushed

1/2 pt. whipping cream,
   whipped
1 small pkg. Dream Whip,
   prepared
3/4 c. nuts, finely chopped

Mix cream and Dream Whip, marshmallows, nuts and mints; spread over crumbs.

Note: Mints heated in oven crush easier by rolling pin.

Maryann Skelton, Duluth, Mn.

PINEAPPLE DESSERT

Boil in top of double boiler till thick 2 egg yolks and 1 tablespoon cream. Take from double boiler; add 1/4 cup pineapple juice and steam. Cream:

1 c. sugar   1/2 c. butter or margarine

Add to above mixture and cook till thick. Beat 2 egg whites till stiff; add to above mixture and also 1 cup crushed pineapple. Pour in small pan or sherbet dishes, alternating with layers of graham crackers, crushed fine. Refrigerate till served. Makes 6 servings. May be topped with whipped cream when served.

Norma Haugerud, Montevideo, Mn.

PINEAPPLE JEWEL SQUARES

1 c. fine graham cracker
   crumbs
1 (8 3/4 oz.) can (1 c.)
   crushed pineapple
1 1/4 c. boiling water
1 (3 oz.) pkg. cream
   cheese, softened
1/4 tsp. grated orange peel

2 Tbsp. sugar
1/4 c. butter or margarine,
   melted
1 (3 oz.) pkg. orange-pineapple flavored gelatin
3 Tbsp. sugar
1/2 tsp. vanilla
1 c. dairy sour cream

Mix crumbs, sugar and butter; press into bottom of 8x8x2 inch baking dish. Chill. Thoroughly drain pineapple, reserving 1/2 cup syrup. Dissolve gelatin in boiling water; add pineapple syrup. Cool. Blend cream cheese with 3 tablespoons sugar, vanilla and orange peel. Stir 1/2 cup gelatin into drained pineapple; set aside. Gradually blend remaining gelatin into cream cheese mixture; stir in sour cream. Pour into crust; chill until firm. Spoon pineapple mixture evenly over cream cheese layer. Chill 4 to 6 hours. Makes 6 to 9 servings.

Mrs. Emma Buhl, Minneapolis, Mn.

PISTACHIO DESSERT

2 c. crushed Ritz crackers 2/3 c. melted butter

Melt the butter; mix in crackers. Pat in 9x13 inch pan; cool in refrigerator.

2 pkg. pistachio instant 2 c. milk
 pudding   1 qt. vanilla ice cream

Mix pudding with milk; fold in softened ice cream. Keep refrigerated.

Grace Locke, St. Paul, Mn.

PISTACHIO DESSERT

Crust:

1 c. flour   1/2 c. chopped nuts
1/2 c. margarine

Mix together into crumbs; press into 9x13 inch pan. Bake at 350° for 15 minutes; cool.

Filling:

1 pkg. cream cheese, 1 c. powdered sugar
 softened

Fold in 1/2 of large container of Cool Whip; spread over crust. Mix 1 package instant coconut cream pudding and 1 package pistachio pudding with 3 cups milk; spread over cream cheese layer. Add the rest of the Cool Whip on top. Sprinkle with nuts; refrigerate.

Rosalee Wendelbo, Grafton, N.D.

PISTACHIO-ORANGE BUNDT CAKE

1 (18 oz.) pkg. white or yellow cake mix (without pudding added)
4 eggs
1 c. orange juice
1/2 c. cooking oil
1 (3 3/4 oz.) pkg. pistachio instant pudding mix
1 tsp. almond flavoring
3/4 c. chocolate syrup

Place cake mix, eggs, orange juice, oil, pudding mix and almond flavoring in mixer bowl. Mix at low speed for 1 minute and at medium speed for 3 minutes or until well blended. Pour 2/3 of batter into a well greased, lightly floured 10 inch Bundt pan. Add chocolate syrup to remaining batter; pour batter over batter in pan. Cut through batter with knife several times to give a marbled effect. Bake in a moderate oven, 350°, for 50 to 60 minutes or until cake tests done. Allow to cool in pan for 10 minutes. Invert onto plate or rack for further cooling. To serve: Sprinkle with powdered sugar or drizzle with a thin powdered sugar icing. A sumptuous addition enhances the pistachio flavor of the cake by adding this topping just before serving.

Pistachio Topping:

1 (3 3/4 oz.) pkg. instant pistachio pudding
1/2 c. milk
1 (9 oz.) ctn. frozen whipped topping, thawed

Combine pudding and milk; fold in whipped topping and frost the cake. Alternative topping recipe for the Pistachio-Orange Bundt Cake -

Brandy Frosting:

1 sq. (1 oz.) semi-sweet chocolate
1 1/2 Tbsp. butter
3/4 c. confectioners sugar
2 Tbsp. brandy

In small saucepan over low heat, melt chocolate with butter, stirring constantly, until smooth. Remove from heat. Add sugar alternately with brandy. Stir until of glaze consistency.

St. Cloud, Mn.

PISTACHIO JELLO

1 (3 1/2 oz.) pkg. pistachio
   instant pudding
1 (8 oz.) container Cool Whip

1 large can crushed
   pineapple, with juice
1/2 c. chopped walnuts

Mix together dry pudding mix and pineapple; fold in Cool Whip. Add nuts and stir. Must set 4 hours before serving.

Mary Ann Dinius, Coon Rapids, Mn.

PLACHENDA

Beat 3 eggs. Add:

1 c. sugar
1/2 tsp. salt

2 c. cream

Sift together flour with 3 teaspoons baking powder. Add enough flour to make soft dough; let rest for 1 hour. Divide dough into small pieces, size of an egg. Roll into squares; put pumpkin mix into center and bring up sides and ends to make rectangle. Prick with fork; sprinkle with sugar and bake at 425° for 10 to 15 minutes.

Pumpkin Mixture: Combine -

4 c. smooth, cooked
   pumpkin
1 1/2 c. sugar

2 eggs
1 tsp. cinnamon
1 tsp. lemon extract

Mix thoroughly. If it is watery, add 2 tablespoons flour.

F. Schwartzbauer, Bismarck, N.D.

GRANDMA OLSON'S POTATO PUDDING

1 c. grated carrots
1 c. grated potatoes
1 c. raisins (optional)
1 c. sugar
2 eggs, well beaten
2 c. flour (more, if needed)
1 tsp. baking soda

1 tsp. cinnamon
1/2 tsp. salt
1/2 tsp. nutmeg
1/2 tsp. allspice
1/4 tsp. ground cloves
3 Tbsp. melted butter or
   margarine

Combine carrots, potatoes, raisins and sugar. Add eggs; combine and stir in well the flour, soda, salt and spices. Add more flour, if needed to make the consistency of a cake batter. Coat all sides of a 2 quart pudding mold or can with butter; pour in batter. Cover tightly with a lid or with aluminum foil, secured with rubber band. Place on a rack in a covered pan; steam for 3 hours. Cool. Store in refrigerator or cover mold with foil and freeze. When ready to serve, reheat in oven. Serve with Old-Fashioned Caramel Sauce.

Mrs. Elmer Wright, Minneapolis, Mn.

POTATO TORTE

2 c. sugar	1 c. riced potatoes (or mashed)
1 c. shortening	1 tsp. soda
1 c. sour milk	1 tsp. cinnamon or cloves, as desired
1 c. raisins	
1 c. nuts	2 sq. melted bitter chocolate
2 c. flour	Dash of salt
5 eggs	

Cream shortening; add sugar, beaten eggs, potatoes, salt, chocolate and sour milk. Add soda, in flour, raisins and nuts. Bake 1 hour in slow oven, 325°. Grease pan extra careful and flour.

Just a few hints: I use vegetable shortening. I use my electric beater and don't beat eggs separately; just add one at a time.

Mrs. Emma Buhl, Minneapolis, Mn.

PUMPKIN PARFAIT SQUARES

Mix:

1 1/2 c. graham cracker crumbs	1/4 c. sugar
	1/4 c. melted butter

Press into 9 inch square pan. Combine:

1 1/2 c. pumpkin	1 tsp. cinnamon
1/2 c. brown sugar	1/4 tsp. ginger
1/2 tsp. salt	1/2 tsp. cloves

Fold in 1 quart vanilla ice cream; pour over crust. Freeze until firm. Top with whipping cream and pecans.

Helen Teeuwen, Minneapolis, Mn.

PUMPKIN PIE SQUARES

1 c. flour
1/2 c. oatmeal
1/2 c. brown sugar
1/2 c. butter

Combine and mix till crumbly; press in 9x13 inch ungreased pan. Bake for 15 minutes at 350°.

1 can pumpkin or 2 c.
1 (13 1/2 oz.) can evaporated milk
2 eggs
3/4 c. sugar
1/2 tsp. salt
1 tsp. cinnamon
1 1/2 tsp. ginger
1/4 tsp. cloves

Combine and beat well; pour over crust. Bake for another 20 minutes at 350°.

Topping:

1/2 c. chopped pecans
1/2 c. brown sugar
2 Tbsp. butter

Combine and sprinkle over dessert; return to oven for 15 minutes or until done.

Jeanette Guzek, Grand Forks, N.D.

APPLE PUDDING

1 1/2 c. sugar
1 1/2 c. flour
3 tsp. baking powder
Pinch of salt

Mix with 1 cup milk; spread in bottom of 9x13 inch pan. Pour 3 cups chopped apples over; sprinkle 1 1/2 cups brown sugar, 1/4 cup butter and cinnamon over apples. Bake at 350° until apples are done.

Ollie Kearney, Rochester, Mn.

BREAD PUDDING

3 c. soft bread cubes, lightly packed
1/2 c. raisins
2 2/3 c. milk
1/4 c. butter
1/2 c. sugar
1 tsp. nutmeg
1/4 tsp. salt
3 eggs, slightly beaten

Combine bread cubes and raisins in a 2 quart casserole. Heat milk, butter, sugar, nutmeg, salt and eggs till butter melts; pour over bread cubes. Bake in 325° oven till knife inserted near edge comes out clean, 45-50 minutes. Best served warm. Serves 6.

Colleen Landwehr, St. Cloud, Mn.

CHOCOLATE CREAM PUDDING

3/4 c. sugar
3 Tbsp. cornstarch
4 Tbsp. cocoa or 2 sq.
  chocolate

1/4 tsp. salt
2 c. milk
1 tsp. vanilla
1 Tbsp. butter

1. Put milk into double boiler. 2. Mix dry ingredients together. 3. Add a little milk to dry ingredients to make a paste. 4. Add mixture to milk. 5. Stir over double boiler for about 10 minutes. 6. Take from fire; add vanilla and butter.

Margaret McKenney, Minneapolis, Mn.

RUTH'S STEAMED CRANBERRY PUDDING WITH BUTTER SAUCE

1 1/3 c. sifted flour
1/2 c. molasses
1/3 c. hot water

2 tsp. soda
1/2 tsp. salt
2 c. raw cranberries, cut in
  halves

Mix all together. Pour into buttered mold; steam 2 hours. Serve with Butter Sauce.

Butter Sauce:

1/2 c. butter
1 c. sugar

1/2 c. whipping cream

Melt butter; add sugar and cream. Cook until sugar is thoroughly dissolved (barely bring to boil). Serve hot.

Marian Vranicar, Parkville, Mn.

Similar recipe submitted by: Helen Teeuwen, Minneapolis, Mn.

DANISH RICE PUDDING (RISALMAND)
(Christmas Eve Dough)

1/4 c. rice, cooked in the milk
1/4 c. almonds, chopped very fine
2 c. milk
2 c. cream, whipped

1 env. gelatin, dissolved in 1/4 c. water
1 tsp. vanilla
5 Tbsp. sugar
1 whole almond (if prize given for finding almond)

Add almonds to cooked rice and dissolved gelatin. When cool, add cream and rest of ingredients. I serve a sauce of whole, frozen raspberries over this.

Martha Fjelstad, Minneapolis, Mn.

MUFFIN PUDDING WITH STRAWBERRY SAUCE

3 English muffins with raisins, split
2 Tbsp. soft butter or margarine
1/2 c. firmly packed brown sugar

6 eggs plus 3 yolks, lightly beaten
1 1/4 c. sugar
2 tsp. vanilla
4 1/2 c. milk, heated
1 pt. fresh strawberries

With sharp knife, trim off outer crusts of each muffin. Butter muffins lightly; cover with brown sugar. Arrange on pan; carefully broil until golden. Set aside. Combine beaten eggs, sugar and vanilla; slowly stir in hot milk. Measure 1 1/4 cups of this custard mixture into top of double boiler; set aside. Pour remaining mixture into 2 quart casserole. Arrange 6 prepared muffin rounds on top. Set casserole in pan of hot water. Bake in preheated 400° oven for 20 to 25 minutes or until knife inserted in center comes out clean. Cool to room temperature. While pudding bakes, cook and stir mixture in double boiler over hot water until it coats a metal spoon; cool. Fold sliced strawberries into cooled sauce. Spoon strawberry sauce over each serving of pudding. Serves 6 to 8.

St. Cloud, Mn.

PRINCESS PEACH PUDDING

1 (2 lb.) pkg. graham cracker crumbs
1/2 c. melted butter or margarine

2 (29 oz.) cans sliced peaches, well drained
1 (12 oz.) container frozen whipped topping, thawed

584

12 maraschino cherries,   Whipped topping
    drained and halved

    In a large bowl, combine graham cracker crumbs and just enough melted butter or margarine to moisten, stirring with a fork to blend. In the bottom of a large clear glass bowl, spread 1 cup of the crumb mixture. Top with a layer of peaches and a thin layer of whipped topping. Repeat layers until all peaches have been used up. Top with additional whipped topping. Arrange cherry halves over topping. Chill 2 to 3 hours before serving. Makes 8 to 10 servings.

                    Bernita Engel, Minneapolis, Mn.

RAISIN PUDDING

Mix together:
1 c. flour	Pinch of salt
3/4 c. sugar	1 c. raisins
2 tsp. baking powder	1/2 c. milk

    Put into a greased baking dish. Combine 1/2 cup brown sugar and 1 cup boiling water; add 1 tablespoon butter or oleo. Pour this mixture over the batter. Bake 40 minutes at 350°. This makes its own sauce!

                    Alice Holman, Grand Forks, N.D.

OLD FASHIONED TAPIOCA PUDDING
(Not Minute Type)

3 c. milk	4 oz. tapioca seeds (dry)
1/3 c. sugar	2 eggs, separated
1/2 tsp. vanilla	Pinch of salt

    Do not wash tapioca, just soak overnight in cold water. Mix egg yolks with small amount of milk, soaked tapioca, sugar, salt and the remaining milk. Cook in top of double boiler until pearl tapioca is clear; remove from heat. Beat egg whites until stiff. When mixture is cooled slightly, fold in egg whites and vanilla. Pour in a dampened dish. Chill and serve with a dab of whipped cream or Cool Whip.

    Note: The tapioca seeds or pearl tapioca is the imported kind and can be purchased at any gourmet shop or International House.

                Helen-May Johnson, Chanhassen, Mn.

TROPICAL DATE PUDDING

1 c. drained, crushed
  pineapple
1 c. chopped dates
1/2 c. chopped walnuts
1/2 c. all-purpose flour
1 tsp. baking powder

1/2 tsp. baking soda
1/2 tsp. salt
3 eggs, separated
1 tsp. vanilla
3/4 c. sugar

    Combine pineapple, dates and nuts in mixing bowl; add flour, baking powder, baking soda and salt. Mix well. Beat egg whites until stiff; beat in 1/4 cup of sugar. Beat egg yolks with vanilla and 1/2 cup sugar. Stir egg yolk mixture into fruit; fold in stiffly beaten egg whites. Bake in greased 8x11 inch pan at 325° for about 40 minutes. Serve warm or cold with whipped cream. Makes 8-10 servings.

                Beverly Fox, Fargo, N.D.

RAISIN-STUFFED APPLES

4 large baking apples
1/2 c. raisins
1/2 c. dry sherry or water
2 Tbsp. chopped walnuts
2 Tbsp. brown sugar
2 Tbsp. chopped mara-
  schino cherries

1/8 tsp. ground cinnamon
1/8 tsp. ground cloves
1/8 tsp. ground nutmeg
1 Tbsp. butter
Vanilla ice cream

    Core apples; place each apple on a 12x18 inch piece of aluminum foil. Combine raisins, sherry or water, walnuts, sugar, cherries and spices. Put equal portions of filling into each apple; dot with butter. Wrap apples loosely in foil. Grill over low coals for about 1 hour. Serve with a scoop of ice cream.

                St. Cloud, Mn.

RASPBERRIES IN THE SNOW

1 c. flour
1/2 c. brown sugar

1/2 c. butter or oleo
1/2 c. walnuts

    Mix; put in 9x13 inch pan. Bake 12-15 minutes at 325°.

    Filling: Mix 1 (8 ounce) package Philadelphia cream cheese with 1 cup sugar. Whip 1 pint of cream; add to cheese and sugar mixture. Add 1 teaspoon vanilla. Fold in

2 cups miniature marshmallows. Pour over crust and re-frigerate. Serve with pie cherries or raspberry glaze.

Glaze:

1 1/2 c. sugar	1/4 c. cornstarch
1 1/2 c. water	

Boil until mixture thickens and clears. Add 1 package raspberry jello; add raspberries and cool. Pour over cheese mixture. Refrigerate overnight.

Va Fyksen, Duluth, Mn.

"RASPBERRY TORTE"

2 (3 oz.) boxes raspberry gelatin	1 Tbsp. lemon juice
2 (3 oz.) pkg. vanilla pudding	1 (9 oz.) ctn. whipped topping
2 c. water	1 qt. raspberries
	1 graham cracker crust

Prepare gelatin as directed on box; let set until jelly like. Mix pudding with water and lemon juice in saucepan. Boil until thick; cool. Add jello and whipped topping, beating with mixer until well mixed. Fold in berries. Pour into prepared graham cracker crust in 9x13 inch pan. Refrigerate.

Julaine Burbach, Winona, Mn.

STRAWBERRY RHUBARB CAKE

Grease with butter or margarine a 9x13 inch cake pan. Dump in 5 cups cut up rhubarb. Sprinkle 1 large (6 ounce) package strawberry jello over rhubarb. Mix yellow cake as on package; pour over rhubarb and jello mixture. (Optional: If desired, 3/4 cup of sugar can be added over jello.) Bake at 350° for 50 to 60 minutes; test for doneness.

Bernita Engel, Minneapolis, Mn.

RHUBARB CRISP

2 c. rhubarb	1 Tbsp. flour or tapioca
1 c. sugar	1/2 tsp. salt
	1/2 tsp. cinnamon

Put in 8x8 inch pan.

Top with:

3/4 c. oatmeal	1/4 tsp. baking powder
3/4 c. sugar (can use	1/2 tsp. soda
brown or white sugar)	1/3 c. butter or margarine
3/4 c. flour	

Bake at 350° for about 1 hour.

Marion Vonesh, Grand Forks, N.D.

RHUBARB CRISP

3 c. diced rhubarb	1/4 c. butter
3/4 c. sugar	3/4 c. brown sugar
1 egg, well beaten	2/3 c. flour
2 Tbsp. flour	Whipped cream
1/4 tsp. mace	

Thoroughly mix rhubarb, sugar, egg, flour and mace. Spread in a 9 inch square pan. Work together with fingers the butter, brown sugar and flour; press mixture over rhubarb. Bake in 375° oven for 30 minutes. Cut into squares. Serve with whipped cream.

Dee Olson, St. Paul, Mn.

RHUBARB-CHERRY CRUNCH

Crust:

1 c. oatmeal	1/2 c. butter
1 c. brown sugar	1 c. flour
Pinch of salt	1/2 c. chopped nuts

Filling:

4 c. diced rhubarb	2 Tbsp. cornstarch
1 c. water	1 can cherry pie mix
1 c. sugar	

Mix above crust; pat 1/2 the mixture into a greased 9x13 inch pan. Put the diced rhubarb on top. Boil the sugar, water and cornstarch together until thick. Remove from stove; add the cherry pie mix and spoon over the rhubarb. Sprinkle the remaining crust over the top; add the nuts. Bake for 45 minutes at 350°. Serve either alone or with whipped cream or ice cream.

Mrs. Gary L. Hagen, Princeton, Mn.

Similar recipes submitted by: Fern Graskreutz, Litchfield, Mn., Jane Bohline, Minneapolis, Mn.

RHUBARB DESSERT

1 c. sugar
3 Tbsp. cornstarch
4 c. rhubarb
1/2 c. water with a little
   red food coloring added*

1/2 c. whipping cream
1 1/2 c. miniature
   marshmallows
1 pkg. instant vanilla
   pudding
Graham cracker crust

Cook first 4 ingredients; let cool. First Layer: Graham cracker crust. Second Layer: Spread cooled rhubarb mixture on crust. Third Layer: Whip cream and marshmallows; put on top of rhubarb. Fourth Layer: Make pudding; put on top. Sprinkle graham cracker crumbs on top and refrigerate. (Use 9x9 inch pan or double recipe for 13x9 inch pan.)
   *Omit if rhubarb is frozen.

                  Anne Aune, Minneapolis, Mn.

RHUBARB DESSERT

Crust:

2 c. flour
1 c. butter

3 Tbsp. sugar

Bake at 350° for 15 to 20 minutes; cool.

First Filling:

7 c. rhubarb
1 c. water

2 c. sugar
6 Tbsp. cornstarch

Cook together until thick like pudding, about 2-3 minutes. Cool; pour over cooled crust. Add a layer of Cool Whip.

Second Filling: Prepare 1 package of instant vanilla pudding using only 1 3/4 cups milk. Put on top of Cool Whip. Add topping of Cool Whip again.
                  Mrs. Carl Granrud, Montevideo, Mn.

RHUBARB DESSERT

Layer as numbered in 9x13 inch pan (make the day before):

   1:

40 Ritz crackers, crushed*   1/4 c. margarine, melted

2: Cook and cool -

2 c. rhubarb   1 c. sugar
3 Tbsp. cornstarch

3: Fold together -

1 (8 oz.) ctn. Cool Whip   1 c. miniature marshmallows

4: Mix 1 (5 1/2 ounce) box instant vanilla pudding as directed. 5: Garnish with crumbs.
*May use 1 1/4 cups graham cracker crumbs; reserve some for top.

Doris Thorson, Glenwood, Mn.

RHUBARB DESSERT

Base:

1 3/4 c. flour   2/3 c. butter or oleo
2 Tbsp. sugar   2 egg yolks
1 tsp. baking powder

Mix above ingredients; press into greased 9x13 inch pan. Bake at 350° for 10 minutes.

Filling:

2 beaten egg yolks   5 Tbsp. flour
1 3/4 c. sugar   4 c. rhubarb, cut fine

Pour filling on top of baked base.

Topping:

4 beaten egg whites   1/2 c. nutmeats (optional)
3/4 c. sugar

Beat egg whites, adding sugar gradually. Blend in nuts; spread on top of filling. Bake 30-40 minutes at 350°.

Jean Kreutzer, Rochester, Mn.

RHUBARB DESSERT

Cover 3 cups of cut up rhubarb with boiling water for 10 minutes; drain. Make crust of:

1 c. flour   1 beaten egg
1 tsp. baking powder   2 Tbsp. milk
1/4 tsp. salt

Roll out and line an 8x8 inch pan or large pie tin. Put rhubarb in crust; sprinkle with 1 package red gelatin (raspberry or strawberry are good). Cover with a streusel of:

1 c. sugar	1/4 c. butter or margarine
1/2 c. flour	

Sprinkle with cinnamon. Bake at 375° for 45 minutes or till crust is baked.

Margaret Hulst, Waltham, Mn.

SPEEDY RHUBARB DESSERT

Cook 5 to 6 cups of cut up rhubarb with 1 1/2 cups water and 3/4 cup sugar. When rhubarb is done, thicken with just enough flour to make a thick paste; let cool. Mix 2 cups graham cracker crumbs with 1 tablespoon melted butter or margarine; press into bottom of 9x13 inch cake pan. Pour cooled rhubarb mixture over crumbs. Mix 1 small container of thawed whipped topping with 2 cups miniature marshmallows. Beat with mixer on low speed for 1 minute; spread over rhubarb mixture. Mix 1 regular size package of instant vanilla pudding according to package directions; spread over topping mixture. Chill in refrigerator until ready to serve. Cut into squares and serve.
Optional: You can sprinkle graham cracker crumbs over pudding, if desired.

Bernita Engel, Minneapolis, Mn.

RHUBARB ICE CREAM

2 c. diced rhubarb	1 1/2 c. miniature
1/3 c. sugar	marshmallows
1/4 c. water	Few drops red food coloring
	2 c. Cool Whip, thawed

In saucepan, combine rhubarb, sugar and water. Cover; simmer 10 minutes or until rhubarb is tender. Add marshmallows; cook and stir over low heat until melted. Stir in food coloring; chill. Fold in Cool Whip. Spread in 3 cup freezer tray. Cover and freeze.

Pam Doyea, Fargo, N.D.

RHUBARB KUCHEN

Crust:

1 (17 oz.) pkg. yellow   1/4 c. butter, melted
    cake mix   2 eggs

Combine until well mixed; pat into ungreased 9x13 inch pan.

Filling: Put 2 cups of cut up rhubarb on crust. Mix -

1 (3 oz.) pkg. strawberry   1/2 c. sugar
    jello (dry)   2 Tbsp. flour

Sprinkle above mixture over rhubarb.

Topping: Mix streusel of -

1 c. sugar   1/2 c. flour
                          1/2 c. butter

Cut up coarsely with pie crust cutter; sprinkle over top, then a few shakes of cinnamon over all. Bake at 350° for 35-40 minutes.

Jan Ferry, Golden Valley, Mn.

RHUBARB LAYER DESSERT

4 c. rhubarb, cut up   1/2 pkg. white cake mix
1 c. sugar   (dry)
3 oz. jello (strawberry or   1 c. water
    lemon)   1/3 c. melted butter

Put cut up rhubarb in 9x11 inch pan. Sprinkle remaining ingredients in order given over rhubarb. Bake at 350° for 1 hour.

Debbie Burgum, Dickinson, N.D.

OPEN FACE RHUBARB DESSERT

1/2 c. butter or margarine   1 c. sifted flour
2 Tbsp. sugar   1/2 tsp. baking powder
1 egg

Cream butter and sugar in small bowl of electric mixer. Add egg; beat thoroughly. Add flour, sifted with baking powder and beat; refrigerate. Turn dough out on lightly floured cloth. Roll to fit 9 inch pan. Place dough in pan;

press to fit bottom. Top with 3 cups sliced rhubarb.
Sprinkle 1 (3 ounce) package strawberry gelatin over all.
Mix 1 cup sugar, 1/2 cup flour and 1/4 cup margarine;
sprinkle over all. Bake at 350° for 50 minutes.

G.W. Seemans, Robbinsdale, Mn.

RHUBARB SAUCE

4 c. rhubarb   1 c. sugar

Cook 10 minutes for sauce; add strawberries or
pineapple.

Vi Geving, Duluth, Mn.

RHUBARB SPECIAL

Mix 1 1/2 cups graham cracker crumbs, 1/4 cup
melted shortening (margarine or butter) and 1/4 cup sugar.
Put in 9x12 inch pan; bake at 350° for 8 minutes. Cook 4
cups rhubarb and 1/2 cup water until rhubarb is soft.
Add 1 cup sugar and 2 tablespoons flour; cool and pour
over crust. Mix 1 large carton Cool Whip and 1 1/2 cups
miniature marshmallows; pour over rhubarb.

Topping: Mix 1 large package instant vanilla pudding
with 2 1/2 cups milk; sprinkle nuts on top.

Norma Stevens, Montevideo, Mn.

RHUBARB TOPSY TURVY

6 c. diced rhubarb   3 tsp. baking powder
1 1/2 c. sugar   1/2 c. milk
240 small marshmallows   2 c. flour
1/2 c. butter or margarine   1/4 tsp. salt
1 c. sugar   1 tsp. vanilla
2 eggs

Put rhubarb, sugar and marshmallows into a greased
9x13 inch pan. Cream butter and sugar well. Add eggs;
beat well. Sift flour, salt and baking powder; add alternately with milk and vanilla to creamed mixture. Spread
over rhubarb mixture. Bake in 350° oven for 1 hour or until cake mixture is done; let cool. When ready to serve,
cut into squares; turn upside down on serving dish. Top
with whipped cream. Serves 20.

LaDonna Dallmann, Faribault, Mn.

RHUBARB TORTE

Crust:

1 c. margarine	2 Tbsp. sugar
2 c. flour	1/2 tsp. salt

Mix as for pie crust; pat in 9x13 inch pan. Bake at 350° for 15 minutes.

Filling:

6 egg yolks, beaten	4 Tbsp. flour
2 c. sugar	5 c. diced rhubarb
1 c. cream	

Mix and pour over crust. Bake 45 minutes at 350°.

Meringue:

6 egg whites, beaten	1 tsp. vanilla
12 Tbsp. sugar	1/4 tsp. salt

Beat well. Bake at 350° for 8-10 minutes. Keeps well in refrigerator.

Norma Haugerud, Montevideo, Mn.

RICE CREAM

Cook 1/4 cup rice in double boiler in 2 cups milk for 1 hour or until rice is soft. Soften 1 tablespoon Knox gelatine with cold water. Add 1/2 cup sugar, pinch of salt and 1/2 teaspoon vanilla. Let cool; when it begins to thicken (or set), fold in 1 cup of cream, whipped. Put in refrigerator.

Sauce:

1 c. raspberry juice	1/4 c. sugar
1/2 c. water	A little almond flavoring
1 tsp. cornstarch	

Mix and cook to thicken slightly.

Anne Aune, Minneapolis, Mn.

GLORIFIED RICE

1 c. rice, cooked
2/3 c. sugar
2 c. mini marshmallows
1 tsp. vanilla

2 c. crushed pineapple,
  undrained
1/2 c. chopped nuts
1 medium container Cool Whip

In large bowl, combine rice, sugar, marshmallows and pineapple. Blend in vanilla, nuts and Cool Whip. Store in refrigerator.

Mrs. Norma Applen, Minneapolis, Mn.

SWEDISH RICE

Boil 1 cup rice in 6 cups of water and a pinch of salt until done; blanch and drain. Add 1 quart milk; boil 3 minutes. Mix 4 teaspoons cornstarch in a little milk; add 5 beaten egg yolks to the rice and 3/4 cup sugar. Make a meringue with the 5 egg whites; add 10 teaspoons powdered sugar. Put on the rice in the casserole. Put in the oven; bake until brown.

K. Otto, Harvey, N.D.

VERY GOOD RICE PUDDING

Cook in double boiler until done:
1/2 c. regular rice   1 1/2 c. water

Heat 3 3/4 cups whole milk; add to rice. Mix together:

3/4 c. sugar   3 heaping Tbsp. cornstarch
1 tsp. salt

Add to above mixture; cook until thickened. Add 4 slightly beaten egg yolks, 1/4 cup milk and 1 teaspoon vanilla. Put into casserole. Top with meringue of 4 egg whites and 4 tablespoons sugar. Brown at 350°.

Emmy Thielmann, Minneapolis, Mn.

RUM BUNDT CAKE

Grease (Crisco) and sugar pan; sprinkle 2 cups chopped pecans in bottom.

1 pkg. yellow cake mix
1 pkg. French vanilla
  pudding mix

1/2 c. water
1/2 c. oil
1/2 c. dark rum

Mix all ingredients together. Add 4 eggs (5 if small) one at a time; beat until smooth. Bake at 325° for 1 hour. Cool cake for 10 minutes. Pierce surface with fork. Pour Rum Sauce over; let set for 20 minutes, then put on plate.

Rum Sauce:

1/2 c. butter	1/4 c. water
1 c. sugar	1/4 c. dark rum

Combine all ingredients in heavy saucepan; boil for 1 minute. Cake tastes better when chilled overnight.

Anne Aune, Minneapolis, Mn.

7-UP DESSERT

1 c. orange juice	1 (10 1/2 oz.) pkg.
1 c. 7-Up	miniature marshmallows
1 pt. whipping cream	Angel food cake

Bring 7-Up and orange juice to boil; add marshmallows and stir until melted. Cool. Whip cream; add to orange juice mixture. Pour over angel food cake, that has been torn and placed in bottom of pan

Anne Aune, Minneapolis, Mn.

SODA CRACKER DESSERT

16 single soda crackers (1 sq.)	1 tsp. baking powder
	1/2 c. walnuts, chopped
1 c. sugar	3 egg whites, beaten

Mix dry ingredients; fold in beaten egg whites. Bake in 8x8 inch pan for 20 to 25 minutes or till light brown. Cool; top with 1/2 pint whipping cream, beaten stiff and sweetened. Spread on top at least 6 hours before serving. Can be spread on night before. Double ingredients for a 9x13 inch pan. Keep in refrigerator.

Liz Tuft, St. Paul, Mn.

STRAWBERRY CHIFFON SQUARES

1/4 c. butter or margarine	3/4 c. boiling water
1 1/2 c. finely crushed vanilla wafers (about 45)	1 (14 oz.) can Eagle Brand sweetened condensed milk (not evaporated)
1 (3 oz.) pkg. strawberry flavored gelatin	

1 (10 oz.) pkg. frozen
strawberries in syrup,
thawed

4 c. Campfire miniature
marshmallows
1 c. (1/2 pt.) whipping
cream, whipped

In small saucepan, melt butter; stir in cookie crumbs. Pat firmly on bottom of 2 quart shallow baking dish, 12x7 inches; chill. In large bowl, dissolve gelatin in boiling water; stir in sweetened condensed milk and undrained strawberries. Fold in marshmallows and whipped cream. Pour into prepared pan. Chill 2 hours or until set. If desired, garnish with additional whipped cream and strawberries. Refrigerate leftovers. Makes 12 servings.

Eileen Rekowski, St. Cloud, Mn.

STRAWBERRY DESSERT

1 c. flour
1/4 lb. margarine

1/2 c. nuts

Mix until crumbly; bake 10 minutes at 350°. Crumble and press into 9x13 inch pan; save 1/2 cup for top. Beat together for 15 minutes:

2 egg whites
1 c. sugar
1 Tbsp. lemon juice

1 box frozen strawberries,
thawed for 1/2 hour

Add 1 cup whipping cream, already whipped. Pour into crust and sprinkle with 1/2 cup topping. Store in refrigerator.

Helen Martin, Fargo, N.D.

MILE-HIGH STRAWBERRY DESSERT

Beat 3 egg whites until they form peaks. Add gradually:

1 c. sugar
1 Tbsp. lemon juice

2 (10 oz.) pkg. frozen
strawberries

Beat mixture together about 3 minutes. Add 1 large container Cool Whip. Beat with mixture for 10 minutes (very important).

Graham Cracker Crust: Add as many crushed graham crackers as you wish with small amount of melted butter to bottom of pan, 9x13 inches or larger. Pat crumb mixture down. Pour strawberry mixture over crumbs; freeze until ready to serve. If desired, reserve a "very little" of crumb mixture to sprinkle on top. Serves 12-16.

Maryann Skelton, Duluth, Mn.

FROZEN STRAWBERRY DESSERT

1 pkg. frozen strawberries, thawed	2 egg whites
1 c. sugar	1/2 tsp. salt

Beat the above ingredients 15 minutes at high speed. Add 1 cup cream, whipped. Pour into graham cracker crust in a 9x12 inch pan; freeze 6 hours or overnight. Keep frozen till served.

Norma Haugerud, Montevideo, Mn.

STRAWBERRY JELLO FLUFF

Drain juice from 1 (10 or 12 ounce) package frozen strawberries into measuring cup; add water to make 1 cup. Bring to boil; add 1 package raspberry jello. Beat 3 egg yolks until light; add hot jello, stirring constantly. Stir in 1/4 teaspoon salt and 1 tablespoon lemon juice. Taste and add more sugar, if necessary. Add berries; chill, stirring occasionally. When slightly stiff, beat 3 egg whites stiff with 1/4 cup sugar. Fold into jello mixture and pour into baked pie shell or dessert glasses. Serve with whipped cream. Can be made the day before.

K., St. Cloud, Mn.

STRAWBERRY MARSHMALLOW WHIP

1 (3 oz.) pkg. strawberry gelatin	1 (1 1/2 oz.) pkg. whipped topping mix, prepared, or
1 c. boiling water	2 c. frozen non-dairy
1 c. cold water	whipped topping, thawed
1 c. miniature marshmallows	1 (8 oz.) can crushed pineapple, drained

Dissolve gelatin in boiling water; add cold water and chill until slightly thickened. Whip until very light and fluffy. Add 1 1/2 cups whipped topping (reserve remainder); fold in marshmallows and crushed pineapple. Chill. Garnish with reserved whipped topping and fresh strawberries, if desired.

598   Marlys Swehla, Albert Lea, Mn.

STRAWBERRY MILE HIGH DESSERT

1/2 c. butter	1 c. flour
1/4 c. brown sugar	1/2 c. nuts

Mix lightly and put in oblong, 9x13 inch, pan. Brown in 400° oven, stirring occasionally, about 10 minutes. Use for bottom and top of dessert.

1 pkg. strawberries, partially thawed	1/2 tsp. salt
	1 Tbsp. lemon juice
1 c. sugar	2 egg whites, unbeaten

In large bowl, place partially thawed berries and rest of the ingredients. Beat 15 minutes at high speed until fluffy and thick. Fold in 1 cup cream, whipped, and 1 teaspoon vanilla. Pour into cooled crust; sprinkle with remaining crumbs. Freeze. Can be served right from freezer.

Mary Fingalson, Detroit Lakes, Mn.

FRESH STRAWBERRY TARTS

Make 12 pastry shells by lining 12 patty shell cups with rich pie crust. Bake at serving time. Spread with Philadelphia cream cheese, blended with cream to soften, over bottom of cooled shells. Cover with 1 pint fresh berries. Make a filling of 1 pint mashed berries, brought to boiling point. Stir in 1 cup sugar, mixed with 3 tablespoons cornstarch; cook for 10 minutes. Cool; pour over uncooked berries in patty shells. Cover with sweetened whipped cream or Cool Whip.

Helen-May Johnson, Chanhassen, Mn.

STRAWBERRY TIFFANY TORTE

3 c. vanilla wafer crumbs	1 (3 3/4 oz.) pkg. instant vanilla pudding mix
1/2 c. margarine, melted	
1 (8 oz.) pkg. cream cheese	1 qt. strawberries, sliced
2 c. milk	1 (2 oz.) pkg. dessert topping mix (or use Cool Whip)
2 tsp. grated lemon rind (optional)	

Combine crumbs and margarine; reserve 1 cup for topping. Press remaining crumb mixture onto bottom of greased 9x13 inch pan. Gradually add 1/2 cup milk to softened cream cheese, mixing until well blended. Add pudding mix, remaining milk and lemon rind; beat slowly 1 minute. Pour over crust; cover with strawberries. Spread prepared dessert topping mix or Cool Whip on top of strawberries. Top with remaining crumbs. Chill several hours or overnight. Makes 12-15 servings.

Marian Pearson, Minneapolis, Mn.

SWEDISH GINGERBREAD

2 eggs	1 tsp. baking powder
1 c. sugar	1 tsp. ground ginger
1 3/4 c. sifted flour	2/3 c. milk or cream
1/2 tsp. salt	

Beat the eggs and sugar together. Sift dry ingredients; add alternately with the milk, beating well after each addition. Pour into a greased loaf pan. Bake at 350° for 45-50 minutes. Let stand to slightly cool, about 15 minutes; turn out of bread pan onto a wire rack to cool completely. Serve with soft butter or margarine on smaller slices, not too thick.

Bernice Fonos, Minneapolis, Mn.

SWEDISH RICE PUDDING

2 1/2 c. water	1 c. rice

Cook until all water disappears. In the meantime, beat 4 eggs and 2 egg yolks in casserole (about 2 1/2 quart) with 1/2 cup sugar, salt and heaping teaspoon of vanilla with 1 cup milk. Put 1/4 cup butter on rice. Fill casserole with milk. Put casserole in pan of hot water. Bake at 350°; stir after 15 minutes. Sprinkle with cinnamon. Bake till knife comes out clean, then done, about 1 hour.

Betty Olson, St. Paul, Mn.

GRASSHOPPER TORTE

24 large marshmallows	1/4 tsp. salt
3/4 c. milk	2 c. whipping cream, whipped
2 Tbsp. white creme de cocoa	Green food coloring (opt.)
2 Tbsp. white or green creme de menthe	1 large angel food cake
	1/2 c. toasted, slivered almonds

600

Place marshmallows and milk in top of double boiler; cook over hot water until melted. Cool; stir in liqueurs and salt. Chill until partly set. Fold in whipped cream. Add food coloring, if desired. Cut cake into 3 layers. Spread mixture between layers, top and sides. Sprinkle almonds over cake. Chill for several hours or overnight.

Betty Cortright, Minneapolis, Mn.

BLITZ TORTE

1/4 c. shortening
1/2 c. sugar
1/4 tsp. salt
4 egg yolks, beaten

1 tsp. vanilla
3 Tbsp. milk
1 tsp. baking powder

Topping:

4 egg whites
3/4 c. sugar
1/4 c. blanched almonds

1 Tbsp. sugar
1/2 tsp. cinnamon

Cream shortening, sugar, salt, yolks, vanilla, milk, flour and baking powder; spread into 2 round cake pans. Beat egg whites until light; add 3/4 cup sugar and spread on unbaked dough. Sprinkle with almonds and rest of cinnamon and sugar. Bake at 350° for 30 minutes. Cool; take out of pans and put a vanilla custard between layers. Grease and flour pans.

Karleen Gerth, St. Paul, Mn.

BROKEN GLASS TORTE

4 pkg. jello (orange, lemon, lime and raspberry)
1 c. hot pineapple juice
1/2 c. sugar
6 c. hot water

1 env. Knox gelatine
2 c. whipping cream
1 tsp. vanilla
1 sponge cake or ladyfingers

Dissolve each package of jello separately in 1 1/2 cups hot water; stir until dissolved. Turn into pans so mixture is about 3/4 inch thick; chill until firm. Cut into cubes about 1/2 inch in width. Soften plain gelatine in cold water and add to hot pineapple juice; cool thoroughly. Add sugar and vanilla to whipped cream, then fold in cold pineapple juice mixture. Carefully fold colored jello cubes into whipped cream mixture. Line spring form pan with sponge cake or ladyfingers; add the jello mixture. Chill in refrigerator until thoroughly set.

1507-82 Mrs. Emma Buhl, Minneapolis, Mn. 601

RHUBARB TORTE

1 c. sugar
3 Tbsp. cornstarch
4 c. sliced rhubarb
1/2 c. water
Few drops red food coloring

1 recipe Graham Cracker
Crust
1 c. whipping cream
2 c. tiny marshmallows
1 (3 3/4 or 3 5/8 oz.) pkg.
instant vanilla pudding mix

Combine sugar and cornstarch; stir in rhubarb and water. Cook and stir till thickened. Reduce heat; cook 2 to 3 minutes. Add food coloring. Spread on cooled graham cracker crust; cool. Whip cream; fold in marshmallows. Spoon on rhubarb mixture. Prepare pudding according to package directions; spread over all. Sprinkle with reserved crumbs; chill. Makes 9 servings. (I use a 9x9 inch pan.)

To make Graham Cracker Crust: Combine -

1 c. graham cracker crumbs
2 Tbsp. sugar

4 Tbsp. melted butter or
margarine

Reserve a few crumbs for top; pat remainder in 9x9 inch pan. Bake at 350° for 10 minutes; cool.

Bev. Jensen, Willmar, Mn.

RITZ CRACKER TORTE

3 egg whites
1 tsp. baking powder
1 c. nuts
1 small Hershey's bar

1 c. sugar
21 Ritz crackers
1 tsp. vanilla
1/2 pt. whipping cream

Beat egg whites until stiff; add 1 cup sugar and baking powder. Crumble Ritz crackers real fine; add with nutmeats and 1 teaspoon vanilla. Grease a 12 inch pie plate or other pan with butter. Pour cracker and egg mixture into the pan. Smooth top; bake in oven at 350° for 25 minutes. Cool. Whip 1/2 pint cream; spread on top of torte. Grate 1 small Hershey's bar on top of cream; refrigerate overnight.

Mrs. Emma Buhl, Minneapolis, Mn.

ENGLISH TRIFLE

Make soft custard out of:

6 eggs	3 c. milk
1/4 c. sugar	Vanilla*

*Vanilla bean should be used if available; use 1 inch. Open and remove seeds; add. Also, cook what is left after seeds are removed with custard. One (3 1/4 ounce) package vanilla pudding mix can be substituted.

1/3 c. raspberry preserves	12 almond macaroons, crushed
2 doz. ladyfingers	
1/4 c. orange liqueur (Triple Sec, Cointreau or Grand Marnier)	1/2 c. whipping cream
	2 Tbsp. powdered sugar
	1/2 tsp. vanilla
1/4 c. cherries	1/2 c. slivered almonds, toasted

Split ladyfingers; place upright around sides of glass bowl. Put together remaining ladyfingers with jam; cover bottom of dish. Mix sherry and liqueur; pour 1/2 over ladyfingers. Pour in 1/2 of cooled custard; sprinkle with 1/2 of crushed macaroons. Repeat layers; allow to set. Spread whipped cream over top; sprinkle with almonds.

Martha Fjelstad, Minneapolis, Mn.

TRIPLE TREAT SQUARES

Sift into bowl:

1 1/4 c. flour	1 tsp. salt
3/4 c. sugar	1/2 tsp. soda

Add 2 unbeaten egg yolks and 1/2 cup water; mix well. Spread batter in bottom of greased 13x9x2 inch pan. Combine 1 can blueberry or cherry pie filling, 1 tablespoon flour, 1 tablespoon lemon rind and 2 tablespoons lemon juice. Drop by teaspoonfuls over batter. Beat 2 egg whites with 1 tablespoon water and 1/4 teaspoon salt until soft mounds form. Gradually add 1/3 cup sugar; beat until stiff peaks form. Fold in 1 cup coconut and 2 tablespoons flour; spread over filling. Sprinkle with 2 tablespoons coconut. Bake at 350° for 35-40 minutes.

Anne Aune, Minneapolis, Mn.

VANILLA PARTY DESSERT

First Layer:

1 c. flour
1/2 c. chopped nuts

1/2 c. butter

Mix until smooth; spread in the bottom of a buttered 9x13 inch pan. Bake 15-20 minutes in a 350° oven, until slightly browned; cool.

Second Layer: Beat and spread over crust -

8 oz. cream cheese
1 c. Cool Whip

1 c. powdered sugar

Third Layer:

2 pkg. instant pudding

3 c. milk (disregard pudding directions)

Beat until thick; spread over cheese mixture.

Fourth Layer:

Cool Whip

1/4 c. nuts or browned coconut

Spread with Cool Whip over all and top with nuts or coconut.

Margaret McKenney, Minneapolis, Mn.

VANILLA WAFER DESSERT

Cream:

1/4 lb. butter

3 egg yolks

Add:

1 c. sugar
1 c. broken walnuts
1 Tbsp. cream

1 c. crushed pineapple, drained
Vanilla wafers

Grease a 7x11 inch pan and line with wafers. Put filling over this; cover with vanilla wafers. Refrigerate. Serve with whipped cream or Cool Whip.

Mary Fingalson, Detroit Lakes, Mn.

VANILLA WAFER DESSERT

1 lb. vanilla wafers, crushed
2 c. whipping cream
2 c. crushed, drained
   pineapple

2/3 c. butter
2 c. powdered sugar
4 egg yolks

Place half of the crushed wafers in a 9x13 inch cake pan. Cream butter and sugar; add egg yolks and beat. This will be a little thick, so add a bit of juice from drained pineapple. Spread over crumbs in thin layer. Put drained pineapple on top of this, then add the whipped cream in another layer. Finally, cover evenly with remaining crumbs. Chill 12 hours. Serves 15 to 18. (Marvelous do ahead recipe.)

Dode Desch, St. Paul, Mn.

ZUCCHINI KRISP

5 c. zucchini, peeled, cut
   like you would apples
1/2 c. sugar

1 tsp. cinnamon
1/4 c. lemon juice
3/4 c. water

Cook 10 minutes; put into 9 inch pan. Mix the following until crumbly:

6 Tbsp. butter
1 c. flour
1/2 c. brown sugar

1 tsp. baking powder
1/2 tsp. salt

Sprinkle over zucchini; bake at 350° for 45 minutes.

Helen Martin, Fargo, N.D.

CARAMEL SAUCE FOR POTATO PUDDING

2 c. sugar
1/2 c. boiling water

1/2 c. heavy cream

In a skillet (heavy) over moderate heat, melt 1 cup sugar; cook until brown. Carefully and gradually stir in water. Cook, stirring, until dissolved. Stir in remaining sugar; stir until dissolved. Blend in cream. If sauce is too thin, thicken with a little cornstarch, made in paste with cream. Yields 1 1/2 cups sauce.

Mrs. Elmer Wright, Minneapolis, Mn.

GEN'S CHOCOLATE SAUCE

3 Tbsp. flour
1 1/2 c. sugar
4 Tbsp. cocoa

1/4 tsp. salt
1 1/2 c. water
Flavoring

Mix dry ingredients and water; cook until thickened. Cool; refrigerate.

Helen Teeuwen, Minneapolis, Mn.

FUDGE SAUCE

1 can Carnation milk
1 1/4 c. sugar

3 sq. chocolate

Stir constantly until thick.

Audrey Fisher, St. Paul, Mn.

HOT FUDGE SAUCE

2 c. sugar
2/3 c. cocoa
1/4 c. flour
1/4 tsp. salt

2 c. water
2 Tbsp. butter
1 tsp. vanilla

Mix sugar, cocoa, flour and salt in heavy saucepan. Add water and butter; cook to boiling. Lower heat; cook for about 8 minutes longer, stirring constantly. Cool; stir in vanilla. Makes about 2 1/2 cups.

Clara O. Johnson, Chanhassen, Mn.

ABE LINCOLN PIE

Mix together:
1/4 c. soft butter
1 tsp. vanilla
1 c. sugar

1 c. applesauce
2 beaten eggs

Bake pie shell till almost done, then pour in mixture. Bake at 350° for 45 minutes.

Pat Ivey, Bismarck, N.D.

DOUBLE WEDDING RING ANGEL CAKE PIES

(Bridal Shower Idea - Decorate the tray with green leaves and blossoms.)

1 (10 inch) angel food cake
2 c. strawberries
1/2 c. sugar
1 env. unflavored gelatin
1/4 c. cold water
2 c. mixed canned or
  fresh fruits
1 Tbsp. lemon juice
1/4 c. orange juice

Pinch of salt
2 egg whites
1 c. whipping cream
Whipped cream for top
1/2 c. shredded coconut
1/4 c. shredded, blanched
  almonds
Whole strawberries for top

Cut cake crosswise into 2 even layers; turn crust side down; hollow each, leaving a 1 inch thick shell. Place on pan or cookie sheet; fill in tube hole with cake pieces. Slice or quarter strawberries; sprinkle with sugar. Let stand a while so you'll have some red juice. Soften gelatin in cold water in small metal cup; melt by setting cup in hot water. Stir into berries. Add the fresh or canned fruit used, lemon and orange juices. Chill until thick, but not set. Add salt to egg whites; beat until stiff. Whip cream till stiff. Fold egg whites, then cream into thickened gelatin. Heap into cake-pie shells. Chill until firm. Place side by side on large tray or platter. Decorate rims with ruffle of whipped cream. Sprinkle with coconut and almonds. Decorate with whole berries. Serves 16.

Dena Stoddard, St. Louis Park, Mn.

APPLE PIE

Make pastry for 9 inch two crust pie. Mix well 6 to 7 cups thinly sliced, tart juicy apples, peeled, quartered and cored with mixture of 3/4 to 1 cup sugar (depending on tartness of apples) and 1 teaspoon cinnamon or nutmeg. Fill pastry lined pie plate; dot with 1 tablespoon butter. Adjust top crust. To seal, see directions for Two-Crust Pies on Crustquick package. Bake 50 to 60 minutes in hot oven, 425°, until crust is nicely browned and apples cooked through (test with fork). Serve warm.

Dutch Apple Pie: Five minutes before baking time is up, remove pie from oven. Pour 1/2 cup heavy cream through slits in top crust. Return to oven and continue baking.

1507-82

"Mince" Apple Pie: Mix with sugar 1 teaspoon cinnamon, 1/2 teaspoon cloves, 1/4 teaspoon mace, 1/8 teaspoon salt, 1/2 cup raisins and 1 teaspoon molasses.

Streusel Apple Pie: In place of top crust, sprinkle over sweetened apples a mixture of 1/2 package Crustquick (about 1 cup), 1/3 cup brown sugar and 1/2 teaspoon cinnamon. Bake as for Apple Pie.

Dena Stoddard, St. Louis Park, Mn.

APPLE PIE FILLING

Blend these ingredients:

4 1/2 c. sugar	1 1/2 tsp. salt
1 c. cornstarch	2 tsp. cinnamon
1/4 - 1/2 tsp. nutmeg	

Stir in 10 cups of water; cook and stir till thickened and bubbly. Add 3 tablespoons lemon juice and 1/4 teaspoon yellow food coloring, if desired. Pack sliced apples into jars; fill with hot syrup and process (20 minutes for quarts; 15 minutes for pints). One quart makes 1 pie or enough for 9 inch square apple crisp.

Karen Ireland, Montevideo, Mn.

APPLE PUDDING PIE

1 c. sugar	1/2 tsp. cinnamon
1/4 c. shortening	1 c. flour
1 egg, beaten (large)	1/2 c. nuts
1/2 tsp. salt (scant)	2 1/2 c. diced apples
1 tsp. soda	

Grease pie plate (10 inch). Bake in 325° oven for 50 minutes. Serve with sauce.

Sauce:

1/2 c. butter	1/2 c. brown sugar
1/2 c. white sugar	1/2 c. cream

Cook until slightly thickened. Serve sauce warm over pie and whipped cream over this.

Vivian Brickson, Detroit Lakes, Mn.

SOUR CREAM APPLE PIE

1 pastry crust
6 apples, peeled and sliced
3 Tbsp. flour
1 c. sugar

1/4 tsp. cloves
1 c. sour cream
1/2 tsp. cinnamon
1 1/2 Tbsp. sugar

Place apples in crust; pour mix of flour, sugar, cloves and sour cream over them. Sprinkle cinnamon and 1 1/2 tablespoons sugar over top. Bake at 375° for 50-60 minutes.

Fern Raddant, Minneapolis, Mn.

VERNON'S APPLE PIE
(Revised by B. Klinke)

1 1/2 c. brown sugar
1/4 tsp. salt
3/4 c. water
1 Tbsp. vinegar

2 Tbsp. butter
1 tsp. vanilla
Apples
Cinnamon
Juice of 1 lemon

Mix first 4 ingredients together; cook until thick. Add butter and vanilla; cool on unbaked pie crust. Pour over sliced, heaped apples. Sprinkle with cinnamon. Cover with latticed top crust. Bake at 425° for 25 minutes, then at 350° for 15 minutes in electric oven.

Pie Crust:

1 c. lard
1 egg, beaten
1 tsp. vinegar

3 c. sifted flour
5 Tbsp. water
1 tsp. salt

Mix shortening and flour well. In separate bowl, mix the egg, water, vinegar and salt. Combine the mixtures and chill in refrigerator (not freezer) until ready to use.

Bonnie Sovick, Marshall, Mn.

APPLE-RHUBARB PIE

Pastry:

2 c. all-purpose flour
1/2 tsp. salt
6 Tbsp. butter

6 Tbsp. lard
6-8 Tbsp. milk

Filling:

1 1/4 c. sugar
3 Tbsp. quick cooking
  tapioca
1/2 tsp. cinnamon
1/2 tsp. nutmeg
1/4 tsp. salt

3 c. sliced, peeled cooking
  apples
2 c. rhubarb, cut in 1/2 inch
  pieces
1/2 c. chopped nuts
1 Tbsp. butter

For pastry, combine flour and salt; cut in butter and lard until mixture resembles coarse crumbs. Sprinkle in milk, mixing until flour is moistened. Divide dough in half; wrap each in wax paper and refrigerate while preparing filling. For filling, combine sugar, tapioca, cinnamon, nutmeg and salt in mixing bowl. Add apples, rhubarb and nuts; toss gently to coat fruit and nuts. Let mixture stand 15 minutes. Preheat oven to 375°. Roll out pastry to fit 9 inch pie plate; trim bottom crust to 1/2 inch beyond edge of pie plate. Roll out rest of dough; cut into 1/2 inch strips. Place fruit mixture in pie plate; dot with butter. Lay strips atop filling. Fold bottom strips over crust. Bake 50 minutes; put tin foil over edges for 25 minutes, then take off and bake 25 minutes more.

Lydia Skaret, Austin, Mn.

BANANA MARSHMALLOW PIE

Mix 1 cooked vanilla pudding package, using 1 3/4 cups milk; cool. Add 1 cup whipped cream and 1 1/2 cups miniature marshmallows to the cooled pudding. Slice 2 bananas in bottom of a cooked pie crust. May garnish top with whatever you like.

Irene Mittelstadt, Campbell, Mn.

QUICK BANANA PEANUT BUTTER PIE

In an 8 inch graham cracker crust pie shell, slice 2 bananas over crust. Place contents of 3 ounce package of instant pudding mix in blender; add 1 1/2 cups cold milk and 1/4 cup peanut butter. Blend at low speed for 30 seconds. Pour into a bowl; add 1 1/2 cups whipped topping. Spoon into pie shell over bananas. Refrigerate for 1 hour.

Esther Mungovan, Duluth, Mn.

HAWAIIAN BLUEBERRY PIE

1 (9 inch) unbaked pie crust
1 (12 oz.) jar pineapple
   ice cream topping
1/2 tsp. grated lemon peel
4 c. fresh or frozen
   blueberries
1 Tbsp. butter
3 Tbsp. flour

Combine pineapple topping, flour and lemon peel; fold in blueberries. Pour into pie shell. Dot with butter. Bake at 400° for 35-40 minutes.

                        Irene Faber, St. Paul, Mn.

BROWNIE PIE

Beat until frothy:
3 egg whites
1/2 tsp. vanilla
                  Dash of salt

Add 3/4 cup granulated sugar gradually until meringue is very stiff and glossy. Fold in 3/4 cup chocolate wafer crumbs and 1/4 cup walnuts. Butter a 9 inch pie plate; spread egg white mixture into pie plate. Bake 35 minutes at 350°; remove from oven and cool. Whip 1/2 pint whipping cream; add small amount of granulated sugar and vanilla, if desired. Refrigerate 3 to 4 hours before serving.

                Delina Sherette, St. Paul, Mn.

FRENCH CHERRY PIE

1 baked pie shell
1 (3 oz.) pkg. Philadelphia
   cream cheese
1 tsp. vanilla
1 c. cream, whipped
1/2 c. powdered sugar
1 can cherry pie filling mix

Cream together cheese and sugar; add vanilla. Fold in cream. Spread on pie shell; let set for a while in refrigerator. Carefully spread on pie filling. Chill in refrigerator until set.

            Pearl Paulsrud, Montevideo, Mn.

*   *   *   *   *

PASTRIES
"The loveliest hands
in Masculine eyes
Are the hands that make
the loveliest pies."

CHERRY PIE SUPREME

9 inch unbaked pie shell
1 (1 lb. 5 oz.) can cherry
   pie filling
4 (3 oz.) pkg. soft cream
   cheese

1/2 c. sugar
2 eggs
1/2 tsp. vanilla extract
1 c. dairy sour cream

1. Preheat oven to 425° F. 2. Prepare pie shell. Spread half of cherry pie filling in bottom; set rest of filling aside. 3. Bake shell 15 minutes, or just until crust is golden. Remove from oven. 4. Reduce oven temperature to 350° F. 5. Meanwhile, in small bowl, with portable electric mixer, beat cheese with sugar, eggs and vanilla until smooth. 6. Pour over hot cherry pie filling. Bake 25 minutes (filling will be slightly soft in center). 7. Cool completely on wire rack. 8. To serve: Spoon sour cream around edge of pie. Fill center with remaining cherry pie filling. Makes 8 servings.

Blueberry Pie Supreme: Follow above recipe, substituting 1 (1 pound 5 ounce) can blueberry pie filling for cherry pie filling.

Blanche B. Masica, Minneapolis, Mn.

AMAZING COCOANUT PIE

2 c. milk
3/4 c. sugar
1/2 c. biscuit mix
1 c. cocoanut

1/4 c. margarine or butter
1 1/2 tsp. vanilla
5 eggs

Combine milk, sugar, biscuit mix (flour) and vanilla in electric blender on low speed for 3 minutes. Pour into greased 9 inch pan; let stand 5 minutes, then sprinkle on cocoanut. Bake at 350° for 40 minutes.

Elizabeth Redmond, Long Prairie, Mn.

AMAZING COCONUT PIE

Some poeple call it the Impossible Pie because it even makes its own crust. Just mix, bake and serve.

2 c. milk
3/4 c. sugar
1/2 c. biscuit mix
4 eggs

1/4 c. butter or margarine
1 1/2 tsp. vanilla
1 c. Baker's Angel Flake
   coconut

Combine milk, sugar, biscuit mix, eggs, butter and vanilla in electric blender container. Cover; blend on low speed for 3 minutes. Pour into greased 9 inch pie pan. Let stand about 5 minutes, then sprinkle with coconut. Bake at 350° for 40 minutes. Serve warm or cool.

Margaret McKenney, Minneapolis, Mn.

BLENDER COCONUT PIE

2 c. milk or buttermilk
4 eggs
1/2 c. Bisquick
1/2 c. sugar

1 tsp. vanilla
1 c. flaked coconut
1/4 c. margarine
1/2 tsp. salt

Whirl in blender 2 minutes. Pour into greased and floured 9 inch pie pan. Bake at 350° for 45 minutes.

Vi Geving, Duluth, Mn.

COCONUT ICE CREAM PIE

1/4 c. butter, melted
2 c. coconut
1 qt. strawberry ice cream

1 (4 1/2 oz.) container Cool Whip, thawed
Easy Chocolate Fudge Sauce

Add butter to coconut, mixing lightly; press evenly into an 8 inch pie pan. Bake at 300° for 20-30 minutes or until golden; cool. Alternate spoonfuls of ice cream and about half of the sauce in crust for a ripple effect; freeze until firm. Spread whipped topping over the top; freeze again. Sprinkle with toasted coconut and serve with remaining sauce, if desired.

Easy Chocolate Fudge Sauce: Combine 1 (4 ounce) package German's sweet chocolate, 3/4 cup evaporated milk and 8 marshmallows in a saucepan. Cook and stir over low heat until chocolate and marshmallows are melted. Remove from heat; add 1/2 teaspoon vanilla. Cool. Makes 1 1/2 cups.

Anne Aune, Minneapolis, Mn.

COOKIE CRUST FRUIT PIE

Cookie Crust Pastry
  (recipe follows)
1/2 c. sugar
3 Tbsp. Argo or Kingsford
  cornstarch

1 1/2 c. fruit juice*
1 tsp. grated lemon rind
1/4 c. lemon juice
6 c. assorted sliced or cut
  up fresh fruit**

1507-82

*For juice you can use apple juice or any fruit juice from canned fruit. (When making jello or salads, I save the juices and put in a covered jar for making puddings.)

**Such as apples, pears, strawberries, grapes, bananas or drained mandarin oranges.

In saucepan, mix sugar and cornstarch. Gradually stir in juice; mix until dissolved and smooth. Stirring constantly, bring to a boil over medium heat; boil 1 minute. Remove; stir in lemon rind and lemon juice. Cool completely. Fold into fruit. Turn into pastry shell; chill 4 hours until set.

Cookie Crust Pastry: Stir 1/4 cup Mazola margarine to soften; mix in 1/4 cup sugar and 1 egg yolk. With pastry blender or 2 knives, gradually mix in 1 cup flour until crumbs form. Press firmly into bottom and sides of a 9 inch pie plate. Bake at 400° F. for 8-10 minutes, until edge is browned; cool.

Helen-May Johnson, Chanhassen, Mn.

CRAZY CRUST APPLE PIE
(Makes its own crust as it bakes. Impossible? Try it.)

1 c. Pillsbury's Best all-purpose flour
1 tsp. baking powder
1/2 tsp. salt
1 Tbsp. sugar
1 egg

2/3 c. shortening (I used Crisco)
3/4 c. water
1 (1 lb. 5 oz.) can apple pie filling
1 Tbsp. lemon juice
1/2 tsp. apple pie spice

In small mixer bowl, combine flour, baking powder, salt, sugar, egg, shortening and water; blend well. Beat 2 minutes at medium speed of mixer. Pour batter into 9 inch pie pan. Combine pie filling, lemon juice and spice; pour into center of batter. Do not stir. Bake at 425° F. for 45 to 50 minutes. Makes 6 servings.

*If you use Pillsbury's Best self-rising flour, omit baking powder and salt.

Helen-May Johnson, Chanhassen, Mn.

CREME-DE-MENTHE PIE

Crust:

14 Hydrox cookies, crushed   2 Tbsp. butter

Dissolve 24 marshmallows with 1/2 cup milk; cool. Mix 1/2 jigger creme de cocoa and 2 tablespoons creme de menthe. Whip 1/2 pint cream. Mix all together and place in cookie crust; chill.

Mary Jean Voss, Owatonna, Mn.

CUSTARD PIE

1 unbaked pie shell
2 large or 3 small eggs
1/2 c. sugar (white)

1 tsp. vanilla
3 c. whole milk

Beat eggs well; add sugar, vanilla and milk. Mix until sugar is about melted, then pour into crust. Bake at 350° until knife comes out clean when inserted in the middle. Sprinkle cinnamon on top.
Note: Don't overbake.

Ruth Bates

COCOANUT CUSTARD PIE

Put into blender:
2 c. milk
3 eggs
1 tsp. butter
1 tsp. vanilla

1/2 c. Bisquick
3 1/2 - 4 oz. coconut
1/2 c. sugar

Blend a few seconds. Pour into greased 9 inch pie plate; bake at 350° for 40-45 minutes. Cool well.

Alice Gudknecht, Faribault, Mn.

15 MINUTE VELVETY CUSTARD PIE

4 slightly beaten eggs
1/2 c. sugar
1/4 tsp. salt

1 tsp. vanilla
2 1/2 c. milk, scalded
9 inch unbaked pastry shell

Roll out to a little less than 1/8 inch, thin crust. Thoroughly mix egg, sugar, salt and vanilla; slowly stir in hot milk. At once, pour into unbaked pastry shell. On top, sprinkle cinnamon and nutmeg. Bake in very hot oven, 475°, for 5 minutes. Reduce heat to 425°; bake 10 minutes or until knife comes out clean.

Gloria Smith, Jackson, Mn.

CUSTARD PEACH PIE

6-8 peaches
1 unbaked pie shell
1 c. sugar
1/4 c. flour

1 tsp. vanilla
3/4 c. cream
1 egg, beaten
Cinnamon

Peel and pit peaches; slice into pie shell. Combine sugar and flour. Combine vanilla, cream and eggs. Blend flour and egg mixture; pour over peaches. Sprinkle with cinnamon. Bake at 350° for 1 hour.

Mrs. Robert Sloneker, Chisholm, Mn.

DATE PIE

Beat 2 egg yolks with 1 tablespoon flour, 1 teaspoon baking powder, 1 cup powdered sugar and 1 1/2 cups milk. Beat 2 egg whites until almost stiff; fold in date mixture. Pour into unbaked shell. Bake at 350° until silver knife comes out clean.

Ava S. Day, St. Paul, Mn.

FOURTH OF JULY PIE

Pastry:

1 c. corn meal
1 1/2 c. sifted flour
1 1/4 tsp. salt

3/4 c. shortening
6-8 Tbsp. cold water

Filling:

1 (1 lb. 5 oz.) can cherry pie filling
1 (1 lb. 5 oz.) can blueberry pie filling

1 (1 lb. 5 oz.) can apple pie filling

Preheat oven to 425°. For pastry, sift together dry ingredients; cut in shortening. Add water, a tablespoon at a time, until dough holds together; shape into a ball. Set aside 1/5 of the dough. Roll out remainder to fit into a 10x15 inch jelly roll pan, covering sides and outside lip of pan. Trim edges. Spoon pie filling into 1/3 of the shell

616

with apple in the center. Roll out remaining 1/5 of dough; cut out 15 stars with a cookie cutter. Arrange on top of filling. Bake 35-40 minutes or until golden brown and bubbly; cool before serving. Cut into 15 squares. Serve with ice cream.

K., St. Cloud, Mn.

FRENCH MINT PIE

1 c. powdered sugar	1/4 stick butter
2 eggs	2 sq. unsweetened chocolate
1/4 tsp. mint flavoring	

Melt chocolate; cool. Beat sugar and butter till smooth. Add eggs, one at a time; beat well after each addition. Add chocolate, then mint. Spread into a graham cracker crust. Chill several hours.

Dee Olson, St. Paul, Mn.

FRUIT SALAD PIE

1 baked pie crust or crumb pie crust	1/2 c. maraschino cherries, halved and drained
1 1/2 c. sliced bananas	3 Tbsp. lemon juice
1 c. sliced peaches, well drained	3 Tbsp. honey
1/2 c. miniature marshmallows	1/2 c. whipping cream
	2 Tbsp. crushed cheese crackers

Mix fruit, lemon juice and honey; chill until serving time. Beat whipping cream until thick; fold into fruit mixture. Spoon into baked shell. Sprinkle with cheese crackers and serve.

Dee Olson, St. Paul, Mn.

FREEZER PIE

Use any type crust you like, graham or butter. Thaw a 6 ounce can of frozen concentrate (orange or lemon). Mix in 14 ounces of sweetened condensed milk and 4 ounces of Cool Whip. Spoon into crust and store in freezer. Cover.

Jolaine Farley, Sartell, Mn.

GRAHAM CRACKER PIE

18 graham crackers,
   rolled fine
1 tsp. flour

1/3 c. sugar
1 tsp. cinnamon
1/3 c. melted butter

Mix as for pie crust; line pie plate with 3/4 of mixture.

Custard Filling:

2 egg yolks
1/2 c. sugar
2 c. milk

1 tsp. vanilla
2 tsp. cornstarch

Blend sugar and cornstarch. Add beaten eggs to milk; stir into dry ingredients. Cook until mixture coats a spoon. Add vanilla; pour into pie shell. Beat egg whites and a little sugar; cover custard. Spread remainder of graham cracker crumbs on meringue. Bake in slow oven.

Marlys Swehla, Albert Lea, Mn.

MY MOM'S GRAHAM CRACKER PIE
(9 Inch)

1 tsp. vanilla
2 Tbsp. flour
1/2 c. sugar

2 egg yolks
1 c. milk (good sized)
1/2 tsp. salt

Mix; add milk and everything. Put in pan and beat until thick (over heat), then use spoon until done. Slice bananas on top of custard. Use graham cracker crust.

Mrs. Kermit A. Haugen, Clarkfield, Mn.

GRASSHOPPER PIE

Crust:

20 Hydrox chocolate
   cookies, crushed

3 Tbsp. melted oleo

Mix together and pat into pie pan.

24 marshmallows

1/3 c. milk

Melt marshmallows in the milk in top of double boiler; cool.

1 jigger creme de cacao
1 jigger creme de menthe

1 c. whipped cream

618

Add to cooled marshmallow mixture; pour into crust. Sprinkle a few cookie crumbs on top; chill.

Carolyn Brudevold, Fargo, N.D.

GREEN TOMATO PIE

Slice 3 cups green tomatoes very thin; let drain. Mix 3 tablespoons flour, 1 1/4 cups sugar, 1 teaspoon salt, 1/2 teaspoon nutmeg and 1/2 teaspoon cinnamon. Place tomatoes in unbaked pie shell; cover with sugar mixture and dot with 1 tablespoon butter. Sprinkle with 1 tablespoon mild vinegar. Cover with top crust; bake 10 minutes at 475° for 50 minutes.

Norma Stevens, Montevideo, Mn.

IMPOSSIBLE PIE

Combine in the blender:

4 eggs	1/4 c. butter
2 c. cold milk	Dash of salt
3/4 c. sugar	1 tsp. vanilla
1/2 c. flour	1 c. cocoanut

Blend at 10 counts. Slowly turn off. Pour into well greased pie plate. Bake in 350° oven for 45 minutes.

Esther Mungovan, Duluth, Mn.

JEWEL BOX PIE

1 c. Bisquick	1 pkg. cherry or strawberry
1 Tbsp. granulated sugar	jello
1/4 c. soft butter or oleo	1/2 pt. whipped cream
3 Tbsp. boiling water	3/4 c. milk
1 pkg. lime jello	1 pkg. instant vanilla
	pudding

Preheat oven to 425°. Mix Bisquick, sugar and butter. Add boiling water; mix with fork until dough forms a ball and cleans the bowl. Pat evenly into a 9 inch pie pan, fluting edges. Bake 8 to 10 minutes. Prepare the jello according to directions on package; pour each color into 9 inch square pans. Chill until firm; cut into cubes with a sharp knife. Whip cream until stiff. Put milk into a bowl; add pudding mix. Beat with egg beater about 1 minute. Immediately fold into whipped cream. With a spatula, turn

1/2 of the red and 1/2 of the green jello cubes into the pudding; stir carefully to mix. Garnish with some of the remaining cubes. Refrigerate until serving time.

Dorothy Bowe, Minneapolis, Mn

KENTUCKY PECAN PIE

1 c. white corn syrup
1 c. dark brown sugar
1/3 tsp. salt
1/3 c. melted butter (or margarine)

1 tsp. vanilla
3 whole eggs, slightly beaten
1 heaping c. shelled whole pecans

Combine syrup, sugar, salt, butter and vanilla; mix well. Add slightly beaten eggs. Pour into a 9 inch unbaked pie shell. Sprinkle pecans over all. Bake in preheated 350° oven for approximately 45 minutes. When cool, you may top with whipped cream or ice cream...but nothing tops this.

Margaret McKenney, Minneapolis, Mn.

LEMON PIE

Bring to a boil in saucepan on direct heat:

1 c. water
3/4 c. sugar

1/4 tsp. salt
1 tsp. grated lemon peel

Blend 5 tablespoons cornstarch with 1/2 cup cold water; add. Cook over low heat until thickened; remove from heat. Add separately, mixing well after each addition:

2 well beaten egg yolks
1 Tbsp. butter

6 Tbsp. lemon juice

Pour into 8 inch baked shell; top with meringue made of 2 egg whites, beaten stiff with 4 tablespoons sugar. Fold in 1 teaspoon lemon juice. Brown 15 minutes in 325° oven. Serves 5 or 6.

Fran Basch, White Bear Lake, Mn.

LEMON PIE

1 graham cracker crust
1 (6 oz.) can frozen, thawed lemonade

1 (14 oz.) can sweetened condensed milk
1 (8 or 9 oz.) ctn. Cool Whip, thawed

Mix lemonade and milk, then add Cool Whip. Put pie in refrigerator until firm, about 2 or 3 hours.

620   Liz Tuft, St. Paul, Mn.

BEST LEMON PIE

Grate the rind from 3 large lemons; boil rind and drain. Mix 1 tablespoon flour with 3 tablespoons cornstarch and 1 1/2 cups sugar. Add 3 beaten egg yolks to lemon rind and the juice and pulp of the 3 lemons. Add 1 1/2 cups water; mix well. Stir constantly while cooking until clear and thick. Let cool before pouring in cooked crust to decorate with Cool Whip, or into unbaked crust if you want meringue. (Instead of all water, drain a small can of crushed pineapple and add water to make 1 1/2 cups.)

Ava S. Day, St. Paul, Mn.

ANGEL ORANGE LEMON PIE

4 eggs
1 c. sugar
2 Tbsp. water

Juice of 1 orange and 1/2 lemon

Beat egg yolks thoroughly; add orange and lemon juices and water and all but 4 tablespoons sugar. Cook in a double boiler until thick. Remove from stove; add 2 egg whites, which have been beaten until stiff, and 2 tablespoons sugar. Mix well; pour into a baked pie shell. Cover with meringue made from the remaining 2 egg whites and sugar. Brown in a slow oven.

Clara Omlid Peterson, Minneapolis, Mn.

LEMON LOVIN' CREAM PIE

1 stick pie crust mix
1 1/2 tsp. sugar

1 tsp. nutmeg
2 Tbsp. sour cream

Filling:

1/2 c. (3 3/4 oz.) pkg. instant lemon pudding
1 1/4 c. milk

3/4 c. dairy sour cream
1 Tbsp. powdered sugar

In small mixing bowl, combine top 6 ingredients; roll out pie shell. Flute edge and prick crust. Bake in 450° oven for 8 to 10 minutes; cool and prepare filling. Pour filling into cooled crust; refrigerate 1 hour at least. Serve with whipped cream.
Filling: In medium bowl, combine pudding with 1 1/4 cups milk; beat as directed on package. Fold in sour cream and powdered sugar.

Elaine Aaberg, Minneapolis, Mn.

NEVER FAIL LEMON PIE

Into a blender, place the following:

1 1/4 c. water
1/2 c. lemon juice
1 1/4 c. sugar

1/4 c. cornstarch
3 egg yolks
Dash of salt

Cover; blend 20 seconds. Pour into a saucepan with 1 tablespoon butter; cook over low heat until thickened, stirring constantly. Pour into 9 inch baked pie shell.

Meringue:

3 egg whites
1/4 tsp. cream of tartar

6 Tbsp. powdered sugar

Beat egg whites and cream of tartar until soft peaks form. Add powdered sugar gradually; beat into stiff peaks. Put on pie; make sure meringue covers edges of pie. Bake at 325° for 12-15 minutes.

Mrs. Norma Applen, Minneapolis, Mn.

UNBELIEVABLE LEMON PIE

1 (14 oz.) can sweetened
    condensed milk (not
    evaporated)
1 c. water
1/2 c. reconstituted lemon
    juice

1/2 c. biscuit baking mix
3 eggs
1/4 c. butter or margarine,
    softened
1 1/2 tsp. vanilla extract
1 c. flaked coconut

Preheat oven to 350°. In blender container, combine all ingredients, except coconut; blend on low for 3 minutes. Pour mixture into greased 10 inch pie plate. Let stand 5 minutes; sprinkle coconut over top. Bake 35 to 40 minutes or until knife inserted near edge comes out clean. Cool slightly. Serve warm or cold. Refrigerate leftovers. Makes one 10 inch pie.

Marie Capen, Duluth, Mn.

KEY LIME PIE

1 can sweetened condensed
    milk

2/3 c. lime juice
4 egg yolks

Beat egg yolks and condensed milk; gradually add to lime juice. Pour into a baked pie shell.

Virginia Miller, Anoka, Mn.

622

MARTHA'S MANDARIN PIE

3 egg whites
1/2 tsp. cream of tartar
1 c. sugar (granulated)
1/2 c. Rice Krispies
1/2 c. chopped nuts
1 env. Dream Whip

1/2 c. powdered sugar
3 Tbsp. instant vanilla
  pudding
1 c. mandarin oranges,
  drained
3/4 c. flaked coconut

Beat egg whites until stiff; add granulated sugar and cream of tartar. Beat again. Stir in cereal and nuts. Bake at 325° F. for 25 minutes in ungreased 9 inch pie pan; let cool. Prepare Dream Whip as directed on package. Add powdered sugar, instant pudding, oranges and coconut. Spread over crust; refrigerate. Top with whipped cream. Okay to prepare this the day before serving.

Harlene Swenson, Minneapolis, Mn.

MARSHMALLOW PIE

30 marshmallows
1/2 c. milk
24 graham crackers

6 Tbsp. butter, melted
1 pt. cream, whipped
6 sq. semi-sweet chocolate

First, crush crackers; mix with butter. Line a cake pan, 13x9x2 inches, with the crumbs. Cook marshmallows and milk over low heat until melted; set aside to cool. Whip cream; add the chocolate, that has been grated. Add marshmallow mixture. Pour into pan lined with crumbs. Refrigerate for several hours before serving.

Mrs. Kermit A. Haugen, Clarkfield, Mn.

MILE-HI PIE

Crust: Melt 1/4 cup butter in 9x13 inch pan. Add 1 1/3 cups crushed corn flakes and 2 tablespoons sugar. Bake for 8 minutes in 350° oven.

In large bowl, combine 1 (10 ounce) package partially defrosted strawberries, 1 cup sugar, 1 tablespoon lemon juice, 2 egg whites and 1/4 teaspoon salt. Beat for 15 minutes, till thick and creamy. In separate bowl, whip 1 pint whipping cream till thick; combine with strawberry mixture. Pour into corn flake crust. Place in freezer till ready to serve.

Esther Mungovan, Duluth, Mn.

MILLIONAIRE PIE

Cream together:

1 c. powdered sugar	1/4 tsp. salt
1/2 stick margarine	1/4 tsp. vanilla
1 egg	

Beat; spread in baked shell. Chill. Whip 1 cup cream without sugar; fold in 1 cup drained pineapple and 1/2 cup chopped pecans. Spread this over the first mixture. Refrigerate.

Marilyn Johnson, Albert Lea, Mn.

OATMEAL PIE
(Tastes just like good old Pecan)

3/4 c. sugar	1/2 c. coconut
3/4 c. dark corn syrup	1/2 c. melted butter
3/4 c. quick cooking oatmeal	2 eggs, well beaten

Use a 9 inch pie shell (try the No-Roll crust for this one; works well). Combine sugar, syrup and oatmeal. Blend in coconut, melted butter and beaten eggs. Pour into the unbaked pie shell; bake 45 to 50 minutes in 350° oven. (No top crust needed, but you may serve each piece with a dollop of Cool Whip.)

Mrs. Norma Applen, Minneapolis, Mn.

Similar recipe submitted by: Colleen Landwehr, St. Cloud, Mn.

ORANGE PIE

Graham cracker crust	1 (8 oz.) pkg. cream cheese,
1 c. powdered sugar	softened

Cream powdered sugar and cream cheese; add:

1/2 c. orange juice (the straight with no water added)	3 Tbsp. lemon juice
	1 orange rind, grated
	1 large ctn. Cool Whip (no, the extra large)

Put this in the crust and refrigerate. Best if you can do for overnight.

Elsa Ditty, St. Cloud, Mn.

PEACHES AND CREAM PIE

4 c. miniature marshmallows   1 Tbsp. lemon juice
2 Tbsp. orange juice

Heat until marshmallows are melted; chill. Fold in 1 cup whipped cream and 1 cup drained, crushed fresh peaches. Pour into baked pie shell; chill. Makes 1 pie.

Gemma Pierson, St. Cloud, Mn.

FRESH PEACH PIE

1 c. sugar   1 Tbsp. butter
3 Tbsp. cornstarch   6 peaches (large)
1/2 c. water

Mix sugar and cornstarch; add water and butter. Bring to a boil. Add 3 diced peaches; simmer 5 minutes or until thick, then let cool. Slice remaining peaches into pie shell; pour mixture over top. Serve plain or with whipped cream.

Jan Farley, Sartell, Mn.

FRESH PEACH PIE

Butter Crunch Crust: Mix -

1 c. flour   1/4 c. brown sugar
1/2 c. butter   1/2 c. walnuts

Line pie pan; bake at 375° for 10 minutes.

Filling:

3/4 c. granulated sugar   1 env. unflavored gelatin
6 fresh peaches, sliced   1/4 c. cold water
1 Tbsp. lemon juice   1/2 c. boiled water
Dash of salt   1 c. heavy cream, whipped

Mix sugar, peaches, lemon juice and salt. Soften gelatin in cold water; dissolve in boiling water. Mix into peach mixture. Fold in the whipped cream. Pour into baked pie shell; refrigerate until ready to serve. This may be made a day ahead. Top with whipped cream when serving.

Caroline 'Cari' Bennett, Apple Valley, Mn.

SOUR CREAM PEACH PIE

2 Tbsp. flour
2 c. sliced peaches
3/4 c. sugar
1 egg, beaten

1/2 tsp. vanilla
1/4 tsp. salt
1 c. sour cream

Stir the above ingredients well; place in an unbaked pie shell.

Topping:

1/3 c. sugar   1/3 c. flour

Cut in 1/4 cup margarine. Crumble on top of pie and also sprinkle 1 teaspoon cinnamon on top. Bake for 15 minutes at 450°, then for 30 minutes at 350°.

Judy Rieger, Grand Forks, N.D.

PEANUT PIE

2 c. crushed graham
   crackers
1/4 c. sugar
1/3 c. melted butter
1/2 c. light corn syrup

1 qt. vanilla ice cream,
   softened
1/3 c. creamy peanut butter
2/3 c. dry roasted peanuts,
   chopped

Mix together first 3 ingredients for crust. Press half of softened ice cream into unbaked crust. In a small bowl, stir syrup and peanut butter until well blended. Pour half of mixture over ice cream; sprinkle with half of nuts. Repeat; freeze.

Anne Aune, Minneapolis, Mn.

PEANUT BUTTER PIE

1 pkg. Dream Whip   1 box instant vanilla pudding
2 c. milk

Whip together; stir in 3 tablespoons peanut butter. Put in graham cracker pie shell. Keep in refrigerator.

Lucille F. Anderson, Grand Forks, N.D.

PECAN PIE

Mix together:

4 Tbsp. butter, melted   1 c. brown sugar

Stir in:

3 eggs, beaten   1/8 tsp. salt
1 c. white corn syrup   1 c. whole pecans
1 tsp. vanilla

Pour the mixture into 8 or 9 inch unbaked pie crust. Bake at 450° for 10 minutes; lower to 325° for 25 minutes or longer, until set. Better overbaked than under. Eight inch pie crust works better for the amount of ingredients.
Dorothy Savig, Minneapolis, Mn.
Similar recipes submitted by: Mrs. Neva Kost, Fairmont, Mn., Anne Aune, Minneapolis, Mn., Helen-May Johnson, Chanhassen, Mn., Mary Jean Voss, Owatonna, Mn.

PUMPKIN CHIFFON PIE

1 env. unflavored gelatin   3/4 c. firmly packed brown
1/2 c. cold water   sugar
2 eggs, separated   1/2 tsp. each salt, nutmeg
1 c. evaporated milk   and cinnamon
1 1/4 c. mashed, cooked   1/4 tsp. ginger
    pumpkin   1 (9 inch) baked pie shell

Sprinkle gelatin on cold water in top of double boiler to soften. Add egg yolks, evaporated milk, pumpkin, 1/2 cup of the brown sugar, salt and spices. Cook over boiling water 10 minutes, stirring constantly; remove from heat. Cool, stirring occasionally. Beat egg whites until stiff, but not dry. Gradually add remaining 1/4 cup sugar; beat until very stiff. Fold into pumpkin mixture; turn into pie shell. Chill until firm. If desired, garnish with whipped cream. Makes one 9 inch pie.
Dena Stoddard, St. Louis Park, Mn.

EASY PUMPKIN PIE

1 c. Dream Whip, whipped   1 c. pumpkin
1 pkg. instant Jell-O vanilla   1/2 tsp. cinnamon
    pudding   1/4 tsp. salt
2/3 c. milk

Mix all together 1 minute in mixer; do not mix longer

than 1 minute. Pour into baked pie shell; top with rest of
Dream Whip. Refrigerate 2 hours to set.

Patricia Larson, Grafton, N.D.

FROZEN PUMPKIN PIE

9 inch baked pie shell
1 c. cooked or canned
   pumpkin
1 1/4 c. sugar
1/2 tsp. salt

1/2 tsp. ginger
1/4 tsp. nutmeg
1 c. whipping cream,
   whipped
1 pt. vanilla ice cream

Mix pumpkin, sugar, salt and spices; fold into whipped
cream. Spoon ice cream into baked pie shell. Top with
pumpkin-cream mixture. Freeze at least 2 hours or
overnight.

Rhea Layne, Sauk Rapids, Mn.

PUMPKIN PIE
(No Crust)

Grease a pie tin generously with butter; dust generously with flour. Don't shake the pan too hard, but also
don't leave too much flour in the pan. This forms the
"crust".

4 eggs
1/2 c. brown sugar, packed
1/2 c. white sugar
1 tsp. cinnamon
1/2 tsp. salt
1/4 tsp. cloves

1/4 tsp. nutmeg
1/4 tsp. ginger
1 (No. 300) can (1 3/4 c.)
   pumpkin
1 (14 1/2 oz.) can evaporated
   milk

Beat eggs; mix in remaining ingredients. Pour into pie
tin; bake in moderately hot oven, 375°, for 45 minutes or
until knife inserted in center comes out clean. (If you don't
like making pie crust, this is for you.)

Clara O. Johnson, Chanhassen, Mn.

PUMPKIN PIE

1 c. sugar
1 egg
1/2 Tbsp. salt
1/4 tsp. cloves

1/4 tsp. nutmeg
1/4 tsp. ginger
1 (No. 2) can pumpkin
2/3 c. milk
1 tsp. cinnamon

Pour into unbaked shell. Bake until knife inserted in middle comes out clean, 425° for 15 minutes, then 375° until done.

Marie Capen, Duluth, Mn.

Similar recipes submitted by: Helen Martin, Fargo, N.D., Mrs. Knute Andal, Henning, Mn.

SELF CRUST PUMPKIN PIE

2 eggs
1/2 tsp. ginger
1/4 tsp. cloves
1 can pumpkin
2 tsp. butter, melted
1/2 tsp. salt

1 (13 oz.) can evaporated milk, plus water to make 2 c.
1 tsp. cinnamon
3/4 - 1 c. sugar
1/2 c. Bisquick
1/4 tsp. nutmeg

Combine in blender; blend 2 minutes. Grease and flour glass pie pan. Bake at 350° for 1 hour.

Vi Geving, Duluth, Mn.

RAISIN FESTIVAL PIE

1/4 c. butter
3 eggs
1 1/2 c. seedless raisins
1 stick pastry mix

3/4 c. sugar
1 tsp. vanilla
1/2 c. chopped walnuts
Whipped cream

Beat butter and sugar together until creamy. Beat in eggs and vanilla; add raisins and walnuts. Crumble in pastry stick, stirring until well blended. Turn into 9 inch pan. Bake in 325° oven for about 35 minutes until set. Cool before cutting. Garnish with whipped cream.

Colleen Landwehr, St. Cloud, Mn.

SOUR CREAM RAISIN PIE

2 1/4 c. raisins
3/4 c. sour cream
3/4 c. buttermilk
3 Tbsp. cornstarch
3/4 tsp. salt
3/4 c. sugar

1 tsp. cinnamon
3 eggs, separated
1/2 c. milk
3/4 tsp. nutmeg
9 inch baked pastry shell

Combine raisins with cream, buttermilk, cornstarch,

salt, sugar and spices in saucepan; stir until well blended. Bring to boil; cook until thick. Remove from heat. Beat egg yolks and milk together. Add to hot mixture, stirring briskly. Return to heat; cook until thickened, stirring the mixture while cooking, about 2 minutes. Pour into baked pie shell; cover with meringue.

Pie Meringue:

3 egg whites
1/4 tsp. cream of tartar

6 Tbsp. sugar
1/2 tsp. vanilla

Beat egg whites and cream of tartar until foamy. Beat in sugar, 1 tablespoon at a time. Continue beating until stiff and glossy; do not underbeat. Beat in vanilla. Bake in preheated oven, 400°, for 10 minutes.

Marion B. Standring, Big Lake, Mn.

SOUR CREAM RAISIN PIE

1 c. sour cream
2 eggs
1 c. sugar

1 tsp. cinnamon
1/2 tsp. cloves
1 c. raisins

Bake in unbaked crust at 350° until knife comes out clean.

Ollie Kearney, Owatonna, Mn.

RASPBERRY PIE

Fill 1 baked pie crust with berries. Top with glaze made of:

1 c. sugar
2 Tbsp. cornstarch

1 c. water

Cook until thick; add 2 tablespoons raspberry jello. Cool. Serve with whipped cream.

Variation: Use only 1 tablespoon jello instead with 1/2 cup crushed berries when cooking glaze.

Mary Paul, Minneapolis, Mn.

RHUBARB PIE

3 c. flour	1 c. shortening (lard is
1 egg	good)
1 tsp. vinegar	5 Tbsp. water
	1 tsp. salt

Mix flour, salt and lard until crumbly. Beat in 1 egg and 1 teaspoon vinegar. Add 5 tablespoons water; add this liquid mixture to flour and lard mixture. Roll out to make 4 pie crusts (these freeze well).

Filling:

8 Inch Pie	9 Inch Pie
2 egg yolks	3 egg yolks
2 tsp. milk	2 Tbsp. milk
1 1/2 c. sugar	2 c. sugar
3 Tbsp. flour	1/4 c. flour
3 c. rhubarb	4 c. pink rhubarb
2 tsp. butter	Dot with 1 Tbsp. butter

Mix together; put into pie crust. Bake at 400° for the first 15 minutes, then at 350° for 45 more minutes. Cover with meringue.

Meringue (practically foolproof):

3 egg whites	1 c. (1/2 jar) Kraft
Dash of salt	marshmallow creme

Beat egg whites and salt until soft peaks form. Add gradually the marshmallow creme, beating until stiff peaks form. Spread over pie filling, sealing to edge of crust. Bake at 350° for 12-15 minutes or until lightly browned; cool.

La Donna Dallmann, Faribault, Mn.

RHUBARB PIE

Two Crust Shell:

1 1/2 c. flour	3/4 c. Crisco (or 1/2 each
1/2 tsp. salt	margarine and Crisco)
1/2 tsp. baking powder	

Cut and mix. Add 5 tablespoons cold water or 4 tablespoons cold water and 1 tablespoon vinegar for flakier crust. Sprinkle sugar and cinnamon over top before baking.

Filling:

1 1/2 c. (or more; I use 2 c.) rhubarb	2 eggs
1 c. sugar (less if rhubarb is not sour)	1 Tbsp. flour
	1 Tbsp. butter
	Grated rind of 1 orange

Bake at 350° for about 1 hour.

Marion Vonesh, Grand Forks, N.D.

RHUBARB PIE

1/3 c. sour cream	1/8 tsp. salt
2 egg yolks	1 tsp. grated orange rind
1 1/3 c. sugar	2 Tbsp. flour
3 c. rhubarb, cut fine	

Combine all above ingredients; pour into unbaked pastry shell. Bake 45 minutes at 350°. Top with meringue made with the 2 egg whites, which have been beaten with 4 tablespoons sugar added. Bake another 12 to 15 minutes until meringue is brown. (An additional egg may be added for richer filling and higher meringue.)

Mae Styrlund, Edina, Mn.

RHUBARB CREAM PIE

Melt 3 tablespoons butter; add 3 cups diced rhubarb and 1 1/2 cups sugar. Cook slowly until rhubarb is tender. Combine 1/2 cup sugar, 3 tablespoons cornstarch, 3 egg yolks, beaten well, 1/2 cup light cream and 1/4 teaspoon salt; cook with rhubarb until thick. Cool; pour in a baked pie shell. Cover with meringue; brown in oven.

Bette Thistle, Minneapolis, Mn.

RHUBARB CUSTARD PIE

9 Inch Tin	8 Inch Tin
1 unbaked pie shell	1 unbaked pie shell
4 1/2 c. rhubarb	3 c. rhubarb
1 1/2 c. sugar (depending on rhubarb)	1 c. sugar (depending on rhubarb)
4 Tbsp. flour	2 Tbsp. flour
1/2 tsp. cinnamon	1/2 tsp. cinnamon
Pinch of salt	Pinch of salt
2 eggs, beaten separately*	2 eggs, beaten separately*
1 tsp. lemon juice	1 tsp. lemon juice

632

*Save whites for meringue.

Sift together sugar, flour, cinnamon and salt. Beat egg yolks. To beaten yolks, add lemon juice and as much flour mixture as eggs will absorb without getting too dry. To this, add rhubarb and any remaining flour mixture; mix well. Put in unbaked pie shell; bake in slow oven (like for apple pie), about 350°-375° F., for about an hour or until rhubarb tests done. Remove from oven; cover with meringue made as follows:

2 egg whites, beaten stiff but not dry

4 Tbsp. cane sugar
1 tsp. vanilla

Put under broiler until meringue is a light brown.

Clara O. Johnson, Chanhassen, Mn.

RHUBARB ORANGE CREAM PIE

3 eggs, separated
1/4 c. soft butter
3 Tbsp. frozen orange juice
  concentrate
1/4 tsp. salt

1/3 c. chopped pecans
1/4 c. flour
1 1/4 c. sugar
2 1/2 c. rhubarb, cut in
  pieces

Beat egg whites till stiff; add 1/4 cup sugar gradually. Add butter and orange juice to egg yolks; beat thoroughly. Add remaining cup of sugar, flour and salt; beat well. Add rhubarb to yolks; mix well. Gently fold in meringue. Pour into unbaked pie shell; sprinkle with nuts. Bake 15 minutes at 375° and 45 to 50 minutes at 325°.

Marion Round, Faribault, Mn.

RUM PIE

14 graham crackers
4 Tbsp. butter
4 eggs
2 c. milk
1 1/2 Tbsp. cornstarch
1/2 c. sugar
1 1/4 Tbsp. Knox gelatine

2 Tbsp. cold water
1/4 tsp. cream of tartar
1/2 c. sugar
5 Tbsp. rum
1/2 pt. whipping cream
2 Tbsp. powdered sugar

Mix the graham crackers, which have been rolled fine, with the melted butter; pat into pie pan. Bake 10 minutes in 350° oven. Cook the egg yolks, milk, cornstarch and first 1/2 cup of sugar until thick; allow to cool. Dissolve gelatine in cold water. Beat egg whites to froth; add cream of tartar and other 1/2 cup sugar. Beat until stiff; add rum. Fold into cooled custard. Let it almost congeal before pouring into crust. Top with cream, which has been whipped stiff with powdered sugar. Sprinkle grated bitter chocolate over top; refrigerate.

Dorothy Bowe, Minneapolis, Mn.

ANN'S SHOO-FLY PIE
(Pennsylvania Dutch)

1/2 c. Karo syrup (dark)	1 tsp. soda (put in water)
1/2 c. Brer Rabbit (green label)	1 c. sugar
1 1/2 c. boiling water	Juice of 3/4 lemon, plus rind of 1 grated lemon

Crumbs:

2 c. flour	1 c. sugar
1/4 c. shortening	

Put about 2/3 of crumbs in batter, saving out enough for tops of pies. Bake at 425° for about 10 minutes. Reduce heat to 375° for about 20-25 minutes. Bottom of pie should be soft. Makes 2.

Helen Teeuwen, Minneapolis, Mn.

SODA CRACKER PIE

Beat 4 egg whites and 1/4 teaspoon cream of tartar until stiff. Add:

1 c. sugar	16 crushed soda crackers
1 tsp. vanilla	1/2 c. chopped nuts

Pour into a greased pie pan. Bake 35 to 40 minutes at 325°. When cool, fill with ice cream or fresh fruit or pie filling. Very good!

Bette Thistle, Minneapolis, Mn.

SODA CRACKER PIE

4 egg whites	1/2 c. chopped dates
1 tsp. baking powder	1/2 c. chopped nuts
1 c. sugar	3/4 c. soda crackers
1 tsp. vanilla	

Separate eggs· beat whites until foamy. Add baking

powder and beat stiff. Add sugar and vanilla; fold in dates, nuts and cracker crumbs. Bake 25 minutes at 350° in 9 inch pie tin.

Marge Pye, St. Paul, Mn.

OLD FASHIONED SOUR CREAM PIE

2 eggs	1/4 tsp. cloves
3/4 c. sugar	1 c. sour cream
1/4 tsp. salt	1 c. raisins
3/4 tsp. cinnamon	

Beat eggs; add sugar, salt and spices. Combine with cream and raisins. Pour into unbaked pie shell. Bake at 375° for 30 minutes.

Marion Iverson, Bismarck, N.D.

SOUTHERN PIE
(Pecan Pie "Southern Style" Without Pecans)

1/2 c. Post Grape-Nuts cereal	1 c. dark corn syrup
1/2 c. warm water	3 Tbsp. butter, melted
3 eggs, well beaten	1 tsp. vanilla
3/4 c. sugar	1/8 tsp. salt
	1 unbaked (9 inch) pie shell

Combine cereal and water; let stand until water is absorbed. Meanwhile, blend eggs with sugar; add syrup, butter, vanilla and salt. Fold in softened cereal. Pour into pie shell. Bake at 350° for 50 minutes, or until filling is puffed completely across top; cool. Serve with prepared cream whipped toppings, if desired. (If you are allergic to nuts and love pecan pie, try this.)

Helen-May Johnson, Chanhassen, Mn.

STRAWBERRY PIE

1 baked pie shell	4 c. fresh strawberries, sliced

Place in cooled pie shell; set aside. Combine in saucepan 1 1/2 cups water, 3/4 cup sugar and 2 tablespoons cornstarch. Cook over medium heat, stirring constantly, until mixture comes to a boil. Continue cooking over low heat 2 more minutes or until clear. Add 1 (3 ounce) package strawberry jello; stir until jello is dissolved. Pour cooked mixture over strawberries while still hot; chill until set. Serve with whipped cream.

Inez Wagner, Austin, Mn.

Similar recipe submitted by: Fran Basch, White Bear Lake, Mn.

FRESH STRAWBERRY PIE

1 c. sugar   3 Tbsp. cornstarch
1 c. water

Boil until clear in color; add 3 tablespoons of strawberry jello. Pour over fresh sliced strawberries in a baked pie shell. Serve with Cool Whip or whipped cream.

Goldie Mikish, Staples, Mn.

FRESH STRAWBERRY PIE

1 baked (9 inch) pie crust   3 Tbsp. cornstarch
1 c. sugar   1 qt. fresh strawberries
1 (8 oz.) pkg. cream cheese   1 c. whipping cream

Bring cheese to room temperature; whip. Add a few drops of cream if needed to soften enough to spread. Carefully spread over bottom and sides of cooled pie shell. Place half of the berries in cheese (halve them). Mash and strain the remaining half of berries; you should have 1 1/2 cups. Add water to make that amount. Heat to boiling; stir in sugar and cornstarch, which are mixed together. Cook, stirring until mixture starts to boil. Remove from heat; cool thoroughly. Spoon over berries in shell; chill. At serving time, whip and sweeten cream; spoon on pie. Decorate with a few halved strawberries.

Nancy Fechtner, Fargo, N.D.

FRESH STRAWBERRY PIE

3/4 c. crushed strawberries   2 Tbsp. cornstarch
3/4 c. sugar   2 tsp. lemon juice
1/4 c. water   Red food coloring

Combine first 4 ingredients in a saucepan; cook, stirring constantly, until thick. Blend in lemon juice and food coloring. Cover; cool until ready to use. Fill pastry shell with fresh strawberries; pour glaze over berries. Serve with whipped cream.

636

Suzie Brainard, Minneapolis, Mn.

OLD FASHIONED STRAWBERRY PIE

1 c. sugar
3 Tbsp. cornstarch
1/2 tsp. salt
1 (7 oz.) bottle lemon-lime
  carbonated (7-Up)

Red food coloring
3 c. strawberries, sliced
1 baked Butter Pecan Crust
  (9 inch)

Combine sugar, cornstarch and salt in a saucepan; stir in lemon-lime carbonated beverage (7-Up). Cook on medium heat, stirring constantly, until thickened. Add food coloring, a few drops at a time, to tint glaze the same shade as strawberries; cool slightly. Arrange strawberries in cooled pie crust. Pour glaze evenly over berries. Chill until set. Makes one 9 inch pie.

Butter Pecan Crust:

1/2 c. butter or margarine
1/4 c. brown sugar
1/4 c. shredded coconut

1 c. flour, sifted
1/4 c. pecans, finely
  chopped

Cut butter into brown sugar and flour with a pastry blender or fork until mixture resembles coarse corn meal. Add pecans and coconut; stirring until evenly distributed through mixture. Place mixture into 9 inch pie pan. Press the mixture with the back of a spoon evenly around the bottom and sides of pie pan. Bake in 375° oven for 12 to 15 minutes or until browned.

                       Irene Faber, St. Paul, Mn.

MY OWN STRAWBERRY-RHUBARB PIE

1 baked pie shell
1 pt. strawberries, washed
  and sliced
2 c. cut up rhubarb

3/4 c. water
1/3 c. sugar
1 pkg. strawberry jello
1/2 pt. whipping cream

Cook rhubarb, water and sugar. When cooked to a sauce, remove from heat; stir in jello. Chill until jelled. Pour sliced strawberries into pie shell; pour cooled rhubarb sauce over berries. Refrigerate. Whip cream and frost pie and serve.

                     Sigrid Johnson, Hibbing, Mn.

STRAWBERRY RHUBARB PIE

1 1/2 c. sugar	1/4 tsp. nutmeg
3 Tbsp. tapioca	1 lb. rhubarb
1/4 tsp. salt	1 c. fresh strawberries

Put in large bowl; let stand 20 minutes. Bake in pie crust at 400° for 35 to 40 minutes.

Ollie Kearney, Owatonna, Mn.

TEXAS PIE

Melt 1 stick margarine; combine with 1 cup flour and 1 cup chopped pecans. Press into 9x13 inch pan. Bake at 350° for 15 minutes; cool completely. Combine 1 cup powdered sugar and 1 (8 ounce) package Philadelphia cream cheese; fold in 2 cups Cool Whip. Spread over cooled crust. Let set in refrigerator for 10 minutes. Mix small package of instant chocolate pudding and 1 package instant vanilla pudding with 3 1/2 cups milk; add 1/2 teaspoon vanilla. Pour over cooled cream layer; let set in refrigerator for 10 minutes. Spread 2 cups Cool Whip over all. Top with 1/2 shaved Hershey's bar. Let set at least 30 minutes in refrigerator.

Grace Locke, St. Paul, Mn.

MA'S WHIPPED CREAM PIE

1/2 c. milk	24 large marshmallows

Put in top of double boiler over hot water; beat until the marshmallows are melted. Cool; add 1 pint of cream, whipped stiff. Add 2 squares of semi-sweet chocolate, grated. Pour into graham cracker crust. Use 4 ounces of Hershey's milk chocolate, grated, instead of semi-sweet chocolate, if desired.

Graham Cracker Crust: Combine -

1 1/4 c. graham cracker crumbs	1/4 c. sugar 1/3 c. soft butter or margarine

Press firmly in bottom and sides of 8 or 9 inch pie pan.

Jim Tuft, St. Paul, Mn.

OLD-FASHIONED APPLE PIE

Prepare pastry for a 2 crust pie.

Filling:

3/4 - 1 c. sugar	1/4 tsp. salt
2 Tbsp. flour	6-7 c. sliced, peeled apples
1 tsp. cinnamon	(2 - 2 1/2 lb.)
1/8 tsp. nutmeg	2 Tbsp. butter or margarine

Combine sugar, flour, cinnamon, nutmeg and salt. Mix this lightly through the apples (sliced 1/4 inch thick). Heap in pastry lined 9 inch pie pan; dot with the butter. Adjust top crust and flute edges; cut vents. Bake in hot oven, 425°, for 50 to 60 minutes or till crust is browned and apples are tender.

Note: Amount of sugar you will need varies with the tartness of the apples. The Minnesota cooking apples in the fall are so good for pies!

Bernice Fonos, Minneapolis, Mn.

PIE CRUST HINTS

Easy, helpful tips that give you the light, flaky pie and pastry crusts you want:

1. Always have shortening very cold before using.
2. Use about 1/3 as much shortening as flour.
3. Mix crust dough the day before baking and leave in refrigerator.
4. Roll pastry lightly, using as little flour as possible.
5. Roll from the center of the dough out and up, not back and forth.
6. If possible, use pastry cloths over the board and rolling pin. These lessen the amount of flour needed.

Donna Hoff, Fargo, N.D.

BEST EVER PIE CRUST

3/4 - 1 c. Crisco   1 Tbsp. milk

Mix these two in bowl; add 1/4 cup boiling water and whip with a fork. Add 2 cups flour and 1 teaspoon salt; stir with a fork. Form dough into 2 balls; roll out between wax paper. Enough for 2 shells or 1 double crust pie. Bake according to pie directions.

Marilyn McPhee, St. Cloud, Mn.

CEREAL CRUST

4 c. Country corn flake
   cereal, crushed (1 2/3 c.)
1/4 c. sugar

1/3 c. butter or margarine,
   softened
1 tsp. cinnamon

Heat oven to 375°. Mix cereal, sugar, butter and cinnamon; press mixture firmly and evenly against bottom and side of a 9 inch pie plate. Bake 8 minutes. For filling you can use any pudding mix. 1. Try vanilla pudding mix with instant cherry pie filling (Wilderness). 2. Try Philadelphia cream cheese filling: Use 1 (8 ounce) package softened Philadelphia cream cheese, mixed with 1/2 cup milk, mixing until well blended. Add vanilla instant pudding mix and another 1 1/2 cups milk (2 cups milk in all). Beat slowly until smooth. Pour into shell and refrigerate until ready to use. Top with whipped topping.

Helen-May Johnson, Chanhassen, Mn.

COOKY PIE CRUST

1/2 c. soft butter
1/4 c. sifted powdered sugar

1/2 tsp. vanilla
1 c. sifted flour
1/8 tsp. salt

Mix butter, sugar and vanilla thoroughly. Sift flour and salt; add to butter and blend. Chill 30-45 minutes. Heat oven to 400°. Pat dough evenly into ungreased 9 inch pie pan. Flute edge; prick evenly with fork. Bake 10-12 minutes. Cool and fill with ice cream.

Dee Olson, St. Paul, Mn.

NEVER FAIL PIE CRUST

2 c. flour
6 Tbsp. Crisco
6 Tbsp. butter

3 Tbsp. water
3 Tbsp. cream
Pinch of salt

Blend flour, salt, Crisco and butter together, using fingers to mix until crumbly. Add cream and water. Mix with fingers until the dough holds together in a ball. Roll out on a floured board. Makes 4 shells. Bake until golden brown.

Donna Hoff, Fargo, N.D.

640

NEVER FAIL PIE CRUST

1 c. lard   1/2 c. hot water

Pour water over lard. When cool, add 1 teaspoon salt and 2 1/2 cups flour. Mix well with hands and roll out. This will keep in refrigerator.

Esther Mungovan, Duluth, Mn.

NO-ROLL PIE CRUST

Sift before measuring:
1 1/2 c. flour   1 level tsp. salt
1 1/2 tsp. sugar

Sift the above into a pie tin (or Pyrex pie plate). Add 1/2 cup oil plus 2 tablespoons milk. Mix this well with a fork; use the fork tines to press into the tin and against the sides. Bake 12-15 minutes at 425°. If you want a two crust pie, merely use the recipe below as the "top" crust, then you don't have to roll out any pie crusts:

1/2 c. butter, softened   1 c. flour
1/2 c. brown sugar

Mix well with your fingers; sprinkle over the pie filling, be it mince, cherry, apple, etc.

Mrs. Norma Applen, Minneapolis, Mn.
Similar recipes submitted by: Ruth Eberlein, Luverne, Mn., Mary Fingalson, Detroit Lakes, Mn.

PIE CRUST

3 c. flour   1 egg
1 1/4 c. lard   5 Tbsp. cold water
1 tsp. salt   1 Tbsp. vinegar

Mix flour, lard and salt together well. Beat egg, water and vinegar; add to first mixture. Chill 20 minutes; roll. Makes 2 double crust pies. Two tablespoons of butter may be substituted for 2 tablespoons lard for a richer crust. This crust is better if frozen before baking. It need not be rolled before freezing, but divided in amounts for one crust and then frozen.

Norma Stevens, Montevideo, Mn.
Similar recipes submitted by: Mary Lempe, St. Cloud, Mn., Laura Schloeder, Litchfield, Mn.

OAT PIE SHELL

Put 1/3 cup butter or margarine in 9 inch pie pan; set in preheated 350° F. oven until melted. Add 1/3 cup packed brown sugar and 1 1/4 cups rolled oats (not instant). Heat in oven, stirring once or twice, 10 minutes. With spoon, press onto bottom and sides of pan.

Lorraine Follrath, Anoka, Mn.

BASIC SHORTCRUST PASTRY

2 c. hard wheat white flour
   (preferably unbleached)
1/2 tsp. salt
1/2 tsp. sugar

3/4 c. butter
Lemon juice
1-3 Tbsp. ice water

Mix flour, salt and sugar in a bowl. Cut in the butter, using 2 knives or a pastry cutter, until the mixture resembles coarse corn meal. Sprinkle over it a few drops of lemon juice and a very small amount of ice water, absolutely no more than 3 tablespoons; toss lightly until it begins to come together. Form it quickly into a ball; chill before rolling it out. Roll it out quickly on a lightly floured board, making 2 circles slightly larger than the pie dish. This recipe makes two 9 inch crusts or one double crust. If the pie shell is to be prebaked (or baked "blind"), prick the bottom with a fork in several places. Put a piece of foil in the center and about 1 cup of dried beans on the foil. Bake it for 12 to 15 minutes in a hot oven, 425°. Remove the foil and store the beans, which may be used over and over again for this purpose.

Joan Billadeau, St. Cloud, Mn.

CANDY
SNACKS
JELLY
PRESERVES

TEMPERATURE TESTS
FOR CANDY MAKING

There are two different methods of determining when candy has been cooked to the proper consistency. One is by using a candy thermometer in order to record degrees, the other is by using the cold water test. The chart below will prove useful in helping to follow candy recipes:

TYPE OF CANDY	DEGREES	COLD WATER
Fondant, Fudge	234 - 238°	Soft Ball
Divinity, Caramels	245 - 248°	Firm Ball
Taffy	265 - 270°	Hard Ball
Butterscotch	275 - 280°	Light Crack
Peanut Brittle	285 - 290°	Hard Crack
Caramelized Sugar	310 - 321°	Caramelized

In using the cold water test, use a fresh cupful of cold water for each test. When testing, remove the candy from the fire and pour about ½ teaspoon of candy into the cold water. Pick the candy up in the fingers and roll into a ball if possible.

In the SOFT BALL TEST the candy will roll into a soft ball which quickly loses its shape when removed from the water.

In the FIRM BALL TEST the candy will roll into a firm but not hard ball. It will flatten out a few minutes after being removed from water.

In the HARD BALL TEST the candy will roll into a hard ball which has lost almost all plasticity and will roll around on a plate on removal from the water.

In the LIGHT CRACK TEST the candy will form brittle threads which will soften on removal from the water.

In the HARD CRACK TEST the candy will form brittle threads in the water which will remain brittle after being removed from the water.

In CARAMELIZING, the sugar first melts then becomes a golden brown. It will form a hard brittle ball in cold water.

ALMOND BARK-NUT KRISPIES

2 1/2 lb. almond bark
2 c. dry roasted peanuts
2 c. miniature marshmallows
3 c. Rice Krispies
2 c. chunky peanut butter

(Oven melt.) Heat oven to 200°. In large pan, melt almond bark for 20-25 minutes. Remove pan; add peanut butter, peanuts, Rice Krispies and marshmallows. Mix well and fast drop onto wax paper. If it should start to set up, put back in oven to warm up. Scoop fast! This makes a big batch.

Harriet Haggard, Anoka, Mn.

CHOCOLATE BONBONS

3 1/2 Tbsp. melted paraffin
1 (12 oz.) pkg. chocolate
  chips
4 Tbsp. melted butter
2 c. powdered sugar
2/3 c. peanut butter or 1 (8
  oz.) pkg. cream cheese
1 c. chopped nuts
1 c. coconut, chopped fine
12 maraschino cherries,
  chopped fine

Melt paraffin in top of double boiler. Add chocolate chips; melt. In a mixing bowl, mix melted butter and peanut butter together; add powdered sugar. Stir in chopped nuts, coconut and cherries; mixture will be stiff. Roll in balls; place on cookie sheet, lined with waxed paper. Chill and dip into melted chocolate; chill again. Makes about 4 dozen.

Anne Aune, Minneapolis, Mn.

CATHEDRAL WINDOWS

1 (6 oz.) pkg. chocolate
  chips
2 Tbsp. butter or margarine
1 egg, beaten
1 c. sifted powdered sugar
1 c. walnuts
2 c. colored miniature
  marshmallows
1/2 c. flaked coconut

Melt chocolate and butter over low heat. Remove from heat; blend in egg. Stir in sugar, nuts and marshmallows, blending well. Sprinkle coconut over sheet of waxed paper; drop mixture on top of coconut. Roll into log shape; chill, then slice into thin pieces. Makes 48 pieces.

1507-82 Betty Goebel, Williston, N.D. 643

FREIDA'S CANDY

1 c. chopped walnuts or
   pecans
1/2 c. butter

3/4 c. brown sugar
1 (6 oz.) pkg. chocolate
   chips

Spread chopped nuts in 8x8 inch pan. Boil butter and brown sugar for 5 minutes, stirring constantly; pour over nuts. Spread chocolate chips over mixture. Cover with bread board to melt chocolate chips. Keep in refrigerator.

CARAMELS

2 c. white sugar
1 c. brown sugar
1 c. whipping cream

1 c. light corn syrup
1 c. milk
1 c. butter

Cook on medium heat; turn down and cook slowly to 248°. Stir frequently for about 1 1/2 hours. Add 4 teaspoons vanilla. Pour into greased 7x11 inch pan.

Suzie Brainard, Minneapolis, Mn.

CARAMEL CHEWS

28 caramels
3 Tbsp. margarine
2 Tbsp. water
1 (3 oz.) can chow mein
   noodles

1 c. peanuts
1/2 c. semi-sweet chocolate
   chips
1 Tbsp. water

Melt caramels with margarine and 2 tablespoons water in pan over low heat; stir occasionally until sauce is smooth. Add noodles and peanuts; toss until well coated. Drop by rounded teaspoonfuls onto greased cookie sheet. Melt together the chocolate chips and 1 tablespoon water in small saucepan. Top caramel chews with mixture; chill until firm. Makes about 2 1/2 dozen.

Joan Dinius, Coon Rapids, Mn.

CARAMELLOWS

1 stick oleomargarine
1 can Borden's condensed
   milk

1 pkg. Kraft caramels
1 pkg. regular marshmallows
Rice Krispies

Melt margarine, milk and caramels over low heat in

644

large saucepan, stirring frequently. Dip marshmallows into mixture, then roll in Rice Krispies. Dry on waxed paper until firm. If mixture gets too thick, add a bit of cream or milk and reheat. These can be frozen after they become firm.

Mrs. Norma Applen, Minneapolis, Mn.

CHOCOLATE PIZZA

8 oz. unsweetened baking	1 c. miniature marshmallows
chocolate	1 c. nuts (broken pieces)
1 lb. white almond bark	Maraschino cherries
1 c. toasted rice cereal	Shredded coconut

In a 2 quart mixing bowl, melt chocolate and 7/8 of the almond bark; microwave at High 3 to 4 minutes, or until melted. Mix together rice cereal, marshmallows and nuts; add to chocolate mixture. Mix well. Spread onto buttered pizza pan. Top with maraschino cherries (tomatoes). Melt remaining almond bark at 60% for 1 to 2 minutes, or until melted. Drizzle over cherries (Mozzarella cheese). Sprinkle with coconut; chill to set. Cut in small pieces, or break out in FAT!

Marlene Barton, Grand Forks, N.D.

DIABLOS DULCES
(Deviled Sweets)

1 1/2 c. 4X powdered	1/2 tsp. salt
sugar	1/4 tsp. cloves
2 Tbsp. cornstarch	1/4 tsp. allspice
1 tsp. cinnamon	1/4 tsp. chili powder

Slightly beat 1 egg white; add 2 tablespoons water and selection of nuts. Sift above mixture over nuts; place in flat pan. Bake in oven until crispy and light brown.

Clara O. Johnson, Chanhassen, Mn.

DIVINITY

4 c. sugar	3 egg whites
1 c. corn syrup	1 tsp. vanilla
3/4 c. water	1 c. chopped nuts

Bring sugar, syrup and water to a boil. Boil until

hard ball stage or 255° on candy thermometer. Beat egg whites until stiff, but not dry. Slowly pour hot syrup mix into egg whites, beating constantly. When thick, pour in vanilla and nuts. Beat until candy dropped from teaspoon onto waxed paper holds its shape. Drop rest from teaspoon. Let candy dry before storing.

Mary Paul, Minneapolis, Mn.

BERTHA'S DOUBLE DIVINITY

Mixture 1:

3 c. sugar
3/4 c. water

1 c. white corn syrup

Mixture 2:

1 c. sugar

1/2 c. water

Mixture 3:

3 egg whites
1 tsp. vanilla

1 c. nuts

Place mixture 1 in saucepan; stir until sugar dissolves. After syrup comes to a boil, cover for a few minutes so that sugar crystals do not form on sides of pan. Uncover; continue boiling until temperature on candy thermometer reaches 246°. When mixture 1 starts to boil, start beating egg whites in electric mixer, using large bowl. As soon as mixture 1 is cooked, place mixture 2 on heat. Pour mixture 1 very slowly over egg whites, beating constantly. Continue beating until mixture 2 has reached 255°. Pour mixture 2 very slowly over the egg white mixture; continue beating until the candy will not adhere to your figure when gently touched. Add vanilla and nuts; drop quickly on waxed paper. Store in tightly covered container; freezes well.

Carolyn Brudevold, Fargo, N.D.

DIVINITY FUDGE

2 1/2 c. sugar
1/2 c. corn syrup
1/2 c. water

2 egg whites
1 c. walnuts

Mix sugar, syrup and water; boil until mixture forms a firm ball when dropped in cold water. Beat egg whites stiff. Pour hot mixture over egg whites. Beat until stiff enough to drop by teaspoon on waxed paper. (Can add red or green food coloring, if desired.)

Marlys Swehla, Albert Lea, Mn.

FUDGE

4 1/2 c. sugar

1 can Carnation evaporated milk

Bring to boil and boil 6 minutes; add:

1/2 lb. butter
2 c. chopped nuts

1 (8 oz.) pkg. chocolate chips

Pour into buttered cake pan.

Sue Hetland, Grand Forks, N.D.

CREAMY FUDGE

1 lb. mik chocolate
(Hershey's bars)

1 lb. semi-sweet chocolate chips
1 pt. marshmallow cream

Put in bowl; chop and let stand. Stir together:

4 1/2 c. sugar

1 large can condensed milk
Butter the size of walnut

Bring to a boil; boil for 4 1/2 minutes, stirring constantly. Pour over chocolate mix; stir until smooth. Add nuts; put in buttered pan, 12x17 inches. Cool before cutting into squares.

Jo Nell Murack, Fargo, N.D.

KERRIE'S YUMMY FUDGE

Mix 2/3 cup undiluted Carnation evaporated milk (small can) with 1 2/3 cups sugar and 1/2 teaspoon salt in a saucepan over low heat. Heat to boiling; reduce heat and cook 5 minutes, stirring constantly. Remove from heat; add:

1 1/2 c. mini marshmallows
1 1/2 c. chocolate chips

1 tsp. vanilla
1/2 c. chopped nuts

Stir 1 to 2 minutes until marshmallows melt. Quickly pour into a buttered 9 inch square pan; cool and cut.

Kerrie C. Applen
Mrs. Norma Applen, Minneapolis, Mn.

CHOCOLATE BUTTER FUDGE

3 c. sugar
1 env. Knox gelatine
1 c. milk
1/2 c. (scant) white syrup

3 sq. unsweetened chocolate
1 1/4 c. oleo
2 tsp. vanilla
1 c. chopped nuts

Butter a 9 inch pan. Mix sugar and gelatine in a saucepan. Add milk, syrup, chocolate and oleo; cook over a medium heat, stirring frequently, until candy reaches soft ball stage or forms a soft ball when tested in cold water. Remove from heat; pour into a large bowl. Add vanilla; cool 15 minutes. Beat until candy thickens. Add nuts; spread in buttered pan.

Alice Holman, Grand Forks, N.D.

BAVARIAN MINT FUDGE

3 c. chocolate chips
1 (1 oz.) sq. unsweetened
  chocolate
1 Tbsp. butter

1 (14 oz.) can sweetened
  condensed milk
1 tsp. mint flavoring
1 tsp. vanilla

Place chocolate chips, unsweetened chocolate and butter in medium saucepan; put over low heat. Stir frequently. Melt until just smooth. Remove from heat; add milk and flavorings. Beat with electric mixer for 1 minute on low speed. Refrigerate for a total of 15 minutes. Every 5 minutes, beat by hand for a few seconds. After refrigerating the last 5 minutes, beat with electric mixer at high speed for 2 minutes. Spread in greased 8 inch square pan; cool. When firm, cut in small squares. Store in cool place.

Rosie Schudar, Fargo, N.D.

PEANUT BUTTER FUDGE

Melt 2 cups (12 ounce package) peanut butter chips and 14 ounce can sweetened condensed milk in top of double boiler over hot water; stir occasionally. Remove from heat; stir in 1 teaspoon vanilla. Spread evenly into wax paper lined 8 inch square pan. Cover; chill 2 hours or until firm.

648 Mrs. Gary L. Hagen, Princeton, Mn.

BEST PEANUT BUTTER FUDGE EVER MADE

1 lb. white almond bark 1 c. peanut butter (creamy or chunk)

Melt almond bark in top of double boiler over hot water; stir in peanut butter. Pour into buttered pan. Cool; cut into squares.

Dee Olson, St. Paul, Mn.

CHOCOLATE PEANUT BUTTER CANDY
(Small Batch)

Melt:
1/2 c. white syrup 1/4 c. butter
1 c. sugar

Add 1 cup crunchy peanut butter. Add 1 1/2 to 1 1/4 cups crushed corn flakes. Top with 1/2 small bag chocolate chips.

K., St. Cloud, Mn.

EASY PEANUT BUTTER CHOCOLATE FUDGE

1 (12 oz.) pkg. peanut butter flavored chips 1/4 c. butter or margarine
1 (14 oz.) can Eagle Brand sweetened condensed milk (not evaporated) 1/2 c. chopped peanuts (optional)
  1 (6 oz.) pkg. semi-sweet chocolate morsels

In large saucepan, melt peanut butter chips, 1 cup sweetened condensed milk and 2 tablespoons butter; stir occasionally. Remove from heat; stir in peanuts. Spread mixture into wax paper lined 8 inch square pan. In small saucepan, melt chocolate morsels, remaining sweetened condensed milk and butter. Spread chocolate mixture on top of peanut butter mixture; chill 2 hours until firm. Turn fudge onto cutting board; peel off paper and cut into squares. Tightly cover any leftovers. Makes about 2 pounds.

Georgine Isakson, Fargo, N.D.

TWO-TONE FUDGE

2 c. brown sugar
1 c. sugar
1 c. evaporated milk
1/2 c. butter
1 (5-10 oz.) jar
  marshmallow

1 tsp. vanilla
1 c. (6 oz.) butterscotch
  chips
1/2 c. chopped walnuts
1 c. (6 oz.) chocolate chips
1/2 c. chopped walnuts

Combine brown sugar, white sugar, milk and butter in saucepan; bring to full boil, stirring constantly. Remove from heat. Add marshmallow and vanilla; stir till smooth. To 2 cups of mixture, add butterscotch chips and 1/2 cup walnuts. Stir till chips melt. Pour evenly into 9 inch square pan. To remaining mixture, add chocolate chips and 1/2 cup walnuts; stir till chips melt. Pour over butterscotch mixture in pan; chill.

K., St. Cloud, Mn.

PRETTY PARTY FUDGE

2 c. sugar
1/2 c. sour cream
1/3 c. light corn syrup
2 Tbsp. butter
1/4 tsp. salt

2 tsp. vanilla
1/4 c. candied cherries, cut
  into eighths
1 c. cut up nuts

Combine first 5 ingredients in saucepan; bring to a boil slowly, stirring until sugar dissolves. Boil without stirring over medium heat until a little mixture dropped in cold water forms a soft ball. Remove from heat; let stand 15 minutes. Do not stir. Add flavoring; beat until mixture starts to lose its gloss, about 8 minutes. Stir in cherries and nuts; pour into buttered 8 inch square pan. Cool; cut into squares.

Colleen Landwehr, St. Cloud, Mn.

MILLION DOLLAR FUDGE
(Mamie Eisenhower's)

4 1/2 c. sugar
Pinch of salt
2 Tbsp. butter
1 tall can evaporated milk
1 pt. marshmallow cream

12 oz. semi-sweet chocolate
  (chocolate bits)
12 oz. German's sweet
  chocolate
2 c. nutmeats

650

Boil together 6 minutes the sugar, salt, butter and evaporated milk. Put remaining ingredients in a large bowl; pour boiling syrup over these. Beat until chocolate is all melted; pour into pan. Let stand a few hours before cutting. Store in a tin box.

Helen-May Johnson, Chanhassen, Mn.

OATMEAL FUDGE

1 c. white sugar	1/2 c. margarine
1 c. brown sugar	1/2 c. milk

Boil 2 minutes; take off stove. Add 1 cup quick oatmeal; stir. Wait 3 minutes. Put in 1 cup chocolate chips, 1 cup miniature marshmallows, 1 teaspoon vanilla and 1 cup walnuts. Put in 8x8 inch pan; let set a while.

Laurel Pavek

GOLDEN NUT CRUNCH

12 oz. dry roasted peanuts	1/4 tsp. Italian seasoning
1/4 c. butter, melted	1/4 tsp. celery salt
1/4 c. Parmesan cheese	4 c. Golden Grahams cereal
1/4 tsp. garlic powder	

Mix nuts and melted butter in bowl; add cheese and spices. Toss until well coated. Spread on ungreased pan. Bake 15 minutes. Stir in cereal; cool. Store in airtight container.

Geri Running, St. Paul, Mn.

GRANOLA

4 c. rolled oats	1 c. sunflower seeds
1 1/2 c. unsweetened coconut	1/2 c. sesame seeds
	1/2 c. bran
1 c. wheat germ	1 c. ground, toasted soy beans
1 c. chopped nuts	

Heat:
1/2 c. oil	1-2 tsp. vanilla
1/2 c. honey	

Add to dry ingredients. Bake at 375° for 20-30 minutes, stirring now and then.

Tom and Marsha Leubner, Litchfield, Mn.

GUMDROP BARS

4 eggs
2 c. light brown sugar
2 c. flour
1 tsp. vanilla

1/4 tsp. salt
1/2 c. chopped nuts
1 c. finely chopped gumdrops
(lemon and orange)

Beat eggs until light and thick; add sugar gradually. Continue beating until thick. Add nuts, gumdrops and flour (mix all together before adding so nuts and gumdrops are coated with flour); blend well. Spread 3/4 inch thick in greased pan, 9x12 inches. Bake 20-30 minutes at 325°.

Bessie Wilke, Detroit Lakes, Mn.

PEANUT BUTTER CANDY BARS

Heat to 140° (use a candy thermometer):

1 1/2 c. corn syrup (light)
1 1/2 c. granulated sugar

2 Tbsp. water

Stir constantly to prevent sticking. Add 2 1/2 cups peanut butter (chunky style); cool. Add 2 cups Wheaties, 2 teaspoons vanilla and 2 1/2 cups peanuts (if you use the plain peanut butter, but if you use the chunky style, only use 1 1/2 cups unsalted peanuts). Cool in pan, 17x11 inches, or a large cookie sheet. Frost with chocolate frosting.

Mrs. B.V. Feller, Excelsior, Mn.

MASHED POTATO CANDIES

3/4 c. mashed potatoes
1 lb. (4 c.) flaked coconut

1 lb. (4 3/4 c.) confectioners
sugar
1 tsp. almond extract

Combine ingredients; roll into balls. Chill for 1/2 to 1 hour. Coat with the following, melted in double boiler:

12 oz. chocolate chips

1/2 bar paraffin wax

Debra Tollefson, Fargo, N.D.

M.M.M. MINTS

3 oz. cream cheese
2 1/2 c. powdered sugar

1 tsp. flavoring
  (peppermint or almond)

Mix all ingredients; knead. Add food coloring, if desired. Roll into desired shapes or use mold. May be coated with chocolate coating.

Mrs. Gary L. Hagen, Princeton, Mn.

MINTS

1/3 c. prepared frosting
  mix

1/3 c. plus 1 Tbsp.
  powdered sugar

Mix together; put into molds that have been sugared. Use various flavored frosting mixes.

Marion Round, Faribault, Mn.

NUT CLUSTERS

Melt in double boiler:
12 oz. chocolate chips

12 oz. butterscotch chips

Add 1 cup creamy peanut butter; stir till creamy. Add 2 cups Spanish peanuts. Drop by spoonfuls on waxed paper. Chill in refrigerator. Need not refrigerate after set.

Adeline Jasken, St. Cloud, Mn.

PEANUT BRITTLE

Line electric fry pan with aluminum foil; set at 375°. Pour into fry pan:

1 c. sugar
1/2 c. water

1/4 c. light corn syrup
1 tsp. margarine

Cook, stirring occasionally, until light golden brown. Stir in 1 cup peanuts; continue stirring until mixture turns medium brown. Add 1/8 teaspoon soda; stir vigorously. Remove foil containing candy from pan; cool. Break into pieces.

Helen Martin, Fargo, N.D.

1507-82

PEANUT BRITTLE

1 1/2 c. white sugar	2 c. peanuts
1/2 c. white syrup	1 1/2 tsp. soda
1/4 c. water	1/4 tsp. salt

Combine sugar, syrup and water; bring to a boil. Stir in peanuts gradually; do not lose the boil. Keep at a rolling boil until peanuts pop and turn brown. Remove from heat; add salt and soda. Pour on a well greased cookie sheet. Allow room for candy to spread. When cold, break into pieces.

Gemma Pierson, St. Cloud, Mn.

PEANUT CLUSTERS

2 lb. white bark	1 (12 oz.) pkg. sweet
1 (12 oz.) pkg. semi-sweet	chocolate bits
chocolate bits	4 (12 oz.) cans Planter's
12 oz. German's chocolate	peanuts

Place bark, chocolate bits and German's chocolate in large ovenproof bowl. Place bowl in 200° oven to melt ingredients together. Remove from oven; stir in peanuts. Drop mixture from spoon onto waxed paper. Makes about 5 dozen.

Pearl Paulsrud, Montevideo, Mn.

CARAMEL CORN

1 bag Old Dutch puffcorn	1 c. packed brown sugar
curls	1/4 c. light Karo syrup
1/2 c. butter	1/4 tsp. salt

Later, add:

1/4 tsp. soda	1 tsp. vanilla

Butter deep 9x13 inch pan; spread corn evenly in it and place in oven. In 2 quart pan, melt butter slowly. Add sugar, syrup and salt; stir constantly until it boils. Keep at slow boil for 5 minutes, without stirring. Remove from heat; quickly stir in soda and vanilla. Remove corn from oven; pour mixture over. Bake 1 hour at 250°; stir at least every 15 minutes. Remove from oven and stir as it cools to separate.

Jan Ferry, Golden Valley, Mn.

SUMMERTIME SNACK

3 c. granola cereal
1/2 c. semi-sweet chocolate
   flavored chips

3/4 c. unsalted peanuts
1/2 c. seedless raisins
1/2 c. diced, dried apricots

Combine all ingredients; store in airtight container. Makes 5 cups.

Marion Round, Faribault, Mn.

SUGAR AND SPICE NUTS

Add 2 tablespoons water to 1 slightly beaten egg white. Stir in 1/2 cup sugar, 1/2 teaspoon salt, 1/4 teaspoon cinnamon, 1/4 teaspoon cloves and 1/4 teaspoon allspice; mix well. Add 2 cups nuts (pecans and almonds are very good); stir to coat. Place on ungreased cookie sheet; bake at 250° for 1 hour. Turn or stir every 15 minutes.

Fran Toler, Minneapolis, Mn.

NUTS AND BOLTS
(Original Spice Islands Recipe)

1 (13 oz.) pkg. Cheerios
1 (13 oz.) pkg. Rice Chex
1 (13 oz.) pkg. Wheat Chex
2 c. pretzel sticks
1 Tbsp. Spice Islands Beau
   Monde seasoning salt
1 Tbsp. Spice Islands
   smoke flavored salt
1 tsp. Spice Islands marjoram

1 tsp. Spice Islands summer
   savory
1/2 tsp. Spice Islands garlic
   powder
1/2 tsp. Spice Islands onion
   powder
1/8 tsp. Spice Islands
   cayenne pepper
2 cans salted peanuts
3/4 lb. butter

In large baking pan, carefully mix cereals, pretzels and nuts. Hand pulverize marjoram and savory; blend with other seasonings, then blend with cereals. Cut butter in small chunks over entire surface. Place in 250° oven for 45 minutes. Stir during toasting period, being careful to keep cereals whole. May be stored in refrigerator in airtight containers. Heat as used.

Note: This makes a large amount but the best Nuts and Bolts I have tasted. These are all spices which you use in everyday cooking for soups, meats, etc., but if you don't use them, then this recipe would be a bit expensive.

Helen-May Johnson, Chanhassen, Mn.

BARBECUE PECANS

4 c. whole pecan halves
1/4 c. butter

4 Tbsp. Worcestershire sauce
1 Tbsp. garlic salt
1/2 tsp. Tabasco sauce

Stir together the last 4 ingredients; mix with nuts. Spread on cookie sheet; toast for 20-30 minutes at 325°. Stir once or twice. Watch so they don't get too brown; cool.
Fran Toler, Minneapolis, Mn.

MRS. KINGSLEY'S POPCORN BALLS
(Second Grade, Eastwood, West Fargo, N.D.)

3/4 c. butter or margarine
6 c. tiny marshmallows
1 (3 oz.) pkg. flavored jello

6 qt. unsalted popcorn (kept hot in 200° F. oven)

In medium saucepan, melt butter over medium-low heat. Add marshmallows; stir until melted. Blend in dry gelatin. Pour over popcorn, mixing well; form balls. Makes about 20 medium balls.
Rosie Schudar, Fargo, N.D.

CARAMEL POPCORN BALLS

5 qt. popped corn
4 Tbsp. butter or margarine
1 c. brown sugar
1/2 c. light corn syrup

2/3 c. (1/2 of 15 oz. can) sweetened condensed milk
1/2 tsp. vanilla

In saucepan, combine butter, sugar and syrup; stir well. Boil over medium heat. Stir in sweetened condensed milk. Simmer, stirring constantly, till mixture forms a soft ball, 234°, when dropped in cold water. Stir in vanilla when done. Pour over popped corn; stir till kernels are well coated. Makes about 15 balls (3 1/2 inches in diameter).
Mary Jean Voss, Owatonna, Mn.

POPCORN BALLS

Pop enough corn to make 6 cups. Boil together until medium ball stage:

1 c. dark Karo syrup
1/2 tsp. cream of tartar

2 Tbsp. butter

After reaching medium ball stage, remove from heat; add 1/4 teaspoon soda and stir until foamy. Pour over popcorn; mix well and form into balls.

Ruth Rehschuh, Minneapolis, Mn.

POPCORN BALLS

1 c. corn syrup	1/4 tsp. soda
1/2 c. sugar	1 or 2 Tbsp. butter
1 tsp. cream of tartar	4 qt. popped corn

Boil syrup, sugar and cream of tartar to a soft ball stage; add butter and soda. Pour over popped corn; shape into balls.

Mildred Nelson, St. Paul, Mn.

POPCORN CAKE RING

4 qt. cooked popcorn	1 can peanuts
1 large bag marshmallows	1 pkg. gumdrops or jelly
1/2 c. butter or margarine	beans

Melt marshmallows and butter together; pour over popcorn, peanuts and gumdrops. Press in well greased Bundt pan or angel food pan.

Mabel Gunner, Minneapolis, Mn.

POPPYCOCK
(A Light Caramel Corn)

1 c. unpopped popcorn	Oil

Pop the popcorn; set aside in a large baking pan.

1 stick margarine or butter	1 c. white sugar
1/2 c. white syrup	1/2 tsp. salt

Melt butter; stir in syrup, sugar and salt. Boil slowly, about 5 minutes. Pour over popcorn; mix until popcorn is well coated. Stir in 1 cup of mixed nuts or salted peanuts. Bake in oven at 250° for 1/2 hour, stirring occasionally.

Claudia Farley, Sartell, Mn.

BEET JELLY

3 c. beet juice	4 c. sugar
1 pkg. Sure-Jell	1 box jello (any flavor; I use
3 Tbsp. lemon juice	raspberry)

Heat beet juice; add Sure-Jell and lemon juice. Bring to a boil; add sugar and 1 package jello. Boil 6 minutes or less if it boils hard. Put in jars; seal with wax.

Kathryn Otto, Harvey, N.D.

CINNAMON APPLE JELLY

1 qt. bottled apple juice	1-2 Tbsp. red cinnamon
1 pkg. powdered pectin	candies (red hots)
4 1/2 c. sugar	

Combine juice and pectin in large pan; bring to full rolling boil. Add sugar and candies, stirring; return to boil. Boil 2 minutes. Remove from heat; skim off foam. Pour into hot jelly glasses; seal. Store in cool, dry place.

Dee Olson, St. Paul, Mn.

CRANBERRY JELLY
(A Thanksgiving Must)

Cook cranberries until soft, with 3 cups water for each 8 cups of berries. Strain the juice through a jelly bag. Measure juice; heat to boiling point. Add 1 cup sugar for each 2 cups juice; stir until sugar is dissolved. Boil briskly for 5 minutes. Pour into glass jars and seal.

Clara O. Johnson, Chanhassen, Mn.

"CHRIS" GREEN PEPPER JELLY

3 hot peppers and 3/4 c.	6 1/2 c. sugar
bell pepper, put through	1 (6 oz.) bottle Certo
grinder or blender	Green food coloring
1 1/2 c. cider vinegar	

Mix; bring to a boil. Cook 10 minutes; add Certo. Put in jars; seal. (Do not double recipe unless you have a huge kettle, as it boils over when Certo is added.) Great served with cream cheese and crackers.

Helen Teeuwen, Minneapolis, Mn.

SUGARLESS ORANGE JAM

1 env. unflavored gelatin
1/4 c. cold water

1 (6 oz.) can frozen orange juice, thawed

Sprinkle gelatin over cold water; let stand 5 minutes. Add orange juice to gelatin mixture; heat to boiling, stirring constantly. Pour into jar and store in refrigerator.

Esther Mungovan, Duluth, Mn.

PEACH BUTTERSCOTCH JAM

1 3/4 c. prepared peaches
2 Tbsp. lemon juice
1 tsp. ascorbic acid
4 c. white sugar

1/4 c. brown sugar
3/4 c. water
1 box powdered pectin

Peel, pit and grind peaches; measure amount into a large bowl. Add lemon juice and ascorbic acid to peaches. Mix in the sugars. Bring water and pectin to a boil; boil 1 minute. Stir pectin into fruit; stir until sugar is dissolved, about 3 minutes. Ladle into sterilized jars. Let stand until set, then freeze.

Dee Olson, St. Paul, Mn.

PEACH PRESERVES

8 large peaches, peeled
3 lemons, unpeeled

3 oranges

Grind all together; add 1 medium can pineapple. Weigh and add equal weight of sugar; cook until thick. Stir and stir over low heat. Pour into sterilized jars; cover with paraffin.

Ava S. Day, St. Paul, Mn.

SPICED PRUNE JAM

5 c. ground prunes
1 c. sugar
1/4 c. lemon juice

1 Tbsp. cinnamon
1 Tbsp. cloves
About 1 box powdered pectin

Bring to rolling boil and boil 5 minutes. Skim foam and put into jars.

Ellie Cox, Rochester, Mn.

RHUBARB JAM

5 c. rhubarb, cut fine	1 pkg. frozen strawberries
5 c. sugar	1 1/2 pkg. wild strawberry jello

Cook rhubarb and sugar over low heat until rhubarb is done; stir in jello and frozen strawberries. Stir often over low heat as it scorches easily. Bottle and keep in refrigerator.

Myrtle Bohline, Gamaliel, Ar.

Similar recipe submitted by: Bettie Mallon, Minneapolis, Mn.

RHUBARB-APRICOT JAM

6 c. cut up rhubarb	1 can apricot pie filling
4 c. sugar	1 small pkg. orange Jell-O

Combine rhubarb and sugar; let stand 4 hours or overnight, then boil for 10 minutes. Add apricot pie filling and boil 1 minute more. Stir in orange Jell-O. Put in jars and refrigerate.

Bettie Mallon, Minneapolis, Mn.

RHUBARB APRICOT JAM

4 c. finely cut rhubarb	2 c. sugar

Let stand overnight; boil about 5 minutes. Add 1 junior size jar of apricot baby food; bring to a boil. Remove from heat and add 1 package of apricot jello; stir well. Pour into jars; place in refrigerator or freezer.

Mary Trogstad, Rochester, Mn.

RHUBARB-CHERRY JAM

6 c. cut up rhubarb	1 can cherry pie filling
4 c. sugar	6 oz. cherry jello

Bring rhubarb and sugar to a boil; boil 8 minutes. Add cherry pie filling; boil for an additional 2 minutes. Remove from heat; add gelatin. Stir until dissolved. Pour into glasses; refrigerate or seal as you prefer.

Phyllis Mathe, St. Paul, Mn.

Similar recipe submitted by: Paula Earhart, Jackson, Mn.

RHUBARB CONSERVE

7 c. rhubarb   1 lb. orange slices
4 c. white sugar

Cut rhubarb and candy fine; mix with sugar. Let stand overnight. Boil until thick, low heat, for about 1 hour, more or less.

K., St. Cloud, Mn.

NO-COOK STRAWBERRY JAM

Wash, hull and fully crush 1 quart ripe strawberries, one layer at a time; measure 1 3/4 cups. In 4 quart bowl, stir together fruit, 3 cups sugar and 1 cup Karo light corn syrup until well blended. Let stand 10 minutes. In small bowl, mix 2 (3 ounce) pouches liquid fruit pectin and 2 tablespoons lemon juice; stir into fruit mixture. Stir vigorously 3 minutes. Ladle into clean 1/2 pint freezer containers, leaving 1/2 inch head space. Cover tightly. Let stand at room temperature until set, up to 24 hours. Makes 6 containers. Store freshly made jam in freezer up to 1 year. For best results, keep jar in use in refrigerator up to 3 weeks.

Gloria Smith, Jackson, Mn.

FREEZER RASPBERRY OR STRAWBERRY JAM

Pour boiling water over 4 cups berries; drain. Add 1 cup sugar; boil 2 minutes. Add 2 cups sugar; boil 3 minutes. Remove from burner. Add a bit of butter and 1 teaspoon lemon juice. Let stand overnight; stir occasionally. Do not double. Very natural flavor.

Adeline Hortsch, St. Cloud, Mn.

RASPBERRY OR STRAWBERRY JAM

4 c. berries   4 c. sugar
1/4 c. lemon juice

Wash, drain and hull berries. Place in layers in kettle, covering each layer with sugar. Let stand 4 hours or overnight. Bring to a full rolling boil; boil 8 minutes. Add lemon juice; again bring to a boil. Boil 2 minutes. Skim jam; pour into sterilized jars and seal.

Suzie Brainard, Minneapolis, Mn.

STRAWBERRY JAM

1 qt. strawberries   2 Tbsp. lemon juice
4 c. sugar

Wash and cut up strawberries. Boil 2 cups sugar with strawberries for 1 minute. Add remaining 2 cups sugar; boil for 3 minutes. Add lemon juice; set in shallow pan for 8 hours or overnight. Stir occasionally. Fill jars to within 1/2 inch of top; cover with a thin layer of paraffin wax, 1/8 inch thick. Makes 2 pints.

Helen H. Clark, Grand Forks, N.D.
Similar recipe submitted by: Mary Paul, Minneapolis, Mn.

STRAWBERRY JAM

5 c. crushed strawberries   1 pkg. Sure-Jell

Mix together and bring to a good boil; stir in 6 1/2 cups white sugar. Bring to rolling boil that can't be beaten down. Boil for 1 minute; stir constantly. Seal in hot jars with hot lids. Ready to use when cool. Makes 4 pints.

Ruth Preble, Rochester, Mn.

STRAWBERRY FREEZER JAM

1 qt. hulled strawberries,   1 qt. granulated sugar
    packed firmly, not   2 Tbsp. strained lemon juice
    mashed

Put berries and 2 cups of sugar into a large, broad kettle or saucepan; jam cooks more evenly this way. Heat berries and sugar to boiling, stirring constantly. Boil 2 minutes, stirring. Add remaining sugar; again heat to boiling and boil, stirring, 3 minutes. Stir in lemon juice. Pour into shallow bowl and stir occasionally. Let stand overnight. Spoon jam into jars and freeze. Makes 2 pints of jam (thick, but not too stiff). Make additional batches rather than double recipe.

Barbara Wixon, Milroy, Mn.

STRAWBERRY RHUBARB JAM

6 c. rhubarb, chopped
4 c. sugar
1 can strawberry pie filling

2 (3 oz.) or 1 (6 oz.) pkg.
strawberry or raspberry
jello

Mix together the rhubarb and sugar; let set over-night. Next morning, bring to boil and boil for 10-15 minutes. Add the pie filling; boil another 5 minutes. Remove from heat; stir in jello till dissolved. Pour into jars and store in refrigerator or freezer.

Gordy and Elaine Sneva, Brainerd, Mn.

FRIEDA'S STRAWBERRY PRESERVES

Put 4 heaping cups of washed, stemmed strawberries in large kettle; add 5 cups of sugar and 1 tablespoon vinegar. Let stand 30 minutes. Put over low heat and slowly bring to a boil. When they begin to boil, start timing and boil 12 minutes. Remove from heat; put in large flat pan (cake pan). Stir carefully several times while cooling. Let stand about 24 hours. Seal in sterilized jars.

Careadell Richter, Detroit Lakes, Mn.

TOMATO CONSERVE

5 c. tomatoes (after
   chopped)
4 c. sugar

1 c. chopped dates
2 oranges (grated rind of 1)
1 lemon, cut up and grated

Cook until thick. Put in hot jars and seal. Delicious.
M. Wills, Austin, Mn.

TOMATO JAM

Cook 15 minutes:
2 1/2 c. sugar

3 c. cooked tomato pulp

Add 1 (3 ounce) package lemon jello; cook 5 minutes more. Pour into jars and seal. Very good and different.
Maryann Skelton, Duluth, Mn.

RIPE TOMATO JAM

7 lb. ripe tomatoes
2 lemons, with peel

6 lb. sugar (2 1/4 c. equals 1 lb.)

Peel and cut up tomatoes. Slice lemons thin. Bake at 400° for 2 1/2 to 3 hours. Add sugar; bake 1/2 to 1 hour. Makes 7 pints.

Mrs. Neva Kost, Fairmont, Mn.

ZUCCHINI JAM

6 c. ground, raw zucchini, peeled
6 c. sugar
1/2 c. lemon juice

1 c. crushed pineapple with its juice
1 (6 oz.) pkg. orange gelatin

Boil ground zucchini until clear, about 6 minutes; drain. Add sugar, lemon juice and crushed pineapple with juice. Boil for 6 minutes. Remove from heat; add gelatin and stir until dissolved. Seal hot in jars; top with paraffin, if desired.

Emmy Thielman, Minneapolis, Mn.

Similar recipes submitted by: Elsa Ditty, St. Cloud, Mn., Marlys Swehla, Albert Lea, Mn.

LOW CALORIE
MICROWAVE

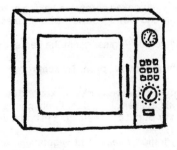

MICROWAVE HINTS

1. Place an open box of hardened brown sugar in the microwave oven with 1 cup hot water. Microwave at high for 1½ to 2 minutes for ½ pound or 2 to 3 minutes for 1 pound.
2. Soften hard ice cream by microwaving at 30% power. One pint will take 15 to 30 seconds; one quart, 30 to 45 seconds; and one-half gallon 45 seconds to one minute.
3. One stick of butter or margarine will soften in 1 minute when microwaved at 20% power.
4. Soften one 8-ounce package of cream cheese by microwaving at 30% power for 2 to 2½ minutes. One 3-ounce package of cream cheese will soften in 1½ to 2 minutes.
5. Thaw frozen orange juice right in the container. Remove the top metal lid. Place the opened container in the microwave and heat on high power 30 seconds for 6 ounces and 45 seconds for 12 ounces.
6. Thaw whipped topping...a 4½ ounce carton will thaw in 1 minute on the defrost setting. Whipped topping should be slightly firm in the center but it will blend well when stirred. Do not overthaw!
7. Soften jello that has set up too hard—perhaps you were to chill it until slightly thickened and forgot it. Heat on a low power setting for a very short time.
8. Dissolve gelatin in the microwave. Measure liquid in a measuring cup, add jello and heat. There will be less stirring to dissolve the gelatin.
9. Heat hot packs in a microwave oven. A wet finger tip towel will take about 25 seconds. It depends on the temperature of the water used to wet the towel.
10. To scald milk, cook 1 cup milk for 2 - 2½ minutes, stirring once each minute.
11. To make dry bread crumbs, cut 6 slices bread into ½-inch cubes. Microwave in 3-quart casserole 6-7 minutes, or until dry, stirring after 3 minutes. Crush in blender.
12. Refresh stale potato chips, crackers or other snacks of such type by putting a plateful in the microwave oven for about 30-45 seconds. Let stand for 1 minute to crisp. Cereals can also be crisped.
13. Melt almond bark for candy or dipping pretzels. One pound will take about 2 minutes, stirring twice. If it hardens while dipping candy, microwave for a few seconds longer.
14. Nuts will be easier to shell if you place 2 cups of nuts in a 1-quart casserole with 1 cup of water. Cook for 4 to 5 minutes and the nut meats will slip out whole after cracking the shell.
15. When thawing hamburger meat, the outside will many times begin cooking before the meat is completely thawed. Defrost for 3 minutes, then remove the outside portions that have defrosted. Continue defrosting the hamburger, taking off the defrosted outside portions at short intervals.
16. To drain the fat from hamburger while it is cooking in the microwave oven (one pound cooks in 5 minutes on high), cook it in a plastic colander placed inside a casserole dish.
17. Cubed meat and chopped vegetables will cook more evenly if cut uniformly.
18. When baking large cakes, brownies, or moist bars, place a juice glass in the center of the baking dish to prevent a soggy middle and ensure uniform baking throughout.
19. Since cakes and quick breads rise higher in a microwave oven, fill pans just half full of batter.
20. For stamp collectors: place a few drops of water on stamp to be removed from envelope. Heat in the microwave for 20 seconds and the stamp will come right off.
21. Using a round dish instead of a square one eliminates overcooked corners in baking cakes.
22. When preparing chicken in a dish, place meaty pieces around the edges and the boney pieces in the center of the dish.
23. Shaping meatloaf into a ring eliminates undercooked center. A glass set in the center of a dish can serve as the mold.
24. Treat fresh meat cuts for 15 to 20 seconds on high in the microwave oven. This cuts down on meat-spoiling types of bacteria.
25. A crusty coating of chopped walnuts surrounding many microwave-cooked cakes and quick breads enhances the looks and eating quality. Sprinkle a layer of medium finely chopped walnuts evenly onto the bottom and sides of a ring pan or Bundt cake pan. Pour in batter and microwave as recipe directs.
26. Do not salt foods on the surface as it causes dehydration (meats and vegetables) and toughens the food. Salt the meat after you remove it from the oven unless the recipe calls for using salt in the mixture.
27. Heat left-over custard and use it as frosting for a cake.
28. Melt marshmallow creme in the microwave oven. Half of a 7-ounce jar will melt in 35-40 seconds on high. Stir to blend.
29. Toast coconut in the microwave. Watch closely as it browns quickly once it begins to brown. Spread ½ cup coconut in a pie plate and cook for 3-4 minutes, stirring every 30 seconds after 2 minutes.
30. Place a cake dish up on another dish or on a roasting rack if you have difficulty getting the bottom of the cake done. This also works for potatoes and other foods that don't quite get done on the bottom.

BEEF VEGETABLE LOAF

1 lb. lean ground round
3 medium carrots, shredded
1 egg
1/2 tsp. basil

1 c. (8 oz.) cream style
  cottage cheese
1 small onion, chopped
1 tsp. salt
1/4 tsp. pepper

Mix all ingredients lightly in a bowl; shape into a loaf in the middle of an ungreased shallow baking pan. Bake in moderate oven, 350°, for 50 minutes or until firm and lightly browned on top. Makes 12 slices; 171 calories each.

Diane Haan, Bismarck, N.D.

CANTONESE BURGERS IN RED SAUCE

1 1/2 lb. ground lean beef
  round
1 (1 lb.) can bean sprouts,
  drained
2 Tbsp. instant minced onion
2 Tbsp. finely chopped
  pepper

1/4 tsp. ground ginger
1/4 c. catsup
1/4 c. dry sherry
1/4 c. soy sauce
1 1/2 c. water
2 Tbsp. cornstarch

Lightly combine ground beef with 1 cup bean sprouts, onion and ginger; shape into 12 patties. Broil first until brown on both sides. Combine catsup, sherry, soy sauce, water and cornstarch in saucepan; cook over medium heat, until sauce thickens and bubbles. Add burgers to sauce; heat sauce to boiling and lower heat. Cover; simmer for 10 minutes. Add green pepper; simmer 10 minutes longer. Skim fat from sauce, if necessary. Heat the remaining bean sprouts; arrange burgers over bean sprouts. Serve with the sauce. Combine all into one dish. One-half cup serving of instant rice adds 92 calories per serving. Per serving, 231 calories.

Diane Haan, Bismarck, N.D.

SAN FRANCISCO BARBEQUED CHICKEN
(No salt or fat is added.)

Cut up 2 chickens; remove all skin. Sprinkle with paprika. Put on baking sheet and brown in oven 1 hour at 350°. While browning, put together Barbeque Sauce.

Barbeque Sauce:

1 jar prepared sauce (Uncle Ken's or similar)
1/3 c. brown sugar
1/2 c. ketchup
2 tsp. Worcestershire sauce
1/2 lemon or 1/4 c. lemon juice
1/4 green pepper, chopped
1/2 onion, chopped
Garlic powder
1/4 tsp. pepper

Put browned chicken in large casserole. Cover with sauce; cover with foil. Bake 1 hour at 325°. Very tender and juicy. Salt lovers may add their own salt.

Jean Schwartz, Owatonna, Mn.

NO NOODLE LASAGNE

1 lb. lean ground beef
1 (15 oz.) can tomato sauce
1 1/2 tsp. garlic salt
1 tsp. basil
1 tsp. oregano leaves
1 (12 oz.) ctn. (1 1/2 c.) dry cottage cheese
1/4 c. grated Romano cheese
1 egg
1 1/2 lb. zucchini, cut lengthwise into 1/4 inch slices
2 Tbsp. flour
1 (4 oz.) pkg. shredded Mozzarella cheese
1/4 c. grated Romano cheese

Heat oven to 350°. Cook and stir meat in large skillet until brown; drain off fat. Stir in tomato sauce, garlic salt, basil and oregano leaves; heat to boiling. Reduce heat and simmer, uncovered, until mixture is consistency of spaghetti sauce, about 10 minutes. Use baking pan, 9x9x2 inches, with nonstick finish or coat regular baking pan with vegetable spray-on for cookware. Mix cottage cheese, 1/4 cup Romano cheese and the egg. Layer 1/2 each of zucchini, flour, cottage cheese mixture, meat sauce and Mozzarella cheese; repeat. Sprinkle 1/4 cup Romano cheese on top. Bake, uncovered, 45 minutes; let stand 20 minutes before serving. Makes 9 servings; 240 calories each. If you are on a low calorie food plan, this is an excellent meal in itself. Take it from one who has eaten a lot of this.

Laura Donahue, Arden Hills, Mn.

666

SHRIMP OVER RICE
(Low Calorie)

2 cans shrimp or 1 pkg. frozen
2 c. celery, sliced
1 can water chestnuts, sliced and drained
2 cans of bouillon

1 Tbsp. cornstarch and 2 Tbsp. water, mixed into a paste
1 Tbsp. Worcestershire sauce
1 tsp. soy sauce
White or long grain rice

Saute celery; add bouillon, soy sauce, Worcestershire sauce and cook until tender. Add flour paste, mushrooms, water chestnuts; cook until mixture thickens. Add shrimp and heat. Serve over desired rice. Serves 3-4.

Lynn Cooch, Minneapolis, Mn.

CASSEROLE SAUCE MIX: LOW CALORIE

Combine:
2 c. instant non-fat dry milk crystals
3/4 c. cornstarch
1/4 c. instant chicken bouillon granules

2 Tbsp. dried onion flakes
1/4 tsp. pepper
1 tsp. dried basil, crushed (optional)
1 tsp. thyme, crushed (optional)

Mix well and store in an airtight container. To substitute for one 10 1/2 ounce can of creamed soup use 1/3 cup sauce mix and 1 1/4 cups water. Combine in a saucepan; cook and stir till thickened. If desired, add 1 teaspoon margarine. This recipe makes the equivalent of nine 10 1/2 ounce cans of creamed soup. This recipe will also cut your caloric intake by 235 calories. Canned soup will add 330 calories to your dish and this mix will add only 95.

Audrey Glidden, Bloomington, Mn.

HERB BLEND FOR MEATS AND VEGETABLES

1 tsp. dried basil
1 tsp. thyme
1 tsp. dried parsley
1 tsp. ground cloves
1 tsp. black pepper
1/4 tsp. cayenne pepper

1 tsp. marjoram
1 tsp. oregano
1 tsp. summer savory
1 tsp. mace
1/4 tsp. ground nutmeg

Place all ingredients in tightly covered jar; store in a cool place up to 6 months. Makes about 1/4 cup. May be used for salads, meats, vegetables or any other uses one has for spices and herbs. No calories and no sodium.

Lorraine H. Follrath, Anoka, Mn.

CRANBERRY SALAD

4 c. fresh cranberries
2 c. boiling water
1 tsp. sweetener
Juice of 1 orange
3 Tbsp. unflavored gelatin

1/2 c. cold water
1 apple
1 c. finely sliced celery
1 c. chopped walnuts

Cook cranberries in boiling water about 10 minutes; put through sieve. Stir in sweetener and orange juice. Soften gelatin in cold water. Add to hot cranberries; stir until dissolved. Chill until slightly thickened. Dice unpeeled apple; combine with celery and nuts. Fold into gelatin mixture. Pour into 5 cup mold. Chill until set.

Mankato, Mn.

FROZEN FRUIT SALAD

Dissolve 2 cups sugar and 2 cups water. Add 2 cans frozen orange juice, not thawed. Add 1 (No. 2) can crushed pineapple and juice, 2 (No. 2) cans apricots, cut up, and juice, 6 mashed bananas and 2 tablespoons lemon juice; mix all together. Line muffin tins with paper cups; fill. Freeze; take out 20 minutes before serving. Makes about 40.

Mary R. Jones, Spirit Lake, Ia.

LO-CAL LIME GELATIN SALAD

2 packets dietetic lime
  gelatin
1 c. hot water
1 c. cold water (use juice of
  pineapple, plus water to
  make 1 c.)
1 Tbsp. lemon juice
1 (3 oz.) pkg. cream cheese

1 small can water packed
  crushed pineapple, well
  drained
1 small can evaporated milk,
  chilled
1/2 c. chopped celery
1/2 c. chopped nuts, if
  desired

Dissolve lime gelatin in hot water; add juice of

pineapple, water and lemon juice. Chill, till it just starts to set. Whip evaporated milk, till the consistency of whipped cream; beat in cream cheese thoroughly. Fold cheese mixture into gelatin mixture along with pineapple, nuts and celery gently, but thoroughly. Chill till firm. May be molded, if desired.

Mankato, Mn.

SUPER SALAD - LOW CALORIE

Use amounts desired of:

Cut up cauliflower	Fresh cherry tomatoes
Cut up broccoli	(leave whole)
Cut up radishes	Fresh mushrooms
Cut up celery	Olives (stuffed green)
Cut up green pepper	Olives (black, pitted)

Marinate overnight in 1 bottle Wish-Bone salad dressing (light Italian). Will keep for a long time in refrigerator.

Marilyn Radakovich, Duluth, Mn.

LOW-CALORIE SOUP

1 (48 oz.) can tomato or V-8 juice	2 c. water (add another cup of water if you wish)
1/2 head cabbage, chopped	6 chicken or beef bouillon cubes
3 medium onions, chopped	
3 or 4 stalks celery, chopped	1 bay leaf (take out after soup cooks)
	Salt and pepper

Simmer 2 hours; freezes well. (Thirty calories per cup unless you add beef or chicken. Add the meat after the soup has cooked.)

Optional: Carrots, beef, chicken.

Dode Desch, St. Paul, Mn.

LOW-CAL VEGETABLE SOUP

1 large onion	3 or 4 stalks of celery
1/2 head cabbage	6 bouillon cubes
1 (46 oz.) can tomato juice	Salt and pepper to taste
3 c. water	1 bay leaf
3 or 4 carrots	

1507-82

Chop vegetables and combine all ingredients; simmer 1 hour. About 30 calories per cup.

Elynor Pederson, Minneapolis, Mn.

CRISP PICKLE CHIPS

15 medium cucumbers	2 1/2 c. granulated sugar
4 large white onions	substitute or 5 Tbsp.
1 large sweet pepper	liquid sweetener
1/4 c. salt	1 Tbsp. mustard seed
2 1/2 c. cider vinegar	1/4 tsp. whole cloves

Slice cucumbers thin. Chop onions and pepper; combine with cucumbers and salt in a large bowl. Let stand at least 3 hours; drain. Combine sweetener, vinegar and spices in large kettle; bring to a boil. Add drained vegetables and heat thoroughly, but do not boil. Pack in clean, hot jars; seal at once. Yield: 7 pints.

Mankato, Mn.

SACCHARINE PICKLES

Brine:

1 gal. weak vinegar	Piece of alum size of hickory
1 c. coarse salt	nut
1/2 c. ground mustard	1 tsp. liquid sweetener

Wash small pickles. Drop into the brine; set in cool place. Ready to eat after 1 week.

Mankato, Mn.

CAKE

2 c. sifted flour	4 drops yellow food coloring
3 tsp. baking powder	2 egg whites
1/4 tsp. salt	1 (8 oz.) jar orange
1/3 c. soft butter	marmalade for frosting
3/4 c. skim milk	(any other type jello or
4 tsp. liquid sweetener	jam can also be used)

Sift dry ingredients in bowl; add butter at low speed of mixer. Beat 3 to 5 minutes. Combine milk, sweetener and food coloring. Add all but 1/4 cup liquid; beat 1/2 minute. Add remaining liquid; beat 1 minute. Add unbeaten egg whites; beat 1 minute. Bake in 8 inch pan at 375° for 20 minutes. Frost with marmalade or jam.

Mankato, Mn.

MOCK CHEESE CAKE
(Low Calorie)

1 angel food cake, prepared
1 large container Cool Whip

1 can cherry pie filling or
thawed strawberries

Combine in a large bowl the Cool Whip and small pieces of cake; stir and pack in a jello ring. Seal; freeze overnight. Unmold; top with fruit (cherries or strawberries).
Mary Jones, Spirit Lake, Ia.

LOW CALORIE LEMON CAKE TOP PUDDING

3 Tbsp. flour
1/4 tsp. salt
1/8 tsp. nutmeg or mace
2 Tbsp. softened butter or
margarine
1/3 c. sugar

3 eggs, separated
1/2 tsp. finely grated lemon
peel
1/4 c. fresh lemon juice
1 1/4 c. water

Sift flour, salt and nutmeg together; set aside. Mix butter and sugar, beating until light and fluffy. Add egg yolks one at a time, beating well after each addition. Fold in flour mixture, blending well. Add grated lemon peel, juice and water, mixing well. Beat egg whites until they hold in stiff peaks; fold lightly into lemon mixture. Spoon into custard cups, filling each 3/4 full. Place in shallow pan containing 1 inch hot water. Bake at 350° for 30 to 35 minutes or until tops are firm. Makes 6 servings.
Mankato, Mn.

PINEAPPLE SAUCE

1/4 c. water packed
pineapple
1/4 c. water

6 drops liquid sweetener, or
sweeten to taste
1 tsp. cornstarch

Place pineapple and water in pan; stir in sweetener and cornstarch. Cook over medium heat, stirring constantly until thick. Place over simmering water and cook 10 minutes more. Chill. Serve over cake.
Mankato, Mn.

LOW CALORIE ALMOND MERINGUE DROPS

3 egg whites
1/4 tsp. cream of tartar

32 drops of liquid sweetener
3 c. popped rice cereal

Beat egg whites, cream of tartar and sweetener until meringue forms peaks. Fold in cereal and 1/4 cup blanched, chopped almonds. Drop by rounded spoonfuls onto lightly greased cookie sheets. Bake at 350° for 15 minutes.

Mankato, Mn.

LOW CALORIE APPLESAUCE COOKIES

1 3/4 c. cake flour
1/2 tsp. salt
1 tsp. cinnamon
1/2 tsp. nutmeg
1/2 tsp. cloves
1 tsp. baking soda
1/2 c. butter or margarine

1 Tbsp. liquid sweetener or
    24 tablets, crushed
1 egg
1 c. water packed applesauce
1/3 c. raisins
1 c. All-Bran

Sift together the dry ingredients. Mix butter, sweetener and egg until light and fluffy. Add flour mixture and applesauce alternately, mixing well after each addition. Fold in raisins and All-Bran. Drop by level tablespoonfuls onto greased cookie sheet, about 1 inch apart. Bake at 375° for 20 minutes. Makes 4 dozen cookies; each contains 39 calories.

Mankato, Mn.

COCONUT MACAROONS

2 c. shredded coconut
2 Tbsp. cake flour
1/4 tsp. baking powder

2 egg whites
1/4 tsp. cream of tartar
4 tsp. liquid No-Cal
    sweetener

Combine coconut, flour and baking powder. Beat egg whites till foamy; add cream of tartar and sweetener. Beat till peaks form. Fold egg mixture into coconut mixture. Drop by teaspoon onto a lightly greased cookie sheet. Bake 12 to 15 minutes at 350° till golden brown. (31 calories each.)

Mankato, Mn.

LEMON BUTTER COOKIES
(Low Calorie)

1 c. sifted cake flour
1/2 tsp. baking powder
1/2 tsp. salt
1/4 c. margarine
12 drops sweetener

1 egg
1 Tbsp. lemon juice
1 tsp. grated lemon rind
1/2 tsp. vanilla
2 Tbsp. shredded coconut

Preheat oven to 400°. Measure 1 cup sifted cake flour and place in sifter. Add baking powder and salt; stir lightly, then sift twice. Cream butter in small bowl at high speed on electric mixer. Add sweetener, egg, lemon juice, lemon rind and vanilla; mix well until blended. Stir in coconut. Gradually stir sifted flour mixture into butter and egg mixture. Shape into roll about 2 inches in diameter. Wrap in waxed paper and chill; cut into 26 thin slices. Bake on ungreased cookie sheet for 10-12 minutes.

Mankato, Mn.

SUGARLESS COOKIES

Boil for 3 minutes, then cool:
3 Tbsp. shortening
2/3 c. water
3/4 c. raisins

1/4 tsp. nutmeg
1 tsp. cinnamon

Beat 1 egg and 1 teaspoon liquid sweetener. Dissolve 1/8 teaspoon soda in 1 tablespoon water; add to egg mixture, then add 1 cup flour, 1/8 teaspoon salt and 1/2 teaspoon baking powder. Drop by spoonful on greased cookie sheet. Bake for 15 minutes at 350°.

Mankato, Mn.

SUGARLESS DROP COOKIE

1/2 c. margarine
1 egg
2 Tbsp. condensed orange
  juice
4 tsp. liquid sweetener
1 Tbsp. orange rind

1/2 tsp. vanilla
1 1/4 c. flour
1/4 tsp. salt
1 tsp. baking powder
1/2 tsp. soda
1/2 c. buttermilk

Cream shortening. Beat egg, orange juice, sweetener, orange rind and vanilla together; add to shortening. Reserve 1 tablespoon flour. Sift flour, salt, baking powder and soda; add alternately with buttermilk. Mix 1 tablespoon flour with finely chopped nuts or a few chopped raisins. Drop by tablespoons on greased baking sheet; bake at 375° for 15 minutes.

Mankato, Mn.

LOW CALORIE APPLESAUCE PUDDING

1 c. milk
1 egg, slightly beaten
12 drops liquid sweetener
1/2 tsp. cinnamon

Few grains of salt
1 tsp. vanilla
2 c. water packed applesauce

Scald milk. Combine egg, sweetener, cinnamon and salt; add hot milk slowly, stirring constantly. Cook over hot water, stirring constantly. Cook until mixture coats a spoon. Remove from heat; add vanilla and chill. Fold custard and applesauce together; sprinkle with nutmeg. Serves 6.

Mankato, Mn.

LOW CALORIE CHOCOLATE PUDDING

3 Tbsp. cornstarch
Pinch of salt
3 Tbsp. cocoa

2 c. skim milk
1/4 tsp. Sweeta
1 tsp. vanilla

Combine cornstarch, salt and cocoa. Add milk gradually; stir until well blended. Cook and stir over medium heat until smooth and thick. Remove from heat; stir in Sweeta and vanilla. Serves 6.

Mankato, Mn.

CHOCOLATE CHIFFON DESSERT
(Dessert for Dieters - Chocolate Dish, 110 Calories)

To some dieters, the craving for chocolate becomes almost manic. Should this be your situation and you have taken to gnawing on the edge of the table in frustration, Chocolate Chiffon Dessert is a compromise. The dessert yields 8 servings at 110 calories per serving.

1 env. unflavored gelatin
1/2 c. sugar
1/8 tsp. salt

1/3 c. unsweetened cocoa
3 eggs, separated
1 1/2 c. skim milk
1 tsp. vanilla

Mix together gelatin, 1/4 cup sugar, salt and cocoa in saucepan. Beat together egg yolks and milk; stir into gelatin mixture. Place over low heat; stir constantly until gelatin dissolves and mixture thickens slightly, about 5 minutes. Remove from heat; stir in vanilla. Chill, stirring occasionally, until consistency of unbeaten egg white. Beat egg whites until stiff but not dry; gradually add remaining 1/4 cup sugar and beat until very stiff. Fold into chocolate mixture. Turn into 4 cup mold or individual molds. Chill until firm.

Margaret McKenney, Minneapolis, Mn.

BAKED CUSTARD

2 c. skim milk
2 eggs
12 drops sweetener

1 tsp. vanilla, nutmeg or
cinnamon

Preheat oven to 300°. Scald milk over hot water in double boiler. Beat eggs frothy. Add sweetener and vanilla; stir. Strain into lightly greased custard cups; sprinkle with nutmeg or cinnamon. Set cups in flat pan containing 1 inch of water. Bake about 1 hour.

Mankato, Mn.

STRAWBERRY DESSERT
(Low Calorie)

1 c. water
1/2 c. sugar
3 Tbsp. quick cooking
   tapioca
Dash of salt
1/2 c. non-fat dry milk

1/2 c. ice water
1 Tbsp. sugar
Dash of salt
2 Tbsp. lemon juice
1 1/2 c. strawberries

Combine first 4 ingredients in a pan; bring to a boil. Stir constantly; cool. Combine next 5 ingredients; beat until stiff peaks form. Fold in tapioca mixture and strawberries; chill. Garnish with sliced berries. Peaches or raspberries may be used.

Mankato, Mn.

ORANGE AND LEMON SNOW
(Low Calorie)

2 tsp. unflavored gelatin
5 Tbsp. cold water
1 c. unsweetened orange
  juice
1 tsp. lemon juice

12 drops liquid sweetener
1 egg white, beaten stiff with
  3 drops sweetener
4 graham crackers, crushed

Place gelatin and 5 tablespoons cold water in top of double boiler; let stand 5 minutes. Place over hot water; stir until gelatin is dissolved. Remove from heat; stir in orange juice, lemon juice and sweetener. Chill until it starts to thicken. Fold in the stiffly beaten egg white. Rinse four 1/2 cup molds; spoon in the mixture. Chill until firm. Unmold and coat well with crushed graham crackers. Serves 4; 64 calories per serving.

Mankato, Mn.

ORANGE STRAWBERRY SPONGE

2 Tbsp. unflavored gelatin
2 c. cold, fresh orange
  juice
2 Tbsp. lemon juice
1 tsp. vanilla

1/8 tsp. salt
1 c. fresh orange sections
2 c. sliced strawberries
1 egg white

Slice berries and orange sections for garnish. Soften gelatin in 1/2 cup orange juice; set in a pan of hot water to melt. Add to the remaining juice the vanilla and salt. Chill until the mixture is about as thick as unbeaten egg white. Fold in fruit. Beat egg white until it stands in soft peaks; beat in sugar. Fold into gelatin mixture, then fold into a 5 cup mold and chill until firm. Unmold onto a serving plate and garnish with fresh strawberries and orange sections.

Mankato, Mn.

TAPIOCA CREAM
(Low Calorie)

2 Tbsp. quick cooking
  tapioca
2 c. milk
6 drops sweetening
Pinch of salt

2 egg yolks
1 tsp. vanilla
2 egg whites, beaten stiff
  with 6 drops sweetener

676

Cook tapioca with milk in double boiler until well softened. Add sweetener and salt to egg yolks; beat lightly. Add hot tapioca and milk mixture slowly to egg yolks, stirring constantly. Return to double boiler; cook over simmering water, stirring frequently, until mixture is thick. Remove from heat; stir in vanilla. Fold in egg whites; chill. Makes 6 servings; 91 calories per serving.

Mankato, Mn.

LOW CALORIE LEMON SPONGE PIE

1 Tbsp. soft butter
Grated peel of 1 lemon
1/2 tsp. liquid sweetener
3 eggs, separated

2 Tbsp. flour
1 c. milk
5 Tbsp. lemon juice

Combine butter, lemon peel, sweetener, egg yolks, flour and milk; beat well. Stir in lemon juice. Beat egg whites stiff; fold in. Pour into 8 inch baked pie shell and bake at 375° for 30 minutes.

Mankato, Mn.

LOW-CAL PUMPKIN PIE

9 inch unbaked pastry
  shell
2/3 c. instant non-fat
  dry milk
1 1/4 c. water
3 eggs

1 (15 oz.) can pumpkin
3 1/2 tsp. liquid Sweet 10
1 1/4 tsp. cinnamon
1/2 tsp. salt
1/2 tsp. cloves
1/2 tsp. nutmeg

In mixing bowl, combine dry milk and water; add remaining ingredients. Beat well with rotary beater or electric mixer; pour into pie shell. Bake at 400° for 50 to 60 minutes or until knife inserted in center comes out clean; cool. One-eighth of pie equals 150 calories. One-sixth of pie equals 200 calories. One piece of pie also equals 2 fruit exchanges, 1 fat exchange and 1 meat exchange.

Liz Tuft, St. Paul, Mn.

PEACH CUSTARD PIE

Water packed or fresh
  peaches to fill 1 unbaked
  (10 inch) pie shell
1/3 c. grated coconut
4 eggs

1/2 tsp. salt
2 tsp. vanilla
1/2 tsp. sweetener
2 2/3 c. skim milk

Arrange sliced peaches in pie shell; scatter coconut over peaches. Combine eggs, salt, vanilla and sweetener; beat until blended. Stir in milk; mix well. Pour into pie shell. Bake at 425° for about 40 minutes or until filling puffs up; chill.

Mankato, Mn.

LOW CALORIE SPICY PUMPKIN PIE

1/4 tsp. mace
1/2 tsp. allspice
1 tsp. cinnamon
1/4 c. browned butter

1 (1 lb.) can pumpkin
1/2 tsp. Sweeta
1 c. skim milk
1 unbaked (9 inch) pie shell

Stir spices into pumpkin; mix well. Stir in Sweeta, milk and butter; pour into unbaked pie shell. Bake at 425° for 15 minutes. Lower heat to 350° and bake 45 minutes longer.

Mankato, Mn.

BACON APPETIZERS

6 slices bacon, cut into
  thirds

18 stuffed olives or
  maraschino cherries

Wrap bacon around olives and/or cherries; secure with a toothpick. Place on roasting rack or paper towel lined plate. Cook on High for 5 to 6 minutes, turning over halfway through.

Marge Johnson, Minneapolis, Mn.

BEEF JERKY

1 lb. beef round steak
1/8 tsp. pepper

1 1/2 tsp. salt
1 tsp. liquid smoke

Trim fat from meat; cut across grain into 1/8 inch strips, about 5 inches long. Layer 1/3 each of the meat, salt, pepper and liquid smoke in loaf pan, 9x5x3 inches; repeat 2 times. Refrigerate 8 hours. Arrange 1/3 of meat strips on microwave roasting rack in oblong baking dish. Cover with paper towel and microwave 7 minutes. *Turn strips. Cover and microwave until crisp, 2-3 minutes. Repeat with remaining meat. Makes 8-10 servings.

Note: If you don't have roasting rack, place strips on paper plates.

*At least 9 minutes per side with full bacon rack.

Diane Haan, Bismarck, N.D.

ALL-IN-ONE CASSEROLE

1 lb. ground beef
1 chopped onion
1 (16 oz.) can green beans, drained
1 (8 oz.) can tomato sauce

Salt and pepper
2 c. hot mashed potatoes
Parmesan cheese
Paprika

Brown ground beef and onion in 2 quart casserole for 5 to 7 minutes on High, stirring once; drain. Stir in green beans and tomato sauce. Season to taste with salt and pepper. Microwave on High for 5 minutes. Top with mashed potatoes; sprinkle with Parmesan cheese and paprika. Serves 4 to 6.

Marge Johnson, Minneapolis, Mn.

ALMOND CHICKEN

4 chicken breasts, skinned and boned (about 1 1/2 lb. after boning)
1/2 tsp. seasoned salt
1/2 tsp. pepper

4 slices bacon
1 (10 3/4 oz.) can condensed cream of chicken soup
1/4 c. dry sherry
1/4 c. sliced almonds, toasted

Wrap each chicken breast with a bacon slice; season. Arrange in baking dish; cover with wax paper. Cook on High (9) for 4 to 5 minutes. Combine soup and wine; pour over chicken. Continue to cook, uncovered, on High (9) for 4 to 5 minutes. Allow to stand 5 minutes; top with almonds before serving. Serves 4. Total cooking time: 10 minutes. Use 9 inch square glass baking dish.

Marge Johnson, Minneapolis, Mn.

HAPPY CHICKEN

2 whole chicken breasts, split and skinned (about 1 lb. each)
1 c. mayonnaise

2 tsp. prepared mustard
1 tsp. Worcestershire sauce
Paprika

Arrange chicken in flat casserole, bone side down and thicker areas to outside of dish. Cover with wax paper and microwave on High for 7 minutes; drain. Combine mayonnaise, mustard and Worcestershire sauce; spread over chicken. Recover; microwave on Medium High for 10 to 11 minutes or until chicken is tender. Let stand for 5 minutes; sprinkle with paprika. Makes 4 servings.

Marge Johnson, Minneapolis, Mn.

POLYNESIAN CHICKEN

2-3 lb. frying chicken, cut in serving size pieces
1 (6 oz.) can orange juice concentrate
1 Tbsp. cornstarch

1 Tbsp. lime juice
1 tsp. salt
1/4 tsp. cinnamon
1/2 c. sliced almonds
1/2 c. coconut, toasted

Arrange chicken in glass baking dish, skin side down with meatiest pieces toward outside. Cover with wax paper; cook on High (9) for 10 minutes; turn pieces over. Mix juice concentrate, cornstarch, lime juice, salt and cinnamon; pour over chicken. Continue to cook on High (9) for 10 to 12 minutes. Add almonds; cover with wax paper. Let stand 5 minutes before serving. Garnish with toasted coconut. Serves 4 to 6. Total cooking time: 22 minutes. Use 12 x 7 1/2 inch glass baking dish.

Marge Johnson, Minneapolis, Mn.

SEASONED CRUMB CHICKEN

1/4 c. butter or margarine
3/4 c. crushed rich round crackers (about 16 crackers)
1/2 c. grated Parmesan cheese

1 Tbsp. dried parsley flakes
1/2 tsp. garlic powder
1/8 tsp. pepper
2 1/2 - 3 lb. frying chicken, in pieces

Place butter in 2 quart (12x7 inch) glass baking dish. Microwave about 1 minute on Roast, until melted. Combine remaining ingredients, except chicken, in flat dish. Roll

680

chicken in butter, then in seasoned crumbs. Place chicken pieces, skin side up and thick pieces toward outside, in buttered baking dish; sprinkle with remaining crumbs. Microwave for 19 to 21 minutes on high, or until meat cut near bone is no longer pink. Let stand 5 minutes before serving. Makes 4 to 6 servings. (Takes a little longer on roast for 3 pound chicken.)

HERB SAUCED FISH

1/4 c. celery slices
1/4 c. chopped onion
3 Tbsp. margarine
3 Tbsp. flour
1/4 tsp. salt
Dash of pepper

1/4 tsp. tarragon leaves, crushed
1 1/4 c. milk
1 c. (4 oz.) shredded Casino brand natural Monterey Jack cheese
1 lb. fish fillets

Microcook vegetables and margarine in 2 quart casserole 4 to 5 minutes or until vegetables are tender, stirring after 2 minutes. Blend in flour and seasonings. Gradually add milk, stirring constantly. Cover; microcook 4 to 5 minutes or until sauce boils and thickens, stirring once each minute. Add cheese; stir until melted. Arrange fillets in 11 3/4 x 7 1/2 inch baking dish; top with cheese sauce. Cover; microcook 4 1/2 minutes, turning after 2 minutes. Let stand, covered, 2 to 3 minutes before serving or until fish flakes easily with fork. Makes 4 servings.
Variation: Add 1 tablespoon sherry to cheese sauce.

HAMBURG "NESTS"

2 Tbsp. butter or margarine
1/4 c. onion, chopped
1/2 green pepper, chopped
1 lb. ground beef
2 c. soft white bread crumbs
Salt and pepper

1 Tbsp. prepared mustard
Milk
Cereal crumbs (about 1/4 c.)
4 small eggs
1/4 c. shredded Swiss cheese

1. Preheat small browning skillet 2 1/2 minutes. Place butter, onion and green pepper in small browning skillet; cook in oven 1 minute. Stir once. Mix with beef, bread crumbs and seasonings. 2. Form meat mixture into four doughnut shaped rings, about 4 inches in diameter. Brush with a little milk; coat with cereal crumbs. Chill (rings will hold shape and be easier to handle if cold, but

this is optional). 3. Arrange meat nests in a greased shallow baking dish; cook in oven 2 minutes. Turn dish around 180°; cook 2 minutes more. 4. Break an egg into each "nest" (remember to pierce yolk); top with cheese. Cook in oven 3 to 4 minutes or to desired doneness for eggs. Let stand 2 to 3 minutes. 5. Serve with shredded lettuce and pickle garnish. Makes 4 servings.

SPECIAL HOT DOGS

1 lb. wieners
1/2 c. grated Cheddar
  cheese
1/3 c. crushed corn chips

2 Tbsp. minced onion
1 tsp. Worcestershire sauce
10 strips of bacon

Carefully slit wieners lengthwise, being careful not to cut in halves. In mixing bowl, combine cheese, corn chips, onion and Worcestershire sauce. Stuff each wiener with about 2 tablespoonfuls of the cheese mixture; wrap with a strip of bacon. Arrange wieners on a microwave roasting rack cut side up. Loosely cover with wax paper and microwave on Medium High for 7-9 minutes or until cheese has melted and bacon has browned. Serve plain or in heated buns.

Marge Johnson, Minneapolis, Mn.

PUFFY PEACH OMELET

2 peaches, peeled and
  sliced
2 Tbsp. honey
1/8 tsp. pumpkin pie spice
4 eggs, separated

1/4 c. water
1/2 tsp. sugar
1/4 tsp. salt
1/4 tsp. cream of tartar

1. In small microwaveable bowl, combine sliced peaches, honey and spice, stirring to coat peaches evenly. Microwave on High 1 to 2 minutes or until peaches are tender and mixture comes to a full boil. Cover with plastic wrap to retain heat; set aside. 2. In large mixing bowl, beat egg whites, water, sugar, salt and cream of tartar until stiff but not dry, just until whites no longer slip when bowl is tilted. 3. In small mixing bowl, beat egg yolks at high speed until thick and lemon colored, about 5 minutes. Gently, but thoroughly, fold yolks into whites. 4. Pour omelet mixture into lightly buttered 9 inch pie plate; gently smooth surface. Microwave on Defrost 8 minutes or until top of

omelet feels firm when lightly touched. Quickly, but carefully, turn out onto serving plate or platter. Spoon peaches and sauce over top of omelet. Cut in wedges and serve immediately. Makes 3 to 4 servings.

STUFFED PEPPER POT
(To be prepared on baking sheet.)

4 large green peppers	1 (8 oz.) can tomato sauce
1 lb. lean ground beef	2 Tbsp. chopped celery
1 small chopped onion	1 tsp. salt
2 c. cooked rice	Dash of pepper

Cut thin slice from stem end of pepper; remove seeds with teaspoon. Discard. In 1 1/2 quart glass casserole, combine onion and ground beef; place in microwave oven and cook 2-3 minutes on Full power or until onion becomes transparent and beef slightly browned. Add remaining ingredients, except peppers; mix well. Stuff peppers with mixture; place on baking sheet. Cover with plastic wrap; microwave 12-15 minutes on 2/3 power (Medium High).

For conventional oven: Combine onion and hamburger in skillet; brown lightly on stove top at medium high heat. Assemble as directed. Bake at 350° F. for 45 minutes. Serves 4.

Marge Johnson, Minneapolis, Mn.

MAKE AHEAD PIZZA

Keep pizza in your freezer for quick snacks and fast meals. It's easy and delicious when you use hot roll mix for the crust.

1 pkg. hot roll mix	Pizza toppings
1 (12 oz.) can pizza sauce	

Preheat oven to 425°. In large bowl, dissolve yeast in 1 cup warm water. Stir in hot roll mix. With greased fingers, pat out dough in greased 14 inch pizza pan or 15x10 inch jelly roll pan. Spread pizza sauce over dough; top with your favorite pizza toppings. Bake on bottom rack of oven at 425° for 20 to 30 minutes until edges are golden brown; cool. Cut into slices; wrap and freeze.

To defrost: Place pizza slices on napkin and microwave 1 to 1 1/2 minutes on High.

PORK STRATA

3/4 c. pork sausage
5 eggs, slightly beaten
1 1/2 c. milk
3/4 tsp. dry mustard

1/2 tsp. salt
2 slices white bread, cubed
3/4 c. grated cheese

1. Brown sausage; drain on paper towel. Mix eggs, milk, mustard and salt. Add bread, sausage and cheese. Pour mixture into 8 inch round baking dish. 2. Cover and refrigerate overnight. 3. Microwave, uncovered, at 80% power for 18 minutes or until eggs are almost set. Turn dish once. Let stand 10 minutes before serving. Makes 4 servings.

MICROWAVE SCAMPI

1 lb. raw shrimp
1/4 c. butter
1 clove garlic, minced
2 Tbsp. lemon juice

1/2 tsp. salt
1/8 tsp. pepper
1 Tbsp. minced parsley

Peel shrimp; split along the back curve, cutting deep to butterfly it. Press almost flat. Melt butter in 2 1/2 quart baking dish; pour in garlic and lemon juice. Add shrimp; coat with butter mixture. Cover; cook 1 minute. Uncover; stir it and cook another 2 minutes. Sprinkle with salt, pepper and parsley. Do not overcook.
Dee Olson, St. Paul, Mn.

SCOTCH EGGS

1 1/2 lb. bulk pork sausage
3 Tbsp. snipped parsley
1/2 tsp. rubbed sage
1/4 tsp. rosemary

1/2 tsp. crushed dried thyme
1/4 tsp. black pepper
12 hard cooked eggs, peeled

Combine sausage, parsley, sage, rosemary, thyme and pepper in mixing bowl. Shape mixture into 12 thin patties (about 4 to 5 inches in diameter). Wrap one pattie around each egg. Place eggs in 12x7 inch baking dish; cover with plastic wrap. Microwave on Medium High for 13 to 15 minutes. Drain and serve hot or cold.
Marge Johnson, Minneapolis, Mn.

SHEPHERD'S PIE
(Microwave)

1 lb. ground beef	1/2 tsp. salt
1 medium onion	1/4 tsp. basil
1 (10 oz.) pkg. frozen	1/8 tsp. pepper
green beans, thawed,	3 c. hot mashed potatoes
or mixed vegetables	(instant works great)
1 can tomato or cream soup	1 c. shredded Cheddar
1 tsp. Worcestershire sauce	cheese

Crumble ground beef into 2 quart casserole; add chopped onion. Microwave on High 4-6 minutes, until meat loses its pink color. Break up meat; drain. Stir in soup and seasoning. Sprinkle with vegetables. Spoon mounds of potatoes over; microwave on High 6 minutes. Top with cheese and microwave 2 more minutes until melted.

Linda Landsman, Bloomington, Mn.

SHRIMP IN GARLIC BUTTER
(For Microwave Oven)

1/4 c. butter or margarine	1 (12 oz.) pkg. frozen,
1/2 tsp. garlic powder	peeled, deveined quick
2 tsp. parsley flakes	cooking shrimp (makes
	1 1/2 - 2 c. shrimp)

Place butter in custard cup; microwave on High 30 to 45 seconds until melted. Stir in garlic powder and parsley flakes. Separate shrimp; place in a 9 or 10 inch diameter dish. Pour butter mixture evenly over shrimp; cover tightly. Microwave 5 to 8 minutes, until shrimp is opaque, stirring every 2 minutes. Let stand covered for 1 to 1 1/2 minutes to finish cooking.

Elaine L. Rolerat, East Grand Forks, Mn.

CHICKEN SPAGHETTI

2 Tbsp. butter or margarine	1/4 tsp. garlic powder
1 small onion, chopped	Salt and pepper to taste
3-4 c. cooked chicken, diced	1 c. grated Cheddar cheese
1 can cream of celery soup	1 (2 oz.) jar pimientos,
1 can cream of mushroom	drained
soup	Cooked spaghetti

Place butter and onion in a 7x12 inch casserole; microwave on High until onion is lightly browned, stirring twice.

Add chicken, soups, garlic powder, salt and pepper to taste. Microwave on Medium for 12 to 15 minutes while cooking spaghetti, stirring once. Stir in cheese and pimientos and serve over spaghetti. Makes 8 servings.

Marge Johnson, Minneapolis, Mn.

SPANISH RICE

1 lb. ground beef
1/2 c. chopped onion
1/4 c. chopped green pepper
1 1/2 tsp. salt
1/2 tsp. black pepper

1 (8 oz.) can tomato sauce
2 Tbsp. chili powder
2 c. water
1 c. long grain rice

In a 2 1/2 quart casserole, place ground beef, onion, green pepper, salt and pepper. Microwave on High for 5 to 7 minutes or until meat is browned, stirring twice. Drain off fat. Stir in tomato sauce, chili powder, water and rice; cover. Microwave on High for 4 to 5 minutes or until boiling. Stir; reduce heat to Medium. Cover and microwave for 15 to 20 minutes. Let stand, covered, for 10 minutes.

Marge Johnson, Minneapolis, Mn.

CRUNCHY TUNA CASSEROLE

1 c. (8 oz.) elbow macaroni
1 (10 oz.) can cream of
  mushroom soup
1/2 c. milk
1 Tbsp. lemon juice
1/2 tsp. Worcestershire
  sauce
1/2 tsp. salt

1/4 tsp. pepper
1 tsp. parsley
1 (6 1/2 oz.) can tuna,
  drained
1 (16 oz.) can cut green
  beans, drained
1 c. dry roasted peanuts
1 Tbsp. pimientos

Cook macaroni in boiling, salted water until tender; drain. Combine soup, milk, lemon juice, Worcestershire sauce, seasonings and macaroni; stir in tuna and green beans. Pour into 1 quart casserole. Top with peanuts and pimientos. Microwave on Medium High for 12-15 minutes. Let stand 5-10 minutes. Makes 4 servings.

Marge Johnson, Minneapolis, Mn.

SCRAMBLED EGGS

6 eggs   6 Tbsp. milk
2 Tbsp. margarine or butter

Melt margarine. Beat eggs and milk with fork; pour in casserole with melted margarine. Cook 2 minutes and 25 seconds, covered, stirring after 2/3 cooked. Stir again when cooked another minute and 25 seconds. Season to taste.

Mary Lempe, St. Cloud, Mn.

WAKE-UP SPECIAL

1 Tbsp. butter or margarine   1/2 (10 3/4 oz.) can
1/3 c. chopped green pepper   condensed cream of
6 eggs   chicken soup
6 slices cooked, crumbled   Salt and pepper
  bacon

1. Place butter in 2 quart casserole with green pepper; saute 30 seconds. 2. Stir eggs and soup together; blend into sauteed mixture. Cook 4 1/2 to 5 minutes on High or 9 to 10 minutes on Medium; stir every 2 minutes. 3. Crumble bacon on top. Season with salt and pepper to taste. Makes 3 servings.

Micro-Wave Tip: Mix remaining soup with 1/2 cup milk; heat 1 1/2 to 2 minutes. Use as sauce for eggs.

FRENCH ONION QUICHE

4 eggs   1/2 c. shredded Cheddar
1 (4 oz.) pkg. plain   cheese
  refrigerated fresh dough   1/2 env. onion soup mix
1/2 (7 oz.) can evaporated   1/4 c. grated Parmesan
  milk   cheese

1. Roll each square of refrigerated dough out to a 6 inch square; gently fit each square into a 9 ounce custard cup. Microwave at 1/2 power (or Medium setting) for 4-5 minutes; let dough cool. 2. Beat together eggs, evaporated milk, Cheddar cheese and soup mix. Pour 1/2 cup egg mixture into each dough lined custard cup. Sprinkle 1 tablespoon Parmesan cheese over top of each dish. Microwave at 80% power for 10-12 minutes or until knife inserted near center comes out clean. Turn or rotate dishes if

1507-82   687

necessary. 3. Remove from custard cups. Serve warm or chilled. Makes 4 servings.

QUICHE LORRAINE

9 inch unbaked pie shell, at room temperature
4 eggs
1 c. cream (half & half)

1 c. shredded Swiss cheese
6 slices bacon, cooked and crumbled
1/4 tsp. salt

1. Prick pastry lightly, but thoroughly, with fork. Microwave 4 minutes on High. 2. Sprinkle cooked bacon and cheese over bottom of baked shell. 3. In medium mixing bowl, beat eggs with fork or whisk; stir in cream and salt. 4. Microwave on High for 5 minutes, turning halfway through. Stir and cook for an additional 3 - 3 1/2 minutes on High. Let stand for 10 minutes before serving. Makes 4 servings.

CHEESE SAUCE

2 Tbsp. butter or margarine
2 Tbsp. flour
1/4 tsp. salt

Dash of white pepper
1 c. milk
1/2 c. grated Cheddar cheese

Place butter or margarine in 2 cup glass measure and microwave on High for 45 seconds. Stir in flour, salt and pepper; mix well. Add milk; stir. Microwave on High for 1 1/2 to 2 minutes or until thickened, stirring twice. Stir in cheese until melted and smooth.

Marge Johnson, Minneapolis, Mn.

SPICY BARBECUE SAUCE

1 Tbsp. lard or shortening (lard tastes better)
1 medium onion, coarsely chopped
2 cloves garlic, minced
3 (8 oz.) cans tomato sauce
3 Tbsp. brown sugar

3 Tbsp. Worcestershire sauce
2 Tbsp. honey
1 Tbsp. lemon juice
2 tsp. dry mustard
1 1/2 - 3 tsp. chili powder (more or less to taste)

Combine lard, onion and garlic in a microwave saucepan; cover with wax paper and micro 5 minutes on high, stirring once, or until onion is slightly soft. Add all other

688

ingredients; cover with wax paper and micro 8 to 9 minutes on high, stirring once, or until boiling. Use for either ribs or chicken.

For Ribs: Place 4 to 5 pounds country style pork ribs in a microwave 3 quart shallow casserole in two layers perpendicular at right angles to each other. Cover tightly with plastic wrap and micro 12 minutes on high, reversing and rearranging positions halfway through. Pour off any drippings; turn ribs fat side up and coat well with sauce. Sprinkle fat with Microshake if desired (powdered browning agent); cover with wax paper and micro 10 minutes on high, rearranging if necessary for even cooking.

For Chicken: Place a 3 pound fryer, cut into quarters, skin side down in a microwave 3 quart shallow casserole. Pour enough sauce over the chicken to coat well. Cover with wax paper and micro 12 minutes on high. Turn pieces over, rearranging if necessary for even cooking; baste with more sauce and sprinkle with Microshake (powdered browning agent) if desired. Recover and micro 10 to 12 minutes on high. Repeat with one or more chickens, if needed.

Note: To finish either the ribs or chicken on your grill, reduce microwaving by 3 minutes and quickly brown on a very hot grill.

ARTICHOKES

Clip off tips of leaves of artichokes and place 3 or 4 thin lemon slices between leaves to prevent browning and to accent the natural flavor. Place each artichoke in a custard cup; cover with plastic wrap. Microwave on High. Check for doneness at minimum time; if leaf is easily removed, artichoke is done. Serve with your favorite sauce.

Time: One takes 6-9 minutes; 2 take 9-13 minutes; 4 take 15-18 minutes.

Marge Johnson, Minneapolis, Mn.

QUICK BAKED BEANS

1 (16 oz.) can pork and beans
1/4 c. chopped onion
1 tsp. prepared mustard
1 tsp. Worcestershire sauce
3 Tbsp. molasses
1 Tbsp. brown sugar

Combine all ingredients in a 1 quart casserole. Top

with 2 slices cut up bacon. Cover and microwave at Medium High for 12 to 14 minutes; let stand 5 minutes. Makes 4 servings.

Marge Johnson, Minneapolis, Mn.

BROCCOLI AND RICE CASSEROLE

1 (10 oz.) pkg. frozen,
  chopped broccoli
2 c. cooked rice
1 small onion, chopped

1/4 c. margarine
1 small jar Cheez Whiz
1 can cream of mushroom
  soup

Cook broccoli in covered container on High for 8 to 9 minutes, stirring halfway through; drain. Melt margarine in 12x7 inch casserole for 1 to 2 minutes on High. Add onion; saute on High for 2 to 3 minutes. Stir in remaining ingredients. Microwave at High for 5 to 6 minutes; let stand 5 minutes. Makes 6 servings.

Marge Johnson, Minneapolis, Mn.

GRANDMA B'S CABBAGE CASSEROLE

4 c. chopped or shredded
  cabbage
1/4 c. water
1/4 c. chopped onion

1/2 c. butter or margarine
2 c. saltine cracker crumbs
2 beaten eggs
1/4 tsp. pepper

Place cabbage and water in 2 quart casserole. Cover and cook at High for 8 minutes. Place onion and margarine or butter in small dish; saute for 2 to 3 minutes at Medium High power. Stir onion, cracker crumbs, eggs and pepper into cabbage. Cover with wax paper; microwave at Medium High for 15 to 18 minutes or until set. Let stand 5 to 10 minutes. Makes 6 to 8 servings.

Marge Johnson, Minneapolis, Mn.

CINNAMON CARROTS

1 lb. carrots
3 Tbsp. butter or margarine

1 tsp. sugar
Cinnamon

Peel and grate carrots. Melt butter or margarine in a glass pie plate for 1 to 2 minutes on High; stir in sugar and carrots. Toss to coat with butter; arrange in a circle. Cover with plastic wrap; vent and cook for 5 to 6 minutes on High. Let stand 2 to 3 minutes; sprinkle with cinnamon. A delightful taste treat! Makes 4 servings.

690   Marge Johnson, Minneapolis, Mn.

MICROWAVED CORN ON THE COB

Soak 8 ears of corn (husks and silk intact) in salt water for 30 minutes to remove any unwanted insects. Drain and shake off excess water. Place on the floor of the microwave, tip to toe, and micro 16 to 20 minutes on high, depending on the size of each ear. Larger ears will take the longer time. When corn is just cool enough to handle, pull back husks, remove silk and spread with butter or desired spread. Replace husk; secure with a rubber band or piece of yarn and serve immediately.

Note: If corn has to be reheated, micro all ears at one time another 2 to 3 minutes of high.

Garlic-Cheese Spread: Combine 1/2 pound butter or margarine, whipped with 2 cloves of garlic, finely minced and 1/2 cup grated Parmesan or Romano cheese.

Green Chili Spread: Combine 1/2 pound butter or margarine, whipped with 1 (4 ounce) can chopped green chilies, 1/2 teaspoon ground cumin seed and 1 tablespoon (or more to taste) chili powder.

Herb Spread: Combine 1/2 pound butter or margarine, whipped, with 4 tablespoons each fresh chives and parsley, minced, and 1 teaspoon dried tarragon leaves.

ONIONS PARMESAN

2 Tbsp. butter or*	1 Tbsp. flour
2 large (1/2 lb.) yellow onions	1/2 tsp. salt
	1/8 tsp. pepper
2 strips bacon, cooked and crumbled	1/4 tsp. seasoned salt
	1/2 c. light cream
1/4 c. Parmesan cheese	Paprika

Slice onions into 1/4 inch slices. In 1 quart casserole, melt butter. Place 1/2 of onions in casserole; top with 1/2 of cheese and bacon. Add rest of onions and cheese. Mix flour, salt, pepper, seasoned salt and cream until smooth; pour over onions. Cook, covered, 8-10 minutes. Dust with paprika.

*If desired, fry bacon in casserole dish; use 2 tablespoons drippings instead of butter in recipe. This can be doubled for family size servings.

FRESH PEAS

2 c. peas, shelled 2 Tbsp. water
1 qt. casserole, covered

    Cook 7-8 minutes; stir once. Season to taste.
                  Mary Lempe, St. Cloud, Mn.

POLYNESIAN PINEAPPLE PORK

1 lb. cubed fresh pork
1 medium onion, sliced,
  separated into rings
1-2 fresh pineapples
2 c. fresh broccoli flowerets
1 c. sliced almonds
1 (2 oz.) jar sliced pimento

2 Tbsp. cornstarch
2 Tbsp. packed brown sugar
1 tsp. salt
1 tsp. ginger
2 Tbsp. soy sauce
2 Tbsp. dry sherry or water

    Microwave pork and onion in 3 quart casserole, cov-
ered, on Roast for 20 minutes. Meanwhile, cut pineapple in
half, keeping leaves intact and cutting through them.
Loosen and remove pineapple from shells; core and cut into
chunks. Measure 2 cups of chunks. Stir pineapple chunks,
broccoli, almonds and pimento into pork mixture. Combine
remaining ingredients in small bowl until smooth; pour over
pork mixture. Cover; microwave about 15 minutes on Roast
or until meat is fork tender. Let stand, covered, 5 minutes.
Divide between pineapple halves and serve. Makes 4-5
servings.

CHEESY POTATO BAKE

1 (10 3/4 oz.) can
  Cheddar cheese soup
1/2 c. milk

5 c. potatoes, sliced
1 c. onion, diced
Paprika

    Mix together soup and milk. Place half of potatoes in a
2 quart casserole. Top with half of onion and half of soup
mixture; repeat process. Sprinkle with paprika, as desired.
Microwave, covered, at 80% power for 20 to 25 minutes, or
until tender. Serves 6 to 8.
    Note: No short cuts; must mix as directed.
                  Marlene Barton, Grand Forks, N.D.

MASHED POTATOES

When your family eats in shifts, you can still serve piping hot mashed potatoes. Here's the way to make a single serving right in a serving dish. Great for babies and toddlers, too.

To make one 2/3 cup serving:

1/2 c. water	1/8 tsp. salt
2 Tbsp. milk	1/2 c. potato flakes
2 tsp. butter or margarine	

Microwave first 4 ingredients in small serving bowl 1 1/2 to 2 minutes. Stir in potato flakes.

QUICK SCALLOPED POTATOES

4 large baking potatoes, peeled, thinly sliced	1 1/2 c. milk
2 Tbsp. flour	Salt and pepper
2 Tbsp. milk	Butter

Place potatoes into a buttered 12x7 inch casserole. Mix together flour and 2 tablespoons milk to form a paste. Stir paste into remaining milk. Pour over potatoes; season with salt and pepper and dot with butter. Cover with wax paper and microwave on High for 12 to 14 minutes. Let stand 8 to 10 minutes before serving. Makes 6 servings.

Note: To add extra flavor, sprinkle 1/2 - 1 cup grated cheese over potatoes after removing from oven. Cheese will melt during the standing time without becoming stringy.

Marge Johnson, Minneapolis, Mn.

SWEET POTATO SPECIAL

4 medium sweet potatoes	1/3 c. honey
1/4 c. margarine	1 tsp. vanilla
2 eggs, slightly beaten	1/8 tsp. salt
1 (6 oz.) can coconut	

Topping:

1/2 c. flour	6 Tbsp. margarine
1/2 c. brown sugar	1/2 c. nuts

Bake sweet potatoes for 8 to 10 minutes on High; let

1507-82

stand for 5 minutes. Peel and mash in a 1 1/2 quart casserole. Stir in remaining ingredients; mix well. Prepare topping by cutting sugar and flour into margarine until crumbly. Add nuts; sprinkle over potato mixture. Microwave at High for 6 to 8 minutes; let stand for 5 minutes. Serves 8.

Marge Johnson, Minneapolis, Mn.

HERBED VEGETABLE RING

1 c. grated carrots
1 c. grated zucchini
3 Tbsp. butter or margarine

Dill weed or fines herbs
seasoning

Place butter and seasoning in pie plate; microwave on High for 1 to 2 minutes. Stir in vegetables; arrange in a circle. Cover with plastic wrap; vent and microwave on High for 4 to 5 minutes. Let stand 5 minutes. Makes 4 servings. Allow 6 to 7 minutes per pound on High when microwaving fresh, cut up vegetables. When vegetables are grated, allow 4 to 5 minutes per pound.

Marge Johnson, Minneapolis, Mn.

RATATOUILLE PYRENEES

2 medium zucchini, sliced
1 medium eggplant, peeled,
   cubed
1 medium onion, sliced

1 green pepper, cut in strips
3/4 c. French dressing
1 pt. cherry tomatoes, halved

Combine ingredients, except tomatoes, in 3 quart casserole; mix lightly. Cover; microcook 12 to 14 minutes or until vegetables are crisp-tender, stirring after 5 minutes. Add tomatoes. Cover; microcook 2 or 3 minutes or until hot. Serve hot or cold. Makes 10 to 12 servings. Ratatouille will keep in the refrigerator, covered, for several days and is delicious served cold.

BISCUIT RING

1/3 c. margarine
1/2 c. brown sugar
3 Tbsp. corn syrup (dark
   or light)

1/4 c. nuts, coconut, raisins,
   cherries or crushed pineapple (select 1-3 items)
1 can refrigerated biscuits

Melt margarine in pie plate on High for about 1 minute.

Stir in remaining ingredients, except for biscuits. Arrange biscuits in a circle on top of mixture. Microwave on Medium for 6-7 minutes or until biscuits appear dry on the surface. Let stand for 5 minutes on a flat surface; invert on a serving plate.

Marge Johnson, Minneapolis, Mn.

WHITE BREAD
(Basic Recipe)

Here's an easy yeast bread recipe that takes a minimum of kneading, plus variations for whole wheat bread and cinnamon rolls. Bake it in your conventional oven and freeze it when you are in a baking mood, then look forward to freshly baked bread thawed in just 4 to 5 minutes in the microwave.

2 1/2 c. unbleached or   1/4 c. sugar
   all-purpose flour*   1 Tbsp. salt
2 pkg. active dry yeast

Lightly spoon flour into measuring cup; level off. Combine in large mixer bowl; blend.

1 c. water   1/4 c. cooking oil
1 c. milk

Heat in saucepan over low heat until very warm, 120°-130° F. Add 2 eggs and warm liquid to flour mixture. Blend at low speed until moistened; beat 3 minutes at medium speed. With spoon, stir in an additional 3 to 3 1/2 cups flour to form a sticky dough. In bowl or on board, gradually add 1/2 to 1 1/2 cups more flour, kneading or working with hands until dough is smooth, pliable and no longer sticky, about 5 minutes. Place dough in greased bowl; cover. Let rise in warm place until light and doubled in size, about 45 minutes. Punch fist into dough several times to remove all air bubbles; divide in 2 parts. Form dough into 2 loaves; place in greased bread pans. Cover; let rise in warm place until light and doubled in size, about 30 minutes. Bake at 375° for 35 to 45 minutes or until loaf sounds hollow when lightly tapped. Immediately remove from pan; cool.

*If using self-rising flour, omit salt.

WHOLE WHEAT BREAD

Follow White Bread basic recipe. After beating with the mixer, stir in 3 cups whole wheat flour instead of white flour. Knead in 3/4 to 1 1/4 cups white flour. To defrost: Place frozen loaves on a paper towel and microwave 4 to 5 minutes on High.

QUICK BREADS

Darker colored bread mixes, such as banana, oatmeal raisin and applesauce spice make the most attractive finished products because the microwave does not brown. Placing the loaf pan on top of an inverted glass pie pan helps insure even baking.

Lightly grease bottom only of 9x5 or 8x4 inch glass loaf pan. Prepare batter according to package directions. To microwave: Place loaf pan on top of an inverted glass pie pan and bake as directed, rotating pan 1/4 turn every 2 minutes during baking.

	8x4 inch pan	9x5 inch pan
Banana	low: 7 1/2 minutes high: 2-3 minutes high only: 6 - 6 1/2 minutes	low: 10 minutes high: 2 1/2 - 3 minutes high only: 7 - 7 1/2 minutes
Oatmeal Raisin	low: 8 minutes high: 2-3 minutes	low: 10 minutes high: 2 1/2 - 3 minutes
Applesauce Spice	high only: 6-7 minutes	high only: 6 1/2 - 7 1/2 minutes

Cool on flat surface 15 minutes; remove from pan. Cool completely before slicing.

Muffins: Freeze extra muffins, baked conventionally, for hot muffins in seconds. To defrost muffins: One muffin, 15 seconds; 2 muffins, 30 seconds; 3 muffins, 45 seconds; 4 muffins, 1 minute; 5 muffins, 1 minute 15 seconds; 6 muffins, 1 minute 30 seconds.

CRUNCHY COFFEECAKE

1/2 c. crunchy peanut butter
1/2 c. brown sugar
1 can refrigerated biscuits

Mix peanut butter and brown sugar in a small dish; microwave on High for 1 minute. Spread about 1 tablespoon of mixture on top of each biscuit; arrange biscuits in a ring in a lightly buttered pie plate. Cover with waxed paper and microwave on Medium for 5-7 minutes. Let stand 3-4 minutes. Great with a glass of milk or a cup of coffee!

Marge Johnson, Minneapolis, Mn.

PUMPKIN MUFFINS

1 1/2 c. flour
1/2 c. sugar
2 tsp. baking powder
3/4 tsp. cinnamon
3/4 tsp. salt
1 egg, slightly beaten
1 c. canned pumpkin
1/3 c. squeeze margarine
1/4 c. milk
1/2 c. raisins

Combine dry ingredients. Add remaining ingredients; mix well. Line plastic muffin tray or custard cups with paper liners. Spoon batter into 6 cups, filling each cup 1/2 full. Microcook 3 to 5 minutes or until tops are set, turning once each minute. Remove muffins from tray or cups immediately. Cool on wire rack. Repeat with remaining batter. Makes approximately 1 dozen.

CINNAMON STREUSEL SWIRL

Cinnamon Streusel Swirl is an excellent cake for the microwave, with the topping included in the package adding an attractive crust. Plan Ahead Tip: Serve one cake square warm for dessert or for brunch. Freeze the other for spur-of-the-moment entertaining.

Prepare batter according to package directions. Use two 8 inch glass pans. Pour 1 1/2 cups batter in each pan. Sprinkle 1/4 of packet 2 (about 1/4 cup) over each layer. Spread 1 1/2 cups batter over filling; top each layer with remainder of packet 2. Wrap one layer with plastic wrap · freeze remaining batter up to 3 weeks. Microwave other layer as directed below, rotating pan 1/2 turn after 4 minutes.

To microwave: Place cake pan directly on floor of oven. Low: 4 1/2 minutes; high: 4-5 minutes;

high only: 4 1/2 to 5 1/2 minutes. To defrost: Microwave, covered with plastic wrap, for 5 minutes on Low, rotating 1/2 turn every minute. Remove plastic wrap and microwave 5 to 6 minutes on High. Cool on flat surface; glaze.

Note: Leftover glaze may be stored tightly covered in refrigerator until frozen layer is used.

APPLESAUCE CAKE

1/2 c. finely chopped nuts	2 c. applesauce
1 (18 oz.) pkg. yellow	2 eggs
cake mix	1 tsp. cinnamon

Grease a microwave plastic or glass tube pan and sprinkle bottom with nuts. Mix together remaining ingredients; pour into pan. Microwave on Medium for 12-15 minutes until cake tests done, rotating pan 2-3 times. Let stand on flat surface for 8-10 minutes before removing from pan. Makes 10-12 servings.

Marge Johnson, Minneapolis, Mn.

CARROT CAKE

1 pkg. yellow cake mix	1/3 c. firmly packed brown
3 eggs	sugar
1/3 c. oil	2 c. shredded carrots
1/2 c. water	1/2 c. raisins
2 tsp. cinnamon	1/2 c. chopped nuts

Glaze:

1 c. powdered sugar	1-2 Tbsp. milk
1 1/2 oz. cream cheese,	1 tsp. vanilla
softened	

Grease and sugar a 12 cup fluted plastic or ceramic tube pan. In large bowl, blend the first 6 ingredients until moistened. Beat 2 minutes at highest speed. Fold in shredded carrots, raisins and nuts; spoon into pan. To microwave: Rotate pan 1/2 turn every 5 minutes. Defrost*: 11 minutes; High: 5 1/2 minutes or High only: 12 minutes. Cool upright in pan for 10 minutes; turn onto serving plate. Cool completely. Blend glaze ingredients in small bowl until smooth. If needed, add a few more drops of milk for desired consistency. Refrigerate leftovers. Makes 10 inch ring cake.

*Defrost refers to 30% to 50% power.

CREAMY MALLOW CHEESECAKE

1/4 c. margarine
1 c. vanilla wafer crumbs
4 c. miniature marshmallows
1/3 c. milk
2 (8 oz.) pkg. cream cheese

2 Tbsp. lemon juice
2 tsp. grated lemon rind
1 tsp. vanilla
1 c. heavy cream, whipped

Microcook margarine in small bowl 45 seconds or until melted. Blend in crumbs; reserve 1/4 cup for topping. Press remaining crumb mixture onto bottom of 9 inch spring form pan. Combine marshmallows and milk in large bowl; toss to coat marshmallows with milk. Microcook 1 to 1 1/2 minutes or until smooth when stirred, stirring every 30 seconds. Chill until slightly thickened. Mix until well blended. Microcook cream cheese in bowl 30 to 45 seconds or until soft. Add lemon juice, rind and vanilla, mixing at medium speed on electric mixer until well blended. Beat in marshmallow mixture; fold in whipped cream. Pour over crust; sprinkle with reserved crumb mixture. Chill. Garnish with mandarin orange segments, strawberry halves or peach slices, if desired.

CHOCOLATE CHERRY CAKE

1 pkg. Pillsbury Plus dark
  chocolate or devils food
  cake mix
3 eggs

1 (21 oz.) can cherry fruit
  pie filling
1 tsp. almond extract

Glaze:

1/2 c. semi-sweet chocolate
  chips
1-2 Tbsp. milk

1 Tbsp. margarine or
  butter, softened
1/2 c. powdered sugar

Grease and sugar 12 cup fluted plastic or ceramic tube pan. In large bowl, blend first 4 ingredients until moistened. Beat 2 minutes at highest speed. Pour into pan. To microwave: Rotate pan 1/2 turn every 5 minutes. Defrost*: 11 minutes; High: 6 minutes or High only: 13 minutes. Cool upright in pan 10 minutes; turn onto serving plate. Cool completely. In 2 cup glass measure, microwave first 3 glaze ingredients for 2 minutes until chocolate chips melt. Stir in powdered sugar. Add additional milk if necessary for desired consistency. Spoon over cooled cake. Makes 10 inch ring cake.
   *Defrost refers to 30% to 50% power.

QUICK DESSERT CAKE

Use Quick Bread Mix for a speedy dessert cake, stirred together right in the baking pan.

1 pkg. oatmeal raisin or applesauce spice quick bread mix

1 c. water
1 egg

Combine above ingredients in 8 inch <u>glass</u> square baking pan; stir about 60 strokes with a fork. Microwave on an inverted glass pie pan 10 minutes on Low and 3 minutes on High or 7 minutes on High. Rotate pan 1/2 turn every 3 minutes. Cool on flat surface. Frost with Pillsbury frosting supreme or dust with powdered sugar.

LEMON POPPY SEED CAKE

1 pkg. lemon cake mix
3 eggs
1/3 c. oil

1 c. water
2 Tbsp. poppy seed

Glaze:

1 c. powdered sugar
1 Tbsp. lemon juice
1 Tbsp. milk

1 Tbsp. margarine or butter, softened
2-3 drops yellow food coloring

Grease and sugar 12 cup fluted plastic or ceramic tube pan. In large bowl, blend first 5 ingredients until moistened. Beat 2 minutes at highest speed; pour into pan. To microwave: Rotate pan 1/2 turn every 5 minutes. Defrost*: 11 minutes; High: 5 1/2 minutes or High only: 12 minutes. Cool upright in pan for 10 minutes; turn onto serving plate. Cool completely. Blend glaze ingredients in small bowl until smooth. If needed, add a few more drops of milk for desired consistency. Spoon over cooled cake. Makes 10 inch ring cake.

LEMON POUND CAKE

1 (18 oz.) pkg. lemon cake mix
1 (3 3/4 oz.) pkg. instant lemon pudding mix

4 eggs
1 c. water
1/4 c. oil

Mix together ingredients; pour into a greased

microwave plastic or glass tube pan. Microwave at Medium for 13-17 minutes until cake tests done, rotating 2-3 times. Let stand on flat surface for 5-10 minutes before inverting to cool. Makes 10-12 servings.

For dainty tea cakes or muffins in a jiffy, place miniature cupcake liners in spaces of an egg carton. Twelve will bake in about 2 minutes on High. Quick Petit Fours!

When microwaving a cake, cover with a paper towel and it will rise more evenly.

Marge Johnson, Minneapolis, Mn.

MARDI GRAS PARTY CAKE

1 c. water
1/2 c. butterscotch chips
3 eggs

1 pkg. Pillsbury Plus yellow
  cake mix
1/3 c. oil

Frosting:

1 pkg. coconut pecan
  frosting mix
1/4 c. margarine or butter,
  softened

3/4 c. milk
1 c. whipping cream,
  whipped and sweetened

Place water and butterscotch chips in 2 cup glass measure; microwave 2 minutes on High. Stir to dissolve chips. Combine butterscotch mixture with cake mix, eggs and oil in large mixing bowl; blend until moistened. Beat 2 minutes at highest speed. Divide batter evenly between two 8 inch round glass pans, lined with paper towel. Microwave each layer separately 4 minutes on Defrost and 5 minutes on High. Rotate pan 1/2 turn after 4 minutes. Cool 10 minutes on flat surface. Remove cakes from pans and cool completely.

Frosting: Combine frosting mix, margarine and milk in small bowl; microwave 2 1/2 minutes on High. Stir until margarine is melted. Spread while frosting is warm between layers and on top of cake. Frost sides with sweetened whipped cream.

ORANGE COCONUT RING CAKE

1/4 c. margarine or butter
3/4 c. orange marmalade
1/2 c. flaked coconut

1 pkg. lemon cake mix
3 eggs
1/3 c. oil
1 c. water

Grease and sugar 12 cup fluted plastic or ceramic tube pan. In 2 cup glass measure, microwave margarine until melted. Add marmalade and coconut; mix well. Spread evenly on bottom of pan. In large bowl, blend cake mix, eggs, oil and water until moistened. Beat 2 minutes at highest speed. Pour batter over marmalade mixture in pan. To microwave: Rotate pan 1/2 turn every 5 minutes. Defrost: 11 minutes; High: 5 1/2 minutes or High only: 12 minutes. Cool upright in pan 10 minutes; turn onto serving plate. Spoon any remaining marmalade in pan onto cake; cool completely. Makes 10 inch ring cake.

PEPPERMINT BONBON CAKE

1 pkg. fudge marble
  cake mix
3 eggs
1/3 c. oil
1 c. water

1 oz. (1 sq.) unsweetened
  chocolate, grated
1/2 tsp. mint extract
5-6 drops green food coloring

    Glaze:

1 c. powdered sugar
2 Tbsp. unsweetened cocoa
2 tsp. vanilla

2 Tbsp. margarine or butter,
  softened
2-3 Tbsp. water

Grease and sugar 12 cup fluted plastic or ceramic tube pan. In large bowl, blend first 4 ingredients until moistened. Beat 2 minutes at highest speed. Pour 1/4 of batter into small bowl; set aside. To the 3/4 remaining batter, add grated chocolate, mint flavoring and food coloring; blend well. Pour into pan. To reserved 1/4 batter, add marble pouch and 2 tablespoons water; blend well. Pour over batter in pan. Marble the layers with a knife in a folding motion, turning the pan while folding. To microwave: Rotate pan 1/2 turn every 5 minutes. Defrost*: 11 minutes; High: 5 1/2 minutes or High only: 12 minutes. Cool upright in pan 10 minutes; turn onto serving plate. Cool completely. Blend glaze ingredients until smooth. If needed, add a few more drops of water for desired consistency. Spoon over cooled cake. Makes 10 inch ring cake.
    *Defrost refers to 30% to 50% power.

PINEAPPLE RIGHT SIDE UP CAKE

1 pkg. lemon cake mix
2 Tbsp. margarine or butter
1/2 c. firmly packed brown
   sugar
6 maraschino cherries

1 (8 1/4 oz.) can pineapple
   slices, drained (reserve
   juice)
3 eggs
1/3 c. oil
1 c. water

Grease and sugar 12 cup fluted plastic or ceramic tube pan. In 1 cup glass measure, microwave margarine until melted; stir in brown sugar until well mixed. Press brown sugar mixture into bottom of pan. Cut pineapple slices in halves; place 6 halves on top of the brown sugar to form a ring. Cut each of the remaining pineapple halves into 3 pieces. Place 1 piece between each pineapple half. Place cherry in center of each pineapple half. In large bowl, blend cake mix, eggs, oil and water until moistened. Beat 2 minutes at highest speed; pour into pan. To microwave: Rotate pan 1/2 turn every 5 minutes. Defrost: 11 minutes; High: 5 1/2 minutes or High only: 12 minutes. Cool upright in pan for 5 minutes; turn onto serving plate. Cool completely. Makes 10 inch ring cake.

PUMPKIN CAKE

1 pkg. Pillsbury yellow
   cake mix
3 eggs

1/2 c. water
1 c. pumpkin pie filling
2 tsp. pumpkin pie spice

   Glaze:

1 c. powdered sugar
1 1/2 oz. cream cheese,
   softened

1 Tbsp. milk
1 tsp. vanilla

Grease and sugar 12 cup fluted plastic or ceramic tube pan. In large bowl, blend first 5 ingredients until moistened. Beat 2 minutes at highest speed; pour into pan. To microwave: Rotate pan 1/2 turn every 5 minutes. Defrost: 11 minutes; High: 5 1/2 minutes or High only: 12 minutes. Cool upright in pan 10 minutes; turn onto serving plate. Cool completely. Blend glaze ingredients in small bowl until smooth. If needed, add a few more drops of milk for desired consistency. Spoon over cooled cake. Refrigerate leftovers. Makes 10 inch ring cake.

1507-82

ROCKY ROAD CAKE

1 pkg. devils food or dark chocolate cake mix
3 eggs
1/3 c. oil
1 c. water

1 (6 oz.) pkg. (1 c.) semi-sweet chocolate chips
1 c. miniature marshmallows
1/2 c. chopped nuts

Glaze:

1 c. powdered sugar
2 Tbsp. unsweetened cocoa
2 tsp. vanilla

2 Tbsp. margarine or butter, softened
2-3 Tbsp. water

Grease and sugar a 12 cup fluted plastic or ceramic tube pan. In large bowl, blend first 4 ingredients until moistened. Beat 2 minutes at highest speed. Fold in chocolate chips, marshmallows and nuts; pour into pan. To microwave: Rotate pan 1/2 turn every 5 minutes. Defrost: 11 minutes; High: 5 1/2 minutes or High only: 12 minutes. Cool upright in pan for 10 minutes; turn onto serving plate. Cool completely. Blend glaze ingredients in small bowl until smooth. If needed, add a few more drops of water for desired consistency. Spoon over cooled cake. Makes 10 inch ring cake.

SUGAR CRUSTED MAPLE CAKE

1 pkg. yellow cake mix
3 eggs
1/3 c. oil

1 c. water
1/2 c. sugar
1/2 c. maple flavored syrup

Grease and sugar 12 cup fluted plastic or ceramic tube pan. In large bowl, blend first 4 ingredients until moistened. Beat 2 minutes at highest speed; pour into pan. To microwave: Rotate pan 1/2 turn every 5 minutes. Defrost: 11 minutes; High: 5 1/2 minutes or High only: 12 minutes. In 2 cup glass measure, microwave sugar and syrup until mixture boils and sugar is melted. Pour around edges of hot cake. Cool upright in pan 15 minutes; turn onto serving plate. Serve warm or cool. Makes 10 inch ring cake.

LEMON BUTTER SAUCE

1 c. sugar
1/2 c. water
1/2 c. butter or margarine

1/4 c. lemon juice
2 Tbsp. cornstarch

Combine above ingredients in 4 cup glass measure or medium sized glass bowl. Microwave 5 1/2 to 7 minutes on High, until mixture boils. Stir occasionally during the last 3 minutes of cooking time. Makes 1 1/2 cups sauce.

WHATCHAMACALLIT BARS

1/2 c. light corn syrup
1/2 c. brown sugar, packed
1/2 c. peanut butter
4 c. toasted rice cereal

1 (6 oz.) pkg. chocolate chips
1 (6 oz.) pkg. butterscotch chips

Microwave corn syrup and brown sugar in a 2 quart bowl at High for 1 1/2 to 2 minutes, or until mixture boils and sugar dissolves, stirring once. Stir in peanut butter; mix well. Add toasted rice cereal; mix till well coated. Pat evenly into a 12x8 inch baking dish. Let stand until cool and set. Place chocolate and butterscotch chips in a 1 quart bowl. Microwave at 60% power for 3 to 3 1/2 minutes, or until melted; stir until smooth. Spread evenly on bars. Chill until set. Cut into squares.

Marlene Barton, Grand Forks, N.D.

BROWNIES

Microwave brownies are fast and easy...just be sure not to overbake. Top will appear moist. (Brownies continue baking when removed from the microwave.) Placing baking pan on inverted pie pan helps brownies bake more evenly.

Regular Size (15 1/2 ounces): Grease bottom only of 8x8 inch square glass dish. Prepare brownies according to package directions. To microwave: Place pan on inverted glass pie pan and bake as directed, rotating 1/4 turn every 2 minutes.

Fudge Brownie Mix: Low - 8 minutes; High - 2 to 2 1/2 minutes; High only - 6 to 6 1/2 minutes (fudgy recipe). Cake-like recipe: Low - 8 minutes; High - 2 1/2 to 3 minutes; High only - 5 1/2 to 6 minutes.

Walnut Brownie Mix: (fudgy recipe) Low - 8 minutes;

High - 2 1/2 to 3 minutes; High only - 6 1/2 to 7 minutes.
Cake-like recipe: Low - 8 minutes; High - 2 1/2 to 3 minutes; High only - 5 1/2 to 6 minutes. Cool on flat surface, not a wire rack.

Family Size (22 1/2 ounces): Grease bottom only of Corning Ware 10 inch skillet or 9x12 inch glass baking pan. Prepare brownies according to package directions. To microwave: Place pan on inverted glass pie pan and bake as directed, rotating pan 1/4 turn every 2 minutes.
Fudge Brownie Mix (Fudgy recipe): Low - 8 minutes; High - 6 to 6 1/2 minutes; High only *. Cake Like recipe: Low - 8 minutes; High: 5 to 5 1/2 minutes; High only: *.
Walnut Brownie Mix (Fudgy recipe): Low - 8 minutes; High - 5 1/2 to 6 minutes; High only - 10 to 10 1/2 minutes. Cake Like recipe: Low - 8 minutes; High - 4 to 4 1/2 minutes; High only - 9 1/2 to 10 minutes. Cool on flat surface, not a wire rack.
*Not recommended.

CUSTARD

1 3/4 c. milk	1/8 tsp. salt
3 eggs	1 tsp. vanilla
1/4 c. sugar	Nutmeg

1. Place four individual glass custard dishes, 6 to 8 ounce capacity, into 9x9x2 inch pan. 2. Pour milk into glass measuring cup; heat in microwave on High until scalded, about 3 1/2 minutes. 3. While milk heats, beat eggs slightly; stir in sugar gradually. Blend well. Stir in salt, scalded milk and vanilla. 4. Pour custard into dishes; sprinkle with nutmeg. Bake about 4 1/2 minutes on High, turning dishes every 30 seconds or about 13 1/2 minutes on Low, turning dishes every 3-5 minutes. (Custards do not require baking in a dish of water when baked on Low.) Custard will barely set. Cool at room temperature. Chill, if desired.

GINGERBREAD

You mix it right in the pan. Serve it warm with ice cream, whipped cream or Lemon Butter Sauce.
Prepare mix according to package directions, mixing it in an 8x8 inch square glass pan. To microwave: Place pan on top of inverted glass pie pan and bake as directed,

rotating pan 1/2 turn after 3 minutes. Serve warm.
Low: 9 minutes; High: 3 1/2 to 4 minutes or High only:
7 to 7 1/2 minutes. Cool on flat surface, not a wire rack.

SUNDAE SUPREME DESSERT

For a quick hot fudge sauce to top almost any cake,
just melt fudge frosting supreme in your microwave. It
stays creamy smooth and liquid in the refrigerator, so you
can keep it on hand for ice cream toppings or to turn
Pillsbury Plus devils food into Sundae Supreme Dessert.

Hot Fudge Sauce: Microwave fudge frosting supreme
in a 2 cup glass measuring cup for 1 minute on High; stir.
Store in refrigerator. Serve over leftover devils food
slices, topped with ice cream.
Note: Cake slices may be heated on High for 8 to 10
seconds.

WALNUT PIE

3 eggs	1/2 c. chopped walnuts
1 c. sugar	1/2 tsp. vanilla
1 c. graham cracker crumbs	Dash of salt

Beat eggs until thick and lemon colored. Add sugar;
beat well. Fold in crumbs, walnuts, vanilla and salt. Pour
into greased 9 inch pie plate. Microwave at Medium High
for 8-9 minutes, rotating twice. Cool, then chill. Serve
with whipped cream. Makes 6-8 servings.

Marge Johnson, Minneapolis, Mn.

PIE CRUST MIX

Fresh apple pie hot from the oven in 20 minutes!
Other fresh fruit pies in less than half the time, using this
combination microwave and conventional oven method.
(The conventional oven bakes the bottom crust and browns
the top crust.)
Plan Ahead Tip: Freeze unbaked pies for thawing
and baking later. For a quick dessert, try Easy No Roll
Pie on the label.
Unfilled Pie Crust: Prepare crust according to package directions, using a 9 inch glass pie pan. Microwave
directly on floor of oven 4 to 5 minutes on High, rotating
1/2 turn after 2 minutes.

Easy No Roll Pie: Prepare pie according to package directions, using an 8 or 9 inch glass pie pan. Microwave directly on floor of oven until filling is bubbly, 6 1/2 to 7 1/2 minutes on High. Rotate 1/2 turn after 4 minutes. (Preheat conventional oven while microwaving.) Bake at 450° for 10 minutes until crust is golden.

PUMPKIN PIE

Crust: Prepare crust according to package directions in 9 inch glass pie pan.

Filling:

2 eggs, slightly beaten	1 tsp. cinnamon
1 (16 oz.) can prepared	1/2 tsp. salt
pumpkin	1/2 tsp. ginger
1 1/3 c. evaporated milk	1/4 tsp. cloves
3/4 c. sugar	

Blend filling ingredients; pour into unbaked pie shell. Microwave directly on floor of oven until edges bubble, 6 1/2 to 7 1/2 minutes on High. Rotate 1/2 turn after 4 minutes. (Preheat conventional oven while microwaving.) Bake at 450° for 15 to 20 minutes, until knife inserted in center comes out clean. Refrigerate leftovers.

Two Crust Pies: Fresh Fruit Pies - Prepare pie according to package directions, using an 8 or 9 inch glass pie pan. Microwave directly on floor of oven until filling is bubbly, 8 to 10 minutes on High. Rotate 1/2 turn after 4 minutes. (Preheat conventional oven while microwaving.) Bake at 450° for 10 to 12 minutes, until crust is golden.

Frozen Fruit Pies - Microwave directly on floor of oven unbaked pies straight from the freezer 14 to 16 minutes on High. Rotate 1/2 turn after 6 minutes. (Preheat conventional oven while microwaving.) Bake at 450° for 15 to 17 minutes until crust is golden.

MICROWAVE PEANUT BRITTLE

1 c. raw peanuts	1 tsp. baking soda
1 c. sugar	1 tsp. vanilla
1/2 c. white corn syrup	1 tsp. butter
1/8 tsp. salt	

In a 1 1/2 quart casserole, stir together peanuts,

sugar, syrup and salt. Cook 8 minutes at High, stirring well after 4 minutes. Add butter and vanilla; cook 1 minute longer at High. Add baking soda; quickly stir until light and foamy. Immediately pour onto lightly buttered baking sheet; spread out thin. When cool, break into pieces. Store in airtight container.

Gretchen Marquart, Fargo, N.D.

Similar recipes submitted by: Arlene Carlson, Lake Park, Mn., Marion Round, Faribault, Mn.

GRANOLA
(Microwave)

1/4 c. water	1/4 c. honey
3/4 c. brown sugar	1/2 tsp. cinnamon
1/2 c. oleo or butter	1 tsp. salt

Microwave above ingredients 8-10 minutes at full power. Stir after 4 minutes or cook until slightly thickened. Add:

3 c. oatmeal (old fashioned or minute)	1 c. or more raisins
	1 c. flaked coconut
1/2 c. wheat germ	1 c. salted peanuts
1 c. nuts or slivered almonds	1 c. salted sunflower nuts

Microwave all together for 8-12 minutes more at 50% power till slightly browned; stir every 3 minutes. Spread on waxed paper and let cool.

Mary Jean Voss, Owatonna, Mn.

PARTY MIX
(Microwave)

3 Tbsp. butter	2 c. Wheat Chex
4 tsp. Worcestershire sauce	2 c. Rice Chex
1/2 tsp. garlic powder	2 c. Cheerios (or Corn Chex)
1/2 tsp. onion powder	1 c. pretzels (optional)
1/2 tsp. seasoned salt	1 c. peanuts (optional)

In large glass mixing bowl, melt butter on High 1 - 1 1/2 minutes. Add seasonings; stir well. Add cereal; toss until all are evenly coated. Microwave on High 5 1/2 - 6 minutes, stirring after each 2 minutes. Drain and cool on paper towels.

Linda Landsman, Bloomington, Mn.

BEVERAGES
MISCELLANEOUS

FOOD QUANTITIES FOR 25, 50, AND 100 SERVINGS

FOOD	25 SERVINGS	50 SERVINGS	100 SERVINGS
Rolls	4 doz.	8 doz.	16 doz.
Bread	50 slices or 3 1-lb. loaves	100 slices or 6 1-lb. loaves	200 slices or 12 1-lb. loaves
Butter	½ pound	¾ to 1 pound	1½ pounds
Mayonnaise	1 cup	2 to 3 cups	4 to 6 cups
Mixed Filling for Sandwiches (meat, eggs, fish)	1½ quarts	2½ to 3 quarts	5 to 6 quarts
Mixed Filling (sweet-fruit)	1 quart	1¾ to 2 quarts	2½ to 4 quarts
Jams & Preserves	1½ lb.	3 lb.	6 lb.
Crackers	1½ lb.	3 lb.	6 lb.
Cheese (2 oz. per serving)	3 lb.	6 lb.	12 lb.
Soup	1½ gal.	3 gal.	6 gal.
Salad Dressings	1 pt.	2½ pt.	½ gal.
Meat, Poultry or Fish:			
Wieners (beef)	6½ pounds	13 pounds	25 pounds
Hamburger	9 pounds	18 pounds	35 pounds
Turkey or chicken	13 pounds	25 to 35 pounds	50 to 75 pounds
Fish, large whole (round)	13 pounds	25 pounds	50 pounds
Fish, fillets or steaks	7½ pounds	15 pounds	30 pounds
Salads, Casseroles, Vegetables:			
Potato Salad	4¼ quarts	2¼ gallons	4½ gallons
Scalloped Potatoes	4½ quarts or 1 12×20″ pan	8½ quarts	17 quarts
Mashed Potatoes	9 lb.	18-20 lb.	25-35 lb.
Spaghetti	1¼ gallons	2½ gallons	5 gallons
Baked Beans	¾ gallon	1¼ gallons	2½ gallons
Jello Salad	¾ gallon	1¼ gallons	2½ gallons
Canned Vegetables	1 #10 can	2½ #10 cans	4 #10 cans
Fresh Vegetables:			
Lettuce (for salads)	4 heads	8 heads	15 heads
Carrots (3 oz. or ½ c.)	6¼ lb.	12½ lb.	25 lb.
Tomatoes	3-5 lb.	7-10 lb.	14-20 lb.
Desserts:			
Watermelon	37½ pounds	75 pounds	150 pounds
Fruit Cup (½ c. per serving)	3 qt.	6 qt.	12 qt.
Cake	1 10×12″ sheet cake	1 12×20″ sheet cake	2 12×20″ sheets cakes
	1½ 10″ layer cakes	3 10″ layer cakes	6 10″ layer cakes
Whipping Cream	¾ pint	1½ to 2 pints	3 pints
Ice Cream:			
Brick	3¼ quarts	6½ quarts	12½ quarts
Bulk	2¼ quarts	4½ quarts or 1¼ gallons	9 quarts or 2½ gallons
Beverages:			
Coffee	½ pound and 1½ gal. water	1 pound and 3 gal. water	2 pounds and 6 gal. water
Tea	1/12 pound and 1½ gal. water	1/6 pound and 3 gal. water	1/3 pound and 6 gal. water
Lemonade	10 to 15 lemons, 1½ gal. water	20 to 30 lemons, 3 gal. water	40 to 60 lemons, 6 gal. water

ANISETTE

1 qt. vodka	1 1/2 Tbsp. ground
3 Tbsp. aniseed, crushed	coriander
1 pinch of ground cinnamon	2 1/2 c. sugar

1. Into the vodka, pour the aniseed, cinnamon and coriander. Let infuse in a closed glass container for 1 month. 2. Melt the sugar in a small amount of water. Mix together with the vodka mixture. Strain through several layers of cheesecloth or through coffee filter paper. Pour into bottles. Yield: About 7 cups.

Lorraine H. Follrath, Anoka, Mn.

BRUNCH BLOODY MARYS

1 (46 oz.) can V-8 or	3 drops of Tabasco sauce
tomato juice	1/2 tsp. salt
2 c. vodka	1/2 tsp. celery salt
2 Tbsp. lemon juice	1 Tbsp. brown sugar
1 Tbsp. horseradish	1 tsp. Worcestershire sauce

Mix and chill overnight. Serve with celery stick dill pickle spear or large stuffed olives Rub rim of glass with lime and dip in celery salt.

Ann Christensen, Litchfield, Mn.

HOT CIDER DRINK

1 qt. apple cider	1 pt. orange juice
1 pt. cranberry juice	

Put in coffee urn. In basket, put:

1 tsp. whole allspice	3 sticks cinnamon
1 tsp. whole cloves	1/2 c. sugar

Run through urn cycle.

Emogene Homan, Minneapolis, Mn.

BERKELEY HOT SPICED CIDER

3 pieces of stick cinnamon
1/2 tsp. ground cinnamon
1 c. sugar
1/2 c. lemon juice

2 tsp. whole cloves
8 c. apple cider
2 c. orange juice
1/2 c. apple brandy

Tie cinnamon, cloves and nutmeg in a small piece of cheesecloth. Combine with cider and sugar in a large saucepan; simmer 15 minutes. Remove spice bag. Stir in orange juice and lemon juice; heat just until bubbly hot. Pour into heated punch bowl. Add small oranges, studded with whole cloves for garnish if you wish. Mix in apple brandy.

Joan Norton, Hibbing, Mn.

HOMEMADE CREME DE MENTHE

3 c. sugar
2 c. water
1 lemon, thinly sliced
1 1/3 c. 100 proof vodka

1/2 tsp. peppermint extract
2 tsp. vanilla extract (pure)
Green food coloring

Combine sugar, water and lemon in medium sized pan. Bring to a boil, stirring constantly. Lower heat; simmer 5 minutes without stirring. Strain; cool. Stir in remaining ingredients. Cover tightly and mellow at least 2 weeks.

Dee Olson, St. Paul, Mn.

PERCOLATOR GROGG

3 qt. cranberry juice cocktail
1 bottle dry red wine
1 Tbsp. whole cloves
6 sticks cinnamon

12 whole cardamom pods, cracked
1 c. sugar

Put juice and wine into 30 cup percolator. Put spices and sugar into percolator basket; perk as for coffee. Makes 25 six ounce servings.

Maryann Skelton, Duluth, Mn.

712

BAILEY'S IRISH CREME

1 can Eagle Brand sweetened
   condensed milk
1 pt. half & half
1 heaping tsp. cocoa
1 scant tsp. instant coffee

1/2 tsp. coconut flavoring
   (more if desired)
1 c. Canadian Club or
Windsor

Makes 1 quart. Mix cocoa and coffee in a little water. Put all ingredients in blender to mix. Store in empty bottle in refrigerator.

R. Mielke, Chisholm, Mn.

"BAYLEES" IRISH CREME

1 1/2 c. blended whiskey
1 can Eagle Brand milk
1 pt. whipping cream
2 eggs

3-4 Tbsp. Hershey's
   chocolate syrup
1/2 Tbsp. vanilla
3-4 Tbsp. water

Mix in blender; store in refrigerator. (I use Canadian Windsor.) Makes about 1 1/2 fifths.

June Szymczak, Duluth, Mn.

RASPBERRY LIQUEUR

3 c. sugar
3 c. water

1 qt. fresh raspberries
1 qt. whiskey or brandy

Simmer sugar with water until sugar is dissolved; cool. Pour over fresh raspberries in a wide mouthed jar; add liquor. Cover loosely and set aside for 3 months. Pour off through a sieve and put in decanter.

Susie Brainard, Minneapolis, Mn.

PERFECT MARGARITAS

6 oz. frozen limeade
   concentrate
6 oz. tequila

3 oz. triple sec
2 egg whites

Put all ingredients in blender; fill to top with ice and blend until smooth. Serve in salt rimmed glasses; garnish with lime wedge.

Denise Daeger, Minneapolis, Mn.

ORANGE SHRUB

1 pt. orange sherbet   1/2 qt. ginger ale
1/2 c. vodka

 Combine in blender; pour over ice. Serves 10.
      Marlys Swehla, Albert Lea, Mn.

PUNCH

 Mix 7-Up and sherbet together.
      Virginia Miller, Anoka, Mn.

PUNCH

1 (6 oz.) can concentrated 1 pkg. half thawed
 orange juice (half frozen) strawberries
1 (6 oz.) can concentrated 1 qt. ginger ale
 lemonade (half frozen) 1 qt. club soda
          1 pkg. ice cubes

 Combine ingredients; place in a punch bowl. Float thin sliced orange slices on top.
      Jean Taylor, Grand Forks, N.D.

CHRISTMAS PUNCH

1 c. sugar   2 c. unsweetened pineapple
1 c. water   juice
4 c. bottled cranberry juice Ice ring or chunk of ice
1 1/2 c. lemon juice   2 (28 oz.) bottles ginger ale
2 c. orange juice

 In a saucepan, combine sugar and water. Bring to a boil, stirring until sugar dissolves. Cover; boil over low heat, without stirring, for about 5 minutes. Mix this syrup with all the fruit juices; chill thoroughly. Just before serving, place the ice ring or block of ice in punch bowl. Pour in the fruit juices. Ladle over ice until well chilled. Add ginger ale. Makes about 30 punch cup servings. (For color, you might add red and green maraschino cherries.)
      Helen-May Johnson, Chanhassen, Mn.

GOOD LUCK PUNCH

1 qt. fresh chopped rhubarb
Water to cover (you will
   want to end up with 3 qt.
   rhubarb juice)
3 c. sugar
2 c. water

Juice of 6 lemons or 1 (6 oz.)
   can frozen lemonade
   concentrate
1 c. pineapple juice
1 qt. carbonated beverage,
   such as 7-Up

Cook rhubarb until mushy; strain. Simmer sugar and water for 10 minutes to make syrup; cool. Mix all juices. Pour over ice in punch bowl. Add carbonated beverage. Makes 5 quarts or 40 four ounce servings.
Bettie Mallon, Minneapolis, Mn.

HOT CIDER PUNCH

1 gal. apple cider
2 (6 oz.) cans frozen
   orange juice

6 juice cans of water
1 c. sugar
3 cinnamon sticks

Simmer 1/2 hour before serving.
Paula Earhart, Jackson, Mn.

DAIRY PUNCH

1 qt. milk
1 qt. vanilla ice cream

1 (6 oz.) can frozen orange
   juice
Dash of nutmeg

Blend and serve immediately.
Marlys Swehla, Albert Lea, Mn.

FROZEN PUNCH

2 pkg. cherry Kool-Aid
1 pkg. orange Kool-Aid
3 c. sugar
3 ripe bananas, mashed
1 qt. 7-Up

1 1/2 qt. water
Juice of 3 lemons (can
   substitute ReaLemon)
1 large can pineapple juice

Mix all ingredients, including 7-Up; freeze. Thaw 1 to 2 hours before serving. Should be slush when served.
Mary J. Sward, New Hope, Mn.

FRUIT PUNCH

4 c. sugar
6 c. water
5 bananas
1 c. orange juice
2 Tbsp. frozen lemonade
concentrate

1 large can unsweetened
pineapple juice
2 small boxes frozen
strawberries, thawed
Red food coloring
2 liters 7-Up

Boil sugar and water for 6 minutes; let cool. In a blender, put bananas, orange juice, lemonade concentrate and pineapple juice; blend until smooth. Add sugar-water; stir well. Blend strawberries and food coloring; stir into fruit mixture. Put mixture in freezer for 1 to 3 days before serving. Take out 2 hours before serving to soften.

Minneapolis, Mn.

GOLDEN FRUIT PUNCH

1 pt. sugar
1 c. lemon juice
1 c. orange juice
1 pt. pineapple juice

1 qt. ginger ale
1 qt. cracked ice
1 doz. cherries

Mix together.

K., St. Cloud, Mn.

ICEY PARTY PUNCH

Dissolve 1 large package jello in 2 cups* boiling water and 2 cups sugar. Add to above:

1 (12 oz.) can frozen
lemonade
1 (12 oz.) can frozen
orange juice

1 (46 oz.) can pineapple juice
1 1/2 pkg. Kool-Aid (23 oz.
for 1 pkg.)
1 1/2 gal. water less 2 c.*
used for jello

Mix together; freeze in milk cartons. Take out 4 hours before serving. Add 2 quarts ginger ale just before servings. Colors: Orange, use orange Kool-Aid and jello; Green, use lime Kool-Aid and jello; Pink, use strawberry Kool-Aid and jello; Grape, use grape Kool-Aid and jello.

M. Paul, Minneapolis, Mn.

716

LEMONADE PUNCH

2 large cans lemonade
  concentrate (add water
  as directed)
1 large can Dole unsweet-
  ened pineapple juice

1 large bottle ginger ale
  (cold), poured in just
  before serving
Ice cubes (made before hand
  of lemonade or pineapple
  juice)

Garnish with lemon slices, if desired.
K., St. Cloud, Mn.

PARTY PUNCH

2 1/2 qt. cold water
4 (9 oz.) cans Awake
Ice cubes

4 (1 pt.) bottles cranberry
  juice cocktail
2 large bottles chilled ginger
  ale

Combine 2 1/2 quarts cold water with four 9 ounce cans Awake and four 1 pint bottles cranberry juice cocktail; stir and chill. Just before serving, add 2 large bottles of chilled ginger ale and ice cubes. Makes about 7 quarts or 50 servings.
Gerri Ruprecht, St. Cloud, Mn.

RASPBERRY PUNCH

2 pkg. raspberry Kool-Aid
  (unsweetened)
2 c. sugar

2 qt. water
2 large cans frozen lemonade

Mix the above together; add 2 packages frozen rasp berries, thawed, and 4 quarts of chilled ginger ale.
Colleen Grapentin, St. Cloud, Mn

RASPBERRY SHERBET PUNCH

1 1/2 gal. raspberry sherbet
5 qt. ginger ale

5 qt. orange juice
1 pt. lemon juice

Mix ginger ale, orange juice and lemon juice to taste. Mix in part of sherbet; put the rest in the punch bowl. Serves 40-50.
K., St. Cloud, Mn.

RECEPTION PUNCH

1/2 gal. sherbet (any kind)   4 qt. chilled ginger ale

Cut sherbet into good sized chunks; mix with ginger ale. Ice is not needed, but can be added. Makes about 50 servings.

Helen-May Johnson, Chanhassen, Mn.

ROSIE'S PUNCH

3 c. sugar   6 c. water

Boil 5 minutes; cool 15-20 minutes. Combine:

1 (6 oz.) can lemonade   46 oz. unsweetened pineapple
2 (6 oz.) cans orange juice   juice
                              5 ripe, mashed bananas

Mix and freeze in three 2 quart containers. Two hours before serving, remove from freezer. Just before serving, add 3 quarts club soda.

Maryann Skelton, Duluth, Mn.

SANGRIA WINE PUNCH

1 bottle Sangria wine   1 bottle 7-Up
1 can Hi-C orange juice   1 can Hawaiian Punch
1 can fruit juice

Mix everything together, except 7-Up. Pour 7-Up in just before serving.

Liz Tuft, St. Paul, Mn.

SPARKLING WINE PUNCH

1 (6 oz.) can frozen   1 c. sugar
  lemonade concentrate,   1 (750 ml. or 4/5 qt.) bottle
  thawed   dry white wine, chilled
1 (6 oz.) can frozen orange   2 (28 oz.) bottles carbonated
  juice concentrate, thawed   water, chilled
1 (46 oz.) can unsweetened   Strawberry slices
  pineapple juice, chilled   Lime slices

Combine lemonade, orange and pineapple juices; stir in sugar and wine. Keep chilled. At serving time, pour into a large punch bowl. Gently stir in carbonated water. Garnish top with strawberry and lime slices. Makes about 3 1/2 quarts or 28 punch cup servings.

Blanche B. Masica, Minneapolis, Mn.

YOUTH DELIGHT PUNCH

1 (46 oz.) can pineapple juice
1 (46 oz.) can grapefruit juice
1 can apricot juice
2 c. granulated sugar

3 pkg. raspberry flavored Kool-Aid
2 oranges, sliced
2 lemons, sliced
1 lime, sliced
1 (2 liter) bottle 7-Up

Combine pineapple juice, grapefruit juice, apricot juice, Kool-Aid and sugar; stir until Kool-Aid and sugar are dissolved. Chill thoroughly. If desired, part of this mixture can be poured into a ring mold and frozen for use in the punch bowl. Just before serving, float slices of orange, lemon and lime in punch and add 7-Up to make it sparkle. Makes 4 gallons.

St. Cloud, Mn.

HOT BUTTER RUM MIX

Batter:

1 lb. butter
1 qt. vanilla ice cream

1 lb. powdered sugar
1 lb. brown sugar

In large bowl, whip softened butter. Add softened ice cream; add sugar. Mix well; freeze. To serve. In 10 ounce mug, place 3 tablespoons batter, 1 ounce dark rum and fill with boiling water.

Cathy Rudolph, Grand Rapids, Mn.

HOT BUTTERED RUM

1 lb. powdered sugar
1 lb. brown sugar

1 stick butter
1 qt. vanilla ice cream

Mix above very slowly together; store in freezer. To serve: Use 1 large spoon of above, 1 jigger of rum and fill rest of the cup with hot water; stir.

1507-82   Jan Ferry, Golden Valley, Mn.   719

BONNIE'S HOT BUTTERED RUM

Batter:

1 pt. vanilla ice cream
1 lb. brown sugar
3 sticks butter

1 lb. (2 c.) granulated white
   sugar
2 Tbsp. vanilla

Drink:

1 Tbsp. batter
1 jigger rum
Hot water

Cinnamon
Nutmeg

Cook 20 minutes in double boiler; start timing when melted. Batter keeps a long time in refrigerator.

Barb Discher, Bismarck, N.D.

HOT BUTTERED RUM BATTER

2 c. brown sugar
1 c. white sugar
1 lb. butter

2 qt. vanilla ice cream
3 tsp. vanilla

Beat sugar with softened butter; add the rest. Keeps 2 months in refrigerator or freeze in freezer. Add to cup of boiling water and a shot of rum.

Jeanette Guzek, Grand Forks, N.D.

SANGRIA

1 (25.4 oz.) bottle burgundy
   or other dry red wine,
   chilled
1/2 c. sugar

1 orange, thinly sliced
1 lemon, thinly sliced
1 (10 oz.) bottle club soda,
   chilled

Combine first 4 ingredients in a large pitcher, stirring to dissolve sugar. Add club soda just before serving. Serve over ice. Yield: About 1 quart.

Sylvia Disciario, Irving, Tx.

720

SLUSH

1 (6 oz.) can orange juice
1 (6 oz.) can lemonade
1 (6 oz.) can lemon juice

1 c. (or more) Southern Comfort

Freeze. Mix with 7-Up, as much as you like.

Debra Tollefson, Fargo, N.D.

SHARON'S SLUSH
(Vodka)

1 c. water
1 1/2 pt. cranapple juice
1 (6 oz.) can limeade

1 (6 oz.) can lemonade
1 1/2 c. vodka

Mix well; freeze overnight. Serve with a glass of 7-Up.

Linda Landsman, Bloomington, Mn.

FRIENDSHIP TEA

2 c. sugar or less
2 c. orangeade mix
3/4 c. lemonade mix

2 c. instant tea
2 tsp. cloves
2 tsp. cinnamon

Combine all ingredients. Store in airtight container. Use 1 cup boiling water per 1 tablespoon mixture.

Rosie Schudar, Fargo, N.D.

LEMONY ICED TEA

2 c. boiling water
6 heaping tsp. black tea
1 c. (scant) sugar
Juice of 2 lemons

Cold water
Juice of 1 orange or lime, if desired

Pour boiling water over tea; let steep 6 minutes. Strain into a 2 quart container; add sugar. When sugar is dissolved, mix in lemon juice. Fill container with cold water. Save space for adding orange or lime juice. Makes 8 to 10 servings.

Adeline Hortsch, St. Cloud, Mn.

TOM AND JERRY'S
(As served at the Waldorf-Astoria Hotel)

Separate whites and yolks of 4 eggs. Beat the egg yolks with 1/4 pound confectioners sugar until thick and creamy and sugar is dissolved. Add 1 teaspoon baking powder; beat the whites to stiff froth. Add yolks to whites; stir well. Chill in refrigerator. Put 2 teaspoons of the mixture in a cup or mug. Add 1/2 jigger of rum and 1/2 jigger of brandy; stir well. Add boiling water. Sprinkle nutmeg on top. Serve hot. Makes about 12 drinks.

Helen-May Johnson, Chanhassen, Mn.

TOM AND JERRY'S

6 eggs, separated   1 (1 lb.) box powdered sugar

Beat eggs separately; add 1/2 of sugar to beaten yolk mixture. Add sugar to beaten white mixture. Mix the two mixtures together; beat. Add 3 drops of oil of cinnamon and 3 drops of oil of cloves. Put 1/3 of mixture into cup; add 1/2 jigger rum and 1/2 jigger brandy. Add nutmeg to top of mixture before serving.

Liz Tuft, St. Paul, Mn.

TOM AND JERRY BATTER

Use 2 separate bowls to prepare batter in. Take as many eggs as desired. Break the whites into one bowl and the yolks into another bowl. Beat whites to a stiff broth; add enough powdered sugar gradually until it's a real stiff batter. Beat egg yolks until thick; fold into white batter, adding some cream of tartar. To serve drink:

1 large spoon of batter   1/2 jigger of rum
1/2 jigger of brandy

Fill with hot water. Put nutmeg on top.

Mary Perron, Rochester, Mn.

HOT TOMATO JUICE

1 qt. tomatoes (whole)
2 (10 1/2 oz.) cans chicken
   broth (or your own)
1/2 c. celery tops, cut
   quite small

4 sprigs of parsley
6 whole black peppers
1 small bay leaf
1 Tbsp. sugar
Salt to taste

Bring to a boil; simmer 30 minutes. Strain in colander. Put 3 or 4 drops of red food coloring. Serve hot. Serve in glass cups.

Pearl Paulsrud, Montevideo, Mn.

HOMEMADE VAN DER MENTHE

1 lb. dark brown sugar
1 c. white sugar
2 1/2 c. water
1 vanilla bean, split
   lengthwise

3/4 c. cocoa
1 1/2 tsp. pure peppermint
   extract
1 qt. 100 proof vodka

In medium pan, combine first 4 ingredients. Bring to a boil, stirring occasionally; boil rapidly 10 minutes. Remove from heat; at once, stir in cocoa, blending until dissolved. Cool. Add extract and vodka. Pour into jars with tight fitting lids. Let stand 2 weeks, then pour off clear liquid, discarding the sediment.

Note: If vanilla bean is unavailable, 4 teaspoons pure vanilla extract can be added with the vodka.

Dee Olson, St. Paul, Mn.

BEET WINE

12 fairly large beets or
   more small ones
1 lb. raisins
6 c. sugar

Pinch of pepper
1 slice of toast
1 cake compressed yeast

Wash beets; cook with enough water to have a gallon of juice when cooked and strained. Put juice in crockery jar; dissolve sugar in it. Add raisins and pepper. Spread yeast on toast; let it float, yeast side down, on top of juice. Cover with cloth; let stand 1 week. Strain and pour into jug; leave it open. Let this work for several weeks. More sugar may be added if not sweet enough. Strain several times after it works. Cork it; store in cool place.

1507-82   Mary Paul   723

RHUBARB WINE

1 lb. sugar
1 qt. boiling water

1 qt. rhubarb
Raisins
Yeast

Pour boiling water over rhubarb; let stand 25 hours. Strain; add sugar and 2 handfuls of raisins. Stir in 1/2 cake of yeast. Work for 1 month (Fleischmann's or brewer's yeast). Double recipe makes 2 1/2 quarts.

Phyllis Christenson, Brooklyn Center, Mn

COOKING HINTS

Freeze leftover tea in ice cube trays for use in iced tea; these will not dilute tea flavor.

Sprinkle cake plate with granulated sugar to prevent cake from sticking when serving.

Use sifted powdered sugar instead of flour on your work surface with rolling out sweet dough.

To make instant candle holders for your cakes, use miniature marshmallows, maraschino cherries or gumdrops.

Always tear lettuce   Cutting causes the edges to turn brown

Thicken soups, gravies and sauces by gradually adding potato flakes. Flakes never lump when added directly as flour and cornstarch do and they add to the texture

Save those vitamins for soup   Save the water in which you boil your vegetables like carrots, celery, cabbage, onions and potatoes and store in a covered jar in refrigerator. When you want a cup of soup, heat what you need and add a teaspoon of beef or chicken concentrate soup mix or a bouillon cube

HOUSEHOLD HINTS

A small nick in the rim of a glass can be smoothed with an emery board.

When one glass is stuck inside another, do not force them apart. Fill the top glass with cold water and dip the lower one in hot water. They will come apart without breaking.

Scratches on glassware will disappear if polished with toothpaste

Helen-May Johnson, Chanhassen, Mn.

724

HOMEMADE DEODORANT

Stir well:

2 Tbsp. alum   1 pt. warm water

Add small amount of cologne for lady; add small amount of after shave for men.

Marion Round, Faribault, Mn.

PANEL CLEANER
(Wood)

1 part boiled linseed oil   1 part turpentine
1 part vinegar

Mix together. Rub on walls and buff with a dry cloth.

Suzie Brainard, Minneapolis, Mn.

SALADS, DRESSINGS, SAUCES

1507-82

BREADS, COFFEE CAKES,
ROLLS, SANDWICHES

1507-82

1507-82

This Cookbook is a perfect gift for Holidays, Weddings, Anniversaries and Birthdays.

Cookbook Publishers, Inc. are pleased to have the privilege of publishing this fine cookbook.

Would you like a personalized cookbook for your own favorite organization? For complete information write to:

COOKBOOK PUBLISHERS, INC.
13550 W. 108th Street
Lenexa, Kansas 66212